KEOS I

KEPHALA

JOHN E. COLEMAN

KEOS

VOLUME I

KEPHALA

Pottery decorated with pattern burnishing

KEOS

RESULTS OF EXCAVATIONS CONDUCTED BY
THE UNIVERSITY OF CINCINNATI
UNDER THE AUSPICES OF
THE AMERICAN SCHOOL OF CLASSICAL STUDIES AT ATHENS

VOLUME I

KEPHALA

A LATE NEOLITHIC SETTLEMENT AND CEMETERY

BY
JOHN E. COLEMAN
WITH A FOREWORD BY
JOHN L. CASKEY

AMERICAN SCHOOL OF CLASSICAL STUDIES
PRINCETON, N.J.
1977

PUBLISHED WITH THE AID OF A GRANT FROM THE CLASSICS FUND, A GIFT OF LOUISE TAFT SEMPLE IN MEMORY OF HER FATHER, CHARLES PHELPS TAFT

Library of Congress Cataloging in Publication Data

Coleman, John E 1940–
Kephala: a late Neolithic settlement and cemetery.

(Keos, results of excavations conducted by the University of Cincinnati; v. 1)
Includes bibliographies and index.
1. Kephala site, Greece. I. Title. II. Series.
GN776.22.G8C64 949.9 76-13187
ISBN 0-87661-701-1

PRINTED IN GERMANY *at* J. J. AUGUSTIN, GLÜCKSTADT

FOREWORD

Excavation at Kephala began in 1960 with a few probings on a single day, July 31. We had been led to explore the place by references in an excellent article by Kathleen Scholes (1956), in which she reported the presence of early sherds and obsidian. The site seemed not very promising, being sorely denuded in its exposed position, but was perhaps worth further examination. Therefore a series of tests followed during thirteen days in 1961.

Graves were discovered not unlike those of Syros and other islands (Tsountas, 1898, 1899) and of Ayios Kosmas (Mylonas, 1959). House walls were sparse. Pottery and objects showed Neolithic qualities but certain of them looked as if they might be related to Bronze Age types. After preliminary inspection it was charily stated in 1961 that they might "be assigned tentatively to the Early Cycladic period, and quite possibly to a very early stage." Then digging was resumed in 1963, and at the end of that season we reported that "the presence of late Neolithic cultural elements seems reasonably certain." This statement was unnecessarily guarded. Kephala was by that time recognizable as something new and important, the first Neolithic settlement to be excavated in the Cyclades. It ought to have received closer attention from the start.

The omission, such as it was, came partly from preoccupation with our major undertaking, excavation of the Bronze Age site at Ayia Irini. Let me pay tribute to the diligence and determination of the men who tramped the rough path over the hills to Kephala in the first seasons, P. H. Auerbach, E. G. Carlson, T. W. Jacobsen, A. C. Renfrew, and J. C. Overbeck. They did the work well.

A more consecutive program of digging and studies began in 1964 when J. E. Coleman, the author of this book, took charge of the operation. He excavated representative parts of the site during that season and, with Katherine Coleman, in 1966. In 1965 and within the years 1967–1973 he spent longer or shorter periods on the island, making small tests for verification at Kephala, exploring other regions, and examining the materials found. He with L. E. Cotsen and R. L. Holzen, architects of the expedition, collaborated in surveying the whole headland and producing coordinated plans and sections of the various areas where excavation had been done. Visitors and other members of the staff consulted with them and gave much practical help from time to time. The book speaks for itself. I must offer my own special thanks, along with those of all our colleagues in the undertaking, to Mr. Coleman, now Associate Professor at Cornell, for carrying this part of the whole task to its conclusion.

Keos and the Cyclades

Since this is the first volume in a series of definitive reports on all aspects of our excavations in Keos it may be appropriate to give here a brief account of what has been accomplished, besides the work at Kephala, up to now.

In 1960 the Bronze Age in the Cyclades was known chiefly from the work done by Tsountas in Syros and other islands and by the British School in Melos: exceedingly good work and well published, but long ago. French and German studies of Thera, Rubensohn's excavation in Paros, and many other limited investigations had added modest bits of useful information. Meanwhile and thereafter, much more extensive work in Crete, on the Greek mainland, and at sites on the eastern shores of the Aegean was producing objects of Cycladic origin or derivation. Museums in many countries held excellent pieces which illustrated the early arts of the islands but gave no secure evidence of relative chronology or local provenience. New examination of a Cycladic site seemed to be wanted.

The late Professor N. Kontoleon, who had served as Ephor of Antiquities in the islands, encouraged us and helped with good advice. We visited a number of places, and ultimately chose to make tests on the small peninsula of Ayia Irini within the great natural harbor of Keos. This was already known to have been inhabited in the Bronze Age; stratified deposits of very considerable depth could be seen in the banks, and potsherds were plentiful. The situation, well protected and on one of the principal shipping lanes in the Aegean, suggested that maritime people and traders might have chosen to live here. Circumstances were propitious for us. The University of Cincinnati approved of the venture and provided financial support; the American School at Athens gave its sponsorship and the Greek Archaeological Service its authorization; the German Archaeological Institute graciously surrendered such claims as it had through the studies conducted previously by G. Welter; and the owners of the property, the Michalinos Coaling and Shipping Company of Piraeus, not only encouraged us to excavate but freely and voluntarily offered living and working quarters in their disused buildings near the site. In one of the large walled coal depots we were allowed to build storerooms with shelves, benches, and generous space for tables on which pottery and other objects could be laid out, mended, and studied.

Ayia Irini

The enterprise began at Ayia Irini with digging of trenches in twelve days of July and August, 1960. These soundings were designed to test the site and determine whether a modest survey or more extensive excavations would be justified. The results were promising, more provocative, in fact, than we had dared to hope. Good luck played a part: segments of the fortification walls were seen; the largest trench opened central rooms in House A, which was ultimately to be revealed as the principal building of the settlement; another trench uncovered the excellent masonry of House C; and still another (only 2 m. by 5 m.) came down upon the Bronze Age temple, even producing three fragments, scarcely recognizable at the time, of large free-standing terracotta statues. Pottery and other objects recovered in all parts of the site showed that people had lived here throughout most of the Bronze Age and that they had had close contact with major centers of Aegean civilization.

Work was therefore resumed in 1961 on a larger scale. Areas where the trenches had been opened were expanded and outlines of some buildings began to be visible. In House A the effects of a violent earthquake were evident, walls being displaced and debris of all sorts, including shattered frescoes, having fallen into cellar rooms. Many vases of Late Minoan I and early Mycenaean styles could be put together. House C was cleared, and deep soundings near it brought up sherds of pots that belonged to the Early and Middle Bronze Ages. New tests in the northern parts of the site uncovered further stretches of the fortifications and in some places gave hints of industrial activities, metal working included. The southeastern rooms of the temple were excavated to a certain depth; more pieces of statues were found; there was clear evidence that the space had been used at the very end of the Bronze Age (LH III C), but there were signs of earlier occupation also and the state of the remains was puzzling, sometimes misleading. Results achieved in the two initial campaigns were described in our first preliminary report in *Hesperia* (Caskey, 1962).

No work was undertaken in 1962 but a long campaign followed in 1963 (Caskey, 1964a). Deep digging in Area C revealed parts of a fine building of the Early Bronze Age which lay well preserved under the remains of Middle Bronze Age houses, and our sampling of materials, local and imported, from both periods was greatly increased. Excavations in the northern areas were extended. House A continued to yield rich deposits, chiefly from the period of the great destruction but also some earlier and a few later. A graffito on a potsherd, comprising two Linear A signs, was found with LM I B and LH II vases in the earthquake debris. Within the temple the northwestern rooms were now cleared and the whole plan became visible. The innermost compartment on the left, toward the western corner of the building, was of particular interest since here on the floor lay dozens of fragments of the big terracotta statues whose presence had been signaled by scattered finds in 1960 and 1961. Furthermore, to reach this heap of fallen statues we had dug through a long series of stratified floor deposits which showed that this small room had been used repeatedly, probably without interruption and probably always for religious purposes, from a time around 1000 B.C. through the Classical Greek period.

The campaign of 1964 gave further information about the plan of the town and the chronological sequence of its constructions. Lines of the fortifications were determined in the northern and northeastern sectors and it became clear that the rooms running out to the northeast tower had been added beyond the original course of the wall; the earlier construction went back at least to the time of MM III, the rest being datable probably in that of LM I. Farther south, we began to uncover the main gateway and lines of big walls which continue southeastward to the shore. Near and under the fortifications on either side of the site graves were discovered, some containing pots and ornaments. More rooms of House A were cleared. The northern part of another large building, House F, was excavated. Deep digging in the temple, below water level, showed that its walls were bedded much lower than we had guessed, and that its history of building and rebuilding had begun in an early phase of the Middle Bronze Age. Excavation was suspended in 1965, when the whole season at Ayia Irini was devoted to sorting, mending, and study of the finds and their association with the architectural sequences. Pottery, now overcrowding the storerooms, required much attention; statues from the temple, fresco fragments, miscellaneous objects, human and animal bones were examined and recorded. The work of these two seasons is outlined in our third preliminary report (Caskey, 1966).

By this time we had a fairly clear picture of the general scheme of the site, the sequence of settlements, and the types of objects associated with them. Uncertainties remained, however, and excavation on a moderate scale was carried forward in the seasons of 1966, 1967, and 1968. In 1966 we investigated a complex of ruins at the summit of a "troullos," about half a kilometer northwest of Ayia Irini, where a watchtower or small sanctuary may have stood. After 1968 digging was limited to stratigraphical tests and trimming of areas that had been opened previously. More and more, emphasis was centered on study of the collections. Provisional but comprehensive reports on the topography and architecture, and on the chronology as seen in the pottery, were published in *Hesperia* (Caskey, 1971a, 1972). The principal advances made in the years 1966–1971, as there recorded, include examination of well-preserved rooms which belong to two major phases of the Early Bronze Age, in the western sector; in the same region, houses and an important system of fortifications with a gateway and flanking tower, of the Middle Bronze Age; further clearing of the greater defensive works of the succeeding period from the western to the eastern shore; clearing of the main gateway; discovery of large tombs, smaller graves, a subterranean spring chamber and an early potter's kiln outside the walls; further excavation in and around Houses A, F, and L; investigation of regions south and southwest of the modern church (Areas Q and R); deep digging in the southeastern parts of the temple and in the roadways on either side of it.

Since 1971 attention has been devoted almost wholly to study and publication. Small test-pits excavated in houses and near the fortifications helped to advance the analysis of architecture and pottery sequences, which occupied most of the staff. All periods received attention, from certain very early deposits (probably overlapping those of Kephala) through the whole Bronze Age and down to Classical Greek times. Special topics taken up in these years include frescoes, graves, human and animal bones, potters' marks, small fire-boxes (often called incense burners), sealstones and sealings, evidence of metallurgy, and various classes of objects made of stone and of lead. Mending, conservation, and study of the terracotta statues continued throughout. By the end of the season of 1974 the collection of pottery comprised some 4330 single items, that of miscellaneous objects some 3825, and besides these, many hundreds of pieces individually recorded but not numbered in the general inventory and, of course, many thousands of potsherds. Meanwhile the foreman and a few of our regular workmen, who are competent practical masons, have systematically reinforced the ancient walls where necessary by underpinning, filling, and buttressing. Retaining walls and paths have been built and trees, shrubs, and flowering plants have been set out.

Staff

An excavation of this sort must be collaborative. Many people have taken part in the work in Keos; all have made valuable contributions. To describe or classify the activities of each would be inappropriate, but to dismiss them with an anonymous acknowledgment would curtail and distort the record. Briefly, therefore, those who have spent weeks and months at the site from 1960 through 1975 are listed here alphabetically, with note of the years in which they served: Katherine Abramovitz (Coleman) '65–'67, '70, '71, '73; S. Andreou '75; J. L. Angel '65, '69, '72; Mrs. Angel '72; P. H. Auerbach '61; Aliki Bikaki '61, '63, '65, '72–'75; Susan Bird '71; Tucker Blackburn '63, '69–'75; Stella Bouzaki '68–'75; Kathryn Butt '66, '69, '71, '75; Jill Carington Smith '70; E. G. Carlson '61; Elizabeth G. Caskey '60, '61, '63–'65; J. L. Caskey '60, '61, '63–'75; K. Chionatos '68, '70–'73; A. J. Christopherson '68; J. E. Coleman '64–'67, '69–'71, '73; L. E. Cotsen '61, '63, '65–'68, '70, '71, '73–'75; Jennie Coy '65,

'67–'69, '71, '72; W. W. Cummer '70, '72–'75; Mrs. Cummer '74; J. L. Davis '74, '75; Mrs. Davis '75; Chr. Doumas '61, '63; Mary Eliot '68–'75; Miriam Ervin (Caskey) '63–'75; Alice Fäthke '71–'73, '75; Alison Findlay '71–'74; Rose Gathorne-Hardy '69; Hara Georgiou '74, '75; Evelyn Harrison '63; G. Hellner '74; R. L. Holzen '64, '66–'69, '71, '73; T. W. Jacobsen '63; P. de Jong '65; J. H. Kaimowitz '67; P. Kallios '60, '61, '63–'75; W. G. and Mrs. Kittredge '61, '63, '64–'72, '74; J. Lavdas '65–'67, '70; Eleni Lazaridou '64–'75; Maria Lilibaki '75; S. Maras '61, '63–'65; T. M. Mathews '66; F. R. Matson '65; Elizabeth Milburn (Schofield) '61, '64, '68, '69, '71, '75; J. D. Muhly '73; A. E. and Mrs. Osborne '64, '66–'69; J. C. Overbeck '63, '72–'75; Mrs. Overbeck '72–'75; D. Papaioannou '60, '61, '63, '64, '66–'75; P. Petrakis '71; V. Pigott '73; I. Pini '71; M. R. Popham '70, '71, '73; Leslie Preston '68–'71; Lynne Radcliffe '65; A. C. Renfrew '63; B. Schmaltz '74; Eva Stehle '67; H. Tessmann '71; N. Tountas '73; Ann Trovinger '74; Metaxia Tsipopoulou '75; R. F. Tylecote '73; Karen Vitelli '70, '73; Anastasia Voutsina '68–'73; Mary Webb '71, '73, '74; T. A. Wertime '73; C. K. Williams, II '64, '65; S. Yapitzopoulos '71; J. G. Younger '69–'71; Karen Younger '70, '71.

Sponsorship

Permission to excavate was granted by the Greek Government through its Archaeological Service. We think with special gratitude of the successive Directors, J. Papadimitriou, Chr. Karouzos, Sp. Marinatos, and more recently N. Kontoleon, J. Kontis, and D. Lazarides; and of the Ephors N. Zapheiropoulos, Mrs. Zapheiropoulou, and J. Tzedakis. Chr. Doumas, as Epimelete, helped us in the early campaigns; Eleni Lazaridou worked with us through many seasons, and Maria Lilibaki and Metaxia Tsipopoulou in 1975, as representatives of the Service.

As mentioned above, we are greatly indebted to the Michalinos Coaling and Shipping Company, which owned the property at Ayia Irini, for generous permission to conduct the excavation and for ready help voluntarily given on many occasions. Mr. N. Michalos, director of the company, has shown friendly interest and understanding of the archaeological enterprise. The area of the site on the promontory, except the private chapel, was bought from the Company in 1967 for the Greek State. Excavation at Kephala was carried on by permission of the owner, K. Maroulis, without formalities. M. Dalarettos allowed us to make the brief investigation on the "troullos" above Ayia Irini.

All the work has been sponsored from the beginning by the University of Cincinnati and conducted under the auspices of the American School of Classical Studies at Athens. Our debt to the Directors and administrative officers of the University and to our colleagues in its Department of Classics is acknowledged with warm thanks. Similar thanks are extended to the Directors and other colleagues at the School.

Financial support was provided in 1960 by a grant from the Taft Memorial Fund of the University. In 1961 we had the backing of a group of generous private donors in Cincinnati, among whom should be mentioned particularly Mr. and Mrs. W. G. Kittredge and the late Lucien Wulsin. Supplementary grants were given by the American Philosophical Society and the Wenner Gren Foundation. Since 1962 the undertaking has been financed in large measure by the Classics Fund, a gift of Louise Taft Semple in memory of her father Charles Phelps Taft. Trustees of the Taft and Semple funds have given strong support to this venture. We would acknowledge also a grant provided in 1965 by the Wallace K. Harrison Architectural Foundation of New York; the scholarly contributions of advanced students holding the Olivia James Fellowship of the Archaeological Institute of America and stipends awarded by the American School and other institutions; and important collaboration by volunteers who have come to the excavations at their own expense.

Plan of Publication

Preliminary reports of the annual campaigns of excavation and several brief studies of objects found have appeared in *Hesperia* and other journals.[1] Similar papers will be published from time to time. Those of provisional character will of course be superseded by the definitive reports.

[1] These are cited in *Hesperia* 31, 1962, p. 263, note 1; 35, 1966, p. 363, note 2; 40, 1971, p. 359, note 1; 41, 1972, p. 357, note 2. Among subsequent publications are: K. A. Coleman, "Frescoes from Ayia Irini, I," *Hesperia* 42, 1973, pp. 284–300; J. L. Caskey, "The Early Bronze Age at Ayia Irini," *Bronze Age Migrations in the Aegean*, London, 1974, pp. 29–31; "Addenda to the Marble

The first of these "final" volumes is presented herewith, inaugurating the series appropriately with an account of the earliest remains uncovered in any appreciable quantity in the course of our excavations. In issuing succeeding reports we shall not insist on following a chronological order, but shall offer them as each is ready for publication.

The volumes are being written by various members of the staff, most of whom have taken active part in the digging and have personally followed the sorting, mending, and recording of the materials found. Undoubtedly it is a slow process, but continuity of involvement in the whole enterprise also brings important advantages.

Publication is to be achieved under a collaborative agreement between the University of Cincinnati and the American School, each meeting a part of the cost. Speaking for the University and my immediate colleagues, I would express warm thanks to Lucy Meritt, editor for many years of the School's publications, and to Marian McAllister, the present editor, for careful scholarly attention to all aspects of the production, and to J. J. Augustin, Inc., and the Meriden Gravure Company for the printing and engraving.

AYIA IRINI, AUGUST 1975 JOHN L. CASKEY

Figurines," *Hesperia* 43, 1974, pp. 77–79; W. W. Cummer, "Photogrammetry at Ayia Irini," *Journal of Field Archaeology* 1, 1974, pp. 385–387; annual notices in *Archaeological Reports* 18, 1972, pp. 18–19; 19, 1973, pp. 23–24; 20, 1974, pp. 28–29; "Chronique des fouilles," *B.C.H.* 96, 1972, pp. 766–768; 97, 1973, pp. 369–371; Ἐπετηρὶς τῆς Ἑταιρείας Κυκλαδικῶν Μελετῶν, 1971 (1974), pp. 694–717.

TABLE OF CONTENTS

Concordances

ABBREVIATIONS

PERIODICALS

A.J.A.	*American Journal of Archaeology*
Anat. Stud.	*Anatolian Studies*
Arch. Anz.	*Archäologischer Anzeiger* (accompanying *Jahrbuch des deutschen archäologischen Instituts*)
Ath. Ann. Arch.	*Athens Annals of Archaeology*
Ath. Mitt.	*Mitteilungen des deutschen archäologischen Instituts, athenische Abteilung*
B.C.H.	*Bulletin de correspondance hellénique*
B.S.A.	*Annual of the British School at Athens*
Δελτ.	Ἀρχαιολογικὸν Δελτίον
Ἐφ. Ἀρχ.	Ἐφημερὶς Ἀρχαιολογική
I.L.N.	*The Illustrated London News*
Πρακτικά	Πρακτικὰ τῆς ἐν Ἀθήναις Ἀρχαιολογικῆς Ἑταιρείας
Proc. Preh. Soc.	*Proceedings of the Prehistoric Society*

TERMS

av.	average
D.	diameter
est.	estimated
H.	height
L.	length
max.	maximum
pres.	preserved
rest.	restored
Th.	thickness
W.	width
Wt.	weight
EBA	Early Bronze Age
EC	Early Cycladic
EH	Early Helladic
LH	Late Helladic
LM	Late Minoan
LN	Late Neolithic
MM	Middle Minoan
MN	Middle Neolithic
NM	National Museum
cm.	centimeters
gm.	grams
km.	kilometers
m.	meters
mm.	millimeters

All dimensions in Catalogues and Appendices are metric if not otherwise specified.

GENERAL BIBLIOGRAPHY

(Specialized bibliographies follow Appendices 2–5)

Angel, J. L. (1971), *Lerna*, II, *The People*, Princeton (issued separately as *The People of Lerna, Analysis of a Prehistoric Aegean Population* by the Smithsonian Institution Press, Washington).

Atkinson, T. D. *et al.* (1904), *Excavations at Phylakopi in Melos* (Society for the Promotion of Hellenic Studies, Supplementary Paper No. 4), London.

Belmont, J. S. and Renfrew, C. (1964), "Two Prehistoric Sites on Mykonos," *A.J.A.* 68, pp. 395–400.

Benton, S. (1947), "Hagios Nikolaos near Astakos in Akarnania," *B.S.A.* 42, pp. 156–183.

Biesantz, H. (1959), "Bericht über Ausgrabungen in Thessalien 1958: II. Die Ausgrabung bei der Soufli-Magula," *Arch. Anz.* 74, pp. 56–74.

Blegen, C. W. (1928), *Zygouries, a Prehistoric Settlement in the Valley of Cleonae*, Cambridge, Mass.

— (1935), "Excavations at Troy 1934," *A.J.A.* 39, pp. 6–34.

— (1937), *Prosymna, the Helladic Settlement Preceding the Argive Heraeum*, Cambridge.

Blegen, C. W., Caskey, J. L., Rawson, M. and Sperling, J. (1950), *Troy*, I, *General Introduction, The First and Second Settlements*, Princeton.

Bossert, E.-M. (1960), "Die gestempelten Verzierungen auf frühbronzezeitlichen Gefäßen der Ägäis," *Jahrbuch des deutschen archäologischen Instituts* 75, pp. 1–16.

— (1967), "Kastri auf Syros," Δελτ. 22, Α':Μελέται, pp. 53–76.

Caskey, J. L. (1957), "Excavations at Lerna: 1956," *Hesperia* 26, pp. 142–162.

— (1958), "Excavations at Lerna, 1957," *Hesperia* 27, pp. 125–144.

— (1959), "Activities at Lerna, 1958–1959," *Hesperia* 28, pp. 202–207.

— (1962), "Excavations in Keos, 1960–1961," *Hesperia* 31, pp. 263–283.

— (1964a), "Excavations in Keos, 1963," *Hesperia* 33, pp. 314–335.

— (1964b), "Chalandriani in Syros," *Essays in Memory of Karl Lehmann*, New York, pp. 63–69.

— (1966), "Excavations in Keos, 1964–1965," *Hesperia* 35, pp. 363–376.

— (1971a), "Investigations in Keos, Part I: Excavations and Explorations, 1966–1970," *Hesperia* 40, pp. 358–396.

— (1971b), "Marble Figurines from Ayia Irini in Keos," *Hesperia* 40, pp. 113–126.

— (1972), "Investigations in Keos, Part II: A Conspectus of the Pottery," *Hesperia* 41, pp. 357–401.

Caskey, J. L. and Caskey, E. G. (1960), "The Earliest Settlements at Eutresis: Supplementary Excavations, 1958," *Hesperia* 29, pp. 126–167.

Coleman, J. E. (1967a), *Kephala in Keos*, Unpublished Ph.D. Dissertation, University of Cincinnati.

— (1967b), "Excavations at Kephala in Ceos," *A.J.A.* 71, p. 185 (abstract).

— (1974), "The Chronology and Interconnections of the Cycladic Islands in the Neolithic Period and the Early Bronze Age," *A.J.A.* 78, pp. 333–344.

Dawkins, R. M. and Droop, J. P. (1910–1911), "Excavations at Phylakopi in Melos, 1911," *B.S.A.* 17, pp. 1–22.

Delibrias, G., Guillier, M. T. and Labeyrie, J. (1974), "Gif Natural Radiocarbon Measurements VIII," *Radiocarbon* 16, pp. 15–94.

Doumas, Ch. (1961–1962), «Ἀνασκαφαὶ ἐν Νάξῳ», Δελτ. 17, Β': Χρονικά, pp. 272–274.

— (1963), «Νάξος», Δελτ. 18, Β': Χρονικά, pp. 275–281.

— (1964), «Κέρος, Νάξος», Δελτ. 19, Β': Χρονικά, pp. 409–412.

— (1968), *The N. P. Goulandris Collection of Early Cycladic Art*, Athens.

— (1973), "Grave Types and Related Burial Practices During the Cycladic Early Bronze Age," *The Explanation of Culture Change: Models in Prehistory* (ed. C. Renfrew), London, pp. 559–563.

Dümmler, F. (1886), "Mittheilungen von den griechischen Inseln," *Ath. Mitt.* 11, pp. 15–46.

Edgar, C. C. (1896–1897), "Prehistoric Tombs at Pelos," *B.S.A.* 3, pp. 35–51.

Evans, A. J. (1921), *The Palace of Minos at Knossos*, I, London.

— (1928), *The Palace of Minos at Knossos*, II, Part 1, London.

Evans, J. D. and Renfrew, C. (1968), *Excavations at Saliagos near Antiparos* (British School of Archaeology at Athens, Supplementary Volume No. 5), Oxford.
Forbes, R. J. (1950), *Metallurgy in Antiquity*, Leiden.
Furness, A. (1956), "Some Early Pottery of Samos, Kalimnos and Chios," *Proc. Preh. Soc.* 22, pp. 173–212.
Fürst, C. M. (1932), "Über einen neolithischen Schädel aus Arkadien," *Lunds Universitets Årsskrift*, N.F. Avd. 2, Bd. 28, Nr. 13, pp. 1–12.
Goldman, H. (1931), *Excavations at Eutresis in Boeotia*, Cambridge, Mass.
Hauptmann, H. and Milojčić, V. (1969), *Die Funde der frühen Dimini-Zeit aus der Arapi-Magula Thessalien* (*Beiträge zur ur- und frühgeschichtlichen Archäologie des Mittelmeer-Kulturraumes* 9), Bonn.
Heidenreich, R. *et al.* (1935–1936), "Vorgeschichtliches in der Stadt Samos," *Ath. Mitt.* 60–61, pp. 112–200.
Heurtley, W. A. (1937), *Prehistoric Macedonia*, Cambridge.
Holmberg, E. J. (1944), *The Swedish Excavations at Asea in Arcadia*, Lund.
— (1964), *The Neolithic Pottery of Mainland Greece* (*Göteborgs Kungl. Vetenskaps-och Vitterhets-Samhälles Handlingar*, Följd. 6, Ser. A, Bd. 7, Nr. 2), Göteborg.
Hood, S. (1965), "Excavations at Emporio, Chios, 1952–55," *International Congress of Prehistoric and Protohistoric Sciences*. 6th, Vol. 2, Rome, 1962, pp. 224–228.
Immerwahr, S. A. (1971), *The Athenian Agora*, XIII, *The Neolithic and Bronze Ages*, Princeton.
Jacobsen, T. W. (1969), "Excavations at Porto Cheli and Vicinity, Preliminary Report, II: The Franchthi Cave, 1967–1968," *Hesperia* 38, pp. 343–381.
— (1973), "Excavations in the Franchthi Cave, 1969–1971, Part II," *Hesperia* 42, pp. 253–283.
Koşay, H. and Sperling, J. (1936), *Troad'da dört yerleşme yeri*, Istanbul.
Krukoff, S. (1971), "Les ossements humains," Part IV in N. Lambert, "Grotte de Kitsos (Laurion)," *B.C.H.* 95, pp. 725–726.
Lamb, W. (1932), "Schliemann's Prehistoric Sites in the Troad," *Prähistorische Zeitschrift* 23, pp. 111–131.
— (1936), *Excavations at Thermi in Lesbos*, Cambridge.
Lambert, N. (1969), "Grotte de Kitsos," *B.C.H.* 93, pp. 956–966.
— (1970), "Grotte de Kitsos (Laurion)," *B.C.H.* 94, pp. 755–764.
— (1971), "Grotte de Kitsos (Laurion)," *B.C.H.* 95, pp. 703–735.
— (1972a), "Grotte de Kitsos (Laurion)," *B.C.H.* 96, pp. 817–844.
— (1972b), "Grotte d'Alépotrypa (Magne)," *B.C.H.* 96, pp. 845–871.
Lawn, B. (1971), "University of Pennsylvania Radiocarbon Dates XIV," *Radiocarbon* 13, pp. 363–377.
Lloyd, S. and Mellaart, J. (1962), *Beycesultan*, I, *The Chalcolithic and Early Bronze Age Levels*, London.
Matson, F. R. (1967), "Could Pottery Have Been Made at Kea?" *A.J.A.* 71, p. 191 (abstract).
Milojčić, V. (1959), "Ergebnisse der deutschen Ausgrabungen in Thessalien, 1953–1958," *Jahrbuch des Römisch-Germanischen Zentralmuseums Mainz* 6, pp. 1–56.
Mussche, H. *et al.* (1967), *Thorikos 1965: Rapport préliminaire sur la troisième campagne des fouilles*, Brussels.
Mylonas, G. E. (1959), *Aghios Kosmas, an Early Bronze Age Settlement and Cemetery in Attica*, Princeton.
Papathanasopoulos, G. A. (1971a), «Σπήλαια Διροῦ: Αἱ ἀνασκαφαὶ τοῦ 1970–1971», *Ath. Ann. Arch.* 4, pp. 12–26.
— (1971b), «Σπήλαια Διροῦ, 1971», *Ath. Ann. Arch.* 4, pp. 289–304.
Plassart, A. (1928), *Les Sanctuaires et les cultes du Mont Cynthe* (*Délos* XI), Paris, pp. 11–50.
Preziosi, P. G. and Weinberg, S. S. (1970), "Evidence for Painted Details in Early Cycladic Sculpture," *Antike Kunst* 13, pp. 4–12.
Psyllas, I. (1920), Ἱστορία τῆς Νήσου Κέας, Athens.
Ralph, E. K., Michael, H. N. and Han, M. C. (1973), "Radiocarbon Dates and Reality," *MASCA Newsletter* 9, No. 1, University Museum, University of Pennsylvania.
Renfrew, C. (1967), "Cycladic Metallurgy and the Aegean Early Bronze Age," *A.J.A.* 71, pp. 1–20.
— (1969), "The Development and Chronology of the Early Cycladic Figurines," *A.J.A.* 73, pp. 1–32.
— (1970), "The Tree-Ring Calibration of Radiocarbon: An Archaeological Evaluation," *Proc. Preh. Soc.* 36, pp. 280–311.
— (1971), "Sitagroi, radiocarbon and the prehistory of south-east Europe," *Antiquity* 45, pp. 275–282.
— (1972), *The Emergence of Civilisation: The Cyclades and the Aegean in the Third Millennium B.C.*, London.
Renfrew, C., Cann, J. R. and Dixon, J. E. (1965), "Obsidian in the Aegean," *B.S.A.* 60, pp. 225–247.
Sackett, L. H. *et al.* (1966), "Prehistoric Euboea: Contributions toward a Survey," *B.S.A.* 61, pp. 33–112.
Schachermeyr, F. (1955), *Die ältesten Kulturen Griechenlands*, Stuttgart.
Scholes, K. (1956), "The Cyclades in the Later Bronze Age: A Synopsis," *B.S.A.* 51, pp. 9–40.
Stuckenrath, R., Jr. and Lawn, B. (1969), "University of Pennsylvania Radiocarbon Dates XI," *Radiocarbon* 11, pp. 150–162.

Theochares, D. (1951), «'Ανασκαφὴ ἐν Παλαιᾷ Κοκκινιᾷ Πειραιῶς», Πρακτικά, pp. 93–127.
— (1953–1954), «'Ασκηταριό», 'Εφ. 'Αρχ., Part 3, pp. 59–76.
— (1956), "Nea Makri. Eine große neolithische Siedlung in der Nähe von Marathon," *Ath. Mitt.* 71, pp. 1–29.
— (1959), «'Εκ τῆς προϊστορίας τῆς Εὐβοίας καὶ τῆς Σκύρου», 'Αρχεῖον Εὐβοικῶν Μελετῶν 6, pp. 279–328.
Tsountas, Ch. (1898), «Κυκλαδικά», 'Εφ. 'Αρχ., cols. 137–212.
— (1899), «Κυκλαδικά», 'Εφ. 'Αρχ., cols. 73–134.
— (1908), «Αἱ προϊστορικαὶ ἀκροπόλεις Διμηνίου καὶ Σέσκλου», Athens.
Tylecote, R. F. (1962), *Metallurgy in Archaeology*, London.
Ucko, P. J. (1968), *Anthropomorphic Figurines of Predynastic Egypt and Neolithic Crete*, London.
Wace, A. J. B. and Thompson, M. S. (1912), *Prehistoric Thessaly*, Cambridge.
Weinberg, S. S. (1937), "Remains from Prehistoric Corinth," *Hesperia* 6, pp. 487–524.
— (1962), "Excavations at Prehistoric Elateia, 1959," *Hesperia* 31, pp. 158–209.
— (1970), "The Stone Age in the Aegean," *Cambridge Ancient History*[3], I, Part 1, pp. 557–618.
Welter, G. (1937), "Aiginetische Keramik," *Arch. Anz.*, pp. 19–26.
Wertime, T. A. (1964), "Man's First Encounters with Metallurgy," *Science* 146, No. 3649, pp. 1257–1267.
Wolters, P. (1891), "Marmorkopf aus Amorgos," *Ath. Mitt.* 16, pp. 46–58.
Zervos, Ch. (1956), *L'Art de la Crète*, Paris.
— (1957), *L'Art des Cyclades*, Paris.
— (1963), *Naissance de la civilisation en Grèce*, Paris.

LIST OF PLATES

(In the illustrations of objects the scales are in centimeters except where otherwise noted.)

LIST OF TABLES

ACKNOWLEDGMENTS

Many people have had a direct hand in the excavation and study of Kephala. For their work in the field I am particularly grateful to the excavators John L. Caskey (1960), Philip H. Auerbach and Eric G. Carlson (1961), Thomas W. Jacobsen, Colin Renfrew and John C. Overbeck (1963) and Katherine Abramovitz Coleman (1966) and to the architects Lloyd E. Cotsen and Roger L. Holzen. Mr. Holzen also prepared the final architectural drawings in this report (Pls. 1–21).

Thanks are due the following for exercising their talents in the drawing of finds in the workrooms in Keos: Aliki H. Bikaki, Stella Bouzaki, Caryl F. Kittredge, Marilyn A. Ross, Eva M. Stehle (all pottery), Karen D. Vitelli (pottery and objects of stone), Mary Webb (obsidian) and Alice Fäthke (terracotta). Barbara J. Blackwell is to be thanked for inking these drawings in the United States, Diana Wardle for the drawings reproduced as Plate 46, E–K, and Arthur Wimberly for some last-minute changes in several drawings. Professor Caskey took most of the photographs reproduced in this report.

For technical help I am grateful to the following: Reuben G. Bullard, for analysis of sherds, mineral samples, and slags; J. A. Charles, for metallurgical analyses which, although not mentioned explicitly in this report, provided welcome confirmation of metallurgy at the site; R. C. Koeppen, for the examination of a sample thought by the excavator (erroneously, as it turned out) to be wood; Thomas F. Lynch, for reading and making helpful comments on the general discussion of chipped stone tools; Frederick R. Matson for information about pottery and for conducting a firing experiment in which Kephala material was included (p. 10); Martin Oosterom for the identification of the material of **38*** and **77*** (p. 5); Elizabeth K. Ralph for the C 14 determination carried out on seeds from Area K; James D. Muhly, Theodore A. Wertime and Ronald F. Tylecote for discussion of metallurgical questions, the latter in particular for reading and making helpful comments on the metallurgical sections of this report; and C. Conophagos, Jill Carington Smith, Jane Renfrew, Jennie P. Coy and J. Lawrence Angel for contributing Appendices 1–5 respectively.

I have been much helped by discussion of the site and finds with visitors to Keos. I would particularly like to thank the following: Sara A. Immerwahr (1965), who contributed much helpful information about the Athenian Agora Neolithic; Colin Renfrew (1965), who also enlisted the aid of Martin Oosterom and J. A. Charles; Rainer Felsch, Sinclair Hood, Nicole Lambert, and Jerome Sperling (all 1969), who shared with me the results of their work at Tigani in Samos, Emborio in Chios, the Kitsos cave, and Kum Tepe respectively.

A preliminary study of the site was presented to the University of Cincinnati as a Ph.D. dissertation in 1967. I am much obliged to Elizabeth G. Caskey and Katherine Abramovitz Coleman for advice and help when the work was in its early stages.

Typescripts of the present report were read for errors by Frederick L. Williams, Norman A. Campbell, Ilene B. Sterns and Tucker Blackburn. Miss Blackburn has the author's warm gratitude for help in many other matters too numerous to list in detail; in particular her patient and critical reading of the manuscript at various stages has contributed greatly to its accuracy and clarity.

My greatest debt is to Professor Caskey, Director of the Cincinnati Excavations in Keos and General Editor of the series of which this is the first volume. It was he who began the excavations at Kephala and gave me the opportunity to take part in them. He has helped in many ways while the work was in progress, and provided advice and guidance throughout. Finally, he and the other members of the Department of Classics of the University of Cincinnati are greatly to be thanked for providing the financial resources which enabled the work to be carried to completion.

I. INTRODUCTION

DESCRIPTION OF THE SITE

The small promontory of Kephala is situated on the northwestern coast of Keos, twenty minutes' walk north of the island's main anchorage in the bay of Ayios Nikolaos (Pls. 1, 2). Exposed to the prevailing northerly and northwesterly winds, the promontory has been much eroded and is now almost devoid of vegetation and soil (except for the low, thorny scrub which clings stubbornly, if sparsely, to all but the steepest surfaces). The view from the outer ridge is spectacular: the island of Makronesos (ancient Helene), some 15 km. to the west, is almost always visible, and the hills of Attica, the tip of Euboea, and the northwestern end of Andros may often be made out. It is significant that there are at least two Late Neolithic sites roughly contemporary with Kephala within this area,[1] and it is not surprising that the main cultural affinities of the site are with Attica, Euboea and the Saronic Gulf rather than with the other Cyclades.

Geologically the promontory, like much of the island, consists of a green or gray-green schist with occasional outcrops of a gray-brown or rust-colored gossan. Layers of limestone or marble, light blue or gray, also occur less than one kilometer to the southeast. The schist is fairly soft and has been much weathered in places; it splits easily into irregularly shaped slabs.

In plan the promontory resembles the head and neck of a horse with mouth pointing towards the southwest (Pl. 3). Its maximum length on the major northeastern-southwestern axis is about 250 m. To the south there is a small bay, bordered by cliffs or steep slopes except at the isthmus of the promontory, where there is a beach of fine sand. The bay has a sandy bottom and is well sheltered from all but the southwesterly winds; it is ideal for the beaching of small ships, and may have been one of the greatest attractions of the site for its prehistoric inhabitants.

The most prominent feature of the outer part, or "head", of the promontory is a high ridge parallel to the major axis and sloping gently down towards the southwest (Pl. 47). The highest point of the ridge (about 43 m. above our datum zero at sea level) is near the northeastern end; on it is a modern cairn of stones. The southern side of the promontory, which faces the island, is steep, but with a fairly even grade, and it was extensively built upon in prehistoric times. The other sides are more forbidding: there are abrupt drops to the sea on the northern and northeastern sides where huge masses of rock have been gradually breaking away and slipping into the water; the northwestern side is also very steep and exposed, and hardly suitable for habitation.

The narrow isthmus of the promontory consists, to the east, of a spine of rock which has a maximum height of about +10 m. and, to the west, of a low sandy area bordering the bay (Pl. 48). Leading into the sandy area from the south is a narrow ravine with a stream bed which is dry for most of the year. This ravine provides the easiest approach to the site from the hills to the south. On several of the nearby hills are traces of Classical or later remains but no indication of prehistoric occupation contemporary with that of Kephala; only 2.5 km. to the east, however, is a contemporary site, Paoura, which is visible from the top of the ridge of Kephala.[2]

Three Areas dug in the southern part of the low-lying sandy area (A, B, and C; Pl. 3) were carried down to water level through a deposit almost completely devoid of ancient remains. The deposit has been produced by natural processes of erosion, and sea level has risen in relation to the land.[3] Thus we

[1] Thorikos: Mussche *et al.*, 1967, pp. 24–27; the Kitsos cave: Lambert, 1969, 1970, 1971, 1972a. Two other sites in Keos are described in Appendix 6. For further discussion of nearby sites see Chapter IV.

[2] Pls. 52, e, 53, c; see Appendix 6.

[3] This is apparent from the excavations at Ayia Irini. Remains of many buildings originally above ground have been found at depths of more than 1 m. below present sea level. The bottom of the subterranean springhouse in Area J is 3.78 m. below present sea level and it is now filled with salt water: see Caskey, 1971, pp. 365–367.

cannot be sure of the prehistoric conformation of this part of the isthmus, or whether it was built upon.

Even before excavation had begun it was evident that the prehistoric settlement at Kephala was of considerable extent. Here and there the eroded walls of houses could be made out, and pieces of obsidian, pottery, and other debris were scattered over the ridge and southern slope of the promontory. The ancient remains have suffered greatly from erosion, which is proceeding at an ever increasing rate. The terracing which must have supported most of the houses has long since washed away, spreading debris over the hillside below, and the depth of soil and debris now rarely exceeds 0.20 or 0.30 m. anywhere on the promontory. The two most rewarding areas tested were near the top of the ridge, just beneath its crown, where rock scarps were used for shelter (Areas K and L); even here the evidence for the architecture was scanty, and other nearby areas were not very productive (Areas H and J). Remains in the areas tested lower down on the slopes (Areas D, E and G) were preserved largely because they were located where the hillside formed natural terraces. Since most surviving walls in the excavated parts of the settlement were founded on bedrock, and the bedrock had also been trimmed in places to provide floors, it is safe to assume that the promontory had no great depth of soil even in antiquity.

The cemetery (Area F) was prominently situated at the base of the headland, where anyone ascending to the settlement would be bound to pass. The easiest route now, and probably also in ancient times, passes close by the westernmost graves; it is possible that Wall 6 in the Upper Cemetery (Pls. 8, 64, a) was built to delineate a path as much as to enclose part of the cemetery.

Near the northern end of the isthmus there is a modern well which, until it recently became filled with sand, provided a supply of water for grazing animals. Similar wells, scooped out of sandy beaches close by the sea, are common on the island and the water they provide is drinkable, if brackish. Since no other perennial water supply has been found at or near the site, it is probable that the ancient inhabitants used similar wells at least for those times of the year when there was no rain.

The prehistoric settlement lasted only for a hundred years or so (see pp. 44, 54). The site seems never again to have been occupied, although a few sherds found at the surface testify that it was visited occasionally (pp. 24, 43, 83). There are only a few signs of recent activity, which has evidently been restricted to the grazing of sheep and goats:[4] the cairn and the well mentioned above, a sheep shed on the isthmus, and a sheep wall, now in disrepair, across the base of the headland.[5]

One can understand why people chose to live at Kephala: the harbor is excellent, the narrow isthmus would have been easy to defend, if necessary,[6] and even the strong wind, which often hampered excavation, may have been welcomed in antiquity as a help in firing pottery and smelting copper (see Appendix 1).

HISTORY OF EXCAVATIONS AND STUDIES

The excavations at Kephala were part of a larger project of archaeological investigations on Keos which has been undertaken by an expedition from the University of Cincinnati under the general direction of Professor J. L. Caskey.[7] Work began at Kephala in 1960. On July 31 of that year Professor Caskey and two workmen excavated a jar burial (Grave II[8]) and tested another grave (I) which had been partly exposed by erosion. As a result of this preliminary operation, the need for further excavation was recognized.

[4] Andonis Maroulis of Vourkari, Keos, the present owner of the site and its environs, still uses the land occasionally for this purpose.

[5] This wall is not shown on the general plan. It extends from near the northeastern end of the bay to a point just south of Area G, passing between Area F (the cemetery) and Area D, and to the south of Area E. It is indicated at the right side of Sections a–a and b–b through Area G on Plate 6.

[6] The possibilities of defense were probably a consideration in the location of several contemporary sites near Kephala: e.g. Paoura and Sykamia on Keos (see Appendix 6) and Thorikos (Mussche *et al.*, 1967, pp. 24–27).

[7] See the Foreword. The major effort of the expedition has been the excavations at the Bronze Age site at Ayia Irini. Preliminary reports of the expedition have been published in *Hesperia*; the latest are Caskey, 1971 (where earlier reports are listed on p. 359, note 1) and 1972.

[8] In this paragraph, and those which immediately follow, the graves are referred to by the Roman numerals which were originally assigned them; see Concordance 3 which gives the Arabic numbers used in the catalogue of graves in Chapter III.

In 1961 Philip H. Auerbach and Eric G. Carlson continued work in the cemetery from July 10 to August 2 (preliminary report for 1960–1961: Caskey, 1962); they directed three to four workmen and excavated ten more graves (Graves III–XII). They also excavated Areas A, B and C in the sandy ground at the isthmus, and two parts of the settlement (Areas D and E) on the slope not far above the cemetery.

There was no work on the site in 1962. In 1963, from June 10 to July 5, the major excavation of what was to become known subsequently as the Lower Cemetery was carried out by Thomas W. Jacobsen (preliminary report: Caskey, 1964a). He was assisted by Colin Renfrew from June 10 to June 19 and by John C. Overbeck from June 24 to July 3. Two to three workmen were employed and nineteen more graves were excavated (Graves XIII–XXIX, XXXI, XXXII; XXX turned out not to be a grave, and the number was reassigned in 1966), bringing the total to thirty-one.

In 1964, from June 22 to June 30, the author conducted excavations with three to four men (preliminary report: Caskey, 1966). A new part of the cemetery was discovered which was designated the Upper Cemetery. Four graves were excavated (Graves XXXIII–XXXVI) and five new areas in the settlement were tested (Areas G, H, J, K and L).

The summer of 1965 was devoted to study of the pottery. In 1966, from June 22 to July 6, the author excavated five more graves in the Upper Cemetery (Graves XXX, XXXVII–XL), bringing the total to forty, while Katherine Abramovitz Coleman, from June 22 to June 30, conducted excavations in Area L. In December, 1966, a paper on the work to date was presented at the annual meeting of the Archaeological Institute of America (Coleman, 1967b).

In spring, 1967, a preliminary study of the site was presented as a doctoral dissertation to the Graduate School of the University of Cincinnati (Coleman, 1967a). That study, after extensive revision, formed the nucleus of the present work, which should be regarded as wholly superseding it; the most important change has been in the manner of dealing with the pottery, but there have been many lesser changes as well. In the summer of 1967, from August 21 to August 23, the author conducted a clean-up operation in Area L with one workman.

Further study of the finds took place at the expedition's workrooms near Ayia Irini during the summers of 1968 to 1971. The Greek Archaeological Service is preparing a new museum at Chora in Keos and all the finds from the Cincinnati expedition will eventually be transferred to it; at the time of writing (1975) the finds are still housed in the workrooms.

The site was referred to in print only once before the Cincinnati expedition began:[9] Scholes (1956, p. 10, note 6) mentioned in passing that after the abandonment of Kephala "its inhabitants may have been absorbed into the settlement at Ayia Irini"; she assumed, erroneously, that Kephala was an EC site.

CLASSIFICATION AND SUMMARY OF OBJECTS

In the catalogues of objects the following order of materials is observed: metal (including fragments of furnaces or crucibles and slag from metalworking activity), stone, bone, terracotta, and pottery. Catalogue numbers appear in boldface; objects which are not described in detail are listed under the appropriate headings after the catalogued objects. An asterisk after a catalogue number indicates that the object was found at or near the surface and must be regarded as unstratified; all other objects are from stratified contexts. It is the belief of the author, unless otherwise stated, that all the finds in the catalogues, both stratified and unstratified, can plausibly be assigned to the single period of prehistoric occupation.

METAL

Copper and Copper Working

All objects of copper are surface finds. Four pieces can be recognized as tools or artifacts (Pls. 22, 66): a pin (**28***), two fragments of sharp-edged tools (**82***, **147***), and a fragment with a narrow but blunt end (**83***). **147*** has been analyzed (Appendix 1, No. 7) and was found to consist of almost pure copper.

[9] I. Psyllas, a local antiquarian, did not mention it in his history of Keos (1920), although he listed many other ancient sites.

There can be no doubt that the copper objects, regardless of their provenance, are contemporary with the period of prehistoric occupation of Kephala; not only do they resemble early copper tools from elsewhere (see Chapter IV, p. 108) but, as the following discussion will show, there is evidence for the production of copper at the site.

Of exceptional interest are fragments of burnt clay from furnace-linings or crucibles (Pls. 22, 66) and pieces of slag which testify that copper was actually extracted from ore at Kephala (see Appendix 1). There are seven fragments of burnt clay (five from stratified contexts) which are certainly or probably connected with copper working (**76*, 107, 148*, 174, 175, 203, 204**); two others may possibly be connected (**15, 108**). Two of the fragments were found in the settlement (**15** in Area G, **76*** in Area L); the rest were found in the cemetery (Area F, many of the finds from which were not of funerary character; below, p. 53). Three of the burnt clay fragments have deposits of slag adhering to them, **174** (see catalogue entry), **76*** and **175** (Appendix 1, Nos. 6 and 5). The other fragments are included because they resemble those with slag deposits; like them they show signs of having been subjected to intense heat, and two were pierced in the same way as two of the fragments with slag deposits.

The burnt clay fragments are all small. The fabric resembles that of the coarser pottery; it is red towards the exterior and gray or gray black towards the interior. The outer surface is generally rough, the inner surface pitted and fused from being subjected to intense heat. The thickness of the fragments with slag deposits varies from about 0.01 to 0.02 m. not counting the deposits, which vary in thickness from about 0.002 to 0.005 m. Some of the other fragments probably connected with metalworking are thicker (for example, **148***: max. Th. 0.03 m.). The deposits are gray black or black with a rough pitted surface; small beads of oxidized copper can be seen embedded in the deposit on **175**.

The fragments are probably from the linings of furnaces in which ore was reduced, or from crucibles; the exact purpose of these cannot be determined because the fragments are very small. None is strongly curved, which suggests that the objects may have been of fairly large diameter. One fragment (**148***) preserves part of a rim which is broad and flat on top; there is a hole pierced through the side below the rim. Three other fragments have holes of about the same diameter (0.02 m.); the holes may have been for the insertion of tuyeres (i.e. nozzles of bellows, which would probably have been needed to raise the temperature sufficiently to reduce the ore).[10]

15 and **107** cannot with certainty be associated with the other burnt clay fragments; but they do not resemble in profile any of the pots from the site, and both have been subjected to intense heat.

Fragments apparently of slag from copper working have been found at various places on the hillside in surface contexts in Areas D, E, G and the cemetery. Analyses of characteristic samples are given in Appendix 1, where Professor Conophagos concludes that the slag comes from the reduction of ore rather than the simple melting of metallic copper.[11]

The source of the copper ore has not been identified. If there were sources in Keos itself, they have not yet been found. It is equally possible that ore was brought in from elsewhere; no great quantity would have been needed, to judge by the small scale of the metalworking operations (see Chapter IV, p. 108).

Surface finds from Paoura in Keos (see Appendix 6) suggest that it too may have been an early copper-working site, although the evidence is less secure than that from Kephala. A fragment of a crucible with a metallic deposit was also found in one of the earliest deposits at Ayia Irini (Caskey, 1972, p. 360, no. A 47; cf. below, p. 108).

Lead

A lead object (**84***) was found on the surface near Area D and probably dates to the time of prehistoric occupation of the promontory. It resembles one side of the clamps used in the Bronze Age for mending broken pottery. Some of the pottery from Kephala was evidently mended in antiquity, since holes bored after firing occur on either side of ancient cracks (see below, p. 10); but there is no evidence that clamps of lead were inserted in the holes.

[10] I am indebted to R. F. Tylecote for examining the Kephala material, commenting on the metallurgical processes involved, and undertaking further technical studies of the copper tools. For general information about the equipment and processes of early copper metallurgy see Forbes (1950), Tylecote (1962) and Wertime (1964).

[11] For the suggestion that some of the slag collected on the surface may not be as early as the LN period see the further note at the end of Appendix 1.

STONE

Vessels

Two complete vessels and fragments of three others were found, all of marble (Pls. 23, 67). The stones used vary in grain from fine (**16, 103**) to coarse (**47**) and in color from brilliant white (**47**) to gray white (**16**). The vessels may all have been imported from outside the island; there is no evidence for local manufacture and although marble does occur locally, its color is generally a blue gray unlike that of any of the vessels.

There are two types: a tall pointed rhyton and a simple shallow bowl; the one complete example of each shape has a pair of vertically elongated lugs, horizontally pierced, placed on the upper body of the rhyton (**103**), and at the rim of the bowl (**171**).

Celts

Six celts of polished stone were found (Pls. 24, 68), two from well-stratified contexts and the rest from excavation and exploration at the surface. Four are of stones of various shades of gray or green (**1*, 29*, 65, 66**); the other two are of a compact, black stone identified by Dr. Martin Oosterom as emery (**38*, 77***).[12] All have cutting edges which pass through or near the main axis but beyond this the forms vary considerably: all but one (**66**) are small: **1*** and **29*** are fairly long and narrow; **38*** and **77*** are broader, but both were probably considerably longer than they were wide; **65**, the most finely finished, is broad and stubby. **66**, which is considerably larger and heavier than any of the others, is also unique in form; it has a broad blade and pointed butt and belongs to Type A in the system of Tsountas (1908, cols. 307–309). None of the others may be readily classified by this system.

Flint

Six chipped stone tools of material other than obsidian were found (Pl. 68) and this material may be loosely described as flint or chert. Three are of red-brown, almost chocolate-colored stone (**48, 85*, 172**), one is white (**110**), one is honey colored, weathered white at the surface (**86***), and one is gray white, where broken, and gray brown at the surface (**111**). The tools were probably imported ready-made. None of the varieties of flint has been observed to occur naturally in Keos and no waste pieces were found. The finest of the tools (**86*, 172**) are very well made and surpass in quality most of the products of the local obsidian industry.

The flint tools may be grouped in two categories. The first comprises pointed tools, of which there are two nearly complete (**85*, 110**) and a fragment probably of a third (**111**). All are triangular in section. **85*** is pointed at the base (cf. **91***, a similar tool of obsidian); the base of **110** is probably missing. These may have been projectile points; there are no rotary marks at the tips to suggest that they were used for drilling. The second category comprises scrapers or knives with bifacial working. There are three: **86*** and **172** are more or less triangular in outline, **48** leaf-shaped. **86*** and **172** were finely finished with pressure retouch; **172** is, furthermore, finely serrated at both edges. **48** was somewhat more crudely finished, almost certainly by direct percussion.

Obsidian

Fragments of obsidian were found in large quantities everywhere on the promontory,[13] and it is obvious that the substance was worked on the spot. All the pieces found are apparently from Melos. They vary in color from milky gray to black and the surface is lustrous; most pieces are opaque, but some few are translucent and have natural dark striations. There is one piece (**51**), a fragment of an exceptionally wide blade, which is opaque and mottled red and black; obsidian of this type is also occasionally found in Melos (Renfrew, Cann and Dixon, 1965, p. 232).

The greater amount of the obsidian found was apparently waste material (Pl. 70).[14] Waste pieces vary greatly in size, but in general they are large; more than half are over 0.02 m. in length, many are

[12] The identification was made possible through the help of Colin Renfrew. I am grateful both to him and to Dr. Oosterom.

[13] See Table 1. From stratified lots a total of 2636 pieces were recorded; from unstratified lots and collecting on the surface (including all obsidian from Areas J and K), a total of 1193 pieces were recorded. One hundred eleven of the best preserved and most characteristic pieces were inventoried and are presented in detail in the catalogues.

[14] As shown in Table 1, waste comprised 85% of all obsidian recorded. Since only the best pieces were collected from the surface the true proportion of waste to tools must have been still greater.

0.03 m., and pieces over 0.05 m. in length are not unusual. Many are irregular in shape. Others resemble to a greater or lesser extent the blades and flakes classified below as tools, but show no evidence of further working or use after detachment from the core. Fragments of cores are not uncommon in the waste; sometimes they are of considerable size (**93***: Wt. 126 gm.; **94***: Wt. 225 gm.; **95***: Wt. 314 gm.). The fragments of cores suggest that they might be classified as blade cores (e.g. **95***) or flake cores (e.g. **61**), although there is no clear line of division between the two types. In general, one receives the impression from the waste that obsidian was a relatively cheap commodity. On the other hand, some tools of obsidian appear to have been valued enough to be deposited in graves (e.g. **100, 101**).

For the purposes of this discussion, tools are distinguished in general from waste pieces by the presence of retouching or of some other sign of further working or use after detachment from the core, such as notching or chipping of the edges. Chipping which had resulted from ancient use was difficult to distinguish from later damage and sometimes a fairly arbitrary decision was made. A notable characteristic of many of the tools, and some of the waste pieces as well, is the presence of large flat striking platforms. The area of these platforms is sometimes as big as the nail of the little finger, and a maximum length of 0.01 m. is not at all unusual.

The secondary working was usually not elaborate, although some flat flaking as well as steeper retouch did occur. In general, one receives the impression that the industry was crude and not highly specialized, especially as compared to that of Saliagos (Evans and Renfrew, 1968, pp. 46–61). Two pieces are considerably better than the rest in the quality and extent of retouching (**72, 90***). They may be compared to some of the finely worked pieces collected on the surface at Paoura (see Appendix 6).

The worked tools are classified, according to their function, into six categories: 1, blades (1 a, parallel sided or 1 b, irregular); 2, flake tools; 3, scrapers; 4, pointed tools; 5, used cores; 6, other used pieces. The categories are listed in order of frequency, except the last, which is a miscellaneous category.

The distribution of the various categories is indicated in Table 1;[15] it is immediately apparent that we are dealing with a blade and flake industry (40% and 32% respectively of the total number of worked pieces) and that obsidian was only rarely worked into other types of tools. There appear to be no significant differences in the distribution of the tools and waste in the various Areas and strata; the working of obsidian does not appear to have been a centralized activity.

TABLE 1. DISTRIBUTION OF OBSIDIAN BY CATEGORIES

Provenance		1 a	1 b	2	3	4	5	6	Waste	% Waste	Total
B		1	0	0	0	0	0	0	0	0%	1
C		1	0	0	0	0	0	0	0	0%	1
D	Stratified	0	7	2	0	0	0	12	66	76%	87
	Unstratified	5	2	10	0	0	0	11	71	72%	99
E	Stratified	2	0	1	0	0	0	0	28	90%	31
	Unstratified	1	0	2	0	0	0	1	13	76%	17
G	Stratified	14	1	21	0	0	3	8	403	90%	450
	Unstratified	5	1	4	0	0	1	1	66	85%	78
H	Stratified	0	0	4	0	0	0	1	21	81%	26
	Unstratified	2	0	2	0	0	0	3	10	59%	17
J		0	0	1	0	0	0	0	6	86%	7
K		1	0	14	0	0	0	2	55	76%	72
L	House Y	18	13	28	0	0	0	20	452	85%	531
	House Z	19	14	17	1	1	0	18	452	87%	522
	Unstratified	6	7	18	0	0	0	12	558	93%	601
F	Lower: Central	32	7	11	2	0	0	10	290	82%	352
	Lower: Eastern	5	1	1	0	0	0	0	16	70%	23
	Lower: Unstratified	17	1	18	3	2	0	11	168	76%	220

[15] The figures for the cemetery (Area F) include obsidian found within as well as around the graves. As already mentioned, one blade and perhaps another were deliberately deposited in graves; the other pieces found in graves were probably all intrusive, having found their way in with the earth and pebbles which filled the graves in the course of time.

	Provenance	1 a	1 b	2	3	4	5	6	Waste	% Waste	Total
F	Upper: Early Deposit	0	0	0	0	0	0	0	1	100%	1
	Upper: Western	20	8	21	1	0	1	15	360	85%	426
	Upper: Eastern	6	2	5	1	0	0	8	163	88%	185
	Upper: Unstratified	6	2	0	1	0	0	6	58	79%	73
Surface		1	0	0	2	2	0	0	4	44%	9
Totals		162	66	180	11	5	5	139	3261	85%	3829

1. BLADES

a) *Parallel sided* (Pls. 25, 69). This is the more common type of blade. One hundred sixty-two pieces were recorded, of which 26 were inventoried. The sides are nearly parallel, although they may converge slightly, usually towards the distal end. Where the proximal end is preserved, a flat striking platform is usually apparent. In section they vary from triangular to trapezoidal, sometimes on the same blade. The width varies from 0.025 **(51)** to 0.008 m. **(52)**, wider ones being more common. Only a few are preserved to nearly their original length (shortest, **141**: 0.053 m.; longest, **117**: 0.076 m.). Many of the narrower ones may have been shorter than **141** and some others may have been longer than **117** (e.g. **112**: L. pres. 0.07 m., both ends missing). So far as could be determined, short pieces of broken blades were not used in antiquity.

At least nine parallel-sided blades had been retouched to some extent to serve as side or end scrapers (e.g. **116**: one side; **67**: both sides; **100**: both sides and end); most of these were more or less pointed at one end (**117** very markedly). Chipping was also noted on one or both sides of many pieces.

b) *Irregular* (Pls. 25, 69). Sixty-six pieces were recorded, of which 14 were inventoried. Many were oval in outline and relatively broad in comparison with their length, and these are either triangular or trapezoidal in section. A few others become wider at one end. All the pieces included here are relatively thin; thicker tools of oval outline were classified as scrapers (category 3).

At least four had been retouched to some extent to serve as side scrapers (e.g. **179**: one side; **121**: both sides). Many pieces were chipped along the edges.

2. FLAKE TOOLS (Pls. 25, 69)

This category comprises pieces with a length less than twice their width. One hundred eighty pieces were recorded, of which 29 were inventoried. They are generally oval or oblong in outline and fairly thin. Most are small and crude and might be considered used waste, although we cannot know how they were regarded by their users. Six are larger and more carefully fashioned **(13, 19, 56, 122, 143, 182)**; two of these have secondary working at the edges **(19, 143)** and another **(56)** has a crudely serrated edge.

All the flake tools probably served for some kind of scraping, with the exception of **56**, which may have been for sawing.

3. SCRAPERS (Pls. 25, 70)

This category comprises pieces which are longer than twice their width but which cannot be readily classified as blades because they are too short and thick. Eleven were recorded, all of which were inventoried. They vary in length from 0.036 **(71)** to 0.076 m. **(155*)**. Six are more or less pointed at one end and five are more or less rounded at both ends. All have considerable retouching around their periphery.

4. POINTED TOOLS (Pls. 25, 70)

There are five pieces, all of different appearance; the category is thus a catch-all. One, probably originally tanged, is likely to have been a true projectile point **(72)**. The others are: **157***, a narrow tool (borer or awl?); **91***, a tool pointed on both ends resembling the flint tool **85***; **158***, a flat piece with a notched base; and **90***, a fragment with bifacial retouching (knife?).

5. USED CORES (Pls. 25, 70)

Three fragments of cores **(20, 30***, and one uninventoried) have chipping on their edges, which suggests that they were used for rubbing or grinding. Two other pieces, apparently from the ends of cores, had been fashioned into disk-like artifacts **(21, 186)**.

6. OTHER WORKED PIECES (Pl. 70)

This category comprises pieces which cannot be placed in the above categories; most are too fragmentary, but there are a few slightly worked pieces which are unusual in form. One hundred thirty-nine pieces were recorded, of which nine were inventoried.

OTHER STONE OBJECTS

The only other stone objects (Pls. 22, 68) are a bead of green stone (**191**), a small disk of schist (**23**), a piece of schist with grooves cut in it (**192**), a small stone with worn edges which had been used perhaps for rubbing (**96A***), two larger stones used probably as grinders (**8, 14**), and a piece of chalky mineral (**126**).

BONE

Only five pieces of worked bone were found (Pl. 71); in each case the artifact is fragmentary. One (**193**), the only piece which has part of a finished end preserved, was evidently a chisel or gouge. Two other fragments (**208, 209**) may be from similar chisels (or points?). **194** is a fragment of a rib with grooves on it and **195** is a fragment of a tibia with similar grooves; in both cases the grooves may have been for decoration.

TERRACOTTA

FIGURINES

There are fragments of eight (Pls. 26, 71–73). All but one (**96B***) were found in the cemetery, where they may have been used in funerary ceremonies; none was clearly associated with a skeleton in a grave, and they may originally have been thrown into grave pits after the graves were closed or placed on platforms such as were found above some of the graves (below, pp. 45–47, 52–53). All were made of coarse clay similar to that of the pottery and they were also fired in a similar way. There are no traces of any substance applied to their surfaces. They may be grouped into three types, which will be briefly described in order of frequency of occurrence.

The first type comprises small, crudely modeled, female figurines, of which four were found (**127, 196, 197, 198**). Precise interpretation of the pose is difficult, since all are fragmentary. They evidently had both arms outstretched (except possibly **127**, which may have had only one arm outstretched) and they should probably be thought of as standing or lying since there is no indication that the legs were bent. **127**, which is apparently nearly complete at the bottom, seems to have terminated a short distance below the torso, but even here there is no indication of a seated posture. The legs were evidently not distinguished from one another and the sex is made clear only by the presence of small pellet-like breasts. **196** and **198** are somewhat flattened from front to back; **198** is also curved as if the arms were flung back.

The second type comprises heads. Two are small and very similar to one another (**128, 202**). The neck is round in section and the face is a flattened, roughly triangular surface sloping backward from the neck. At the top of the face there is a projecting knob to represent a nose, and at the back a corresponding knob. **128** has holes at the upper corners. The necks spread slightly at the bottom and the undersurface is uneven; the heads cannot easily be made to rest on a flat surface. Presumably they were originally attached to bodies which had been made separately. Bodies similar to those of the first type of figurine might be suitable for these small heads, but the necks of the surviving heads are larger than those of all but one of the surviving bodies. It is also possible that the bodies were of material other than terracotta.

A third head (**96B***), a surface find in the settlement, is similar in general to the others; it is unusual, however, for its large size and the use of supports, probably of wood, in its construction.

There is only one figurine of the third type, **160***, an ithyphallic male. The body terminates at the bottom in a manner probably similar to that of **127**, but the featureless head is very different from those of the second type.

Other Terracotta Objects

The only other objects of terracotta (Pls. 26, 71) are a fragment of a spoon-like object (**168**), a spindle whorl or button (**145**), a fragment possibly of a loomweight (**129**), two small crude objects like knuckle bones (**26, 81***; perhaps struts from the handles of pots?) and sixteen worn sherds of various shapes which were used as rubbing-tools. Most of the last are easily recognizable as fragments of pottery; two still have lugs attached to them (**130, 161***), one is a fragment of a base (**162***), and one was originally part of a bowl with pattern burnishing inside (**24**). One of the rubbing-tools has a bored hole in it (**32***).

POTTERY

The pottery was in general very poorly preserved, in part because it was not well fired and in part because of the corrosive effects of weathering and, probably, of the soil itself. From the whole site it was possible to inventory only fourteen vessels with full profile preserved; the remaining twenty-eight items in the pottery inventory are either large fragments of pots or sherds of special interest such as those with cloth impressions.

Fabric and Technique

The fabric is remarkably uniform and all the pottery was certainly made locally. Professor F. R. Matson has demonstrated the feasibility of making pottery from the local clay beds of Keos (Matson, 1967). Furthermore, most of the mineral inclusions are obviously weathered bits of the local bedrock of green-to-gray schist. Not a single sherd was found which is definitely or even probably from an imported pot.

All the pottery may be described as coarse, although the degree of coarseness has a certain range. Some of the smaller, thinner-walled vessels might be regarded as semi-coarse, but many of the smaller vessels are as coarse as any of the pottery. The primary descriptive categories are therefore based on shape rather than on fabric.

The clay is rich in iron, very micaceous, and tempered with pieces of schist and quartz. The size of the inclusions is not uniform; they are generally small, but a sherd of a medium degree of coarseness may have several inclusions with a length of 0.002 to 0.003 m. and the coarsest sherds have inclusions with a length of 0.005 to 0.008 m. or more. Vegetable material seems never to have been added deliberately as tempering although it may sometimes have been present in the clay; at least one seed impression was noted, and a few sherds (e.g. Pl. 91, H) have pockmarked surfaces which suggest that a combustible and perhaps organic material may have burned out during the firing.

The preparation of the clay was evidently rudimentary, although it must have been washed to some extent to produce the fabric of the less coarse vessels. The fired pottery is gritty to the touch and not very hard; the surfaces of all but the most well burnished sherds tend to disintegrate, and sherds dropped on a hard surface make a dull thud rather than a ringing sound. Most sherds of any size may be broken in the hands. The surface color of the fired pottery is usually red to red brown; the cores are sometimes roughly the same color as the exterior and sometimes gray or black. Sometimes one surface is red and the other gray or black, often with a clear line of demarcation in the core between the two colors. Often the surface of a vessel, while generally red in color, is mottled or streaked with gray or black. A few sherds, usually from small vessels, are altogether gray or black; no complete example is preserved and it is uncertain whether the color was deliberate or whether it was the result of accidental firing under reducing conditions. The dark-colored sherds are generally of good quality in fabric and burnish.

The only notable variations in fabric are a few red-to-purple sherds which feel slippery to the touch (e.g. Pl. 32, F = Pl. 77, AS) and a few sherds of a soft, tan fabric, sometimes gray at the core (e.g. Pl. 28, N = Pl. 75, Q).

The potter's wheel was not in use at Kephala. Some large vessels were made in broad horizontal rings (e.g. p. 24), the edges of which were sometimes beveled or roughened. The flat bottoms of large vessels were often made separately as disks to which the walls of the pot were then joined (e.g. Pl. 85, BK, BL). Ring bases, too, were often made separately. Impressions of woven mats are occasionally found on the bottoms of pots (see Appendix 2); either the mats were used to turn them while they were being fashioned or the finished but unfired pots were stored or transported on mats. One base with a leaf impression was also found (Pl. 90, K). Unlike some of those from Saliagos (Evans and Renfrew, 1967, pp. 71–72) all the mat impressions found were evidently on exposed surfaces.

In three instances, impressions of finely woven fabric were observed within the walls of a pot parallel to its surface (**167*, 201, 213***; for the nature of the cloth see Appendix 2). The fabric had evidently been used as a modeling aid for the wet clay and had then been concealed by a final layer of clay which was smoothed over it. This use of cloth, which has not been recognized at any other site, may have been more frequent at Kephala than was observed, since it is only recognizable when the surface layer of clay breaks off. Perhaps it will some day be recognized at other sites; it may, however, have been a local peculiarity.

Handles and lugs were usually applied to the surface of the vessel; occasionally handles were attached with plugs thrust through the pot wall (e.g. Pl. 38, C = Pl. 84, BD).

The finishing process was generally not elaborate. The surfaces of many vessels, even small ones, appear to have been merely smoothed in a cursory manner. Scoring, which was evidently part of the process of manufacture rather than a decorative technique, is frequently observed on one or both surfaces of large vessels or on the inside of small vessels (Pl. 91, E–G, J). It was produced when the surface was wiped or rubbed while still in a soft state, and it consists of groups of marks roughly parallel to one another. Usually, although by no means invariably, the scoring runs horizontally; sometimes groups of marks meet at various angles; sometimes only a part of the surface is scored (e.g. Pl. 81, A). Generally surfaces with scoring were not burnished, or, if scored, the marks were practically obliterated by the burnishing. Occasionally a pot was scored after burnishing, perhaps when a slight irregularity in shape was noticed by the potter after the pot was nearly finished. Burnishing, if carried out at all, was the last step in the finishing process. It occurs on the outside of closed vessels and on both surfaces of bowls. A small blunt tool was used, perhaps a pebble or sherd (see above, p. 9, for worn sherds used as rubbing-tools). The burnished surface usually has a low rather than a high sheen. The burnishing is usually fairly regular; sometimes individual strokes of the burnishing tool make a scribble of small lines on the surface, but this does not seem to be a deliberate effect. For a discussion of pattern burnishing, which is fairly common, see below, pp. 11–12. There is no reason to suppose that a slip was ever applied before burnishing.

Occasionally small holes were bored through the walls of pots after firing, apparently for mending cracks. That this was the purpose of the holes is clear in **170** where they occur on either side of an ancient crack, and **136**, where three holes occur in close proximity to one another. Whatever was threaded through the holes (leather thongs?) has not survived. In the Bronze Age clamps of lead were often used for mending but there is no evidence that they were used at Kephala (unless **84*** is part of a clamp: see below, p. 42).

No significant differences were recognized between the pottery found in the settlement and that found in the cemetery, either in shape or in decoration; pottery from all parts of the site is therefore discussed together in the following general description.

Quantities of pottery are estimated in the catalogues in tinfuls; the tins measure *ca.* 0.23 × 0.23 × 0.35 m. and contain five American gallons (four Imperial gallons).

Decoration

Crusted

The potters of Kephala seem never to have used a true paint in the sense of a substance applied before firing. Nevertheless red and white coloring materials apparently similar to those of the crusted wares of Thessaly[16] were sometimes applied after firing. It is certain that the red material, at least, would not have stood up to firing; a fragment from a bowl (**138**) which has crusted red over its entire inside surface was placed in a small kiln during experiments conducted by Frederick R. Matson (1967). Even at the

[16] I.e. Γ1γ, Γ1δ: Tsountas, 1908, cols. 244–249; Wace and Thompson, 1912, pp. 17–18.

low firing temperature obtained in the kiln, the crusted red turned a powdery white. A sample of red coloring material was examined by Reuben G. Bullard, Department of Geology, University of Cincinnati, and found to consist primarily of hematite (see below, p. 28).

Crusted red occurs more frequently than white. It varies from bright red to red orange, and often has a granular appearance. In some instances it was applied liberally up to 0.001 m. thick and has often partially flaked or rubbed off. In other instances it was apparently much more thinly applied and appears as a mere wash through which the coarse surface of the pot is clearly visible; the thinness may sometimes be due, however, to the generally worn condition of the pottery.

Crusted red occurs on both small and large vessels. Since it is rarely well preserved, little can be said about its use as a decorative element except that broad surfaces of pots were often covered. There is no definite instance in which it was applied in a pattern but, since it is often observed on and around handles, at rims, and on pedestals, there may have been some conventions for its use which cannot now be recognized. Crusted red and pattern burnishing sometimes occur on the same vessel (see below, p. 28).

Crusted white decoration has survived on only a few vessels; it was apparently used much less often than red. One bowl (**62**) from House Y in Area L seems to have been completely coated on the outside, and there is a fragment of another vessel from the same house (below, p. 37) on which white also occurs independently. In two other instances (**106, 138**) the white substance was covered over with red, but only scanty traces of the decoration have survived. A sample of white coloring material from **62** was examined by Bullard and found to consist of magnesium carbonate, applied after firing (see below, p. 37).

PATTERN BURNISHED (Frontispiece; Pls. 40–43, 86–88)

The common occurrence of this distinctive decorative technique is one of the most striking characteristics of the pottery from Kephala. It occurs (in descending order of frequency) on the inside of shallow bowls, on the outside of steeper-sided bowls (both category A 2), on the outside of large jars (B 2) and on the outside of small jars (category B 1). Very rarely it is found on both sides of bowls (e.g. Pl. 42, F = Pl. 87, H; Pl. 42, G = Pl. 87, G). The process was like that recognized and most fully described at Tigani in Samos (Heidenreich, 1936). The surface of the leather-hard vessel was smoothed, but without pressure; those parts of the design which were to be darker in color were then rubbed with the burnishing tool. Many strokes were probably necessary to produce even narrow lines. When the vessel was fired, a marked contrast in appearance was produced between the lighter-colored, duller red surfaces of the unburnished areas and the darker-colored, more shiny surfaces of the burnished areas. The patterns were generally executed with considerable care, and smudging or blurring is rare; in a few instances, however, the decoration on large vessels is rather careless (e.g. **105**) and the burnished lines so closely spaced that they are difficult for the eye to distinguish.

Pattern burnishing was apparently used as an overall decoration and no instance has been recognized where it is restricted to a zone or panel; its boundaries are those imposed by the pot itself, i.e. the neck, rim, foot or handles. The basic units of the pattern are usually groups of three or more parallel lines, and these units are juxtaposed, often at oblique angles. Where groups of parallel lines meet, they sometimes cross over one another to some extent, but normally they form discrete units of pattern. Sometimes a triangular area is burnished at the juncture of two lines from different groups (e.g. Frontispiece H = Pl. 41, L = Pl. 86, P). Occasionally the space between two roughly parallel lines is hatched or crosshatched (e.g. Frontispiece J = Pl. 41, G = Pl. 86, S; **164***). In at least three instances, motifs of a more complex type were introduced into the decoration: Frontispiece N (= Pl. 42, E = Pl. 86, AO) has a meandroid pattern; Frontispiece M (= Pl. 42, A = Pl. 86, AN) has interlocking hooks; and Plate 41, B (= Pl. 86, AA) preserves part of a curving line or area.[17]

[17] The possibility has been considered, and rejected, that the more complex motifs, as well as some of the other decoration described as pattern burnished, were originally executed in white paint which has completely disappeared, leaving the darker lines as "ghosts" where it had been. A fugitive matt white paint was used on Late Neolithic red burnished pottery found in excavations near the Athenian Agora (Immerwahr, 1971, pp. 4–9, 11); since the surface which had originally carried white paint was dulled and sometimes even gouged out, however, an opposite impression to that of pattern burnishing has been created. Furthermore, if a paint had been used at Kephala which protected the burnished surface beneath it, it surely would have survived in a few instances. Crusted red and white were not observed to have left "ghosts" of their former presence where they had partially disappeared.

A few general observations may be made about the syntax of the decoration. It seems often to have been applied in a random way, without regard to symmetry either within itself or in relation to the axis of the pot. Occasionally the axis may have been emphasized by a predominance of vertical or nearly vertical lines (e.g. **75, 105**). Some vessels (e.g. Pl. 42, D = Pl. 86, R) may have had a nearly symmetrical arrangement of lines within a rectangular framework. Except in a very few instances (e.g. Pl. 41, C = Pl. 86, Z) there is no deliberate contrast between broader and narrower lines.

Only one vessel, **164***, is sufficiently complete to warrant a possible reconstruction of the overall decoration (Pl. 42).

INCISED AND GROOVED

Decoration of this kind is most commonly restricted to a horizontal band on the outside of the rims of bowls and large, fairly open jars (e.g. Pl. 44, A–H; Pl. 88, A–AL); it never occurs on the inside of a rim. The rims were often thickened on the outside by the addition of a plastic strip. The decorated band varies from about 0.015 m. to 0.04 m. in width. The predominant pattern is a continuous series of multiple chevrons, usually executed with a fairly pointed instrument and sometimes set off by shorter lines or punctations in the triangular spaces (e.g. Pl. 88, P, R, S, W). The incised band is sometimes interrupted by vertical plastic bands (e.g. Pl. 44, B = Pl. 88, A; Pl. 88, Q). Most of the bowls with incised rims could be classified under category A 2 (see below, p. 14) but for convenience they are all grouped together in the catalogues under the heading "A 1 and A 2: Incised Rims." Large, fairly open jars with incised rims fall into category B 2.

Incised bands are also found occasionally on the outside of offset necks or collar-necks of jars, both large (e.g. Pl. 46, D = Pl. 80, A) and small (e.g. Pl. 32, F = Pl. 77, AS; Pl. 32, G = Pl. 77, AR; Pl. 32, M=Pl. 77, AQ).

Incision and grooving also occur on the bodies of vessels small and large, of which most, if not all, are probably jars (e.g. small jars: Pl. 32, A = Pl. 77, AA; Pl. 77, AU). Sometimes the decoration is confined to a narrow, horizontal band, either on the surface of the vessel (e.g. Pl. 88, AQ) or on a plastic strip (e.g. Pl. 44, M = Pl. 89, S). More often the decoration is more extensive (e.g. Pl. 44, J = Pl. 88, AN; Pl. 44, K = Pl. 88, AO; Pl. 44, L = Pl. 88, AR). The patterns are generally rectilinear, but there are at least eight examples of curvilinear elements: Plate 44, J (= Pl. 88, AN; curving lines); Plate 44, L (= Pl. 88, AR; complex pattern); Plate 44, M (= Pl. 89, S; hook); Plate 44, N (= Pl. 89, L; hook or circle); Plate 88, AS (spiral?); Plate 89, X–Z (curving lines). A few other fragments of bodies or rims with slightly curving lines may also have had curvilinear motifs (e.g. Pl. 88, U, Z, AT).

Incised decoration also occurs frequently on the handles and struts of scoops, which are described in detail below, pp. 16–17. There is at least one instance of a curvilinear motif (Pl. 36, F = Pl. 83, AG); meandroid motifs occur on **98**, which has the most complex decoration of any vessel surviving from Kephala.

Incision is also found occasionally on handles (e.g. Pl. 84, AO, AP), and once on the inside of a vessel (Pl. 39, V = Pl. 89, AD).

In one instance incised decoration was evidently filled with a white substance (see below, p. 38).

PLASTIC

The most frequent type of plastic decoration is formed of raised bands, impressed at more or less regular intervals. Such bands decorated many of the large vessels and some of the small ones. That they were thought of, at least in some instances, as imitating rope is clear from **146** and **170**, where they are arranged as if the vessels were trussed for lifting, and they often occur on other pots near the handles. The impressions were usually made with a finger, and occasionally the mark of the nail shows clearly. Plate 89, BC–BP give an idea of the range of size and type of impressed bands. There is one instance (Pl. 89, BL) of a broad band with two parallel rows of impressions. In at least three examples (**11***, Pl. 89, BJ, BK) raised bands were decorated with incised diagonal lines, another way of simulating rope.

Bands or strips without further embellishment also occur, although less frequently than those with impressions, often in connection with handles (e.g. on **74, 134**) or lugs (e.g. Pl. 84, BO–BR, BT, BU). In two instances there are two plastic strips which curve away from each other (Pl. 46, B = Pl. 89, AS;

Pl. 89, AT), and in one instance there seems a deliberate contrast between a higher, more prominent strip and a lower strip (Pl. 89, AW). One sherd (Pl. 89, AV) has a unique arrangement of short strips in an interlocking pattern which may, like the impressed bands, also have been inspired by rope.

Knobs and disks were occasionally applied to pot walls (Pl. 89, AF–AP); sometimes these have depressed centers (e.g. Pl. 89, AL–AP). Knobs were also used to decorate handles (see below, p. 18). It is not clear whether Plate 89, AX, which has a vague and perhaps fortuitous resemblance to the terracotta-figurine heads, was originally connected to a handle or lug.

Shapes

The pottery has been grouped by shapes into four main divisions: bowls (A), jars (B), miscellaneous (C), and other sherds.[18] The first three divisions are subdivided into categories (designated by Arabic numerals). These categories do not comprise distinct "types" except in a few cases (e.g. C 1, scoops), but rather include a considerable range, partly because the shapes show great variety and individuality, and partly because of the special difficulties of sorting and description posed by the very fragmentary state of the pottery. Furthermore, one shape often ranges continuously into another so that, for example, bowls of category A 1 are often difficult to distinguish from those of category A 2, or even from small jars which are fairly open. In such cases an arbitrary dividing line was chosen.[19]

A 1: Bowls with upright sides (Pls. 27, 74, 75)

The defining characteristic of this category is that the diameter of the rim is roughly equal to that of the bottom. There are four examples in which the profile is preserved from rim to bottom (**62, 99, 138** and Pl. 27, E), and fragments from the rims of at least twenty others; this category is much less common than A 2. The sides of some vessels (e.g. **99**) converge somewhat towards the rim and these resemble to some extent the hole-mouthed jars in B 1 (e.g. Pl. 31, A–C). The rims are all plain. The four vessels which are preserved from rim to base all have flat bottoms: three have a rounded transition from the side of the pot to the bottom, while the fourth (**62**) has an angular transition. Lugs were evidently placed on the upper part of the body, either outside (e.g. **99**) or inside (**62**). Crusted red occurs on the inside (e.g. **99, 138**) and crusted red and white on the outside (**62, 138**). Some of the rims decorated on the outside with incision may have been from bowls of this category (e.g. Pl. 44, C = Pl. 88, W; Pl. 44, E = Pl. 88, P; Pl. 44, D); for convenience, however, they are grouped in the catalogues under "A 1 and A 2: Incised Rims." One fragment has a curving plastic strip (Pl. 27, D = Pl. 75, H).

A 2: Bowls with spreading sides (Pls. 27–30, 38, 74–76)

This category, which is the most frequent and has a great range, comprises bowls which are distinctly broader at the rim than at the bottom, whether conical, rounded or angular. They may have flat bottoms, ring feet or pedestals. Those with the first two types of bases, and fragments which yielded no information about the base, are grouped together in the catalogues under the general heading A 2; those with pedestals are described separately under the heading "A 2: With Pedestals."

There are fragments of several hundred, including six fairly complete examples (i.e. in which the profile is preserved from rim to base).

Many fragments are from simple conical or rounded bowls, among them being four of the fairly complete examples (**27, 34***, Pl. 27, F, G), which all have flat bottoms. Probably some of the fragments of small raised bases and ring feet (listed in the catalogues under Other Sherds) come from similar bowls. Rounded bodies also sometimes have pedestals (e.g. **165***). The type represented by **104**, a shallow vessel with a high ring foot, is more rare, although there is a probable example from the settlement (Area L, below, p. 37) as well as those from the cemetery.

[18] The present system of classification, which was drawn up after a re-examination of all the pottery in the summers of 1969 through 1971, completely supersedes that used in Coleman, 1967a.

[19] Pedestaled bowls posed a special problem: although fragments from the juncture of bowl and pedestal or, in some cases, from the pedestal alone could be recognized as belonging to pedestaled bowls, it was impossible to distinguish rim fragments from those of other similar bowls. It was therefore decided to make those pieces which could be definitely recognized as pedestaled bowls a sub-group of the category (A 2) in which the upper bodies would be classified in the absence of evidence for a pedestal.

Angular vessels (whose profile is bent, but seldom sharply) tend to be fairly shallow, with their angle near the rim (e.g. Pl. 29, B–K). A lug is often placed at or just below the angle. **164***, a fairly deep vessel with a pedestal, is the only piece recognized as having an angle well below the rim, but there were undoubtedly others which were not recognized because of the fragmentary state of the material.

The other pedestaled shapes are either rounded (e.g. **165***), conical (e.g. Pl. 30, A = Pl. 75, AZ), or with slightly flaring rim (e.g. Pl. 30, B = Pl. 75, AY). The pedestals are all roughly conical and relatively low in comparison with many of the "fruitstands" found at other Neolithic sites. Several fragments from pedestals have angular cutouts (e.g. Pl. 30, E = Pl. 75, AV; Pl. 75, BS, BU, BV); these were probably decorations, rather than air vents to facilitate placing the vessel over a fire, since none of the fragments from pedestals are blackened by fire, and some (e.g. **165***) have traces of crusted red which would not have stood up well under the effects of heat.

The rims of nearly all the vessels in this category are plain (except those which are thickened toward the outside and incised: see above, p. 13). Some rims bulge slightly (e.g. Pl. 30, B = Pl. 75, AY), while some have a tab (e.g. **104**; Pl. 29, P = Pl. 75, AX) or notch (Pl. 28, C = Pl. 75, AU) above a lug. One may have had a wavy upper edge (Pl. 29, N = Pl. 75, AP). Another rim, probably from a bowl belonging in this category, is indented at the top at regular intervals (Pl. 75, AO). There is one example with a tubular spout, probably for the feeding of an infant (Pl. 28, G = Pl. 75, AS).

Horizontally pierced lugs or lug handles frequently occur, generally well below the rim. Other types of lugs and lug handles are much more rare: occasional unpierced horizontal lugs (e.g. Pl. 28, F = Pl. 75, Z); very rare vertically pierced lugs (e.g. Pl. 29, K = Pl. 75, AB); one vertical lug handle having its upper end attached to the rim (Pl. 29, E = Pl. 75, AR); and three examples with one horizontally pierced lug or lug handle at the rim and a second beneath it (Pl. 28, A = Pl. 75, AC; Pl. 75, AD; below, p. 29). High-swung handles or tab handles occur in at least five instances. These are of various types: plain, flattened loop handles (e.g. Pl. 38, L = Pl. 85, AK; Pl. 38, M = Pl. 85, AL); broader loop handles with internal struts (e.g. Pl. 38, N = Pl. 85, AN); solid, finger-like projections pierced one or more times parallel to the rim (e.g. Pl. 38, O = Pl. 85, AQ); and tab handles, i.e. more or less rectangular projections pierced parallel or perpendicular to the rim (e.g. Pl. 38, P = Pl. 85, AT). Some of the high-swung handles have knobs at the apex (e.g. Pl. 38, N = Pl. 85, AN).

Crusted red occurs on the inside of many bowls and on the outside of several pedestals. Sometimes bowls with crusted red inside have pattern burnishing on the outside.

Pattern burnishing occurs on the outside of bowls with fairly steep sides, generally rounded or conical (e.g. Pl. 40; Pl. 86, A–N; Pl. 87, A–F). The profiles vary considerably. The full profile of one vessel with a flat bottom has been tentatively reconstructed (Pl. 40, G = Pl. 86, F, L) and there are fragments from the flat bottoms of two others with pattern burnishing outside (Pl. 40, H = Pl. 86, M; Pl. 40, J = Pl. 86, N). **164***, which has an angular body and is supported by a pedestal, also has pattern burnishing outside; it is the only example recognized of a pedestaled shape with pattern-burnished decoration.

Bowls with pattern burnishing inside are about twice as common as those decorated outside. They are generally fairly shallow (e.g. Pl. 41; Pl. 42, A–E; Pl. 86, O–AT) and often have an angle near the rim. There are fragments from the flat bottoms of at least five (e.g. Pl. 42, B = Pl. 86, AQ; Pl. 42, C = Pl. 86, AR; Pl. 42, E = Pl. 86, AO). No other type of base was recognized as belonging to bowls with pattern burnishing inside.

Pattern burnishing occurs on both surfaces of two fragments (Pl. 42, F = Pl. 87, H; Pl. 42, G = Pl. 87, G).

Incised and grooved decoration occur almost exclusively in horizontal bands on the outside of rims which are sometimes thickened; see the general discussion of incised and grooved decoration above, p. 12. Most of the bowls with incised rims can be classified in category A 2; since no profiles are preserved from rim to base, however, they are all grouped together under the heading "A 1 and A 2: Incised Rims." The only certain bowls with incised decoration elsewhere on the body than at the rim are three with angular profile, which have two rows of punctations at the angle (e.g. Pl. 75, AN), and a fragment with curving lines, probably from a bowl of this category (Pl. 88, U). It is possible, however, that some of the body sherds of small vessels with incised decoration, described in the catalogues under Other Sherds, are from bowls of category A 2.

Pedestals are sometimes decorated with incision or grooving. Horizontal lines are common (e.g. Pl. 30, C = Pl. 75, BJ; Pl. 75, BW, BX), sometimes together with punctations (e.g. Pl. 30, D = Pl. 75, BA) or angular cutouts (e.g. Pl. 75, BS, BU, BV). Vertical lines also occur, either singly (e.g. Pl. 75, BK) or in pairs (Pl. 75, BL). Plate 75, BT has deep angular punctations, which are very similar to those on a scoop strut (Pl. 36, C = Pl. 83, AD). The most elaborate examples of decoration are on Plate 30, F (= Pl. 75, AT) which has a vertical line and parallel diagonal lines, and on Plate 75, BQ (if it is from a pedestal) which has a crisscross design.

Applied vertical plastic strips sometimes occur on bowls of this category (e.g. Pl. 75, AH).

B 1: SMALL JARS (Pls. 31, 32, 76, 77)

This category comprises all small closed vessels, of which there are three recognizable types: hole-mouthed jars, jars with up-turned or everted lip, and jars with a distinct neck. In addition there are a few other fragments not readily classifiable.

Since none of the hole-mouthed jars is even fairly complete, the shape can be recognized only from fragments of rims (e.g. Pl. 31, A–M; Pl. 77, A–R). So far as can be determined, these are simple rounded vessels, differing from bowls of category A 1 only in being somewhat more closed. The rims are generally plain, although one has a horizontal incised line on the outside of the rim and a notch in the rim (Pl. 31, L = Pl. 77, L) and one has a slightly rolled rim (Pl. 31, N = Pl. 77, M). Various lugs and lug handles are attached at or somewhat below the rim; whether there were other lugs or lug handles on the belly is not certain. Presumably some of the small bases with pierced ring feet, described in the catalogues under Other Sherds, belong to jars of this type.

Jars with up-turned or everted lip are represented by one example with nearly complete profile (**37**) and many fragments of rims (e.g. Pl. 31, O–V; Pl. 32, A, B; Pl. 77, S–AE). The lip of these vessels is turned upward or outward, either at an angle or in a curve. They often have horizontally pierced lugs, either at the lip or just below it. **37** makes a rounded transition to a flat bottom; it is atypical in that its flaring lip is tall.

Jars with distinct neck (e.g. Pl. 32, F–N; Pl. 77, AK–AS) most often have a low, upright collar-neck. Sometimes the necks are somewhat flaring (e.g. Pl. 32, H = Pl. 77, AN; Pl. 32, J = Pl. 77, AF; Pl. 32, K = Pl. 77, AM). One fragment of a collar-neck had a handle, probably vertical, attached to the collar (Pl. 77, AO). The only other evidence for handles comes from **166***, which is broken at the top, but which may have had a collar-neck; the lower end of the handle was attached at the belly and the upper end near the top of the vessel. It is significant that there are very few other fragments of handles of this type (see the catalogues under Other Sherds); probably most of the jars with distinct neck, if they had any type of handle at all, had small lugs placed somewhere on the belly.

Various fragments cannot be readily assigned to any of the types just described. Some may be thought of as intermediate between vessels with up-turned or everted lip and those with distinct neck (e.g. Pl. 32, C = Pl. 77, AW; Pl. 32, D = Pl. 77, AV; Pl. 32, E = Pl. 77, AH). There is one fragment from a vessel which apparently had a conical neck (Pl. 32, Q). One fragment from a vessel with a pronounced shoulder is unique (Pl. 32, P = Pl. 77, AJ). A few other unusual vessels are described in the catalogues.

The usual types of decoration were employed on small jars. Crusted red sometimes occurs (e.g. Pl. 31, E = Pl. 77, S; Pl. 32, D = Pl. 77, AV; Pl. 32, K = Pl. 77, AM). There are three instances of pattern burnishing (Pl. 43, A = Pl. 87, K; Pl. 43, B = Pl. 87, L; Pl. 43, C = Pl. 87, J). Incision or grooving is found on the outside of collar-necks (e.g. Pl. 32, F = Pl. 77, AS; Pl. 32, G = Pl. 77, AR); probably many of the fragments from small vessels with this kind of decoration, listed among Other Sherds, come from jars (e.g. Pl. 44, J = Pl. 88, AN; Pl. 44, K = Pl. 88, AO). There are examples of raised strips, one curving (Pl. 31, A = Pl. 77, K) and one vertical with finger impressions (Pl. 77, J); and there is one applied disk (Pl. 31, P = Pl. 77, Y).

B 2: LARGE JARS (Pls. 33–35, 78–81)

This is a category with a wide range and very little uniformity. There are several fairly complete vessels: high and closed (e.g. **134**), high and open (e.g. **146, 170**), and low and open (e.g. **74**). The more closed vessels will be discussed first and then the more open ones.

Closed vessels have either a plain rim (e.g. Pl. 34, A; probably **105**), an up-turned or thickened rim (e.g. Pl. 34, B = Pl. 81, Q; Pl. 34, E, F), or a distinct neck, whether a collar-neck (e.g. **10, 134**, Pl. 33, A) or a flaring neck (e.g. **135**). The neck of one very large vessel was apparently conical (Pl. 46, D = Pl. 80, A). The necks are often very narrow (e.g. **134**, D. rim 0.10 m.; **135**, D. rim 0.114 m.) and sometimes quite broad (e.g. **10**, D. rim est. 0.32 m.). The shape of the body of closed vessels varies considerably: **134** is a fairly tall, ovoid vessel; **135** is squatter and has a sagging belly; **97** and **105** are roughly biconical; **11*** and **137** are globular to biconical. Several have strap handles at the widest part of the body, spaced in various ways: **97** has two, one opposite the other; **134** has at least four, fairly regularly spaced; **137**, and probably **135**, have four, grouped in pairs on opposite sides. Lugs are also found in some cases on the upper part of the shoulder: **10** has a T-lug; Plate 33, B (= Pl. 80, B) has a similar lug, but placed obliquely, with a long plastic tail; Plate 81, AM has a vertically pierced lug; Plate 34, A has a simple horizontal lug; **97** has horizontal lugs with long plastic extensions, mounted above the handles; **64** has a complex arrangement of lugs and plastic ridges. One fragment has a vertical lug handle at the rim with finger impressions on it (Pl. 34, B = Pl. 81, Q).

Open vessels vary considerably in height. **74** is very low and broad, narrowing only slightly toward the top; there is a strap handle at the widest point. A fragment from a slightly higher vessel with up-turned lip has a strap handle on the shoulder (Pl. 81, G). Another fragment has a handle resembling a large T-lug near the rim (Pl. 81, S). There are also examples of unpierced horizontal lugs with indented edges (e.g. Pl. 81, AK, AL) and unpierced crescent-shaped lugs with indented edges near the rims (e.g. Pl. 81, C–E, AH, AJ). **146** and **170** are high and widen almost continuously from bottom to top (**170** narrows slightly toward the rim); these two vessels are not only close to one another in shape but also have very similarly organized rope decoration and they should be regarded as forming a distinct type. There is a fragment probably from a similar vessel (Pl. 81, K), and the type may have been fairly common. There is no reason to suppose that vessels of this type were produced specifically for burials (despite the suitability of the shape for this purpose), especially since **170** was apparently mended in antiquity. The shape may have been influenced by basketry.

In addition, there are many rim fragments from jars which are intermediate in openness and height or which are too small to reveal the original form of the vessel (e.g. Pl. 34, C, D, G, H = Pl. 81, T).

The usual types of decoration were employed on large jars. Crusted red sometimes occurs (e.g. Pl. 80, C; around the handles and lugs of **97**). Pattern burnishing was recognized on fragments of at least five vessels (**63, 75, 105**, Pl. 43, D = Pl. 87, R; Pl. 43, E = Pl. 87, N); the decoration is somewhat less careful than that on smaller vessels and there is an emphasis on vertical or nearly vertical lines, sometimes varying in width (e.g. **105**). Incision or grooving occurs on horizontal bands on the outside of rims, sometimes on a thickened strip (e.g. Pl. 34, H = Pl. 81, T; Pl. 34, K = Pl. 81, AA): the predominant pattern is multiple chevrons. Plate 80, A has carefully incised lines on a high, conical neck. Many of the incised fragments from the bodies of large vessels, listed in the catalogues under Other Sherds, must have come from jars. Plastic bands are common, especially around handles; sometimes they are plain (e.g. Pl. 81, AE), but more often they have finger impressions at regular intervals. For various arrangements of this plastic rope decoration see especially **137, 146** and **170**.

C 1: SCOOPS (Pls. 36, 82, 83)

These are vessels of a distinct type; their purpose is not clear and they are called scoops only for convenience. Fragments of at least thirty-six and probably as many as sixty or seventy were found, most in the area of the cemetery but at least six in the settlement.[20] Two nearly complete vessels (**102, 173**) and one handle (**98**) were found in graves.

The two nearly complete vessels show that the body was set on a hollowed disk base; the base of **102** is round, that of **173** is oval. The body is an elongated ovoid, set on its side and cut away obliquely

[20] Assuming the greatest possible dispersal of fragments throughout the cemetery, there are at least 30 different vessels represented: **98, 102** and **173** from graves, and fragments of at least 27 others found around the central group of graves in the Lower Cemetery (below, p. 72). To these we may add at least five different vessels from the stratified deposits in Area G (below, p. 28) and one from House Y in Area L (below, p. 37), making a minimum number for the whole site of 36. Probably there were many more, since such a great dispersal of fragments in the cemetery is unlikely and there is probably no substantial overlap from catalogue to catalogue. If there were no overlap at all, the minimum number for the whole site would be 87.

at the front to form a large mouth; the interior slopes downward from the lower rim to the base, but is too shallow to hold liquid in any quantity while upright. A broad, flat handle rises obliquely from the back; it flattens out at the top where it is supported on either side by a nearly vertical strut. The lower ends of the struts are attached to either side of the upper body near the middle. Most of the struts are round or rectangular in section, but one is made up of two rolls of clay (Pl. 36, A = Pl. 83, R) and others have deep vertical grooves (e.g. Pl. 36, B = Pl. 83, Q).

Crusted red occurs in at least two instances (Pl. 83, C, AQ). Incised decoration occurs mostly on handles and struts. A common pattern is multiple zigzag, arranged in a vertical zone or zones (e.g. **102**, Pl. 83, E, F); one handle (**98**) has a complex pattern with meandroid elements. Struts often have diagonal lines, single or multiple zigzag, one or more vertical lines or some combination of these; occasionally horizontal lines occur (e.g. Pl. 36, D = Pl. 83, V). Two fragments from struts are of special interest: one has deep angular punctations (Pl. 36, C = Pl. 83, AD), the other has interlocking hooks (Pl. 36, F = Pl. 83, AG). Another fragment, probably of a scoop strut, also has a curvilinear incised pattern (below, p. 92). Not all handles and struts are extensively decorated with incision (**173** is almost completely undecorated). Apparently the bodies did not have incised decoration as a rule: there are only two instances in which incised lines were recognized, in each case near the juncture with a strut (Pl. 83, AL, AM). Since small fragments from the bodies of scoops are not always distinguishable from those of other vessels, it is possible that some of the incised body fragments, described in the catalogues under Other Sherds, were from scoops (e.g. Pl. 39, U = Pl. 89, AC). Plastic knobs are occasionally attached at the juncture of handle and strut (e.g. Pl. 36, A = Pl. 83, R; Pl. 83, L, N, O, X). There were also knobs, or perhaps struts of some sort, on the inside surface of a few handles (e.g. Pl. 83, AT, AU).

Several fragments which resemble scoop handles are described under Other Sherds because they exhibit some differences from the fragments recorded as certainly from scoops (below, pp. 73, 93, 96).

The purpose of these curious vessels is still unclear. They must have been in common use, to judge by the number found. Three were found in graves (they are the most frequent type of funerary offering), all certainly or probably associated with the bodies of women. Fragments of many others were found in the earth around the graves. Scoops were not exclusively of funerary character, however, since other examples were found in the settlement. It is unlikely that they were used as braziers or to transport live coals or as lamps or torches, since none of those from Kephala show any evidence of burning (although it is possible that a small quantity of a substance such as incense was burned in them without leaving a trace).[21] They appear unnecessarily complex in form and too fragile to have served in everyday use as scoops for grain, or something similar, as Tsountas suggested (1908, col. 206). Probably they were of ritual character, a purpose supported by the parallels from Elateia and elsewhere (Weinberg, 1962, pp. 190–195), which will be discussed further in Chapter IV. One can only hope that more will be found in circumstances which will make their use clear.

C 2: CYLINDRICAL STANDS (Pls. 37, 83, 84)

There is one complete example (**106**) and fragments of three or more other vessels probably of this shape (Pl. 37, B = Pl. 84, W, X; Pl. 84, Y, Z). **106** is not a perfect cylinder but rather flares toward the bottom and, slightly, toward the top; it has a pair of doubly pierced lugs on the interior opposite one another. The other probable examples may have been more cylindrical (see especially Pl. 37, B); they have interior ledges or lugs, placed closer to the rim than those of **106**.

C 3: BAKING PANS OR HEARTHS (Pls. 37, 84)

These are broad, low-walled vessels, generally crudely made and flat on the bottom. There are only small fragments, which fall into two types. The first, to which the majority of fragments belong, comprises very crudely fashioned vessels of irregular shape (e.g. Pl. 37, F–L; Pl. 84, A–N, R–V), with low walls, rims pierced at more or less regular intervals, and rough bottoms (e.g. Pl. 84, R, U). The walls vary considerably in height, but are never greater than about 0.10 m. and are usually lower; in places they diminish to nothing (e.g. Pl. 84, T). There is sometimes an internal horizontal ledge-like projection

[21] Immerwahr (1971, p. 13) notes that the scoop from Sesklo "preserves clear traces of black discoloration, as if from burning, at the base and inside the bowl." For further discussion of this vessel see Chapter IV, p. 101.

at the top of the wall (e.g. Pl. 37, K; Pl. 84, G); more often, concave horizontal lugs occur a short distance below the rim (e.g. Pl. 37, J = Pl. 84, F; Pl. 84, E, H). The second type, to which only a few fragments may be assigned (e.g. Pl. 37, C = Pl. 84, O; Pl. 37, D = Pl. 84, Q; Pl. 37, E = Pl. 84, P), comprises vessels of more regular outline, either circular or oval, with thick bottoms and very low regular unpierced walls; the bottoms are rough; the upper surface is smooth.

The first type may have served as a sort of retainer for a fire or hearth; sometimes the fragments show traces of burning, and the absence of a wall in places would be convenient for the sweeping out of ashes. The second type may have been for the same purpose, or it may have served as a convenient surface for the preparation of food or other substance.

C 4: STRAINING VESSELS (Pls. 37, 84)

There are a few fragments of flat bottoms pierced at regular intervals; Plate 37, A (= Pl. 84, AJ) is the best preserved.

C 5: LIDS (Pls. 37, 84)

There are a few fragments probably of lids. Most are evidently flat, with plain edges (e.g. Pl. 84, AA–AD) and simple knobs (e.g. Pl. 37, M = Pl. 84, AF; Pl. 37, N = Pl. 84, AG). One fragment is probably from a crown lid with four arms (Pl. 37, O = Pl. 84, AE).

OTHER SHERDS

This category comprises other sherds worth noting. Most, if less fragmentary, might have been assigned to one or another of the preceding categories; a few do not seem to fit any of them. They are grouped in the catalogues under the following headings: Crusted, Pattern Burnished, Incised and Grooved, With Plastic Decoration, Handles, Bases, Oddments. The four types of decoration have already been discussed (pp. 10–13). A few general remarks may be made here about Handles and Bases.

Handles (including lugs). The only commonly occurring handles are strap handles, which are frequent on larger vessels. They are always vertical and are usually placed at or near the widest part of the vessel. Occasionally they are attached by plugs thrust through the pot wall (e.g. Pl. 38, C = Pl. 84, BD; Pl. 84, AT). Plate 84, AK–AP, BE and BF give an idea of their range and variety. Sometimes they have knobs at the apex. Plastic bands with finger impressions are often set around them (e.g. **146, 170**, Pl. 84, AM, AO). Rarely they are decorated with incision (e.g. Pl. 84, AL, AO, AP). There is a small group of vertical ribbon handles of various sizes, similar to strap handles but attached at the upper end to the rim of a vessel (e.g. Pl. 38, F = Pl. 84, BC; Pl. 38, G = Pl. 84, AQ; Pl. 38, H = Pl. 84, AX; Pl. 38, J = Pl. 84, AV; Pl. 84, AW, AY); Plate 84, AR is similar to these but is concave in section. A few fragments of other broad, flat handles are difficult to understand: Plate 38, B (= Pl. 84, BA) is very large and makes an unusual angle with the wall of the pot; Plate 38, A (= Pl. 84, BB) makes an unusually sharp bend and may have been high swung; Plate 84, AZ makes an obtuse angle rather than being rounded; Plate 38, E is a broad, flat handle with very little curve (although it has more than that of any of the certain scoop handles); a few other fragments are generally similar to scoop handles but differ in some details (see above, p. 17).

There are only three possible examples of horizontal ribbon handles (Pl. 84, AU; Pl. 85, W, X).

Simple lugs are almost always horizontally pierced (see Pl. 75, AB, AG; Pl. 84, BS for examples of vertically pierced lugs); the holes are generally small and can only have been string-holes for suspension, if they were functional at all. The term lug handle is used here for those which are larger and have larger holes than usual. Lugs and lug handles are usually longer on either the horizontal axis (e.g. Pl. 75, F, G, W, AA) or the vertical axis (e.g. Pl. 75, AE; Pl. 77, S); hemispherical lugs are almost entirely lacking (Pl. 75, X is nearly hemispherical). One of the most distinctive forms of lug is that referred to in the catalogues as a T-lug (e.g. Pl. 75, Y; Pl. 77, T–W; Pl. 80, A; described as an "elephant-head lug" in some preliminary reports, e.g. Caskey, 1964a, p. 316 and pl. 47, b–d): these are broad at the top and drawn out at the bottom and give the impression of being almost triangular; they are pierced horizontally near the top; sometimes they have long vertical plastic extensions (e.g. Pl. 33, B = Pl. 80, B); in at least one instance (Pl. 84, BN) a large T-lug has a row of finger impressions; otherwise they are generally plain. Sometimes there occur triangular handles (e.g. on **170**) or lug handles (e.g. Pl. 84, BM) which are similar to T-lugs.

Another distinctive form of lug is horizontal or crescent shaped, pierced either vertically or diagonally at the upper corners, and having long plastic extensions depending from either end (e.g. Pl. 39, D = Pl. 84, BR; Pl. 39, E = Pl. 84, BQ; Pl. 84, BO, BP, BT, BU); there is sometimes a triangular plastic extension depending from the middle as well (e.g. **97**, detail of lug on Pl. 78).

Simple unpierced lugs ("ledge lugs"), often with a central indentation, are fairly common (e.g. Pl. 28, F = Pl. 75, Z; Pl. 31, G = Pl. 77, N). Unpierced crescent-shaped lugs (often shaped like an inverted U) are frequent on larger vessels; most have finger impressions at the edge (e.g. Pl. 39, A = Pl. 85, F; Pl. 39, B = Pl. 85, E; Pl. 39, C = Pl. 85, C) but some plain ones occur (e.g. on **146** and **170**); the ends are sometimes drawn out in long extensions and sometimes they are continuous with vertical plastic strips (e.g. on **170**).

High-swung handles, lug handles and tab handles are also fairly common (Pl. 38, K–P; Pl. 85, AD–AV). Where the evidence has survived, the type of vessel is always a bowl of category A 2 (see above, p. 14). Some of the tab handles, however, are quite large (e.g. Pl. 85, AV) and may have come from large jars or some other fairly large vessel.

Bases. There are several types. Representative profiles of all but pedestal bases are shown on Plate 39, F–R; most of these are fairly small, but the larger bases are similar (cf. Pl. 85, BB–BL). Flat bottoms, raised bases (both flat and hollowed), low and high ring feet, and pedestals occur; the pedestals are apparently confined to bowls of category A 2 (see above, p. 13). Ring feet are often pierced, sometimes with a pair of holes side by side (e.g. Pl. 39, R = Pl. 85, BC), sometimes with four holes in pairs opposite each other (e.g. Pl. 39, P = Pl. 85, BB). The holes may have held strings for the suspension of the pot. **104** has a pair of holes aligned with a lug on the upper body (and a tab at the rim) and the holes may often have been aligned with lugs; it is curious, however, that so few of the lugs are vertically pierced. The holes tend to be larger in the case of the larger ring feet (e.g. Pl. 85, BF). Occasionally flat bottoms and bases are oval rather than round (e.g. **138**, **173**, Pl. 27, E = Pl. 75, A; Pl. 39, U = Pl. 89, AC; Pl. 85, BH).

II. THE SETTLEMENT

GENERAL

The domestic structures were not well preserved. Walls were constructed of small to moderate-sized stones, apparently without the use of any kind of mortar; their width varies from about 0.50 to 0.70 m.; they have rarely survived to a height of 0.50 m. and most are less than 0.30 m. The stones were those immediately available: schist and, less often, marble or limestone. The construction of the walls was reasonably careful, although no attempt was made to lay the stones in courses. There is no evidence that mud brick was used, although the possibility cannot be entirely excluded in view of the state of preservation.[1] There are a few possible post-holes (e.g. House Y in Area L) but otherwise there is no evidence for roofing, which was presumably of perishable materials such as wood and clay.

The houses examined were all built on a slope and made use of natural bedrock scarps and ledges. House Z in Area L used a rock scarp for one of its walls and Area K may have been nothing more than a rock shelter; elsewhere the houses probably had built walls on all sides. In several instances the bedrock, which is fairly soft, was trimmed to some extent (e.g. for the floors of Houses Y and Z in Area L).

Recovery of the plans of houses was greatly hindered by the eroded state of the remains. All the structures in the excavated areas apparently had rectilinear plans, and none of the exposed walls elsewhere on the hillside are curved to any great extent. Only two Areas, D and L, are well-enough preserved to yield any further information about the plans. The remains in Area D might be interpreted as those of a single agglutinative structure with rooms at several different levels; it is possible, on the other hand, that they represent several different building phases (cf. Area E, where as many as three building phases were represented). At any rate, we can recognize an open court paved at one time with stones (south of Wall 1), a long narrow enclosed space (Room II) and, probably, other enclosed spaces more nearly square in plan (e.g. Room III). House Z in Area L is essentially a modified rock shelter, triangular to trapezoidal in plan. Its neighbor, House Y, stands in a close relationship with it. House Y is the most impressive building excavated: it has an interior length of at least 6.70 m. (the distance from Wall 3 to Wall 6) and it may have measured as much as 8.20 m. (i.e. from Wall 1 to Wall 6); it probably had posts to support the roof.

Very little evidence for the interior arrangement of the houses has survived. House Y in Area L had a long bench (Wall 7) divided into two parts by a spur (Wall 11; perhaps an interior buttress). House Z in Area L had a rock-cut bench or sleeping area and may also have had an interior spur (Wall 8). There was a sort of niche, perhaps a storage space, next to the northern side of Room I in Area D, and a small cupboard-like space at the corner of Walls 6 and 7 in House Y in Area L.

AREAS A, B, AND C

These small Areas were laid out with long axis east-west in the low-lying sandy part of the isthmus (Pl. 3).

Area A, the easternmost, was 5.00 m. long and 1.00 m. wide. It was excavated to a depth of about 1.00 m. below the surface. The earth was sandy and had been deposited in a series of layers, evidently through the action of water. It was completely devoid of artifacts.

Area B was also 5.00 m. long and 1.00 m. wide, about 5 m. west of Area A. Water was encountered about 2.40 m. below the surface so that further digging was impossible. The deposit was similar to that

[1] Mud brick is used rarely, if at all, in modern times on Keos, whereas structures built completely of stone are common; see, e.g., Caskey, 1971, pl. 73.

found in Area A. Two sherds were found, however, one about 0.30 m. and the other about 1.05 m. below the surface. Both were from wheelmade vessels of the Iron Age or later. One fragment of an obsidian blade (category 1 a) was also found at a depth of about 0.30 m.

Area C was 5.00 m. long and 2.00 m. wide; its southeastern corner was about 5 m. west and 2 m. north of the northwestern corner of Area B. It was excavated to a maximum depth of about 0.60 m. The deposit was similar to that in the other two Areas. The only artifacts found were four sherds, similar to those in Area B, a fragment of gray-green terracotta possibly from a tile, and a fragment of an obsidian blade (category 1 a); all were about 0.20 m. below the surface.

The evidence from these three Areas suggests that the sandy part of the isthmus has been built up considerably through natural processes of erosion since the time of the settlement at Kephala. If there was prehistoric habitation here, all traces are now inaccessible beneath the present water level.

AREA D

Architecture

Area D (Pls. 4, 50) is one of the best preserved parts of the settlement in terms of walls, but almost no floor deposits were intact. It is near the base of the southern slope of the promontory (Pl. 3) about 20 m. due north of the cemetery and about 10 m. higher. A few small ledges, which interrupt the almost continuous slope of the hillside, provided a meager footing for walls. The total area cleared was only 50 or 60 sq. m.; the greatest depth of deposit was about 0.60 m. while the average depth was only about 0.20 to 0.30 m. The excavated area is surrounded by an almost bare hillside with no traces of the continuation of walls.

The surviving walls were founded directly on bedrock, which was probably trimmed in places to provide a bedding. The best preserved wall, Wall 1, survives to a height of only 0.60 m., and few of the others exceed 0.30 m.

The general impression is of several structures built on ascending terraces, although the plan of the surviving remains (Pl. 4) is difficult to interpret in detail. At the southwestern part of the excavated area there was probably a room, Room I, backed to the north against a scarp of rock (Pl. 50, c); only the norethastern corner of this room has survived (Walls 4 and10). There is a narrow space between the northern side of Wall 10 and the bedrock scarp to the north (Section b–b, Pl. 4); within the space were found a number of rounded, water-worn stones (missiles?), about 0.10 to 0.15 m. in diameter. Since there were no traces of burning, the space was apparently not used for a hearth; perhaps it was a storage space. To the east of Room I is a long narrow space marked Room II on the plan; this may have been an unroofed terrace rather than a room. Jutting into this space on the eastern side are fragments of two walls (Walls 8 and 9) which form a right angle and probably belonged to a room or house situated towards the northeast. Several flat slabs were found by the eastern side of Wall 4, some on end as if they had slipped down or fallen from above (Pl. 50, d). There may have been a way of access from the north at the northwestern corner of Room II; Wall 4 makes a jog here and Wall 2, at least as it has survived, did not extend as far as Wall 4.

The northern part of Area D was probably divided into two rooms, Room III to the west and a poorly preserved room to the east (Pl. 50, h); Wall 5 evidently served as a party wall; the fragmentary Wall 6 seems to continue eastward beyond Wall 5, and may have been the southern wall of both rooms. The space south of Wall 6 and north of the line of Wall 2 was possibly a way of access to these rooms from the west; bedrock in this space slopes down somewhat from west to east. The eastern and southern walls of Room III are preserved to some extent (Walls 5 and 6); Wall 3 may have been its northern wall, although it is bedded on a shelf of rock about 1 m. higher and thus may have had no relation to this room. A few stones (at 11 on Pl. 4) may be a continuation of Wall 5, or they may belong to another wall perpendicular to Wall 3 on its northern side. One of the stones at the bottom of Wall 5 juts out into Room III a short distance (at 7 on Pl. 4).

The structures so far described produced only scanty remains of floor deposits, and much of the material collected in them may have been incorporated in fill used for terracing.

The greatest depth of deposit (about 0.60 m.) was found at the southern side of Wall 1, where there was a fairly level space about 6 m. long (roughly east-west) and 2 m. wide (Pl. 50, e). The space may have been an open terrace: there was no trace of an east-west wall on its southern side; a few stones perpendicular to Wall 1 at its eastern end (at 12 on Pl. 4) might belong to a cross-wall, but this could equally well have bordered an unroofed structure. Two floor levels were recognized in the eastern half of the space. The lower floor, almost immediately above bedrock (Pl. 50, f), was made up of carefully laid flat slabs bedded in clay, an unusual practice at Kephala.[2] A stone with a hole bored through its center had been placed among the paving stones just beside Wall 1 (Pl. 50, g);[3] although it resembles the pivot for a door post, Wall 1 continued beside it without a break, and there is no trace of a cross-wall to which it could have been related. The upper floor, of packed earth, was found about 0.10 to 0.15 m. above the paved floor. Fragments of two or more large jars (below, p. 24) were found in the earth between the two floors, but the finds were otherwise meager, and very little pottery was found above the upper floor.

Objects

Since there was so little observable stratification in Area D, the objects are presented in a single catalogue; unstratified objects found at or near the modern surface are so indicated.

COPPER WORKING

One fragment of fine-grained slag (Appendix 1, No. 1), found near surface south of Wall 6 and west of Wall 5.

STONE

1* (Kph.1.3) Celt Pls. 24, 68
Found near the surface west of Wall 5 and south of Wall 3.
Nearly intact; slightly chipped on butt end. L. 0.054, W. 0.019, Th. 0.01.
Gray green; surface polished. Small, long and narrow. Edges taper towards the ends: butt end blunt, blade slightly bowed. Oval in section: one face curved on long axis, the other straight but beveled at the end towards the blade. Very similar to **29***.

2 (Kph.1.16) Obsidian blade (category 1 b) Pl. 69
Found south of Wall 1, within 0.20 m. above the packed earth floor.
One end missing. L. 0.057, W. 0.024, Th. 0.007.
Dark gray; surface shiny. Nearly parallel sided but broadening at preserved end; triangular in section at middle, trapezoidal at end; edges somewhat chipped.

3* (Kph.1.15) Obsidian flake tool (category 2) Pl. 69
Found near surface south of Wall 1.
Intact. L. 0.028, W. 0.02, Th. 0.005.
Dark gray; surface dull. Nearly straight on one edge, curved on other edges; flat on one face; three main facets on the other; bulb of percussion at one end; all other edges chipped.

4* (Kph.1.19) Obsidian flake tool (category 2) Pl. 69
Found near surface south of Wall 6 and west of Wall 5.
Intact. L. 0.027, W. 0.02, Th. 0.007.
Black; surface dull. Roughly oval; edges chipped.

5* (Kph.1.14) Obsidian tool (category 6) Pl. 70
Found near surface.
Intact. L. 0.033, W. 0.032, Th. 0.009.
Dark gray; surface slightly shiny. Thick flake with notches giving a cruciform outline, flattened at one edge. Some chipping around the two notches opposite the flattened edge.

6 (Kph.1.17) Waste core of obsidian Pl. 70
Found near bedrock just west of Wall 4.
Intact. L. 0.032, W. 0.018, Th. 0.011.
Gray; surface dull. Oblong; roughly diamond shaped in section at middle; scars from flaking on one side.

7* (Kph.1.18) Waste core of obsidian Pls. 25, 70
Found near surface at east side of Room II.
One end missing. L. 0.035, W. 0.032, Th. 0.02.
Black; surface shiny. Many-faceted nucleus, pointed at one end and flat where broken at the other; one large flat area has a rough natural surface.

[2] It is possible, however, that some of the stones scattered about in Area K belonged to a similar paving; below, p. 32.
[3] D. of stone *ca.* 0.20 m.; Th. *ca.* 0.06 m. Hole round, with smooth sides tapering from a diameter of about 0.08 m. at the top to 0.04 m. at the bottom.

Obsidian uninventoried (by categories):

	1 a	1 b	2	3	4	5	6	waste	total
Stratified	0	6	2	0	0	0	12	65	85
Unstratified	5	2	8	0	0	0	10	70	95

8 (Kph.1.4) Grinder Pl. 68
Found near bedrock just west of Wall 4.
Intact. L. 0.102, W. 0.068, Th. 0.036.
Gray green; surface fairly smooth but with many small pits. Oval in outline and in section.

TERRACOTTA

9* (Kph.4) Sherd rubbing-tool
Found near surface close to Wall 4.
Mended; one large chip missing. L. 0.059, W. 0.049, Th. 0.018.
Red-brown biscuit. Roughly oval; perhaps originally from the base of a pot.

POTTERY

About three and one-half tinfuls of pottery were securely associated with the excavated structures, and the catalogue is based on this material. An equal amount of pottery was found at or near the surface, and has a probable, though less secure, association with the structures; only a few of these sherds are mentioned, and they are noted as unstratified. Body sherds from coarse vessels comprise the bulk of the pottery.

A 1
Pl. 75, C: rim fragment.

A 2
Rim fragments of 13 or more bowls, at least three with angular profile and two with T-lugs placed near the rim: Pl. 86, J, with pattern-burnished parallel lines on exterior; Pl. 86, V, with angular profile, and traces of pattern burnishing on interior.

Ring base and lower body of a bowl with a small hole bored in the bottom.

B 1
Fragments of five rims including: Pl. 31, G = Pl. 77, N (D. rim est. 0.14) with conical upper body and unpierced horizontal lug on the shoulder; Pl. 31, M = Pl. 77, Q and Pl. 31, S = Pl. 77, T with slightly up-turned lip and T-lug on the shoulder.

Pl. 43, A = Pl. 87, K: up-turned lip; on the shoulder, pattern-burnished groups of parallel lines and a triangular burnished area.

B 2
10 (Kph.27) Fragment of large jar with collar-neck Pls. 33, 80
Found close to bedrock in room (?) east of Room III.
About one third of collar-neck and part of shoulder preserved; consolidated with plaster. H. pres. 0.185, D. rim est. 0.32.
Coarse, orange-brown biscuit; tan accretion on parts of surface. High and nearly vertical collar-neck; gently curving shoulder. One T-lug preserved on shoulder close to base of neck.

11* (Kph.29) Fragment of large closed jar Pl. 80
Found near surface close to Wall 4.
Body fragment, only a small portion of the whole; consolidated with plaster. H. pres. 0.53, Th. 0.012.
Coarse, orange-brown biscuit; surface covered with scoring. Roughly biconical body; at its widest diameter is a large broad strap handle, and beside one end of the handle is part of a horizontal plastic band with diagonal slashes.

Fragments of at least 11 other vessels.

Relatively closed. Pl. 46, D = Pl. 80, A: unstratified; very large vessel with offset conical neck, D. bottom of neck est. 0.44, Th. of wall 0.015; T-lug on shoulder; incised group of slanting parallel lines and a group of vertical parallel lines. Fragments of three vessels with collar-necks, e.g. Pl. 81, R, two of which have T-lugs on the shoulder. Pl. 81, AM: rim of a hole-mouthed jar, D. est. 0.32, with a horizontal lug, vertically pierced, near the rim. Pl. 34, A = Pl. 81, AG: rim of a hole-mouthed jar with an unpierced horizontal lug just beneath the rim.

Relatively open. Pl. 81, Z: a rim with deep punctations in a slanting line on the outside.

Intermediate and indeterminate. Pl. 81, H: slightly thickened rim; slanting impressed band on the body. Pl. 81, L: slightly thickened rim; vertical impressed band. Pl. 87, Q: broad parallel lines of pattern burnishing; a similar sherd is probably from the same vessel. Pl. 81, A: unstratified; large strap handle; next to it is a band of deep scoring, about 0.08 m. wide. Pl. 91, C: the lower part of a large open (?) jar with a slightly raised base, D. *ca.* 0.17, and a mat impression on the bottom (Appendix 2, No. 4).

Many fragments from two or more large jars found above the paving south of Wall 1. Some, e.g. Pl. 91, E, with drilled holes. Some of the fragments are broken in bands with prepared edges, showing that the jars were constructed in horizontal rings, i.e. vertically flattened coils, 0.10 to 0.14 m. in height. Pl. 85, BK: a base, evidently manufactured as a disk to which the lowest ring was then attached. Pl. 91, B and D, from the lower part of an open (?) jar, D. *ca.* 0.40, have the impression of a mat on the flat bottom (Appendix 2, No. 3).

C 1

Fragment of a handle (?) with incised zigzags.

C 3

Rim fragment, perforated.

OTHER SHERDS

Crusted red. One or more vessels.

Pattern burnished. Several sherds with parallel lines.

With plastic decoration. A raised knob on the outer wall of a pot.

Handles and lugs. Several strap handles, one unusually wide (0.065). Several T-lugs; Pl. 84, BN with finger impressions on plastic tail. One rounded lug. Two unpierced horizontal lugs, e.g. Pl. 85, M, one indented in the middle.

Bases. At least seven in addition to those already mentioned. Pl. 90, B: slightly raised base, D. 0.038, from a small open (?) vessel with a mat impression on the bottom (Appendix 2, No. 1).

Oddments. Pl. 45, B = Pl. 75, K: probably from a rim with everted lip; possibly from a pedestal, but well smoothed inside. Pl. 91, J: with deep scoring on the interior, apparently produced by a cloth or brush. Five late unstratified sherds: one wheelmade, with a pattern (?) in red paint, perhaps of Middle or Late Bronze Age; one round leg perhaps from a tripod vessel; three post-Bronze Age sherds, wheelmade, one with combed decoration.

AREA E

ARCHITECTURE

Area E (Pls. 5, 51) is about 15 m. east of Area D and about the same height above sea level. The structures were built on a fairly level ledge in the sloping hillside. Excavation was limited to about 10 sq. m., and the greatest depth of deposit was about 0.80 m. (immediately south of Wall 2). No floor levels, and only very fragmentary plans of structures could be distinguished; nevertheless a probable interpretation of the remains can be suggested.

The earliest structure evidently used the rock ledge for a floor; a short stretch of wall (Wall 1), founded on bedrock at the southern edge of the ledge, was probably part of the southern wall of the structure. The stones forming an L-shape to the south and west of Wall 1 may also have been related to the earliest structure, but they are not arranged in a regular way and are probably not in their original position. The earliest structure fell into disuse or was pulled down, and the ledge became covered with loose stones and debris at least 0.40 m. deep in some places. On top of the debris was built a second structure with a slightly different alignment. Only a part of the northern corner is preserved (Walls 2 and 3; the loose stones and debris beneath Wall 2 are indicated in Section a–a on Pl. 5). It apparently was destroyed in turn and other structures with slightly different alignments were built, represented by Walls 4 and 5. These walls were founded at the same height as Wall 2, or only a little higher, but Wall 2 appears to have been partly dismantled to accommodate Wall 4; this fact, and the different alignments, make it unlikely that Walls 2, 3, 4 and 5 could all belong to the same building phase.

The probable existence of three building phases is of considerable importance since it confirms the evidence from the cemetery that the occupation of Kephala lasted several generations. The only other place where more than one building phase was observed was Area K, which had two phases.

OBJECTS

Since the finds are meager and could not be assigned to the various phases, they are presented in a single catalogue; unstratified finds are so indicated.

COPPER WORKING

One fragment of copper-bearing ore or slag (Keos excavation sample No. 82) found near surface.

STONE

12 (Kph.1.22) Obsidian blade (category 1 a) Pl. 69
From central part of Area E.
Missing: one end and about two thirds of one edge. L. 0.044, W. 0.014, Th. 0.003.
Black; surface somewhat shiny. Trapezoidal to triangular in section; bulb of percussion preserved.

13 (Kph.1.20) Obsidian flake tool (category 2) Pl. 69
From west part of Area E.
One end missing. L. 0.045, W. 0.03, Th. 0.009.
Gray, striated; surface dull. Roughly rectangular; one face and one edge nearly flat; three planes on other face and other edge; preserved end chipped from use.

Obsidian uninventoried (by categories):

	1 a	1 b	2	3	4	5	6	waste	total
Stratified	1	0	0	0	0	0	0	28	29
Unstratified	1	0	2	0	0	0	1	13	17

14 (Kph.1.5) Grinder Pl. 68
From west part of Area E.
One end preserved. L. 0.045, W. 0.068.
Dark blue-gray stone; surface somewhat polished; pitted by use. Rounded end; roughly rectangular in section.

POTTERY

The following list includes all the sherds found, both stratified and unstratified, totaling about one tinful. The material, which was very fragmentary, comprises at least ten small vessels and two large jars.

A 2

Fragments of five or more. At least two have an angular profile, e.g. Pl. 75, AG with a horizontal lug, vertically pierced, set at the angle. Two sherds probably from the same vessel, Frontispiece, A = Pl. 40, G = Pl. 86, F, L, have been reconstructed as a bowl with continuous curve, D. rim 0.15, decorated outside with pattern burnishing. Two other fragments, one on Frontispiece, L = Pl. 86, AL, have pattern burnishing inside. The patterns in all cases consist of groups of parallel or slightly radiating lines that sometimes vary in width.

B 1

A fragment with up-turned lip or collar-neck, and small vertical handle at juncture with shoulder.

B 2

Two plain rims; Pl. 81, J slightly flaring, D. 0.21. Frontispiece, F = Pl. 87, P: a jar (?) with pattern-burnished parallel lines in groups that meet at a right angle. Pl. 90, G: flat base, Th. 0.016, from a large open (?) vessel with a mat impression on the bottom (Appendix 2, No. 14). Pl. 90, C: slightly raised base, D. 0.25, from a large open (?) vessel with a mat impression on the bottom (Appendix 2, No. 16).

C 3

Pl. 37, D = Pl. 84, Q: low curving wall, D. 0.50 if round, burnished on the inside, rough on the bottom. Pl. 37, C = Pl. 84, O: probably from a similar pan.

Other Sherds

With plastic decoration. One sherd with a band.

Handles and lugs. One strap handle. Pl. 38, B = Pl. 84, BA: body sherd (angle uncertain) with a large flat vertical handle that has twin bulges at the top. Pl. 38, A = Pl. 84, BB: a flat vertical handle bent over at the top as if high swung.

Bases. From medium-sized to large vessels: one flat bottom; one raised base; one pierced ring foot.

AREA G

Architecture

This was the easternmost area tested and the one most exposed to the northerly and northeasterly winds (Pls. 6, 51). It is about 15 m. east of Area E and, like Areas D and E, fairly low down on the slope of the promontory. The hill rises toward the northwest in a fairly even grade to the summit (Pl. 6, Section b–b); toward the east and northeast it falls steeply into the sea (Pl. 6, Section a–a). The ancient remains were best preserved beneath Wall 2, where bedrock forms a ledge; the relatively modern, sheep wall extending across the base of the promontory (at the right in Sections a–a and b–b; see above, p. 2) has retained the earth to some extent and contributed to their preservation.

The architectural remains are very scanty because of severe erosion in much of the area. Fragments of three walls have survived (Walls 1–3) but they are too small and scattered to yield any information about the structure or structures to which they belonged. The hillside between the walls was practically devoid of covering. Wall 1 is aligned roughly northeast-southwest, on a narrow shelf of rock (Pl. 51, d; cf. Section a–a). The wall itself is preserved for only about 3.30 m.; the shelf continues at either end, however, and has a total length of at least 7 m. Although very little ancient deposit was found around Wall 1, the copper pin **28*** was found beside it at the surface and is probably to be associated with it. Wall 2 is aligned roughly northwest-southeast (not exactly perpendicular to Wall 1). One end rests against a scarp of rock (Pl. 51, e); otherwise it rests on top of an ancient deposit (cf. Section b–b). Wall 2 was evidently later than the deposit on which it rested, and no floor level could be associated with it. Only a few stones of Wall 3 have survived; it may have been aligned roughly perpendicular to Wall 2, but it was at a considerably higher level.

The most important discovery in Area G was the existence beneath Wall 2 of an ancient deposit of considerable extent; this was explored in two trenches, A and B, laid out on either side of Wall 2. Trench A was roughly 2 m. square (Pl. 51, c). Trench B was about 2 m. (northeast-southwest) by 1 m. The deposit reached a maximum depth of about 0.60 m. (after surface debris had been removed) and rested on a shelf of rock. Two strata were distinguished, the upper lighter colored and the lower darker colored; the change occurred about 0.25 to 0.30 m. above the rock ledge. Both the rock ledge and the two strata sloped down considerably from southwest to northeast. The deposit was fairly uniform, except for the change in color, and consisted of reddish earth with occasional small stones and a moderate quantity of sherds, animal bones and shells. Some large stones were encountered in both strata at the southeastern side of Trench B and some of these were left in place projecting from the trench wall. At the bottom of Trench A was a group of stones which formed a line roughly east-west (Pl. 51, c); they were too loosely arranged to be securely interpreted as part of a wall. Ninety limpet shells (see Appendix 4, p. 132) were found together next to the stones not far above bedrock.

The deposit tested in the two trenches appeared to have been either deliberate fill or, more likely, gradually accumulated debris which had cascaded down from higher up the hillside; it was probably not a floor deposit resulting from a continuous occupation of the spot itself, to judge by its slope and the large quantity of stones it contained.

Stratified Objects

The finds from the stratified deposit beneath Wall 2 are presented in a single catalogue, since no changes were observed among the four parts of the deposit, and since the finds were not sufficiently numerous for a statistical analysis. All other finds from Area G were found at or near the surface and must be regarded as unstratified; they are presented in a second catalogue (below, pp. 28–30).

COPPER WORKING

15 (Kph.4.12) Fragment of terracotta object (perhaps used in metalworking) Pls. 22, 66

From upper stratum of Trench B.

All edges missing. H. 0.024, L. 0.034.

Fairly coarse, light gray biscuit, gray on surface; subjected to intense heat which burned out particles of material and left the surface pitted.

The fragment resembles the flat bottom of a vessel about 0.012 m. thick and with a diameter of about 0.09 m.; the wall of the hypothetical vessel, however, is only about 0.004 m. thick. Perhaps from a lid or cover of some kind. Unlike other pottery shapes from the site and perhaps to be associated with metal-working because of its burned condition.

STONE

16 (Kph.4.10) Rim fragment of a marble bowl Pls. 23, 67

From lower stratum of Trench A.

D. rim est. 0.25, H. 0.035, W. 0.032, Th. 0.01.

Fine-grained, grayish white marble; surface smooth; interior has faint marks of abrasion, both vertical and horizontal. Plain rim; thickness varies from 0.008 to 0.01 m., as if becoming thicker near a lug. Probably from a vessel like **171**, but considerably larger.

17 (Kph.4.15) Obsidian blade (category 1 b) Pl. 69

From lower stratum of Trench A.

One end missing. L. 0.046, W. 0.02, Th. 0.006.

Dark gray; surface shiny.
Oblong; triangular in section, except trapezoidal near end; bulb of percussion preserved; secondary working and chipping along edges.

18 (Kph.4.16) Obsidian flake tool (category 2) Pl. 69
From lower stratum of Trench A.
Intact. L. 0.032, W. 0.02, Th. 0.0045.
Black; surface shiny. Nearly rectangular; roughly trapezoidal in section.

19 (Kph.4.19) Obsidian flake tool (category 2) Pl. 69
From upper stratum of Trench A.
Narrow end missing. L. 0.063, W. 0.039, Th. 0.011.
Black; surface shiny. Edges crudely worked and chipped in places.

20 (Kph.4.44) Core tool of obsidian (category 5) Pl. 70
From lower stratum of Trench B.
Intact. L. 0.025, W. 0.02, Th. 0.011.
Gray; surface dull. Many-faceted lump with marks of use or secondary working along one edge.

21 (Kph.4.45) Core tool of obsidian (category 5) Pl. 70
From lower stratum of Trench A.
Intact. L. 0.025, W. 0.022, Th. 0.008.
Dark gray; surface somewhat shiny. Disk-like; oval to trapezoidal in section; flat flaking on both faces.

22 (Kph.4.18) Waste piece of obsidian Pl. 70
From lower stratum of Trench A.
Narrow end missing. L. 0.046, W. 0.016, Th. 0.008.
Gray; surface moderately shiny. Long, narrow, blade-like piece but with a triangular projection along one edge.

Obsidian uninventoried (by categories):

1 a	1 b	2	3	4	5	6	waste	total
14	0	19	0	0	1	8	402	444

23 (Kph.4.7) Small disk of schist Pl. 68
From upper stratum of Trench A.
Intact. D. 0.019, Th. 0.002.
Dark gray green; surface feels soapy. Purpose uncertain.

TERRACOTTA

24 (Kph.4.40) Sherd rubbing-tool Pl. 71
From upper stratum of Trench B.
Part of one end missing. L. 0.061, W. 0.041, Th. 0.006.
Coarse, orange-brown biscuit; overall burnishing outside and burnished parallel lines inside. Oblong body sherd from a bowl; one edge smoothed and flattened.

25 (Kph.4.41) Sherd rubbing-tool Pl. 71
From lower stratum of Trench B.
Intact. L. 0.053, W. 0.032, Th. 0.008.
Coarse, red-brown biscuit. Oblong, with rounded edges; nearly flat.

26 (Kph.4.11) Object of unknown purpose Pls. 26, 71
From upper stratum of Trench B.
H. 0.022, L. 0.03, W. 0.024.
Coarse, gray-brown biscuit. Very irregular, short concave cylinder, hollowed at one end. Possibly a strut broken from the handle of a pot (cf. Pl. 85, T, U). See also **81***.

POTTERY

The total amount of pottery was only about one tinful. No change or development was noticed from one stratum to the other in the two test trenches. For example, incised decoration occurred in both strata in both trenches, crusted red in all except the upper stratum in Trench B, and pattern burnishing in all except the upper stratum in Trench A. About eighty percent of the sherds are from small vessels.

A 2

27 (Kph.40) Bowl Pls. 27, 74
From upper stratum of Trench A.
About one quarter preserved; restored in plaster. H. 0.088, D. rim est. 0.199, D. base est. 0.062.
Coarse, red-brown biscuit; interior and exterior surfaces preserve shiny traces of burnishing, dark brown to gray. Rounded bowl with plain rim and flat bottom. No evidence for handles.

Fragments of at least 28 rims.
With continuous curve. Many fragments, e.g. Pl. 75, R. One example, Pl. 28, L, with lip slightly turned up, D. *ca.* 0.24. Pl. 41, E = Pl. 86, AG, with similar lip; pattern-burnished parallel lines on the interior. Pl. 86, T: shallow bowl with a small tab on the rim and pattern-burnished parallel lines on the interior; this fragment may have been found in the Upper Cemetery (record unclear).

With angular profile. At least 15, e.g. Pl. 75, V, D. *ca.* 0.16, and Pl. 75, T, U. One has a rounded lug, horizontally pierced, just below the angle and is decorated inside with pattern-burnished stripes. One has a small plastic knob at the angle.

Fragments of at least seven others with pattern burnishing inside; Frontispiece, M = Pl. 42, A = Pl. 86, AN with a design of interlocking hooks, apparently flanked on either side by parallel lines.

A 2: WITH PEDESTALS

Fragments of at least three vessels preserving the junction between body and pedestal.

B 1

Fragments of three or more vessels with slightly up-turned lip, one with a T-lug just below the lip. A fragment from a small collar-neck (?), D. 0.14, with crusted red outside.

B 2

Rim fragments of seven vessels.

Relatively closed. One slightly thickened. Pl. 34, E: slightly up-turned, D. est. 0.26. Pl. 81, AO: offset lip or low collar-neck.

Relatively open. Pl. 81, AL: low horizontal lug with finger impressions on the edge. Pl. 81, C: curving lip; crescent lug with finger impressions. One with a slightly raised horizontal band on the outside on which multiple chevrons are incised. Pl. 81, M: oblique slashes on lip; impressed plastic bands meeting at a right angle near rim.

C 1

Fragments of at least five vessels. One, from a junction of body and handle, has incised horizontal and oblique lines on the handle. Pl. 83, AU: from a scoop (?) handle without incised decoration but with a small plastic lump on the inside. Two small fragments of incised handles. Three fragments of struts, flattened in section.

C 3

Fragments of at least two coarse pans with low walls, e.g. Pl. 84, U. Another, Pl. 84, H, has a horizontal lug inside, near the pierced rim.

C 4

A fragment with flat profile, pierced at regular intervals.

OTHER SHERDS

Crusted red. Fragments of several small vessels with crusted red on one or both surfaces. A sample of the red substance, examined by Reuben G. Bullard, consists of "remnants of a paste (or slip) composed of finely ground hematite (FE_2O_3) containing about 10% fine clay" (memorandum dated May 29, 1973). At least three fragments with crusted red were also decorated with pattern burnishing.

Pattern burnished. Several fragments with groups of parallel lines meeting at various angles. Three vessels have crusted red inside and pattern burnishing outside, e.g. Pl. 40, L = Pl. 87, D, where nearly horizontal stripes flank a plastic band with finger impressions.

Incised and grooved. Pl. 88, AH: a rim fragment with multiple zigzag. Pl. 88, AF, also with multiple zigzag, is either from a rim or perhaps, since its surface is nearly flat, from the handle of a scoop. Several fragments of a rim (?), e.g. Pl. 89, G, with pairs of lines at right angles apparently framing groups of oblique lines; perhaps the original pattern consisted of a horizontal band framed at top and bottom by pairs of horizontal lines and divided into panels by pairs of vertical lines. Pl. 88, K: a slightly thickened rim (?) with multiple chevrons drawn by an instrument with a split tip, probably a stick or reed. A rim fragment, perhaps from a bowl but rough inside, with a horizontal groove outside below the lip. Pl. 39, U = Pl. 89, AC: small vessel (miniature scoop?) with oval raised base, slightly hollowed; the lower body preserves traces of fine incised lines in a rectilinear pattern; for other oval bases see **138** and **173**. Pl. 89, T: large vessel with crude grooving; handle attachment at upper left.

With plastic decoration. Pl. 89, BH: a fragment with a narrow band meeting a raised circle. Pl. 89, AH: a flat disk on the outside. Several fragments have bands with finger impressions.

Handles and lugs. Four vertical strap handles, Pl. 85, Y continuing as a plastic ridge which was pierced horizontally. One T-lug. Two ribbon handles, Pl. 85, W and X, apparently placed horizontally. Three horizontal lugs with two vertical piercings, Pl. 84, BP with plastic ridges depending from the middle and ends. Pl. 85, G: horizontal lug with three finger impressions on the edge; depending from either end is a low vertical ridge, similarly impressed. One unpierced horizontal lug.

Bases. Nine flat bottoms; Pl. 90, E, from a large (?) vessel, Th. 0.015, with a mat impression on the bottom (Appendix 2, No. 13). Three ring bases, one pierced. A fragment probably from a spreading foot.

Oddments. Pl. 45, D: slightly flaring rim, D. est. 0.20, of a bowl or jar with finely burnished red surface both inside and out.

UNSTRATIFIED OBJECTS

The following catalogue contains all finds other than those from the deposit beneath Wall 2.

COPPER

28* (Kph.4.2) Pin or awl Pls. 22, 66
From surface at south side of Wall 1.
Intact. L. 0.073, W. 0.002.
Surface smooth; green patina before conservation. Pointed at one end, blunt at the other; round in section towards the pointed end, otherwise square in section.

STONE

29* (Kph.4.1) Celt Pls. 24, 68
From surface east of Area G.
Butt end missing. L. 0.038, W. 0.017, Th. 0.011.
Dark gray; surface polished. Small, long and narrow; edges almost parallel but converging towards the blade; blade slightly bowed; roughly oval in section but irregular. Very similar to **1***.

30* (Kph.4.46) Core tool of obsidian (category 5) Pl. 70
Found near surface.
Intact. L. 0.036, W. 0.028, Th. 0.014.
Dark gray; surface shiny. Roughly oblong lump with many planes on the surface; in one place a rough natural surface; marks of secondary working and/or use along one edge.

31* (Kph.4.28) Obsidian tool (category 6) Pl. 70
Found near surface west of Wall 2.
Intact. L. 0.035, W. 0.009, Th. 0.005.
Black; surface dull. Long narrow piece, widening slightly at one end; triangular in section except at the wider end, which is flat like a wedge.

Obsidian uninventoried (by categories):

1 a	1 b	2	3	4	5	6	waste	total
5	1	4	0	0	0	0	66	76

TERRACOTTA

32* (Kph.4.37) Sherd rubbing-tool Pl. 71
Found near surface west of Wall 2.
Intact. L. 0.058, W. 0.04, Th. 0.009.
Coarse, orange-brown biscuit, smoothed and brown on outer surface which also has traces of burnishing. Slightly curved body sherd with part of a perforation preserved; one edge smoothed and flattened.

33* (Kph.4.38) Sherd rubbing-tool Pl. 71
Found near surface.
Intact. L. 0.048, W. 0.032, Th. 0.008.
Blackened orange-brown biscuit; well-smoothed outer surface. Body sherd with oval outline; edges rounded and smoothed.

POTTERY

The total amount collected at or near the surface was about one and one-quarter tinfuls. From a count of rim fragments it can be estimated that at least 30 small vessels and one large jar were represented.

A 1
A rim fragment.

A 2
34* (Kph.14) Small conical cup or bowl Pls. 27, 74
Found near surface west of Wall 2.
About one third preserved. H. 0.065, D. rim est. 0.094, D. base est. 0.048.
Coarse, red-brown biscuit; surface tan, speckled with black. Nearly conical, but walls slightly rounded; plain rim; flat bottom.

Fragments of 19 or more rims, at least six from bowls with angular profile, e.g. Pl. 29, C, D. est. 0.024. One bowl with continuous curve has a vertical lug handle, with two loops, descending from the rim (cf. Pl. 28, A = Pl. 75, AC; Pl. 75, AD).

B 1
Fragments of two vessels with up-turned lip or collar-neck, and horizontally pierced vertical lug at junction of rim and shoulder. Another vessel with a small collar-neck.

B 2
A small fragment of a jar with collar-neck and bored hole.

C 1
Fragments of three vessels. Pl. 83, AQ: upper part of a rim with crusted red on the inside. Pl. 83, X: round strut with a small knob where it joins the handle; decorated with vertical groove on the outside and incised oblique lines on the front. Another strut with incised oblique lines.

C 3

Several fragments of at least two pans with pierced rims, e.g. Pl. 37, G = Pl. 84, D. Another, Pl. 37, L = Pl. 84, V, with rim squashed in from the outside, and an unpierced horizontal lug on the inside. Pl. 84, T, with straw-like impressions on the bottom, was not walled around its entire circumference: it preserves part of a finished horizontal edge, at a point where it is beginning to curl up to form the wall of the vessel; the edge has deep punctations, roughly lozenge shaped.

OTHER SHERDS

Incised and grooved. Three fragments, e.g. Pl. 89, B, from two or three large vessels with simple rectilinear designs; one, Pl. 89, N, perhaps from a rim, has multiple chevrons on a slightly raised surface.

Handles and lugs. Several strap handles and lugs. Pl. 85, AD: high-rising lug handle with two horizontal piercings. Pl. 84, AZ: ribbon handle with angular profile. One fragment of a flat vertical handle joining a rim of large diameter. One fragment of an interior lug. Pl. 84, BK: a tab-like knob probably broken from a handle (cf. Pl. 84, BF–BH).

Bases. Fragments of at least 12 including flat bottoms, raised bases and ring bases. Pl. 85, BL: a separately made bottom, broken around the circumference at a surface prepared to receive the walls of the pot.

Oddments. Fragments of an oblong plaque (or lid?) with flat bottom and convex upper surface. Pl. 91, H: sherd with rough, pitted surface.

AREA H

ARCHITECTURE

Area H (Pls. 6, 52), the easternmost of the four near the top of the ridge, lies a short distance southwest of the summit, at an average elevation of about +36.50 m. Remains of two approximately parallel walls (Walls 1 and 2) were visible before excavation. After their tops had been cleared of surface accumulation, a trench was dug between them (about 4 m. [east-west] by 1 m.) in order to test the stratigraphy. Bedrock was reached at a maximum depth of about 0.60 m., sloping down from north to south in accordance with the overall slope of the hillside. The earth was fairly homogeneous, containing a jumble of stones, possibly fallen, and occasional sherds and animal bones. It did not have the character of a floor deposit.

Little can be made of the architecture of Area H. Wall 1 is the most carefully built of all the walls found at Kephala (Pl. 52, c) and it is solidly based on the sloping bedrock. Wall 2 also rests on bedrock, but at a slightly higher level than Wall 1, and survives to a height of only one or two stones. If Wall 1 was the eastern side and Wall 2 the western side of a structure, the floor must have been at a level higher than the modern surface, lost by erosion. It is equally possible, however, that Walls 1 and 2 belonged to different structures.

OBJECTS

Since no significant stratigraphy was observed in the small space excavated, the meager finds are presented in a single catalogue. All objects other than pottery were found beneath the surface and may be regarded as stratified; the same is true of almost all the pottery.

STONE

35 (Kph.4.17) Waste piece of obsidian
Found near bedrock between Walls 1 and 2.
One end missing. L. 0.027, W. 0.009, Th. 0.006.

Black; surface shiny. Long narrow piece, resembling a pointed tool; nearly square in section.

Obsidian uninventoried (by categories):

	1 a	1 b	2	3	4	5	6	waste	total
Stratified	0	0	4	0	0	0	1	20	25
Unstratified	2	0	2	0	0	0	3	10	17

TERRACOTTA

36 (Kph.4.39) Sherd rubbing-tool Pl. 71
Found among stones between Walls 1 and 2.
Intact. L. 0.045, W. 0.038, Th. 0.009.
Coarse, orange-brown biscuit. Oval, with smoothed and rounded edges; nearly flat.

POTTERY

About three eighths of a tinful of pottery was collected, almost all from beneath the surface. At least 11 bowls and one large jar were represented.

A 1

A rim fragment.

A 2

Fragments of at least three vessels, two with pattern burnishing inside, apparently consisting of parallel lines.

B 1

37 (Kph.32) Jar with S-curved wall Pls. 32, 76
Found near bedrock beside north end of Wall 1.
About one seventh preserved. H. pres. 0.072, D. rim est. 0.16.

Coarse, gray biscuit; exterior burnished, gray brown; interior rough. Low broad vessel with curving wall, rounded in lower part and slightly flaring at the lip.

C 1

A fragment probably from the rim of a scoop.

Other Sherds

Crusted red. A small vessel with crusted red inside, burnished outside.

Incised and grooved. Pl. 89, Y: flat profile; deep curving groove.

With plastic decoration. An impressed band.

Handles and lugs. Fragments of at least four strap handles, one of them small. Pl. 84, BH, decorated with crusted red, has a tab-like knob at the top. Another tab-like knob probably broken from a handle. Pl. 85, L: a large unpierced horizontal lug, slightly indented at the middle.

Bases. Three small flat bottoms. One large flat bottom, D. 0.16. One large raised base, concave beneath.

AREA J

Architecture

Area J (Pls. 5; 52, d) is about 20 m. west of Area H at an average elevation of about +35.50 m. The remains lie just south of a large outcrop of rock (see Section b–b on Pl. 5). Beneath a scanty cover of soil were found several east-west walls aligned with the contour of the hill. These are presumably the northern walls of structures whose southern walls and supporting terraces have been swept away. Coherent plans of rooms or houses could not be recognized; the only distinctive feature is the wall, near the middle of the space investigated, which makes a conspicuous jog to the south at an acute angle.

Objects

The finds from Area J must all be regarded as unstratified surface finds.

STONE

Obsidian uninventoried (by categories):

1 a	1 b	2	3	4	5	6	waste	total
0	0	1	0	0	0	0	6	7

POTTERY

Only one sixteenth of a tinful was collected. The material included at least five small vessels and one large vessel.

A 2: WITH PEDESTAL

A fragment from the juncture of bowl and pedestal.

OTHER SHERDS

Pattern burnished. A small vessel with parallel strokes on the outer surface.

Bases. A fragment of a large flat bottom.

Oddments. Pl. 45, G: a small thick-walled vessel with a broad, flat, everted lip. An up-turned or everted rim with indentations on the top.

AREA K

ARCHITECTURE

The remains in Area K (Pls. 5, 52, 53) are situated on a shelf of rock within a triangular space bordered by nearly vertical rock scarps on the northeast and northwest. The scarps rise about 1.50 to 2.10 m. above the shelf and afford excellent protection from the north wind; the northeastern scarp is undercut about 0.80 m. (Section c–c on Pl. 5). The hill slopes down gradually from the other sides of the shelf.

The only considerable ancient deposit was located in the immediate angle formed by the scarps; it reached a maximum depth of about 0.80 m. Toward the south, east, and west the deposit diminished gradually until it almost disappeared, about 2.50 m. from the angle. Two strata were distinguished in the deeper part of the deposit, but they could not be clearly separated toward its edges. The lower stratum appears to have been deposited when a hearth or fireplace was in use. It was immediately contiguous to bedrock and consisted of a layer of dark-colored earth containing many fragments of large jars and a deposit of carbonized seeds. No remains of walls were recognized in the lower stratum; the only noticeable feature was a shallow depression in bedrock immediately beside the angle of the rock scarps; it was about 0.30 m. deep and had a radius of about 0.50 m. (Pl. 53, b). The lower stratum completely covered the depression and extended somewhat beyond it. Several flat stones were found at the edge of the depression and a coarse clay plaster had been set around them; other flat stones were scattered around at the foot of the northeastern scarp at about the same level.[4] The interior of the depression and the stones at its edge showed a marked discoloration from fire. The hearth or fireplace was presumably situated within the depression but its exact arrangement could not be determined. The maximum depth of the lower stratum (including the depression) was about 0.50 m.

More than half a tinful of carbonized seeds was collected in the lower stratum. Most of them were packed together in a roughly oval space about 0.80 m. (north-south) by 1.20 m., in the southern part of the shallow depression and farther south; all lay to the west of the flat stones and plaster. They may have been contained in one of the large jars which were found in this stratum, and they appear to have become carbonized but not to have been burned. They were identified by Jane M. Renfrew as predominantly grass pea with some hulled six-row barley (see Appendix 3). A sample of the material was submitted to the Radiocarbon Laboratory of the University of Pennsylvania for dating (P 1280: Stuckenrath and Lawn, 1969, p. 156). The date arrived at, 2876 $\pm$ 56 B.C. (on the basis of a half-life of 5570 years) is a little later than the date suggested by a comparison with other sites (see Chapter IV).

The upper stratum was very shallow and reached a maximum depth of about 0.30 m.; it was lighter in color than the lower stratum. Within the upper stratum, but resting immediately above the lower one, were a number of flat stones in no orderly arrangement. Remains of a wall aligned northeast-southwest (Pl. 53, a) were found about 0.20 m. above the top of the lower stratum and almost immediately beneath the surface.[5] The wall is about 0.80 m. from the northwestern scarp, and its northeastern end was contiguous with the northeastern scarp. Some stones (not shown on the plan but visible in Pl. 53, a) were found scattered around the southwestern end of the wall and they may originally have belonged to a northwest-southeast wall; if so, the space northwest of the walls, enclosed by the angle of the rock scarps, would have been roughly rectangular and about 1.20 m. in length. This space is too small to have been a room and no remains of other walls were found in the area. Area K may have been a simple open shelter during the time that both strata were deposited.

[4] The stones shown with less dense hatching on Plate 5 are those associated with the lower stratum. It is possible that some of the stones belonged to a paving like that in Area D south of Wall 1 (above, p. 22).

[5] The stones of the wall are shown in more dense hatching on Plate 5.

Objects

STONE

38* (Kph.4.36) Celt Pls. 24, 68
Provenance not recorded in detail.[6]
Missing: both ends and most of one edge. L. 0.053, W. 0.027, Th. 0.016.
Black emery, polished. Small, roughly oval; edges nearly parallel but converging towards the blade; one edge thicker than the other. Probably similar in form to **77***, the only other celt of emery.

39* (Kph.4.20) Obsidian flake tool (category 2) Pl. 69
Intact. L. 0.027, W. 0.024, Th. 0.0055.
Gray; surface shiny. Small; roughly triangular in outline and in section; several flake scars on one face; edges chipped.

40* (Kph.4.21) Obsidian flake tool (category 2) Pl. 69
Intact. L. 0.025, W. 0.025, Th. 0.004.
Black; surface shiny. Small, nearly round; several flake scars on one face; edges chipped to some extent.

41* (Kph.4.22) Obsidian flake tool (category 2) Pl. 69
One edge missing. L. 0.027, W. 0.028, Th. 0.0075.
Black; surface shiny. Small, rounded in outline but flat on the broken edge; edges chipped to some extent.

42* (Kph.4.23) Obsidian flake tool (category 2) Pl. 69
Intact. L. 0.02, W. 0.02, Th. 0.0075.
Gray black. Small, nearly triangular; several flake scars on one face; edges chipped to some extent.

43* (Kph.4.24) Obsidian flake tool (category 2) Pl. 69
Intact (?). L. 0.021, W. 0.019, Th. 0.0055.
Black with light and dark striations; surface shiny. Small; irregular in outline, triangular in section; edges chipped to some extent.

44* (Kph.4.27) Obsidian tool (category 6)
Intact (?). L. 0.018, W. 0.013, Th. 0.004.
Gray; surface dull. Small, triangular; edges chipped to some extent.

45* (Kph.4.25) Waste piece of obsidian Pl. 70
Intact. L. 0.024, W. 0.009, Th. 0.0035.
Black; surface shiny. Small, blade-like; triangular in section.

46* (Kph.4.26) Waste piece of obsidian Pl. 70
Intact. L. 0.03, W. 0.009, Th. 0.003.
Black; surface shiny at one end, elsewhere dulled by exposure. Small, blade-like; triangular in section.

Obsidian uninventoried (by categories):

1 a	1 b	2	3	4	5	6	waste	total
1	0	9	0	0	0	1	53	64

POTTERY

The total amount was about one tinful; body sherds of large jars make up the bulk of it. The pottery is presented in one catalogue because the two strata could not be isolated at the edge of the excavated area; it may be observed, however, that the sherds in the lower stratum were almost exclusively from large jars, described under B 2, a fact which suggests that the lower stratum represents a short period of specialized use.

A2

Rim fragments of at least six vessels; Pl. 28, H = Pl. 75, AK, with incised line outside below the lip. One body fragment with burnished stripes inside.

B 2

Relatively closed. A rim fragment possibly from a hole-mouthed jar.

Intermediate and indeterminate. Many fragments from two to four vessels. Rims include: Pl. 34, C, D. est. 0.44; Pl. 34, G, D. est. 0.42; Pl. 81, F, D. est. 0.46; Pl. 81, G, D. est. 0.42, with a bored hole below rim and a strap handle below that. Pl. 84, AN: a broad strap handle. At least two flat bottoms, D. est. 0.12 and 0.15. Most of the fragments are scored or rough on the inside and smoothed on the outside, and are gray as if burned.

Other Sherds

With plastic decoration. A fragment with a crude impressed band.

Oddments. Pl. 84, BL: a large tab-like knob, separately applied, presumably broken from a handle.

[6] The same is true of all nine inventoried objects of stone.

AREA L

GENERAL

Area L (Pls. 7, 53, 54) was the most rewarding of the areas excavated in the settlement because it produced both architectural remains and floor deposits. It lies about 30 m. west of Area K and at a slightly lower elevation. Two houses were excavated: the eastern one, House Y, is situated on the southern brow of the ridge where the rock has a fairly even slope; the western one, House Z, lies in the shelter of two rock scarps, a little further south and at a lower level than House Y. Wall 1 forms a link between the two levels, since its foundations slope down considerably from north to south. The architecture and contents of each house are described; then follows a short catalogue of unstratified objects found throughout the area during surface excavation.

HOUSE Y

Architecture

House Y (Pls. 7, 53) was a large structure built on a shelf of rock. It was roughly rectangular, to judge by the existing walls, with long axis northeast-southwest. The interior length must have been at least 6.70 m. (the distance from Wall 3 to Wall 6; see Pl. 7) and it may have been as great as 8.20 m. (the distance from Wall 1 to Wall 6). The interior width was probably 3.30 m. or more.

The walls of the house have survived to some extent on the northeast, northwest, and southwest, but have been altogether lost through erosion on the southeast. The walls which have survived are all founded on bedrock. The best preserved is Wall 6, which has a maximum height of about 0.50 m.; the others survive to only 0.20 to 0.30 m. The floor in the northern corner of the house, and along much of the northwestern side, is of bedrock, which was probably trimmed and leveled to some extent.

Wall 6 is the outer wall on the northeast. It is preserved for at least 4.20 m., resting for much of its length on an outcrop of rock about 0.35 m. higher than the bedrock floor (Section a–a on Pl. 7). The southwestern face of the outcrop was apparently trimmed smooth, but in a line somewhat oblique to Wall 6, with the result that it juts into the house a short distance (Pl. 53, d, e). Wall 6 is best preserved at its northwestern end; only a few stones have survived southeast of the outcrop, so that the original length of the wall is uncertain.

Wall 2, the outer wall along much of the northwestern side (Pl. 53, d), is also fragmentary. It is preserved to a length of about 5.30 m. It was founded about 0.50 m. higher than the level of the bedrock floor, in part on a narrow ledge of rock (Section a–a on Pl. 7; Pl. 53, d, e). At the northeast it is bonded with Wall 6; towards the southwest it curves somewhat and comes to an end about 1.40 m. from the line of Wall 3. It gives the impression of being carelessly built; the preserved width is only about 0.30 to 0.40 m., considerably less than the outer walls of the house, but it is probable that what is preserved is only the footing for a wider wall.

The arrangement of the western corner of the house is not clear. Wall 2 as preserved stops short of the corner. A few stones (at 10 on Pl. 7) may have belonged to the continuation of Wall 2 as far as Wall 1, but they are not in exact alignment with what is preserved of Wall 2. It is therefore uncertain whether Wall 1 was the outer wall of the house on the southwest (in which case the space encompassed by Walls 1, 3, 9, and the stones at 10 was an interior enclosure), or whether Wall 3 was the outer wall (in which case the space encompassed by Walls 1, 3, 9, and the stones at 10 was an exterior appendage such as a lean-to).

Wall 1 is preserved for more than 6.50 m. (measured horizontally). Since it was built on the sloping rock, its southeastern end is about 2 m. lower than the northwestern end. Whatever its exact relationship with House Y, it probably projected to the southeast beyond the strict limits of House Y, and by meeting Wall 5 it is also linked to House Z (below, p. 38). Walls 3 and 9 are too fragmentary to reveal their function; Wall 3 seems to meet the end of the bench which is retained by Wall 7 (see below), and, as already mentioned, Walls 1, 3, 9, and the stones at 10 evidently formed an enclosure, roughly rectangular, about 2.80 m. by 1 m.

House Y was at least 3.30 m. wide, to judge by the preserved length of Wall 6. Considerable terracing would have been required to bring the floor in the southern part of the house up to the level of the bedrock floor in the northern corner and along the northwestern side, but no traces of a wall or terrace on the southeastern side have survived.

The roof was presumably of light construction. Since the main part of the house was fairly large, there may have been some interior supports. Three possible post-holes were noted in the course of excavation (Pl. 7). The one farthest to the northeast (about 3.10 m. southwest of Wall 6 and 2.20 m. southeast of Wall 7) was an arrangement of three stones which may have been used to wedge the bottom of a post in place; the space between the stones is approximately 0.10 m. square. The other two are holes in bedrock. The larger had a rim diameter of about 0.40 m. and was some 0.30 m. deep; the smaller had a rim diameter of about 0.25 m. and was some 0.10 to 0.20 m. deep. If these three features were indeed post-holes, their proximity makes it unlikely that they were in simultaneous use.

The interior arrangement on the northwestern side of House Y is of considerable interest. A low wall, Wall 7, is apparently preserved to its full height of 0.20 to 0.30 m. It served as a retaining wall for a bench of hard-packed earth which extended alongside the outer wall of the house. The width of the bench varies from about 0.50 to 0.80 m. (being greatest where Wall 2 curves toward the northwest). Resting on the bench about 2.40 m. southwest of Wall 6 is a short spur, Wall 11, which comes to an end at the front of the bench. Wall 11 may have served to buttress Wall 2, which, as already mentioned, seems carelessly built. On the other hand, it may have served only to divide the bench into two parts. At the northern corner of the house a small structure was built, partly on the bench and partly on the outcrop that projects from beneath Wall 6: two low spur walls, one projecting from Wall 2, the other immediately in the corner, with a flat stone placed on them as a cover. The space between them was about 0.40 m. square and 0.30 m. high. The small structure was presumably for storage; nothing was found within it but earth.

The floor of House Y was best preserved in the northern corner (Pls. 53, d, e) and consisted of bedrock which had been carefully trimmed to a fairly level surface. The bedrock floor continued alongside Wall 7 almost as far as its juncture with Wall 3, although it narrowed to a width of only about 1.20 m. in places; it continued alongside Wall 6 for about 3 m. Towards the center of the house the bedrock falls away, at first gradually in a series of small steps, and then more rapidly; the floor in the southern part must have been created by fill, which subsequently disappeared through erosion. If the floor was originally level throughout the house, considerable terracing would have been necessary on the southern side; perhaps the floor was not entirely level.

Most of the finds from House Y come from a layer of compact reddish earth, with occasional large and small stones; this layer was only about 0.20 m. deep, and lay immediately above the bedrock floor; it could not be clearly distinguished everywhere. The earth above it contained many scattered stones, apparently fallen when the walls of the house collapsed. There were no indications of burning. The maximum depth of the entire deposit was nowhere more than about 0.75 m. The rather small number of finds suggests either that the floor was frequently swept or that the house was not occupied for very long.

Objects

STONE

47 (Kph.6.14) Fragment of marble bowl Pls. 23, 67

From north corner just above bedrock floor.

Fragment of base and wall. D. base est. 0.08, H. 0.027, W. 0.065.

Coarse-grained, white marble (Naxian?), yellowish brown at surface; surface smooth; worn to thin sharp edges where broken, perhaps through re-use since the smooth surface continues to the broken edges. Flat bottom, slightly offset; sieds curved, more nearly upright than those of **171**.

48 (Kph.6.16) Pointed scraper of flint Pl. 68

From north corner just above bedrock floor.

Intact. L. 0.057, W. 0.029, Th. 0.007.

Red brown with tan patches. Leaf-shaped: one end pointed, the other rounded; thickest in the middle, tapering in section towards the edges; fairly crude bifacial working, almost certainly the result of direct percussion (cf. **172**). Similar in general form to **86*** and **172**; perhaps also to obsidian tool **90***.

49 (Kph.6.11) Obsidian blade (category 1 a) Pls. 25, 69

Found among stones in north corner about 1 m. southwest of Wall 6.

Intact except for some chipping, probably recent. L. 0.056, W. 0.017, Th. 0.004.

Black; surface shiny. Narrow; triangular to trapezoidal in section; bulb of percussion at one end.

50 (Kph.6.15) Obsidian blade (category 1 a) Pl. 69

From north corner just above bedrock floor.

Both ends missing. L. 0.049, W. 0.01, Th. 0.004.

Black; surface dull. Narrow; trapezoidal in section; one edge chipped a little.

51 (Kph.6.28) Obsidian blade (category 1 a) Pl. 69

Found among fallen stones in north corner.

One end missing. L. 0.055, W. 0.025, Th. 0.002.

Dark red with black mottling; surface dull. Very broad; roughly trapezoidal in section but upper facet concave; bulb of percussion preserved; edges slightly chipped.

52 (Kph.6.32) Obsidian blade (category 1 a)

Found among stones in north corner.

Both ends missing. L. 0.022, W. 0.008, Th. 0.002.

Gray black; surface shiny. Narrow; triangular in section; one edge scarred from secondary working or from use.

53 (Kph.6.10) Obsidian blade (category 1 b) Pl. 69

Found among fallen stones in north corner.

Intact. L. 0.068, W. 0.025, Th. 0.007.

Gray black with light and dark striations; surface shiny. Broad blade with one edge nearly straight, the other irregular; triangular to trapezoidal in section; the irregular edge has several different planes and surfaces.

54 (Kph.6.12) Obsidian blade (category 1 b) Pls. 25, 69

Found among fallen stones about 1.30 m. southeast of Wall 7 and about 1.30 m. southwest of Wall 6.

Intact. L. 0.057, W. 0.026, Th. 0.0065.

Gray black with light and dark striations; surface shiny. Oval; flat on one face, five main facets on the other; edges chipped to some extent. Differs from most other blades in that the upper surface is more complex.

55 (Kph.6.29) Obsidian blade (category 1 b) Pl. 69

Found in southwest part of house among scattered stones.

Intact. L. 0.062, W. 0.019, Th. 0.004.

Gray; surface shiny except for a rough natural surface at one end and on one plane of one face. One edge nearly straight, the other converging towards it; trapezoidal in section; bulb of percussion at narrow end; one edge slightly chipped from use.

56 (Kph.6.39) Obsidian flake tool (category 2) Pl. 69

From north corner just above bedrock floor.

Intact except for small breaks made by pick during excavation. L. 0.059, W. 0.04, Th. 0.014.

Gray; surface slightly shiny. Large, teardrop-shaped; striking platform 0.018 by 0.005 at narrow end; one face roughly flat with two flat flakes removed; roughly triangular in section, higher near one edge, sloping toward the other; four notches along the thinner edge form a serrated edge, probably intended for sawing or scraping; some secondary working around narrow end, perhaps to facilitate hafting.

57 (Kph.6.40) Obsidian flake tool (category 2) Pl. 69

Found among fallen stones in north corner.

Intact. L. 0.036, W. 0.018, Th. 0.008.

Gray; surface slightly shiny. Roughly triangular; one edge has a broad flat surface, probably a striking platform; other edges serrated from use and probably secondary working.

58 (Kph.6.41) Obsidian flake tool (category 2) Pl. 69

Found among stones by southeast face of Wall 7.

Intact. L. 0.023, W. 0.022, Th. 0.007.

Gray; surface slightly shiny. Roughly triangular; broad bulb of percussion at base; other edges chipped from use.

59 (Kph.6.42) Obsidian flake tool (category 2) Pl. 69

Found among stones by southeast face of Wall 7.

L. 0.036, W. 0.021, Th. 0.004.

Gray with black striations; surface shiny. Roughly oval; bulb of percussion at one end, partly obliterated by the removal of a flat flake; one edge with broad notch perhaps modern; edges chipped from use.

60 (Kph.6.33) Waste piece of obsidian Pl. 70

Found among stones in north corner.

L. 0.034, W. 0.005, Th. 0.002.

Gray black, translucent, with light and dark striations; surface shiny. Very thin, narrow, blade-like; triangular in section.

61 (Kph.6.43) Waste core of obsidian Pl. 70

Found among stones by southeast face of Wall 7.

L. 0.032, W. 0.032, Th. 0.018.

Gray black; surface shiny. Many-faceted lump, apparently a worked-out core; probably from flake production since it is worked from many different angles.

Obsidian uninventoried (by categories):

1 a	1 b	2	3	4	5	6	waste	total
14	10	24	0	0	0	20	450	518

POTTERY

A total of about one and one-third tinfuls of pottery was collected in close association with House Y; most of it was found in a very fragmentary state immediately above the rock floor, but a few sherds came from among the fallen stones at a higher level. The catalogue is confined to material securely associated with the house.

A 1

62 (Kph.31) Bowl with crusted white on exterior Pls. 27, 74

Found just above bedrock floor beside southwest end of Wall 7.

About one fifth preserved; restored in plaster. H. 0.089, D. rim est. 0.118, D. base est. 0.104.

Bowl with nearly upright, slightly curving wall; plain rim; angular transition to a flat bottom. A vertically pierced lug is partially preserved inside near the rim.

Coarse, orange-brown biscuit; a fairly soft, matt, crusted white substance, applied after firing, is preserved on much of the exterior; interior rough.

A sample of the white substance was examined by Reuben G. Bullard (memorandum dated May 29, 1973): "White material (treated) is composed of very finely ground magnesium carbonate (probably derived from local magnesian dolomite or marble rock sources). The material contains less than 10% calcium. This material was added to the ceramic surface after the pottery was fired; post-firing abrasion on the ceramic surface occurs under the coating material."

A similar crusted white was found on one other sherd from the same floor deposit (below, Other Sherds), and there are traces on **106** and **138**, where it is combined with crusted red.

A 2

A fragment with angular profile, having a rounded lug, horizontally pierced, just above the angle.

A large fragment of a ring base, D. 0.12, pierced by two holes, from a vessel like **104**; other fragments from the same vessel have a plain rim with a horizontally pierced lug handle set beneath it.

A 1 or A 2

Fragments of at least seven rims. Pl. 88, M: thickened band on exterior with incised chevrons. Another rim (?) fragment has similar incised decoration.

B 1

Rim sherds from three vessels with up-turned lip, e.g. Pl. 31, Q = Pl. 77, AB.

B 2

63 (Kph.41) Fragment of large jar Pl. 87

From just above bedrock floor at northwest side of house.

Fragment of shoulder and belly, consolidated with plaster. H. pres. 0.17, D. body est. 0.45–0.50.

Coarse, red-brown biscuit. Large closed pot. At top of fragment, beginning of offset rim or collar-neck (cf. **10**). Burnished pattern, less careful than those on smaller vessels, made up of broad areas and parallel stripes; the latter of differing widths and drawn at various angles.

64 (Kph.28) Fragment of large jar Pl. 80

From southwest part of house among scattered stones.

Fragment of upper body, consolidated with plaster. H. 0.22, Th. av. 0.01.

Large closed vessel. Beginning of offset rim or collar-neck (cf. **10**). Two small lug handles, horizontally pierced, just beneath juncture of neck and shoulder. Beneath one of the upper lug handles are fragments of a lower lug handle; this has a long plastic extension beneath it, and is flanked on either side by vertical plastic ridges beginning just below the level at which the lug handle is pierced.

Relatively closed. Pl. 33, B = Pl. 80, B: large vessel with nearly conical shoulder and offset neck; T-lug with a long, narrowing, plastic extension set obliquely on the shoulder; marks of scoring in several places on the outside.

Intermediate and indeterminate. Rim fragments of at least five other vessels, e.g. Pl. 81, AR; another, Pl. 81, V, with a horizontal band of incised multiple chevrons.

C 1

Two small fragments perhaps from the same vessel: a strut with one vertical incised line, and an incised handle.

C 2

Pl. 84, Y: from the rim (?) of a cylindrical vessel with a ledge on the inside (cf. Pl. 37, B).

C 3

Rim fragment probably from a pan.

C 4

Pl. 84, AH: a fragment with flat profile, but with broad shallow grooves on one side; pierced at fairly regular intervals.

C 5

Pl. 84, AB: one of two fragments having rounded edge and flat profile, probably from a lid.

OTHER SHERDS

Crusted white. One sherd from a large jar (?), white on the outside.

Incised and grooved. Several small fragments from a large vessel: deep red burnish on exterior; incised lines, meeting one another at oblique angles, and groups of punctations (cf. Pl. 44, K = Pl. 88, AO); a few traces of a white substance within the incisions suggest that they may have been white filled.

With plastic decoration. One fragment with an impressed band.

Handles. Fragments of at least six strap handles; Pl. 38, C = Pl. 84, BD was attached by plugs thrust through the pot wall.

Bases. Fragments of at least five flat bottoms.

HOUSE Z

ARCHITECTURE

House Z (Pls. 7, 54) made more extensive use of the natural rock for shelter than any other structure excavated. In plan it may be roughly trapezoidal (with base at the northeastern side); the length (northeast-southwest) is about 4 m. and the maximum width about 2.50 m. The entire northwestern side of the house consists of a rock scarp without built elements. The maximum height of the scarp is about 1.70 m. It was apparently trimmed smooth at the bottom; toward the southeastern end it had a considerable overhang (Section b–b on Pl. 7). The northeastern side of the house also consists of a rock scarp, nearly vertical and apparently also trimmed smooth at the bottom. At the top are some large stones (at 4 on the plan). These are probably natural rather than having been moved into place in ancient times; they are identical in appearance to the bedrock and were apparently part of the mass of rock which became cracked and eroded but remained more or less in place. The maximum height of the northeastern scarp, including the stones, is about 1.60 m. Wall 5 formed the entire southeastern side of the house. It is about 0.50 to 0.60 m. wide, at least 6 m. long and was preserved to a maximum height of about 0.30 m. A few stones which project toward the northwest from near the southwestern end of Wall 5 probably mark the position of a wall at the southwestern side of the house (Pl. 54, e); although practically nothing survives of this wall, the carefully dressed rock floor comes to an end at this point.

The entrance to the house was probably at the eastern corner; the scarp which forms the northeastern wall of the house slopes down toward the eastern corner, and there is apparently a gap between it and Wall 5. Wall 5 apparently extended toward the northeast as far as Wall 1 and blocked access from the south and east. The entrance was probably therefore approached from the northwest, down a sloping bedrock path along the southwestern side of Wall 1. Another possible approach would have been from the northeast, if there was originally a gap in Wall 1 (to the northwest of its junction with Wall 5) as the plan perhaps suggests. It would have been necessary to step down about 0.30 m. to enter the house at the northeastern corner.

The floor of the house was of bedrock throughout; it was approximately level and must have been dressed with some care. There was a ledge about 0.20 m. above the rock floor at the western corner of the house, partly beneath the overhang of the northwestern scarp (Section b–b on Pl. 7, and Pl. 54, c, e). The ledge had probably been trimmed to some extent; it formed a more or less oval space about 1.40 m. long (northeast-southwest) by 0.80 m. wide (the inner side of the space is shown in broken lines in Pl. 7). A few stones on the southwestern side of Wall 8 may have formed a continuation of the ledge. It perhaps served as a bench or couch.

One certain interior construction and another possible one were recognized in the course of excavation. Wall 8 is a short spur built against the scarp on the northwestern side of the house (Pl. 54, c, e, f); it is preserved to a height of about 0.60 m. and was perhaps intended as a partial divider of the interior. A pentagonal formation of stones near the southwestern end of Wall 5 (Pl. 54, d) may have been fortuitous, since the stones were found to rest not on the bedrock floor, but a few centimeters above it.

House Z, like House Y, was covered by earth containing many scattered and apparently fallen stones (shown at an early stage of excavation in Pl. 54, a). The stones continued all the way down to the bedrock floor, and a separate floor deposit could not always be clearly distinguished; most of the finds, however, were concentrated near the floor. There was no indication of burning in the house. The deposit was greatest at the western corner, where it reached a maximum depth of about 0.80 m.; elsewhere it had a depth of only 0.20 to 0.40 m.

OBJECTS

STONE

65 (Kph.6.7) Celt Pls. 24, 68

Found beside Wall 5 near its mid-point about 0.10 m. above bedrock floor.

Intact except tiny chip from blade. L. 0.03, W. 0.025, Th. 0.013.

Gray green; very fine stone; surface smoothly polished. Small, broad; butt rounded; edges nearly parallel; thickest towards the middle; both faces rounded except where they are beveled to flat planes, nearly triangular, which meet to form the blade; blade very slightly bowed. This is the most finely worked of the celts found; it is also broader and shorter than the others.

66 (Kph.6.8) Celt Pls. 24, 68

Found beside Wall 5, about 0.50 m. northeast of **65**, near the bedrock floor.

Intact except slight chip at one edge of blade. L. 0.082, W. 0.042, Th. 0.024.

Blue gray; fine stone; surface polished. Large; blade broad and rounded; butt pointed; oval to round in section, both faces rounded. Not closely similar to the other celts.

67 (Kph.6.34) Obsidian blade (category 1 a)

Found near the bedrock floor on northwest side of house.

Both ends missing. L. 0.027, W. 0.013, Th. 0.003.

Black; surface shiny. Small fragment, narrowing slightly towards one end; flat on one face, several planes on the other; extensive secondary working on both edges.

68 (Kph.6.37) Obsidian blade (category 1 a)

Found at southeast side of house near bedrock floor.

One end missing. L. 0.027, W. 0.009, Th. 0.003.

Black; surface fairly shiny. Fairly narrow; trapezoidal in section; one edge chipped from use.

69 (Kph.6.35) Obsidian blade (category 1 b) Pl. 69

Found at southeast side of house near bedrock floor.

Intact. L. 0.054, W. 0.021, Th. 0.005.

Black; surface shiny. Edges nearly parallel but narrowing slightly towards one end; bulb of percussion at broader end; flat on one face; triangular in section at middle; one edge flat for about half its length with rough natural surface; other edges somewhat chipped from use.

70 (Kph.6.30) Obsidian flake tool (category 2) Pl. 69

Found among fallen stones in the house.

Intact. L. 0.03, W. 0.027, Th. 0.006.

Gray; surface shiny. Irregular shape; roughly flat on one face; bulb of percussion at one end; chipped at edges from use and perhaps secondary working; slight notches at two places.

71 (Kph.6.36) Obsidian scraper (category 3) Pl. 70

Found on southeast side of house near bedrock floor.

Intact. L. 0.036, W. 0.014, Th. 0.008.

Gray; surface slightly shiny. Roughly oblong; triangular in section; bulb of percussion at one end; edges chipped from use.

72 (Kph.6.31) Obsidian projectile point (category 4) Pls. 25, 70

Found among fallen stones in the house.

Both ends missing. L. 0.014, W. 0.01, Th. 0.004.

Black; surface somewhat shiny. Small; narrowing slightly towards one end where there is probably the beginning of a tang; oval in section; all surfaces show fine secondary working.

This is the finest obsidian tool from Kephala; no other piece found is comparable in type, and only **90*** is comparable in workmanship; it is closely similar, however, to points from Paoura (see Appendix 6).

73 (Kph.6.38) Obsidian tool (category 6) Pl. 70

Found at southeast side of house near bedrock floor.

Intact. L. 0.031, W. 0.014, Th. 0.004.

Gray; surface dull. Irregular; two notches at one edge; bulb of percussion at one end; edges chipped from use or secondary working.

Obsidian uninventoried (by categories):

1 a	1 b	2	3	4	5	6	waste	total
17	13	16	0	0	0	17	452	515

POTTERY

A total of about four fifths of a tinful of pottery was collected on or near the floor; it was all very fragmentary. A further one-quarter tinful came from among the stones at a higher level. The catalogue is limited to material from near the floor, except one sherd, the context of which is noted.

A 1

A rim fragment.

A 2

Fragments of nine rims, five probably from bowls with continuously curved sides. Fragment of a vessel with angular profile.

A 2: WITH PEDESTALS

Fragment of a vessel with pedestal or high ring base.

B 1

Pl. 31, D = Pl. 77, R: rim, D. est. 0.12, of a hole-mouthed jar with a lug, horizontally pierced and vertically elongated, near the rim.

B 2

74 (Kph.26) Squat open jar Pls. 34, 80

About one seventh preserved; consolidated with plaster. H. 0.26, D. rim est. 0.30, D. base est. 0.11.

Coarse, red-brown biscuit; surface burnished; white accretion in places.

Sides rounded to biconical; plain rim; the bottom evidently flat, but tilted up somewhat at the edges. At greatest diameter, a wide strap handle (perhaps there were originally two); from top of handle, a low plastic ridge extending vertically for a short distance towards the rim.

75 (Kph.35) Fragment of large jar Pls. 43, 88

From southeast side of house.

Part of flat base and curving side of a large closed (?) vessel. H. 0.164, D. base est. 0.14.

Coarse, red-brown biscuit. Scored inside. Burnished decoration outside: many parallel lines in groups, vertical or nearly so; most lines are fairly uniform in width, but a few are wider.

Relatively closed. Frontispiece, G = Pl. 43, E = Pl. 87, N, found among fallen stones at a level higher than the floor: offset lip or collar-neck; burnished stripes radiating down the shoulder. A collar-neck, D. 0.10, with traces of crusted red on the outside.

Intermediate and indeterminate. Fragments from a large vessel of crumbly fabric, broken at the edges of the horizontal rings (flattened coils or bands) by which it was constructed and showing that the rings had beveled edges.

C 4

Four fragments of one (?) flat strainer, pierced at regular intervals.

OTHER SHERDS

Crusted red. Small fragments of at least three vessels.

Handles. One large strap handle; one unpierced horizontal lug; one rounded lug.

Bases. Pl. 39, M: medium-sized raised base, D. 0.11; another, D. 0.14. Pl. 39, P = Pl. 85, BB: ring base, D. 0.073, possibly from a jar, with four holes set in pairs opposite each other.

Oddment. Pl. 91, G: small closed (?) vessel with strongly curved wall and scored interior.

AREA L: UNSTRATIFIED OBJECTS

The following catalogue consists of objects which were found near the surface throughout the area and cannot be assigned with certainty to either house.

COPPER WORKING

76* (Kph.24) Fragment of burnt clay from a furnace-lining or crucible with metallic deposit Pls. 22, 66

Found at southwest end of House Y and above House Z.

Small fragment. Missing: all edges and part of slag deposit. L. 0.036, W. 0.033, Th. with deposit 0.025.

Coarse, orange-brown biscuit; porous and ashy where it meets the slag deposit. Sherd with flat profile, preserving part of a hole about 0.02 m. in diameter. The size of the perforation is comparable to those in **107**, **148***, and **174**. Slag deposit on the inside about 0.005 m. thick; gray black; rough and pitted. For analysis see Appendix 1, No. 6.

Small fragment of mineral kept as a sample (Keos excavation sample No. 22); identified by Reuben G. Bullard as ore or slag.

STONE

77* (Kph.4.8) Fragment of celt Pls. 24, 68

Found near House Z.

Blade end preserved. L. pres. 0.026, W. 0.025, Th. 0.009.

Very fine, smooth, black emery; surface polished. The faces are roughly parallel except where they converge towards the blade; one edge straight, the other slightly curved; thicker near one edge than at the other; blade somewhat bowed. Probably very similar to **38***, the only other celt of emery.

78* (Kph.4.29) Obsidian flake tool (category 2) Pl. 69
Found at southwest end of House Y and above House Z.
One end missing. L. 0.029, W. 0.026, Th. 0.006.
Gray; surface fairly shiny except along one edge which has a rough natural surface. Roughly triangular; two edges chipped from secondary working or use.

79* (Kph.4.30) Obsidian flake tool (category 2)
Found at southwest end of House Y and above House Z.
Intact (?). L. 0.031, W. 0.014, Th. 0.0045.
Gray; surface fairly shiny. Semicircular; the curving edge is chipped from secondary working or use.

80* (Kph.4.31) Obsidian flake tool (category 2) Pl. 69
Found at southwest end of House Y and above House Z.
Intact. L. 0.032, W. 0.019, Th. 0.0065.
Gray with black striations; surface shiny. Irregular outline; one edge chipped from use.

Obsidian uninventoried (by categories):

1 a	1 b	2	3	4	5	6	waste	total
6	7	15	0	0	0	12	558	598

TERRACOTTA

81* (Kph.4.9) Object of unknown purpose Pl. 71
Found at southwest end of House Y.
Intact (?). H. 0.024, D. 0.023.
Coarse, brown biscuit; surface rough. Very irregular, short concave cylinder, hollowed at one end. Possibly a strut broken from the handle of a pot (cf. Pl. 85, T, U). See also **26**.

POTTERY

One third of a tinful of pottery was collected while clearing the surface; the sherds were very fragmentary.

A 2

Pl. 38, O = Pl. 85, AQ: bowl with high-swung lug handle projecting obliquely above the rim.

C 1

Pl. 83, B: top of the handle of a scoop, with the forward edge indented at regular intervals; the top is bordered by the following incised decoration: a row of indentations parallel to the forward edge, a deep groove, another row of indentations, another groove; the main incised decoration evidently comprised groups of parallel lines meeting at oblique angles. Cf. **98**.

A fragment of an incised strut.

Other Sherds

Incised and grooved. Small fragments of two vessels.

With plastic decoration. A fragment with a knob. Several fragments with impressed bands.

Handles. At least four strap handles: one with plastic knob at the apex; one with impressed vertical band at point of attachment. Fragment of round handle or strut with lengthwise groove. Horizontal lug with two vertical piercings, and plastic ridges depending from either end. An unpierced horizontal lug. Pl. 85, AS: large tab handle pierced with two small holes.

Bases. Three raised bases. A fragment probably from a rounded bottom.

SURFACE FINDS FROM UNEXCAVATED AREAS

The objects in the following catalogue were found on the surface but not within the limits of any of the excavated Areas. Where possible their approximate provenance is given.

COPPER AND COPPER WORKING

82* (Kph.9.1) Fragment of small chisel (?) Pls. 22, 66
From surface about 10 m. north of Area E.
Small fragment from blade end. L. pres. 0.011, W. 0.01, Th. 0.003.
Surface smooth; green patina before conservation. Wedge-shaped in section; edges parallel, with sharp blade perpendicular to edges. Similar to **147*** but smaller and lighter.

83* (Kph.9.2) Fragment of small tool Pls. 22, 66
From surface north of Areas E and G.
One end only. L. pres. 0.013, W. pres. 0.009, Th. 0.004.
Surface smooth; green patina before conservation. Part of small tool with blunt end 0.008 m. by 0.0025 m.; the edges apparently converged and the shaft was slightly thinner towards the end.

Three pieces of slag (Appendix 1, Nos. 2, 3, 4).

LEAD

84* (Kph.71.1) Object of unknown purpose Pl. 66
Found about 10 m. east of Area D.
Both ends missing (?): some gouging along edges and one face. L. 0.053, W. 0.01, Th. 0.004.
Gray. Long, roughly rectangular but narrowing slightly at one end, and bent somewhat in the middle; one face flattened, the other rounded.
Similar to one of the two side-pieces of clamps used in the Bronze Age to mend cracked pots; there is no trace of the pins, however, which pass through the wall of the pot and link such side-pieces.

STONE

85* (Kph.4.13) Pointed tool of flint Pl. 68
Found on surface near Area D.
Intact. L. 0.035, W. 0.014, Th. 0.008.
Dark red to brown. Somewhat pointed at both ends but one end narrower and sharper; roughly triangular in section; marks of secondary working on all surfaces. Similar to obsidian tool **91***; perhaps a projectile point.

86* (Kph.3.7) Fragment of triangular scraper of flint Pl. 68
Found between cemetery and settlement.
Pointed end missing. L. 0.029, W. base 0.025, Th. 0.007.
Yellow-gray stone with pinkish white surface. Broad straight base; edges curve towards the pointed end; thickest in the middle, tapering in section towards the edges; careful bifacial pressure flaking. Similar to **172** but without serrated edges.

87* (Kph.0.2) Obsidian blade (category 1 a)
One or both ends missing. L. 0.04, W. 0.01, Th. 0.0035.
Gray; surface dull. Narrow; trapezoidal in section; edges extensively chipped from use.

88* (Kph.0.1) Obsidian scraper (category 3) Pl. 70
One end missing. L. 0.054, W. 0.022, Th. 0.007.
Gray; surface fairly shiny. Roughly oblong, with one end pointed and the other flat; flat on one face, several facets on the other; edges and pointed end reworked and/or chipped to some extent.

89* (Kph.1.13) Obsidian scraper (category 3) Pl. 70
Base end missing. L. 0.04, W. 0.021, Th. 0.008.
Dark gray; surface dull. Roughly triangular in section; edges and the pointed end retouched and/or chipped to some extent.

90* (Kph.1.12) Fragment of pointed tool of obsidian (category 4) Pls. 25, 70
Pointed end only. L. 0.025, W. 0.026, Th. 0.008.
Dark gray; surface shiny. Careful bifacial reworking. Probably from a scraper such as **123** and flint tools **48, 86*** and **172.**

91* (Kph.4.4) Pointed tool of obsidian (category 4) Pls. 25, 70
Intact. L. 0.04, W. 0.016, Th. 0.009.
Dark gray; surface shiny. Oval, but tapering to a point at either end; slight shoulder at one end, as if a tang were intended; triangular in section; sporadic secondary working on each face. Similar to the flint tool **85***; perhaps a projectile point.

92* (Kph.1.11) Waste piece of obsidian Pl. 70
Intact. L. 0.026, W. 0.018, Th. 0.007.
Dark gray; surface slightly shiny. Roughly triangular; probably trimmed off when a core was being rejuvenated.

93* (Kph.1.10) Waste piece of obsidian Pl. 70
Fragment only. L. 0.084, W. 0.059, Th. 0.032.
Dark gray; shiny on most surfaces. Large, nearly pointed end from a nucleus (Wt. 126 gm.); natural rough surface of matrix in two places; scars from flaking parallel to the axis; one single broad curving surface oblique to the axis with striking platform at its lower end. Struck off a large core which had not been extensively worked; probably the knapper's intention was to strike off a smaller piece, but he ruined the original core. Cf. **94*** and **95***.

94* (Kph.5.1) Waste core of obsidian Pl. 70
From surface near the cemetery.
Fragment only. L. 0.065, W. 0.056, Th. 0.037.
Dark gray stone, weathered. Large lump (Wt. 225 gm.); natural, flat, rough surface of matrix on one side; several blade scars on another side; a single broad broken surface extends perpendicular to the direction of the blade scars. Probably discarded as useless when it broke in half after only a few blades had been removed; cf. **93***.

95* (Kph.7.1) Waste core of obsidian Pl. 70
From surface about 10 m. north of Area K.
Fragment only. L. 0.107, W. 0.072, Th. 0.046.

Dark gray; surface shiny in places. Large lump (Wt. 314 gm.) with natural rough surface of matrix over much of it; four broad, shiny flake scars. Evidently lost or discarded before it had been completely prepared for the production of tools. This is the largest and heaviest piece of obsidian found. Cf. **93*** and **94***.

96A* (Kph.4.14) Rubbing-tool Pls. 24, 68

From surface just east of Area E.

Intact except surface deeply pitted in places. L. 0.045, W. 0.023, Th. 0.011.

Dark blue-gray stone. Flat, rectangular with rounded edges; slightly thinner at one end; worn smooth from use.

TERRACOTTA

96B* (Kph.73.1) Head of large figurine Pls. 26, 71

From surface northeast of Area G.

Head and neck preserved; upper edge and surface of face missing; broken at juncture with body. H. pres. 0.12, W. 0.077, Th. 0.048.

Coarse biscuit, brown at core, blackened around hole; a distinct layer of finer red clay 0.003 to 0.004 m. thick on surface (see sections on Pl. 26).

Face apparently roughly triangular with apex at slightly rounded chin; tilted back from bottom to top. Neck oval in section; slightly flaring at bottom.

Vertical hole, D. 0.013, pierced through center; a smaller vertical hole, D. 0.006, depth *ca.* 0.014, near upper right corner of face; only a trace of the bottom of a similar hole remains at the left side (Pl. 26). The central hole was presumably made by a wooden support around which the piece was modeled; the smaller holes may have been made by secondary supports; the wood burned out during firing, leaving the blackened holes.

Considerably larger than **128** and **202** and preserving no evidence for a projecting knob at the back. The use of wooden supports has no parallel at Kephala, but see Immerwahr, 1971, p. 48, no. 220, where it is suggested that the head was made separately, then attached to the body.

POTTERY

Many fragments of pottery were picked up on the surface of the promontory, outside the excavated Areas, within and around the remains of eroded buildings. Almost all are from vessels like those from the excavated Areas and they testify to the widely scattered occupation of the promontory in prehistoric times.

Only four sherds are illustrated. Pl. 89, AU: large open vessel (like **146** and **170**?) with indented rim, and three vertical plastic bands with finger impressions at regular intervals. Pl. 89, AV: large vessel; at top of sherd are curving ridges in an interlocking pattern probably simulating rope. Pl. 84, AO: strap handle with vertical incised lines and a short plastic strip just above it. Pl. 84, BM: lug handle, now detached, shaped like a large T-lug. Only seven sherds appear to be later than the period of prehistoric occupation: one with black slip or polish may date to the Bronze Age; the rest are probably post Bronze Age and include a wheelmade sherd with vitreous green glaze, and a handle fragment probably from a modern water jar. The scarcity of later finds suggests that the promontory was seldom visited after the time of prehistoric occupation.

III. THE CEMETERY (AREA F)

GENERAL

The cemetery was situated near the base of the headland (Pls. 3; 49, d; 55, a) where the slope, which in general rises steadily towards the north, is interrupted by two clefts running along the contour of the hill (Pl. 12, Section C–C). At least forty graves, and perhaps originally many more, were constructed in and around these clefts. The cleft on the south, with its adjacent areas, is at a lower level than the other, and has been designated the Lower Cemetery; the cleft on the north, with its adjacent area, the Upper Cemetery (Plan, Pl. 8). These designations are merely to aid in description; the graves appear in fact to have been built wherever possible, more or less continuously over the whole area.

The two clefts were roughly parallel to one another and were separated by about 2 m. of bedrock which was exposed before excavation began. In the course of our investigations bedrock was also cleared over much of the surrounding slope. The uppermost graves in the clefts had been partly destroyed through erosion, and only traces remained of graves on the adjacent hillside (e.g. Graves 29 and 40). To judge from the eroded graves, there must have been a greater depth of soil, possibly as much as one meter more, over the whole area when the cemetery was in use.

Forty graves were excavated. Many were side by side, although never with a wall in common. Others were built directly above or overlapping one another. The graves were most dense in the central part of the Lower Cemetery. Earlier graves were apparently respected when later ones were built, and there is very little evidence of damage in the course of later activity (Grave 23 may have been slightly disturbed when Grave 24 was built; see below, p. 74). The only constructions in the cemetery besides the graves themselves were five walls in the Lower Cemetery (Walls 1–5; Pls. 8, 9) and one in the Upper Cemetery (Wall 6). Walls 1–4 may have been partition walls dividing a portion of the cemetery into plots (see below, p. 62); they date to a late stage in the use of the cemetery. Wall 6 may have been a boundary wall for part of the cemetery (see below, p. 84). Wall 5 is very fragmentary and its purpose is unclear (see below, p. 78).

Neither the axes of the graves nor the skeletons within them were consistently oriented.

From the archaeological evidence it is possible to form only a rough estimate of the length of time the cemetery was in use and the size of the community it served.[1] The sequence of graves in the central group of the Lower Cemetery provided the best evidence. It is argued below (p. 54) that this part of the cemetery must have been in use for at least 60 years, and probably for 100 years or more. Since there is no way of knowing how many graves have been lost through erosion, no reasonably sure upper limit can be suggested. A guess, based in part on observation of the site as a whole, is that the cemetery was in use for not more than 150 years.

In all, remains of at least sixty-five people were found, including 21 adult men, 25 adult women, five adults of undetermined sex, nine children and five infants. Since bones of the young are more likely to have disappeared completely than those of adults,[2] the proportion of children may originally have been higher. The evidence from the central group of the Lower Cemetery suggests that at one period there were four or more graves in approximately contemporary use (see Table 5 below, p. 55); since this was only part of the cemetery, more graves elsewhere are likely to have been in use during the same period. At a rough guess ten or fifteen families may have been using the cemetery in any one period.[3]

[1] For other estimates see Angel, Appendix 5, pp. 134–135.
[2] See Graves 19 and 27.
[3] Angel, Appendix 5, p. 135, estimates about 10–12 families.

TYPES OF GRAVES

Built Graves

The most common type of grave (35 out of 40) is that in which the walls were constructed of many relatively small stones. The stones were those immediately available, schist and, more rarely, limestone or marble. The walls were constructed of unshaped stones, usually between 0.30 and 0.70 m. in length, interspersed with smaller stones. The width of the walls varies from about 0.20 to 0.60 m. Construction was fairly careful, but no attempt was made to set the stones in courses or in any particular pattern. A clay mortar was used as a bonding substance in at least some instances (e.g. Graves 14 and 20).

The plan varies considerably. Most may be described by the shape of the interior as roughly rectangular (e.g. Grave 20), circular (e.g. Grave 12), or oval (i.e. intermediate between these two extremes, e.g. Grave 9). There seems to be no particular significance in the distribution of different plans, although it is worth noting that there is a slightly higher incidence of multiple burials in rectangular graves than in circular graves (Table 2).

The size also varies considerably. Grave 18, one of the smallest, is only 0.46 m. in interior length; Grave 39, the longest, is 1.58 m.; the average interior length is about 0.90 m. The interior height varies from 0.15 (Grave 27) to 0.85 m. (Grave 3), most being 0.40 to 0.50 m. high. Some graves narrow somewhat towards the top (e.g. Graves 7, 37) but there was no extensive use of corbeling.

Built graves were regularly covered with several large slabs of schist. These were placed either on the longer or the shorter axis of the grave. The longest cover slabs are about 1.50 m. Smaller stones were sometimes wedged beneath the slabs to stabilize them, or were used to fill gaps. Since the schist breaks easily, the cover slabs were often found to have cracked; this had usually occurred after the grave had filled with earth, to judge by the position in which they were found.

In seven instances fairly solid structures of stone, here referred to as platforms, were constructed above the cover slabs.[4] Some of the other graves which have been partly lost through erosion may also have had platforms originally. The platforms were distinctive structures with a height of up to 0.38 m. above the cover (Grave 9). They were not merely a filling of the grave pit, since they are carefully built rather than a jumble of stones. The platforms generally project horizontally beyond the limits of the grave beneath them, and their plan may have been determined by the shape of the shaft dug for the grave; at any rate there is no exact correlation in plan between the platforms and the graves which they surmount. Five of the seven platforms are more or less rectangular or rectilinear in plan but two of these surmount graves which are round in plan. One of the other two (P 8 over Grave 36) was semicircular, having been curtailed on its northern side by a vertical scarp of rock; the other (P 3 over Grave 9) appears to have been constructed in three distinct layers, the lower two roughly circular, the upper quadrilateral. The platform-like structure labeled P 4 on Plate 10 was an anomaly: in form it resembled the other platforms, although smaller than any of them, but no grave was found beneath it. The relationship between the original surface level and the top of the platforms could not be stratigraphically determined, but the platforms are not so high that they are likely to have projected above the ground.

The platforms can have had no structural purpose. They could not have been used to counterbalance the weight of the cover slabs since stones were packed solidly over the whole area of the cover and since the covers almost always extended the full length or width of the grave and were supported by its walls. Thus the platforms differ from the groups of stones or walls used as counterweights at the outer edges of cover slabs at Ayios Kosmas.[5] Possibly they played a part in the burial ritual, perhaps providing a sort of altar where libations might be made and offerings placed for the dead. Many fragments of pots and all the figurines (except possibly **202**) were found in the earth around the graves rather than inside, and some of these may have been offerings made after the graves were closed; no recognizable offering was found in place on the top of a platform, however, and most of the finds made around the graves can be explained in other ways (see below, pp. 52–53). A more remote possibility is that the platforms

[4] P 1, P 2, P 3, P 5, P 6, P 7, and P 8, above Graves 10, 12, 9, 13, 4, 3, and 36 respectively. See Plate 10 for plans, Plates 55, b and 57, a, b for views.

[5] Mylonas, 1959, p. 65. He notes, however, that "over the roof slabs and between the walls which acted as counterweights small stones often were laid, so that the results looked almost like a cobblestone pavement" (see *ibid.*, figs. 74, 82, and 89); this produced an appearance similar to that of the platforms at Kephala.

TABLE 2. TYPES OF GRAVES AND NUMBER OF BURIALS

Number (Excavation No.)	Type	Plan	Platform	Length	Man	Woman	Adult, Sex Undetermined	Child	Infant	Total Burials
Grave 1 (XIX)	Built	Oval	?	1.05	2	3	1	–	–	6
Grave 2 (XXVII)	Cist	Rectangular	?	0.32	–	–	–	1	–	1
Grave 3 (XVIII)	Built	Rectangular	P 7	1.00	–	1	1 or more	–	–	at least 2
Grave 4 (XXII)	Built	Oval	P 6	1.00	1	–	–	–	–	1
Grave 5 (XXI)	Built	Trapezoidal	None	0.70–0.80	–	–	–	–	–	?
Grave 6 (VII)	Built	Circular	None	1.08	1	–	–	–	–	1
Grave 7 (XIII)	Built	Rect.-Oval	?	1.13	5	6	–	2	–	13
Grave 8 (XVII)	Jar	–	None	–	–	–	–	–	1	1
Grave 9 (X)	Built	Oval	P 3	0.96	–	2	–	–	–	2
Grave 10 (XII)	Built	Trapezoidal	P 1	1.04	–	1	–	–	–	1
Grave 11 (IX)	Built	Circular	None	1.00	1	–	–	–	–	1
Grave 12 (XI)	Built	Circular	P 2	0.93	–	1	–	1	–	2
Grave 13 (XX)	Built	Rectangular	P 5	1.23	1	1	–	–	–	2
Grave 14 (I)	Built	Rectangular	?	1.22	2	2	2	–	–	6
Grave 15 (XIV)	Built	Rectangular?	?	?	–	–	–	–	–	?
Grave 16 (VI)	Built	Rectangular	?	1.14	1	1	–	2	–	4
Grave 17 (XV)	Built	Oval	?	0.57	–	–	–	?	–	?
Grave 18 (XVI)	Built	Trapezoidal	?	0.46	–	–	–	?	–	?
Grave 19 (XXXI)	Built	Oval	None	0.67	–	–	–	?	–	?
Grave 20 (V)	Built	Rectangular	?	1.40	3	4	1	1	–	at least 9
Grave 21 (VIII)	Built	Rectangular?	?	1.05	–	–	–	–	–	?
Grave 22 (XXIX)	Built	Circular	None	0.60	–	–	–	1	–	1
Grave 23 (XXXII)	Jar in Cist	Triangular	None	0.42	–	–	–	–	1	1
Grave 24 (XXVI)	Built	Oval	None	1.20	–	1	–	–	–	1

TABLE 2, cont.

Number (Excavation No.)	Type	Plan	Platform	Length	Man	Woman	Adult, Sex Undetermined	Child	Infant	Total Burials
Grave 25 (XXV)	Built	Rectangular?	?	?	1	–	–	–	–	at least 1
Grave 26 (IV)	Built	Rectangular?	?	?	1	–	–	–	–	at least 1
Grave 27 (XXIV)	Built	Rectangular	None	0.50	–	–	–	?	–	?
Grave 28 (XXIII)	Built	?	?	?	–	–	–	–	–	?
Grave 29 (XXVIII)	Built	?	?	?	–	–	–	–	–	?
Grave 30 (III)	Built	Rectangular?	?	0.72?	–	–	–	–	–	?
Grave 31 (II)	Jar	–	?	–	–	–	–	–	2	2
Grave 32 (XXXVIII)	Jar	–	None	–	–	–	–	–	1	1
Grave 33 (XXXIII)	Built	?	?	?	–	–	–	–	–	?
Grave 34 (XXXVI)	Built	Rectangular	?	0.97	–	1	–	–	–	1
Grave 35 (XL)	Built	Oval	? P 9	1.05	1	–	–	–	–	1
Grave 36 (XXXIX)	Built-Cist	Rectangular	P 8	0.73	–	1	–	–	–	1
Grave 37 (XXXV)	Built	Circ.-Oval	None	0.79	–	–	–	1	–	1
Grave 38 (XXXIV)	Built	Circ.-Oval?	?	?	–	–	–	–	–	?
Grave 39 (XXXVII)	Built	Oval	None	1.58	1	–	–	–	–	1
Grave 40 (XXX)	Built	Rectangular?	?	?	–	–	–	–	–	?
Total					21	25	5+	9+	5	65+

were used to mark the position of the grave in some way. Since the platforms themselves probably did not project above ground level it is difficult to imagine that they served merely to support markers which did project. The reason for marking the position of a grave would presumably have been to make it easy to locate for subsequent burials, but only three of the seven platforms (P 3, P 5, and P 7) were found above graves which contained more than one burial, and other tombs with more than one burial were not surmounted by platforms.[6]

The way of access to all the built graves which are reasonably well preserved was through the top and there is no secure evidence of doors or openings in the walls. Grave 7 may have had a doorway in

[6] In the Early Cycladic cemeteries similar platforms are sometimes found: e.g. at Akroteri on Naxos (Doumas, 1963, p. 278; 1973, p. 560); cf. Tsountas, 1898, col. 142. In a few other instances graves were marked by a layer of pebbles: e.g. Ayioi Anargyroi on Naxos (Doumas, 1961–1962, p. 272; 1973, p. 560; the pebbles are wrongly called "flat stones" by Renfrew, 1972, p. 158). Caskey has suggested to me that the platforms at Kephala were constructed through fear of the dead, in the belief that their spirits might thereby be held down and contained. Doumas, 1968, p. 92 has also postulated such a fear in the Early Cycladic period, although without making specific reference to the platforms.

its side, but the evidence is not conclusive because of its damaged condition. A more remote possibility exists that one other damaged grave (Grave 14) had a doorway.[7]

CIST GRAVES

Only two of the 40 were cist graves. Both were very small. Grave 2 was rectangular in plan and contained the body of a child. Grave 23 was triangular in plan and contained a jar, which in turn held the body of an infant. Cist graves were thus not only rare, but also limited to use for the young. Grave 2 was one of the earliest in the Lower Cemetery. The construction of graves with slab sides was evidently familiar to the people of Kephala, but they chose to use it only rarely and for small graves, perhaps because it was easier to build with smaller, more readily available stones than with large slabs.

JAR BURIALS

There were three other jar burials of infants in which the jars were placed within pits without walls around them. In two instances the vessel was on its side; in the third, upright. In each case a stone was placed against the mouth of the jar. One of the vessels which lay on its side (Grave 32) had a cover of slabs above it which closely resembled those of the built graves; the other (Grave 31) had been damaged by erosion and no evidence of a cover was preserved. The two vessels on their sides (**146, 170**) were very similar in shape, whereas the vessel set upright (**97**) was of a different type. The vessels have close parallels in the settlement; they probably were not manufactured specifically for burials. **170** may have been used for some time before it became a burial jar, since it had been mended.

BURIAL PRACTICES

All the burials were inhumations. The bodies were often laid on specially prepared surfaces of pebbles or small stones. The instances in which the original position of the body could be ascertained[8] show that the bodies were not placed in the graves in any consistent position or orientation. The legs were often doubled up in a contracted position roughly perpendicular to the spine; the small size of the graves would seldom, if ever, have permitted an adult corpse to be fully extended, and this may have been a major determinant for the position of the body. The skeleton was sometimes on its right side (e.g. Grave 3) and sometimes on its left (e.g. Grave 37); the heads were often, although not always, towards the west. In one instance (Grave 39) the skeleton was extended as far as the knees, with the lower legs doubled up, and lay partly on its back with the head placed on a stone pillow. In Grave 35 the skeleton was also extended as far as the knees, with the lower legs doubled up, but here it lay on its face.

Tables 2 and 3 show the number of burials, and whether they were of adult men or women (i.e. fifteen years or older), children, or infants (under one year).[9] This information could be accurately determined for only 25 of the 40 graves. Fifteen of the 25 contained a single burial, five contained two burials and the remaining five contained from four to 13 burials. No distinctions based on sex or age were apparent, except that infants were buried exclusively in jars.

The single burials are not limited to one sex or age group. Nine of the 15 certain single burials were of adults (five men and four women), three were of children and three were of infants.

The graves with multiple burials were probably family tombs (except Grave 31, a pithos containing two infants). They contained the skeletons of men, women, and children. In Graves 1, 3, and 7, two or three distinct burial levels were recognized; this suggests that the burials were made over a considerable length of time and that the graves were closed and reopened.[10] In several cases (e.g. Grave 7) a bedding of pebbles or stones was laid for the different burial levels. Although at least 21 people were

[7] For more detailed discussion see the descriptions of each grave.

[8] The skeletal remains were not, on the whole, well preserved; many of the skeletons were in a state of such disintegration or confusion that it proved impossible to recognize the original position of the body, even when the grave was apparently intact. On the question whether the confused state might sometimes be due to secondary interment, see below, p. 50.

[9] I am indebted to Professor J. Lawrence Angel, Curator of the Division of Physical Anthropology, National Museum of Natural History, The Smithsonian Institution, for the information recorded in Tables 2 and 3, and in the catalogues of graves, concerning the skeletons. For further information on the physical anthropology of the people of Kephala see the complete discussion by Angel in Appendix 5.

[10] There were several skeletons at most of the burial levels and it is possible that some of the burials at these levels were simultaneous.

TABLE 3. DISTRIBUTION OF BURIALS BY GRAVES

Single Burial			More Than One Burial					At Least One Adult	Evidence Insufficient		
Adult	Child	Infant	2	4	6	9	13		Large Grave, Prob. Adult	Small Grave, Prob. Child	Uncertain
Grave 4 (XXII)	Grave 2 (XXVII)	Grave 8 (XVII)	Grave 3 (XVIII)	Grave 16 (VI)	Grave 1 (XIX)	Grave 20 (V)	Grave 7 (XIII)	Grave 25 (XXV)	Grave 15 (XIV)	Grave 17 (XV)	Grave 5 (XXI)
Grave 6 (VII)	Grave 22 (XXIX)	Grave 23 (XXXII)	Grave 9 (X)		Grave 14 (I)			Grave 26 (IV)	Grave 21 (VIII)	Grave 18 (XVI)	Grave 28 (XXIII)
Grave 10 (XII)	Grave 37 (XXXV)	Grave 32 (XXXVIII)	Grave 12 (XI)						Grave 30 (III)	Grave 19 (XXXI)	Grave 29 (XXVIII)
Grave 11 (IX)			Grave 13 (XX)						Grave 40 (XXX)	Grave 27 (XXIV)	Grave 33 (XXXIII)
Grave 24 (XXVI)			Grave 31 (II)								Grave 38 (XXXIV)
Grave 34 (XXXVI)											
Grave 35 (XL)											
Grave 36 (XXXIX)											
Grave 39 (XXXVII)											
Totals: 9	3	3	5	1	2	1	1	2	4	4	5

Grand Total: 40

buried in these three graves, only one skeleton was found in a recognizably articulated state (the burial at the upper level of Grave 1). The later burials had probably often disturbed the bones of the earlier ones and it is possible that grave goods of earlier burials were removed;[11] at any rate, none of the three graves contained any recognizable offerings.

In the other seven graves with multiple burials, the bones of two or more people were found together without any distinction of levels. In all but one instance (Grave 9) the bones were in a confused state and provided little evidence of the sequence, if any, in which the bodies had been buried. In Grave 9 the bones of the second body were found in a more or less articulated state, while the disturbed bones of the first body were found at one end of the grave as if swept aside after decomposition of the flesh.

The statistics on burials suggest that a person, regardless of age or sex, might be buried either in a tomb designed to contain a single burial or in a family tomb. The question arises, however, whether all the graves with single burials were in fact intended as individual tombs.

The three graves which contained single burials of children (Graves 2, 22, 37) were markedly smaller than those containing single adult burials (average length 0.57 m. as opposed to 1.07 m.) and were evidently constructed only large enough for one particular burial.

The graves containing adults, on the other hand, do not present such a clear picture. The nine containing single adult burials were about as large as the nine containing multiple burials with at least one adult (average length 1.07 m. as opposed to 1.12 m.). There is no obvious reason why re-use was intended but did not occur. The final desertion of the site might explain why three graves were not re-used (34, 36, 39) but in the other six cases other graves were built above those with single burials, either immediately (in the case of Graves 4, 6, 24, 35) or with an interval between (as in the case of Graves 10 and 11). It might be argued that the seemingly single graves had, in fact, been re-used but that the bones of other burials had entirely decayed, or been removed when the last interment was made (cf. Angel, Appendix 5, p. 135). Decay alone, however, would not in my opinion have been so selective that traces frequently remain of only one burial when there were originally two or more; nor is it likely that bones of earlier burials were entirely removed in many cases, when they were rmeoved either not at all, or only partly, in other cases. In short, though some ambiguity remains, it is a reasonable assumption, in view of the high proportion of graves in which only one adult was found,[12] that many graves were in fact used only once and that re-use was not always intended.

No graves with multiple burials were found in the Upper Cemetery. This is in marked contrast to the Lower Cemetery, where they have a wide distribution and occur among both earlier and later graves. The difference is a significant one,[13] even taking into account the greater number of graves in the Lower Cemetery and the many cases where the evidence for burials is incomplete or lacking. Two equally plausible explanations may be suggested: the burial customs of those using the Upper Cemetery may have been slightly different (were they of higher social status?); or the Upper and Lower Cemeteries may have been used at different times and burial customs may have changed slightly as time went on. These explanations are not mutually exclusive. There is no stratigraphic evidence for a chronological difference, since the space between the Upper and Lower Cemeteries is devoid of deposit. The less dense spacing of graves in the Upper Cemetery, on the other hand, perhaps suggests that they were used at a different time, if we suppose that the cemetery area was expanded only after the Lower Cemetery became too crowded.

The confused or disturbed state of many of the burials raises a question which is difficult to answer unequivocally in view of the poor preservation of much of the skeletal material: whether all burials were primary or whether some of the graves were used as ossuaries for the secondary burial of bones after the flesh had disintegrated.

It is clear that primary burial was practiced in the graves with a single body: the skeletons were in more or less natural order in many cases, and the graves were large enough (some only barely, e.g.

[11] At least some of the pottery and other objects found within the cemetery may have been discarded grave goods; below, p. 52.

[12] I.e. nearly half of the graves which definitely contained adult burials (leaving aside Graves 25 and 26, where the evidence is ambiguous).

[13] There are nine graves with multiple burials in the Lower Cemetery as opposed to only seven with single burials (leaving infant burials in jars out of consideration as a special case). If roughly the same ratio were maintained in the Upper Cemetery, we would expect two or three of the five graves to have multiple burials.

Grave 36) to accommodate a corpse. The bones in graves with multiple burials, however, tended to be more confused. Angel notes the scarcity of postcranial bones in Grave 7 (Appendix 5, p. 133), which might suggest that some of the skulls were detached from the body before they were placed in the grave. As mentioned above (p. 50), on the other hand, there were two skeletons in a fairly well articulated state in graves with multiple burials (Graves 1 and 9) and these were surely primary burials. Furthermore, the confusion may be explained in other ways than that secondary burial was practiced. In some cases it may have been caused by later burials, during which the bones of earlier ones were scattered or removed; in others by natural causes such as the periodic inundation by ground water and the intrusion of earth and pebbles into the grave. In short, there is no instance in which secondary burial is definite, and it is likely that most if not all burials at Kephala were primary.

The less well preserved burials may be briefly mentioned. Two graves which had been partly damaged by erosion are listed separately in Table 3; each contained at least one adult, but may originally have contained more than one body. Thirteen graves are listed as uncertain. Four of these were intact (Graves 17, 18, 19 and 27) but the bones had completely disintegrated or were otherwise unavailable for study. The other eleven graves were largely destroyed: eight are listed according to size as either probably adult burials (i.e. as containing at least one adult) or probably child burials, while five graves could not be classified even in this crude way.

OFFERINGS

The incidence of grave goods is summarized in Table 4. There may have been other objects which have left no trace in the archaeological record. Of the 27 graves for which there is definite information, only nine contained any offerings whatsoever and only one contained more than one object. This is the record of a poor community. Four of the nine had single burials of adults (Graves 10, 34, 35, 36), and four had more than one burial (Graves 9, 12, 13, 20); no skeleton was preserved from the ninth (Grave 27). Women may have received grave goods more often than men: the recipient was almost certainly a woman in Graves 9, 10, 13, 34 and 36 and probably a woman in Grave 12, whereas in only one instance was the recipient certainly a man (Grave 35, containing a flint scraper); in two cases the sex is uncertain (Grave 20, where the offerings could not be associated with specific burials, and Grave 27, where no skeleton was preserved).

The position of grave goods in relation to that of the body is not generally clear, since only three examples could be associated with more or less articulated skeletons: in Graves 9 and 36 the skeleton was contracted, and a scoop or scoop handle was placed near the knees or feet;[14] in Grave 35 the skeleton was in a unique position, on its front, and the flint scraper was placed by the right humerus. In Grave 34, although the skeleton was not in a clearly articulated position, the marble cup was found next to the remains of the skull near one end of the grave and may originally have been placed by the head of the corpse.

Grave goods consisted chiefly of vessels, two of marble, the rest of pottery. In many cases the only surviving whole pot of a specific shape comes from a grave. Otherwise the vessels are indistinguishable from those found in the settlement and presumably were not manufactured specifically for the grave. The vessels may have originally contained foodstuffs which have left no traces. The size of the clay vessels varies from small bowls (e.g. **99**) to fairly large storage jars (e.g. **105**). The two marble vessels (**103, 171**) may have been considered valuable personal possessions of the dead and hence placed in graves on account of their intrinsic value, not for their contents. Scoops, which are hardly efficient containers, may have had a ritual function (see above, p. 17) which caused them to be appropriate grave furnishings; in one case (Grave 9) only the handle was present. It is noteworthy that two and perhaps all three scoops found in graves were associated with women. Only one object other than vessels of clay and marble can be considered to have been deliberately deposited in a grave: the flint scraper (**172**) in Grave 35. Two obsidian blades (**100** and **101**, from Graves 12 and 13) may also have been offerings, but it is possible that they were intrusive.

[14] The other scoop found in a grave (Grave 13) lay at one end, above fragments of female humeri.

TABLE 4. INCIDENCE OF OFFERINGS

None	Prob. None	One	Four	Uncertain
Grave 1 (XIX)	Grave 7 (XIII)	Grave 9 (X)	Grave 20 (V)	Grave 5 (XXI)
Grave 2 (XXVII)	Grave 31 (II)	Grave 10 (XII)		Grave 14 (I)
Grave 3 (XVIII)		Grave 12 (XI)		Grave 15 (XIV)
Grave 4 (XXII)		Grave 13 (XX)		Grave 16 (VI)
Grave 6 (VII)		Grave 27 (XXIV)		Grave 21 (VIII)
Grave 8 (XVII)		Grave 34 (XXXVI)		Grave 25 (XXV)
Grave 11 (IX)		Grave 35 (XL)		Grave 26 (IV)
Grave 17 (XV)		Grave 36 (XXIX)		Grave 28 (XXIII)
Grave 18 (XVI)				Grave 29 (XXVIII)
Grave 19 (XXXI)				Grave 30 (III)
Grave 22 (XXIX)				Grave 33 (XXXIII)
Grave 23 (XXXII)				Grave 38 (XXXIV)
Grave 24 (XXVI)				Grave 40 (XXX)
Grave 32 (XXXVIII)				
Grave 37 (XXXV)				
Grave 39 (XXXVII)				

OBJECTS FOUND NEAR THE GRAVES

The clefts of both the Lower and the Upper Cemetery appear to have become filled with earth largely after the beginning of prehistoric occupation at Kephala; sherds and other objects were found within them down to the very bottom. The western part of the Lower Cemetery apparently served another purpose before graves were built within it (see the discussion of the *dromos* below, pp. 53–54) and the same may have been true of the western part of the Upper Cemetery.

The many objects found in the earth around the graves are to be regarded as stratified in the sense that they must date to the time of, or earlier than, the latest graves. The deposits around the graves consisted largely of earth, with some small stones, sherds, animal bones, and pieces of obsidian. Occasionally other objects were found, including sherd rubbing-tools, terracotta figurines, bone tools, fragments of crucibles, fragments of flint tools, a stone bead, and several other objects of stone and terracotta.

Possibly some of these objects were funerary offerings which had originally been placed in graves and which were subsequently discarded when later burials were made; others may have been placed on or around graves, or their platforms, during funerary ceremonies. The terracotta figurines may be specifically mentioned in this connection; none can be associated beyond question with a particular grave (**202** near Grave 38 has the likeliest claim), but all were found in the cemetery close to graves.

Most of the objects, however, are not likely to have been funerary offerings. Obsidian and pottery occur in great quantity (e.g. at least 352 pieces of obsidian and fragments of at least 255 pots were found around the graves of the central group of the Lower Cemetery). It is difficult to account for the very fragmentary state of the pottery if we assume that most vessels were whole when they were deposited in the cemetery, even if they were placed outside the graves where they might be more subject to breakage. The deposits in the cemetery are similar to those found in the settlement, and it is more likely that they represent domestic than funerary debris. The cemetery lay at the foot of the steep slope on which the settlement was built and debris must have been continually making its way downhill. This debris would probably have gradually accumulated in any case; possibly it was used deliberately as fill to create a place close to the settlement where there was sufficient depth of earth for graves to be built underground.

THE LOWER CEMETERY

GENERAL

The cleft that forms the Lower Cemetery (Pls. 8, 55) is about 15 m. long. Its axis is not absolutely straight but bends somewhat in the middle, so that the eastern half is aligned roughly east-west and the western half southwest-northeast. The width is greatest at the eastern end where it reaches a maximum of about 3.50 m.; at the western end it is only about 2 m.

On the northern side is a shelf of rock which extends eastward from a point just northwest of Grave 3 to the eastern end of the cleft between Graves 24 and 26. The shelf varies somewhat in level and in distance below the top of the scarp on the northern side; it is narrow on the western end and widens to a maximum of about 1.50 m. at the eastern end of the cleft. Resting on this shelf are Grave 13, the slab beneath Grave 19, the northern part of Grave 11, and the entire eastern group of graves.

The southern side of the cleft is highest at the eastern end and descends westward in a series of ridges which gradually decrease in height. The first ridge terminates just east of Grave 12, the second just east of Grave 9, and a third just east of Grave 6. Outside the cleft in all directions the bedrock slopes at the general angle of the hillside. The sandy area south of the cemetery is only about 1 to 2 m. beneath the level of the southern side of the cleft.

No graves were built immediately above bedrock in the lowest parts of the cleft. In some places the lowest graves were 0.50 to 1 m. above the bottom. At the eastern end, the space between the lowest graves and the bottom of the cleft was filled with earth and occasional small stones. Although sherds continued to be found to the bottom, there was little other sign of human activity. Beneath the level of the lowest grave at the western end of the cleft, on the other hand, evidence of more extensive human activity was found. At the bottom, beyond the point at which the cleft bends to the southwest, bedrock had been artificially cut down and trimmed to form a sort of passageway leading down into the cleft from the west (Pls. 49, e; 55, d, e). This passageway is referred to as the *dromos*, even though its purpose is uncertain. The *dromos* begins just southeast of Grave 29 and Wall 5, and it ends beneath Grave 1 (Pl. 8). The rock scarp on the southern side of the *dromos* rises at an angle of about 45° and reaches a height of about 0.60 to 0.90 m. above the bottom; the northern scarp is very steep, almost vertical in places, and reaches a maximum height of about 2.50 m. (see Pl. 12, Section C–C, and Pl. 14, Section B–B, for sections through the *dromos*). Both of these scarps are fairly smooth and regular and seem to have been trimmed in antiquity. At the bottom is a fairly smooth path or floor, about 4.50 m. long and 0.50 to 0.70 m. wide, which slopes down from about +4.45 m. at its western end to about +3.70 m. at its eastern. At the western end are two low steps (Pl. 55, e). Between the vertical scarp on the northern side and the path at the bottom is a low ledge, only some 0.10 to 0.20 m. high, which is about 0.70 m. wide at the western end and narrows towards the east until it virtually disappears.

The purpose of the *dromos* is a mystery. Only earth and occasional small stones and sherds were found within it. The path at the bottom simply comes to an end at the east against a scarp of bedrock about 0.40 m. high; farther east the natural bottom of the cleft has not been altered. Originally the plan may have been to continue the path to the east; perhaps the labor of cutting rock with primitive tools proved very difficult and the project was therefore abandoned. Possibly the *dromos* was intended to collect water and to serve as a cistern. At any rate, it can have had no connection with the graves found above it, since the lowest level of these graves is about 0.90 to 1.00 m. above the level of the path. The *dromos* may well have preceded the use of this part of the promontory as a cemetery.

CENTRAL GROUP: GRAVES AND OFFERINGS

Twenty-two graves, over one half of the total number excavated, were found in close proximity to one another in the central part of the Lower Cemetery. Graves 11 and 12 are the easternmost and Grave 14 the westernmost of the group (Pls. 8, 9). In many instances graves were built above one another (see Sections on Pls. 12–17) and it is certain that the upper grave was built and used later than the lower. In other instances, when graves are close to or touching one another, probable relationships may be suggested by a consideration of their relative positions and levels. The catalogue of graves gives specific details of the certain and probable chronological relationships. A broader division of the graves into earlier and later has also been adopted for clarity of presentation; the exact dividing line is arbitrary and the division rests on the assumption that activity proceeded at a fairly continuous pace throughout this part of the cemetery. The specific chronological relationships and the broader chronological divisions are shown in schematic form in Table 5. It should be noted that Table 5 cannot be regarded as dependable where relationships are not explicitly indicated and that the uncertainties increase with distance; Grave 14, for instance, may have been made earlier or later than Grave 16 or Grave 2.

From the sequence of graves in this group one may estimate the length of time that the cemetery was in use. There are two almost certain sequences of three graves, in which the lowest went out of use when the next was built (Graves 10, 19, 20; Graves 11, 21, 22). If a period of at least 20 years may be assigned to each grave (a conservative estimate, considering that many of the graves were family tombs), then the cemetery must have been in use for at least 60 years. Probably it was in use for at least 100 years, since it is likely that five or more graves were used in succession.[15]

Earlier Graves

Graves 1–13 are included here. Most are probably about contemporary, but there is one apparent sequence of three graves (4, 5 and 13) and another of two (11 and 12). The graves are described from west to east, or from earliest to latest when there is a sequence.

GRAVE 1 (XIX)[16]

Pls. 56, 62; Plan, Pl. 18; Sections, Pls. 12, 14

A built grave with remains of six people. At nearly the same level as Grave 3 on the east and probably about contemporary. Partly beneath Graves 14 and 15, both of which are assigned to the later series.

Roughly oval in plan; walls of moderate-sized and large stones. Max. interior length (east-west) *ca.* 1.05 m., width *ca.* 0.75 m. Four large cover slabs, two deep at center, set north-south. Interior height *ca.* 0.60 m. A few stones found above the cover (Pl. 62, a) suggest that a platform may have been built over it, though probably not so elaborate as those over some of the other graves.

Burials apparently at three different levels. The lowest had a pebble floor on which a heap of bones was found near the northeast corner of the grave (Pl. 56, a). The heap included fragmentary remains of a skull and two sets of teeth. A very few other bones were scattered about the grave at the lowest

[15] E.g. there is a probable sequence of Graves 4, 5, 13, 20, 22; see Table 5.

[16] In the catalogues, the graves are numbered in arabic numerals in the order in which they are described. They were originally numbered in roman numerals in the order in which they were excavated; those numbers are given in parentheses, since they are used by Angel in Appendix 5 and in preliminary reports. See Concordance 3.

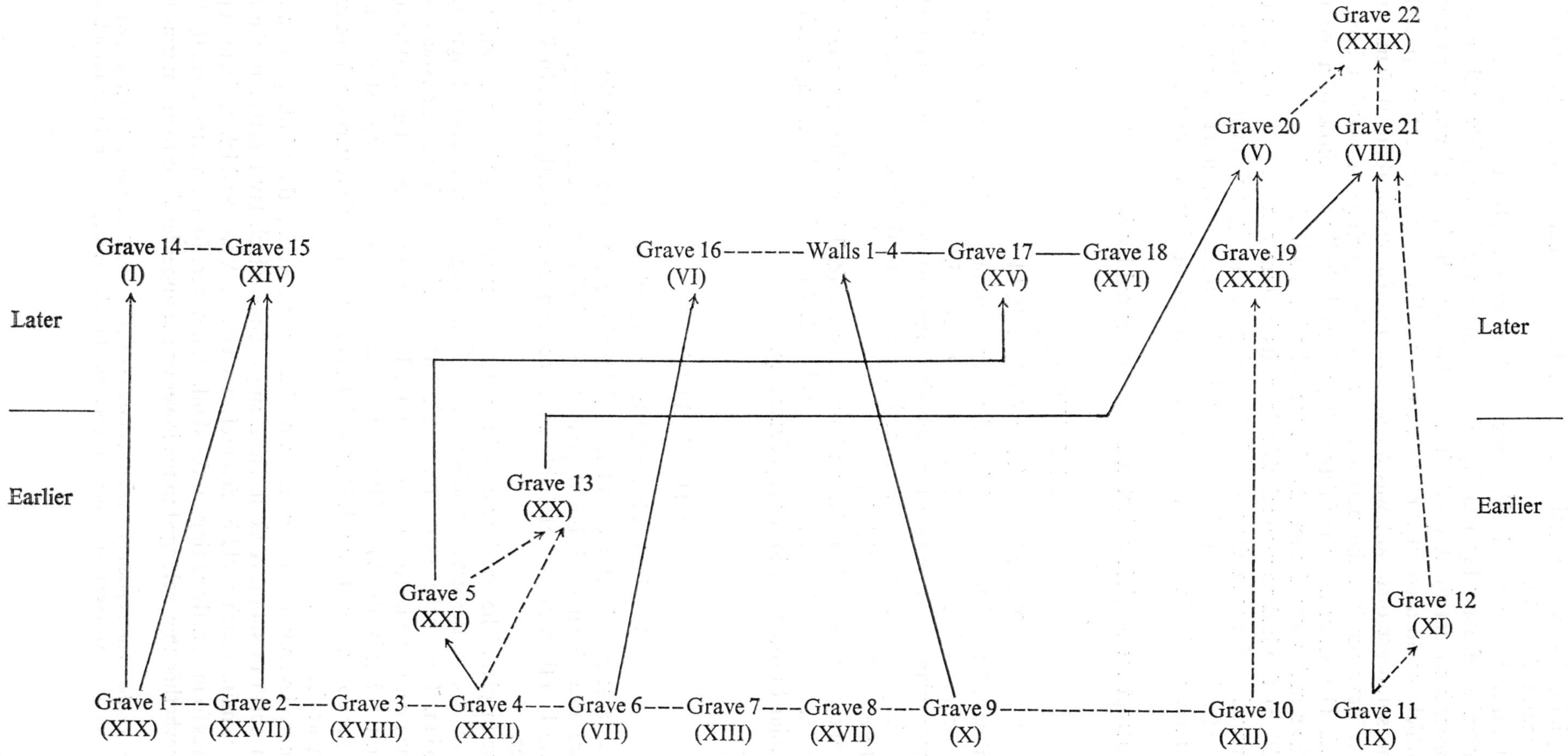

Table 5. Schematic chronological diagram showing graves of the central group of the Lower Cemetery. In general, east is towards the left. Earlier graves are towards the bottom. Solid lines indicate certain chronological relationships; broken lines probable chronological relationships. For clarity, the following relationships have been omitted: Grave 3 is earlier than Wall 4; Grave 4 is earlier than Wall 3 and Grave 17; Grave 10 is earlier than Grave 20; Grave 13 is earlier than Wall 3.

level. The skeletal material included the remains of two adults, one a man about 37 years old (*32 KeK*) and one probably a woman (*32a KeK*).[17]

The second burial level had no recognizable floor. Its bottom was about 0.08 m. above the floor of the lowest level. A number of bones lay near the center of the grave, and a fairly well preserved skull lay in the northeast corner immediately above the heap of bones of the lowest level. A stone was found resting on the skull (which would account for its flattened condition) and projecting upward through the upper level. In the southeast quadrant was an area of reddish earth about 0.20 m. square and 0.05 m. deep; this may have marked the position of an object, perhaps a wooden box, that had completely decomposed. The bones and the fairly well preserved skull were those of a woman about 26 (*31 KeK*). Among the remains were fragments of a second adult skull (*31a KeK*).

The third level (Pl. 56, b) also had no recognizable floor. Its bottom was *ca.* 0.08 m. above the top of the second level. The remains of a man about 40 (*34 KeK*) lay on the right side with head to the west; thighs drawn up perpendicular to trunk and lower legs doubled up. The skull had been smashed; the jaw was lying some distance north of the rest. Also included among the bones were remains of a woman about 31 (*33 KeK*).

No offerings found except the possible object at the second burial level.

GRAVE 2 (XXVII)

Pl. 56; Plan, Pl. 21; Section, Pl. 14

A tiny slab-sided cist with the skeleton of a child. About contemporary with, or perhaps a little earlier than, Grave 3 on the north (Section D–D, Pl. 14). Beneath Grave 15.

Roughly rectangular in plan. A single slab for each side; the eastern one inclines outwards toward the top. Max. interior length (east-west) 0.32 m. (at bottom), width 0.30 m. Cover missing: interior height *ca.* 0.20 m. if the cover had fitted tightly.

Skeleton of a child about 3 years old, perhaps a boy (*39 KeK*). Skull in southeast corner with crown up and face to the northeast. Only a few other bones were found. The body evidently lay on the left side; knees about perpendicular to spine and lower legs drawn up.

No offerings found.

GRAVE 3 (XVIII)

Pls. 56, 57; Plan, Pl. 18; Section, Pl. 14

A built grave with at least two skeletons. Probably slightly later than Grave 2 to the south, since its cover and platform are at a higher level, but the chronological difference cannot be great. At nearly the same level as Grave 1 to the west and probably about contemporary. Partly beneath Wall 4 (Pl. 9), which is therefore later.

Roughly rectangular in plan. The north scarp of the cleft forms much of the north wall; the other walls of moderate-sized stones, the greatest being *ca.* 0.65 m. long. Max. interior length (east-west) *ca.* 1.00 m., width 0.65 m. Three cover slabs (Pl. 56, d), with small stones in the interstices, set north-south and sloping down *ca.* 0.15 m. from north to south. Interior height at center *ca.* 0.85 m.

Rectangular platform P 7 (Pls. 10, 57) solidly built of moderate-sized to large stones, above and of the same extent as the cover. Length *ca.* 1.70 m., width *ca.* 1.50 m., height varying from *ca.* 0.30 m. at the north to 0.20 m. at the south.

Burials at two or more levels.[18] The lower had a pebble floor covering the whole grave and sloping down somewhat from north to south. A skull and a single bone which lay together in the northwest corner were the only remains which could be definitely associated. A stone which projected upwards as far as the upper level was found partly resting on the skull. Bones were found scattered *ca.* 0.15 m. above the floor; it is unclear whether they belonged to the lower or the upper level, or to an intermediate level.

[17] In the catalogues of graves, the numbers given in parentheses for each skeleton are those assigned by Angel; see Appendix 5.

[18] The skeletal material from the grave, except that from the upper burial level, was misplaced and was unavailable for Angel to study.

The upper level was about 0.20 m. above the pebble floor of the lower. No clearly marked floor. Skeleton of a woman about 23 years old (*30 KeK*), fairly well preserved (Pl. 56, e). Body on right side. Head originally near southwest corner; the skull had been displaced, however, and was found at the north side near the base of the spine. A stone at the southwest corner (not shown in the plan) perhaps was a pillow. Knees at an acute angle to spine, lower legs drawn up. Position of arms uncertain; the hands may have been placed near the head to cradle it. Angel records a few scraps of adult bones (*30a KeK*) perhaps from a second burial at the upper level; possibly they are from a burial at a lower level.

No offerings found.

GRAVE 4 (XXII)

Pl. 57; Plan, Pl. 18; Section, Pl. 15

A built grave with a single skeleton. At roughly the same level and probably about contemporary with Grave 8 to the east, Grave 9 to the southeast and Grave 10 to the northeast. Probably also about contemporary with Grave 6, which is at a somewhat lower level to the south. Grave 5 to the west makes use of the edge of P 6 over Grave 4 for one of its sides and it must therefore be a little later. Grave 13 to the north is situated on a shelf of rock at a higher level and may be considerably later.

Roughly oval in plan. A scarp of rock forms the north wall; the other walls of moderate-sized stones. Max. interior length (east-west) *ca.* 1.00 m., width *ca.* 0.80 m. Three or four large cover slabs set east-west. Interior height *ca.* 0.50 m.

Rectangular platform P 6 (Pls. 10; 57, a) solidly built of moderate-sized to large stones above the cover. Length *ca.* 1.30 m., width *ca.* 1.10 m., height *ca.* 0.25 m.

Fragments of a skeleton (Pl. 57, c) of a man about 28 years old (*36 KeK*). Body probably on right side, head to west, with knees drawn up almost to chest and with lower legs drawn up.

No offerings were found within the grave. It is possible that a jar (**135**) found in fragments by the west side, beneath Grave 5, was somehow associated originally with Grave 4.

GRAVE 5 (XXI)

Pl. 57; Plan, Pl. 8

A built grave with few bones preserved. Closely connected with Grave 4 but later, since it was built against the west side of P 6 over Grave 4. At a lower level and probably earlier than Grave 13 to the north. Immediately beneath Grave 17.

Apparently roughly trapezoidal in plan. The west face of P 6 served as the east wall; the north and west walls of small stones; the south wall missing. To judge by the extent of the cover slabs, the max. interior length (north-south) was *ca.* 0.70 to 0.80 m., the width of the south end was *ca.* 0.40 m. and the width at the north end was *ca.* 0.24 m. Two cover slabs set north-south; the larger east slab slightly overlapped the top of P 6. Interior height uncertain but it cannot have been greater than 0.25 m. since a layer of stones was found at that level.

A few bones were found about 0.10 m. beneath the cover; these were discarded and not available for Angel to study.

No offerings were found within the grave. It is possible that a jar (**135**) found in fragments immediately beneath it was somehow associated either with Grave 4 or Grave 5.

GRAVE 6 (VII)

Pl. 57; Plan, Pl. 18; Section, Pl. 15

A built grave with a single skeleton. About contemporary with Grave 7, contiguous on the south, and with Grave 4 on the north; the latter slightly higher but probably at the same depth below the sloping surface of the ground. Directly beneath Grave 16.

Roughly circular in plan; walls of small and moderate-sized stones. Max. interior length (east-west) *ca.* 1.08 m., width *ca.* 0.96 m. Three large cover slabs set north-south. Interior height *ca.* 0.45 m.

Fragments of a skeleton of a man about 30 years old (*16 KeK*); position of body not determinable.

No offerings found.

GRAVE 7 (XIII)

Pl. 59; Plan, Pl. 20; Section, Pl. 15

A large built grave with remains of at least thirteen people. Situated at the south edge of the cleft and possibly built only after the space within the cleft had been largely taken up by other graves. Contiguous with Grave 6 to the north and probably about contemporary; whichever was built first, no apparent damage was done to it when the second was built. Cover and upper part of the walls missing because of erosion.

Rectangular to oval in plan; walls of moderate-sized stones. Max. interior length *ca.* 1.13 m., width *ca.* 0.97 m. The north, east, and west walls incline inward from the bottom.

There was a space *ca.* 0.45 to 0.50 m. wide in the center of the south wall where the stones were at a lower level than the rest of the wall (left unhatched on Pl. 8 and shown in lighter hatching on Pl. 20; see also the photograph Pl. 59, h); perhaps the space was once a doorway, but the evidence is inconclusive because of the damage by erosion. If the stones at the bottom of the space were a threshold, it would have been *ca.* 0.10 m. above the lower burial level, at nearly the same level as the middle burial level and *ca.* 0.15 m. below the upper. A few bones at the upper and middle levels were found within the space (Pls. 20; 59, a–d) but these may have been displaced by erosion rather than deposited in the space.

There were at least three burial levels (see Section E–E, Pl. 15; the skulls shown there are projected into the section). The lowest (Pls. 20; 59, f) had a floor of sand *ca.* 0.02 m. thick; between it and bedrock was a layer of earth. On the floor were the confused remains of at least five people, and slightly above the floor was the skull of a sixth. The skulls were crushed and compressed. Four rested at nearly the same level: S9, of a man about 42 years old (*29 KeK*), near the northwest corner; S8, of a man about 45 (*28 KeK*), near the southwest corner; S7, of a man about 33 (*27 KeK*), just northeast of the center of the grave; S6, of a child just over 2 (*26 KeK*), by the middle of the east wall. S5, the skull of a man about 44 (*25 KeK*), was found northeast of S7 and north of S6, but slightly higher than the floor; although it projected somewhat above the floor of the middle level, it is probably to be associated with the lower level. Among the bones were those of an adult woman (*27a KeK*) which cannot be associated with any of the skulls.

The middle level (Pls. 20; 59, d) was separated from the lower by a floor of small stones (max. length *ca.* 0.15 m.) over much of the grave (Pl. 59, e). The upper surface of the floor was only *ca.* 0.08 to 0.10 m. above that of the lower level; perhaps this floor crushed the skulls below it. On it were the confused remains of at least five people. There were two nearly complete skulls: S4, of a woman about 27 (*24 KeK*), near the east side, and S3, of a child just over 2 (*23b KeK*), near the northwest corner. Among the bones were those of three people which could not be associated with either of the skulls: an adult man (*23 KeK*), and two women, one about 22 (*23a KeK*), and the other an adult of indeterminate age (*24a KeK*).

The upper level (Pls. 20; 59, a, b) was partly lost on the south side owing to erosion. Two pebble layers were found, one at the north side about 0.07 to 0.15 m. above the floor of the middle level, the other in the center and at the east side about 0.14 to 0.18 m. above the floor of the middle level; it was not clear whether they represented two floors or were part of the same floor. Resting on the lower level of pebbles at the north side of the grave were two moderate-sized stones, one laid flat beside the north wall, the other on end at the northeast corner (visible in Pl. 59, a–c); they were apparently deliberately placed in the grave. There were remains of at least two people, including two nearly complete skulls: S2, of a woman about 30 (*22 KeK*), near the northeast corner and S1, of a woman about 24 (*21 KeK*), near the southeast corner. Other bones were scattered around in no discernible order. Since the upper level was encountered almost immediately beneath the modern surface, it is possible that other burials have been completely lost.

No offerings found.

GRAVE 8 (XVII)

Pl. 58; Plan, Pl. 18

A jar with the bones of an infant. Probably about contemporary with the graves which surrounded it: Grave 4 to the west, Grave 9 to the southeast, Grave 10 to the northeast. The cover slab was almost exactly at the same level as the top of P 6 over Grave 4 and nearly at the level of the covers of Graves 9 and 10.

Jar set on its bottom in a pit and covered by a slab (Pl. 58, a, b). Slab roughly 0.20 m. square, thickness *ca.* 0.05 m.

A few fragmentary bones of a girl (?) in the eighth foetal month (*29a KeK*); position of body not determinable.

No offerings found.

97 (Kph.16) Large jar used for burial Pls. 33, 78

Missing: rim, one handle and part of the other, part of one lug, and small parts of the body; partially restored. H. 0.345, D. max. 0.315, D. base 0.13.

Coarse; tan to red brown with patches of dark gray on outer surface; burnished outside; scored inside; traces of crusted red around handles and lugs and on the bottom.

Biconical to rounded in profile; uneven flat bottom; two strap handles opposite one another at widest diameter; on the shoulder above each handle is an elongated horizontal lug, doubly pierced, with a long plastic extension depending from either end, and a shorter triangular extension beneath the middle. The neck may have been a cylindrical collar; cf. the somewhat similar although smaller vessels from Athens (Immerwahr, 1971, nos. 1–18).

The shape is rather like that of **105**, which seems also to have had a similar arrangement of strap handles and lugs. **97** is not particularly similar to any of the other vessels used for burials: **137** is a closed vessel, but more globular and with a different arrangement of handles; **146** and **170** are open vessels and quite different. There is no reason to suppose that any of them was made specifically as a burial jar.

GRAVE 9 (X)

Pl. 58; Plan, Pl. 18; Section, Pl. 16

A built grave with the bones of two people. Situated at the south side of the cleft; one wall abutted the south scarp of rock. At about the same level and probably about contemporary with Grave 10 to the north; probably also about contemporary with Grave 4 to the northwest and Grave 6 to the southwest, although these two were at a slightly lower level. Partly beneath Wall 1 (Pl. 9), which must therefore be later.

Roughly oval in plan. Walls of moderate-sized to large stones. Max. interior length (north-south) at the level of the cover *ca.* 0.96 m., width *ca.* 0.72 m. The area of the grave is lessened somewhat at the bottom by a number of slabs projecting inwards from the walls. Four large cover slabs with smaller stones packed around them. Interior height *ca.* 0.45 m.

A platform, P 3 (Pls. 10; 58, c), solidly built of moderate-sized to large stones above the cover; height *ca.* 0.38 m. Three distinct layers: the lowest roughly circular in plan and extending slightly beyond the area of the cover; the second also circular but slightly smaller in diameter (the two lower levels are unhatched in Pl. 10); the upper level (hatched in Pl. 10) more or less quadrilateral in plan and of lesser extent than the other layers. The variation in plan suggests that not all the layers were intended to project above the ground, although the upper layer may have done so.

A skeleton of a woman about 37 years old (*18 KeK*), largely intact, body on the right side with head to the northwest; thighs raised slightly beyond the perpendicular and lower legs drawn up. A number of other bones lay at the west side in a confused state, including a fragment of the occiput of a second skull, that of an adult, probably also a woman (*18a KeK*).

98 (Kph.2) Handle of scoop Pl. 82

Found broken in three pieces next to southwest wall of grave near knees of skeleton *18 KeK*, with which it is almost certainly to be associated.

Handle and two struts. H. 0.159. Since no other fragments were found, it must have been incomplete when placed in the grave; its size precludes the possibility that it found its way in by accident.

Red-orange to orange-brown biscuit.

One strut preserved to its full height; adhering to its lower surface is part of the body of the vessel, or a plug by which it was attached. The handle and the other strut are broken higher up and preserve no trace of attachment. The surface of the back of the handle is missing at the lower right side. Struts round to oval in section.

Incised decoration. Nine vertical slashes at front edge of handle. Complex pattern on top and back of handle, bordered at each edge by two parallel lines, which turn and run a little way down the struts. The pattern consists of the following elements: a step-like area, unincised, at the upper middle and descending from left to right at the back of the handle; narrow oblique zones of punctations at the upper right; meandroid motifs, either in zones, as between the two zones of punctations, or individually, as in the upper right corner. On the lower parts of the struts are slanting lines, loosely arranged in multiple zigzag. Although individual elements of the pattern are found elsewhere at Kephala, the combinations are never so complex.

GRAVE 10 (XII)

Pl. 58; Plan, Pl. 18; Section, Pl. 16

A built grave with a single skeleton. At about the same level and probably about contemporary with Grave 9 to the south; at a lower level and probably earlier than Grave 19 to the north. Almost directly beneath and at a much lower level than Grave 20.

Roughly trapezoidal in plan: a scarp of rock forms the north wall; the other walls of moderate-sized stones. Interior dimensions: north side 1.04 m.; south 0.63 m.; east 0.68 m.; west 0.76 m. Cover slabs set east-west (Pl. 58, e): two large slabs covered everything except the south side; two small slabs covered the south wall, projecting somewhat north and south of it. Interior height *ca.* 0.50 m.

Rectangular platform P 1 (Pl. 10), solidly built of moderate-sized stones one or two layers high, above the cover; length of north side 1.46 m., south 1.40 m., east 0.84 m., west 0.89 m.; height *ca.* 0.30 m.

A skeleton of a woman about 24 years old (*20 KeK*), partly disintegrated and perhaps disturbed; fragments of skull at the north side, near which was a stone *ca.* 0.23 m. long; a few other bones scattered about.

Fragments of a large closed vessel (**134**) were found during excavations beneath Grave 20, almost immediately above and around the top of P 1; possibly it was a marker or receptacle for offerings, but it cannot be certainly associated with Grave 10.

99 (Kph.1) Bowl Pls. 27, 74

Found just southwest of center of grave (see Pl. 18).

Missing: one lug (point of attachment preserved), restored; and small chips; mended. H. 0.081, D. rim 0.083.

Dark buff-to-black biscuit; traces of crusted red inside. Flat base with rounded transition to sides, which are broadest near bottom and curve inward slightly toward the plain rim. Two lugs, vertically elongated and horizontally pierced, opposite one another near rim: unusual in that they terminate abruptly at the bottom instead of being drawn out in plastic extensions; no others exactly like them were found at the site.

GRAVE 11 (IX)

Pl. 60; Plan, Pl. 19; Sections, Pls. 12, 17

A built grave with a single skeleton. Situated on a shelf of rock at the north side of the cleft. Burial level about 0.60 m. higher than that of Grave 10 to the west. At a slightly higher level than Grave 12 to the south but probably built earlier: stones apparently from the collapsed walls of Grave 11 (left unstippled in Section G–G on Pl. 17) were found beside Grave 12; the lowest of the stones were at roughly the level of the cover of Grave 12; unless its cover was originally about flush with the surface, which is unlikely, Grave 12 must have been built after the partial collapse of Grave 11 and after a rise in ground level. Beneath Grave 21.

Roughly circular in plan; walls of small and moderate-sized stones. Interior diameter *ca.* 1.00 m. The floor on the north side is bedrock, slightly hollowed. One cover slab set east-west over north side; another fallen on end into the grave. Interior height *ca.* 0.50 m. No evidence for a platform above the cover.

Fragments of a skeleton of a man about 34 years old (*17 KeK*); skull near the west side; other bones scattered at the center and on the east side; position of body not determinable. The skull is of special interest; the man had survived not only a serious piercing wound (Pl. 94, j), but also an operation to remove the weapon which caused it (below, Appendix 5, p. 136).

No offerings found.

GRAVE 12 (XI)

Pl. 60; Plan, Pl. 19; Sections, Pls. 12, 17

A built grave with remains of two people. Later than Grave 11 to the north (see above). Probably earlier than Grave 21, also to the north but at a higher level.

Roughly circular in plan; walls of moderate-sized stones; the south wall partly founded on a shelf of rock at the south side of the cleft. Max. interior dimension *ca.* 0.93 m. Five large cover slabs, set northeast-southwest, with smaller stones packed around them. Interior height *ca.* 0.30 m.

A platform, P 2 (Pl. 10), solidly built of moderate-sized stones above the cover; not completely preserved but seems nearly polygonal in plan. Length of northwest side *ca.* 1.25 m., southwest *ca.* 0.95 m.; height as preserved *ca.* 0.15 m. but probably higher originally.

Fragments of two skeletons scattered about in no discernible order, one probably of a woman about 20 years old (*19 KeK*), the other of a child (*19a KeK*).

100 (Kph.1.9) Obsidian blade (category 1 a) Pl. 69

Found at the burial level near west side of grave; probably deliberately deposited and to be associated with the woman's skeleton (*19 KeK*); it is small enough, however, that it might have found its way into the grave by chance.

Intact. L. 0.07, W. 0.015, Th. 0.004.

Dark gray; surface shiny. Triangular to trapezoidal in section; secondary working and/or chipping at both edges and one end; flat striking platform at the other end.

GRAVE 13 (XX)

Pl. 60; Plan, Pl. 19; Section, Pl. 15

A built grave with remains of two people. Situated on a shelf of rock at the north side of the cleft. Considerably higher than Graves 4 and 5 and probably later. Partly beneath Grave 20 and Wall 3.

Roughly rectangular in plan. The north scarp of the cleft, perhaps trimmed to some extent, forms the north wall; the other walls of moderate-sized and large stones. Max. interior length (east-west) *ca.* 1.23 m., width *ca.* 0.70 m. Three large cover slabs *in situ* (Pl. 60, e), two set east-west over the east side, the other set north-south over the west side, leaving a gap over the west part of the grave; smaller stones, which had apparently originally covered the gap, had fallen inside the grave and were found immediately beneath the level of the cover (Pl. 60, c). Interior height *ca.* 0.48 m.

A rectangular platform, P 5 (Pls. 10; 57, a), solidly built of moderate-sized stones above the cover. Dimensions almost exactly the same as the grave; even after the earth had been completely removed it was difficult to distinguish the level of the cover. Length, east-west, *ca.* 1.94 m., width *ca.* 1.20 m., height *ca.* 0.28 to 0.40 m.

Fragments of the skull of a woman about 30 years old (*35 KeK*), near the center and in the southwest corner; a few other bones scattered about, including a fragment from an adult femur, probably male (*35a KeK*), which evidently belonged to an earlier burial.

101 (Kph.3.5) Obsidian blade (category 1 b) Pl. 69

Found at the burial level; probably deliberately deposited and to be associated with the skeleton of *35 KeK*, although it is small enough to have entered the grave by chance.

One end missing. L. 0.061, W. 0.026, Th. 0.006.

Dark gray with darker striations; translucent; surface shiny. Ellipsoid; triangular to trapezoidal in section; sharp edge at one end, flat surface at the other where broken.

102 (Kph.10) Scoop Pls. 36, 82

Found near southeast corner with handle turned towards center of grave, above fragments of female humeri (Pl. 19); almost certainly to be associated with the more nearly complete skeleton of the woman (*35 KeK*).

Missing: about one third of the handle, especially at the left edge and the bottom; part of the upper body and lip, and part of the base; severely worn in places; restored. H. 0.104, H. with handle 0.204, L. 0.198, W. 0.138, D. base 0.098.

Coarse, brown biscuit, red brown on exterior; surface smoothed on the outside and, less carefully, on the inside; possible traces of crusted red on the outside at upper part of mouth and on base.

Shallow body, roughly ovoid, but sheared off obliquely; plain rim, at an angle of about 40° from the horizontal; hollowed disk base, round as seen from below; broad, flat handle rising obliquely from the back of the body and curving to form a nearly flat surface at the upper end; the upper front edge of the handle makes a smooth curving transition to the nearly vertical struts, which are rectangular to oval in section; lower ends of struts attached on either side of the upper part of the body, near the mouth of the vessel. Indentations at the front edge of the handle, two of which are preserved. Incised decoration: handle bordered at the top by a line parallel to the front edge and at the right side by a single line. The pattern on the back of the handle was evidently divided into two parts by two vertical lines near the center; at the right is a multiple zigzag; at the left the missing decoration was presumably similar. Multiple zigzag on the struts. The only other nearly complete scoop is **173**, which has a slightly larger body and almost no decoration.

LATER GRAVES

Graves 14–22 are included here. The division of the central group into earlier and later graves is necessarily somewhat arbitrary. As a dividing point I have chosen a series of walls (1, 2, 3, and 4 on Pl. 9) which overlay some of the earlier graves or their platforms. Wall 3 was built in part above P 5 over Grave 13, and Wall 4 was built in part above P 7 over Grave 3. The walls appear to have been directly connected with at least three graves (16, 17, 18). Walls 2, 3, and 4 were built of small to moderate-sized stones, laid flat for the most part; their height as preserved was only 0.20 to 0.30 m. They partly enclosed Graves 17 and 18, but Walls 2 and 3 continued beyond the graves. Wall 1 consisted of moderate-sized stones set on edge; it appears to have been connected with Grave 16. Wall 1 must have been about contemporary with the other walls, to judge by its level. The exact purpose of the walls is obscure; they may have been intended to divide the available space into family plots or they may have merely marked off a space around individual graves.

The other six graves were found at a relatively high level and appear to have been among the latest surviving graves in the Lower Cemetery; all overlay earlier graves which have already been described.

GRAVE 14 (I)

Pl. 60; Plan, Pl. 19; Section, Pl. 13

A built grave with remains of at least six people. Partly overlapping and thus later than Grave 1. At nearly the same level as Grave 15 to the east, and probably about contemporary.

Roughly rectangular in plan: north and south sides somewhat rounded; the rock scarp forms the north side except at the top, where there are two or three rows of stones; the other walls of moderate-sized and large stones with white clay for a bonding substance.[19] Max. interior length (east-west) *ca.* 1.22 m., width *ca.* 1.00 to 1.05 m. Cover and west part of south wall missing because of erosion.

The stones of the south wall which are unhatched on Plate 9 and lightly hatched on Plate 19 may possibly have been part of a threshold of a doorway *ca.* 0.05 m. below the level of the pebble floor; at the east side three surviving rows of stones make a vertical face *ca.* 0.20 m. high (a jamb?); at the west side the wall is missing through erosion (cf. Grave 7). The arrangement may, however, be the fortuitous result of the partial disintegration of the wall.

Skeletal remains: a man about 30 years old (*1 KeK*); two women, one about 28 (*2 KeK*), the other about 27 (*3 KeK*); and three other adults, probably men, one about 29 (*4 KeK*), the others of uncertain age (*4a* and *4b KeK*). All were found at one level above a pebble floor (Pls. 19; 60, h), most at the east

[19] White clay was also used for Grave 20; see below, p. 64.

side, three skulls in the northeast corner, perhaps piled there during later burials. Other burials may have been lost through erosion.

No certain offerings. A fragment of a scoop, Pl. 83, AV (below, p. 82), found while cleaning in and around the grave, may have been from a vessel originally deposited in the grave.

GRAVE 15 (XIV)

Pl. 62; Plan, Pl. 9; Section, Pl. 14

A built grave with no bones preserved. At nearly the same level as Grave 14 to the east and probably about contemporary. Partly above Graves 1 and 2.

Severely damaged by erosion; parts only of north and west walls, of moderate-sized and large stones; perhaps rectangular in plan since they meet at a right angle. Probably large enough to have contained one or more adults.

No offerings found.

GRAVE 16 (VI)

Pl. 57; Plan, Pl. 19; Section, Pl. 15

A built grave with the remains of at least four people. Immediately above Grave 6, the cover of which served as its floor.

Roughly rectangular in plan; walls of moderate-sized and large stones. Max. interior length (east-west) *ca.* 1.14 m., width *ca.* 0.70 m. Cover and most of south wall missing because of erosion.

A jumbled mass of skeletal remains: a man about 24 years old (*15 KeK*), a woman (?) about 29 (*14 KeK*), a child of 6–8 (*15a KeK*), and a child of 4+ (*15b KeK*); all were found at one level near the east side and in the northeast corner.

No offerings found.

Wall 1, a line of stones set on end (Pls. 9; 61, c), was perhaps intended to delimit a space around Grave 16; at the east end it partly overlapped P 3 over Grave 9.

GRAVE 17 (XV)

Pl. 61; Plan, Pl. 9

A small built grave with no bones preserved. Closely connected with Walls 3 and 4, which were thus contemporary. Later than Grave 3 since Wall 4 partly overlay P 7 over Grave 3. About contemporary with Grave 18 to the northwest, which was also connected with Walls 3 and 4. Almost immediately above the cover of Grave 5 and P 6 over Grave 4.

Roughly oval in plan on the interior; walls of small and moderate-sized stones. The east and south walls were straight on the exterior and met at approximately a right angle. Max. interior length (east-west) *ca.* 0.57 m., width *ca.* 0.49 m. Two cover slabs set north-south. Interior height *ca.* 0.35 m.

Some moderate-sized stones found above and around the edges of the cover may have been part of a platform; possibly unconnected with the grave, since there were a few centimeters of earth between them and the cover.

The grave could have accommodated only a child or children, to judge by its small dimensions.

No offerings found.

GRAVE 18 (XVI)

Pl. 61; Plan, Pl. 9

A small built grave with the bones apparently of a child. Contemporary with Walls 2, 3, and 4, of which it made partial use for north, east, and west sides; since the walls continued beyond the grave, they were probably not built solely for it. About contemporary with Grave 17 to the south, which was also connected with Walls 3 and 4. Later than Graves 3 and 13, since Wall 4 overlay P 7 over Grave 3, and Wall 3 overlay P 5 over Grave 13.

Roughly trapezoidal in plan; a single slab placed on edge for south wall; the other walls built of small and moderate-sized stones. Max. interior length *ca.* 0.46 m., width 0.35 m. Two cover slabs set east-west. Interior height *ca.* 0.42 m.

A few fragments of a child's skull and other small bones found in no discernible arrangement; misplaced after excavation and left out of consideration in the statistics on burials. The small grave could have held only a child or children.

No offerings found.

GRAVE 19 (XXXI)

Pl. 61; Plan, Pl. 8; Section, Pl. 16

A small built grave with the bones presumably of a child. Situated on a large slab which lay on a rock shelf at the north side of the cleft. At a considerably higher level than Grave 10, immediately to the south, and probably later. Partly beneath Graves 20 and 21 and therefore earlier.

Roughly oval in plan; the north scarp of the cleft forms the north wall; the other walls of small stones. Max. interior length (east-west) *ca.* 0.67 m., width *ca.* 0.36 m. A single cover slab with the east end tilted down somewhat into the grave. Interior height *ca.* 0.15 to 0.20 m.

A few fragments of bones, presumably of a child; misplaced after excavation and left out of consideration in the statistics on burials. The small grave could have accommodated only a child or children.

No offerings found.

GRAVE 20 (V)

Pl. 62; Plan, Pl. 19; Section, Pl. 16

A large built grave with remains of at least nine people. At a somewhat higher level than Grave 21 immediately to the east, but probably about contemporary. Partly above Grave 19, P 1 over Grave 10, and P 5 over Grave 13 and therefore later. At a lower level and probably earlier than Grave 22 to the northeast.

Roughly rectangular in plan; walls of moderate-sized stones with white clay as a bonding substance.[20] Max. interior length (east-west) *ca.* 1.40 m., width *ca.* 1.10 m. The cover and the upper part of the walls missing through erotion; only one or two rows of stones were left of the south wall. Interior height at least 0.35 m.

Burials on a pebble floor which sloped down *ca.* 0.10 m. from north to south; a few bones among and immediately beneath the pebbles apparently earlier than the floor. The remains include an adolescent of indeterminate sex (*12a KeK*), and adults ranging in age from 23 to 39: three men (*9*, *10*, and *12 KeK*); three women (*7*, *8*, and *11 KeK*); one probably a woman (*13 KeK*); one indeterminate (*13a KeK*). Bones disturbed; no skeleton in determinable order.

The offerings could not be assigned to specific burials.

STONE

103 (Kph.1.1) Marble rhyton Pls. 23, 67

Found on its side in the southwest corner with rim towards the north; the highest point was at nearly the same level as the top of the floor. Possibly from a burial earlier than the floor; more likely it was deposited at the major burial level and sank slightly into the floor in the course of time.

Upper part broken into many pieces on one side; tiny chips missing; mended. H. 0.168, D. rim 0.068, H. of lugs 0.045.

Fine-grained, white marble with yellowish surface, well smoothed; translucent; marks of rotary drilling or abrasion on lower part of interior for a distance of 0.02 to 0.03 m. from the bottom; vertical marks of abrasion on upper part of interior and whole exterior.

Pointed, nearly conical; plain rim; bottom solid for a height of about 0.035 m.; walls become slightly thinner toward the top. Two lugs, vertically elongated and horizontally pierced, opposite one another on upper body; the lugs are rounded and taper toward

[20] White clay was also used for Grave 14; see above.

the bottom; at the top they rise free of the body, creating a knobbed or eared effect; the holes are near the top, drilled from both sides.

The lugs on the marble bowl **171** are similar except that they lack the eared effect at the top; lugs on pottery, especially T-lugs, have similarly elongated plastic extensions, and are generally pierced horizontally, but they are never partly detached to form ears.

109 is a fragment from a similar but somewhat larger rhyton; for parallels from elsewhere see below, p. 106.

POTTERY

104 (Kph.9) High-footed shallow bowl (A 2) Pls. 28, 76

Found upside down beside west wall near northwest corner.

About four fifths preserved; worn in places; restored. H. to tab 0.12, H. to rim 0.114, D. rim 0.263, D. base 0.095.

Coarse, sandy, orange-brown biscuit, gray at core; surface smoothed; marks of scoring in places; traces of crusted red on exterior. Rim plain; low tab for about one fifth of the circumference; horizontally pierced lug beneath center of tab. High, slightly flaring ring base, pierced twice below the lug.

105 (Kph.8) Fragment of large jar (B 2) Pls. 43, 87

Found on edge near center of grave; it is uncertain whether the jar was complete when deposited because of damage from erosion. Presumably not used for a burial within the grave (cf. Grave 23) since no infant bones were found.

About one fourth preserved. Missing: half of upper body, three quarters of lower body, the base, and possibly the rim; worn; consolidated with plaster. H. pres. 0.28, D. max. 0.36.

Fairly coarse, sandy, hard biscuit, buff to brown, but dark in many places as if burned. Inside tan with mottled orange and dark brown; scored. Outside red brown; pattern burnished; traces of crusted red on one lug.

Biconical body; upper part seems to have a finished rim, but its worn condition allows the possibility that the vessel had an offset neck. Two T-lugs on upper shoulder, placed opposite one another; the lugs were evidently arranged in pairs, since part of another survives 0.03 m. from the one at the right side. Below that pair are attachments for a strap handle, probably matched by another on the opposite side. Pattern-burnished decoration, visible only on shoulder, but probably continued on lower part of vessel: rather careless, consisting of vertical or nearly vertical lines of various widths, sometimes converging at an angle.

106 (Kph.5) Cylindrical vessel (C 2) Pls. 37, 83

Found on its side near west wall just southeast of **104**.

About four fifths preserved; restored. H. 0.125, D. top 0.112, D. bottom 0.132.

Fairly coarse, sandy, dark gray biscuit; surface brownish tan with some gray patches; traces of crusted red and white around upper edge, the red apparently over the white (cf. **138**).

Open at both ends; nearly cylindrical, but flaring toward bottom and, slightly, toward top. Plain, soemwhat rounded rim at top; flat edge at bottom providing a firm footing. Two horizontally elongated lugs, pierced twice vertically, opposite each other inside the vessel about 0.035 m. below the rim; most of one lug is missing. Probably a pot stand; the lugs were presumably to hang it up when not in use. Fragments of similar vessels, e.g. Pl. 37, B, have ledges and/or lugs closer to the rim.

GRAVE 21 (VIII)

Pl. 60; Plan, Pl. 9; Sections, Pls. 12, 17

A built grave, badly damaged by erosion. Directly above Grave 11, into which its west wall had partly collapsed (Pl. 60, b); partly above Grave 19. Lower and probably earlier than Grave 22 immediately to the north.

Probably rectangular in plan. Lower parts of north, east, and west walls preserved, of moderate-sized to large stones; max. interior length (east-west) *ca.* 1.05 m., width probably at least 0.70 m. Interior height at least 0.35 m.

Burial level almost completely missing. Two fragments of bones, near center of grave; discarded at time of excavation and not examined by Angel. The grave was large enough to have contained one or more adults.

No offerings found.

GRAVE 22 (XXIX)

Pl. 62; Plan, Pl. 20; Sections, Pls. 12, 17

A tiny grave, partly built and partly hollowed out of bedrock, with remains of a child. At a higher level and probably later than Graves 20 and 21.

Roughly circular inside. South wall and parts of east and west walls of small and moderate-sized stones; the south and east sides meet approximately at a right angle on the outside (cf. Grave 17); north wall and floor of bedrock, apparently trimmed. Max. interior dimension *ca.* 0.60 m. Two cover slabs set east-west (Pl. 62, c). Interior height *ca.* 0.25 m.

Fragments of the skeleton of a child about 3 years old (*40 KeK*); skull near center of grave, and a few other bones scattered about, but exact position of body not determinable.

No offerings found.

CENTRAL GROUP: OBJECTS NEAR THE GRAVES

The objects in the following catalogue were found in stratified contexts around the graves of the central group of the Lower Cemetery. For a discussion of the significance of the finds made around the graves see the general account of the cemetery, above, p. 52.

COPPER WORKING

107 (Kph.34) Fragment of burnt clay, probably from a furnace-lining or crucible Pls. 22, 66

Found among or beneath the stones scattered around Grave 2.

Small fragment; all edges missing. L. 0.048, W. 0.029, Th. 0.019–0.023.

Coarse fabric; red outside but gray inside as if subjected to intense heat. Outer surface nearly flat; inner surface raised around the edge of a hole, about 0.018 m. in diameter, pierced through the wall. The hole is comparable to those in **76***, **148*** and **174**. In the absence of a slag deposit we cannot be certain that **107** is from a crucible, but it closely resembles other fragments, some of which do have slag deposits.

108 (Kph.3.16) Fragment of terracotta vessel (crucible?) Pls. 22, 66

Found in or around Grave 15.

Trough-shaped, with both ends missing; spreading sides, worn on upper edges. H. 0.029, W. 0.065. Near the middle of the bottom the profile is slightly angular.

Fairly coarse, light gray biscuit, gray on surface; subjected to intense heat, which burned out particles of material and left the surface pitted.

In shape the vessel is unlike the pottery from the site; probably to be associated with metalworking because of its burned condition.

STONE

109 (Kph.1.7) Fragment of marble rhyton Pls. 23, 67

Found about 0.15 m. below pebble floor of Grave 20.

Broken at all edges. H. 0.037, W. 0.03, Th. 0.009 to 0.01.

Fine-grained, white marble; surface smooth. Strongly curved fragment from lower part of a conical rhyton; inner surface has vertical marks of abrasion on its upper part, and horizontal marks of rotary drilling or abrasion on its lower part; outer surface has marks of abrasion, not quite vertical. The vessel was larger than **103**, to judge by the thickness of the wall.

110 (Kph.1.2) Pointed tool of flint Pl. 68

Found about 0.25 m. below pebble floor of Grave 20.

Part probably missing at broad end. L. 0.036, W. 0.01, Th. 0.05.

White with gray streaks. Nearly triangular; one edge curves in slightly towards the broad end; triangular in section; secondary working along edges.

111 (Kph.3.36) Fragment of flint tool Pl. 68

Found near east wall of Grave 14.

Both ends missing; two deep gouges on dorsal face. L. pres. 0.029, W. 0.018, Th. 0.009.

Gray-white stone with dull gray-brown surface. Nearly rectangular; one face flat, the other in three planes; trapezoidal to convex in section; secondary working along edges. Probably from a tool like **110**.

112 (Kph.3.14) Obsidian blade (category 1 a) Pl. 69

Found beneath Grave 21 and above the surviving cover slab over the north side of Grave 11.

Both ends missing. L. 0.07, W. 0.02, Th. 0.005.

Dark gray; surface slightly shiny. Long, broad; trapezoidal in section; chipped along one edge from use or secondary working. This is one of the largest and most impressive of the parallel-sided blades.

113 (Kph.1.25) Obsidian blade (category 1 a) Pl. 69
Found within Grave 9, where it was almost certainly intrusive.
One end missing. L. 0.041, W. 0.026, Th. 0.003.
Black; surface shiny; some striations.
Large, broad, flat; roughly trapezoidal in section; bulb of percussion preserved; one edge chipped from secondary working or use.

114 (Kph.3.18) Obsidian blade (category 1 a)
Found beneath Grave 21 and above Grave 11.
Both ends missing. L. 0.032, W. 0.012, Th. 0.004.
Gray; surface somewhat shiny.
Moderate sized, roughly parallel sided; triangular in section; edges serrated from secondary working or use.

115 (Kph.3.37) Obsidian blade (category 1 a)
From west part of cemetery in or near the *dromos*.
One end missing. L. 0.039, W. 0.014, Th. 0.006.
Black; surface shiny; striated. Moderate sized; roughly parallel sided, but one edge slightly notched; triangular in section; small flake removed from ventral face at end; both edges chipped.

116 (Kph.1.26) Obsidian blade (category 1 a) Pls. 25, 69
Found in excavation above Graves 9, 10, 11, 12 and their platforms, beneath the level of Graves 20 and 21.
Complete except slight modern chipping; mended from two pieces. L. 0.07, W. 0.015, Th. 0.004.
Gray; surface shiny. Long, narrow, with edges gradually converging towards one end; roughly trapezoidal in section; extensive secondary working at one edge and around the narrow end; bulb of percussion at broad end. Blade adapted as side and end scraper; similar to **100**.

117 (Kph.3.6) Obsidian blade (category 1 a) Pls. 25, 69
Found near south side of Grave 15.
Intact. L. 0.076, W. 0.021, Th. 0.006.
Dark, shiny surface, except one face with rough natural surface. Blunt at one end with bulb of percussion; edges curve in to form a point at the other end; triangular in section; extensive secondary working along one edge. Blade adapted as side scrapre.

118 (Kph.3.41) Obsidian blade (category 1 a) Pl. 69
Found during removal of the south side of Grave 11 and excavation to bedrock between Graves 9, 10, 11, and 12.
Both ends missing. L. 0.049, W. 0.014, Th. 0.004.
Gray; surface somewhat shiny. Edges nearly parallel, but narrowing towards one end; triangular to trapezoidal in section; secondary working on both edges. Blade adapted as side scraper.

119 (Kph.3.2) Obsidian blade (category 1 a)
Found just above P 5 over Grave 13.
One end only. L. 0.03, W. 0.017.
Gray with black striations. Pointed tip; triangular in section. Probably from parallel-sided blade adapted as end scraper like **100** and **116**.

120 (Kph.1.24) Obsidian blade (category 1 b) Pl. 69
Found during removal of loose stones around the top of P 2 above Grave 12, P 1 above Grave 10, and the top of Grave 11.
Intact except for a small chip at one end. L. 0.058, W. 0.021, Th. 0.004.
Gray; surface somewhat shiny. Oblong; roughly trapezoidal in section; bulb of percussion at one end.

121 (Kph.3.39) Obsidian blade (category 1 b) Pl. 69
From north part of Grave 11.
Intact except for a chip at one end. L. 0.04, W. 0.018, Th. 0.003.
Gray; surface shiny. Oblong; trapezoidal in section; secondary working and/or chipping on both edges.

122 (Kph.1.23) Obsidian flake tool (category 2) Pl. 69
Found in excavation above Graves 9, 10, 11, 12 and their platforms, beneath the level of Graves 20 and 21.
Intact except for slight chipping. L. 0.054, W. 0.051, Th. 0.01.
Gray; surface dull. Roughly oval but with a sideways projection at one end; striking platform and bulb of percussion at other end; flat on one face, many facets on the other; marks of secondary working and/or use along one edge.

123 (Kph.3.38) Obsidian scraper (category 3) Pls. 25, 70
From west part of cemetery in or near the *dromos*.
About one fifth missing from one edge and one end. L. 0.06, W. 0.025, Th. 0.01.
Gray; surface shiny. Oval, pointed at one end; nearly flat on one face, several planes on the other; bulb of percussion at broader end; secondary working on one edge and the pointed end. Similar in form to **212*** but a little larger.

124 (Kph.3.1) Obsidian scraper (category 3) Pl. 70
Found near north side of Grave 12.
Intact. L. 0.041, W. 0.016, Th. 0.007.
Dark gray; surface fairly shiny. Roughly triangular in outline and in section; secondary working at edges and pointed end.

125 (Kph.1.21) Obsidian tool (category 6) Pl. 70
Found about 0.15 m. below pebble floor of Grave 20.
Intact. L. 0.069, W. 0.032, Th. 0.009.
Gray; surface slightly shiny; striated. Rectangular at one end, narrowing almost to a point at the other; angle along one edge; roughly trapezoidal in section; striking platform and bulb of percussion at the pointed end.

Obsidian uninventoried (by categories):

1 a	1 b	2	3	4	5	6	waste	total
23	4	10	0	0	0	9	290	336

126 (Kph.3.10) Piece of chalky mineral Pls. 22, 68

Found outside the northeast corner of Grave 14 about 0.20 m. above the cover of Grave 1.

Probably intact. H. 0.018, L. 0.037, W. 0.028.

Fairly soft, white. Nearly pyramidal chunk; facets and edges worn by use. Probably used for marking or drawing, or as a coloring agent.

TERRACOTTA

127 (Kph.3.11) Female figurine Pl. 72

Found near east side of Grave 17, about 0.20 m. above the top of P 6 over Grave 4.

Missing: head, one breast, all of one arm, most of the other arm, and perhaps the bottom surface. H. pres. 0.054, W. pres. 0.049, Th. 0.029, W. of neck 0.03, D. of lower body 0.028.

Fairly fine, hard, sandy, red biscuit; surface smoothed but worn, reddish brown.

Roughly modeled. Body nearly cylindrical but flattened in front; neck oval in section; lower body round in section. The left arm was outstretched and roughly oval in section; the right arm was probably outstretched as in the similar figurines **196, 197**, and **198**; there is a possibility, however, that it was at the side, now represented by a bulge which begins near the bottom of the figurine and continues to the height of the breasts. Small pellet breasts, added separately.

128 (Kph.3.13) Head of figurine Pls. 26, 73

Found near east side of Grave 17 about 0.05 m. above the top of P 6 over Grave 4.

Head and neck preserved; perhaps this portion had been made separately and added to the body. H. 0.051, W. 0.049, Th. 0.025, W. of neck 0.032.

Rather coarse, micaceous, reddish brown biscuit.

Neck oval in section. Face roughly triangular with apex at slightly rounded chin, tilted back from bottom to top; projecting knob at top of face for nose, and a similar projection at top of head behind; slight swelling on back beginning below projecting knob and continuing to the neck. Two upper corners of head pierced with holes about 0.003 m. in diameter; axis of the holes roughly in the plane of the face but inclined inwards slightly towards the top. Neck slightly flaring at bottom, with uneven, rough lower surface.

It is possible that the pierced holes were intended to represent ears; more likely, however, they were suspension holes, so that the figurine could be hung somewhere or worn around the neck or body. Similar in general to **202**, but the latter has no pierced holes.

129 (Kph.3.34) Fragment perhaps of a weight Pls. 26, 71

Found beneath Grave 21, above north part of Grave 11.

Coarse, red-brown biscuit.

Part of one edge preserved. H. 0.041, W. 0.044, Th. 0.019.

Fragment with flat profile, curving edge; near the edge, a small perforation 0.005 m. in diameter. Perhaps from a fishing weight or loomweight.

130 (Kph.3.9) Sherd rubbing-tool Pl. 71

Found about 0.05 m. above the cover slabs of Grave 17.

Broken at one side. H. 0.028, D. 0.046.

Rather coarse, dark red-brown biscuit; red surface. Flat disk with lug rising from it; worn around the edges.

131 (Kph.3.32) Sherd rubbing-tool Pl. 71

From west part of cemetery above the *dromos* at about the level of Grave 1.

Intact except chip at one side. L. 0.056, W. 0.043, Th. 0.009.

Coarse, brown biscuit. Flat sherd; oval edges rounded from wear.

132 (Kph.3.33) Sherd rubbing-tool Pl. 71

From west part of cemetery above the *dromos* at about the level of Grave 1.

Intact except chip at one edge. L. 0.039, W. 0.03, Th. 0.01.

Coarse, red-brown biscuit. Fragment originally from the base of a pot; slightly hollowed on both sides.

133 (Kph.4.42) Sherd rubbing-tool Pl. 71

Found between Graves 21 and 22.

One end missing. L. 0.061, W. 0.043, Th. 0.014.

Coarse, orange-brown biscuit, black at core. Flat sherd; oval; edges rounded and smooth from wear.

POTTERY

About 12 tinfuls of pottery were collected around the central group of graves. There were no clearly stratified layers, and no development or change in the pottery could be noted between the lower levels and the higher levels; the material is therefore presented in one catalogue, with a record of the context of the more nearly complete vessels. All the pottery can be regarded as stratigraphically secure, in the sense that it must have found its way into the earth before or during the time when the latest graves were built; much of it may have found its way into the earth after the earliest, lowest graves were built.

It is unlikely, considering not only the quantity of pottery but also the number of different vessels represented, that all the pots were funerary offerings; on the other hand, at least some of the vessels may have been offerings, which either had been discarded at the time of later burials or had been placed in the grave pits above the graves or their platforms (see the general remarks above, p. 52).

From a count of rim fragments of different vessels, it can be estimated that at least 234 small vessels were represented, most of them bowls classified under A 2, but including some 26 small jars. In addition, at least 21 large jars were represented.

A 1

Rim fragments of 11 or more, e.g. Pl. 27, C = Pl. 75, E, D. est. 0.18. Two with lip slightly thickened outside. Pl. 27, E = Pl. 75, A gives a complete profile from plain rim to rounded juncture with bottom; D. 0.28 if round, but probably oval; cf. **138.**

A 2

Rim fragments of at least 159; about 45 with conical or rounded profile and 42 with some degree of angularity.

UNDECORATED

With conical or rounded profile. Pl. 27, F, D. est. 0.16, and Pl. 27, G, D. est. 0.12, are from nearly conical vessels, and preserve complete profiles from rim to juncture with flat bottom; the former example had at least one horizontally pierced lug about midway from rim to bottom. Other fragments, e.g. Pl. 28, D = Pl. 75, AE, D. est. 0.30, and Pl. 28, N = Pl. 75, Q, D. est. 0.32, have similar lugs or lug handles placed closer to the rim. Pl. 28, A = Pl. 75, AC, D. est. 0.12, has a vertically elongated lug handle pierced horizontally near top and bottom (cf. Pl. 75, AD).

At least two bowls have slightly flaring rims, e.g. Pl. 28, E = Pl. 75, Y, D. est. 0.20–0.25, which has a T-lug near the rim. Pl. 28, K, D. est. 0.22, has a broad horizontal groove outside the rim. Pl. 75, S, D. est. 0.24, turns up slightly at the lip (cf. Pl. 28, L) and is intermediate in profile between rounded and angular. Pl. 29, L, D. est. 0.19, is unique in profile: the thick shoulder, although rounded, is very sharply curved, and the delicate rim is slightly everted; it is reminiscent of some of the vessels classified as jars, i.e. Pl. 31, T = Pl. 77, Z; Pl. 31, U = Pl. 77, X; Pl. 31, V = Pl. 77, AG. A fragment, Pl. 29, N = Pl. 75, AP, has a horizontally pierced lug handle placed beneath a notch-like depression in the rim. Another fragment from a large bowl with a curving rim, perhaps rising to form a tab.

Fragments of high-swung lugs, lug handles, or tabs from five vessels, probably bowls with rounded profile: Pl. 38, L = Pl. 85, AK, and Pl. 38, M = Pl. 85, AL are small, flattened loops, the latter with diagonal slashes at top and edges; Pl. 38, N = Pl. 85, AN, and Pl. 85, AM are broader loops with internal struts and knobs at the apex (partly broken on the latter example); Pl. 38, P = Pl. 85, AT is a tab handle pierced with two horizontal holes, one parallel and one perpendicular to the rim.

With angular profile. Rim fragments of at least 42, e.g. Pl. 29, B, D. est. 0.16; Pl. 29, D, D. est. 0.16; Pl. 75, AL; several of them, e.g. Pl. 29, F, D. est. 0.20, Pl. 29, J = Pl. 75, AF, D. est. 0.20 and Pl. 29, G = Pl. 75, AA, have horizontally pierced lugs at or immediately beneath the angle. Pl. 29, K = Pl. 75, AB, D. est. 0.22, has a pair of rounded lugs, vertically pierced, placed side by side just below the angle.

DECORATED

Crusted red. One example decorated on the exterior.

Pattern burnished outside. The following seven fragments, probably all with sides relatively upright and continuously curved. Frontispiece, C = Pl. 40, A = Pl. 86, E, D. est. 0.20: rim with groups of parallel lines at oblique angles. Frontispiece, B = Pl. 40, B = Pl. 86, B, D. est. 0.16: rim decorated as the preceding, with some groups oblique, some perpendicular and some parallel to the rim. Pl. 86, H: rim fragment with burnished stripes parallel to it. Pl. 40, K = Pl. 87, C: body sherd from a bowl (?) with an unpierced horizontal lug with central indentation; pattern of groups of parallel lines at oblique angles (perhaps like that of Pl. 42, D). Pl. 87, E: body sherd from a bowl (?) with part of a vertical plastic ridge, probably the termination of a vertical lug; pattern evidently of groups of parallel lines at oblique angles. Frontispiece, E = Pl. 87, F: similar sherd with part of a ridge and with a similar pattern, apparently arranged symmetrically around the lug. Pl. 40, H = Pl. 86, M: lower part of a bowl with flat bottom; parallel burnished lines oblique to axis.

Pattern burnished inside. Fragments of at least 23 relatively shallow vessels including the following. Pl. 41, A = Pl. 86, Y, D. est. 0.24: rim fragment probably from a bowl with continuous curve; worn; inside of lip undecorated or perhaps solidly burnished; pattern beneath of four roughly parallel lines and one oblique line Pl. 41, B = Pl. 86, AA, D. est. 0.26: rim fragment probably from a bowl with continuous curve, since it is too shallow to have had an angle; groups of parallel lines at oblique angles; part of a curved line or area at lower right. Pl. 41, D = Pl. 86, X, D. est. 0.22: rim fragment with lip turning up at an angle; lug handle outside just beneath the angle; pattern of groups of parallel lines at oblique angles. Frontispiece, J = Pl. 41, G = Pl. 86, S, D. est. 0.16: rim fragment of a very shallow vessel; curve continuous on the inside, but lip set off at an angle on the outside; pattern of horizontal lines and a zone of crosshatching. Pl. 41, H = Pl. 86, U, D. est. 0.21: rim with lip slightly turned up; horizontally pierced lug outside below the lip; lip left undecorated inside; beneath is a pattern of parallel and oblique lines. Frontispiece, K = Pl. 41, J = Pl. 86, W, D. est. 0.18: rim with lip turned up; horizontally pierced lug outside below the lip; pattern apparently includes crude hatching and crosshatching between converging lines. Frontispiece, H = Pl. 41, L = Pl. 86, P, D. est. 0.22: rim with offset, curved lip; groups of parallel lines meeting at various angles; also a small triangular burnished area. Pl. 86, AC: rim with lip turned up; pattern probably of groups of parallel lines meeting at various angles. Pl. 86, AD: rim with lip turned up; compact rectilinear pattern. Pl. 86, AE: rim turned up at an angle (cf. Pl. 41, K); pattern of broad diagonal strokes. Pl. 86, AF: rim turned up; lip solidly burnished inside; beneath are parallel lines nearly perpendicular to rim. Pl. 86, AH: decorated with parallel lines perpendicular to plain rim. Pl. 86, AJ: lip turned up; worn; rectilinear pattern with slanting lines. Pl. 86, AM: body sherd with pattern of straight lines at various angles. Pl. 86, AP: body sherd with pattern of lines at various angles (perhaps similar to Pl. 42, D). Frontispiece, O = Pl. 42, B = Pl. 86, AQ (turned at different angle in photographs from that in drawing): lower part of a bowl with flat bottom; groups of parallel lines meeting almost at right angles. Pl. 42, C = Pl. 86, AR (turned at different angle in photograph from that in drawing), D. est. 0.17: lower part of a large bowl with rounded transition to a flat (?) bottom; pattern partly illegible, apparently groups of parallel lines at oblique angles. Frontispiece, N = Pl. 42, E = Pl. 86, AO, D. est. 0.04: lower part of a small bowl with flat bottom; worn; the pattern includes a meandroid hook. Pl. 86, AS: lower part of a bowl with flat bottom; groups of parallel lines meeting almost at right angles. Pl. 86, AT, D. est. 0.07: lower part of a bowl with flat bottom; pattern probably like the preceding.

Pattern burnished on both sides. Pl. 42, F = Pl. 87, H: from a bowl with slightly flaring rim; worn and partly illegible, the pattern evidently consists of groups of parallel lines at oblique angles.

Incised and grooved. Two fragments of angular bowls with two horizontal rows of punctations on the outside at the angle (cf. Pl. 75, AN). See also below, A 1 and A 2: Incised Rims.

With plastic decoration. Two fragments of rims with vertical ridges; Pl. 75, AH, D. est. 0.16, has a neatly bored hole beside the ridge.

A 2: WITH PEDESTALS

Pl. 30, B = Pl. 75, AY: large fragment preserving the profile of a bowl from rim to juncture with base; the rim rises slightly in a curve, and beneath its highest point is a horizontally pierced lug.

The following fragments of pedestals. Pl. 75, BM: complete from bottom to juncture with bowl. Pl. 75, BU and BV each have an angular cutout not far from the lower edge; beneath the cutout is a groove. Pl. 30, F = Pl. 75, AT: large fragment with an elongated cutout, and vertical and slanting grooves. One with crusted red outside.

Fragments from the juncture of bowl and pedestal of at least ten other vessels, e.g. Pl. 75, BC, BG, BH, BK; the last has widely spaced vertical lines incised on the pedestal.

Pl. 75, BR: from a pedestal (?) with at least two angular cutouts. Pl. 75, BQ: from a pedestal (?) with incised lines in a crisscross pattern.

A 1 AND A 2: BOWLS WITH INCISED RIMS

Pl. 44, B = Pl. 88, A, D. rim est. 0.48: large bowl, well burnished, with a vertical plastic ridge projecting slightly above lip, and a horizontal zone of incised multiple chevrons on outside of rim.

Fragments from 12 other rims, all probably from bowls, incised on outside: seven are plain (Pl. 44, C = Pl. 88, W; Pl. 88, O, T, Z, AC, AD, AK), while five have a thickened band outside (Pl. 88, D, F, J, L, N). The decoration usually consists of slanting lines or multiple chevrons, sometimes set off by indentations or punctations. Pl. 88, Z has slightly curving lines, perhaps part of spirals or concentric circles (cf. Pl. 88, AS) but the fragment is too small to be sure. Pl. 88, AK is decorated with crude horizontal lines.

B 1

Fragments from the rims of at least 25.

Hole mouthed. Fragments of eight or more, as follows. Pl. 31, A = Pl. 77, K, D. est. 0.12, has plastic strip in curving line on shoulder. Pl. 31, E = Pl. 77, S, D. est. 0.18, has vertical lug handle just beneath rim; traces of crusted red around lug handle. Pl. 31, F = Pl. 77, V, D. est. 0.11, has T-lug just beneath rim. Pl. 31, J = Pl. 77, A, D. est. 0.16: nearly conical. Pl. 31, K: rapidly curving belly and low shoulder. Pl. 31, L = Pl. 77, L, D. est. 0.16: like the preceding but with a horizontal incised line just below rim and a semicircular notch in rim. Pl. 31, N = Pl. 77, M, D. est. 0.14: lip rolled slightly upward and outward. Pl. 43, B = Pl. 87, L, D. est. 0.19: pattern-burnished stripes outside, illegible toward lower edge of sherd where surface is worn. Pl. 77, B: lip irregularly fashioned. Pl. 75, G: probably from a hole-mouthed jar (exact angle uncertain) with a broad lug handle, horizontally pierced, on shoulder (cf. Pl. 75, F).

With up-turned or everted lip. Fragments of at least seven, as follows. Pl. 31, T = Pl. 77, Z: sharply curving belly, low shoulder, up-turned lip. Pl. 31, U = Pl. 77, X, D. est. 0.10: rounded belly and shoulder; slightly everted lip. Pl. 31, V = Pl. 77, AG, D. est. 0.24: angular transition from belly to shoulder; low, slightly concave shoulder continuous with rim; T-lug from rim to belly; the lug rises slightly above the level of the rim and the rim is pulled up to meet it. Pl. 32, B, D. est. 0.16: probably shallow, with everted lip. Pl. 77, AC and AD: like the preceding. Pl. 43, C = Pl. 87, J, D. est. 0.20: similar in profile to the three preceding; a zone of pattern burnishing on the shoulder with crude crosshatching; pattern illegible toward lower edge of sherd.

With collar-neck. Fragments of at least ten. Pl. 32, F = Pl. 77, AS, D. est. 0.08: of unusual orange-brown fabric with a slippery surface and more dense inclusions than usual; incised multiple chevrons on collar-neck. Pl. 32, M = Pl. 77, AQ, D. 0.12: incised slanting line on collar-neck, perhaps part of a chevron. One other illustrated: Pl. 32, N, D. est. 0.08.

Other. Pl. 32, O = Pl. 77, G, D. est. 0.16: profile like that of a hole-mouthed jar (cf. Pl. 31, K) but with rim curving slightly upwards. Pl. 32, E = Pl. 77, AH, D. est. 0.16: short, angular shoulder and tall, offset, collar-like rim. Pl. 32, P = Pl. 77, AJ: sharply curving shoulder forming a nearly horizontal surface, and low up-turned rim; broad, flat lug from rim to shoulder. Pl. 32, D = Pl. 77, AV: rounded body and tall, flaring neck; gray fabric (burned?); crusted red inside and out. Pl. 32, C = Pl. 77, AW: profile similar to the preceding, but walls thicker; crusted red inside.

B 2

134 (Kph.6) Closed jar with collar-neck Pls. 33, 78

Found below south half of Grave 20, at a level almost immediately above P 1 over Grave 10 (cf. Pls. 8–10, 16). No bones were found in association with it, and the neck, when complete, would probably have been too narrow for an infant burial. Possibly it was placed as a marker or receptacle for offerings on top of P 1 over Grave 10; on the other hand, in view of its fragmentary state, it may not have been connected with any grave.

About one third preserved, including half the circumference of the neck and most of the bottom; surface severely worn; restored in plaster. H. 0.45, D. collar 0.10, D. base 0.13.

Fairly coarse, sandy, orange-red biscuit, gray at core; surface smoothed; mottled lighter red in places; white accretion in places.

Ovoid body with high shoulder; neck nearly cylindrical at one side, inclining slightly inwards at the other; plain rim; irregular flat bottom; two vertical strap handles on surviving fragment with short vertical plastic ridges extending upwards at the top (cf. **74**). Originally there were probably four handles, irregularly spaced; if the spacing of the surviving handles was maintained there may have been five.

135 (Kph.13) Closed jar with flaring neck Pls. 33, 78

Found in excavations beneath Grave 5 by west side of Grave 4; not securely associated with either grave.

About one quarter preserved, including most of the neck and part of the shoulder and lower body; partially restored in plaster. H. pres. 0.25, D. est. 0.28, D. rim 0.114.

Coarse, red biscuit; surface smoothed. Ovoid body, widest towards the bottom; low, flaring neck; two vertical strap handles are preserved side by side at widest part of belly; presumably there were other pairs of handles around the circumference. Similar pairs of strap handles, although less closely spaced, occur on **137**.

136 (Kph.33) Fragment of a jar Pl. 80

Found during removal of Graves 3 and 5, and excavation of stones scattered around Grave 2.

Only the base and part of lower body are preserved. H. 0.192, D. base 0.11.

Coarse, red-brown biscuit, gray at core; black streak caused by uneven firing on one side; scored inside, burnished outside. Bottom slightly hollowed. Groups of bored holes, three near base within 0.04 m. of one another, indicate that it had been cracked and mended in antiquity.

Uncatalogued fragments from the necks or rims of at least 21 other vessels.

Relatively closed. Pl. 34, B = Pl. 81, Q, D. est. 0.30: slightly up-turned lip; extending above the rim is a large T-lug with finger impressions (cf. Pl. 84, BN); the lip protrudes upwards and outwards to meet the lug. Pl. 33, A: from a collar-neck with horizontally pierced lug handle at juncture of collar and shoulder. A fragment of another collar-neck preserves traces of crusted red on the outside.

Relatively open. Pl. 81, AP: plain rim, rounded on top. Pl. 81, AH, D. est. 0.35: plain rim; beneath it is a large crescent-shaped lug with indented edge. Pl. 81, D: rim with indentations on top; below it is a horizontal plastic ridge with finger impressions, perhaps part of a crescent-shaped lug. Pl. 34, J, D. est. 0.45; a rim thickened in a narrow band toward the outside; indentations at regular intervals on top and on the thickened band.

Intermediate and indeterminate. Pl. 81, AQ: plain rim. Pl. 34, D, D. est. 0.32: a slightly thickened rim. Pl. 81, AF, D. est. 0.30: like the preceding; large T-lug immediately beneath the lip. Pl. 81, AD, D. est. 0.28: plain rim; on the outside is a horizontal zone of incised decoration consisting of irregular multiple chevrons bordered by horizontal lines at top and bottom. Pl. 81, X, D. est. 0.24: plain rim; incised lines outside meeting at various angles. Pl. 81, Y, D. est. 0.30: rim with slightly thickened, broad horizontal band outside; slanting across the band are low ridges formed by grooves; one ridge has finger impressions. Pl. 87, M and O: from a large vessel or vessels with parallel lines in pattern burnishing. Two strap handles, e.g. Pl. 81, B, the edges of which have vertical plastic extensions on the pot wall.

C 1

In all, at least 27 different vessels are represented.

Bodies. Pl. 83, AP: large fragment of lower body and rim. Pl. 83, AM: from a body and strut; a nearly horizontal line of incision is preserved on body; incised multiple chevrons on strut. Pl. 83, AL: similar to the preceding; nearly vertical incised lines on body; incised diagonal line on strut.

Handles. Fragments of at least nine. Five apparently without incised decoration. Pl. 83, A: from the top of a handle. Pl. 83, AT: from the lower part of a handle, probably from a scoop, preserving the point of attachment with body; strut or knob partly broken from inner surface. Fragments from three other handles with knobs on inner surface.

Five handles with incised decoration, including the following. Pl. 83, G: from the lower part of a handle at point of attachment with body; closely placed lines in a vertically oriented multiple-zigzag pattern. Pl. 83, H: broad lines probably making a multiple zigzag. Pl. 83, J: two lines parallel to the edge, approached by a diagonal line (part of multiple zigzag?); the lines were produced by a tool with a split tip.

Pl. 83, K: probably from the handle of a scoop, with incised parallel lines interrupted by short perpendicular lines.

Struts. Fragments of at least 25 different vessels; 13 or more with incised or grooved decoration. Pl. 36, E = Pl. 83, AN: from lower part of a strut, round in section, attached by a plug thrust through the pot wall; vertical incised line on strut leading to an indentation at the bottom opposite the plug. Pl. 83, N: from juncture of strut and handle; strut rectangular in section; knob on top of handle at front edge; incised multiple zigzag on front of strut and handle; vertical incised line on side of strut, evidently continuing on top of handle; other incised lines on top of handle; this vessel may have been even more elaborately decorated than **98**. A fragment of another strut with incised multiple zigzag on the front and a single vertical line on the side. Pl. 36, F = Pl. 83, AG: from a strut, nearly rectangular in section, with incised interlocking hooks. Pl. 36, G: from a strut, round in section, with incised horizontal and diagonal lines and indentations. Pl. 83, AF: from a strut, oval in section, with incised parallel diagonal lines. Fragments of four other struts with incised oblique lines or multiple zigzag. Pl. 83, T: from a strut, round in section, with one vertical incision. Two other struts with one or two vertical incised lines or grooves. A fragment, apparently unincised, with a knob at the juncture of strut and handle.

C 2

Pl. 84, W and X are probably from a single vessel as shown in composite restoration in Pl. 37, B (H. pres. 0.07, D. est. 0.12); just beneath the rim on the inside is a horizontal ledge which evidently continued for much, if not all, of the circumference; the ledge was vertically pierced in at least one place. Pl. 84, Z: from a similar vessel, but its ledge terminates at the left, and was therefore not continuous.

C 3

Fragments from the pierced rims of several coarse, irregular pans, some with interior ledges or lugs. Pl. 37, F = Pl. 84, C preserves profile from rim to flat bottom. Pl. 37, J = Pl. 84, F: from an indented rim; ledge or lug on inside with concave upper surface. Pl. 37, K = Pl. 84, J: a flat ledge or lug on the inside, pierced by four vertical holes which do not quite go all the way through. Pl. 84, K: from a coarse tab, perhaps tilted at an angle, pierced twice horizontally. Pl. 84, S: from a rim with oval protuberance inside. Pl. 84, R: from a flat bottom, tilted up to show the rough lower surface.

Pl. 37, E = Pl. 84, P: from a pan with low wall, flat bottom which is rough underneath, and burnished upper surface.

C 4

Pl. 37, A = Pl. 84, AJ: a flat, slightly raised base, D. est. 0.10, pierced at regular intervals.

C 5

Pl. 37, M = Pl. 84, AF: a fragment preserving a knob with slightly flaring sides; rounded in section; flat on top; the lower surface is flat and the lower edge broken all around. A fragment probably from a similar knob. Pl. 37, O = Pl. 84, AE: probably from the top of a crown lid with four arms; pierced at apex.

OTHER SHERDS

Crusted red. Traces on many sherds.

Pattern burnished. Pl. 89, W: from a fairly small vessel with a T-lug; next to it is a broad, oblique, pattern-burnished stripe or area; beside this are two horizontal incised lines. Pl. 87, A: from the rim of a bowl or jar (angle uncretain) with one broad and several narrow stripes, nearly vertical.

Incised and grooved. Body fragments of at least five small vessels, including the following. Pl. 88, AQ: horizontal band with zigzag, one line above, two below. Pl. 88, AV: fine lines. Pl. 88, AT: three curving lines, punctated dots. Pl. 89, Z: curving groove, crusted red on exterior. Pl. 44, L = Pl. 88, AR: medium-sized vessel with pattern of curves (spirals?) and straight lines, probably in a zone or panel. Pl. 44, M = Pl. 89, S: large vessel with broad horizontal band; on this, oblique grooves, one hooked around a dot; deep scoring below. Pl. 89, Q: zigzag on narrow plastic band. Pl. 44, N = Pl. 89, L: large vessel with parallel lines and curving groove. Pl. 88, AU: triangular impressions (*Kerbschnitt*). Pl. 89, AB: two flat surfaces meeting at an obtuse angle with short strokes above and below. Incised decoration on other vessels, both small, e.g. Pl. 88, AY, AZ, and large, e.g. Pl. 89, A, E, J.

With plastic decoration. Four fragments, e.g. Pl. 89, BJ and BK, with raised bands decorated with short incisions. Many fragments with raised bands decorated by impressions. Pl. 89, BL: a band wider than usual, with two parallel rows of finger impressions. Pl. 89, BC: a raised band perpendicular to a deeply indented or scalloped rim. Pl. 89, BG: a raised band terminating in an oblique, disk-like surface. Three other examples are illustrated: Pl. 89, BD, BN, BP. Several sherds with plain raised bands. Pl. 46, B = Pl. 89, AS: from the belly of a fairly small vessel with two curving ridges. Pl. 89, BB: with two parallel ridges. Pl. 89, AY: with relatively large ridge. Three fragments with small knobs or disks on pot walls: Pl. 89, AJ, AL, AP; the last has a low disk with deep indentation, and traces of crusted red.

Handles. Fragments of at least 50 strap handles from larger vessels, seven with plastic knob at apex. Pl. 84, BE: with a simple plastic knob. Pl. 84, AL: with a knob on which horizontal lines are incised. Three handles, two perhaps from the same pot, have vertical grooves, e.g. Pl. 84, AP. Seven with impressed plastic bands beside or near them (cf. **146** and **170**), in two instances on a very flat pot wall, e.g. Pl. 84, AM.

At least 30 lugs and lug handles with vertical axis, pierced horizontally. Pl. 38, D: from the flaring rim of a bowl or jar with elongated lug; the horizontal hole in the lug partly penetrated the pot wall; on the inside, as if to strengthen the wall, is a rounded protuberance. Another fragment with a lug and protuberance similar to the preceding. Three T-lugs. One vertical lug with long plastic tail on which are slanting grooves. Pl. 84, BS: with two pellet-like lugs, vertically pierced, placed side by side (like breasts?). Two unpierced horizontal lugs: Pl. 85, J, small with central indentation; the other consisting of two linked, knob-like projections. Six horizontal or crescent-shaped lugs with two vertical piercings and long vertical plastic extensions depending from either side: e.g. Pl. 39, E = Pl. 84, BQ, with traces of crusted red; Pl. 39, C = Pl. 85, C; Pl. 39, D = Pl. 84, BR. Three unpierced lugs, e.g. Pl. 39, A = Pl. 85, F and Pl. 85, D, shaped either like a crescent or an inverted U, with indented edges. Pl. 85, H: a crude lug of roughly circular form with indented edge. Pl. 85, T and U: small struts possibly from the interior of handles (cf. **26, 81***).

Unusual forms of handles include the following. Pl. 38, E: broad and flat (original angle uncertain) with greater arch than a scoop handle. Pl. 38, G = Pl. 84, AQ: a fairly flat vertical handle with upper end attached to the rim of a vessel having est. D. 0.18. Fragments of two similar handles. Pl. 84, AR: flat handle, slightly concave in section, arching over at the top to form a smooth transition with a rim. Pl. 84, AS: from a high-swung ribbon handle preserving point of attachment to rim. Pl. 85, AJ: from a high, finger-like tab handle with two holes parallel to rim. Pl. 85, AU: a tab, with a ledge inside near top, pierced twice horizontally perpendicular to rim. A (scoop?) handle or strut, with a deep longitudinal groove, probably made from two rolls of clay (cf. Pl. 36, A = Pl. 83, R).

Bases. Fragments of at least 103 in addition to those already mentioned. Twenty-six large flat bottoms including three with mat impressions on the lower surface: Pl. 91, A, D. 0.15 (Appendix 2, No. 11), probably from a closed vessel; Pl. 90, P, D. 0.20 (Appendix 2, No. 15), probably from an open vessel; Pl. 90, A, D. est. 0.20 (Appendix 2, No. 17), from a vessel of indeterminate size. Three large raised bases including two with mat impressions on the bottom: Pl. 90, N, slightly raised, perhaps from a pan (Appendix 2, No. 9); Pl. 90, J, also slightly raised (Appendix 2, No. 12). Eight large ring bases, e.g. Pl. 85, BJ. Twenty-nine small flat bottoms. Eleven small raised bases: e.g. Pl. 39, G = Pl. 85, AZ, and Pl. 39, J, K, all from almost miniature vessels; Pl. 39, N = Pl. 85, AX, hollowed beneath and resembling a small ring foot; one oval; Pl. 90, K, D. 0.035 and profile like Pl. 39, H, has the impression of a leaf on the bottom. Seventeen small ring bases. Three fragments probably from small rounded bottoms. One other mat impression on a bottom: Pl. 90, H, Th. 0.007 (Appendix 2, No. 7).

Oddments. The following three fragments from spouted vessels. Pl. 77, AY: with open spout, perhaps at a rim. Pl. 77, AZ: with open spout just below a rim; above the spout the rim rises in a notched tab; elsewhere the rim was evidently decorated, on a thickened band outside, with incised oblique lines (zigzag?). Pl. 77, BB: from a spout, probably open on top and pinched in at the end. Pl. 45, M = Pl. 77, BG: from a small, perhaps miniature, vessel which makes an angle at the lower part of the body. Pl. 45, F, a rim of a bowl or jar with everted lip. Pl. 85, AA: a fragment preserving the lower part of a vertical strap handle, from a vessel of smaller diameter than others having strap handles. Pl. 85, Z: with a broad plastic strip, turning up at one end in a finished surface. Pl. 91, K: with a bulbous, tab-like swelling at an edge or rim. Pl. 45, H = Pl. 91, O: possibly from near a rim, with a roughly rectangular depression. Pl. 91, R: from a crude vessel (pan?), with two walls meeting at an acute angle, and indentations on top of the rim. Pl. 91, P: with a fine circular line of dark discoloration (not visible in the photograph), presumably produced in the firing.

EASTERN GROUP: GRAVES AND OFFERINGS

The six graves of this group (Graves 23–28) were situated above a rock shelf at the eastern end of the cleft of the Lower Cemetery. The shelf is a continuation of the ledge which extended along the northern side of the central part of the cleft. The graves can be arranged in a probable chronological sequence (Table 6 and Pl. 13, Section J–J): Grave 23, a small grave built almost immediately on bedrock, was partly built over or disturbed by Grave 24, which must therefore be later; Grave 25 was built above the cover slabs of Grave 24; Grave 26 was probably about contemporary with Grave 25; Grave 27 was at a slightly higher level than Grave 25 and was perhaps a little later; finally, Grave 28 was built directly above Grave 27.

These graves cannot be placed in a definite chronological relationship with any of the graves or sequences of graves in the central group; they are, however, probably later than the earliest graves of the central group if, as is likely, the central part of the cleft was built up with graves first, and then its periphery.

Grave 28
(XXIII)
↑
Grave 27
(XXIV)
↗ (dashed)
Grave 25 ----- Grave 26
(XXV) (IV)
↑
Grave 24
(XXVI)
↑
Grave 23
(XXXII)

TABLE 6. Schematic chronological diagram showing graves of the eastern group of the Lower Cemetery. The conventions are as in Table 5, p. 55.

GRAVE 23 (XXXII)

Pl. 62; Plan, Pl. 21

A slab-sided cist grave containing a jar with an infant burial. Earlier than Grave 24, immediately to the southeast, since the upper part of the north wall of Grave 24 overlapped its cover.

Triangular in plan. A single slab for each side.[21] The slabs meet at the corners except at the north. Max. interior length (northwest side) *ca.* 0.42 m., east side, 0.29 m. (both measured as if the slabs continued to the north corner), south side, *ca.* 0.37 m. Three cover slabs, set northwest-southeast. Interior height *ca.* 0.25 m.

Jar upright on a floor of small stones. The jar was smashed and its pieces partly projected beneath the slab at the northeast side of the grave. After mending, the jar was about 0.16 m. higher than the interior of the grave and its upper part was presumably smashed when the cover was set in place. The building of Grave 24 may also have caused some disturbance of Grave 23.

Fragments of the bones of an infant about 6 months old (*41 KeK*); position of body not determinable.

[21] The plan on Plate 21 shows the grave after the removal of the east slab; Plate 8 shows it in place.

137 (Kph.11) Large jar used for burial Pls. 35, 78

About two thirds preserved; neck or rim missing; partly restored. H. pres. 0.41, D. *ca.* 0.40, D. base 0.135.

Coarse, red-brown biscuit; surface brown with some black patches, smoothed. Globular body; flat bottom. Four strap handles placed in pairs approximately opposite each other at greatest diameter; the two handles of each pair are linked at the upper edges by a horizontal plastic band with finger impressions; impressed plastic bands extend upward from the top of each handle a distance of 0.05 to 0.08 m. A similar pair of handles, although more closely spaced, occurs on **135**. The vertical plastic bands are like the plain bands on **74** and **134**.

This vessel does not resemble the others used for burials: **97** is also a closed vessel but nearly biconical and with a different arrangement of handles; **146** and **170** are open vessels and quite different. There is no reason to suppose that any of them was made specifically as a burial jar.

GRAVE 24 (XXVI)

Pl. 62; Plan, Pl. 8; Section, Pl. 13

A built grave with a single skeleton. Later than Grave 23 to the northwest (see above). Immediately beneath Grave 25.

Roughly oval in plan; walls of moderate-sized and large stones. Max. interior length (northwest-southeast) *ca.* 1.20 m., width *ca.* 0.80 m. One cover slab at the northeast side, set northwest-southeast; a fragment of a second beside it; cover missing at southwest side. Interior height *ca.* 0.45 m.

Fragments of the bones and skull probably of a woman about 33 years old (*38 KeK*), on a floor of small stones; position of body not determinable.

No offerings found.

GRAVE 25 (XXV)

Pl. 63; Plan, Pl. 20; Section, Pl. 13

A built grave with at least one burial. Immediately above the cover of Grave 24. At nearly the same level and probably about contemporary with Grave 26 to the northeast.

Severely damaged by erosion. Parts only of north and west walls, of moderate-sized and large stones; perhaps rectangular in plan, since they meet roughly at a right angle.

Remains of a man about 31 years old (*37 KeK*), on a pebble floor; skull with top uppermost and face towards the south; position of body not determinable. There may have been other burials, lost through erosion.

No offerings found.

GRAVE 26 (IV)

Plan, Pl. 20

A built grave with at least one burial. At nearly the same level and probably about contemporary with Grave 25.

Severely damaged by erosion. Parts of north and west walls, of moderate-sized stones founded on large slabs; perhaps roughly rectangular in plan since they meet at an angle slightly greater than a right angle.

Remains of a man about 34 years old (*6 KeK*); skull apparently facing east; position of body not determinable. There may originally have been other burials, now lost.

No offerings found.

GRAVE 27 (XXIV)

Pl. 63; Plan, Pl. 8; Section, Pl. 13

A small built grave with no bones preserved. At a slightly higher level and perhaps later than Grave 25 to the southwest.

Roughly rectangular in plan; west, south and east walls of small and moderate-sized stones; north side of bedrock, which here slopes down irregularly to the south. Max. interior length (north-south) *ca.* 0.50 m., width *ca.* 0.30 m. One cover slab over northeast corner, another over northwest corner; they were apparently unsupported in the middle, but overlapped the walls of the grave sufficiently to be stable. Cover missing on south side. Interior height *ca.* 0.15 m.

Floor of small stones. No bones found above it; presumably the burial was that of a child, whose bones have completely disintegrated. A few bones found underneath the floor were probably unconnected with the grave.

138 (Kph.20) Small oval bowl Pls. 27, 74

Found in pieces immediately beneath the level of the cover slabs; since the cover was partly missing, it is possible that the bowl found its way in later, and was not a funerary offering deposited in Grave 27.

About two thirds preserved; restored. H. 0.06–0.07, L. 0.11, W. 0.071.

Coarse, brown biscuit; surface fairly rough; patches of fairly thick crusted red inside; patches of crusted white outside (visible at left in photograph) with traces of crusted red in places over the white (cf. **106**).

Oval as seen from above or below. Plain rim, rising at either end; two holes made before firing at one end, irregularly placed; the other end, which is partly missing, probably had similar holes. Rounded transition to flat bottom.

A fragment with crusted red was placed in Matson's experimental kiln (see above, p. 10); the red substance (predominantly hematite; above, p. 28) turned a powdery white, which indicates that it had been applied after firing.

GRAVE 28 (XXIII)

Pl. 63; Plan, Pl. 9; Section, Pl. 13

A few stones roughly forming a segment of a circle were found above the north side of Grave 27. These may once have been part of a grave built above the cover of Grave 27, now almost completely lost through erosion.

No bones or offerings preserved.

EASTERN GROUP : OBJECTS NEAR THE GRAVES

The objects in the following catalogue were found in stratified contexts around the graves of the eastern group of the Lower Cemetery. For a discussion of the significance of the finds made around the graves see the general account of the cemetery, above, p. 52.

STONE

139 (Kph.3.20) Obsidian blade (category 1 a) Pl. 69

Found south of Grave 24.

Both ends missing. L. 0.035, W. 0.014, Th. 0.004.

Gray; surface dull. Moderate sized; triangular in section; edges serrated from secondary working or use.

140 (Kph.3.21) Obsidian blade (category 1 a) Pl. 69

Found south of Grave 24.

One end missing. L. 0.043, W. 0.014, Th. 0.004.

Gray; surface dull. Moderate sized, nearly parallel sided; triangular in section; edges serrated from secondary working or use.

141 (Kph.3.23) Obsidian blade (category 1 a) Pl. 69

Found south of Grave 24.

Intact. L. 0.053, W. 0.013, Th. 0.003.

Gray; surface dull. Moderate sized, nearly parallel sided; triangular to trapezoidal in section; secondary working at edges.

142 (Kph.3.22) Obsidian blade (category 1 b) Pl. 69

Found south of Grave 24.

One end missing. L. 0.052, W. 0.015, Th. 0.0035.

Gray; surface dull. Moderate sized; narrowing towards both ends from widest point near one end; triangular to trapezoidal in section; edges chipped from secondary working or use.

143 (Kph.3.40) Obsidian flake tool (category 2) Pls. 25, 69

From the immediate vicinity of Grave 27.

Slightly chipped at one end; otherwise intact. L. 0.056, W. 0.044, Th. 0.012.

Gray; surface dull. Irregular oval; roughly pointed at one end, struck from the other end; trapezoidal to rounded in section; secondary working along one edge.

144 (Kph.3.19) Waste piece of obsidian Pl. 70

From the immediate vicinity of Grave 27.

L. 0.042, W. 0.025, Th. 0.011.

Gray with black striations, surface shiny. Oval; roughly trapezoidal in section.

Obsidian uninventoried (by categories):

1 a	1 b	2	3	4	5	6	waste	total
2	0	0	0	0	0	0	15	17

TERRACOTTA

145 (Kph.3.35) Spindle whorl (?) Pls. 26, 71

Found during the dismantling of Grave 24.

Intact, but probably worn along one edge. H. 0.015, L. 0.038, W. 0.033.

Coarse, brown biscuit. Button-like object, nearly circular but flattened at one edge; edge slightly concave in section except where flattened; pierced with hole about 0.008 m. in diameter. Flattened edge possibly due to wear during secondary use as a rubbing-tool.

POTTERY

A total of about one and two-fifths tinfuls was collected in excavations beneath the surface around the eastern group of graves. From a count of rim fragments, it is estimated that at least 25 small vessels and one large vessel are represented.

A 1

Rim fragment with black burnished surface inside and out.

A 2

Fragments of at least two rims; Pl. 86, K with pattern burnishing outside, evidently in groups of parallel lines at various angles.

A 2: WITH PEDESTALS

Fragments of at least seven. Pl. 30, G = Pl. 76, A: conical pedestal (D. 0.14) and lower part of bowl. Pl. 30, E = Pl. 75, AV, D. est. 0.14: pedestal with an angular cutout, conjecturally restored. Pl. 30, C = Pl. 75, BJ: from juncture of bowl and pedestal with horizontal groove on pedestal. Pl. 75, BF: from juncture of bowl and pedestal, with unusually large diameter (0.098) at narrowest part.

A 1 AND A 2: INCISED RIMS

Fragments of at least three rims with incision outside. Pl. 88, E: thickened outside in a narrow band which is decorated with oblique lines. Pl. 44, E = Pl. 88, P, D. est. 0.24: multiple chevrons interspersed with impressed dots. Pl. 88, R and S, probably from the same vessel: multiple chevrons with an impressed dot at the upper angle.

B 1

Rim fragment from a jar with up-turned lip. Fragments of three collar-necks: Pl. 32, L = Pl. 77, AP, D. est. 0.11, has broad, carelessly made horizontal grooves outside; one other illustrated, Pl. 77, AL. A fragment probably from a jar, Pl. 75, F (exact angle uncertain, D. rim est. 0.08) with broad lug, horizontally pierced, beneath rim (cf. Pl. 75, G), and two bored holes around the lug.

B 2

Pl. 34, F: rim fragment of a fairly closed vessel; rim slightly thickened and up-turned, D. est. 0.20.

C 1

Fragments of at least three. Pl. 83, AR: from lower part of a handle at juncture with body; incised oblique lines on handle. A fragment of an apparently unincised back with a small plastic knob on the inner surface (cf. Pl. 83, AU). Pl. 83, W: from a round strut with carefully incised multiple zigzag. Another strut with multiple zigzag. Pl. 83, U: from a round strut with vertical incisions. Pl. 83, AO: round in section, with a general resemblance to scoop struts, but more strongly curved; evidently unincised.

C 5

Pl. 84, AD: rounded rim with flat profile, perhaps from a lid.

OTHER SHERDS

Crusted red. Two small fragments, one with red outside, the other inside.

Incised and grooved. Body (?) sherds from three vessels decorated outside with incision, e.g. Pl. 89, K. Pl. 39, V = Pl. 89, AD: from a large angular vessel unique in profile, with crude grooved lines inside. Pl. 89, AE: incised line on the outside of a rounded surface.

With plastic decoration. Fragments of several vessels with impressed bands.

Handles. Twelve strap handles. Pl. 84, BT and BU: horizontal lugs, each with two vertical piercings and with plastic ridges depending from the middle and either end. Pl. 39, B = Pl. 85, E: a large unpierced lug shaped like an inverted U, with indented edge. A small unpierced crescent-shaped lug. Pl. 85, AH: a high-swung lug handle, probably from a bowl; one hole preserved parallel to rim.

Bases. Fragments of at least 15. One large flat bottom. Pl. 85, BF: from a large ring base, pierced at least twice. Two medium-sized flat bottoms. Pl. 39, O: a medium-sized raised base with two carelessly made, horizontal grooves. Four medium-sized ring bases, three of them pierced, e.g. Pl. 85, BG. Two small flat bottoms. One small raised base, pierced. Three small ring bases.

Oddment. Pl. 45, L = Pl. 77, BE: from a miniature jar (?) with a vertical handle, probably oval in section, springing from belly and apparently terminating at or near rim.

ISOLATED GRAVES

The following three graves (Graves 29–31) were built around the edges of the cleft of the Lower Cemetery. Each was in an isolated position and no chronological relationship with any other grave could be determined. The isolated graves may be later than most of those within the clefts of the Lower and Upper Cemeteries if, as appears likely, graves were built on the surrounding hillside only after the clefts themselves had become crowded. The isolated graves are listed from west to east.

GRAVE 29 (XXVIII)

Plan, Pl. 8

A severely eroded grave about 2.50 m. southwest of Grave 14, beyond the southwest end of the *dromos*. Evidently built of small stones, some of which were scattered about; plan not determinable.

A few fragments of bones, not saved for examination by Angel.

Some stones northeast of the grave (at 5 on the plan) may have been part of a wall, but the evidence is inconclusive because of erosion.

GRAVE 30 (III)

Pl. 63; Plan, Pl. 8

A built grave with only a few bones preserved. About 0.50 m. northwest of Grave 14 and at a slightly higher level.

Severely damaged by erosion. One slab about 0.80 m. long marks the position of the northeast wall. Stones perpendicular to it at either end may mark the position of the northwest and southeast walls; if so, the plan may have been roughly rectangular and the interior length of the northeast side *ca.* 0.72 m.

Bedrock apparently formed the floor. A few bones were found, but not saved for examination by Angel. The grave was probably large enough to have contained one or more adults.

GRAVE 31 (II)

Pl. 63; Plan, Pl. 8

A jar with the bones of two infants, located south of the east end of the cleft.

Jar set on its side, mouth to west, in a shallow depression in bedrock. Small stones were used to wedge it in place. Slab *ca.* 0.43 m. in diameter set vertically against mouth. The upper side of the jar had been exposed by erosion and had collapsed; it could not be determined whether there was once a cover (cf. Grave 32).

Skeletal remains of two infants, one about four months old (*5 KeK*), the other newborn (*5a KeK*); position of the bodies not determinable. Angel (Appendix 5, pp. 135, 138) suggests that they may have been twins, one buried a few months after the other.

No offerings found.

146 (Kph.7) Large jar used for burial Pls. 35, 79

About four fifths preserved; missing part of the bottom and other small fragments; restored. H. 0.56, D. rim 0.39, D. base 0.16.

Semi-coarse, sandy, red-brown biscuit. Surface originally smoothed; now mostly worn, with light marks of scoring.

Deep, open, nearly conical body; plain rim; flat bottom. Two strap handles are preserved about halfway from rim to base; originally there were four, spaced somewhat irregularly around the pot; two low, unpierced crescent-shaped lugs opposite one another near rim, nearly centered above two of the handles. The lower edges of the handles are linked by plastic bands with finger impressions; similar plastic bands extend from either side of the tops of the handles to meet near the rim at some point between each pair of handles; the pattern is not entirely regular; in some instances the bands meet about halfway between the handles, in others almost above the handle at the right. The raised bands clearly simulate rope or cord, and they create a fairly realistic impression of a vessel trussed for lifting.

Similar in general to **170**, which, however, has only two handles and a somewhat different arrangement of crescent-shaped lugs and rope decoration. There is no reason to suppose that either was made specifically as a burial jar.

UNSTRATIFIED OBJECTS

The objects in the following catalogue were found during the cleaning of the surface and the excavation of the uppermost levels of the Lower Cemetery, and they must be regarded in general as unstratified. It may be noted, however, that the surface of the cemetery was severely eroded, and that there was certainly a greater depth of soil at the time when the latest graves were built than in recent times; many of the objects included may have found their way into the cemetery before the latest graves were built. For a discussion of the significance of the stratified finds made around the graves see the general account of the cemetery above, p. 52. All the unstratified finds from the Lower Cemetery, with the exception of only two sherds (below, p. 83), apparently date to the time of the prehistoric occupation of the promontory.

COPPER AND COPPER WORKING

147* (Kph.3.15) Fragment probably from a narrow chisel Pls. 22, 66

Found near surface about 0.40 m. above the south wall of Grave 17.

Small fragment of blade end. L. 0.014, W. 0.014, Th. 0.009.

Copper with a small amount of zinc and traces of iron (see Appendix 1, No. 7). Green before conservation; surface somewhat rough from corrosion.

Wedge-shaped fragment with faces converging in a curve towards the blade; the edges were probably roughly parallel, but only one is certainly preserved; the other edge was probably as restored on Plate 22. Similar to **82*** but larger and heavier.

148* (Kph.30) Fragment of burnt clay, probably from a furnace-lining or crucible Pls. 22, 66

Found near surface around Wall 1.

Missing all edges except one. H. 0.046, L. 0.062, Th. 0.02 to 0.03.

Coarse, orange-tan biscuit, blackened by fire. Wall of a thick vessel preserving rim or edge, which is broad and flat on top and thickened on the inside; outer surface nearly flat; inner surface puckered around the edges of a perforation about 0.018 to 0.02 m. in diameter. The perforation is somewhat similar to that of **107**, which also has a raised edge; **76*** and **174** also have perforations of comparable diameter.

Fragment of slag found at the surface (Field No. KF-3.69).

STONE

149* (Kph.3.26) Obsidian flake tool (category 2) Pl. 69

Found at the surface.

Part probably missing from the narrow end. L. 0.031, W. 0.026, Th. 0.006.

Gray; surface shiny. Roughly oval; nearly flat on one face, several facets on the other; secondary working along one edge.

150* (Kph.3.27) Obsidian flake tool (category 2) Pl. 69

Found at the surface.

Part probably missing from the narrow end. L. 0.036, W. 0.029, Th. 0.007.

Black; surface shiny. Roughly oval; nearly flat on one face, three main facets on the other.

151* (Kph.3.28) Obsidian flake tool (category 2) Pl. 69

Found at the surface.

Intact. L. 0.028, W. 0.025, Th. 0.006.

Gray; surface shiny. Nearly circular; thickest at the center, tapering towards the edges; secondary working or chipping at the edges.

152* (Kph.3.29) Obsidian flake tool (category 2) Pl. 69

Found at the surface.

Intact. L. 0.028, W. 0.023, Th. 0.006.

Black; surface shiny. Roughly oval; trapezoidal in section; secondary working or chipping at the edges.

153* (Kph.3.43) Obsidian flake tool (category 2) Pl. 69

Found near surface along east side of Graves 24 and 27.

Intact. L. 0.038, W. 0.023, Th. 0.008.

Gray; surface dull. Oval, slightly pointed at one end; roughly triangular in section; flat flaking on one face, two facets on the other.

154* (Kph.3.24) Obsidian scraper (category 3) Pls. 25, 70

Found during clearing of Grave 28.

Intact. L. 0.061, W. 0.02, Th. 0.0095.

Black; surface shiny. Oblong; nearly flat on one face, several facets on the other; secondary working at the edges. Closely similar to **155***.

155* (Kph.3.44) Obsidian scraper (category 3) Pl. 70

Found near surface north of Grave 21.

Intact except for a few chips; broken by pick and mended. L. 0.076, W. 0.025, Th. 0.009.

Gray brown; surface shiny. Oblong; trapezoidal in section; secondary working along both edges. Closely similar to **154***.

156* (Kph.3.42) Obsidian scraper (category 3) Pl. 70

Found near surface in central part of Lower Cemetery.

Intact. L. 0.05, W. 0.026, Th. 0.009.

Gray; surface dull. Oval; roughly triangular in section; secondary working on the ventral face at both ends, and along one edge.

157* (Kph.3.30) Pointed tool of obsidian (category 4) Pls. 25, 70

Found at the surface.

Intact. L. 0.04, W. 0.01, Th. 0.005.

Black; surface somewhat shiny. Long and narrow; roughly trapezoidal in section. Perhaps used as a drill.

158* (Kph.3.31) Pointed tool of obsidian (category 4) Pls. 25, 70

Found at the surface.

Intact. L. 0.03, W. 0.02, Th. 0.01.

Black; surface shiny. Broad, triangular in outline with basal notch; flat, roughly trapezoidal in section; secondary working around edges.

159* (Kph.3.25) Obsidian tool (category 6) Pl. 70

Found at the surface.

Intact (?). L. 0.078, W. 0.032, Th. 0.01.

Black; surface shiny. Large piece; pointed at one end; flat at one edge, curved at the other; roughly triangular in section.

Obsidian uninventoried (by categories):

1 a	1 b	2	3	4	5	6	waste	total
17	1	13	0	0	0	10	168	209

TERRACOTTA

160* (Kph.3.12) Ithyphallic figurine Pl. 73

From surface above east side of Grave 17.

Mended from two pieces; small chips missing. H. 0.072, W. 0.047, W. bottom 0.021, Th. 0.042.

Coarse sandy biscuit, gray at core, reddish brown at surface; crudely made, slightly smoothed. Head and body continuous from rounded top to flat base without distinction of face, neck, or legs. Arms represented by a single roll of clay which runs from front of left shoulder around back and down at right to the phallus. This stands out prominently.

Cf. a standing male figurine from Sesklo (Tsountas, 1908, pl. 33, 2) having both arms in contact with penis. The pose of both figurines is probably intended to emphasize male potency (and hence be symbolic of fertility and regeneration) rather than to represent the act of urination or masturbation, as the initial impression might suggest.

161* (Kph.1.8) Sherd rubbing-tool Pl. 71

Found near surface south of Graves 20 and 21.

Intact. H. 0.019, L. 0.035, W. 0.034.

Rather coarse, red-brown biscuit with brown surface. Oval sherd with perforated lug; all edges worn smooth.

162* (Kph.3.8) Sherd rubbing-tool Pl. 71

Found near surface about 0.10 m. above the cover slabs of Grave 1.

Intact. H. 0.027, L. 0.07, W. 0.044.

Rather coarse, brown biscuit with red-brown surface. Fragment of lower part of a bowl with ring base or pedestal; worn on all edges.

163* (Kph.3.17) Sherd rubbing-tool Pl. 71

Found near surface on north side of central part of Lower Cemetery.

Intact. L. 0.045, W. 0.038, Th. 0.011.

Rather coarse, brown biscuit with smooth, reddish tan surface. Oval sherd with worn and rounded edges.

POTTERY

The total volume of pottery collected from the surface and in the uppermost levels of the Lower Cemetery was about four and one-half tinfuls. From a count of rim fragments it can be estimated that at least 88 small vessels, including some 17 small jars, and at least 11 large jars are represented.

A 1

Rim fragments of at least two: Pl. 27, B and Pl. 75, D.

A 2

Rim fragments of at least 40, ten or more with angular profile.

UNDECORATED

With conical or rounded profile. Pl. 28, F = Pl. 75, Z: plain rim, D. est. 0.32; beneath it, an elongated horizontal lug with a central indentation. Pl. 28, G = Pl. 75, AS: plain rim, D. est. 0.12, with small tubular spout beneath it (for feeding an infant?). Pl. 28, J = Pl. 75, AJ: plain rim, D. est. 0.09, with small vertical lug, horizontally pierced, beneath it. Pl. 75, AD: plain rim, D. est. 0.16, having a vertically elongated lug handle consisting of two linked parts, terminating at the rim (which curves out slightly to meet it); the upper part of the lug handle is like a strap handle, while the lower part is a lug, horizontally pierced and vertically elongated. Pl. 29, A: incurving rim, D. est. 0.12. Pl. 39, R = Pl. 85, BC: high ring base, D. 0.08, with a pair of holes; probably from a shallow vessel with rounded sides like **104**.

With angular profile. Pl. 29, E = Pl. 75, AR: rim fragment, D. est. 0.16, with small vertical lug handle from lip to shoulder. Pl. 29, H: rim fragment, D. est. 0.18.

DECORATED

Pattern burnished. Fragments of three vessels with fairly upright sides and plain rims, decorated on the outside with groups of parallel lines oblique to rim: Pl. 40, D = Pl. 86, A, D. est. 0.14; Pl. 40, F = Pl. 86, D, D. est. 0.14; Frontispiece, D = Pl. 40, C = Pl. 86, G. Fragments of six fairly shallow vessels decorated on the inside, as follows. Pl. 41, F = Pl. 86, O: plain rim, D. est. 0.25, with pattern of parallel diagonal lines. Pl. 86, AB: similar. Pl. 41, C = Pl. 86, Z: plain rim, D. est. 0.26, with groups of parallel lines at oblique angles; the lines in one group are considerably narrower than the rest. Pl. 41, K = Pl. 86, Q: angular rim, D. est. 0.26, with pattern of nearly parallel diagonal lines. Pl. 86, AK: angular rim; pattern almost illegible. Pl. 42, D = Pl. 86, R: body sherd with angle near rim; groups of parallel lines, perhaps arranged symmetrically, within a nearly rectangular framework defined by three vertical and at least two horizontal lines.

A 2: WITH PEDESTALS

164* (Kph.19) Pedestaled bowl Pls. 42, 76

Found near surface above and north of Grave 18.

About one third preserved; fragments from the upper and lower part do not join, but they overlap at the angle of the bowl; restored in plaster. H. rest. 0.192, D. rim rest. 0.17, D. base 0.094.

Coarse, red-brown biscuit. Nearly biconical bowl; plain rim; conical pedestal; the entire bowl above the pedestal was evidently decorated in pattern burnishing, usually consisting of groups of parallel lines meeting at oblique angles; at one place the lower body has a trapezoidal area filled with crosshatching and bordered at either side by two lines; there is some variety in the width of the lines, those making up the cross-hatching, for example, being narrower.

165* (Kph.18) Pedestaled bowl Pls. 30, 76

Found near surface above and west of Grave 3.

Most of pedestal and about one quarter of bowl preserved; rim missing; consolidated with plaster. H. pres. 0.123, D. base 0.102.

Coarse, red biscuit; inside of bowl burnished; traces of crusted red on outside of pedestal. Conical pedestal; bowl almost hemispherical.

Fragments from the juncture of bowl and pedestal of at least three others; Pl. 75, BP with a hole in the pedestal.

A 1 AND A 2: INCISED RIMS

Fragments of at least four rims with incision outside, as follows. Pl. 44, D, D. est. 0.16: short slanting lines. Pl. 44, F: slanting lines, perhaps part of multiple chevrons. Pl. 44, G = Pl. 88, H, D. est. 0.20: a thickened band with careless slanting lines or multiple chevrons. Pl. 44, H = Pl. 88, C, D. est. 0.38: a thickened band with loosely connected multiple chevrons; impressed dots at angles.

B 1

166* (Kph.36) Small jar Pls. 32, 76

Found near surface west of Grave 25.

About half preserved; top probably missing; restored in plaster. H. pres. 0.135, D. max. rest. 0.16, D. base 0.062.

Coarse, red-brown biscuit with brown surface, blackened in some places; traces of crusted red beside the handle.

Biconical to ovoid. The upper edge, which turns up slightly, is too worn for us to determine whether any part of the rim is preserved; probably it continued higher to form a neck or collar, since there is no trace on the existing surface of the upper attachment of the handle. The bottom, which was evidently flat, was broken away in the middle; the edges at the bottom appear worn as if the vessel continued to be used for some purpose after the bottom was broken. One vertical handle, round in section, partially preserved on the shoulder; it is uncertain how high it extended or whether there was another handle. For a similar handle on a smaller vessel cf. Pl. 77, BA.

Rim fragments of at least 16 others. Pl. 31, C = Pl. 77, P: hole mouthed, D. est. 0.10; T-lug from lip to shoulder. Pl. 31, H: hole mouthed, D. est. 0.18; beneath rim is a lug, vertically elongated and horizontally pierced. Pl. 77, F: hole mouthed; no evidence for lugs or handles. At least eight with up-turned or everted lip, including the following. Pl. 31, O: up-turned lip, D. est. 0.08. Pl. 31, P = Pl. 77, Y: up-turned lip, D. est. 0.15, and plastic disk on shoulder. Pl. 31, R = Pl. 77, W: up-turned lip, D. est. 0.16, and T-lug with vertical groove from lip to shoulder. Pl. 77, U: up-turned lip with T-lug just below it. Pl. 77, AE: everted lip. At least five with offset neck or collar-neck. Pl. 77, AX: collar-neck, D. est. 0.26; on the shoulder is a large tubular spout, inner D. est. 0.034. Pl. 32, H = Pl. 77, AN: slightly flaring neck, D. est. 0.12. Pl. 32, K = Pl. 77, AM: slightly flaring neck, D. est. 0.10; crusted red inside and out. Pl. 32, Q: conical neck, D. base of neck est. 0.10.

B 2

Fragments of at least five.

Relatively open. Pl. 34, K = Pl. 81, AA: rim with thickened horizontal band outside, decorated with oblique grooves, probably part of multiple chevron.

Intermediate and indeterminate. Pl. 34, H = Pl. 81, T: a rim, D. est. 0.20, having a horizontal band with grooved multiple chevrons outside; slanting across the body beneath the band is a plastic strip with finger impressions. Pl. 81, AC: rim with a horizontal band decorated with grooved multiple chevrons. Pl. 45, J = Pl. 81, W: a rim or edge, probably from a jar, with a raised rectangular surface perpendicular to rim, decorated with incised oblique lines. Pl. 80, C: from lower body and ring base (D. est. 0.12) of a large vessel, perhaps closed; the exterior was burnished and covered with crusted red, considerable traces of which remain. Pl. 43, D = Pl. 87, R: body sherd (original angle uncertain; different in photograph and drawing) having a raised band with finger impressions, and two pattern-burnished stripes parallel to it.

C 1

Fragments of at least twelve vessels. Pl. 83, AV: large fragment from the body of a scoop, preserving lower end of back and one strut; found during cleaning in and around Grave 14 and perhaps originally deposited in it; incised oblique lines on back and strut, perhaps part of multiple zigzag. Pl. 83, E: flat fragment, probably from the handle of a scoop; two incised vertical lines with multiple zigzag on either side (cf. **102**). Fragments probably from two other incised handles. Fragments of two scoop (?) handles, apparently unincised, with small plastic knobs on the inner surface (cf. Pl. 83, AU). Fragments of at least eleven struts. Pl. 36, B = Pl. 83, Q: strut broken near junction with handle; nearly round in section but with deep vertical groove on the side near the front edge; oblique grooves on side of strut, other grooves on handle. Pl. 36, D = Pl. 83, V: strut, nearly round in section; oblique grooves on one side, interrupted by two horizontal grooves. Pl. 83, S: strut, nearly round in section; vertical groove. One other strut (Inv. No. Kph.3), round in section, with incised multiple zigzag.

C 3

167* (Kph.12) Fragment with cloth impression Pl. 90

Found near surface in west part of Lower Cemetery.

L. pres. 0.095, W. pres. 0.062.

Coarse, rather soft, orange-brown biscuit.

The fragment preserves a rim or edge and is probably from a pan with low wall; the underside (or outside?) of the sherd is rough and irregular while the inside is generally smooth; where part of the surface has broken away, on the inside and at the edge, the impression of a woven fabric is visible (see Appendix 2); the fabric had originally been laid over a clay core and pressed into place with the fingers, marks of which are visible; a further layer of clay was then smoothed over the fabric. Cf. **201** and **213***.

Several fragments of crudely shaped, pierced rims.

C 5

Pl. 37, N = Pl. 84, AG: a cylindrical knob placed on a flat surface which is broken at all edges.

Other Sherds

Incised. Several fragments not already mentioned. Pl. 44, K = Pl. 88, AO: from the body of a small vessel, curving in sharply towards the bottom; vertical band of decoration with oblique lines and impressed dots, probably part of multiple zigzag, bordered at either side by two parallel vertical lines; on either side of this vertical band are preserved parallel horizontal lines, suggesting that there was an alternation of decoration with vertical and with horizontal axis. Pl. 89, V: from a small vessel with a plastic knob and incised lines. Pl. 89, M: from a large vessel with a raised band decorated with slanting grooves. Pl. 89, O: from a large vessel with horizontal and oblique lines. Pl. 89, D: from a vessel of indeterminate size with one horizontal and several oblique grooves. Pl. 89, P: from a vessel of indeterminate size with a raised band decorated with incised oblique lines; at the left side the band diverges from the surface of the vessel as if it were part of a lug or handle. Pl. 46, A = Pl. 89, U: a flat, handle-like object, L. rest. 0.105; carefully made; rectangular in section; at one end an oblique surface where it was attached; the other end terminates in a finished surface; on one side is a deeply incised pattern of multiple chevrons, with traces of crusted red in the incisions.

With plastic decoration. Many fragments with impressed bands, e.g. Pl. 89, BM. Pl. 89, AW: a high ridge and on either side a lower ridge at an oblique angle. Pl. 89, AZ: ridges perhaps arranged in the same way as the preceding. Four fragments with raised disks of various sizes: Pl. 89, AF, AG, AN, AO.

Handles. Many strap handles, lug handles, and lugs of the usual types. Pl. 84, AK: a large strap handle. Two knobbed strap handles. A strap handle with two vertical incised lines. Pl. 84, AT: round in section; the photograph, taken from the inside, shows that the handle was attached by means of a plug thrust through the pot wall. Pl. 38, K: a small vertical handle, rising slightly above a rim (angle and height of rim uncertain). A large crescent-shaped lug with a vertical plastic ridge adjacent to its top. Pl. 85, AR: a small, flat tab handle with two holes, partially piercing it, perpendicular to the rim.

Bases. Fragments of at least 53. Seven moderate sized or large, including the following three with mat impressions on the lower surfaces. Pl. 90, D: a flat bottom, Th. 0.12, probably from a large vessel (Appendix 2, No. 2). Pl. 90, F: a flat bottom, Th. 0.12 (Appendix 2, No. 5). Pl. 90, O: a slightly raised base, D. 0.21 (Appendix 2, No. 8).

Twenty-five small to medium sized, including Pl. 39, Q, a ring foot, D. est. 0.075. Twenty-one small: two flat bottoms, Pl. 39, F = Pl. 85, AY, D. 0.035; Pl. 39, L, D. 0.06; Pl. 39, H, a raised base, D. est. 0.035.

Oddments. Pl. 46, C = Pl. 77, BC (Kph.4.3): fragment of tube broken at both ends, L. 0.06; irregular; probably a spout but possibly not from a pot (cf. Early Cycladic bone tubes, e.g. Tsountas, 1899, pl. 10, 2–5). Pl. 45, K = Pl. 77, BA: part of small pot; flat bottom, D. est. 0.04; round vertical handle from belly (cf. **166***). Pl. 77, BD: askoid vessel with flat handle. Pl. 39, T = Pl. 91, Q: fragment; crude; stem oval in section, widening to concave forms at either end. Two sherds, one light colored, possibly of Bronze Age or later.

THE UPPER CEMETERY

GENERAL

The cleft of the Upper Cemetery is about 2.00 m. north of that of the Lower Cemetery (Pls. 8–10). The slope of the hillside is steep, and the graves of the Upper Cemetery are on the average about 1.00 to 1.50 m. above those of the Lower Cemetery (see Section C–C, Pl. 12). The length of the cleft from the western side of Wall 6 to the eastern end of Grave 39 is about 9.00 m., considerably shorter than that of the Lower Cemetery. Its greatest width, at the western end, is about 3.00 m.; it narrows at the eastern end until it disappears just beyond Grave 39. The southern side was formed by a fairly regular scarp of rock which gradually becomes higher toward the east (Pl. 11). The northern scarp is more irregular, and varies more than 1.50 m. in absolute height. The cleft was not everywhere dug to its full depth, but it seems to have been deepest at the western end and to have become progressively shallower toward the east. Excavation was concluded at the eastern end (i.e. in Trench B, Pl. 11) when a rocky layer devoid of sherds was encountered; the top of this layer sloped down from about +7.80 m. on the northern side of the cleft to about +7.45 m. on the southern.

About 1.00 to 2.00 m. below the top of the northern scarp in the western part of the cleft there is a fairly level shelf which forms a floor for Graves 34 and 35 (see Section C–C, Pl. 12); its width varies, but it is nowhere more than 1.00 m.

The bottom of the cleft was explored only in Trench A 2 and in the southern part of Trench A 1 (Pl. 11). Its sides were fairly smooth and regular near the bottom; perhaps they had been trimmed. Sherds continued to be found all the way to the bottom. There was a shelf near the top of the southern scarp about 0.50 m. wide, the upper surface of which sloped down from west to east forming a sort of path to the bottom of the cleft. Since the lowest grave discovered here, Grave 32, was about 0.80 m. above the bottom, it is possible that this part of the cleft of the Upper Cemetery, like the *dromos* of the Lower Cemetery, had originally been used for some other purpose; a living area, for instance, would have been easy to construct and well sheltered from the wind. No floor was recognized, however, and the filling at the bottom had the appearance not of domestic debris accumulated on the spot, but of casually accumulated debris which had perhaps washed down from the hillside above.

The bottom of the cleft must rise rapidly at the western end. Trench A 3 was not cleared to bedrock and the exact line of the cleft was not determined, but there is no sign of it west of Wall 6, where the slope of the hillside is uninterrupted. Grave 33 was evidently built just outside the western edge of the cleft; Wall 6, which was partly built above Grave 33, was apparently set at the very edge.

Wall 6 is of special interest since it provides the only evidence for overall planning in the cemetery at Kephala. It clearly defines the western end of the cleft, and only the earlier Grave 33 was built to the west of it. Wall 6 was thus apparently intended to define the western limit of this part of the cemetery. Since the easiest access to the settlement from the isthmus passes along the western side of the cemetery, the traffic may have been considerable, and the wall may have prevented people from straying. The original height of Wall 6 could not be ascertained; it may have been built about the same time as Graves 34 and 35, since its foundations were at approximately the same level.

The chronological relationship between the Upper and Lower Cemeteries could not be determined; at the time of excavation they were separated from one another by a surface of bare rock. Presumably they were in contemporary use. The graves are much less densely placed in the Upper Cemetery than in the Lower, but even here Grave 36 was built over Grave 35 and Grave 38 over Grave 37.

As discussed above (p. 50), none of the graves of the Upper Cemetery for which there is accurate information about burials contained more than one skeleton.

For ease in presentation, the graves are divided into a western group, for which a probable chronological sequence can be suggested, followed by an eastern group together with one isolated grave. The objects found which are not attributable to specific graves are grouped together as follows: those found in the western part of the cleft below the lowest graves; those found around the graves of the western group; those found in the eastern part of the cleft; surface finds. Where further details of finding places are given, it is with reference to the trenches shown on Plate 11. See the introductions to the catalogues for further information.

WESTERN PART OF CLEFT: OBJECTS FOUND BELOW LEVEL OF GRAVES

The following objects were found in the lowest levels of Trench A 2 (i.e. below about +6.60 m.) and in a test made to bedrock in the southern part of Trench A 1 below the level of Grave 32 (Pl. 11). The conformation of the cleft as recorded in these trenches is represented in Section C–C on Plate 12.[22]

STONE

One peice of waste obsidian, uninventoried.

TERRACOTTA

168 (Kph.6.20) Fragment of spoon Pls. 26, 71

Found in Trench A 2.

Most of bowl of spoon preserved. L. pres. 0.047, W. est. 0.033, Th. 0.008.

Rather coarse, red-tan biscuit; inner surface gray brown and smooth. Oval.

169 (Kph.6.19) Sherd rubbing-tool Pl. 71

Found in Trench A 2.

Intact. L. 0.044, W. 0.044, Th. 0.01.

Coarse biscuit with worn surface. Flat, roughly oval sherd with rounded edges.

POTTERY

A total of about two fifths of a tinful was collected here. This pottery must be earlier than any grave discovered within the cleft of the Upper Cemetery. It includes rim fragments of at least nine small vessels.

[22] The section passes through Trench A 1; the conformation of bedrock at the bottom of the cleft as determined in Trench A 2 is partly projected into it.

A 1

A rim fragment with uneven curve (possibly from a scoop rather than a bowl).

A 2

Rim fragments of at least four, two with crusted red on the exterior.

A 2: WITH PEDESTALS

Pl. 75, BX: from a pedestal having a horizontal groove with a cutout above it. Pl. 75, BD: from the juncture of a bowl and pedestal.

B 1

Rim fragment of a hole-mouthed jar.

C 1

A fragment of a strut with a vertical groove.

C 3

Small fragments from at least one coarse pan with pierced rim, e.g. Pl. 84, L. One fragment, Pl. 84, N, preserves part of a curving horizontal lug.

OTHER SHERDS

Crusted red. A few other fragments.

Incised and grooved. Pl. 44, J = Pl. 88, AN: body sherd of a small vessel with gray to black biscuit; three narrow, curving, parallel grooves; another groove near the edge of the sherd suggests that there were other grooves symmetrically placed and curving in the opposite direction (cf. a fragment with plastic ridges, next paragraph).

With plastic decoration. A fragment with oblique incisions on a raised band (cf. Pl. 89, BJ, BK). Fragments of at least two vessels with impressed bands; one unusually large with central ridge: Pl. 89, BE. Two fragments with curvilinear ridges; Pl. 89, AT, from the body of a small vessel, has two ridges curving in opposite directions (cf. Pl. 46, B = Pl. 89, AS, and the incised sherd mentioned just above). Pl. 89, AR: a sherd with an applied ring with a sunken center. A knob, perhaps broken from a pot wall.

Handles. Three strap handles, one with vertical plastic ridge adjoining the top. Two vertical lugs, horizontally pierced.

Bases. One large flat bottom. One large raised base. Three small flat bottoms, two of them rounded to pot wall. Four small raised bases. Four small ring bases; one is pierced through the ring, while another is pierced through the bottom of the vessel.

WESTERN GROUP: GRAVES AND OFFERINGS

The five graves of the western group (Graves 32–36) can be arranged in a probable sequence (shown in schematic form in Table 7). Grave 32 was probably the earliest since it was at a considerably lower level than any other grave. Grave 33 was also probably early since it was partly covered by Wall 6, which was about contemporary with Graves 34 and 35; these two graves were near one another at nearly the same level. Finally, Grave 36 was the latest since it was built above the cover of Grave 35.

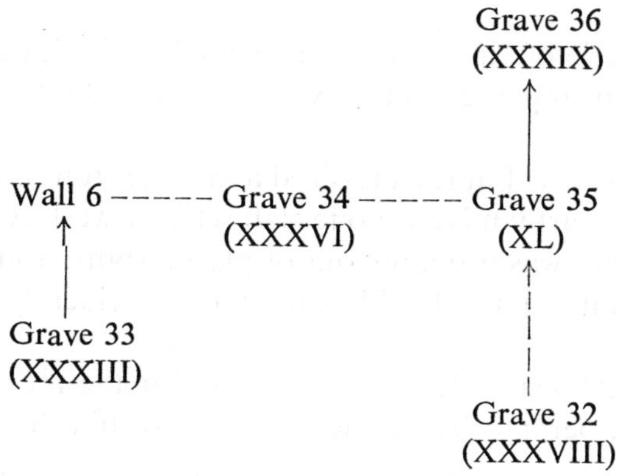

TABLE 7. Schematic chronological diagram showing graves of the western group of the Upper Cemetery. The conventions are as in Table 5, p. 55.

GRAVE 32 (XXXVIII)

Pl. 64; Plan, Pl. 8; Section, Pl. 12

A jar with the bones of an infant, located near the center of the cleft *ca.* 0.80 m. above the bottom (in Trench A 1: see Pl. 11). Cover at nearly the same level as the bottom of Grave 35 and therefore probably earlier.

Jar set on its side in a bedding of pebbles; mouth toward the east, closed by a vertical slab *ca.* 0.38 m. long. Several stones wedged around the upper side and two moderate-sized stones at the south side as a bedding for the cover. Cover of three large and several small slabs (Pl. 64, e) set north-south and extending beyond the area of the jar; the cover closely resembled those of the built graves.

Fragments of the skull of an infant 3 to 11 months old (*69 KeK*); position of body not determinable. No offerings found.

170 (Kph.23) Large jar used for burial Pls. 35, 79

Only a few small fragments missing; restored. H. 0.60, D. max. 0.42, D. rim 0.36, D. base 0.14.

Coarse, red-brown biscuit. Surface brown with patches of black from uneven firing; smoothed.

Deep, open body, conical to ovoid; plain rim; flat bottom. Two vertical handles opposite one another about halfway from rim to base; they are nearly pointed at the lower end and resemble large T-lugs. Two low, unpierced crescent-shaped lugs opposite one another near the rim about halfway between the handles.

A horizontal plastic band with finger impressions extends continuously around the vessel immediately beneath the handles. Similar, nearly vertical bands depend from the ends of each of the crescent-shaped lugs as far as the horizontal band; from the juncture of these bands, four other plastic bands rise obliquely to meet at a point near the rim but not centered over each handle; two triangles are thus formed. In some places the bands have frequent and distinct finger impressions; elsewhere the impressions are fewer and lighter, or completely absent; part of one of the plastic bands is missing (Pl. 79, upper right).

Two bored holes, one on either side of a crack (Pl. 79, upper left), were probably used to mend the vessel after it cracked in antiquity.

Similar in general to **146**, which, however, has four handles and a different arrangement of the crescent-shaped lugs and rope decoration; although the arrangement on **170** is more complex, the illusion of a vessel trussed for lifting is somewhat less realistic. Presumably neither vessel was made specifically as a burial jar.

GRAVE 33 (XXXIII)

Location, Pl. 8

A built grave, severely eroded, just west of the west end of the cleft; partly built over by Wall 6. No bones were found, and the remains were so scanty that no details could be recorded.

GRAVE 34 (XXXVI)

Pl. 63; Plan, Pl. 20

A built grave with a single skeleton, about 0.70 m. east of Wall 6 at roughly the same level. On the same shelf of bedrock and at nearly the same level as Grave 35 to the east and probably about contemporary.

Roughly rectangular in plan; walls of moderate-sized and large stones. Max. interior length (east-west) *ca.* 0.97 m., width 0.65 m. Cover partly missing: one slab set east-west over the north side; another slab, found partly above the south wall, was probably out of place. Many stones *ca.* 0.20 to 0.30 m. in length were found within the grave intermingled with earth; they evidently made their way in after the displacement of the cover.

Remains of a woman about 27 years old (*43 KeK*) lying for the most part in the northeast corner; apparently somewhat disturbed, perhaps by the stones found within the grave.

171 (Kph.4.6) Marble bowl Pls. 23, 67

From northeast corner of grave, partly beneath fragments of the skull.

Intact; rim chipped. H. 0.047, D. rim 0.088, D. base 0.028.

Fine- to medium-grained, grayish white marble, yellowish in places at the surface; originally well smoothed, now somewhat worn; marks of rotary abrasion or drilling inside, vertical abrasion outside.

Nearly conical; plain rim; flat bottom; thick walls. Two lugs, vertically elongated and horizontally pierced, opposite one another at the rim; the lugs are rounded and taper towards the bottom; the holes are near the top and were drilled from both sides.

Similar in shape to some of the pottery vessels of category A 2 (e.g. **34*** and Pl. 27, F); the pots, however, have thinner walls, and their lugs or lug handles are below rather than at the rim. The lugs on the marble rhyton **103** are similar, but are partly detached at the top.

GRAVE 35 (XL)

Pl. 65; Plan, Pl. 21; Section, Pl. 12

A built grave with a single skeleton. On the same shelf of bedrock and at nearly the same level as Grave 34 to the west, and probably about contemporary: at a higher level and probably later than Grave 32 to the south. Immediately beneath Grave 36.

Roughly oval interior. The north side formed by the rock scarp of the cleft, the other walls built of moderate-sized and large stones. The east and south walls are of heavier construction than those of most graves, with a max. width of *ca.* 0.60 m., and their outer faces are nearly straight, meeting at an angle of *ca.* 110°. Max. interior length (east-west) *ca.* 1.05 m., width *ca.* 0.72 m. One cover slab, set north-south, had collapsed into the grave; other slabs may have been removed by the builders of Grave 36. Interior height est. *ca.* 0.40 m.

Fairly well preserved skeleton (P. 65, a) of a man about 33 years old (*71 KeK*); body face down, head to west, extended except that the lower legs were doubled over; left arm apparently extended at the side; right arm folded under the chest.

172 (Kph.6.18) Triangular scraper of flint Pl. 68

Found near north side of grave, partly beneath the right humerus of the skeleton.

Missing: the pointed end and part of one edge. L. pres. 0.048, W. 0.034, Th. 0.007.

Dark red-brown stone. Originally roughly triangular; base slightly concave and edges slightly rounded; lentoid in section; careful bifacial pressure flaking; both edges finely serrated.

Similar to **86***, which also has bifacial working but lacks serrated edges. **48** is somewhat similar, but less carefully worked and with a rounded base.

GRAVE 36 (XXXIX)

Pl. 65; Plan, Pl. 21; Section, Pl. 12

A built grave with a slab-lined interior containing a single skeleton. The burial was made immediately above the one remaining cover slab of Grave 35, presumably after its collapse: the burial level of Grave 36 was 0.20 to 0.30 m. below the original level of the cover of Grave 35, but Grave 36 showed no signs of disturbance such as would probably have occurred if Grave 35 had collapsed after it was built. The builders of Grave 36 may have removed the other cover slabs of Grave 35.

Roughly semicircular in exterior plan, following the line of P 8 (Pl. 10); walls of moderate-sized stones for the most part, the north side formed by the rock scarp of the cleft. Three large slabs, set on edge at the bottom of the interior, form a rectangular burial area that recalls a slab-sided cist grave, but is enclosed within the walls. Plate 21 shows the grave after removal of the exterior walls. Max. interior length (east-west) *ca.* 0.73 m., width *ca.* 0.53 m. Two cover slabs: one over the west side, the other over the center and the east side. Interior height *ca.* 0.45 m.

Semicircular platform P 8 (Pl. 10), solidly built of moderate-sized and large stones, above and of roughly the same extent as the cover. Length, northeast-southwest, *ca.* 1.75 m., height *ca.* 0.20 to 0.30 m.

Fairly well preserved skeleton (Pl. 65, c) of a woman about 38 years old (*70 KeK*); body on left side with head to west; strongly flexed; right arm probably bent at chest, left arm uncertain.

173 (Kph.22) Scoop Pls. 36, 82

Found near northeast corner of grave beside legs of skeleton; it had been placed upright with mouth facing west toward skeleton; the handle and upper part of the body had broken into fragments, most of which had fallen into the vessel.

About two thirds preserved. Missing: upper part of one strut, lower part of handle, the front of rim and part of base. Restored.

Coarse, red-brown biscuit; darker patches on the handle; surface smoothed. H. 0.128, H. with handle 0.216, L. max. rest. 0.23. W. body 0.135, L. base 0.122, W. base 0.086.

Shallow, elongated body, roughly oval but sheared off obliquely; plain rim at an angle of about 40° from the horizontal. Hollowed disk base, oval as seen from below. Broad, flat handle rising obliquely from the back of the body and curving to form a nearly flat surface at the upper end; the front edge of the handle makes a smooth curved transition to the nearly vertical struts, which are oval to circular in section; lower ends of struts attached on either side of upper body, near mouth. The handle and struts lean to one side instead of being in strict alignment with the longitudinal axis.

A single shallow groove on the outside of each strut, passing over the top of the handle, where there is a second groove parallel to the first; otherwise apparently undecorated.

The only other nearly complete scoop is **102**, which has smaller body and more extensive decoration.

WESTERN GROUP: OBJECTS NEAR THE GRAVES

The following objects were found in Trenches A 1, A 2, and A 3 (Pl. 11) in the levels associated with the western group of graves. For a discussion of the nature and significance of the finds made around the graves see the general account of the cemetery above, pp. 52–53.

COPPER WORKING

174 (Kph.25) Fragment of burnt clay from a furnace-lining or crucible Pl. 22

Found in Trench A 1.

Small fragment. Missing: all edges, and part of the slag deposit. L. 0.045, W. 0.037, Th. with deposit 0.013.

Red biscuit with gray core and slightly gray surface; porous and ashy where it meets the slag deposit, as if subjected to intense heat; slag deposit gray black, rough, and deeply pitted. Sherd with flat profile; broken along the edge of a hole, about 0.018 m. in diameter. Slag deposit on the inside 0.002 to 0.004 m. thick. The perforation is comparable in diameter to those in **76***, **107** and **148***. This fragment was found near **175** and is possibly from the same vessel.

According to a spectrographic analysis by Reuben G. Bullard the deposit consisted primarily of iron with smaller quantities of other metals including copper.

175 (Kph.37) Fragment of burnt clay from a furnace-lining or crucible with metallic deposit Pls. 22, 66

Found in Trench A 1.

Small fragment. Missing: all edges, and part of slag deposit. L. 0.039, W. 0.031, Th. with deposit 0.022.

Red biscuit, gray at core and surface; porous and ashy where it meets the slag deposit, as if subjected to intense heat; slag deposit gray black, with rough uneven surface. Sherd with flat profile; slag deposit on the inside 0.0025 to 0.005 m. thick.

Possibly from the same vessel as **174**; the thickness of the clay wall is greater (**175**: Th. 0.013; **174**: Th. 0.010) but the vessel might have been uneven; the slag deposit is very similar. For analysis see Appendix 1, No. 5.

Another fragment of slag or ore (Field No. KF-6.58) was found in Trench A 2.

STONE

176 (Kph.6.6) Obsidian blade (category 1 a) Pl. 69

Found in Trench A 1.

Broader end missing. L. 0.053, W. 0.011, Th. 0.004.

Gray, surface slightly shiny. Roughly parallel sided but pointed at one end; trapezoidal in section; secondary working and chipping on both edges and around pointed end. Blade adapted as a side scraper. Similar to **118**, but a little smaller.

177 (Kph.6.50) Obsidian blade (category 1 a) Pl. 69

Found in Trench A 2.

Both ends missing. L. 0.03, W. 0.012, Th. 0.002.

Gray black; surface somewhat shiny. Moderate sized; triangular to trapezoidal in section; chipping from secondary working or use on both edges.

178 (Kph.4.32) Obsidian blade (category 1 b) Pl. 69

Found in Grave 34 above burial level.

One end missing. L. 0.04, W. 0.021, Th. 0.0035.

Gray, striated; surface slightly shiny. Fragment of blade with spreading end; roughly trapezoidal in section; secondary working and/or chipping from use at edges.

179 (Kph.6.45) Obsidian blade (category 1 b) Pls. 25, 69

Found in Trench A 1.

Intact. L. 0.062, W. 0.018, Th. 0.004.

Gray; surface slightly shiny. Slightly irregular, but nearly parallel sided; rounded at narrower end, which has a bulb of percussion; roughly triangular in section; extensive working on one edge.

180 (Kph.6.53) Obsidian blade (category 1 b) Pl. 69

Found in Trench A 2.

Intact. L. 0.055, W. 0.025, Th. 0.006.

Gray; surface shiny. Parallel sided for part of its length but broadening sharply at one end; bulb of percussion at narrow end; triangular to trapezoidal in section; extensive secondary working along one edge.

181 (Kph.6.55) Obsidian blade (category 1 b)

Found in Trench A 2.

Intact. L. 0.016, W. 0.006, Th. 0.002.

Gray black; surface shiny. Tiny blade, parallel sided for about half its length, then narrowing to a point;

triangular in section; chipping from use along both edges.

182 (Kph.6.4) Obsidian flake tool (category 2) Pl. 69
Found in Trench A 1.
Missing: small part of one side. L. 0.048, W. 0.039, Th. 0.009.
Gray; surface shiny. Large, nearly rectangular, but with rounded corners; flat on one face, four or five main facets on the other.

183 (Kph.6.48) Obsidian flake tool (category 2) Pl. 69
Found in Trench A 1.
Intact. L. 0.039, W. 0.022, Th. 0.006.
Gray; surface shiny. Roughly trapezoidal; triangular in section; bulb of percussion near one edge; chipped from use on the other three edges.

184 (Kph.6.49) Obsidian flake tool (category 2)
Found in Trench A 1.
Intact. L. 0.029, W. 0.019, Th. 0.006.
Gray; surface shiny. Roughly triangular with one edge hollowed; nearly flat on the ventral face, two flake scars on the dorsal face; chipping from use on all edges except the hollowed one.

185 (Kph.6.47) Obsidian scraper (category 3) Pls. 25, 70
Found in Trench A 1.
One end missing. L. 0.054, W. 0.018, Th. 0.008.
Gray; surface shiny. Long, roughly parallel sided, but narrowing towards one end; flat on one face except for a crack where rough original surface shows; triangular to trapezoidal in section; secondary working and chipping from use on both edges and the preserved end.

186 (Kph.6.54) Core tool of obsidian (category 5) Pl. 70
Found in Trench A 3.
Intact. L. 0.024, W. 0.018, Th. 0.007.
Gray; surface shiny. Roughly circular but flattened on two opposite edges; flat on ventral face; roughly triangular in section on long axis; marks of secondary working and use around the whole circumference.

187 (Kph.6.51) Obsidian tool (category 6) Pl. 70
Found in Trench A 2.
Intact. L. 0.05, W. 0.031, Th. 0.009.
Gray; surface shiny. Roughly oval but flat on one end; bulb of percussion at flat end with scars from the removal of two flat flakes; triangular in section; one edge chipped from use.

188 (Kph.6.52) Obsidian tool (category 6)
Found in Trench A 2.
Intact except small chip at one end. L. 0.023, W. 0.012, Th. 0.003.
Gray; surface shiny. Roughly triangular but somewhat rounded at base; bulb of percussion at base; secondary working at the edges.

189 (Kph.6.56) Obsidian tool (category 6) Pl. 70
Found in Trench A 3.
Part may be missing from one end. L. 0.03, W. 0.016, Th. 0.005.
Gray black; surface shiny. Roughly triangular with two edges meeting approximately at a right angle; extensive secondary working on those two edges; oval in section.

190 (Kph.4.33) Waste piece of obsidian Pl. 70
Found in Grave 34 above burial level.
Intact. L. 0.036, W. 0.02, Th. 0.0085.
Black; surface shiny. Roughly oval, but flat on one edge; triangular in section.

Obsidian uninventoried (by categories):

1 a	1 b	2	3	4	5	6	waste	total
18	4	18	0	0	0	12	359	411

191 (Kph.6.13) Bead or button Pls. 22, 68
Found in Trench A 2.
Intact. H. 0.01, D. 0.02.
Fine stone, pale green. Circular; rounded to biconical in section; cylindrical perforation 0.005 m. in diameter.

192 (Kph.6.9) Piece of worked stone Pls. 22, 68
Found in Trench A 2.
Missing at least one side. L. 0.078, W. 0.027, Th. 0.017.
Blue-gray schist; surface very rough and irregular. Long, with irregular outline. On one face are three parallel grooves, and inside them are lightly incised lines in herringbone pattern; the purpose of the grooves is unclear; possibly they were for sharpening a wooden or bone object. Cf. a stone with grooves (without incisions inside) from Palaia Kokkinia (Theochares, 1951, fig. 28, b).

BONE

193 (Kph.6.25) Worked fragment (chisel?) Pl. 71
Found in Trench A 2.
Missing: one end and both edges. L. 0.056, W. 0.008, Th. 0.005.
Gray white with some dark speckles on the surface. Probably from a metaphalange of a sheep or goat, split longitudinally; one end cut nearly perpendicular to the long axis and sharpened. The cut end resembles that of a chisel or gouge; **208** and **209** may be from similar tools.

194 (Kph.6.21) Fragment of tool or ornament Pl. 71
Found in south part of Trench A 1.
Both ends missing; mended. L. 0.082, W. 0.008, Th. 0.006.
Gray white with some dark speckles on the surface. From the rib of a sheep or goat, curved; six shallow grooves, perpendicular to the long axis, cut across one side and one edge; at one end an oblique groove. Somewhat similar to **195**, which, however, is larger, hollow, and has deeper grooves.

195 (Kph.6.22) Fragment of tool or ornament Pl. 71
Found in Trench A 1.
Both ends missing. L. pres. 0.05, W. 0.013, Th. 0.011.
Gray white with dark speckles on the surface. Hollow tibia of sheep or goat, oval in section; two grooves 0.02 m. apart encircle the bone. Cf. **194**, which has somewhat similar grooves.

TERRACOTTA

196 (Kph.6.1) Female figurine Pl. 72
Found in Trench A 1.
Missing: head, left arm and most of the right, lower body. Breasts worn. H. pres. 0.061, W. pres. 0.032, Th. 0.016. W. of neck 0.026, W. of lower body 0.022.
Coarse, brown, blackened biscuit with orange-brown, smoothed surface. Roughly modeled; body somewhat flattened in the middle; neck and lower body oval in section; both arms probably outstretched; small pellet breasts added separately. Similar in general to **127**, **197** and **198.**

197 (Kph.6.5) Female figurine Pl. 72
Found directly above cover of Grave 32.
Missing: head, most of both arms, and part of lower body. H. pres. 0.043, W. pres. 0.035, Th. 0.02. W. of neck 0.02, W. of lower body 0.018.
Coarse, orange-brown, blackened biscuit with slightly smoothed surface. Roughly modeled; body oval in section, narrower towards the front; neck nearly round in section; lower body trapezoidal in section; whole figurine nearly flat behind; arms outstretched; small pellet breasts added separately. Similar in general to **127**, **196** and **198.**

198 (Kph.6.17) Female figurine Pl. 72
Found about 0.40 m. south of the west end of Grave 32, and at a lower level (about +6.42 m.).
Missing: head, one breast, the ends of both arms, and part of the lower body. H. pres. 0.06, W. pres. 0.082, Th. 0.02. W. of neck 0.022, W. of lower body 0.031.
Rather coarse, micaceous, sandy, red-brown biscuit; surface red brown, discolored orange brown in places. Roughly modeled; body flat in middle; neck nearly round in section; lower body oval in section; arms outstretched; the back is hollowed and the arms stretched back so that the whole figurine is curved when seen from above; small pellet breasts added separately. Similar in general to **127**, **196** and **197.**

199 (Kph.6.26) Sherd rubbing-tool Pl. 71
Found in Trench A 3.
Slightly chipped; otherwise intact. L. 0.05, W. 0.038, Th. 0.01.
Rather coarse, tan to red-brown biscuit.
Oval; slightly curved in section; entire edge worn and rounded.

200 (Kph.6.27) Sherd rubbing-tool Pl. 71
From upper levels of Trenches A 1, A 2 and A 3.
Intact. L. 0.04, W. 0.03, Th. 0.006.
Fine, red-brown biscuit. Nearly square; three edges rounded, one flattened.

POTTERY

About six tinfuls of pottery were collected around and within the western graves. The deposits extend from the time of the building of Grave 32, or slightly before, to the time of the use of Grave 36, i.e. from about the level of the bottom of Grave 32 to about the level of the top of Grave 36. No material is included here from the surface levels, which might have been disturbed in the course of time.

A 1

Rim fragments of six vessels probably of this category. Pl. 27, D = Pl. 75, H: plain rim, D. est. 0.25, with a curving plastic ridge depending from it. Pl. 75, AM: a rim, D. est. 0.18, turned out at the top in a projecting flange, with outer edge indented at regular intervals.

A 2

Rim fragments of at least 91, some 13 conical or rounded, and six with angular profile.

UNDECORATED

With conical or rounded profile. Fragments of two plain rims: Pl. 28, B = Pl. 75, W, D. est. 0.16, and Pl. 28, M = Pl. 75, X, both with horizontally pierced lugs beneath. Pl. 28, C = Pl. 75, AU: plain rim, D. est. 0.18; beneath a semicircular notch in rim is a lug, vertically elongated and horizontally pierced. Pl. 29, P = Pl. 75, AX: plain rim, D. est. 0.26; a broad tab at the rim, with oblique indentations on the upper edge, is roughly centered above a T-lug. Two other fragments of plain rims: Pl. 75, O, D. est. 0.20, and Pl. 75, P. Pl. 75, AQ: from a rim rising in a tab with a concave upper edge.

DECORATED

Crusted red. Two fragments decorated inside.

Pattern burnished. At least three with fairly steep walls decorated outside. Pl. 40, E = Pl. 86, C: rim fragment, D. 0.13, from a small bowl with illegible pattern. Pl. 40, J = Pl. 86, N: preserving a rounded transition to a flat bottom, which is burnished; crusted red inside; two pattern-burnished horizontal lines outside. At least two shallower bowls with pattern burnishing inside, including a fragment which preserves part of a flat bottom. Pl. 42, G = Pl. 87, G: from a slightly flaring rim decorated on both sides, evidently with groups of parallel lines at various angles.

Incised. Pl. 75, AN: from a vessel with angular profile; two horizontal rows of punctations at the angle. Pl. 88, U: rim sherd probably from a bowl; on the body are two curving lines, perhaps part of spirals (cf. Pl. 88, AS).

A 2: WITH PEDESTALS

Pl. 30, A = Pl. 75, AZ: from a bowl, D. rim 0.19, preserving a nearly conical profile from rim to juncture with pedestal. Pl. 29, O = Pl. 75, AW: from the lower part of a rounded bowl; the base, which was probably a pedestal, is broken in such a way as to show that it was originally attached at an overlapping surface; vertical lug, horizontally pierced, on body.

Many fragments of conical pedestals. Pl. 75, BN: preserving part of an angular cutout. Pl. 75, BO: with two bored holes near bottom edge. Pl. 75, BS: from near juncture with body; an incised horizontal line below small triangular cutouts. Pl. 75, BT: from near juncture with bowl; three horizontal grooves forming two zones which have deep, angular punctations. Pl. 75, BW: with a horizontal groove.

Fragments from the juncture of bowl and pedestal of 19 other vessels. Pl. 30, D = Pl. 75, BA: with incised horizontal line and impressed dots on pedestal. Pl. 75, BL: with incised horizontal line near juncture; pairs of vertical lines on pedestal. Two others illustrated: Pl. 75, BB, BE.

A 1 AND A 2: INCISED RIMS

At least four rim fragments with incision outside: Pl. 88, V, AJ, and AL from plain rims with multiple chevrons or oblique lines; Pl. 88, G from a rim with thickened horizontal band, incised obliquely. For five other fragments either from bowls or other vessels, see Other Sherds, Incised and grooved, p. 92.

B 1

Rim fragments of at least 27.

Hole mouthed. At least seven. Pl. 31, B = Pl. 77, O: with knobbed T-lug at lip; D. est. 0.10–0.15. Pl. 77, E: with lip slightly thickened. Pl. 77, H: with indented lip. Pl. 77, J: near lip is a vertical plastic ridge with widely spaced indentations.

With up-turned or everted lip. One small shallow vessel.

With offset or collar-neck. Seven examples, including the following. Pl. 32, G = Pl. 77, AR: with slightly flaring collar-neck, D. est. 0.09, decorated outside with grooved multiple chevrons; impressed dot at apex. Pl. 32, J = Pl. 77, AF: with flaring neck, D. 0.09; two lightly incised oblique lines, perhaps decoration, on outside of neck. Pl. 77, AK: with flaring neck. Pl. 77, AO: with low collar-neck; broken surface where a handle or lug was attached at the lip.

Body sherds. Pl. 77, AU: from a small jar; horizontal groove near neck, from which depends a pair of vertical grooves. Fragments of three other small vessels, tall and narrow, with elongated vertical handles: Pl. 77, AT, and Pl. 85, AB, AC.

B 2

Rim fragments of at least 17.

Relatively closed. At least four. Pl. 81, AN: hole mouthed. Pl. 44, A = Pl. 88, B: thickened horizontal band outside rim, decorated with incised multiple chevrons; immediately beneath is a vertical lug handle, horizontally pierced. Pl. 81, N: thickened horizontal band outside rim, beneath which is a partially bored hole. Pl. 81, P: thickened horizontal band outside rim.

Relatively open. Fragments of 14. Pl. 81, AE: vertical handle below lip; oblique plastic ridge adjacent to upper edge of handle. Pl. 81, S: large T-lug or lug handle near rim. Pl. 81, AK: near lip is a small, unpierced horizontal lug with central indentation. Pl. 81, E: near rim is a curving ridge with indented edge, perhaps part of a crescent-shaped lug. Pl. 81, AJ:

lug near rim either crescent shaped or an inverted U. Pl. 81, O: thickened horizontal band outside rim. Pl. 81, K: plain rim, probably from a vessel like **146** and **170**, with vertical plastic band with finger impressions.

C 1

At least 21 different vessels are represented. Pl. 83, AS: from the body and lower part of handle, which has incised horizontal lines. Pl. 83, D: top of a handle preserving upper part of the two struts; a pair of incised lines parallel to front edge of handle, and continuing on the struts (cf. **98**); also on handle are oblique lines (part of multiple chevrons?). Pl. 83, C: top of a handle with a band of incised multiple zigzag bordered by single lines parallel to the edge; traces of other incised lines next to the band; the fragment is lightly covered with crusted red, which extends into the incisions. Pl. 83, F: handle with incised multiple zigzag in two vertical zones, bordered by single lines (cf. **98**). Pl. 83, AK: body sherd with lower part of a strut; oblique incisions on the side of the strut. Pl. 83, AJ: probably from a scoop; body sherd with lower part of a strut or handle; bored hole partly preserved in body. Pl. 83, AH: body sherd with lower part of a strut, apparently without decoration. Pl. 36, A = Pl. 83, R: juncture of handle and strut with two small knobs; the strut consists of two rolls of clay. Four other fragments from the juncture of struts and handles, as follows. Pl. 83, M: vertical groove on strut, continuing on top of handle; oblique grooves on handle. Pl. 83, O: knob at juncture; vertical incised line on strut. Pl. 83, P: vertical groove on strut; other grooved lines on handle. Pl. 83, L: knob at juncture. A fragment, probably from the juncture of strut and handle of a scoop, with traces of incised curvilinear decoration. Fragments from the struts of at least 13 other vessels, as follows. Pl. 36, C = Pl. 83, AD: strut with deep, angular punctations. Pl. 83, Y: round in section; carefully incised multiple zigzag. Pl. 83, AB: round in section; oblique incisions, probably part of multiple zigzag. Pl. 83, AC: oval in section; incised oblique and horizontal lines (cf. Pl. 36, D = Pl. 83, V). Pl. 83, AE: oval in section; incised zigzag. Four other struts decorated with vertical grooves and/or incised zigzag. Four apparently undecorated.

C 2

A fragment probably from a cylindrical stand with a projection inside.

C 3

Fragments of several crude, low-walled pans with pierced rims, e.g. Pl. 84, A. Pl. 84, G and M: with horizontal lug-like projections inside.

C 5

Pl. 84, AA and AC: perhaps from lids; flat in section with curving edges.

Other Sherds

Crusted red. On inside or outside of many body sherds; outside one very large vessel (Th. 0.015) which has a bored hole.

Pattern burnished. A few fragments in addition to those mentioned, one with pattern burnishing outside and crusted red inside.

Incised and grooved. Body sherds from five fairly small vessels with incised decoration outside, as follows. Pl. 88, AM: three nearly vertical grooves, slightly diverging. Pl. 88, AP: similar groove. Pl. 88, AS: curving lines, evidently part of a spiral or similar ornament. Pl. 88, AX: parallel lines, slightly smeared while the clay was soft. Pl. 89, AA: three lightly incised lines. Pl. 89, C and F: body sherds from two large vessels with exterior incision of multiple chevrons next to a horizontal bordering line.

Fragments from the rims or edges of four fairly small vessels, perhaps bowls, but perhaps jars or scoops. Pl. 88, Y: uneven edge; slanting incised lines. Pl. 88, AA: five grooves perpendicular to the edge; next to them are oblique incised lines. Pl. 88, ABs: perpendicular to the uneven edge are two incised lines flanked by deep, angular punctations. Pl. 88, AG: nearly flat edge (scoop handle?) with one incised line parallel to it, approached by several oblique lines.

With plastic decoration. Pl. 89, BF: sherd with a large band (W. 0.035) with a large finger impression. Pl. 89, AM: raised disk. Pl. 89, AQ: elongated raised surface, slightly concave, terminating at a rounded edge.

Handles. Fragments of some 49 strap handles. At least one was applied by a plug thrust through the pot wall. Eight with knobs set on top, e.g. Pl. 84, BF. Pl. 84, AY: concave, with indentations at edges. One with central vertical groove. Two with indented plastic bands near them (cf. **146**, **170**). Two with raised vertical ridges at the middle like those of **74** and **134**. Fragments of at least 20 small lugs or lug handles with vertical axis, pierced horizontally. Pl. 85, V: small vessel with a small horizontal lug, vertically pierced. Three other horizontal lugs, unpierced, two with central indentation, e.g. Pl. 85, K. Six horizontal or crescent-shaped lugs with two vertical piercings and long vertical plastic extensions depending from either side, e.g. Pl. 84, BO. Pl. 85, A and B: unpierced crescent-shaped lugs with indented edges. The following three high-swung lug handles perhaps from bowls. Pl. 85, AF: a solid loop; near the top is a small hole parallel to rim. Pl. 85, AG: a flattened loop, concave at apex, with knob at the middle. Pl. 85, AO: triangular profile, with base upward; small knobs at the two upper corners.

Unusual forms of handles include the following. Pl. 38, J = Pl. 84, AV: strap-like ribbon handle with upper end attached to a rim: exact height of rim uncertain; D. est. 0.10. Pl. 84, AW: similar to the preceding but handle broader. Pl. 84, BG: strap-like ribbon handle, curving sharply at apex and perhaps projecting above a rim or lip; concave at apex with central knob. Pl. 85, N: broad ribbon handle with a low strut between it and the pot wall. Pl. 84, AU: resembling a strap handle, but curving laterally and perhaps horizontally placed (cf. Pl. 85, W, X). Pl. 85, AP: probably a high-swung handle in the form of a flattened loop; unusual in that the inner side of the loop was evidently broader than the outer side.

The following four are puzzling. Pl. 85, O: broad, flat handle; broken at lower end, which is spreading and must be near point of attachment; upper end seems almost complete and terminates in two knob-like projections (cf. Pl. 85, S); inner surface has a round projection, perhaps part of a strut. Pl. 85, P: broad, flat handle, broken at both ends; on the inner surface a vertical loop of clay, partly broken, forms a secondary lug handle. Pl. 85, Q: broad, flat handle, broken at both ends; a projection on the inner surface, partly broken, is perhaps part of a strut or loop like that of the preceding, rather than a knob. Pl. 85, R: broad, flat handle, broken at both ends; the lower end is spreading and must be near the point of attachment; the outer surface slightly concave from edge to edge; a small projection on the inner side, perhaps part of a strut rather than a knob. These four pieces have a general resemblance to scoop handles, especially to those which are unincised and have knobs on the inner surface, e.g. Pl. 83, AT, AU; yet Pl. 85, O, if it is complete at the upper end, cannot be from a scoop; Pl. 85, R is very similar to Pl. 85, O, and the slightly concave surface is unlike any of the pieces which are surely from scoops; the secondary lug handle on Pl. 85, P is unique.

Bases. Fragments of at least 51. Three large flat bottoms, e.g. Pl. 85, BD, D. 0.083. Two large raised bases. Three large, splaying, pierced ring feet, e.g. Pl. 85, BE. Three medium-sized flat bottoms. Ten medium-sized raised bases. Seven medium-sized ring bases, one pierced. Eleven small flat bottoms, e.g. Pl. 85, BA, D. 0.044. Seven small ring bases, three pierced, of which Pl. 85, BH is oval. One small base with a bored hole through the bottom. Pl. 90, L: flat bottom, probably from a closed vessel, with a mat impression (Appendix 2, No. 10).

ODDMENTS

201 (Kph.21) Sherds with cloth impression Pl. 90
Found in Trench A 1.
Four fragments from the same pot, two joining:
A: L. 0.043, W. 0.036, Th. 0.014.
B: L. 0.031, W. 0.021, Th. 0.004.
C: L. 0.02, W. 0.015, Th. 0.004.
D: L. 0.017, W. 0.01, Th. 0.005.

Rather coarse, red-brown clay. Body sherds apparently from a fairly large vessel. The four fragments represent two layers of clay, one thick and one thin, which sandwiched the cloth between them. They are smoothed on the outer surfaces. Fragment A is from the thick layer with a small part of the thin layer still adhering to it; the inner surface, where the thin layer is absent, has furrow-like grooves and bears the cloth impression. Fragment B is from the thin layer; it joins Fragment A, and where the two overlap the impressions of both sides of the cloth are preserved. Fragments C and D are non-joining pieces from the thin layer.

For further discussion of the cloth impression see Appendix 2. Cf. **167*** and **213***.

Pl. 45, A = Pl. 75, M: plain, upright rim, D. est. 0.10, from a deep bowl or jar; two horizontal grooves outside enclose a band with elongated punctations. Pl. 45, E = Pl. 75, N: plain, slightly flaring rim, D. est. 0.10, from a deep bowl or jar similar to the preceding; two horizontal grooves outside. Pl. 39, S = Pl. 91, S: probably from a shallow pan or bowl, D. max. 0.125 if round. Pl. 77, BF: an almost miniature vessel, curving in sharply toward the bottom (cf. Pl. 45, M = Pl. 77, BG). A fragment, Pl. 91, M, from the corner of a roughly rectangular, box-like vessel, H. 0.04 (upside down in photograph). Pl. 91, N: probably from a pedestal or base with two large round holes, side by side, made before firing.

EASTERN AND ISOLATED GRAVES

The following four graves (Graves 37–40) were situated east of the western group. Grave 37 was older than Grave 38. Chronological relationships of the others could not be determined.

GRAVE 37 (XXXV)

Pl. 65; Plan, Pl. 21

A built grave with a single skeleton. Near the southwest edge of the cleft; immediately beneath Grave 38.

Circular to oval in plan; walls of small and moderate-sized stones. Max. interior length (east-west) *ca.* 0.79 m., width *ca.* 0.69 m. The grave narrows somewhat toward the top. Three cover slabs set east-west: two of them had cracked in the middle and fallen part way into the grave; this must have happened after the grave had partially filled with earth, since they rested about 0.30 m. above the burial level. Original interior height *ca.* 0.50 m.

Skeleton of an adolescent about 12 years old, perhaps a boy (*42 KeK*); body on left side with head to west and face to north; thighs perpendicular to spine and lower legs doubled up; arms perhaps folded over chest.

No offerings found.

GRAVE 38 (XXXIV)

Pl. 65; Plan, Pl. 9

A built grave partly above Grave 37 but extending farther to the north. Severely eroded; parts only of north and west sides, of moderate-sized stones. Perhaps circular to oval in plan.

202 (Kph.4.5) Head of figurine Pls. 26, 73

Found during removal of west side of Grave 38 and probably originally deposited in it; possibly, however, an offering placed above the cover of Grave 37; it is also possible that it had no connection with either grave.

Head and neck preserved; perhaps this portion had been made separately and added to the body. H. 0.047, W. 0.032, Th. 0.022, W. of neck 0.028.

Rather coarse, reddish gray biscuit and surface.

Neck roughly oval in section; face triangular with apex at chin, tilted back toward top; projecting knob at top of face for nose; similar projection behind top of head; back of head slightly hollowed; neck flares slightly at the bottom and has an uneven, rough lower surface, perhaps where broken off from the body.

Similar in general to **128**, but without holes at upper corners of head.

GRAVE 39 (XXXVII)

Pl. 65; Plan, Pl. 21

A built grave with a single skeleton, at east end of cleft.

Roughly oval in plan; south and west sides of moderate-sized and large stones, of heavier construction than most graves, with a max. width of *ca.* 0.60 m. North side and east end formed by nearly vertical scarps of rock. Max. interior length (east-west) *ca.* 1.58 m., width *ca.* 0.60 m. Seven moderate-sized cover slabs (Pl. 65, h) set north-south; most were broken in the center and tilted down into the grave from both ends; since they rested some 0.35 m. above the burial, they probably broke only after the grave had partly filled with earth. Original interior height *ca.* 0.60 m.

Fairly well preserved skeleton of a man about 32 years old (*68 KeK*); body on its back but inclined toward the left side; head to west on a stone pillow; face probably to north; thighs extended; lower legs doubled under; arms fully extended at sides.

No offerings found.

GRAVE 40 (XXX)

Plan, Pl. 8; Section, Pl. 12

A built grave, severely damaged by erosion on the sloping hillside about 1.90 m. east of Grave 39. Parts only of northwest and northeast walls, of moderate-sized stones; they meet nearly at a right angle, so the plan may have been rectangular. Probably large enough to have contained one or more adults.

EASTERN PART OF CLEFT: OBJECTS FOUND

The following objects were found in Trench B (Pl. 11) in deposits either contemporary with, or earlier than, Graves 37, 38, and 39. For a discussion of the nature and significance of the finds made around the graves, see the general account of the cemetery above, p. 52.

COPPER WORKING

203 (Kph.39) Fragment of burnt clay probably from a furnace-lining or crucible Pl. 66

Found in Grave 39 at the burial level.

Small fragment. Missing: all edges and the outer surface. L. 0.018, W. 0.015, Th. 0.007.

Rather fine, tan biscuit, red toward the outside, gray black toward the inside; inner surface fairly smooth. This fragment is very small and must have found its way into the grave along with earth and other sherds after the burial.

204 (Kph.38) Fragment of burnt clay probably from a furnace-lining or crucible Pl. 66

Found in Trench B.

Missing: all edges. L. 0.04, W. 0.035, Th. 0.016.

Coarse, tan biscuit, red on one side, gray on the other. Small fragment resembling other fragments from crucibles, and apparently subjected to intense heat.

STONE

205 (Kph.6.44) Obsidian blade (category 1 a)

Found in earth just above cover of Grave 39.

One end missing. L. 0.049, W. 0.021, Th. 0.005.

Gray with some darker striations; surface shiny.

Broad, roughly parallel sided; trapezoidal in section; bulb of percussion preserved; one edge has a broad and a narrow notch; the other edge chipped from use.

206 (Kph.4.47) Obsidian scraper (category 3)

Found during clearing of Grave 38 and removal of its west side.

Intact. L. 0.048, W. 0.023, Th. 0.003.

Gray with darker striations; surface dull.

Roughly triangular; flat in section; bulb of percussion at pointed end; secondary working on dorsal face and at edges around the pointed end.

207 (Kph.6.46) Obsidian tool (category 6) Pl. 70

Found in Grave 39 at the burial level.

One end missing. L. 0.03, W. 0.013, Th. 0.008.

Black; surface shiny.

Roughly oval but narrowing towards one end; diamond shaped in section; chipping from secondary working and/or use around narrow end. This small broken piece must have found its way into the grave along with earth and other objects after the burial.

Obsidian uninventoried (by categories):

1 a	1 b	2	3	4	5	6	waste	total
5	2	5	0	0	0	7	163	182

BONE

208 (Kph.6.23) Worked fragment Pl. 71

Found in earth just above cover of Grave 39.

Both ends missing. L. 0.058, W. 0.01, Th. 0.004.

Gray white with dark speckles on the surface. From a metaphalange of a sheep or goat, split longitudinally; smoothed along the edges. Perhaps from a tool like **193.**

209 (Kph.6.24) Worked fragment Pl. 71

Found in Trench B.

Both ends missing. L. 0.037, W. 0.007, Th. 0.003.

Gray white with dark speckles at the surface. From a long bone, probably of a sheep or goat; split longitudinally; smoothed along the edges. Perhaps from a tool like **193.**

POTTERY

A little more than two thirds of a tinful was collected around and within the graves of the eastern group. The catalogue comprises material either contemporary with or earlier than the latest graves. No material from the surface levels is included.

A 1

Pl. 27, A = Pl. 75, B: rim fragment.

A 2

Rim fragments of fifteen or more, at least one conical or rounded and one angular. A fragment with crusted red inside. A fragment with pattern burnishing inside. Pl. 86, T: pattern burnished inside; found either here or in Area G (see p. 27). Rim fragment with oblique impressions on top.

A 2: with Pedestals

Fragments from the juncture of body and pedestal of at least two. Several fragments from pedestals (?) with horizontal grooves and/or angular cutouts, one of which also has crusted red outside.

A 1 and A 2: Incised Rims

Fragments of two rims with incision outside. Pl. 88, Q: rim indented on top; vertical plastic band with finger impressions depending from lip; beside it a horizontal band of oblique lines, probably part of multiple chevrons, bordered below by a horizontal line. Pl. 88, X: oblique lines, probably part of multiple chevrons.

B 1

Pl. 77, C: rim fragment of a small hole-mouthed jar, curving upward at lip.

B 2

Pl. 81, AB: rim with incisions on thickened band outside. Another rim.

C 1

Fragments of struts from at least eight. Pl. 83, Z: oval in section; on the side is a vertical groove bordered by zigzags. Pl. 83, AA: oval in section; two vertical grooves on the side; a broken vertical line on one edge. Five other struts with vertical grooves or incised zigzag.

C 3

Several fragments, e.g. Pl. 37, H = Pl. 84, B, from coarse, low-walled pans with pierced rims. Pl. 84, E: rim with an interior lug, horizontal and slightly concave, pierced twice vertically.

OTHER SHERDS

Pattern burnished. A fragment of a small vessel with decoration outside.

Incised and grooved. Pl. 88, AE: from a rim or edge, possibly of a scoop handle; oblique lines near edge, probably part of multiple zigzag; two lines next to them, parallel to edge. Pl. 89, X: perhaps from a flat bottom, with two curving grooves.

With plastic decoration. Several fragments with impressed bands. Pl. 89, R: crude raised ridges making an angular design; two crude incised lines at upper right of sherd. Pl. 91, L: rim of a small vessel with a vertical ridge turning out to form a projection at the lip. Pl. 89, AX: small, nearly triangular projection with a knob at the center of one edge, giving a fortuitous (?) resemblance to the figurine heads **128** and **202**.

Handles. At least 11 strap handles, one with a knob on top. Three vertical lugs, horizontally pierced. Fragments of two unpierced lugs, either horizontal or crescent shaped, with long plastic extensions depending from either end (cf. Pl. 84, BO–BR, BT, BU), one large. A large flat handle with knob or strut inside, possibly from a scoop (but cf. p. 93). Pl. 84, BJ: a tab-like knob probably broken from a handle.

Bases. Fragments of at least 12. Two large flat bottoms, one with a row of bored holes. Four medium-sized flat bottoms. One medium-sized ring base. Four small flat bottoms. One small raised base.

Oddments. A fragment with flat profile and exceptional thickness, 0.025 m., perhaps from a hearth or pan.

UNSTRATIFIED OBJECTS

The objects in the following catalogue were found during the cleaning of the surface and the excavation of the uppermost levels of the Upper Cemetery, and they must be regarded in general as unstratified. It may be noted, however, that the surface of the cemetery was severely eroded and that there was certainly a greater depth of soil at the time when the latest graves were built than in recent times; many of the objects may have found their way into the cemetery before the latest graves were built. For a discussion of the significance of the stratified finds made around the graves, see the general account of the cemetery above, p. 52. All the unstratified finds from the Upper Cemetery apparently date to the time of the prehistoric occupation of the promotory.

STONE

210* (Kph.4.35) Obsidian blade (category 1 a)

Found near surface in west part of cleft. Pls. 25, 69

One end missing. L. 0.06, W. 0.016, Th. 0.0035.

Gray with dark striations; surface shiny. Moderate sized; trapezoidal in section; bulb of percussion preserved; extensive secondary working along one edge.

211* (Kph.4.43) Obsidian blade (category 1 a)

Found near surface in west part of celft.

Both ends missing. L. 0.032, W. 0.01, Th. 0.004.

Gray; surface somewhat shiny. Small, nearly parallel sided, but narrowing towards one end; roughly triangular in section; secondary working along both edges.

212* (Kph.4.34) Obsidian scraper (category 3)

Found near surface in west part of cleft. Pls. 25, 70

Intact. L. 0.055, W. 0.026, Th. 0.0065.

Dark gray with lighter striations; surface fairly shiny. Pointed oval; triangular in section; bulb of percussion at blunt end; secondary working along most of one end and part of the other. Similar to **123** but a little smaller.

Obsidian uninventoried (by categories):

1 a	1 b	2	3	4	5	6	waste	total
4	2	0	0	0	0	6	58	70

POTTERY

About one and two-thirds tinfuls of pottery were collected from the uppermost levels.

A 1

Pl. 75, J: rim of a thick-walled vessel, indented on top.

A 2

Rim fragments of eight or more, at least one conical or rounded and at least one angular. Two with vertical lugs, horizontally pierced, below the rim. One with a thickened band outside the rim. One with crusted red inside. Pl. 87, B: body sherd of a relatively steep-walled bowl with a vertical lug, horizontally pierced; pattern burnishing outside, almost illegible, includes parallel oblique lines. A fragment with pattern burnishing inside. Pl. 75, AO: rim with indentations on top.

A 2: WITH PEDESTALS

Fragments from the juncture of body and pedestal of at least three. A fragment of a pedestal (?) with a horizontal groove.

B 1

Pl. 77, D: hole-mouthed rim. Pl. 32, A = Pl. 77, AA: shallow jar with out-turned lip, D. est. 0.22; indentations on top of lip; oblique incisions on shoulder. One slightly flaring lip. A fragment of a jar (?) with vertical lug handle at the rim.

B 2

Pl. 38, F = Pl. 84, BC: strap handle attached at the rim, D. est. 0.22. Pl. 81, U: rim with grooves outside forming multiple zigzag.

C 1

Struts of at least two, one decorated with a vertical groove. A fragment with incised oblique lines, probably from the back of a scoop.

C 3

A fragment probably from a coarse pan with pierced rim.

OTHER SHERDS

Incised and grooved. Fragments of two rims with multiple zigzag outside. Pl. 89, H: with multiple zigzag bordered by a horizontal line. Pl. 88, AW: perhaps from a pedestal (turned 90° in photograph) with a tall multiple-zigzag pattern.

With plastic decoration. Several fragments with raised bands with finger impressions. Pl. 89, BO: three impressed bands, nearly parallel, terminating at different heights. Pl. 89, BA: two parallel raised ridges.

Handles. Seven strap handles, two with impressed bands near them. An unpierced crescent-shaped lug with indented edge. Pl. 38, H = Pl. 84, AX: a strap-like ribbon handle attached to a rim, D. est. 0.15. Two medium-sized flat handles with knob or strut on inner surface, perhaps from scoops (but cf. Pl. 85, O–R). Pl. 85, AE: high-swung lug handle consisting of a flat loop, solid inside except for two (or more) small holes parallel to rim. Pl. 85, AV: large tab handle pierced twice at upper edge perpendicular to rim. Pl. 85, S: crudely fashioned, high tab handle (broken only at the bottom); slightly narrowing toward the top, where it terminates in two knob-like projections.

Bases. Fragments of at least 15. Pl. 90, M: large bottom, D. 0.25 m., from an open vessel with a mat impression (Appnedix 2, No. 6). Another large bottom. Four moderate-sized flat bottoms. One moderate-sized ring base. Two small flat bottoms. Two small ring bases; Pl. 85, AW, with crusted red outside, pierced by two opposed pairs of holes.

ODDMENTS

213* (Kph.17) Sherd with cloth impression Pl. 90

Found near surface above central part of cleft.

L. 0.06, W. 0.035, Th. 0.012.

Coarse, dark gray biscuit, red brown at surface.

Body sherd from a fairly large vessel; the cloth impression is visible where a thin layer of clay has split away from one side (Appendix 2). Cf. **167*** and **201**.

Pl. 45, C = Pl. 75, L: rim of a deep bowl or jar, D. est. 0.12. Pl. 29, M = Pl. 89, AK: bowl or jar with upward curving rim; small plastic disk on shoulder.

IV. INTERPRETATION

INTERCONNECTIONS

In the following pages an attempt is made to view the settlement at Kephala within its broader cultural context. This is no easy task; although from the outset it was clear that the site was to be dated to a time near the transition between the Neolithic period and the Early Bronze Age, it is only since excavations began that comparative material has become available to indicate its essentially Neolithic character and show that it belonged before rather than after the transition. There are still no sites known in the Cyclades except in Keos which are clearly contemporary with Kephala. We shall therefore begin with comparative material of earlier date from the Cyclades, then consider remains contemporary with Kephala from the Greek mainland; finally we shall turn to the EC culture, which is later for the most part, although there may be some slight overlap.[1]

Since excavations began at Kephala in 1960, a whole new phase of occupation belonging to an earlier time than Kephala has become known in the Cyclades, largely through the work of Renfrew. Sites from this phase, apparently closely related to one another, are known in Melos (Renfrew, 1972, p. 507), Mykonos (Belmont and Renfrew, 1964), and Antiparos (Evans and Renfrew, 1968; Renfrew, 1972, pp. 508–509). Excavations on the present-day islet of Saliagos, apparently a promontory connected with Antiparos in Neolithic times, have provided a fairly full picture of this earlier phase (Evans and Renfrew, 1968).

There are remarkable few similarities between Kephala and Saliagos. Saliagos provided a low-lying, fairly level situation for buildings. There were some small structures, both rectilinear and circular in plan (*ibid.*, figs. 6 and 7), but in the latest stage the site was dominated (at least in the excavated space) by a large rectangular building complex (*ibid.*, fig. 10). The architecture at both Kephala and Saliagos is so fragmentary that it provides scant basis for comparison. It may be noted, however, that nothing was found at Kephala comparable in scale to the rectangular building complex at Saliagos, nor is there any evidence for circular structures. Funerary practices cannot be compared since no burials are yet known from the Saliagos phase.

The pottery from Kephala is in general very different from that at Saliagos. In shape there are only rough similarities;[2] many characteristics of Kephala pottery do not occur at all at Saliagos[3] and some characteristics of Saliagos pottery do not occur at Kephala.[4]

There is a great contrast also in decoration. One of the most distinctive features at Saliagos is the frequent use of a matt white paint on a dark ground in a variety of rectilinear and curvilinear patterns

[1] Domestic architecture is largely left out of consideration because the evidence at Kephala is so fragmentary. Since the possibilities for buildings were greatly restricted by the steep slope of the hillside, the types of houses, at any rate, may have resulted from adaptation to local conditions rather than being determined by cultural tradition.

[2] These include flat-bottomed bowls (cf. Pl. 27 with Evans and Renfrew, 1968, fig. 35), vertical strap handles, sometimes knobbed (cf. especially Pl. 84, AK–AP, BE–BH with *ibid.*, figs. 44, 45), unpierced horizontal lugs (cf. Pl. 28, F = Pl. 75, Z; Pl. 31, G = Pl. 77, N; Pl. 34, A = Pl. 81, AG; Pl. 85, J–M with *ibid.*, fig. 46, nos. 8, 10–14, 16, 17), and plain, unpierced crescent-shaped lugs (cf. those on **146** with *ibid.*, fig. 47, nos. 1, 2). Although pedestaled bowls occur at both sites, the pedestals at Saliagos are often high, with curved profile, rather than low and conical as at Kephala (cf. Pl. 30, with *ibid.*, figs. 31–33). Other characteristics of shape which are somewhat similar but have no exact correspondence include lugs and lug handles, which were vertically pierced much more often at Saliagos than at Kephala (cf. the general discussion, p. 18); and crescent-shaped lugs, which at Kephala often have finger impressions at the edges, but at Saliagos apparently never do.

[3] E.g. scoops (category C 1), cylindrical stands (category C 2), baking pans (category C 3), T-lugs and other lugs with long vertical plastic extensions (as e.g. on **97**). Ring feet, which are common at Kephala, are almost completely absent at Saliagos (*ibid.*, p. 38).

[4] E.g. various types of specialized handles (*ibid.*, pp. 39–40, fig. 58, nos. 14–24 and pl. XXXII). Bowls with flaring rims, which are common at Saliagos (*ibid.*, p. 37) are virtually absent at Kephala (Pl. 28, E = Pl. 75, Y and Pl. 30, B = Pl. 75, AY have a slight flare).

(*ibid.*, pp. 40–42). White paint was not found at Kephala, nor is there any close similarity between the patterns in white paint at Saliagos and those in other decorative techniques at Kephala. Crusted red occurs sporadically at Saliagos (usually in combination with white paint, *ibid.*, p. 42) but it is used differently from the way it is used at Kephala (cf. the general discussion pp. 10–11). Pattern burnishing also occurs at Saliagos (*ibid.*, p. 44) but it is very rare and not necessarily closely related to the type found at Kephala.[5] The few pieces with incised decoration from Saliagos (*ibid.*, pp. 43–44) have pointillé bands, which were not found at Kephala, and the plastic decoration from Saliagos (*ibid.*, pp. 42–43) is not very similar to that from Kephala.[6]

The other finds from Saliagos confirm the impression made by the pottery. The obsidian industry (*ibid.*, pp. 46–61) is unusually fine with many well-worked artifacts, among which tanged points are especially frequent and characteristic. The cruder industry of Kephala, in which blades and flakes predominate, provides almost no parallels; only the possibly tanged point **72** and a fragment of another tool with bifacial working (**90***) are of workmanship comparable to that of the well-worked tools of Saliagos.[7] Similar kinds of flint are represented in the tools found at both sites (cf. above, p. 5 with *ibid.*, p. 47), but the types of the finished artifacts are not similar. There are no close similarities between the figurines or the other small finds from the two sites, with the possible exception of emery celts (which have a general resemblance: cf. **38*** and **77*** with *ibid.*, fig. 79, nos. 2–4), and sherds used as rubbing-tools (cf. Pl. 71 with *ibid.*, fig. 83).

The great differences in material culture between Saliagos and Kephala are clearly due, in part at least, to their chronological separation. Saliagos, as I have argued elsewhere (Coleman, 1974, pp. 333–335), may be placed in the early part of the LN period on the basis of a comparison of the pottery with that of the Greek mainland; although curvilinear decoration (including concentric circles) occurs fairly frequently, there are no spiral or meander patterns such as are associated with the fully developed Dimini wares of the later part of the LN period (Milojčić, 1959, especially pp. 16–24). Five C-14 dates from Saliagos bear this out (Evans and Renfrew, 1968, p. 144); they range from about 4200 to 3700 B.C.[8] The chronological evidence for Kephala suggests that it cannot be dated earlier than the middle of the fourth millennium (below, pp. 109–110).

Two sites in Keos known from surface finds, Paoura and Sykamia, were probably inhabited at the same time as Kephala (see Appendix 6). They suggest that the people of Kephala were not a single isolated group. The site at Ayia Irini was first occupied on a large scale in the middle phase of the Early Bronze Age (Caskey, 1971a, pp. 368–372; 1972, pp. 362–369); two small and enigmatic deposits of earlier date, however, merit brief attention (Caskey, 1972, pp. 360–362). They are not floor deposits, but are described as fillings in depressions in bedrock; each was put there all at once, although they contain finds "not necessarily of the same stage" (*ibid.*, p. 362). The fabric of much of the pottery is like that from Kephala, except slightly better washed and fired. Fragments of bowls (*ibid.*, A 4–13), jars (A 26, 27), baking pans (A 15–25, 62–63) and the forms of some of the lugs and handles are similar; however, the long tubular horizontal lugs, pierced and unpierced (A 14, 32–34), are not found at Kephala, nor is there any parallel for the few painted sherds (A 1, 2, 48), or the closed bowl with vertical ridges (A 3), or the vessel with legs (A 61). Scoops were not represented. If, as seems likely, the bulk of the pottery from the Ayia Irini deposits is all of one date, it must be slightly later than the time of Kephala, to judge by the tubular lugs. It is noteworthy that this pottery has little in common with that of the EC culture.

Except for the sites in Keos just discussed, no sites contemporary with Kephala have yet been discovered (or identified) in the Cyclades. We therefore turn now to a consideration of the Greek mainland.

[5] Pattern burnishing has not been found elsewhere in the Cyclades. The single sherd illustrated by Schachermeyr (1955, fig. 35 no. 4) is probably not in this technique: see Renfrew, 1972, p. 509.

[6] Cf. the general discussion above, p. 12. At Saliagos horizontal rows of finger impressions or blobs are common at rims whereas at Kephala there is only one example (Pl. 34, J); bands or "cordons" are very rare at Saliagos, whereas they are one of the most common forms of decoration at Kephala; curvilinear plastic ridges are found at both sites, but at Saliagos they occur more frequently and are more elaborate (cf. *ibid.*, fig. 43, nos. 1–8 with Pl. 46, B = Pl. 89, AS).

[7] Some of the tools from Paoura, on the other hand, particularly the tanged arrowheads, are very like those of Saliagos; see Appendix 6.

[8] All the C-14 dates discussed in this report are calculated on the basis of the shorter half-life (5568 or 5570 years) and, except where stated, are without further adjustment.

With the publication of the Neolithic material from the Agora excavations at Athens (Immerwahr, 1971) and the excavations at the Kitsos cave near Laurion (Lambert, 1969, 1970, 1971, 1972a), it has become increasingly clear that the site at Kephala was fairly closely related to LN Attica and its environs. Pottery provides the main evidence for the relationship: the material from the Athenian Agora all comes from wells, and there was little building activity in and around the Kitsos cave;[9] the only Neolithic burials from this area which may be compared with those at Kephala are some enigmatic deposits of skeletal remains in the Kitsos cave (below, p. 103).

Red pottery decorated with pattern burnishing in overall patterns, like that from Kephala, has been found in some quantity in excavations on the acropolis at Thorikos (Mussche *et al.*, 1967, pp. 24–27) and in the Kitsos cave (Lambert, 1969, pp. 961–962 and fig. 17; 1970, pp. 758, 763; 1971, p. 711; 1972a, p. 821 and fig. 7); sherds are also known from Athens (Immerwahr, 1971, p. 7 and no. 35), Aegina (Welter, 1937, pp. 20–23) and Askitario (Theochares, 1953–1954, p. 66). Simple bowls like those from Kephala are apparently the predominant shape so decorated[10] and the meandroid motif on one of the Kephala sherds (Pl. 42, E = Pl. 86, AO) is roughly paralleled at Thorikos (Mussche *et al.*, 1967, fig. 21). Farther afield, a generally similar ware is known from Corinth (Weinberg, 1937, pp. 511–512) and Prosymna (Blegen, 1937, pp. 375–376). The Kephala type of pattern-burnished ware was probably a simple development from that employed on black burnished wares dating to a late stage of the MN period or an early stage of the LN period (see e.g. Hauptmann and Milojčić, 1969, pl. 1, 18–33, pl. 2, *et passim*). At any rate, regardless of its origin, the distribution of this decoration suggests that there was a fairly close cultural link between Kephala and Attica, and weaker links with other parts of the mainland of Greece.

There is much other ceramic evidence for a link with Attica. Bowls and jars from Kephala have a general similarity in shape to those from the Agora excavations in Athens, where open bowls of rounded or angular profile, and biconical or ovoid jars with collar-necks, are common in red burnished ware (Immerwahr, 1971, nos. 1–55). The handles and lugs on the vessels from Athens are similar to those from Kephala,[11] and there are many other parallels.[12] The correspondence, however, is not complete: red and white crusted decoration, which is fairly frequent at Kephala, was not noted at Athens; the black burnished, fluted vessels (*ibid.*, no. 70–75) and painted wares (*ibid.*, nos. 85–98) from Athens do not occur at Kephala. The Agora material may cover a greater time span than the Kephala settlement (although Immerwahr, *op. cit.*, p. 21, suggests only about 200 years); the more varied material from Athens may also be due to its less isolated situation, which encouraged more extensive contacts with other parts of Greece.

The Kitsos cave and Thorikos have not yet been published in sufficient detail for extensive comparisons. As with the Agora excavations, a general similarity is apparent; the few profiles published from Thorikos are strikingly similar to some of those from Kephala (cf. especially Pl. 32, P = Pl. 77, AJ with Mussche *et al.*, fig. 25). Parallels may also be cited between Kephala and the cave of Pan at Marathon (e.g., cf. Pl. 44, B = Pl. 88, A with Zervos, 1963, fig. 830).

[9] But see Lambert, 1971, p. 720 for a well-built wall outside the cave which cannot be closely dated.

[10] E.g. Immerwahr, 1971, no. 35; Lambert, 1971, p. 711; probably Mussche *et al.*, 1967, fig. 22. The bowls from Aegina were probably also similar to these, rather than as reconstructed by Welter (1937, figs. 1–6). A notable difference in the finds from the Kitsos cave is that at least some of the bowls with decoration inside have an internally thickened or rolled rim (Lambert, 1971, p. 711), a characteristic which never occurs at Kephala.

[11] Cf. especially the doubly pierced lugs with vertical plastic extensions on **97** (shown at a large scale on Pl. 78) and Pl. 39, D = Pl. 84, BR, Pl. 39, E = Pl. 84, BQ, Pl. 84, BO, BP, BT, BU with Immerwahr, 1971, nos. 1, 3, 7, 12, 13. Also similar are knobbed and grooved strap handles (cf. Pl. 84, AL, BE–BH with *ibid.*, no. 205 and Pl. 84, AO, AP with *ibid.*, no. 207), crescent-shaped lugs, either plain (cf. those on **146** and **170** with *ibid.*, no. 201), or with impressed edges (cf. Pl. 39, A = Pl. 85, F, Pl. 39, B = Pl. 85, E, Pl. 39, C = Pl. 85, C, Pl. 85, A, B, D, G with *ibid.*, nos. 162, 163).

[12] They include scoops (below, p. 101), pedestals with cutouts (cf. Pl. 30, E = Pl. 75, AV, Pl. 30, F = Pl. 75, AT, Pl. 75, BR, BU, BV with *ibid.*, no. 57), large ribbon handles, some with internal struts (cf. Pl. 38, A = Pl. 84, BB, Pl. 38, B = Pl. 84, BA, Pl. 85, N–R with *ibid.*, nos. 60–63), horizontal bands with incision on the outside of rims (cf. Pl. 44, A = Pl. 88, B, Pl. 44, B = Pl. 88, A, Pl. 44, C = Pl. 88, W, Pl. 44, E = Pl. 88, P, Pl. 44, G = Pl. 88, H, Pl. 44, H = Pl. 88, C, Pl. 44, D, F, Pl. 88, D–G, J–O, Q–V, X–AL with *ibid.*, nos. 103, 104), raised incised bands (cf. Pl. 44, M = Pl. 89, S, Pl. 89, Q with *ibid.*, no. 132), plastic ridges, either plain (cf. Pl. 46, B = Pl. 89, AS, Pl. 89, AT, AV, AW, AY–BB with *ibid.*, nos. 149–156), or with slashes or impressions (cf. Pl. 89, AU, BC–BP with *ibid.*, nos. 158–161, 164–170), and baking pans, some with internal lugs (cf. Pl. 37, C = Pl. 84, O, Pl. 37, D = Pl. 84, Q, Pl. 37, E = Pl. 84, P, Pl. 37, F = Pl. 84, C, Pl. 37, G = Pl. 84, D, Pl. 37, H = Pl. 84, B, Pl. 37, J = Pl. 84, F, Pl. 37, K = Pl. 84, J, Pl. 37, L = Pl. 84, V, Pl. 84, A, E, G, H, K–N, R–U with *ibid.*, nos. 184–188).

The head of a terracotta figurine from Athens (Immerwahr, 1971, no. 220) provides yet another specific link with Kephala. The Athens head is remarkably similar to **128** (Pls. 26, 71); both have projecting noses (set lower on the Athens head), projections at the back of the head, and holes at the upper edges. The hole at the bottom of the Athens head does not occur on **128** and **202** (Pls. 26, 71), but it may be compared with the holes in **96B*** (Pls. 26, 71). Another terracotta figurine from Athens (*ibid.*, no. 221), although female, has a general similarity to **160*** (Pl. 73); the arms of each are formed by a horizontal roll of clay.

Scoops (category C 1) also points to a cultural interrelationship between Kephala and Attica. They were made locally at Kephala in considerable quantity. Fragments of "at least four and probably several more" are now known at Athens (Immerwahr, 1971, p. 12, note 64; see nos. 111–123) and the shape is also reported at the Kitsos cave (Lambert, 1970, p. 758; 1971, p. 711). Those from Athens, although probably made there, are remarkably similar to the ones from Kephala (cf. especially **98** with Immerwahr, 1971, nos. 111, 121).

A scoop found long ago at Sesklo, apparently in a Thessaly B context (Tsountas, 1908, pl. 16, no. 3; Zervos, 1963, figs. 383–384; Immerwahr, 1971, pl. 8), has important implications, and has been much discussed. Opinions about its place of manufacture differ. Tsountas (*op. cit.*, cols. 206–208) assigned it to a small group of vases, including another complete vessel of a different shape and two sherds from Dimini, and considered that it was "an example of the style of some other locality."[13] Weinberg (1970, p. 605) regards it as an import from the Cyclades and suggests that it and other vessels like it were one of the means by which Cycladic motifs (i.e. the spiral and the meander) were transmitted to Thessaly and adopted in Dimini ware. Milojčić (1959, p. 22, note 57), on the other hand, compares it to the incised ware of the Otzaki phase in Thessaly; his views are followed by Holmberg (1964, p. 31), who evidently regards it without question as a Thessalian product, and Immerwahr (1971, p. 12), who stresses the close relationship between it and other Thessalian pottery.

The Sesklo scoop, while similar in general to those from Kephala, differs in three respects: it has incised decoration not only on the handle and struts but also on the body and the base, whereas the Kephala scoops are generally decorated only on the handle and struts;[14] the incision is white filled, whereas that on the Kephala scoops never is;[15] it has rows of angular perforations on the handle and the upper part of the body and string holes near the top of the handle, whereas such perforations are never found on the Kephala scoops.[16]

These differences are enough to suggest that the Sesklo scoop was not made at Kephala itself. We may further note that the other complete vessel which Tsountas grouped with the scoop (1908, pl. 16, 2) does not have any close parallels at Kephala. Whether or not the Sesklo scoop was imported into Thessaly from elsewhere will be proved only by further study (clay analysis?) and publication of Late Neolithic Thessalian pottery. At any rate, since it cannot be regarded as an import from Kephala, one may question whether it necessarily indicates any connection between Thessaly and the Cycladic islands.

In general, the distribution of scoops, so far as it is now known, suggests that they may have been primarily a mainland rather than a Cycladic type.[17] It has been noted (Caskey, 1964a, p. 317; Holmberg, 1964, p. 21) that they may have been related to the four-legged vessels with open diagonal mouths and high basket handles found at Corinth and in Phocis (Weinberg, 1962, pp. 190–195). These in turn, as Weinberg has shown, are practically identical to vessels from Yugoslavia which were used for cult purposes. The four-legged vases from Greece apparently belong to an earlier context than the Kephala scoops. They were found in the bothros in trench 3 at Elateia, which Weinberg dates to the MN period *ibid.*, pp. 179–181). Fragments from others are known, however, some with curvilinear incised patterns,

[13] Tsountas had some misgivings about the early date of the Sesklo scoop because it was found at the side of the mound although "at a sufficient depth" (*ibid.*, col. 207). Those misgivings may now be laid to rest in view of the context of the other scoops known.

[14] In two instances the bodies were at least partly decorated with incision: Pl. 83, AL, AM. Cf. Immerwahr, 1971, no. 117.

[15] Only one probable example of white-filled incision was noted on any vessel from Kephala (above, p. 38). White filling may in some cases have completely disappeared.

[16] There were angular cutouts on some of the handles from Athens: Immerwahr, 1971, nos. 120, 121.

[17] In addition to the examples already mentioned, a fragment with incised decoration, probably from the strut of a scoop, was found on the surface of a Euboean site (Sackett *et al.*, pl. 19, a, upper right, from Yimnou; cf. Pl. 36, G). Euboea was primarily a cultural offshoot of the mainland; some other possible links to Kephala are mentioned below.

which, although unstratified, should be recognized as Late Neolithic (*ibid.*, pp. 192–193). Scoops have several characteristics in common with four-legged vessels (e.g. high-swung handles and oblique mouths, which made them unsuitable as containers of fluids) and they too may have been of ritual usage.[18] If they represent a modification of the four-legged vessels in the later part of the LN period, an origin on the mainland would seem likely.

Some possible links between Kephala and Euboea have already been mentioned. Although Neolithic remains in Euboea are known so far only from surface survey, the pottery from at least seven of the sites thus recognized has possible affinities to that of Kephala, and at least some of them may have been occupied at the same time.[19]

The cultural connections with Attica and its environs discussed in the foregoing paragraphs are closer than those with any other area of the mainland; some differences have also been noted. In spite of the fairly close ties, it seems premature, in view of the incomplete state of the evidence, to attempt to isolate an "Attic-Kephala Culture" as Renfrew does (1972, pp. 75–76).[20] The ties are strong enough, on the other hand, to suggest that Kephala may have been part of a cultural continuum which also included Attica.

We now turn to comparisons with other areas of the Greek mainland.

The scoop from Sesklo, which has already been discussed, provides a chronological, and probably also a cultural link between Kephala and Thessaly. Kephala vessels other than scoops, on the other hand, are not closely paralleled in Thessaly. Certain features are shared, e.g. the use of crusted decoration, which in Thessaly is especially common in the Rachmani phase (Wace and Thompson, 1912, pp. 25–53); there is nothing at Kephala, however, to compare with the Thessalian painted wares, and in general Kephala pottery is much more simply decorated. Curvilinear and meandroid motifs, which are a distinctive feature of the later phases of Neolithic pottery in Thessaly, are rare, although not entirely absent, at Kephala.[21] In short, nothing except scoops was found at Kephala that offers much support to Weinberg's suggestion (1970, pp. 604–605) that the Dimini culture of Thessaly was influenced by or originated in the Cyclades. If anything, one might suggest that the rare examples of curvilinear and meandroid decoration at Kephala were the result of Thessalian influence.

[18] No traces of burning have been reported on four-legged vessels and they are often decorated with crusted colors, which would not readily withstand the effects of fire. The Kephala scoops also show no evidence of burning. Therefore, in spite of the possible traces of burning noted by Immerwahr on the Sesklo scoop (1971, p. 13), I doubt that scoops were generally used as ritual braziers or incense burners, as she suggests. A vessel with diagonal mouth and high-rising handle, somewhat like our scoops but with no base, was found at Eutresis during supplementary excavations (Caskey and Caskey, 1960, II.43). It dates either to the latest phase of the Neolithic period or the earliest phase of the Early Helladic period. As the Caskeys point out, it is roughly paralleled by vessels from Asea, although those apparently stood upright (Holmberg, 1944, fig. 84, a, b). The Eutresis vessel appears to be a utilitarian object and was probably actually used as a scoop. If it is related to the scoops from Kephala, Attica and Sesklo, it would offer some support to Tsountas' suggestion (see general discussion of scoops above, pp. 16–17) that the Sesklo scoop was used for grain, or a similar substance.

[19] The basic survey work is that of Sackett, Hankey, Howell, Jacobsen (who was responsible for Neolithic and EBA finds), and Popham (Sackett *et al.*, 1966). The sites are here listed with some possible comparisons to Kephala. No. 3, Yaltra: gray-black pattern-burnished sherd (*ibid.*, fig. 18, no. 26). No. 22, Limni: gray-black pattern-burnished sherd (*ibid.*, fig. 18, no. 27). No. 29, Katheni: rim with grooved and punctated decoration (*ibid.*, pl. 19, a, upper left = fig. 19, no. 2; cf. Pl. 44, E = Pl. 88, P). No. 32, Psachna (Varka Psachnon): pattern-burnished sherds of category Γ1α 2 (Theochares, 1959, fig. 10, 1–2). No. 59, Magoula: rim and vertical handle from bowl with pink crusted decoration (Sackett *et al.*, pl. 19, b, center left = fig. 18, no. 31; cf. Pl. 29, E = Pl. 75, AR); knobbed handle (*ibid.*, pl. 19, b, upper left; cf. Pl. 84, BE–BH). No. 61, Yimnou: fragment with incised decoration, probably from the strut of a scoop (*ibid.*, pl. 19, a, upper right; cf. especially Pl. 36, G); thickened and incised rim (*ibid.*, pl. 19, a, center right = fig. 19, no. 4; cf. especially Pl. 44, G = Pl. 88, H and Pl. 44, H = Pl. 88, C); at least two body sherds with crusted decoration (*ibid.*, p. 86). No. 62, Amarynthos: rim and vertical handle from bowl with crusted decoration like that from no. 59 (*ibid.*, pl. 17, b, center right = fig. 18, no. 29). A site at Lambousa, no. 71, may also be about contemporary with Kephala, to judge by the discovery of a rim fragment with incised decoration (*ibid.*, fig. 19, no. 3). The pattern-burnished sherds from nos. 3, 22 and 32 are probably more closely related to the MN to LN gray or black burnished wares of Thessaly and Central Greece than to the red pattern-burnished pottery of Kephala.

[20] Renfrew's definitions of "cultures" in the Aegean raise methodological questions which cannot here be discussed in detail. In general they seem to me to be more likely to hinder than to aid our understanding of the Prehistoric Aegean; see further discussion in Coleman, 1974, p. 340.

[21] Curvilinear. Pattern burnished: Frontispiece M = Pl. 42, A = Pl. 86, AN; Pl. 41, B = Pl. 86, AA. Incised on bowls and/or jars: at least eight examples (above, p. 12). Incised on scoop strut: Pl. 36, F = Pl. 83, AG; cf. also p. 92. Plastic: Pl. 46, B = Pl. 89, AS; Pl. 89, AT; Pl. 89, AV (interlocking curvilinear elements).

Meandroid. Pattern burnished: Frontispiece N = Pl. 42, E = Pl. 86, AO. Incised: **98**.

The terracotta figurines have a general resemblance to the later Neolithic ones from Thessaly. One may compare our type of female figure with outstretched arms to several figurines from Sesklo.[22] Other figurines found at Dimini (Tsountas, 1908, pl. 35, nos. 1–3, 6–8; pl. 36, nos. 4, 6) Rachmani (Wace and Thompson, 1912, fig. 26, n), and Zerelia (*ibid.*, fig. 109) also bear some similarity. Heads with flat faces like **96B***, **128** and **202** (Pls. 26, 71, 73) are also found in Thessaly (e.g. Tsountas, pl. 35, no. 6) although none has projections at front or back nor is any of such a size as **96B***.

Male figurines are also known from Thessaly. A standing one from Sesklo dating to the Thessaly A phase (Tsountas, 1908, pl. 33, no. 2) is roughly similar to **160*** (Pl. 73), but there need be no direct connection between them.

Little material from Central Greece and the Peloponnese has yet been published which may be dated to the latest stage of the Neolithic period. The pattern-burnished sherds from Corinth and Prosymna have already been mentioned. At Prosymna, in the same deposit as the pattern-burnished sherds, were found bowls with incised rims closely comparable to the ones from Kephala (cf. Blegen, 1937, figs. 633, 635, with Pls. 44, 88). Blegen tentatively assigned the deposit to his first phase (*ibid.*, p. 374); it now appears more likely that it dates to a time near the end of the Neolithic period. Vessels from two LN pit graves at Lerna have a fairly close similarity to Kephala pottery.[23] Sherds decorated with pattern burnishing and crusted decoration have also been found in the latest LN levels at the Franchthi cave (Jacobsen, 1969, p. 370; 1973, pp. 273–275); a terracotta figurine from the same levels (Jacobsen, 1973, pl. 53) has a general resemblance to **127**, **196**, **197**, and **198** (Pl. 72).

There is a marked contrast between funerary practices at Kephala and those on the mainland in the Neolithic period. The almost universal practice in the EN and MN periods was interment in simple pits dug within or near the settlement (Weinberg, 1970, pp. 579, 593–594): most of the burials were primary, but secondary burial was sometimes practiced.[24] In a rock shelter at Prosymna two skeletons were found in pits within the lower stratum, dating probably to the MN period. The bodies had apparently been cremated (Blegen, 1937, pp. 25–28). Three skulls and scattered bones were also found in the upper stratum, dating to the MN or LN period; Blegen (1937, p. 28) suggested that these may have been from secondary burials.

There is not a great deal of evidence for the LN period, but what has been found suggests that there was considerable diversity in funerary practices. Human remains have been found in two caves. In a large cave at Alepotrypa near Diros in the Mani, remains of both primary and secondary interments have been found (Papathanasopoulos, 1971a, 1971b; Lambert, 1972b); work is continuing at the site and further elucidation of the burial customs may be expected. In the Kitsos cave near Laurion a number of bones have been found in LN contexts (Lambert, 1969, 1970, 1971). In one place in the cave a well-preserved cremation was found in place on a hearth (Lambert, 1969, p. 965); elsewhere the bones are scattered and the skeletons incomplete. Some, but not all, of the scattered bones show evidence of burning (Lambert, 1969, p. 965; 1970, p. 758) and the possibility has even been raised that anthropophagy was practiced (Krukoff, 1971). A few other LN burials have been found within or near open settlements. At Lerna two primary burials of adults in pits and at least one child's burial came to light within the area of the settlement. At Elateia the burial of a child, evidently intramural, was found in one of the uppermost levels. At Rachmani the jar burial of an infant was found in stratum II, which dates to the Thessaly B period. At Servia the skeleton of a woman was discovered at the bottom of a shaft beneath an ash layer. Finally, at Souphli Magoula a cemetery of cremation urns was found near the settlement.[25]

[22] Tsountas, 1908, pl. 34, nos. 3, 4, 7, all with applied pellets for breasts. The Sesklo figurines are rounded, more symmetrical and better made than the Kephala ones; Tsountas only illustrated the better-formed ones, however, and he noted (*ibid.*, col. 284) that the earlier terracotta figurines were more naturalistic and the later more schematic.

[23] Grave HTN.1 contained a high pedestaled bowl with crusted white and red on the outside (Caskey, 1959, pl. 41, d; for the shape cf. **164***) and two rounded bowls, one burnished and one plain (Caskey, 1958, pl. 37, a and b; cf. category A 2). Grave JC.1 contained a jar with a high-swung ribbon handle and crusted red on the outside (Caskey, 1959, pl. 41, b; for the shape of the body cf. **166***). For the burials in these graves see below, footnote 25.

[24] E.g. at Ayioryitika: Fürst, 1932. Blegen, who is quoted on p. 1 of Fürst's report (followed by Weinberg, 1970, p. 593), describes this grave as a "cist" although it was not slab sided or walled with stone.

[25] Lerna: Grave HTN.1, Caskey, 1958, pp. 136–137, Angel, 1971, p. 40 (*240 Ler*); Grave JC.1, Caskey, 1959, p. 205, Angel, 1971, pp. 40–41 (*242 Ler*); Grave HJT.1, Angel, 1971, p. 41 (*225 Ler*). Angel also mentions skull fragments of a foetus (1971, p. 41, *223 Ler*) perhaps from another burial. For the pottery associated with the Lerna graves see above, footnote 23. Elateia: Weinberg, 1962 p. 163. Rachmani: Wace and Thompson, 1912, p. 41. Servia: Heurtley, 1937, pp. 54–55. Souphli Magoula: Biesantz, 1959.

This diversity in funerary practices presumably represents considerable cultural diversity, if not ethnic change, on the mainland in the LN period.

The contrast between the funerary practices of the mainland and those of Kephala is obvious. Special places were rarely set aside as cemeteries on the mainland, and when they were (e.g. at Souphli Magoula and possibly Prosymna) the corpses were treated in a completely different way. Graves with artificially constructed walls are the rule at Kephala, whereas they do not occur on the mainland. The burial of infants in jars was a regular practice at Kephala, whereas jar burials (except for the cremation urns at Souphli Magoula) are rare on the mainland.[26] The continued use of individual graves as family tombs, which was common at Kephala, is so far unknown on the mainland. The possibility cannot be excluded, in view of the incomplete state of the evidence, that LN cemeteries similar to that at Kephala will one day be found on the mainland; at present, however, the available evidence does not suggest any close link in funerary practices between Kephala and the mainland.

The interconnections with Attica, and to a lesser extent with other parts of the mainland, leave no doubt that Kephala belongs to the LN period as defined on the mainland. Kephala had little in common with the earliest and still rather poorly documented phase of the EH period as recognized, for example, at Eutresis (Goldman, 1931; Caskey and Caskey, 1960), nor does it have much in common with the deposit from Palaia Kokkinia in Attica, which probably dates to EH I.[27]

We now turn again to the Cyclades, and to the difficult question of the relationship between Kephala and the EC culture.[28]

EC settlements are often situated like Kephala, Paoura and Sykamia, on promontories and hilltops close to the sea. Very few have been excavated and studied in detail and there is very little evidence for or against any general relationship with the settlement at Kephala. In contrast to the scattered and apparently unfortified settlement at Kephala, both Chalandriani in Syros (Tsountas, 1899, cols. 115–130; Bossert, 1967) and Panormos in Naxos (Doumas, 1964, pp. 411–412) were close-knit architectural complexes surrounded by fortification walls. The settlement on Kynthos in Delos (Plassart, 1928, pp. 11–50) was similar to Chalandriani, although no trace of fortification walls has survived. The settlement of Phylakopi I was evidently scattered over a wide area, but in a somewhat less precipitous location than Kephala.

Much more is known about EC cemeteries.[29] They were usually located near the settlements they served. The number of graves in each varies from a very few to several hundred; since the graves were usually close to the surface, erosion and looting may have reduced the number of recognizable graves in many cemeteries. The graves are usually spaced less densely than those at Kephala and do not overlap one another; they do not have any particular orientation, except as determined by the lie of the land where the cemetery was located. The graves are of two types: slab-sided cist graves and built graves.

Slab-sided cists constitute the most common type of EC grave. Hundreds have been excavated by archaeologists and many more plundered. Most have a quadrilateral plan (rarely rectangular) with a length of about 1.00 m. The width varies greatly; the narrowest, which are infant burials, are about 0.30 m. wide. The sides consist of slabs set on edge; sometimes one side is built of small stones (Tsountas, 1898, col. 142). The graves are regularly covered by several slabs, and platforms of stones are sometimes found above the covers (above, p. 47, note 6). Almost all the graves contain single burials. Very rarely, more than one burial was made at the same level; Tsountas (1898, cols. 143–144) noted only seven

[26] In addition to the jar burial from Rachmani, there is a MN infant burial in a bowl or beaker at Lerna: Caskey, 1957, p.159 and pl. 48, f. A skull was placed in a vessel at Alepotrypa; see Lambert, 1972b, p. 850.

[27] Theochares, 1951. The only close parallel is the grooved stone (*ibid.*, fig. 28, β) which resembles **192** (Pls. 22, 68). The Cycladic features of the Palaia Kokkinia deposit are often overstressed (e.g. *ibid.*, p. 116; Immerwahr, 1971, p. 8). Specifically mentioned in this regard are spherical pyxides (Theochares, 1951, figs. 24, 25) and fragments of pans and lids with stamped and incised decoration (*ibid.*, fig. 26). The Cycladic character of the pyxides is open to question, since Neolithic forerunners are known from Thessaly (e.g. Tsountas, 1908, col. 214, pl. 21, no. 3), and they do not have the characteristic EC "herringbone" incised decoration. One of the pans with stamped decoration is also probably of mainland type (cf. Renfrew, 1972, pp. 536–537) even if the shape may ultimately have originated in the Cyclades; Bossert (1960) has shown that the mainland probably took precedence over the Cyclades in stamped decoration.

[28] For some recent discussions of the EC culture see Caskey (1964b), Bossert (1965; 1967), Renfrew (1972) and Coleman (1974). I prefer to use the traditional terminology for the successive phases, i.e. the Pelos phase, the Syros phase and the Phylakopi I phase.

[29] The following summary of EC burial practices is drawn mainly from the classic studies of Tsountas (1898, 1899).

instances among the hundreds of graves he excavated in Amorgos, Paros, Antiparos and Despotikon. Burials at different levels in double-tiered graves (e.g. Tsountas, 1898, cols. 144–145) are slightly more common. The bodies were usually, though not always, laid out in a contracted position on the right side. The graves from Pelos in Melos (Edgar, 1896–1897), which many scholars consider among the earliest EC graves, were of this type.

Built graves (i.e. with sides constructed of small stones) are much less common than slab-sided cist graves. Those of simpler form, without entrances, are known from several islands; Tsountas found some at Akrotiraki in Siphnos (1899, col. 74) and one at Dokathismata in Amorgos (1898, col. 146). Their plans and dimensions are said to resemble those of cist graves (Tsountas, 1899, col. 74) and at least one of those in Siphnos was double tiered (grave 145). Other built graves of more complex form, with a small doorway at one side, are largely confined to Syros (Tsountas, 1899, cols. 79–84), although there may have been some at Diakophtis in Naxos (Belmont and Renfrew, 1964, pp. 397–398).[30] The Syros graves vary in plan from polygonal to circular, but many are quadrilateral; the greatest dimension is usually about 1.50 m. or less, and the walls are frequently corbeled inward. Almost all were the tombs of individuals; only ten out of more than 600 excavated by Tsountas (1899, col. 83) contained multiple burials. The body was generally laid out in the same manner as in the cist graves.

At Ayios Kosmas in Attica, a site with a close relationship with the EC culture, built graves were found side by side with cist graves (Mylonas, 1959, pp. 64–120); many graves of both types had doorways. In contrast to the Cycladic practice, most of the 32 graves contained multiple burials (*ibid.*, p. 117).

Pithos burials of EC date are so far unknown in the Cyclades except possibly in the cemetery at Kapsala in Amorgos, and at Phylakopi in Melos, where they were intramural.[31]

Grave goods in the Early Cycladic cemeteries include: vessels of pottery, marble and occasionally silver; obsidian blades; marble figurines; copper weapons, tweezers and pins; shells; and a few other objects of silver, lead, bone and stone.

The similarities between the burial practices at Kephala and those just described are striking. Particularly noteworthy is the use in both cases of a communal cemetery comprising graves with artificial walls.[32] The two instances of slab-sided cists (Graves 2 and 23) show that the type was known at Kephala, and the Kephala built graves have very close EC parallels. The platforms of stones found above some of the Kephala graves also have parallels in EC cemeteries, and it is possible that one or two graves at Kephala (Graves 7 and 14) had doorways such as are found in the Syros graves. The correspondence is not exact.[33] Nevertheless the similarities are sufficiently numerous to suggest that there may have been a close relationship between the burial practices at Kephala and those of the EC culture.

Another possible link is provided by the terracotta figurine heads from Kephala (**96B***, **128**, **202**, Pls. 26, 71, 73), which have a striking resemblance to the heads of EC marble figurines (Caskey, 1971b, nos. 16–23; Zervos, 1957, *passim*). The faces of EC figurines are usually set off more from the neck than the Kephala ones, the noses are lower than the knobs on **128** and **202**, and there are no knobs at the back; nor do EC figurines ever have string holes as on **128**. The greatest difference is that of the material; EC figurines are never made of terracotta, although occasionally of shell (e.g. Renfrew, 1967, p. 18, nos. 26, 27) or lead (Edgar, 1896–1897, fig. 18; cf. Renfrew, 1967, p. 18, no. 1). It is especially

[30] It is not clear whether the built graves investigated by Doumas at Lionas in Naxos had doorways (1963, p. 279). The cemetery was plundered; although Doumas does not mention doorways, he compares the graves to the built graves at Chalandriani and Siphnos. Renfrew (1972, p. 179) implies that the graves at Lionas did have doorways.

[31] In two places at Kapsala, Tsountas found fragments of large open vessels with upright slabs beside them; although he found no proof of it, he suggested that these may have been for the burial of small children (1898, col. 153). For the pithos burials at Phylakopi see Dawkins and Droop, 1910–1911, pp. 6–9 (cf. Atkinson *et al.*, 1904, p. 15); these date to the time of Phylakopi I and may therefore be of early MC date; like those from Kephala they were probably all burials of children. This was also the case with many of the MC pithos burials at Ayia Irini (Caskey, 1971a, p. 373).

[32] Such graves may have been in part a natural response to the environment of the Cyclades; soil cover deep enough for pit graves is rare and stones are abundant.

[33] EC cemeteries are not so crowded as that of Kephala, nor are graves (except for double-tiered ones) built on top of one another; graves with multiple burials are less frequent in the EC cemeteries, the bodies are more consistently oriented, grave goods are more varied and perhaps more numerous (although it should be noted that many EC graves contained none; the publications of Tsountas may give a misleading impression, since he did not describe the great number of graves he excavated which were without grave goods), and pithos burials are rare or absent.

noteworthy that Neolithic figurines are practically never of such large size as **96B***, which must have been about 0.50 m. high when complete, whereas several EC figurines of this size or larger are known.[34]

The resemblance of the figurine heads poses a minor chronological problem. The EC figurines with well-defined, flat faces and projecting noses are almost all of the folded-arm type. According to the chronology of figurines suggested by Renfrew (1969) and Preziosi and Weinberg (1970) the folded-arm type does not occur until the middle phase of the EC period (the Syros phase); the figurines assigned to the earlier phase (the Pelos phase) are mostly of schematic type with featureless rods or knobs for heads. The Louros type, which has a flat face (Renfrew, 1969, p. 8; called "schematic" in Preziosi and Weinberg, 1970) may possibly represent an intermediate stage; it is comparatively rare, however, and lacks a projecting nose.[35] Perhaps EC figurines of the Pelos phase will eventually be found, or recognized, which illustrate better the development from Kephala heads to the later EC heads; at any rate, the Kephala heads must be related to the EC type.

The marble vessels from Kephala pose a problem in interpretation different from those of burial practices and figurine heads since they may not have been locally produced in Keos (above, p. 5). They have a general resemblance to EC marble vessels, even though there are no exact parallels from secure contexts. In particular, the string-hole lugs are of the same general type as those on EC jars with conical necks (*kandiles*; e.g. Zervos, 1957, figs. 6–8, 16) and beakers (e.g. *ibid.*, figs. 1, 2).

A conical rhyton like **103** and **109** (Pls. 23, 67), in the Copenhagen Museum (inv. 4762; Renfrew, 1972, pl. 1, 2), is said to come from Naxos, but nothing else is known about its context. The only other example known to me is a fragment almost certainly from the lower part of such a rhyton which was found at Kum Tepe in the I c level;[36] since it is only a fragment, it could be a stray from an earlier phase. More relevant to the present discussion is the presumable development from the pointed rhyton to the EC beaker. A beaker in the Goulandris collection (Doumas, 1968, no. 57), which is tall, narrow at the bottom, and has lugs partially detached at the top like those of **103**, can be assigned to an intermediate phase in the development.[37]

The shallow marble bowls, of which **171** (Pls. 23, 67) is the best preserved example, have general parallels in both Neolithic and EC contexts, although the arrangement of the lugs on **171** cannot be exactly matched.[38] The shape is such a simple one that no definite conclusions can be drawn from it; nevertheless, as already noted, the form of the lugs appears to provide a link with the EC culture.

The question was raised above whether the funerary practices of Kephala are related to those of the EC culture. The figurine heads tend to support such a relationship. When we turn to the pottery, however, great differences are to be seen. The pots usually considered typical of the EC culture are often gray

[34] The largest complete one is from Amorgos and is about 1.50 m. high (Athens NM 3978; Zervos, 1957, fig. 297). Two heads (*ibid.*, figs. 159–161, 177–178) must come from examples over 1 m. high. Other complete figurines over 0.50 m. high include *ibid.*, figs. 113, 162, 296, 300–301; Doumas, 1968, nos. 257, 280, 281, 282, 304. The largest figurine from Ayia Irini in Keos is represented by a head (Caskey, 1971b, no. 24; H. pres. 0.14 m.) which is roughly the same size as **96B***. The only figurine I know of from the mainland before the Mycenaean period which is comparable in size to **96B*** is the seated ithyphallic terracotta one from Thessaly (Wace and Thompson, 1912, fig. 30; H. 0.48 m.; date uncertain but probably Neolithic).

[35] The Louros type has projecting stumps at the shoulders which were perhaps intended to represent outstretched arms; cf. the pose of **127**, **196**, **197** and **198** (Pl. 72).

[36] I.e. contemporary with Troy I; for this information I am indebted to Jerome Sperling.

[37] Doumas records two projections on one side near the top of the Goulandris vessel. They may be compared with the breasts of an anthropomorphic beaker in the Ashmolean (Renfrew, 1972, pl. 1, 1). Both vessels perhaps had ritual significance; cf. a seated figurine in the Goulandris collection (Doumas, 1968, no. 286), which grasps a beaker in what may be a ritual gesture.

[38] General parallels for the shape in the Neolithic period include a rim fragment of marble from Saliagos (Evans and Renfrew, 1968, fig. 22, no. 2) and a complete marble bowl from Kum Tepe which was found in a grave of the I a phase (Blegen, 1935, p. 34). A rim fragment of a conical marble bowl from Elateia is probably Neolithic, although found in topsoil (Weinberg, 1962, pl. 69, g). Neolithic stone vessels rarely have pierced lugs, and I know of none similar to those on the Kephala vessels. Theochares mentions a fragment with a pierced lug from the LN levels at Nea Makri (1956, p. 26; not illustrated). A vessel from Sparta has rounded lugs which are partially pierced vertically (Wolters, 1891, p. 52, no. 4). A fragment from the Franchthi cave with a horizontally elongated lug, doubly pierced vertically, is from a mixed surface context (Jacobsen, 1969, pl. 98, c, lower right).

Simple bowls of marble are common in EC contexts, particularly during the Syros phase. Shallow ones without handles (*phialai*) are evidently the most frequent (e.g. Tsountas, 1898, pl. 10, no. 9; Zervos, 1957, figs. 4–5. Doumas, 1968, lists more than 30) but taller, handleless bowls also occur (e.g. Tsountas, 1898, pl. 10, no. 8). Bowls with four unpierced, horizontally elongated projections at the rim are also common (e.g. Tsountas, 1899, fig. 25; Zervos, 1957, figs. 21–22). Vertical lugs or lug handles, on the other hand, are known on only a few bowls; unlike those on **171** they are always placed below rather than at the rim, and they are often single rather than in pairs. Examples are: Tsountas, 1898, pl. 10, no. 6 (with a pair of unpierced lugs); *ibid.*, nos. 7 and 10 (both apparently with single lugs); Dümmler, 1886, Beil. 1, E.1 (incurving rim; single lug); Doumas, 1968, no. 61 (grooved rim; single lug).

or black rather than red, and they have many other differences both in shape and decoration.[39] The differences could be partly chronological; although the upper limit of the Pelos phase has not yet been securely established, Kephala is undoubtedly earlier than most, if not all, known EC sites. The difference in the pottery, on the other hand, is greater than one would except if the settlement at Kephala were culturally ancestral to the EC culture. The pottery of the earliest EC phase appears rather to have developed from a Neolithic tradition different from that represented at Kephala; Benton (1947, pp. 165–170) and Weinberg (1970, pp. 604–605) have pointed out its affinities to the pottery of LN Thessaly, and Renfrew (1972, pp. 161–169) its affinities to that of the Eastern Aegean and Western Anatolia.

How then can the apparent relationship between Kephala and the EC culture be explained? Only tentative suggestions can yet be made. Keos was surely not the only Cycladic island inhabited in the later stages of the LN period. Some of the other islands were probably occupied by people who were either in the earliest phase of EC culture or in a phase immediately ancestral to it. These people may have provided their neighbors in Keos with marble vessels and perhaps other commodities (obsidian?) by trade or exchange, and they may also, as a result of such contact, have influenced their burial practices and the style of their figurines.

At this point we may briefly summarize. The cultural (and ethnic?) affinities of Kephala were primarily with the LN mainland, particularly Attica and its environs. There are, in contrast, almost no affinities with the mainland in the EH period. While Kephala has practically nothing in common with the clearly earlier Saliagos phase in the islands, the evidence of burial customs, figurine heads and marble vessels suggests a relationship between Kephala and the EC culture. Although this relationship cannot be clearly defined, the evidence suggests that Kephala was not ancestral to the EC culture as we now understand it;[40] perhaps Kephala was in contact with people in an early stage of the EC culture on other islands.

We may now turn briefly to the less direct interrelations with the Eastern Aegean and Western Anatolia.

Pattern burnishing provides a general link. It is known at Tigani in Samos (Heidenreich *et al.*, 1935–1936, pp. 128–130) and at Besika Tepe (Lamb, 1932) and Kum Tepe[41] in the Troad; a few sherds were also found at Beycesultan (Lloyd and Mellaart, 1962, p. 91). The organization of the decoration is somewhat different from that found at Kephala: fine and broad lines were frequently used together,[42] often in a sort of herringbone pattern, and the decoration was often confined to panels within solidly burnished areas. The pattern-burnished decoration from Tigani, Besika Tepe and Kum Tepe links them closely together and suggests that there may have been a general cultural relationship with Kephala. Tigani, the only site of the three from which a substantial amount of material has been published, provides some other parallels to Kephala as well.[43] The similarities, however, should not be overly emphasized, since there are also many differences; white painted decoration, for instance, does not occur at Kephala; scoops, T-lugs, horizontally elongated lugs with vertical plastic extensions depending

[39] Bowls with incised rims, jars with collar-necks, scoops, T-lugs and pattern burnishing do not occur in the EC repertoire. Bowls with tubular, horizontally pierced lug handles and rims thickened and rolled toward the inside, pedestaled jars with conical necks (*kandiles*), globular and cylindrical pyxides and herringbone incised patterns, to confine the list to characteristics of the EC pottery generally regarded as the earliest (cf. Renfrew, 1972, pp. 153–161), do not occur at Kephala. Vessels with conical necks, which are among the commonest EC shapes, are extremely rare at Kephala (e.g. Pl. 32, Q; Pl. 46, D = Pl. 80, A).

[40] Renfrew, 1972, pp. 166–169, suggests that there may have been a continuous evolution in the Cyclades from the culture represented at Saliagos to the Pelos phase of the EC culture (i.e. his "Grotta-Pelos culture").

[41] Unpublished except in brief preliminary reports (Blegen, 1935; Koşay and Sperling, 1936), but often referred to; see e.g. Renfrew, 1972, p. 162. (Publication by Sperling forthcoming in *Hesperia* 45, 1976, fasc. 4.–Ed.)

[42] Such a contrast between fine and broad lines occurs very rarely at Kephala; e.g. Pl. 41, C = Pl. 86, Z; possibly **105** (Pl. 43).

[43] *Aufgemaltes Rot* (class G: Heidenreich *et al.*, 1935–1936, p. 130; Furness, 1956, pp. 187–188, where it is called "red slipped ware") is probably akin to crusted red. Bowls with rims decorated with incised multiple chevrons (grouped here under A 1 and A 2: Incised Rims) are common at Tigani (e.g. Heidenreich *et al.*, 1935–1936, p. 133, F 5 to F 17). A rare type of thick-walled pottery has deep incisions or grooving in spiraliform or meandroid patterns (*ibid.*, pp. 137–139) which resemble to some extent those from Kephala and elsewhere (above, p. 12). "Gefäße zur Käsebereitung" (*ibid.*, pp. 139–141) are similar to baking pans (category C 3). Flattened, high-swung handles occur at both places (cf. *ibid.*, F 19–20 with Pl. 38, L = Pl. 85, AK, Pl. 38, M = Pl. 85, AL, Pl. 38, K). There is also a general resemblance between some of the open bowls and pedestaled bowls of Tigani (e.g. *ibid.*, F 6–17, F 42–68; pl. 29, 1) and bowls of category A 2. A fragment of a vessel (or figurine?) with spiraliform or meandroid decoration like that from Tigani was also found at Kalymnos (Furness, 1956, pl. XIX, 19). The material from Tigani has lately been restudied and some further excavation carried out by Rainer Felsch.

from either end, and the extensive use of rope-like plastic decoration are not found at Tigani. The marble rhyton from Kum Tepe mentioned above suggests contact with the Cyclades, and not necessarily with Keos. The evidence, in short, is not sufficient to indicate any direct cultural relationship or exchange between Kephala and these Eastern sites.

Kephala, in common with the Greek mainland in the LN period, has almost no close parallels with Crete. The female figurines of terracotta have a general similarity to some of those from Crete (e.g., cf. **197**, Pl. 72, with Ucko, 1968, fig. 101), but not so close as to suggest any direct relationship. Pedestaled bowls are known in Crete in the Neolithic period, but they are apparently most common at the beginning of the Early Bronze Age; "Pyrgos style" goblets of this phase are often decorated with pattern burnishing (e.g. Zervos, 1956, figs. 83–86). The pedestals are usually higher and more flaring than those at Kephala, and there is often a projecting ring at the juncture of bowl and pedestal; the patterns, while extending over a broad area, are simpler and have more in common with those of the Eastern Aegean and Western Anatolia than with Kephala. Nearly conical vessels of clay with a single handle from LN (?) Knossos (Evans, 1921, fig. 6, no. 9; Zervos, 1956, figs. 68, 69) may have a remote connection with the marble rhyta from Kephala (**103**, **109**, Pls. 23, 67), but perhaps only to the extent that both were inspired by animal horns.

The evidence of copper metallurgy at Kephala need come as no surprise. Three objects of copper from Neolithic contexts in the Aegean have long been known and discussed: two chisels or axes from Sesklo (Tsountas, 1908, figs. 292–293) and an axe from Knossos (Evans, 1928, fig. 3, f). To these we may now add some copper objects from Emporio in Chios (Hood, 1965, p. 228), a copper pin or awl from the Kitsos cave (Lambert, 1971, fig. 31) and some copper objects from phases II and III at Sitagroi (Renfrew, 1970, pp. 298, 300 and pl. XLIII, upper). Two copper awls from near the surface of the mound at Sesklo (Tsountas, 1908, pl. 4, nos. 4, 5) should probably be added to the list, since they are of an early type. Evidence of actual copper working (slag) has also been found at Sitagroi in phase III (Renfrew, 1970, p. 300), for the earlier stage of which there are five C-14 dates ranging from about 3850 to 3150 B.C. (Renfrew, 1971, p. 277).

Comparisons of the types of copper objects, while not conclusive because of the scantiness of the evidence, suggest that the Kephala copper working (Pls. 22, 66) was in a common Aegean and Western Anatolian tradition. The awl **28*** is very similar to the one from the Kitsos cave and those from Sesklo, and is close in type to several found in a Chalcolithic hoard at Beycesultan (Lloyd and Mellaart, 1962, fig. F8, nos. 7–10); **82*** and **147*** may have been from narrow chisels like one found in the same hoard at Beycesultan (*ibid.*, fig. F8, no. 4); I know of no close parallel for **83***, but the small size of the fragment makes even its identification difficult.

The existence of slag at Kephala is especially important, since it demonstrates that copper was actually worked at the site (see Appendix 1). The evidence for metallurgy is not extensive and there is no reason to think that copper working was particularly important to the inhabitants. Copper may also have been worked at Paoura (see Appendix 6, **P 45-P 47**), and there is a fragment of a crucible from the earliest deposits at Ayia Irini (Caskey, 1972, p. 360, A 47), which may be only slightly later than those from Kephala.

The source of the copper ore is not certainly known, but it probably comes from within the Aegean area.[44] Conophagos points out (Appendix 1) that small quantities of copper ores are known from Laurion. It is entirely possible that the abundant sources of silver at Laurion, which were exploited at least as early as the beginning of the Late Bronze Age,[45] were already being exploited in the LN period. Extraction of both copper and silver from their respective ores might have gone hand in hand. The close ties between Kephala and Attica have already been stressed. The discovery of an object of lead at Kephala (**84***) also suggests a connection with Laurion and silver working, as lead is a by-product in the extraction of silver from ore; since it is a surface find, however, it cannot be definitely associated with the period of prehistoric occupation of the site.

[44] In the Cyclades, Paros and Syros have been mentioned as having deposits of ore; Tsountas, 1898, col. 192; Forbes, 1950, p. 303.

[45] Litharge, which presupposes silver metallurgy, has been found at Thorikos in a level dated by Servais to approximately the end of the 16th century B.C.; Mussche *et al.*, 1967, pp. 23–24.

CHRONOLOGY

A relative chronology is suggested by the interconnections discussed in the preceding section (Table 8). In general, Kephala belongs to the later stages of the LN in the Aegean. The stratigraphic sequence from the Kitsos cave, when it is fully published, may clarify still further the chronological position of Kephala. We may note here that in Sondage 2, pattern-burnished decoration, scoops, and a copper awl were found together in level III (Lambert, 1970, pp. 758–761); pattern burnishing continued in level II and the period of the occupation of Kephala probably fell within the time represented by these two levels. In Sondage 1, pattern burnishing is also recorded in level III (Lambert, 1969, p. 961; it is not clear from the preliminary reports whether levels may be equated from one Sondage to the other). The C-14 dates from these levels will be considered below (cf. Table 9).

The Sesklo scoop, which must be about contemporary with those from Kephala, indicates that Kephala may be equated in general terms with LN Thessaly. The stratigraphic associations of the Sesklo scoop were not recorded in detail; Milojčić (1959, p. 22, note 57) compares it to the coarse incised ware of the Otzaki phase (i.e. Dimini III on Table 8), which precedes the classic Dimini phase, and Holmberg (1964, p. 31) regards it without question as belonging to the Otzaki phase. These views may be confirmed, or perhaps modified, when more Thessalian material is published; in the meantime, the Sesklo scoop may be tentatively considered earlier than the latest phases of the Neolithic period in Thessaly.

TABLE 8. CHRONOLOGICAL CHART

	THESSALY	S. GREECE	CYCLADES	ASIA MINOR	
4000	Dimini I	Kitsos	Saliagos		4900
	II	*LATE*	*LATE*		
	THESS.	*NEOL.*	*NEOL.*		
	B III				
			Kephala	*KUM TEPE Ia*	
	IV				
				Ib	
3000	Larissa	Cave			3700
			PELOS PHASE		
	Rachmani	*E H I*	Kampos	*TROY I*	
	E. THESS.	*E H II*	*SYROS PHASE*		
			Kastri	*TROY II–V*	
			Temple Lane		
2000	*M. THESS.*	*E H III*	*PHYLAKOPI I PHASE*		2600
		M H	*M C*	*TROY VI*	

The dates given on the left are based on a half-life of 5570 years; those on the right are according to the calibrations proposed by Ralph, Michael and Han (1973).

Recent excavations at the Franchthi cave suggest that in the Peloponnese the earlier phases of the LN period, when matt-painted pottery was in use, were succeeded by a phase in which coarse ware is the common pottery and crusted decoration occurs (Jacobsen, 1973, pp. 266–275). The absence of painted pottery at Kephala, and the presence of crusted decoration, suggest that it should be equated with this later phase. Kephala must also be about contemporary with the deposit at Prosymna containing pattern-burnished and incised pottery (above, pp. 100, 103), and with the LN graves of Lerna (above, p. 103).

The only absolute date from Kephala itself was the C-14 determination from the deposit of seeds in Area K (above, p. 32): 2876 ± 56 B.C. (P 1280). In Table 9 this is compared with some other C-14 dates from the Aegean area which are significant for Kephala. Those from Saliagos, which range from about 4200 B.C. to 3700 B.C., support the view that it was appreciably earlier than Kephala. The date from Kephala is a little later, however, than might be expected when it is compared with those from the Franchthi cave and the Kitsos cave. The latest Neolithic stages in the Franchthi cave are dated to well before the end of the fourth millennium. GIF 1610 from level II in Sondage 2 at the Kitsos cave (the later of the two levels which appear to have affinities with Kephala) is at least 250 years earlier than the Kephala date; GIF 1280 from level III in Sondage 1 (which also has affinities with Kephala) is at least 400 years earlier, and both are consistent with the other dates from the cave.

Two explanations can be proposed for the apparent discrepancy between the date from Kephala and those from elsewhere: either the relative chronology proposed above is faulty or the Kephala date is erroneously low.[46] In my opinion, the latter explanation is the more likely. The carbon sample from Kephala was found near the surface and could have been slightly contaminated. Furthermore, the date from the site is an isolated one and need not carry the same weight as a consistent series of dates. I therefore suggest that the C-14 date from Kephala be largely disregarded and that the site be considered to date (as I have ventured to show it on Table 8) to about 3300–3200 B.C. in terms of the conventional radiocarbon chronology. This date, when calibrated according to the system proposed by Ralph, Michael and Han (1973), would fall near the beginning of the fourth millennium B.C.

TABLE 9. PERTINENT RADIOCARBON DATES OF VARIOUS SITES

Saliagos[1] (half-life 5568)		
P 1311	Dark soil (not ascribed to a specific stratum)	4222 ± 74 B.C.
P 1396	Spondylus shell from Stratum 1	4124 ± 79 B.C.
P 1333	Spondylus shell from upper levels of Stratum 1	3825 ± 84 B.C.
P 1368	Spondylus shells (not ascribed to a specific stratum)	3959 ± 87 B.C.
P 1393	Spondylus shells. Probably Stratum 3	3766 ± 85 B.C.
Kitsos Cave[2] (half-life 5570)		
GIF 1612	Carbon from Sondage 2, Level IV	3750 ± 140 B.C.
GIF 1670	Carbon from Sondage 2, Level IV	3600 ± 150 B.C.
GIF 1610	Carbon from Sondage 2, Level II	3400 ± 200 B.C.
GIF 1280	Carbon from Sondage 1, Level III	3520 ± 150 B.C.
Kephala[3] (half-life 5570)		
P 1280	Seeds	2876 ± 56 B.C.
Franchthi Cave[4] (half-life 5570)		
P 1662	Early Late Neolithic or Late Middle Neolithic	4741 ± 81 B.C.
P 1661	Late Neolithic	4206 ± 70 B.C.
P 1630	Late Neolithic	4160 ± 86 B.C.
P 1660	Late Neolithic	3311 ± 64 B.C.
P 1659	Very Late Neolithic	3213 ± 78 B.C.

[1] Evans and Renfrew (1968), p. 184.
[2] Lambert (1970), p. 761; cf. Delibrias, Guillier and Labeyrie (1974), pp. 54–55, where several other dates from the Kitsos cave are also reported.
[3] Stuckenrath and Lawn (1969), p. 156.
[4] Lawn (1971), pp. 364–365.

[46] A third possibility, that the dates from elsewhere are in error, can, I think, be discounted, given their number and consistency with one another.

SUMMARY

A small group of people, probably no more than 50 in number, settled on the rocky but easily defensible headland of Kephala toward the end of the fourth millennium. Similar groups of people evidently settled elsewhere on Keos at Paoura and Sykamia about the same time (Appendix 6). The settlers may have come from Attica or from elsewhere on the mainland of Greece (were they refugees, driven out by the unsettled conditions which attended the final breakdown of Neolithic culture?).

In the course of time the settlers at Kephala built their houses over much of the promontory, especially on the southern slope, sheltered from the prevailing wind. The walls of the houses were probably built entirely of stones (except where bedrock scarps were utilized). Some houses may have had several rooms, usually small and rectangular in plan. Occasionally rooms were of quite large dimensions (House Y in Area L).

The people of Kephala kept domestic sheep, goats, pigs and cattle; shell fish, and probably other fish as well, formed an important part of their diet (Appendix 4), and may have contributed to the excellence of their teeth (Appendix 5). They also raised crops of barley and grass peas (Appendix 3).

The dead were buried in a cemetery near the base of the headland. The graves are the earliest with built walls known in the Aegean region. Infants were buried in jars; all others were buried either in single graves or in family tombs. The bodies were not consistently oriented. Grave goods, which testify to a belief in an afterlife, were not rich, but included two marble vessels.

Physically the people were probably mixed in type, as were other prehistoric Aegean groups (Appendix 5). Life expectancy may have been about 20 years at birth but adults often lived to 30 or 40 years. The settlement was evidently no troubled by malaria. One man survived a serious head wound and a subsequent operation.

The major communications of the people of Kephala were by sea. They obtained abundant supplies of unworked obsidian from Melos and manufactured crude, if serviceable, tools at the site. Copper ore was another raw material probably obtained elsewhere, perhaps at Laurion, and processed into simple tools (Appendix 1); Kephala is one of the earliest copper-working sites known in the Aegean. Marble vessels were probably imported ready-made from other Cycladic islands; flint tools may also have been imported ready-made.

Pottery, a few tools of stone and bone, and a few objects of terracotta were locally produced. A fine woven cloth, probably from woolen thread, and various types of reed mats are also attested at the site (Appendix 2).

Little can be said about social and religious customs. Burial customs suggest that the social unit was the family. The terracotta figurines, like those from other sites, testify to a belief in supernatural forces which can somehow affect the life of man, particularly in the matter of fertility. The enigmatic scoops, the most characteristic type of vessel from the site, may also have had a religious purpose.

The settlement at Kephala came to an end a century or so after it began. The archaeological record has left no trace of the cause of its demise. Perhaps people simply decided that living conditions were unfavorable at the spot and moved away; no other settlement, at any rate, was ever established there in later times. The first human activity at Ayia Irini, a more hospitable site near by, probably comes soon after the end of the settlement at Kephala.

APPENDICES

APPENDIX 1: EXAMINATION OF EVIDENCE FOR METALLURGY

Four pieces of slag, fragments of two crucibles, and one fragment of a copper tool were examined in November, 1971. Qualitative analysis was carried out by the X-ray fluorescence method. The results are as follows:[1]

1. Slag (Keos excavations sample no. 80). From Area D, unstratified. The graph indicates the presence of a considerable amount of iron (Fe) and a small amount of copper (Cu).

2. Slag. From surface, about 10 m. northwest of Area E (notebook XXVI, p. 142, no. 3). Iron and copper as in No. 1.

3. Slag. From surface, near Area D (notebook XXVI, p. 142, no. 2). Iron and copper as in No. 1.

4. Slag. From surface, about 25 m. north of Area D (notebook XXVI, p. 142, no. 4). Highly ferruginous, with a small amount of copper.

5. Fragment of crucible **175** (Kph.37). Pls. 22, 66. From Upper Cemetery; see above, p. 88. Slag adhering to the surface of the sample was analyzed and found to contain iron and copper. Tin (Sn) was not found.

6. Fragment of crucible **76*** (Kph.24). Pls. 22, 66. From Area L; see above, p. 40. Slag on the surface of the sample is ferruginous, with copper present in very small quantity.

7. Fragment of copper tool **147*** (Kph.3.15). Pls. 22, 66. From Lower Cemetery; see above, p. 79. Analysis showed this to be of copper, without tin but with a small amount of zinc (Zn) and traces of iron.

Conclusions

Slag in samples 1–6 was clearly not produced by a simple melting of metallic copper in crucibles, since in that process the slag on the surface of the molten material, even when flux is added, is not ferruginous and is very rich in copper, owing to the presence of copper oxide in large quantities. Slag of the latter kind may be expected to contain about 30% of copper oxide and pyritic acid from the pyritic fluxes.

Since the slag here in question is ferruginous, even within the crucibles, we must conclude that it came from the reduction of rich copper ore. One must suppose that the inhabitants brought in small quantities of such ore in the form of oxidized copper minerals and reduced it in crucibles at the site.

This supposition is supported by the following considerations: (a) slag was found adhering to the surfaces of crucibles; (b) the use of small crucibles indicates that the ore was rich; (c) since only small quantities of slag were found in this place, metallurgy would seem not to have been practiced on a large scale.

If original ores contain iron, the slag may also be ferruginous.

Supplement

In order to verify the analyses by the X-ray fluorescence method, Mr. M. Petris, chemist, also made for us quantitative analyses of samples No. 3 and No. 4 by standard chemical methods, with the following results:

	No. 3	*No. 4*
Insoluble (SiO_2)	67 %	56.30%
Fe	20 %	28.90%
Cu	0.5%	1.16%
Pb	0	0

[1] Copies of the original graphs and reports are on file at the Departments of Classics of Cornell University and the University of Cincinnati, where they may be consulted. [J.E.C.]

The copper is in the form of oxide. The quantity of copper is indeed small; this might be explained as a result of very intense reduction, i.e. through the use of much charcoal and heating to a high temperature.

C. Conophagos
National Technical University of Athens
Professor of Physics of Metals

Notes

A. In subsequent correspondence Professor Conophagos provided notes which may be summarized as follows:

It is clear that we are dealing with the working of copper at Kephala. The product cannot have been bronze, since tin is lacking. The small amount of zinc which was observed in sample No. 7 may be considered natural, present here by chance. Laurion was probably the source of the copper ore; even today azurite and malachite are to be found there, though in small quantities. In later times, as is well known, the mines at Laurion were exploited chiefly for silver-bearing galena, but copper ores may also have been recognized. If this was the case in our much earlier period, the copper-bearing substances might well have been carried to Kephala. The discovery of litharge in recent excavations at Thorikos seems to indicate that metals were worked there at least as early as the Bronze Age (above, p. 108, note 45).

B. Since this report was prepared, further technical studies have been undertaken on the copper objects and slags by R. F. Tylecote, Department of Metallurgy, University of Newcastle-upon-Tyne (cf. above, p. 4, note 10) and by Strathmore R. B. Cooke, Department of Geology and Geophysics, University of Minnesota. Professor Cooke examined two samples of slag collected on the surface at Kephala. In his opinion, the metallurgical processes which produced them are more advanced than would be expected at such an early date as the LN period. Thus it is possible that some of the slags were not so old as is suggested above. This does not, however, invalidate the evidence for LN metallurgy (stratified fragments of crucibles or furnace-linings; above, p. 4). It is hoped to carry out further technical examinations of the slags and to publish the results. [J.E.C.]

APPENDIX 2: CLOTH AND MAT IMPRESSIONS

The excavation of Kephala has made a valuable contribution to our knowledge of the textile arts in prehistoric Greece. Seventeen sherds with mat impressions have been found, while three bear the impression of cloth. Mat impressions are known from a number of sites in the ancient world, from the Neolithic period onwards, but cloth impressions are rare, and, in view of the paucity of actual remains of fabric in the Aegean area, are of especial interest.

THE CLOTH IMPRESSIONS

Techniques

The cloth impressions of Kephala cannot be profitably discussed without an understanding of some weaving terms and techniques.

Woven fabrics consist of two sets of parallel threads which are interlaced at right angles. The warp is the first set of threads, stretched out on the ground or on the frame of a loom. The weft is the second set of threads, woven in and out of the first set; the weft is usually in fact one long continuous thread doubled back and forth. The weft is sometimes called the woof, both words coming from the same root as the verb to weave. The selvedge is the edge formed at each side of the cloth by the weft, when it is turned back to be woven in the opposite direction.

A plain or tabby weave is the simplest, the earliest known, and still probably the most popular of all cloth weaves. A single weft thread passes over and under alternate warp threads, as in darning. The second weft thread passes over those warps which the first weft went under, and under those which the first weft went over. The third weft repeats the action of the first, and the fourth the action of the second (Pl. 46, E).

A loom can be mechanized by the use of a shed rod and heddle. The shed rod is a stick which divides the warps into two groups. Alternate threads are placed before and behind it, so as to preserve one of the necessary divisions or openings ("sheds") of the warp which are required for the weft to pass through. Half of the warps are thus in front of the shed rod, and half behind it. When the alternative division of the warps is needed for the second row of the weft, the warp threads at the back of the shed rod can be drawn forward, in front of the front ones, by means of a series of fine loops or leashes attached to another rod, the heddle. The heddle is movable, having two positions: one allows the back group of warp threads to remain in their natural position at the back; the other brings them to the front of the front group. If the weaver does not alter the position of the heddle after each weft row, two consecutive wefts will pass through the same opening of the warps, causing a mistake like that in **167*** (Pl. 90).

A shed rod and a single heddle are sufficient to produce a plain weave on a simple loom, such as a horizontal ground loom or a vertical two-beam loom, while the heddle alone is all that is required for a semi-upright warp-weighted loom. (For illustrations of these looms and the working of heddles, see Crowfoot, 1954, p. 426, fig. 269).

Examples from Kephala

167* (Kph.12; Pl. 90; see above, p. 82)

This sherd carries a negative impression[1] of a textile in plain or tabby weave, which had a count of approximately 11 × 14 threads per sq. cm. (28 × 35 per sq. in.). The cloth was perhaps slightly finer, though less regularly woven, than the cloth used in the other Kephala sherds, and it bears evidence of a mistake in the weaving which is of great interest. Two threads lying side by side may be seen running across the center of the impression. As the selvedge of the cloth does not appear, the mistake may be either in the warp or in the weft, but whichever is the case it provides information about the stage of mechanization reached by the loom on which the cloth was woven.

If each weft thread were being woven in by hand, as in darning, the weaver would have been obliged to look closely at the work, and a mistake such as two consecutive weft threads being passed over and under the same warps would have been noticed at the beginning of the second row, and corrected immediately.

If, however, the comparative sophistication of a shed rod and heddle had been achieved, a moment's distraction would have been sufficient to make the weaver forget to alter the position of the heddle for the next throw of the weft, and the mistake could have passed unnoticed until it was too far back in the work to be corrected.

In the same way, if a weaver, laboriously darning in the weft, thread by thread, had picked up two warps instead of one, the mistake would have been immediately observed, but if two warp threads were passed through one loop or leash of the heddle, it would have been possible to weave a reasonable length of cloth before the mistake was noticed. Even when the warp threads are correctly attached to the heddle, if they are close-set, two warps may stick together for a time, and this can easily escape observation.

It seems likely therefore that the loom used at Kephala was at least partially mechanized, and indeed some mechanization is to be expected with cloth of this quality. It would be possible to make cloth as fine as this on an unmechanized loom, but it would be remarkably tedious.

[1] Cloth impressions can be of two kinds—negative or reverse impressions, such as are left when an object is pushed into a matrix and then decays or is removed, leaving a mold; and positive impressions, which are those in which the fabric, while retaining the appearance of the original textile, has actually been replaced by a metal oxide or carbonate of lime (for examples see Henshall, 1950, pp. 130–131).

201 (Kph.21; Pl. 90; see above, p. 93)

Four fragments are inventoried under this number: a comparatively large body sherd, **201** A, and three smaller sherds, **201** B, C and D. The three smaller sherds have flaked away from the surface of the larger one, disclosing the impression of the cloth which was sandwiched between two layers of clay. We thus have a negative impression of each side of this piece of cloth.

The two larger of the sherds which flaked off, **201** B and C, show a fabric in a plain, rather open weave of very fine yarn, with approximately equal numbers of threads in the warp and weft (9–10 × 11 threads per sq. cm. = 23–25 × 28 threads per sq. in.). It is again impossible to decide which set of threads is the warp and which the weft, as no impression of the selvedge is preserved.

The smallest sherd, **201** D, bears the impression of an apparently thicker thread and closer weave, with a count of 11 × 12 threads per sq. cm. (= 28 × 30 per sq. in.), but the count may be inaccurate because the sherd is so small.

The impression on the large sherd, **201** A, is that of the other side of the fabric, and here again the individual threads appear thicker and the weave closer, as though the cloth had become rather felted or matted on this side. The thread count varies, being sometimes as high as 10–12 × 14 threads per sq. cm. (= 25–30 × 35 per sq. in.) but this is not a major discrepancy, and the count on handwoven cloth is likely to exhibit slight variations.

The small sherds **201** B and C bear considerably deeper and clearer impressions than the other two, and the casts taken from them should probably be regarded as the best indicators of the original appearance of the fabric.

The sherds **201** A and B each have two marks left by individual threads as well as the impression of the cloth, and this suggests that the fabric had been ripped or torn, and had loose threads hanging from it when it was built into the body of the pot.

213* (Kph.17; Pl. 90; see above, p. 97)

The cloth which left its impression on this sherd was also a plain or tabby weave of fine thread, evenly woven, very similar to the textile used in the **201** sherds, above. The impression is somewhat indistinct, but the cloth appears to have had a count of approximately 12 × 12 threads per sq. cm. (= 30 × 30 per sq. in.). Again there is no selvedge. The illustration shows clearly how the cloth impression is enclosed within the sherd, and has only been exposed by a fortunate break.

Cloth in Prehistoric Greece

The cloth impressions are a welcome addition to the small body of direct evidence for cloth in pre-Classical Greece, as the climatic conditions of the country do not favor the preservation of textiles.

At present, this evidence consists of a Middle Neolithic cloth impression from Sitagroi, not yet fully published (Renfrew, 1972, p. 351); a scrap of cloth adhering to a bronze dagger from an Early Cycladic tomb in Amorgos[2] (Tsountas, 1898, col. 154, T.14, pl. 12, 8 for the dagger, and Zisis, 1954, p. 587, note 2 for the cloth); remains from textiles used to wrap pottery, utensils and weapons, and scabbards in the two grave circles at Mycenae (Mylonas, 1973, pp. 22, 32, 38, 49, 88, 171, 172, 314, 326, pls. 20, β, 25, 148, β, 150, α, β, γ; Schliemann, 1878, p. 283; Karo, 1930, pp. 71, 137, 142, 145, 251, 284, pls. LXXII, CXLVI, CXLVII); cloth found in a lamp in a chamber tomb at Dendra (Persson, 1931, pp. 77, 94, pl. XXXII, 4); textile remains from a tholos tomb at Kazarma in the Argolid (Protonotariou-Deïlaki, 1969, p. 4); a blanket, cloak, or mat (blue with red borders) placed under a skeleton in the tholos tomb at Routzi in Messenia, which was a mere film of color when found[3] (Marinatos, 1967, p. A 16, and note 68); a scrap of cloth adhering to a sword in the Chieftain's Grave at Zafer Papoura near Knossos (Evans, 1935, p. 866, fig. 852); and a scrap of canvas found in the Granary at Mycenae (Wace, 1921–1923, p. 55).

Finds of cloth in later times include those from Late Geometric Eretria (Bloesch and Mühletaler, 1967, p. 130); Geometric and Orientalizing Fortetsa near Knossos (Brock, 1957, pp. 86, 87, 97, 136, 137); and Classical Eleusis, Trachones (Zisis, 1954) and Koropi (Beckwith, 1954, p. 114).

[2] The dagger is on display in the National Archaeological Museum, Athens, Case 72, no. 4720.

[3] This may have been a rush mat; see Marinatos, 1957, p. 540.

Weave

The plain or tabby weave used in the Kephala textiles is the predictable one at such an early date. All the Greek prehistoric textile remains which are published in detail[4] are in this weave, as are most of the later ones.[5]

The same is true for finds farther afield. Plain fine weaves predominated amongst the world's earliest textiles, those from the Early Neolithic Anatolian site Çatal Hüyük, although other techniques were also employed[6] (Mellaart, 1967, p. 218, pls. 116–118). The earliest Egyptian textiles, from the Fayum (Caton-Thompson and Gardner, 1934, pp. 40, 46, 49, pl. XXVIII, no. 3; quoted by Crowfoot, 1954, p. 431, pl. 11A) and Badari (Midgley, 1928, pp. 64ff., pls. LIX, LX) are plain weaves, and it has been stated that all the fine linen of Egypt and the East was plain weave till *ca.* 2500 B.C. (Crowfoot, 1954, p. 431). The small quantities of fabric preserved in Cyprus throughout the Bronze Age are generally, when identified, in this same weave (Pieridou, 1967, pp. 26, 28; Åström, 1964, p. 112). Some of the earliest European cloth remains, those from the Swiss Lake Villages, are plain weaves, though others show a twined basketry technique (Vogt, 1937, p. 12, figs. 15–17; Crowfoot, 1954, p. 435).

The advantage of plain weave is that it is the easiest to mechanize, requiring only a single heddle, or a heddle and shed rod, whereas even such a comparatively simple weave as twill requires at least three heddles. This does not mean that a plain weave need be considered primitive; it is still one of the most popular in use today.

Quality and Fineness

The Kephala textiles were so fine and, except for the one mistake, well woven, that they do not suffer by comparison with either the scrap of cloth on the Amorgos dagger (the find chronologically and geographically closest to them in Greece) or with any but the finest of the Mycenaean textiles. Their thread counts are similar to that of the Fayum textile, 20–25 × 25–30 threads per sq. in. (Caton-Thompson and Gardner, 1934, pl. XXVIII, no. 3; Crowfoot, 1954, p. 431) and to those of the earlier Badarian textiles, the counts of which vary from 20 × 20 to 34 × 22 per sq. in., but they cannot match those of the finest of the predynastic Badarian examples, one of which has a count of 88 × 50 threads per sq. in. (Midgley, 1928, pp. 64ff.). The counts from the Swiss Lake Village fabrics, two of which were 30 × 30 and 48 × 35–37 per sq. in., (Crowfoot, 1954, p. 435), are also cmparable to those from Kephala.

Raw Materials

Four major types of natural fiber were known in the ancient world: wool, flax (and other bast fibers), cotton and silk; the last two may be discounted as possibilities at Kephala.

Although cotton was used very early in India (Mackay, 1931, p. 585), it was a novelty in Assyria as late as the end of the eighth century B.C. (King, 1909, pp. 339–343; Goossens, 1952, pp. 167–176), and although occasionally used, was not grown in Greece even in Classical times (Zisis, 1954, pp. 591, 593).

Silk, though it may have been introduced from Persia in the fifth century B.C. (Richter, 1929, pp. 32–33), is first mentioned in Greek literature by Aristotle, who seems to have regarded it as an innovation (*Hist. Anim.*, V, 19, 551, b, 13).

The use of either flax or wool, however, would have been practicable.

The world's oldest textiles, those from Çatal Hüyük, may be made of wool or mohair (Mellaart, 1967, p. 219; Helbaek, 1963, pp. 43, 44; Burnham, 1965, pp. 169ff.), although there is some disagreement about this (Ryder, 1965, pp. 175ff.). If these are of wool, the fineness of the thread and weave of the Kephala textiles need not preclude their use of wool, since the cloth from Çatal Hüyük is equally fine (Burnham, 1965, p. 171; see also Mellaart, 1963, p. 197, figs. 4, 5). Fleeces of some kind were available

[4] There are no details available for Dendra, Kazarma, and Routsi.

[5] No details available for Fortetsa; a textural variation in a basic plain weave at Eleusis; a plain weave afterwards embroidered with a pattern of lions in a diamond lattice at Koropi.

[6] These were "net-like" fabrics which were produced by matting rather than true weaving techniques (Burnham, 1965, p. 171, and figs. 1, 2).

at Kephala, as is indicated by the bones of sheep found at the site, and if the inhabitants of seventh-millennium Çatal Hüyük could utilize wool or mohair from their flocks and herds for spinning and weaving, there seems no reason why the people of Kephala at the end of the fourth or early third millennium could not have made similar use of the fleeces from theirs.

Flax, from the fibrous stems of which linen thread is made, is thought to be descended from a plant which is native to certain mountainous parts of the Near East and elsewhere (Helbaek, 1960, pp. 115–116; *idem*, 1970, pp. 211–213). It was being cultivated in Iran and Mesopotamia as early as the sixth millennium B.C. (Helbaek, 1970, pp. 211–213; Renfrew, 1969, pp. 151, 154–156), and in Egypt at the beginning of the following millennium (Caton-Thompson and Gardner, 1934, p. 49; Crowfoot, 1954, p. 431). Flax seeds occurred at Early Helladic Lerna in the Argolid (Hopf, 1962, p. 4), and, while they were not found at Kephala, it seems reasonable to suppose that flax could have been grown in Greece at that time.

Flax may be cultivated for the linseed oil obtainable from its seeds, as well as for its fibers, and therefore flax seeds alone are not sufficient proof for the existence of linen, but from the fifth millennium onwards there are remains of actual linen textiles from Egypt. The Fayum textile is of linen (Caton-Thompson and Gardner, 1934, pp. 40, 46, 49; Crowfoot, 1956, p. 431), and those from Badari are made from flax or an unidentified plant fiber (Midgley, 1928, pp. 64–67). The Swiss Lake Village textiles are linen (Vogt, 1937, pp. 45ff. Crowfoot, 1954, p. 435). Those samples of Cypriote cloth which have had the fiber identified are of the same material (Pieridou, 1967, pp. 26, 28; Åström, 1964, p. 112).

The same is true of prehistoric Greece. In each case where the material of a textile has been specified, it is said to be of linen. The cloth remains from Amorgos, Grave Circles A and B at Mycenae, and Zafer Papoura at Knossos are all so identified (Zisis, 1954, p. 587, note 2; Mylonas, 1973, pp. 22, 38, 49, 88, 171, 172, 326; Schliemann, 1878, p. 283; Karo, 1930, p. 71, no. 228, p. 142, no. 784, p. 145, no. 816; Evans, 1935, p. 866), although the method used for identification is given in only one case.[7] Although there is no direct evidence, I believe that the cloth which left its impression on **201**, as typified by **201** B and C, may have been of linen. This is suggested by the fineness and apparent smoothness of the individual threads, some of the impressions of which seem to show a slight "S" twist under 10 × magnification—but this is very faint, and cannot be claimed with any certainty. The "S" or anticlockwise twist is the one usually employed when spinning flax, as it follows the natural bias of the fiber (Crowfoot, 1955, p. 19). Furthermore, the rather open nature of the weave, with its approximately equal numbers of threads in the warp and weft, is an indication of linen—in fact, when a plain weave has equal numbers of threads in the warp and weft, it is known as a "linen weave" (Crowfoot, 1954, p. 428, fig. 270, A, p. 429). This suggestion is very tentative indeed; **201** and the other Kephala textiles could have been of either linen or wool.

The fact that fine cloth was built into the walls of coarse pots, presumably as a form of temper to strengthen the vessels, is an interesting commentary on the commonplace status of such textiles at the end of the Late Neolithic period in Greece.

Cloth impressions on potsherds may not be so unusual a phenomenon as they appear to be at present. Since they occur within sherds rather than upon them, and have only been exposed by accidental breakages, it is impossible to tell how many other sherds, or even whole pots, may be concealing other impressions. As one can scarcely advocate a squirrel-like cracking of sherds on the chance of finding a kernel of cloth impression, this must remain an enigma.

THE MAT IMPRESSIONS

Techniques

The crafts of weaving on the one hand, and basketry and matting on the other, are closely connected. The principles employed are similar, but because the materials used for making baskets and mats are much coarser than those used for cloth, results may be obtained much more quickly. Therefore it is

[7] The Grave Circle B cloth was submitted to microscopic examination by Papademetriou (Papademetriou, 1951, p. 203; Mylonas, 1973, pp. 22, 32).

often more economical and convenient to do all the work by hand, without any form of mechanization.[8] It is this factor which must have made comparatively complicated weaves possible in these media at a very early date. Thus, while the Kephala cloth was all in plain weave, the mats exhibited four different techniques.

Simple Twine[9] (Pl. 46, F)

To produce twined matting, a number of warps, consisting of either single strands or bundles, are laid out parallel to each other. Two strands are employed for each row of the weft. One of these is passed behind the first warp, and the other in front of it. They are crossed over, then passed one in front of and one behind the next warp, and so on.

This crossing of the two weft strands gives each twist of the weft a characteristic slant, which is of use when trying to establish whether an impression has been left by a plain weave or a twine.

Three good examples of this technique at Kephala are Nos. 7, 8 and 9.

Split Twine (Pl. 46, G)

This is a more interesting variant of simple twine. The warps must be arranged in bundles containing at least two strands each. The first two weft strands pass before and behind the first bundle of warps, cross, and pass before and behind the next bundle, as in simple twine. In the next weft row, however, the warp bundles are split, half of one warp bundle being caught together with half the next warp bundle. This produces a series of triangular openings in the warp, and the repetition of these two weft rows gives a pleasing overall "honeycomb" effect which is best seen in an open weave like that in No. 1.

Plain Weave[10] (Pl. 46, K)

Plain-weave matting is made on exactly the same principle as plain- or tabby-woven cloth described above (p. 115), although the use of warp bundles and multiple wefts, instead of single threads, may result in a different appearance (Pl. 46, K). This weave was not popular at Kephala, occurring twice at most. No. 15 is a possible and No. 16 a probable example. If No. 16 is a plain weave, it is what is known as a weft-faced weave, one in which the wefts are so closely packed that they almost obscure the warps.

Coiled Matting[11] (Pl. 46, H, J)

This technique, which was probably one of the earliest to be invented, has remained one of the most popular, and is still in use in many parts of the world today.

[8] For an exception, see Crowfoot, 1934, pp. 195ff.

[9] Twined weaves probably go back to at least the Mesolithic era (Clark, 1952, pp. 43–44, pl. II, b, c). Early occurrences in settlements include sixth-millennium Nea Nikomedeia (Rodden, 1964, pp. 605–606, fig. 9), fourth-millennium Tarkhan in Egypt (Petrie, Wainwright and Gardiner, 1913, p. 27, pl. XXV, 207), the Swiss Lake Villages (Keller, 1866, pp. 323ff., pls. LXXXIII-LXXXIV; Vogt, 1937, pp. 12ff.; Crowfoot, 1954, p. 421) and the Neolithic Cueva de los Murciélagos, Spain (Góngora y Martinez, 1868, pp. 31ff.; Ebert, 1925, p. 338, pls. 169, 170). They are in common use today.

[10] It would be natural to suppose that this simple weave would have been one of the most common in the ancient world, but on present evidence this does not appear to be the case. The mats on the house floors at Jarmo in Iraq seem to have been of this type (Braidwood and Braidwood, 1950, p. 193; Crowfoot, 1954, p. 418). Plain weave, but with four strands in both warp and weft, was used for bed webbing at mid-fourth millennium Tarkhan (Petrie *et. al.*, 1913, p. 24, pl. VIII, 8) and for mats (*ibid.*, p. 25, pl. X, 10). There are examples from the Swiss Lake Villages (Keller, 1866, pl. LXXXII, 3; Crowfoot, 1954, pl. 9, D) and Italy (Montelius, 1895, p. 46, pl. 2, no. 22). For an example of the great conservatism of matting techniques, and of continued use of plain-weave matting, see Petrie *et al.*, 1913, p. 25, pl. X, nos. 10, 11.

[11] Coiled matting and basketry are again probably pre-Neolithic in origin (Clark, 1952, pp. 227–229) and occur in the earliest Neolithic sites, like pre-pottery Jericho (Kenyon, 1956, pp. 504, 506, figs. 7, 9) and Çatal Hüyük (Mellaart, 1963, p. 198, fig. 10; Helbaek, 1963, p. 45). They continued to be used at Jericho (Ben-Dor, 1936, pls. XXXII, 33B, XLII, b, 33A; Crowfoot, 1938, pl. I, nos. 1–3) and at other Chalcolithic Palestinian sites like those at Ghassūl (Mallon, Koeppel and Neuville, 1934, pp. 91–92, pl. 39, 2, I and 4, II; Crowfoot, 1938, pl. I, no. 4) and those in the Wady Ghazzeh (MacDonald, Starkey and Harding, 1932, p. 5, pl. XXXIV, 10). Finds at Late Neolithic and Chalcolithic Hacılar show their continuance in Anatolia (Mellaart, 1970, Vol. 1, p. 165). They were found at many of the early Egyptian sites, e.g. the Fayum (Caton-Thompson and Gardner, 1934, pp. 42, 53; Crowfoot, 1954, p. 418), Badari (Midgley, 1928, pl. LX, nos. 10–15), and Tarkhan (Petrie *et al.*, 1913, p. 25, pl. X, nos. 1, 2). They were used in the Neolithic and Early Bronze Ages in Cyprus (Dikaios, 1953, p. 273, pl. LXXXII, no. 1180; Crowfoot and Crowfoot, 1950, pp. 380–383, figs. 274, 275). In Europe the technique was used in the Swiss Lake Villages (Vogt, 1937, pp. 9–11; Crowfoot, 1954, pp. 420–421; Keller, 1866, pl. LXXXII, nos. 3, 4), the Cueva de los Murciélagos, Spain (Góngora y Martinez, 1868, pp. 31ff.; Ebert, 1925, p. 338, pls. 169, 170), the Orkneys (Henshall, 1950, pp. 131, 152), etc. It is still commonly used today.

Mats and baskets of this kind are made by taking a long, flexible roll or core of grass, fibers or similar material, and coiling it around and around upon itself in a spiral, each new turn of the coil being attached to the preceding one by being sewn or bound to it—a factor which makes this technique far more akin to sewing than to weaving. The sewing "thread" or wrapping strip may be employed in several different ways. It may (a) pass around the latest coil and pierce a small section of the previous coil *between* the earlier stitches (Pl. 46, H); (b) it may pierce the preceding coil *through* the preceding stitches; (c) it may wrap right around the preceding coil instead of piercing it; or (d) it may repeatedly be passed around a single coil and knotted as in buttonhole stitch; then the sewing strip that attaches the next coil is passed through the loops formed by the previous sewing strip, and does not pierce the coil itself (Pl. 46, J).

The only certain impression of coiled matting from Kephala, No. 17, is not clear enough to indicate which of these four methods has been used, but the first (a) is the simplest, the most usual, and the most likely.

Examples from Kephala

There are seventeen mat-impressed sherds from Kephala. The techniques used to make eight of these mats can be identified with a reasonable amount of certainty: four are of split twine, three of simple twine, and one of coiled matting. For six of the remaining impressions a possible identification can be given: two seem to be of split twine, three of simple twine, and one a plain weave.

This indicates that the people of Kephala preferred various twined methods of mat making, although they were acquainted with other techniques. For warps they generally used bundles of soft, fine strands, perhaps very fine grasses, or plant fibers, and for wefts they used single, double (or split?), and sometimes triple, strands of reeds or grasses.

All counts of warps and wefts are approximate, both because the samples are often too small to give an accurate count to the square unit, and because of the comparatively large size of both warps and weft; also, the tension of the work may vary considerably within a single mat.

Split Twines

1. (Pl. 90, B; from Area D; see above, p. 24)

A very open split twine. The warp bundles each consist of four fine strands, which are divided into pairs. The weft strands are single. A gap of approximately 1 cm. is left between the rows of the weft. 2 bundles of warps (4 strands in each) × 2 twists of weft × 1 weft row per sq. cm. (5 × 5 × 2.5 per sq. in.).

2. (Pl. 90, D; from Lower Cemetery; see above, p. 83)

A very clear example of split twine. The fine warp strands are arranged in pairs. The wefts are thicker, and display in each twist the typical slant of twined work. The gap left between the weft rows is slightly wider than the thickness of the actual weft row, giving a very pleasing decorative effect. The whole is a fine piece of work. 2 warps (of 2 strands each) × 2 weft twists × 2 weft rows per sq. cm. (5 × 5 × 4.5 per sq. in.).

3. (Two fragments: Pl. 91, B, D; from Area D; see above, p. 24)

Exactly as No. 2, but slightly finer. Also displays workmanship of high quality. 2 warps (2 strands in each) × 2 weft twists × approximately 3 weft rows per sq. cm. (5.5 × 5.5 × 6 per sq. in.).

4. (Pl. 91, C; from Area D; see above, pp. 23–24)

Split twine with warps consisting of thin bundles of fine fibers, and a doubled weft. 2 warp bundles × 2 weft twists × 2 weft rows per sq. cm. (5 × 5 × 5 per sq. in.).

5. (Pl. 90, F; from Lower Cemetery; see above, p. 83)

The impression is faint, but possibly of a split twine with a double weft. 1.5 warp bundles × 1.5 weft twists × 2 weft rows per sq. cm. (3.5–4 × 3.5–4 × 5 per sq. in.). Possibly part of a twined circular mat.

6. (Pl. 90, M; from Upper Cemetery; see above, p. 97)

Uncertain, but a possible split twine similar to Nos. 2 and 3. 2 warp bundles × 2 weft twists × almost 3 weft rows per sq. cm. (5 × 5 × 6.5 per sq. in.). It is not possible to determine whether the warps consist of bundles or merely pairs.

Simple Twines

7. (Pl. 90, H; from Lower Cemetery; see above, p. 73)

Simple twine with double wefts. Mistake near top where one warp has been split shows that warp bundles consisted of two or more thin stalks of grass or similar material. Weft rows are closely packed, and have the typical twisted slant. 1.5 warp bundles × 1.5 weft twists × 2.5 weft rows per sq. cm. (3.5–4 × 3.5–4 × 6–6.5 per sq. in.).

8. (Pl. 90, O; from Lower Cemetery; see above, p. 83)

Simple twine with double wefts. Warp consists of bundles of soft fine strands. 1.5 warp bundles ×

1.5 weft twists × 1.5 weft rows per sq. cm. (3.5–4 × 3.5–4 × 4 per sq. in.).

9. (Pl. 90, N; from Lower Cemetery; see above, p. 73)

Simple twine with triple wefts with the characteristic slant to each twist. Warps again consist of bundles of fine strands. 1 warp bundle × 1 weft twist × 1.5 weft rows per sq. cm. (2.5 × 2.5 × 3.5–4 per sq. in.).

10. (Pl. 90, L; from Upper Cemetery; see above, p. 93)

Very worn. Could be either simple or split twine. Warps consist of bundles of soft fine strands. Double wefts. 2 warp bundles × 2 weft twists × 2 weft rows per sq. cm. (5 × 5 × 5 per sq. in.).

11. (Pl. 91, A; from Lower Cemetery; see above, p. 73)

Very worn. May have been a coarse simple twine. From circular mat?

12. (Pl. 90, J; from Lower Cemetery; see above, p. 73)

Very worn. Possibly a simple twine. Approximately 2 warp bundles × 2 weft rows per sq. cm. (5 × 5 per sq. in.).

13. (Pl. 90, E; from Area G; see above, p. 28)

A probable simple twine with double wefts; the impression is not clear. 2 warps × 2 weft twists × 2 weft rows per sq. cm. (5 × 5 × 5 per sq. in.).

14. (Pl. 90, G; from Area E; see above, p. 25)

A probable simple twine with double wefts, but again the impression is far from clear. 2 warps × 2 weft twists × 2 weft rows per sq. cm. (5 × 5 × 5 per sq. in.).

15. (Pl. 90, P; from Lower Cemetery; see above, p. 73)

Either a simple twine with a triple weft, or a plain weave; the impression is only two warps wide, so that it is impossible to decide which. 1 warp bundle × 1 weft twist (?) × 2 weft rows per sq. cm. (2.5 × 2.5 × 5 per sq. in.).

Plain Weave?

16. (Pl. 90, C; from Area E; see above, p. 25)

A possible plain weave. It could also be a simple twine, but the wefts do not appear to have quite the usual slant. The warps are apparently the usual bundles of soft fine strands, and the wefts are double and rather thick. 1 warp bundle × 2 weft rows per sq. cm. (2.5 × 5 per sq. in.).

Coiled Matting

17. (Pl. 90, A; from Lower Cemetery; see above, p. 73)

The core of the coil, which is visible in places, was made of several strands of soft fine grass or similar material. The sewing strip is broad in comparison, and seems to have been of a flexible material, often showing vertical creases where the stitches have been pulled tight. The stitches appear to pass around each coil and pierce the previous coil between its stitches, but the impression is not perfectly clear; see method (a) under heading "Coiled Matting" above; method (d) is the other possibility. 2 rows of coil × 2.5 stitches of the wrapping strip per sq. cm. (5 coils × about 6 stitches per sq. in.).

Purpose

Remains of both mats and baskets have been found in the very earliest settled communities, such as pre-pottery Jericho, in Palestine (Kenyon, 1956, pp. 504, 506, figs. 7, 9), Jarmo in Iraq (Braidwood and Braidwood, 1950, p. 193), Çatal Hüyük in Anatolia (Mellaart, 1967, pl. 119; *idem*, 1963, pp. 196–198, figs. 6, 10; Helbaek, 1963, pp. 44–45) and Nea Nikomedeia in Macedonia (Rodden, 1964, pp. 605–606, figs. 9, 10). Their origins probably go back earlier still, to the traps and nets of Mesolithic times (Clark, 1952, pp. 43–45, 226–227, 229, pl. II).

Pottery developed later, since heavy and breakable containers have no place in a nomadic existence. Even with the establishment of settled communities, there was often an aceramic or pre-pottery stage, when containers were of wood or basketry (Mellaart, 1967, pp. 215–216).

The older craft became serviceable to the younger when potters found it convenient to build their pots upon mats, and it is therefore poetic justice that much of our knowledge of basketry and matting is derived from their impressions on pottery.

There have been many discussions[12] on how and why potters made this use of mats; one school of thought maintains that the vessels were merely stood on mats to dry after they had been formed; the other maintains that mats were used as a primitive forerunner of the potter's wheel. While some of the lighter impressions may have been caused by the former use, it seems probable that the more common,

[12] See Myres, 1898, p. 179; Bosanquet, 1896–1897, pp. 61 ff.; Edgar, 1904, pp. 95–96; Tsountas, 1898, cols. 182–184; Crowfoot, 1938, pp. 3 ff.

clear and deep impressions were occasioned by building the pots upon a mat, whether the mat were used as a turntable or not. This would account for some very distinct impressions left on the bases of vases from the site of Phylakopi in Melos, which were frequently set down "quite away from the centre" upon circular mats of considerable diameter (Edgar, 1904, p. 96). It would explain why the majority of Kephala impressions show mats with straight warps, and would also provide a reason for the clear, deep impressions often left on pot bases by leaves. Where a pot has been centered upon a small circular mat, as was the case with No. 17 and possibly Nos. 5 and 11, the mat must surely have been turned like a simple forerunner of the wheel, a practice which has continued into this century (Crowfoot, 1938, pp. 5ff.).

Distribution

Mat impressions seem to have no geographical limits. Examples have been found from China (Ward, 1954, p. 133; Chang, 1965, pp. 507, 515)[13] and India (Dales, 1965, pp. 259–260) to the Orkneys (Clark, 1952, p. 228 and note 155; Henshall, 1950, p. 152). They have been discovered in Chalcolithic levels at the Palestinian sites of Jericho (Ben-Dor, 1936, p. 87, pl. XXXII, 33B, pl. XLII, 33A), Teleilāt Ghassūl (Mallon, Koeppel and Neuville, 1934, pl. 39, fig. 40, pp. 91–92) and in the Wady Ghazzeh (MacDonald, Starkey and Harding, 1932, pp. 5, 7, pl. XXXIV, nos. 10–12); in Neolithic Cyprus at Chirokitia (Dikaios, 1953, p. 273, pl. LXXXII, no. 1180); and in Late Neolithic Anatolia at Mersin (Garstang, 1953, pp. 34. 36, fig. 20, no. 14). In Europe, various settlements in Bulgaria (Petkov, 1960, p. 47, fig. 3, no. 4), Rumania, Yugoslavia, Hungary, Poland, (Clark, 1952, pp. 230–231) and the Swiss Lake Villages (Crowfoot, 1954, p. 421, pl. 9, D) adopted or invented the idea in their respective Late Neolithic stages, and at least one example is known from Bronze Age Italy (Montelius, 1895, p. 46, pl. 2, no. 22).

Turning to Greece and the Aegean,[14] the earliest mat impressions found in the area, and indeed some of the earliest anywhere, are those from Nea Nikomedeia, the sixth-millennium B.C. site in Macedonia. Another early northern example was found in a Middle Neolithic context during excavations in 1973 at Servia on the Haliakmon river.[15]

The practice really came into its own in the Late Neolithic period and the beginning of the Early Bronze Age. This fact is illustrated by finds from Tigani in Samos, Grotta in Naxos, Saliagos, and also in levels below the Athenian Agora (Immerwahr, 1971, pp. 5, 6, 23, 43, 44, pl. 1, no. 6).

It continued to flourish throughout the Early Bronze Age. Among the Cyclades, impressions have been found in Amorgos, Paros, Syros, and Melos (where the practice may have continued into the Middle Cycladic period). On the mainland, examples are known from Orchomenos, Eutresis, and Galaxidi in Central Greece; from Rafina in Attica (Theochares, 1951, p. 91, fig. 18); and from Corinth, Zygouries, Tiryns, and Asine in the Peloponnese.

A mat impression from Lianokladi in Thessaly belongs to a rather later period, having been found with both handmade matt-painted pottery and wheel-turned Gray Minyan ware.

The notable omission from this list is Crete. Edgar mentions one mat impression found at Knossos, presumably in 1903 or 1904, but says, "it has not yet been ascertained whether they are common in Crete" (Edgar, 1904, p. 96, note 1). They do not appear to be. Sir Arthur Evans makes no mention of them, nor are they apparent in any other publications of Cretan sites. In particular, none occurred at the completely excavated and very fully published Early Minoan II settlement at Myrtos, although one leaf impression was found (Warren, 1972, p. 239, pl. 83, D). At this site, however, a number of disks identified as potters' turntables were discovered (Warren, 1972, pp. 213ff., pl. 75); perhaps the Early Bronze Age Cretans had already progressed beyond the stage of building pots on mats.

The Kephala mat impressions are a valuable addition to the Aegean material in that they are among the earliest of the Cycladic finds, and show a greater variety of techniques than those from any of the other sites except Phylakopi in Melos.

[13] It is not clear from the text whether these impressions were only on pot bases or elsewhere on the vessels, but see also Crowfoot, 1954, p. 419.

[14] Specific references for most of the sites mentioned immediately below will be found in the succeeding section on comparisons.

[15] Mentioned here by kind permission of K. Romiopoulou and C. Ridley, co-directors of the excavations.

COMPARISONS WITH OTHER GREEK SITES

Having established the nature of the Kephala matting as far as possible, it may be interesting to see how it compares with the material from the other Greek sites.

The Islands

Tigani, Samos. Two impressions (Heidenreich, 1935–1936, p. 139, pl. 35, nos. 2, 3) were made by mats which had triple wefts like Nos. 9 and 15, but the warps, where visible, look as though they may have been single units. The weave may have been a kind of twill, but it is difficult to tell without casts from the impressions. The other two examples are too faint for identification (*ibid.*, pl. 35, no. 1; pl. 39, no. 7).

Grotta, Naxos. (Kondoleon, 1949, fig. 13). This appears to be a simple twine in a double weft, similar to No. 7 but circular.

Saliagos. All six impressions are of coiled matting; two at least appear to have had a soft core of fine strands, like No. 17 (Evans and Renfrew, 1968, pp. 71–72, pl. LV, nos. 6–11).

Chalandriani, Syros. This specimen (Bosanquet, 1896–1897, pp. 62–63, pl. V, no. 1), from an island comparatively close to Keos, is unlike any of the Kephala mats. It shows a "loosely woven fabric with a warp of thick single straws or rushes, crossed more or less at right angles by a thinner woof," i.e. probably a plain weave.

Amorgos was apparently the first place in the Aegean to have a mat impression published (Dümmler, 1886, p. 38).[16] J. L. Myres found another at the site called Τζή βίγλαις in 1893 (Myres, 1897, pp. 178ff., pl. XII). His description would classify it as a plain weave on a radial warp,[17] but in his illustration the mat appears to have been in twined work, probably split twine. Since, however, this judgment is based only on a photograph, whereas Myres had the actual sherd to work from, his opinion should not be discounted. The double weft, which so often appears at Kephala, was also used here.

Tsountas published another mat impression from Amorgos before the turn of the century (Tsountas, 1898, col. 167, pl. 9, no. 24)[18] and this does show twined work on a radial warp. It also appears to be split twine, but the weave is somewhat irregular, probably the result of adjustments to accommodate the increasing circumference of the circular mat. Like so many of the Kephala specimens, it had warps consisting of bundles of strands, and a double weft. Tsountas mentions that he found eight mat-impressed sherds in Amorgos and Paros, and these generally showed circular mats with radial warps (*ibid.*, pp. 182–183). His description agrees well with Myres'. Tsountas also published a leaf impression from Amorgos (*ibid.*, col. 155, pl. 9, no. 11a) and has one of the best discussions on the reasons for their occurrence (*ibid.*, col. 184).[19]

There are only two possible examples of twined work on a radial warp from Kephala, but No. 5 is so small and No. 11 so faint that both are uncertain.

Phylakopi, Melos, has produced the most interesting collection of mat impressions in the Aegean. As they were contemporary with Edgar's "geometric" pottery (Edgar, 1904, p. 95), which may continue into the early stages of the Second City at Phylakopi, some could be of rather later date than the other Cycladic impressions.

Circular mats, often of considerable size, were in use here also, and Edgar's description of the radiating warp concurs with those of Myres and Tsountas. Those illustrated by Edgar were made in a closely packed plain weave or simple twine, using a narrow single weft (*ibid.*, pl. VI, nos. 1, 3–5, 9).

Mats woven on straight warps also left their impressions. One of these, a probable plain weave in a double warp (*ibid.*, 1904, pl. VI, no. 2), is very similar to No. 16. Another, apparently a simple twine using a double weft (*ibid.*, pl. VI, no. 7), is reminiscent of Nos. 7 and 8. A rather open split twine using a single warp (*ibid.*, pl. VI, no. 6) is somewhat like No. 2.

[16] This excludes Schliemann's Besika Tepe (Schliemann, 1880, p. 667) as being outside the Aegean area proper.

[17] A radial warp is one in which the warps radiate out from a central point, like spokes from the hub of a wheel. It is used when circular mats or baskets are required.

[18] On display in the National Archaeological Museum, Athens, Case 72, no. 4726.

[19] For two leaf impressions from Naxos see Zervos, 1957, pls. 89, 91.

Another Phylakopi impression which shows a strong resemblance to the Kephala material is published in Bosanquet, 1896–1897, pp. 62–63, pl. V, no. 2. This again appears to be a simple twine with double wefts like Nos. 7 and 8.

Triple wefts were also used at Phylakopi (Edgar, 1904, p. 95).

The Mainland

Eutresis has two mat impressions on Early Helladic I pottery (Goldman, 1931, p. 88, fig. 111). Both show double wefts, and one is a probable plain weave, like No. 16; the other is either a split twine or an irregular plain weave on a radial warp, and does not resemble any of the Kephala examples.

The two Galaxidi impressions (Vatin, 1964, p. 562, fig. 3; p. 565, fig. 6) are the counterparts of the Eutresis ones, and the same remarks apply.

The only identifiable impression of those from Orchomenos (Kunze, 1934, pl. XXXIV, no. 6) seems to be a split twine[20] with a double weft and multiple warps (containing at least six strands each), which is not really similar to any of the Kephala finds.

Early Helladic levels at Corinth (Kosmopoulos, 1948, p. 61, fig. 45) produced a fine plain weave unlikely any of the Kephala specimens, a simple twine with a triple weft like No. 9, and a leaf impression.

Zygouries (Blegen, 1928, pp. 116–117, fig. 109) appears to have both simple- and split-twine matting on straight warps and also twined matting on a radial warp; single, double and triple wefts seem to have been used, double predominating; as the illustrations are an artist's impression, rather than a photograph, the identifications must be very tentative.[21]

The Tiryns impression (Müller, 1938, pl. II, no. 3) shows simple twine or plain weave in a single fine weft on a radial warp, similar to many of the Phylakopi specimens, and unlike any from Kephala.

Asine, in its latest Early Helladic levels, has clear examples of coiled matting like No. 17 (Frödin and Persson, 1938, fig. 172, no. 8), an impression of what seems to be a simple twine in double wefts on a radial warp, and another too faint for identification (*ibid.*, fig. 168, nos. 1, 2).

The open split twine displayed on the Lianokladi base (Wace and Thompson, 1912, p. 187, fig. 136) is very like that on No. 1, giving the same honeycomb effect—but the Lianokladi mat had a radial warp, and a fine double weft was used.

Nea Nikomedeia is rather far removed from Kephala, both geographically and chronologically, for a comparison between the matting of the two sites to have much validity. They are alike only in their preference for twined weaves. Twenty-eight of the thirty-one impressions from Nea Nikomedeia were of twine (Rodden, 1964, p. 605). One (*ibid.*, fig. 9) shows a simple twine on widely spaced warps, with its narrow doubled or twisted weft more closely packed than any of the simple twines from Kephala. The only other impression illustrated (*ibid.*, fig. 10) shows a flat twill weave[22] using the same material in both warp and weft, and possibly produced by plaiting, which is quite unlike anything at Kephala, or indeed any of the other Greek material.[23]

SUMMARY

This comparison shows many similarities between the Kephala mat impressions and those from other Aegean sites. The most obvious of these is the use of double and triple wefts. Bundles of fine warps are also very common, and the twined weaves were generally popular.

It is surprising that only one impression was found from a circular coiled mat, since this type is ideal for use as a primitive turntable (Crowfoot, 1938, pp. 3ff., pl. I, nos. 1, 2, pl. II, nos. 1, 2, pl. III, no. 2) and was the type favored at Saliagos (Evans and Renfrew, 1968, pl. LV, nos. 6–11).

[20] The other possibility is a 6/4 twill.

[21] But the artist is Piet de Jong.

[22] A twill weave is one in which the weft passes over and under set numbers of warps in a certain, changing order, instead of merely over and under single warps as in plain weave. This gives a twill or "herringbone" effect.

[23] This kind of weave was used at many early sites: Chalcolithic Jericho, Ghassūl, and the Wady Ghazzeh sites (Crowfoot, 1938, pp. 3ff., pl. I, nos. 5–7); Early Neolithic Çatal Hüyük (Mellaart, 1963, pp. 196–197, fig. 6; Helbaek, 1963, p. 44); Chalcolithic Hacılar (Mellaart, 1970, Vol. I, pp. 164–165, Vol. II, fig. 189, a); Early Bronze Age Beycesultan (Lloyd and Mellaart, 1962, p. 43, figs. 13, 16); and Late Neolithic sites in Bulgaria, Rumania, Yugoslavia, Hungary and Poland (Clark, 1952, pp. 230–231; Petkov, 1960, p. 47 fig. 3, no. 4). It is considered to have spread into Europe from the southeast, and to have remained an east European characteristic (Clark, 1952, pp. 230–231). It is interesting that no other examples of this flat twilled rush matting have been found in Greece or the Aegean except in the north, close to the geographical connection between Anatolia and southeast Europe.

Also missing from the Kephala repertory is the close-packed single-weft twine or plain weave on a radial warp, of which examples were found at Tiryns (Müller, 1938, pl. II, no. 3) and Phylakopi (Edgar, 1904, pl. VI, nos. 1, 3), which is again well adapted for use as a primitive potter's wheel.

These factors, and the straight warps which the majority of Kephala impressions display, suggest that the settlement's potters were inclined to regard matting merely as a convenient surface upon which to build their vessels, although they may sometimes have used small circular mats (those on No. 17 and perhaps Nos. 5 and 11) as turntables.

In doing so, they had reached a stage in the development of their craft which had been, or was to be, attained by their colleagues in many parts of the ancient world.[24] It is an open question whether the idea spread from one civilization to another, or whether it was independently invented in different centers. Whichever was the case in the Cyclades, the comparatively large amount of material that has been found in these sparsely excavated islands indicates that the practice was a very prevalent one in this region in the Late Neolithic and Early Bronze Ages.

As for the mats themselves, our knowledge of them in prehistoric Greece is confined to the random sample which has been preserved on pot bases, but this is sufficient to give a picture of variety in materials, versatility in techniques, and a degree of skill which, by the time Kephala was inhabited, needed no improvement.

With such craftsmanship at their command, the settlers at Kephala must have been able to equip their dwellings with floor matting, wall hangings, screens, baskets, and containers of whatever kind and in whatever quantity they desired.

October, 1973 — Jill Carington Smith

BIBLIOGRAPHY

Åström, P. (1964), "Remains of Ancient Cloth from Cyprus," *Opuscula Atheniensia* 5, pp. 111–114.

Beckwith, J. (1954), "Textile Fragments from Classical Antiquity," *I.L.N.*, Jan. 23, 1954, pp. 114–115.

Ben-Dor, I. (1936), "Pottery of the Middle and Late Neolithic Periods," pp. 77–90 in J. Garstang, "Jericho: City and Necropolis," *Annals of Archaeology and Anthropology, University of Liverpool* 23, pp. 67–100.

Blegen, C. W. (1928), *Zygouries, a Prehistoric Settlement in the Valley of Cleonae*, Cambridge, Mass.

Bloesch, H. and Mühletaler, B. (1967), "Stoffreste aus spätgeometrischen Gräbern südlich des Westtores von Eretria," *Antike Kunst* 10, pp. 130–132.

Bosanquet, R. C. (1896–1897), "Notes from the Cyclades, III: Textile Impressions on Aegean Pottery," *B.S.A.* 3, pp. 61–63.

Braidwood, R. J. and Braidwood, L. (1950), "Jarmo: A Village of Early Farmers in Iraq," *Antiquity* 24, pp. 189–195.

Brock, J. K. (1957), *Fortetsa, Early Greek Tombs near Knossos*, Cambridge.

Burnham, H. B. (1965), "Çatal Hüyük — The Textiles and Twined Fabrics," *Anat. Stud.* 15, pp. 169–174.

Caton-Thompson, G. and Gardner, E. W. (1934), *The Desert Fayum*, London.

Chang, K. C. (1965), "Relative Chronologies of China to the End of Chou," *Chronologies in Old World Archaeology* (ed. R. W. Ehrich), Chicago, pp. 503–526.

Clark, J. G. D. (1952), *Prehistoric Europe, the Economic Basis*, London.

Crowfoot, G. M. (1934), "The Mat Looms of Huleh, Palestine," *Palestine Exploration Quarterly*, pp. 195–198.

— (1938), "Mat Impressions on Pot Bases," *Annals of Archaeology and Anthropology, University of Liverpool* 25, pp. 3–11.

— (1954), "Textiles, Basketry, and Mats," in C. Singer, E. J. Holmyard and A. R. Hall, *A History of Technology*, I, Oxford, pp. 413–447.

— (1955), "The Linen Textiles," in D. Barthélemy, O. P. and J. T. Milik, *Discoveries in the Judaean Desert*, I, *Qumran Cave*, I, Oxford, pp. 18–38.

Crowfoot, G. M. and Crowfoot, J. (1950), "Impression on a Bronze Age Potsherd from Vounous, Cyprus," Appendix 8 in E. and J. Stewart, *Vounous, 1937–38*, Lund, pp. 380–383.

[24] Also in the New World (Myres, 1897, p. 179).

Dales, G. F. (1965), "A Suggested Chronology for Afghanistan, Baluchistan, and the Indus Valley," *Chronologies in Old World Archaeology* (ed. R. W. Ehrich), Chicago, pp. 257–284.
Dikaios, P. (1953), *Khirokitia*, London.
Dümmler, F. (1886), "Mittheilungen von den griechischen Inseln," *Ath. Mitt.* 11, pp. 15–46.
Ebert, M. (1925), *Reallexikon der Vorgeschichte*, II, 2, Berlin.
Edgar, C. C. (1904), "The Pottery," in T. D. Atkinson *et al.*, *Excavations at Phylakopi in Melos* (Society for the Promotion of Hellenic Studies, Supplementary Paper No. 4), London, pp. 80–176.
Evans, A. J. (1935), *The Palace of Minos at Knossos*, IV, London.
Evans, J. D. and Renfrew, C. (1968), *Excavations at Saliagos near Antiparos* (British School of Archaeology at Athens, Supplementary Volume No. 5), Oxford.
Frödin, O. and Persson, A. W. (1938), *Asine, Results of the Swedish Excavations, 1922–1930*, Stockholm.
Garstang, J. (1953), *Prehistoric Mersin*, Oxford.
Goldman, H. (1931), *Excavations at Eutresis in Boeotia*, Cambridge, Mass.
Góngora y Martinez, M. de (1868), *Antiguëdades Prehistóricas de Andalucía*, Madrid.
Goossens, G. (1952), "Le coton en Assyrie," *Annuaire de l'Institut de Philologie et d'Histoire Orientales et Slaves* 12, pp. 167–176.
Heidenreich, R. (1935–1936), "Vorgeschichtliches in der Stadt Samos: Die Funde," *Ath. Mitt.* 60–61, pp. 125–183.
Helbaek, H. (1960), "The Paleoethnobotany of the Near East and Europe," in R. J. Braidwood and B. Howe, *Prehistoric Investigations in Iraqi Kurdistan*, Chicago, pp. 99–118.
— (1963), "Textiles from Catal Huyuk," *Archaeology* 16, pp. 39–46.
— (1970), "The Plant Husbandry of Hacılar," in J. Mellaart, *Excavations at Hacılar*, Edinburgh, pp. 189–244.
Henshall, A. S. (1950), "Textiles and Weaving Appliances in Prehistoric Britain," *Proc. Preh. Soc.* 16, pp. 130–162.
Hopf, M. (1962), "Nutzpflanzen vom Lernäischen Golf," *Jahrbuch des Römisch-Germanischen Zentralmuseums Mainz* 9, pp. 1–19.
Immerwahr, S. A. (1971), *The Athenian Agora*, XIII, *The Neolithic and Bronze Ages*, Princeton.
Karo, G. 1930), *Die Schachtgräber von Mykenai*, Munich.
Keller, F. (1866), *The Lake Dwellings of Switzerland and Other Parts of Europe* (transl. J. E. Lee), London.
Kenyon, K. M. (1956), "The World's Oldest Known Township: Excavating the Jericho of 7000 Years Ago, and Earlier," *I.L.N.*, May 12, 1956, pp. 504–506.
King, L. W. (1909), "An Early Mention of Cotton: the Cultivation of Gossypium Arboreum or Tree Cotton in Assyria in the Seventh Century B.C.," *Proceedings of the Society of Biblical Archaeology* 31, pp. 339–343.
Kondoleon, N. M. (1949), «Ἀνασκαφὴ ἐν Νάξῳ», Πρακτικά, pp. 112–122.
Kosmopoulos, L. W. (1948), *The Prehistoric Inhabitation of Corinth*, Munich.
Kunze, E. (1934), *Orchomenos*, III, *Die Keramik der frühen Bronzezeit* (*Abhandlungen der Bayerischen Akademie der Wissenschaften*, Philosophisch-historische Abteilung, Neue Folge, Heft 8), Munich.
Lloyd, S. and Mellaart, J. (1962), *Beycesultan*, I, *The Chalcolithic and Early Bronze Age Levels*, London.
MacDonald, E., Starkey, J. L. and Harding, L. (1932), *Beth Pelet*, II, *Prehistoric Fara*, London.
Mackay, E. J. H. (1931), "Ivory, Shell, Faience, and Other Objects of Technical Interest," in Sir John Marshall, *Mohenjo-Daro and the Indus Civilization*, II, London, Chap. XXVIII, pp. 562–588.
Mallon, A., Koeppel, R. and Neuville, R. (1934), *Teleilāt Ghassūl*, I, *Compte rendu des fouilles de l'Institut Biblique Pontifical*, 1929–1932.
Marinatos, S. (1957), "A Magnificent Find of Homeric Gold and Gems from an Unplundered Tomb at Nestor's Pylos, including Superb Inlaid Daggers," *I.L.N.*, April 6, 1957, pp. 540–543.
— (1967), "Kleidung, Haar- und Barttracht," (*Archaeologia Homerica*, I, A' und B'), Göttingen.
Mellaart, J. (1963), "Catal Huyuk in Anatolia: Excavations which Revolutionise the History of the Earliest Civilisations. Part III – Pottery and Textiles," *I.L.N.*, Feb. 9, 1963, pp. 196–198.
— (1967), *Çatal Hüyük, a Neolithic Town in Anatolia*, London and New York.
— (1970), *Excavations at Hacılar*, Edinburgh.
Midgley, T. (1928), "The Textiles and Matting," in G. Brunton and G. Caton-Thompson, *The Badarian Civilisation and Predynastic Remains near Badari*, London, Chap. XX, pp. 64–67.
Montelius, O. (1895), *La civilisation primitive en Italie*, I, Stockholm.
Müller, K. (1938), *Tiryns*, IV, *Die Urfirniskeramik*, Munich.
Mylonas, G. E. (1973), Ὁ ταφικὸς κύκλος Β' τῶν Μυκηνῶν (Βιβλιοθήκη τῆς ἐν Ἀθήναις Ἀρχαιολογικῆς Ἑταιρείας, 73), Athens.
Myres, J. L. (1898), "Textile Impressions on an Early Clay Vessel from Amorgos," *Journal of the Anthropological Institute of Great Britain and Ireland* 27, pp. 178–180.

Papademetriou, I. (1951), «'Ανασκαφὴ λακκοειδοῦς τάφου ἐν Μυκήναις», Πρακτικά, pp. 197–203.
Persson, A. W. (1931), *The Royal Tombs at Dendra near Midea*, Lund.
Petkov, N. (1960), "Contribution à l'étude de la préhistoire de la plaine de Sofia," Археология, год. II, КН. 4, pp. 44ff.
Petrie, W. M. F., Wainwright, G. A. and Gardiner, A. H. (1913), *Tarkhan I and Memphis V*, London.
Pieridou, A. (1967), "Pieces of Cloth from Early and Middle Cypriote Periods," *Report of the Department of Antiquities, Cyprus*, pp. 25–29.
Protonotariou-Deïlaki, E. (1969), «Θολωτὸς Τάφος Καζάρμας», *Ath. Ann. Arch.* 2, pp. 3–6.
Renfrew, C. (1972), *The Emergence of Civilisation: The Cyclades and the Aegean in the Third Millennium B.C.*, London.
Renfrew, J. M. (1969), "The Archaeological Evidence for the Domestication of Plants: Methods and Problems," in *The Domestication and Exploitation of Plants and Animals* (edd. P. J. Ucko and G. W. Dimbleby), London, pp. 149–172.
Richter, G. M. A. (1929), "Silk in Greece," *A.J.A.* 33, pp. 27–33.
Rodden, R. J. (1964), "A European Link with Chatal Huyuk: the 7th Millennium Settlement of Nea Nikomedeia in Macedonia. Part II, Burials and the Shrine," *I.L.N.*, April 18, 1964, pp. 604–607.
Ryder, M. L. (1965), "Report of Textiles from Çatal Hüyük," *Anat. Stud.* 15, pp. 175–176.
Schliemann, H. (1878), *Mycenae, a Narrative of Researches and Discoveries at Mycenae and Tiryns*, London.
— (1880), *Ilios; the City and Country of the Trojans*, London.
Theochares, D. (1951), «'Ανασκαφὴ ἐν 'Αραφῆνι», Πρακτικά, pp. 77–92.
Tsountas, Ch. (1898), «Κυκλαδικά», 'Εφ. 'Αρχ., cols. 137–212.
Vatin, C. (1964), "Un site helladique ancien à Galaxidi," *B.C.H.* 88, pp. 559–568.
Vogt, E. (1937), *Geflechte und Gewebe der Steinzeit*, Basel.
Wace, A. J. B. (1921–1923), "Excavations at Mycenae, 2, The Granary," *B.S.A.* 25, pp. 38–61.
Wace, A. J. B. and Thompson, M. S. (1912), *Prehistoric Thessaly*, Cambridge.
Ward, L. (1954), "The Relative Chronology of China through the Han Period," *Relative Chronologies in Old World Archaeology* (ed. R. W. Ehrich), Chicago, pp. 130–144.
Warren, P. M. (1972), *Myrtos, an Early Bronze Age Settlement in Crete* (British School of Archaeology at Athens, Supplementary Volume No. 7), London.
Zervos, Ch. (1957), *L'Art des Cyclades*, Paris.
Zisis, B. G. (1954), «Βαμβακερά, καννάβινα καὶ λινᾶ ὑφάσματα τοῦ 5ου π.Χ. αἰῶνος. 'Αποδίπλωσις καὶ συντήρησις αὐτῶν», Πρακτικὰ τῆς 'Ακαδημίας 'Αθηνῶν 29, pp. 587–593.

APPENDIX 3: SEEDS FROM AREA K

A large deposit of seeds was found associated with a hearth in the Neolithic settlement at Kephala in excavations of 1965 (above, p. 32). Professor Caskey kindly allowed me to examine a sample of this deposit, which consisted of 22 grains *Hordeum vulgare* L. (hulled six-row barley; Pl. 92, a) and 300 seeds *Lathyrus sativus* L. (grass pea; Pl. 92, b).

The following measurements were obtained from these seeds:

		Length	*Breadth*	*Thickness*
H. vulgare	Maximum	6.0	3.0	2.6 mm.
	Minimum	5.5	2.5	2.0 mm.
	Average	5.7	2.9	2.2 mm.
L. sativus	Maximum	5.2	4.1	3.9 mm.
	Minimum	3.5	3.2	2.5 mm.
	Average	4.5	3.7	3.2 mm.

The find of hulled six-row barley is most interesting; in the earlier phases of the Neolithic in Greece emmer wheat was the chief cereal cultivated. Barley cultivation became much more common in Greece in the Late Neolithic and especially in the Bronze Age. It was the chief cereal crop at the Late Neolithic settlement at Saliagos near Antiparos (Renfrew, 1968); and the hulled six-row form occurred in quantity at Pyrasos in the plain of Almiros, Thessaly, in late Dimini contexts. The naked form of six-row barley was found also in Reinerth's excavations at Magoula Visvikis, Thessaly (Renfrew, 1966). In the Plain of Drama hulled six-row barley was cultivated in Late Neolithic times at Dikili Tash and at Sitagroi (Renfrew, unpublished). Today barley is the chief cereal cultivated on the islands of the Aegean.

It is interesting to find that the bulk of this deposit consists of grass peas—*Lathyrus sativus*. This is not a very common pulse crop in palaeoethnobotanical finds, although it is reported from Jarmo (Helbaek, 1965, p. 32) in the early seventh millennium, from the Early Bronze Age levels of the Aggtelek cave in Hungary (Neuweiler, 1905, p. 116), and from Neolithic sites in Switzerland (Helbaek, 1956, p. 292). It was found also in Troy II (Buschan, 1895, p. 208), at Lachish in Palestine (Helbaek, 1958), at Salamis in Cyprus (Renfrew, 1970) and in Italy in the Late Iron Age of pre-urban Rome (Helbaek, 1956, p. 292). It is also reported from the Ur III period at Tell Bazmosian in Iraq (Helbaek, 1965, p. 32).

The seeds of *Lathyrus sativus* are rather variable in shape: those in the middle of the broad, flat pod are truncated at both ends: those at the ends have one flattened end—towards the middle of the pod—and the other end is rounded or slightly pointed in profile. All the seeds are approximately triangular in cross section. The intermediate seeds have a greater breadth than length; the terminal seeds are often longer than they are broad. Helbaek (1965, p. 33) gives the following measurements for fresh seeds of these two forms:

Intermediate seeds		*Terminal seeds*	
Length	Breadth	Length	Breadth
2.66	3.16 mm.	2.50	2.58 mm.
4.00	4.66 mm.	5.25	4.41 mm.
4.66	5.09 mm.	5.92	4.61 mm.

On this basis it would appear that the Kephala seeds are mainly of the terminal kind—and perhaps that only two or possibly three seeds commonly ripened in the pods of the grass peas cultivated here. The 1½—2 inch long pods of this plant usually contain from two to five seeds.

In early deposits these seeds are often found as an admixture or cultivated in another leguminous crop: in Switzerland mixed with field peas, in Italy with horsebeans (Helbaek, 1965, p. 33); the only site found so far where they appear to have been cultivated as a separate crop is Tell Bazmosian. Here in Keos they may have been grown with the barley in a mixed crop of maslin. The seeds contain a dangerous alkaloid, and if not carefully boiled before eating, may give rise to the disease of lathyrism: paralysis of the lower limbs.

Thus we have evidence for the cultivation of both cereal and pulse crops in the Late Neolithic of the Cycladic Islands.

Jane Renfrew

BIBLIOGRAPHY

Buschan, G. (1895), *Vorgeschichtliche Botanik der Kultur- und Nutzpflanzen der alten Welt*, Breslau.

Helbaek, H. (1956), "Vegetables in the Funeral Meals of Pre-urban Rome," Appendix I in E. Gjerstad, *Early Rome*, II, *Acta Instituti Romani Regni Sueciae*, Ser. 4, 17:2, pp. 287–294.

— (1958), "Plant Economy in Ancient Lachish," Appendix A in O. Tufnell, *Lachish*, IV, London, pp. 309–317.

— (1965), "Isin-Larsan and Horian Food Remains at Tell Bazmosian in the Dokan Valley," *Sumer* 19, pp. 27–35.

Neuweiler, E. (1905), "Die prähistorische Pflanzenreste Mitteleuropas mit besonderer Berücksichtigung der schweizerischen Funde," *Vierteljahresschrift der naturforschenden Gesellschaft in Zürich*, pp. 23–134.

Renfrew, J. M. (1966), "A Report on Recent Finds of Carbonized Cereal Grains and Seeds from Prehistoric Thessaly," Θεσσαλικά 5, pp. 21–36.

— (1968), "The Cereal Remains," Appendix X in J. D. Evans and C. Renfrew, *Excavations at Saliagos near Antiparos*, Oxford, pp. 139–141.

— (1970), "Carbonized Seeds and Fruits from the Necropolis of Salamis," Appendix IX in V. Karageorghis, *Salamis*, 4, *Excavations in the Necropolis of Salamis*, II, Nicosia, pp. 318–328.

APPENDIX 4: ANIMAL REMAINS

All bone and shell fragments found at Kephala were examined, and the resulting identifications are shown in Table 1. With the exception of the important find of red-deer antler, all surface material has been excluded from this report although most of it is probably of the same origin.

TABLE 1. Numbers of fragments and individuals

Species	number of fragments	minimum number of individuals[1]	probable number of individuals
CATTLE	85	5 (calcaneum)	31
SHEEP + GOAT	883	38 (L. humerus)	132
including: SHEEP	55	7 (R. radius)	36
GOAT	63	9 (L. humerus)	38
PIG	99	6 (scapula & mandible)	42
RED DEER	1 group[2]	1	
FISH	1 vertebra	1	
MOLLUSCS	250	229	

[1] The bone used to calculate the minimum number is given in parentheses.
[2] This "group" is a collection of fragments probably all from the same antler.

The bones were often firmly encrusted with rock and soil. At first a very dilute solution of acetic acid was used to dislodge this, but later a solution of citric acid was found to be more effective. The removal of the encrustation is necessary where measurements are needed, and it sometimes reveals cuts and scratches on the bones which suggest that many of the bones are the remains of butchery and meals. Where not encrusted the bones are often in good condition and the drying which must have occurred after excavation does not seem to have harmed them. Other bones, however, are very fragmentary and worn (see detailed note below).

Minimum Number of Individuals

The second column in Table 1 shows the minimum number of individual animals which could be represented by the fragments, followed by the name of the bone which yielded this information. It is usual in reports of this kind to quote a "minimum number of individuals" for each species in an area by taking the number of the most common bone (e.g., the number of left humeri). Adjustments are made where there is additional evidence of animals' ages from this and other bones of the body, to make sure that each individual for which there is some evidence is included in the minimum number.

With such small numbers of cattle and pig bones there is little significance in such figures and it seems unwise to work out percentages for the various species. The evidence points, however, to roughly equal importance for the sheep and goat, and to their numerical superiority over the other domestic species.

Probable Number of Individuals

Many fragments are small and much worn. It is quite possible that some of them spent a long time on the surface before becoming buried, and were thus trodden on, kicked around, and acted upon by the elements, just as are the bones on the surface today in and around any rural community. Sometimes a more concentrated collection of bones is found which does not appear to have been subjected to this treatment. These facts and the distribution of the bones in the excavated area have been used to calculate a third figure for each species (see Table 1), called here the "probable number of individuals." It would be difficult to calculate a comparable figure for the material from a larger site where it might be impossible to view all the material at once and it is therefore little more than a personal estimate of the actual number of animals represented, arrived at after a detailed study of the bones themselves and the groupings in which they were found. It presumes that each animal at Kephala is represented by a very small number of bones, and that bones of the four species suffered in similar circumstances.

On some sites this is clearly not so; for example, the bones of the pig on some sites tend to disappear more readily than those of cattle, sheep, and goats—only the mandibles and foot bones may remain. At Kephala, however, all regions of the pig's body are represented. Table 2 shows the regions of the body represented in the remains.

TABLE 2. Distribution of identified bones

	cattle	sheep	goat	sheep or goat[1]	pig
horn core and skull	5 + 2 groups[2]	3	5	29	24
mandibles	1	1	1	63	18
loose teeth	–	–	–	72	–
ribs and vertebrae	13	–	2	62	9
forelimb	11	33	34	134	22
metacarpus	12	7	8	26	–
hindlimb	15	2	6	128	11
metatarsus	7	5	3	25	6
phalanges	10	4	4	17	6
other fragments	11	–	–	209	3
TOTALS	85 + 2	55	63	765	99

[1] The "sheep or goat" column here includes only those fragments which could not be assigned to one or the other species, unlike the "sheep + goat" column in Table 1 which contains all the sheep and goat bones found.
[2] These "groups" are of fragments which in each case were from a single skull.

A brief account of each species follows:

Cattle

Some bones are large for domestic animals, although a fuller analysis must wait for the processing of results from the Bronze Age material from Ayria Irini, which has recently yielded some large bones. A left distal humerus (Pl. 92, c, right) and a metacarpus fragment (Pl. 92, d, left), both found among the western group of graves in the Upper Cemetery, and a metacarpus fragment found among the central group of graves of the Lower Cemetery (not illustrated) are all just large enough to be possible examples of wild aurochs (*Bos primigenius.* Bojanus). They compare with material described from Lerna (Gejvall, 1969), Argissa (Boessneck, 1962) and other sites in Thessaly (Boessneck, 1956) as possible aurochs and are somewhat heavier in nature than the other bones.

There are two possible explanations for the large size of the Kephala cattle bones. First, Neolithic cattle tend to be larger than those of the Bronze Age and some of the domestic animals of Kephala may have been so. The later domestic cattle of Ayia Irini are by modern standards very small (a typical humerus is shown on Pl. 92, c, left, and a typical metacarpus on Pl. 92, d, center) and we must not be misled into thinking that these larger bones from Kephala represent enormous animals. They could be from just one larger individual—possibly a bull or draught animal.

The second possibility, that wild aurochs existedon Keos, can not yet be ruled out. These bones could represent small wild cattle or a transitional form. Keos and other Cycladic islands have an indigenous mammalian fauna which probably arrived there before the land bridges disappeared. What seems certain, however, is that once man became established on the island he would rapidly threaten the survival of such wild ungulates by deforestation and by the introduction of domestic species. These could have come with him or could have been descendants of the wild stock already there. We are coming to realize that much local domestication did occur and that often it was the idea of domestication which spread with man, not always the domestic animals themselves.

The measurements of the large bones are given below with comparisons from Ayia Irini. Figures in parentheses are approximations. All measurements are taken according to the methods of Duerst (1930) and are in millimeters.

TABLE 3. Cattle bones

HUMERUS	maximum distal width	width of trochlea
Upper Cemetery (Pl. 92, c, right)	(95)	84
large bone from Ayia Irini	(91)	85
usual range of Ayia Irini material	62–79	51–71 (Bronze Age domestic cattle)

METACARPUS	maximum proximal width	maximum proximal depth	maximum distal width	maximum distal depth
Upper Cemetery (Pl. 92, d, left)	(73)	(47)		
Lower Cemetery (not illustrated)			67	38
Large bone from Ayia Irini			(68)	36.6
usual range of Ayia Irini material	45–61	26–38.6	43–62.5	23–31
smaller Kephala bones:				
Upper Cemetery (Pl. 92, d, right)	55	36		
Lower Cemetery (not illustrated)			(57)	32.5

Of the individual animals represented there are two adults of at least 3½ years according to the fusion of the epiphysis of the heel bone. Another of less than 1½ years is represented by a mandibular fragment bearing the second and third milk premolars. The large bones mentioned above may represent at least two further adult individuals.

Sheep and Goat

The two species seem to be present in about equal numbers, but distinction of the bones was much hindered by their fragmentary nature. Whereas 100 % distinction is now possible for some bones from Ayia Irini, using the methods of Boessneck, Müller, and Teichert (1964), this has not been possible at Kephala, where definite identifications to one or the other species have been rare. The animals are comparable with Bronze Age domestic animals in their size and build, coming within the range of those found at Ayia Irini. Both sheep and goat were slender limbed. The two species were probably both well adapted to the hilly island and contributed in no small degree to vegetational changes.

The single male horn core of goat, found among the central group of graves in the Lower Cemetery, is of interest as, unlike the later material from Ayia Irini, it shows absolutely no twisting (Pl. 92, e, f). This type of horn core, called scimitar- or saber-shaped, is similar to that of the wild ancestor of the goat, the bezoar (*Capra hircus aegagrus*). That this particular horn core belongs to a domestic animal there can be little doubt: it has the almond-shaped cross-section described by Zeuner (1963) compared to the typical sub-quadrangular section for the bezoar. This horn core has an approximate basal circumference of 148 mm. The only other goat horn core found was a smaller, untwisted female one with a somewhat more flattened inner surface. The absence of twisting in a female horn core is of less significance, but it is interesting that the only goat horn cores we have from Kephala are of this more primitive type, as this may help to throw more light on the origin of those with twisted horns.

The most extensive evidence for the age of the individual animals comes from the mandibular fragments, but it has not always been possible to separate sheep from goat for these. The tooth eruption data for the left jaw shows one animal with the third molar heavily worn (4–6 years), 2 with medium wear (3–4 years), 12 individuals with the third molar (at least 2 years—some may be more), 1 with the second molar in wear (at least 15 months), and 9 with milk premolars in place (less than 18 months). One of the last group was probably less than 6 months old. The tooth eruption estimates are those of Silver (1963).

Pig

Pigs and piglets are probably domestic. This rapidly breeding animal is very important in the later Bronze Age economy of the island, and the measurements obtained from the Kephala bones are all in the range of those from the later site. It is not yet possible to rule out completely the presence of wild pigs. One or two of the Kephala measurements are high up in the range for Keos, but the key bones for the distinction of wild and domestic pigs are not present.

If wild pigs are represented they must have been considerably smaller than their Central European or Thessalian counterparts.

From the evidence of tooth eruption, three of the pigs represented were at least 2 years old and two were about 6 months old.

Red Deer

There was only one find, of antler, and this was not stratified. There is no reason why this find could not be of the Kephala period. Antler fragments are also common in the Bronze Age levels at Ayia Irini. In the absence of any deer bones to date there is no evidence that red deer lived in Keos. The antler could have come from the mainland or Euboea, where deer were probably numerous.

Shells

The 250 fragments of marine shell represent at least 229 individual marine molluscs, most of which were probably used as food or bait for fishing. Exact identifications are difficult because of the worn state of most of the shells, and because the soft parts are necessary for the identification of some species. A full account of the molluscs of Ayia Irini is being undertaken and a revision of some of the names given in Table 4 may become necessary if better preserved examples come to light.

Some of the species found are common inhabitants of the rocky shore on Keos today, and are used as bait by fishermen—notably the topshell and limpet. The limpets are often broken at one side, which suggests that they were pried from rocks: 90 limpets were found together in Area G (see above, p. 26). Many of the other shell fragments are small. This might mean that they were hit with a stone and the animal removed for bait—a common practice on Keos today.

The cowrie, penshell and *Murex trunculus* can all be caught by diving, or in fishing nets in the bays. Both murex could be used for purple extraction. Other shellfish such as Spondylus, a spiny, oyster-like species (Pl. 92, g), appear to live in deeper water, and it is not clear how these people obtained the shells. Even if the live animal were not within easy reach (and storms could dislodge species which live in deeper waters), shells might be gathered from the beaches and used as tools. Some shells show signs of wear as if used in this way and in the Bronze Age large shells of Spondylus were sometimes made into objects.

Triton remains are relatively common (Pl. 92, h, j) and would provide food (if these were caught locally) and a tough shell with many potential uses as containers or even as lamps. Small fragments of triton shell were used for scraping.

In conclusion, the animal material from Kephala sheds a little more light on the economy of what seems to have been a simple farming/fishing community. We are seeing an incomplete picture as far as the animal remains are concerned: bones of fish and those of very young mammals have almost completely disappeared so that it is impossible to guess at the relative importance played by the different types of food. All we can say is that at that time the land was rich enough to support domestic cattle, pigs, sheep and goats which showed some interesting differences from those in later periods on Keos.

Jennie Coy

TABLE 4. Marine molluscs

Species		number of fragments
LIMPETS	*Patella caerulea* L.	94
	Patella lusitanica Gmelin	53
	Patella sp.	7
MUREX	*Murex trunculus* L.	11
	Murex brandaris (L)	3
TRITON	*Charonia* sp.	31
TOPSHELL	*Monodonta turbinata*	10
HORNSHELL	*Cerithium vulgatum* L.	3
COWRIE	*Cypraea lurida* L.	1
ABALONE	*Haliotis lamellosa* Lamarck	1
	Spondylus gaederopus L.	9
PEN SHELL	*Pinna nobilis* L.	3
ARK SHELL	*Arca noae* L.	2
	Barbatia barbata L.	1
COCKLES	*Acanthocardia tuberculata* (L)	1
	Cerastoderma edule (L)	1
	cockle sp.	2
OYSTER	*Ostrea edulis* L.	1
OTHER BIVALVES	*Glycymeris violacescens* Lamarck	2
	Lima (*Lima*) *lima* (L)	1
	Venus (*Venus*) *verrucosa* L.	1
	Venerupis decussata (L)	1
	Unidentified shell fragments	11
	Total number of fragments	250

BIBLIOGRAPHY

Boessneck, J. (1956), "Zu den Tierknochen aus neolithischen Siedlungen Thessaliens," *Bericht der Römisch Germanischen Kommission* 36, pp. 1–51.

— (1962), "Die Tierreste aus der Argissa-Magula vom präkeramischen Neolithikum bis zur mittleren Bronzezeit," *Die deutschen Ausgrabungen auf der Argissa-Magula in Thessalien*, I (*Beiträge zur ur- und frühgeschichtlichen Archäologie des Mittelmeer-Kulturraumes*, 2), Bonn, pp. 27–99.

Boessneck, J., Müller, H.-H. and Teichert, M. (1964), "Osteologische Unterscheidungsmerkmale zwischen Schaf (*Ovis aries* LINNÉ) und Ziege (*Capra hircus* LINNÉ)," *Kühn-Archiv* 78, pp. 1–129.

Duerst, J. U. (1930), "Vergleichende Untersuchungsmethoden am Skelett bei Säugern," *Handbuch der biologischen Arbeitsmethoden* (ed. E. Abderhalden), Abt. VII, Berlin.

Gejvall, N.-G. (1969), *Lerna*, I, *The Fauna*, Princeton.

Silver, I. A. (1963), "The Ageing of Domestic Animals," in *Science in Archaeology* (edd. D. Brothwell and E. S. Higgs), London, pp. 250–268.

Zeuner, F. (1963), *A History of Domesticated Animals*, New York.

APPENDIX 5: HUMAN SKELETONS

Through the kind invitation of Professor John L. Caskey, Director of American Excavations on the island of Keos, and of Professor John E. Coleman, chief excavator of the Late Neolithic site of Kephala, I had the chance to study the human skeletons from this site for one week in August 1965 and 3 days in August 1969. For 2 days in 1965 Argyris Marinis mended skulls and in 1969 my wife helped as recorder. Grants from the American Philosophical Society (Penrose Fund No. 3750), the Wenner-Gren Foundation, and the Smithsonian Institution (Aleš Hrdlička Memorial Fund) supported these field trips, as well as Professor Caskey's generous provision of living and working space. I thank these people and institutions for their help and support.

We worked under an outdoor shelter with good space and light, using Alvar and Butvar solutions for mending. But as Plates 93–94 indicate, we could not restore completely, since the bones are much broken as well as incomplete; usually the ends of long bones, vertebrae and upper face bones are missing. This is a direct result of burials, often multiple, in graves on a rocky hillside and gulley area, as well as the time lapse of 5,000 years. If the soil had been less sandy and more acid there might have been no bones at all; as it is, only 13 out of 40 graves (about 1/3) produced no bones. Seventeen graves produced only one skeleton each. Only 5 graves contained 2 skeletons each. One grave, VI (16),[1] contained 4 skeletons. Two graves, I (14) and XIX (1), held 6 skeletons apiece. One grave, V (20), held 9 skeletons. And one grave, XIII (7), held 13 skeletons. The average (65 skeletons in 27 graves) is 2.4 skeletons per grave. This is almost certainly a slight underestimate. At Lerna (Middle Bronze Age in intramural burials) only 10 % of 235 graves lacked skeletons (Angel, 1971a) and at Karataş (Early Bronze Age pithos burials) only 24 % of 454 pithoi lacked bones (Angel, 1970). Hence preservation of bone at Kephala is measurably worse than at these somewhat later prehistoric sites and about what one expects in most archaeological contexts.

Demography and Health

At Kephala, Grave II (31), a disturbed jar burial, produced an apparently 4-month infant, *5 KeK* (with porotic hyperostosis) and a third temporal bone apparently of a newborn (*5a KeK*). Three other infants were single jar burials: *29a KeK*, an 8-month foetus from Grave XVII (8), and *41* and *69 KeK*, 6- to 8-month-old infants from Graves XXXII (23) and XXXVIII (32). Thus no infants came from graves with children or adults, and only 2 out of 5 were newborn: the number of infants (and the proportion newborn) are fewer than the 15–30 infants one would expect (Angel, 1969a, b, 1971a) in a prehistoric cemetery with 51 adults: I wonder what happened to infants when they died. Of the 13 empty graves, 4 are unmeasurable. One, Grave XXI (5), measures 70–80 cm. long and presumably contained either an adolescent or an adult, since the largest child grave, XXXV (37), is 79 cm. long and contained a 12-year-old, while the smallest adult grave, XXXIX (36), is 73 cm. long. Four of the empty graves are of adult size: III (30), VIII (21), XIV (15), and XXX (40). The remaining four empty graves, averaging 55 cm. long, are of child-adolescent size: XV (17), XVI (18), XXIV (27), and XXXI (19). One of these latter (XVI) measures 46 cm. and another (XXIV) measures 50 cm., but neither contained a jar for an infant. I suspect that, as apparently at Karataş, most newborn infants who died, presumably before any naming ceremony, were not buried formally in a grave, unlike the apparent situation at Lerna in the Middle Bronze cemetery.

There are 9 children in 7 graves and only 3 of these are single burials: XXVII (2) and XXIX (22) with young children, and XXXV (37) with a 12-year-old boy (?). Considering that there are over 2.5 adults per grave and under 1.5 children per grave (+.7 children in adult graves) the 4 (or 5) adult and 4 (or 5) juvenile graves lacking bones would add 10–12 adults and 6–8 children. Almost certainly the 9:51 ratio or 16 to 62 ratio of children to adults underestimates the true proportion of child to adult deaths by a factor of at least 2. Both child and infant bones last less well in the ground than adult bones, so there is no way to reconstruct the true rates of juvenile deaths. I think it quite likely that the infant:child:adult death ratio at Kephala was under 5:5:10 (1:2–3:10 observed) and that the Late Neolithic island pioneers were indeed healthier as children than the Early Neolithic people at Nea Nikomedeia (5?:8:10) or Middle Bronze Age people at Lerna (8:5:10).

Among the 51 adults, 4 females and 7 males come from 11 single graves. The remaining 40 adults come from 9 multiple graves: I (14), V (20), VI (16), X (9), XI (12), XIII (7), XVIII (3), XIX (1), and

[1] The enumeration of graves by Roman numerals is retained in this Appendix because the skeletons were studied, and numbered, in the order in which the graves were excavated. The Arabic enumeration, which follows the order in which the graves are described in Chapter III, is given in parentheses. Each skeleton has been assigned a number followed by *KeK*, which stands for Keos, Kephala. (The skeletons from Ayia Irini are designated *Kea*.) [J.E.C.]

XX (13). Since four of these graves (V, VI, X, and XIII) also include 6 children it is logical to assume that all 9 of these are family burials. The adult single burials are in graves averaging 107 cm. and multiple burials in graves averaging 112 cm. long. Hence it seems likely that many of the single burials might have held other family members not found because of decay of bone: at least 7 single graves are large enough to have been used as family graves, and 2 others, IV (26) and XXV (25), whose dimensions are uncertain, may actually have held more than one person. Of the 13 empty graves perhaps 5 might have been family graves. This guesswork suggests 22 families (9 +8 +5). If family graves were used for 2 or 3 generations and the period of occupation of the site was 4–6 generations and the average nuclear family size was 5 people, then there would be 10–12 families and about 55 people alive in the village. If at any one time 10 women were producing children at 2- to 3-year birth intervals it is possible that two infants could be born (and die) close enough together to explain jar grave II (31). These might also be twins, both severely anemic, with one living 4 months longer than the other. Population size, using Acsadi and Nemeskeri's Table 9 (1970) and assuming over 100 skeletons in 40 graves and a life expectancy around 20 years, would be less than half that estimated above.

Of the adults I can estimate the sex of 25 females and 21 males and can estimate sex and age of 21 females and 19 males (Table 3). The average adult age at death is 28.7 for females and 34.7 for males. This is a bigger sex difference than expected and male longevity may have been greater and female longevity less than at Nea Nikomedeia. Life expectancy at birth might be under 20. As Tables 1 and 3 show, there are surprising lacks of subadults 15–19 years old (though *19 KeK* is perhaps in this range) and of adults above 45. The accumulation of 13 females but only 3 males dying in the 3rd decade is striking and suggests strongly that death in childbirth is the reason for reduced female lifespan. There are no female pubic symphyses and only 2 male symphyses, so age determinations rest on suture closure and exostoses plus bone surface changes, and are less certain than is desirable. For the same reason no estimates of parity or fertility are possible, nor data on pelvis depth.

Body size is an indicator of healthy growth. Males *9 KeK* at 170 cm., *68 KeK* at 168.2 cm., and *71 KeK* at 166.6 cm., and female *2 KeK* at 152.9 cm. fit the upper part of the range at Karataş and at Lerna (Angel, 1970, 1971a). Apparently the Early Neolithic stature of 170 cm. (28) and 156 cm. (21) at Çatal Hüyük and 168 cm. (9) and 155.5 cm. (9) at Nea Nikomedeia (for males and females) was greater than the stature in late 4th-3rd millennium B.C. Greece of 162.6 cm. (7) and 150.1 cm. (8) at Nea Nikomedeia, Servia, Ayios Kosmas, Corinth, Lerna, Ayioryitika and Astakos. The male robusticity index (13.1) on 2 femora is normal; bones are not slender. Enamel growth arrests occur on only 1 skull, *68 KeK*.

Disease and Injury

At other early sites in the Eastern Mediterranean the skulls, and sometimes also the infant or young child long bones, show signs of porotic hyperostosis suggesting thalassemia or sicklemia related to presence of falciparum malaria (Angel, 1966, 1968, 1971a, b; Bruce-Chwatt, 1965; Allison, 1964). The mutation-producing *Plasmodium falciparum* is a recent one, perhaps even post-Neanderthal, and hence this parasite of red blood cells is poorly adjusted to its host and often fatal to children before they can develop their own antibody defenses. The various forms of abnormal hemoglobin impede this plasmodium's entrance into the red cell, but if through inheritance from each parent of genes for hemoglobin S (for example) there is too much abnormal hemoglobin, the red cells will tend to collapse and the person will be extremely anemic so that the bone marrow-space enlarges and sometimes death from anemia occurs. Deaths from falciparum malaria and from anemia balance: the abnormal hemoglobins are balanced polymorphisms. The (Mesolithic) latest hunters and (Early Neolithic) first farmers in the Eastern Mediterranean tended to build villages outside the forest areas and near water or marshes, especially with the water-level changes of the post-Pleistocene glacial melting (Butzer, 1971). Hence they were in a position to support populations of anopheline mosquitos, probably *A. sacharovi* or *A. superpictus* in sweet or brackish marshes or flowing streams respectively. At Franchthi cave, Çatal Hüyük, and Nea Nikomedeia (Angel, 1966, 1969c, 1971a, b) in the 8th to 6th millennia B.C., porotic hyperostosis (anemia) occurs in 33 % (2 of 6), 41 % (59 of 143), and 60 % (12 of 20) of adults respectively, though it is only slight in 1 plus 50 plus 6 of these 74 adults; among children and infants porotic hyperostosis is absent at Franchthi (1 young child), 22 % (2 marked and 7 slight of 40) at Çatal Hüyük, and 56 % (4 marked and 9 slight of 23) at Nea Nikomedeia. It is less by the Early Bronze Age: 0 marked and 7 slight (including 2 with only cribra orbitalia) of 14 adults (36–50 %) and 2 marked and 2 slight of 7 children (57 %) at Cheliotomylos, Corinth; 0 marked and only 3 slight of 24 adults (12 %) at Ayios Kosmas on the southwest coast of Attica; and 3 marked and 27 slight of 243 adults (i.e. 11 %), and 6 marked and 10 slight of 143 children plus infants (i.e. 11 %) at Karataş. At Middle Bronze Age Lerna porotic hyperostosis is clear-cut in 3 and slight in 8 of 73 adults (15 %) and marked in 7 and slight in 14 of 84 children plus infants (25 %). Yet at Early Neolithic Chirokitia in a rocky location in south-central Cyprus porotic hyperostosis is marked in 0 and slight in 4 of 36 adults. Its frequency lessens with advances in farming, and also a drop in sea level during the third to first millennia B.C., and also lessens at sites separated from obvious marshes or other breeding places for anopheline mosquitos.

On this basis I would expect a low frequency at Kephala, on a rocky headland with no obvious marsh even with higher sea level. The only definite example of porotic hyperostosis is the 4-month-old infant *5 KeK* from Grave II (31) (11 % of 9 children + infants). Diploë is thickened (4 mm. thickness above right orbit), the left humerus (incomplete 67 → [75] mm. long and 8 × 7 mm. midshaft) shows inflated marrow-space with narrow central cavity surrounded by unremodeled trabeculae as seen in Plate 94, k, and an ulna fragment also shows an unremodeled inner shell, as in infants at Nea Nikomedeia (Angel, 1966) and at Lerna (Angel, 1971a, pl. 23, *204 Ler*). Two or 6 % of 31 available adults (male *6 KeK* from Grave IV [26] and female *70 KeK* from Grave XXXIX [36]) show frontal and occipital diploic thickness of about 5 mm. They are each incomplete skulls without porosity on the preserved pieces so that they at most represent a trace of anemic change. There is some thickening also in *1* and *2 KeK*. Although the simplest explanation for anemia of severe and trace degrees in an infant and adults at Kephala may be thalassemia from marriages with people from an endemic malarial area, other causes are possible: hookworm, amebiasis, iron deficiency, erythroblastosis fetalis from incompatible blood-type.

Vertebrae are rarely preserved. Slight vertebral body arthrosis occurs in 3 of 6 males and 2 of 5 females—a 46 % frequency, perhaps less than expected. Limb joint arthritis is even harder to judge. It may be lacking. *71 KeK* does show a right ankle injury, consisting of button and socket exostoses on tibia and fibula at the back part of their syndesmosis, from a ligament tear or more likely from a wound. There are no healed skeletal fractures at all on the preserved fragments.

Out of about 31 skull vaults complete enough to judge, 2 show wounds, both males. *29 KeK* shows a shallow depression 16 × 18 × .5 mm. (deep) just to the left of obelion in the rear of the vertex area of the vault. And *17 KeK* shows a serious penetrating wound (Pl. 94, j) just medial to and above the right frontal boss. The small hole 8 × 11 mm. in size lies in the center of a 25 mm. diameter depression and has healed cuts all around it, as if to remove a projectile point. The frontal bone behind this is locally thickened to 12–14 mm. (Pl. 94, j, right) from lamellar and diploic bone added to the inner table of the skull, apparently as a healing response after an extra-dural hemorrhage and blood clot. This inner thickening and the local remodeling of the outer surface place the injury a considerable time before the man's death in his middle thirties. Hostile action is much more likely as the cause than a sailboat accident or similar hazard. If the injuring weapon had penetrated the dura it is likely that infection in the subarachnoid space or in the brain would have been fatal.

Dental disease is conspicuous by its rarity. If I double all data where only a jaw or only a palate is available and include all specimens with 12 or more alveoli preserved (6 or more for the 16 jaws or palates) there are 20 adult mouths useable with the following average results per mouth:

Number of alveoli available	22.95
Number of teeth lost after death	9.65
Loss of teeth in life	.90
Carious teeth	.15
Abscessed teeth	.05
Dental lesions total	1.05
M_3s suppressed	.20
Teeth unerupted	.10
Teeth available to observe caries	11.9

Thus only 1 tooth per mouth is diseased in contrast to 3.2 at Çatal Hüyük, 4.7 at Nea Nikomedeia, 5.3 on mainland Greece (Late Neolithic plus Early Bronze), and 5.0 at Early Bronze Karataş. Since from 30 to 27 alveoli are available for the other sites, the percentage of lesions among them goes from 11 % (Çatal Hüyük) to 18.4 % (Karataş) while it is 4.7 % at Kephala—not quite so great a contrast as the average numbers show. The reason for this dental health may be largely dietary. Fish have a relatively high fluoride content and in later periods may be the factor balancing the supposedly fairly high levels of selenium in Greek diet (Hadjimarkos and Bonhorst, 1962), as deduced from tooth-chemistry sampling. It is tempting to infer that the Kephala Late Neolithic diet was based on fish. But it is also possible that the soil of Keos is low in selenium and high in fluoride. High dietary protein (fish or meat) also promotes healthy tooth formation. Teeth wear averages medium (+), suggesting no excess of abrasive food. Only 1 skull (*71 KeK*) shows moderate periodontal disease; 2 show only slight disease and 6 show none at all, matching the rarity of dental disease.

Occupation

With regard to stress from occupation we have few data from joint areas (flexion effects at knee and ankle, extension effects at hip, etc.). But the low platymeric index at 74.6 (19) indicates strong hip-balancing and climbing muscles, the fairly high pilastric index at 109.8 (28) indicates strong quadriceps or knee-straightening muscles, and the rather low cnemic index at 65.9 (12) suggests strong deep calf muscles. The humerus, with maximum and minimum shaft thicknesses of 22.1 mm. and 19.1 mm. for 7 males and 19.2 mm. and 15.7 mm. for 10 females, is as robust as one would expect in a fishing plus farming group; the thickness averages only .4 mm. less than the considerably longer modern U.S. humerus and the humerus flatness index at about 84 is 5 units higher than the modern U.S. average at 79. Approximate U.S. averages for platymeric, pilastric and cnemic indices are 87, 109.5 and 70.0.

Morphology and Comparisons

The extremely fragmentary and broken condition of the bones means that there is one complete skull, difficult to restore, out of 10 (8 males and 2 females), which I can describe in terms of morphologic type as listed in Tables 1 and 3 and seen on Plates 93 and 94. Six of these 10 are Basic White (A), one Mediterranean (B1) with low-headed Eastern Alpine (C5) influence, one low-headed Eastern Alpine (C5), and two Mixed Alpine (E) with some A trend. This is only one fifth of the adult population and much too small a sample for the comparisons in Table 2 to be meaningful. The general Aegean trend for the fourth and third millennia B.C. (Angel, 1969b) is for smallish and only medium robust skull with medium breadth and height proportions, medium-wide forehead, small and rather linear face, intermediate nose, variably low orbits, and light jaw sometimes with rather deep chin. This is Mediterranean except for the laterality of the skull vault, and hence shows some parallelism with the divergence from the west and south found in Lower Egypt (Woo, 1930; Morant, 1925; Angel, 1972). There is much local variation. A really linear trend with low face is strong in Minoan Crete; Cyprus is probably more lateral, and Lycia is virtually identical with the general Aegean trend; all of these are peripheral perhaps. The Central Cycladic region is on the edge of being short-headed in comparison with greater linearity elsewhere on the islands, as I have stressed before (Angel, 1951, 1971a).

In this context Kephalans as seen in Table 2 are fairly large-headed, low-headed, deep-jawed, and rugged, suiting the predominance of Type A. Regionally they are a little more comparable to the Early Bronze people of Ayios Kosmas on the southwest coast of Attica than to those of the Central Cyclades (Angel, 1959). It is obvious from the demographic data for Kephala that each rather isolated and small island population of first settlers like Kephalans may not be a random sample of its source group (founder effect) and may change in a few generations through all the forces of microevolution, including mixture and random change (genetic drift) as well as selection. Subjectively, Kephalans seem fairly homogeneous, yet with the expected family similarities within each grave group; they seem less variable than the people of Ayios Kosmas (Angel, 1959). It is possible that the Kephalans are basically a blend of the mainland Middle to Late Neolithic population with whatever groups (South Cypriote or Anatolian?) gave rise to the Central Cycladic Early Bronze people. But data are simply too few.

DESCRIPTIVE NOTES, EXPANDING TABLES 1, 3 AND 4

Grave I (14)

1 KeK is apparently a short and quite robust male with divided chin form; ramus breadth is 31 (?) mm. *4 KeK* is less muscular, and *4a* and *4b KeK* are duplicating shaft pieces of femora and tibiae. *2 KeK* is an average-size female with a slight extra thickness of diploic marrow-space on 1 piece of skull vault; she has slight ankle flexion facets and sinuous tibia and bowed slender humerus. *3 KeK* is apparently a quite short female, fairly slender boned. 3 of the 4 useable occiputs are only slightly curved: the family might have been more like the Central Cycladic norm.

Grave II (31), Jar

5 KeK is an infant about 2 months old on the basis of left humerus length, incomplete, of 67+ mm. (perhaps 75-restored) but 4–6 months on the basis of almost complete milk-tooth crown formation but without roots beginning. Perhaps this is an undersized 4-month baby. Skull fragments are few but include both temporal bones and show diploic thickness of 4 mm. above the right orbit (porotic hyperostosis). The humerus is thickened and almost filled with unremodeled trabeculae (Pl. 94, k) and a fragment of ulna shows an unremodeled inner shell. The obvious interpretation is hemolytic anemia, most probably thalassemia or sickle-cell anemia as discussed earlier. *5a KeK* is a smaller temporal bone of approximately newborn development. If this plus tiny fragments are all that is left of the first or original jar burial, *5 KeK* could be a twin who died several months later, although very sick, and whose introduction disturbed the original burial. Both should have had the anemia, of course, in that case.

Grave IV (26)

6 KeK is a male with thickened diploë (trace of porotic hyperostosis) of the frontal but with the outer table too eroded for measurement; parietal thickness is only 5+. There is a pit at inion; the left coronoid process indicates a high ramus. The broken axis vertebra has upper lateral facet size 19 × 16 and very slight arthritic lipping of the odontoid's facet for the atlas; the lateral mass of the atlas is 20 mm. high and the upper lateral facet measures 13 × 25 mm. The rest of the skeleton is absent.

Grave V (20)

9 KeK is a muscular middle-aged male 170 cm. tall according to the left humerus, although femur and tibia guess-estimates suggest smaller size. Opposite ends of clavicles, with *ca.* 1/3 shaft overlap, suggest clavicle length (165) above average. Lumbar vertebrae 2, 3, 4 have anterior heights 26, 26, and 27 mm., posterior heights 28, 26, and 25 mm., and trace degree of lipping; size is average rather than large and curve average or less (vertical lumbar index 95–102). Right ischial and pubic lengths are 85? and 73? mm.; iliac breadth is 161? mm.; iliac brim and posterior segments are 57? and 62 mm. above extremely narrow sciatic notch; pubic symphysis is at phase VII (35–39 years old) transitional to VIII. Auricular surface is 60 mm. Calcaneus length is 78 mm. Ankle flexion facets occur on right tibia and neckridges, but no facets on the tali, indicating climbing or squatting. The robust low and ovoid skull vault (Pl. 93, k–m) has very narrow forehead and jaw and deep chin of median form, ramus 33– mm. wide with projecting coronoid, squarish angle (116°); and the missing face might have been narrow: type A3 (verging on F?).

10 KeK is a less muscular and younger man (pubic symphysis late phase V—27–30), possibly rather short. Ankle flexion facets are absent. The broken skull has average bosses, size and proportions (?), with deep, bilateral and average chin, ramus breadth 33 mm., perhaps type A (or E?). No teeth are preserved.

12 KeK is a slightly more massive, just middle-aged male with bony outgrowths just starting on the ilium, but not on the 5th lumbar vertebra (anterior and posterior heights 29 and 25 mm.). Auricular surface is 55 mm. Preauricular sulcus is absent. The low and sphenoid skull vault (Pl. 93, q) has narrow forehead above probably lowish upper face, possibly relatively broad nose, and very deep triangular-form chin: type C5 (tending toward F3). In the region of right stephanion there is an oval hole 23 × 33 mm. in size with the inner edge bitten out evenly but no external marks: clearly a post-mortem injury, though the cause is not clear.

7 KeK is a young female with thin skull fragments, arm fragments and strong gluteal crest and fossa. *8 KeK* is a young female, not short, with thick but not muscular bones and left clavicle 135? mm. The humerus head is 42 mm. Lipping is absent on the glenoid surface and 5th cervical vertebra. *11 KeK* is a slightly smaller and older female with olecranon perforation at the elbow and definite third trochanter. Left metatarsal I measures 57 mm. The chin is median, not low, and there is slight alveolar prognathism. *13 KeK* is a middle-aged female including a small rugged right molar, a right acromion process measuring 39 mm., phalanges, and scraps. *13a KeK* includes a right jaw ramus, breadth 30, with long coronoid. *12a KeK* includes humerus and tibia fragments of adolescent (or child?) size.

Grave VI (16)

15 KeK is a young adult male, not short, with many bone fragments. The oval glenoid surface is slightly lipped. Lumbar vertebrae 3, 4, and 5 have anterior heights 27, 28+ and 29+ mm., posterior heights 26?, 26, and 24? mm., and only a trace of lipping;

lumbar curve may be more than average (index 93–98). Acetabulum is large, with no arthritic change. Right metatarsal I is 62 mm. The low, long, linear and broad-based vault may have surmounted a lowish face: type A2? There is no prognathism.

14 KeK is a largish young adult female? with femur head 44 mm., tibial flexion facets at ankle, and slight lipping on neck vertebrae including average-size axis (A–P 50 mm., height 32? mm., odontoid 15? mm., facet 15 × 18 mm.). Lumbar vertebrae 3, 4, and 5 have anterior heights 26, 29 and 30 mm., posterior heights 25?, (25) and 24? mm., and no lipping. Lumbar curve is sharp (index 89–96). Skull fragments include a small right malar with strong marginal process, jaw with deep and triangular chin, definite alveolar prognathism and long coronoid and 4+–4–4 molar cusp count.

15a KeK, a child of 6–8, includes a lower right femur with breadth of 41 and a lumbar vertebra (anterior and posterior heights 17 and 17? mm.) with arch recently fused to body. *15b KeK*, a younger child, includes right ilium with brim and posterior segments measuring 22 and 34.

Grave VII (6)

16 KeK is a young adult male with rather deep left jaw corpus and molar cusp count 5–4–5.

Grave IX (11)

17 KeK is an almost middle-aged male, fragmentary, with a massive and well-filled ellipsoid skull vault and deep mouth area (nasospinale-menton is 70? mm.), triangular non-prominent chin, and slight overbite: type E2. Molar cusp counts are upper 4–4–3 and lower 5–4–4+. The healed 8 × 11 mm. hole in a depression above the right frontal boss (Pl. 94, j) I have already described (above, p. 136) as the likely effect of removing a projectile point which had produced extradural hemorrhage now seen as bone added to the inner surface (12–14 mm. thick). There are also post-mortem holes on each parietal bone.

Grave X (9)

18 KeK is a barely middle-aged female, with slight lipping on thoracic vertebrae, plus lipping on oval glenoid surface. The sacrum is homobasal and average in breadth (110 mm.). Skull fragments show an occiput with only trace crest. *18a KeK* is a second occiput.

Grave XI (12)

19 KeK is a very young female, with smallish and extremely fragmentary bones. *19a KeK* includes a skull fragment too thin to be adolescent or adult.

Grave XII (10)

20 KeK is a very fragmentary female skeleton with humerus head recently fused.

Grave XIII (7)

23 KeK includes odd male fragments, a bowed femur, a big radius with strong interosseous crest and metacarpal I 49 mm. long. *25 KeK* (S5) includes bone fragments of male massiveness with pronounced sciatic spine, and average-size low and linear ovoid skull vault with wide forehead (and face?). Chin is triangular: type A1? This resembles *27 KeK* (S7), a larger and high linear ellipsoid and gabled vault: type A2. *28 KeK* (S8) is an extremely fragmentary older skeleton, occiput, and right jaw corpus whose four posterior teeth were lost in life. *29 KeK* (S9), about the same age, has a comma-shape glenoid with slight lipping. The ovoid, gabled, well-filled skull vault (Pl. 93, g–j) has a broad forehead, huge mastoid processes, and average jaw with median non-projecting chin and molar cusp count 5–4–0: type E1. A depression 16 × 18 × .5 mm. just to the left of the obelion is a possible wound.

21 KeK (S1) is a young female. Metacarpal II measures 59. The skull includes little more than the right half, lacking the jaw, so that breadths are careful guesses. The ovoid and low vault, rather wedge-shaped in profile with deep cerebellar region, surmounts a low face, probably squat hexagonal in form, with average nose and ellipsoid orbits and possible edge bite (Pl. 93, n–p): type B1 with strong C5 influence, i.e. intermediate between the peripheral and central Cycladic trends. *22 KeK* (S2) is the skull vault and broken palate, only, of a young adult female. It is ovoid, fairly high, apparently type A3. Inion is a pit in form. Molar cusp count is 4–4–3; they are rather compressed mesio-distally. An edge bite is likely. The upper left Pm_2 is rotated 90°. *23a KeK* includes a very small neck vertebra and small tibia of a very young female. *24 KeK* (S4) is a young adult female represented by light long-bone and skull fragments. With its slight occipital curve and average bilateral chin and size, bigonial (92), the skull might resemble *21 KeK*. Third molars apparently were lost in life (?). *24a KeK* includes parts of another occiput and jaw and a heavier femur, not short, with strong gluteal attachment and third trochanter. Metacarpal 3 measures 62, metatarsal 1 58 mm. *26a KeK* is an adult right metatarsal 3 found with the child skeleton *26 KeK*; it probably comes from *23* or *24 KeK*. *27a KeK* is a female right ilium fraction with wide notch and medium preauricular sulcus, and left talus measuring 48, 38, 30 mm. (length, breadth, height) and lacking flexion facets.

23b KeK (S3) includes skull vault fragments with 2–3 mm. thickness apparently from a very young child. *26 KeK* (S6) likewise is just fragments of an apparently normal young child, with milk dentition complete and an M_2 with well-developed Carabelli cusp; permanent M_1 crowns are visible in their crypts.

It is remarkable that Grave XIII (7) contains so few postcranial bones. Did the need to bury many people lead the Kephalans to discard them?

Grave XVII (8), Jar

29a KeK includes scattered long bones and skull fragments (no teeth) of a foetus shortly before term; the right ilium brim and posterior segments measure (14) and (14) and the notch is wide.

Grave XVIII (3)

30 KeK is a young female of little under average size and average muscularity. Lumbar vertebrae 1–5 have anterior heights 23, 26, 26, 27, 29 mm. and posterior heights 28, 29?, 26?, 27, 21 mm., showing average size and fully compensating "straight" curve (index of 100.0). There are no arthritic or stress outgrowths on these or thoracic or cervical vertebrae or ilium or scapula. Sacral breadth is 110? mm. and form homobasal. The back part of the skull, preserved, shows average curves, average mastoids and crest, and fits types A or E. *30a KeK* includes adult scraps.

Grave XIX (1)

32 KeK is a male (middle-aged?) represented by long-bone scraps too lime-coated to measure, and fairly thick and not strongly curved skull fragments showing strong constriction above the orbits and average maxilla (type C??). *34 KeK*, a middle-aged male, has fragments of large long bones, unmeasurable, and of a skull with wide forehead and average jaw with triangular chin and bigonial breadth guessed as (104) mm.

31 KeK, a young adult female, includes much-broken long bones and thin skull fragments showing rather flat occiput, jaw with projecting triangular-form chin, and ramus breadth 31 m. (type C??). *31a KeK* includes palate and jaw fragments of a second skull. *32a KeK* includes bones too coated to measure, a right metacarpal 4 53 mm. long, and occipital and other skull fragments and a maxilla with very marked alveolar prognathism. *33 KeK* is a young-to-middle-aged, almost tall female whose fragmentary long bones include a right tibia with marked retroversion at the knee (17°)—a rough-country gait adaptation—right metacarpal 4 of 53 mm., and skull fragments with rather flat forehead and definite postcoronal depression.

Grave XX (13)

35 KeK is a young adult female, fairly short, with humerus and femur fractions and skull fragments with flat frontal bone, and upper molar cusps 4–3–3. *35a KeK* is a lower femur fragment too massive to be female (?).

Grave XXII (4)

36 KeK is a young adult male including crushed slivers of skeleton and skull and a jaw with low and median chin, some alveolar prognathism, bimental 46 mm., bigonial (98) mm., molar cusps 5–4–4, and a retained right milk m_2.

Grave XXV (25)

37 KeK is a young adult male with only slivers of scapula and other bones, and a robust skull having a pinched forehead and very strong lateral browridges and malar process, low and sharply curved occipital, massive mastoids: perhaps type A2 (or C5).

Grave XXVI (24)

38 KeK is a young (?) adult female with light, slender, and very scrappy bones and rather deep left jaw corpus.

Grave XXVII (2), Cist

39 KeK is a child of about 3 with completed milk dentition and no measurable bones. The relatively complete skull is warped in the ground, increasing its posterior flattening. Minimum frontal is 86 mm., bigonial 69 mm., bicondylar breadth 81 mm., bimental 36 mm. and ramus breadth 25+ mm.

Grave XXIX (22)

40 KeK is a child of similar developmental stage including a broken ilium and thoroughly crushed partial skull vault, quite thin.

Grave XXXII (23), Jar in cist

41 KeK includes femur, tibia, and right orbit fragments of an infant about 6 months old; milk incisor crowns are complete.

Grave XXXV (37)

42 KeK is an adolescent, possibly male sinc seciatic notch is medium or less in width and skull fragments fairly robust. The acetabular synchondroses are still unfused, M_2 erupted but lower canines still in crypts and upper canines starting to erupt.

Grave XXXVI (34)

43 KeK is a young adult female, much broken. Occiput is well curved with scarcely a trace of crest or inion, and sutuers starting to close. The left jaw corpus (height 30 mm.) is average. Molar cusps are 4–4–4.

Grave XXXVII (39)

68 KeK is a late young adult male (pubic symphysis just reaching phase 6, 31–34 years; Pl. 94, h) of average size and robusticity. Right clavicle measures 150 (?) mm., femur head 47+ mm., calcaneus 80 × 40 × 46 mm., metatarsal 1 62 mm., and lumbar vertebrae 2, 3, 4 have anterior heights of 28, 29 and 28 mm. Ankle flexion facets are clear-cut on tibia and talus. Arthritis is absent on vertebrae and limb joints and trace at metacarpo-phalanegal joints. The skull has an average-size ovoid vault (Pl. 93, a–f), not low, above a rather low square face (face breadth 129 mm., face height 114 mm., upper face 65? mm.) with tilted chewing plane (*ca.* 13°) and average jaw except for broad ramus (36 mm.). Orbits are rectangular and not high, (height 31– mm., breadth 39 mm.), palate large ([55] × 71 mm.) and nose intermediate (23– × 47 mm.). This fits type A3 with E1 and D3 trends, and is quite comparable with the Karataş population. There is slight jaw-joint arthritis; there is probably a slight overbite. Molar cusps are 4–4–3 upper and 5–4–4 lower. There are slight shovel incisors. Frontal boss thickness is 7 mm. with normal diploë 3.5 mm. thick. There are slight lines of growth arrest on the upper incisors (Pl. 94, g): 4 lines in 2 pairs, suggesting illnesses perhaps in the 3rd-to-4th year of childhood. The lower left 1st incisor alveolus shows a healed abscess with loss of the tooth.

Grave XXXVIII (32), Jar

69 KeK consists of only skull fragments of an infant 3–11 months old. Sutures show some denticulation but fragments are thin, 2.5 mm. near the sutures.

Grave XXXIX (36)

70 KeK, a middle-aged female, includes parts of humerus and femur and of skull with sharply curved occipital bone 8.5 mm. thick (diploë 5.0 mm.), suggesting only trace degree of porotic hyperostosis.

Grave XL (35)

71 KeK is a late young adult male with pubic area showing incipient bony growths and advanced sagittal suture closure. Size and robusticity are average; the calcaneus measures (80) × (44) mm.; metacarpals 1, 2, and 3 are 48, 70 and 71 mm. and show some asymmetry. The (left) patella has a marked supero-lateral notch (as often at Çatal Hüyük). There is little tibia tilt at the knee (9°), and flexion facets are clear at the ankles on tibia and talus. Button and socket exostoses at the back part of the right tibio-fibula syndesmosis suggest an ankle wound or perhaps a severe strain. There is no arthritis otherwise. The skull vault fragments are sharply curved except for the flattish occiput with sharply projecting inion. The jaw (after restoring a gap at the left of the chin) is remarkably wide (Pl. 94, e, f): bicondylar (130) mm. and bigonial 120? mm.! The jaw angle is obtuse (133°) and the muscular angles extremely everted (++++). There is a definite mandibular torus at M_{2-3} position. The deep and bilateral chin shows average prominence and the ramus is fairly wide: breadth 34 mm., height 54 mm. Bimental is 47? mm. Type C5 is possible, or perhaps F3. Teeth are healthy and not large, but periodontal disease is clear-cut, especially between the molars. Molar cusps are 5–4–4.

The Smithsonian Institution

J. LAWRENCE ANGEL

TABLE 1. INDIVIDUAL SKULL MEASUREMENTS FROM LATE NEOLITHIC KEPHALA

Grave number	I (14)	V (20)			VI (16)	IX (11)	XIII (7)		
Skull number	*1 KeK*	*9 KeK*	*10 KeK*	*12 KeK*	*15 KeK*	*17 KeK*	*25 KeK*	*27 KeK*	*29 KeK*
Sex	M	M	M	M	M	M	M	M	M
Estimated age (sutures)	30??	(45)	31?	(35)	25	34	44	33	42
Horiz. circum.		528??		515??		543?	520??	526*	
Sagittal arc		(379)		(330)			(365)	(390)	(370)
Frontal arc		128??		(120)		(133)	120??	135?	(130)
Parietal arc		137		(105)	120	140	120	139?	134
Occipital arc		(114)		(105)	118		(125)	(116)	(106)
Vault length, gl.-op.		185?	(185)	171?	(197)	194??	187?	198	185??
Height, auric.-vert.		111?		105	111??	(123)	110?	123??	119?
Vault breadth		141??	(140)	142	136	146	135?	133*	144+
Minimum frontal br.		91??		94		105	97??	97*	105
Bigonial breadth		(94)							(100)
Minimum ramus br.	31?	33+	33						
Chin height	36??	38	38	40+		39	33+?		33–
Cranial index		76.22??	(75.7)	83.04	(69.04)	75.26??	72.19	67.17?*	77.84??
Mean auricular		68.10		67.09	(66.67)	(72.35)	68.32??	74.32*	72.34??
Fronto-parietal		64.54??		66.20		71.92	71.85	72.93*	72.92
Morphology		A3		C5	A2	E2	A1	A2	E1

TABLE 1, cont.

Grave number	XIII (7)			XVIII (3)	XIX (1)	XXII (4)	XXXVII (39)	XL (35)
Skull number	*21 KeK*	*22 KeK*	*24 KeK*	*30 KeK*	*34 KeK*	*36 KeK*	*68 KeK*	*71 KeK*
Sex	F	F	F	F	M	M	M	M
Estimated age (sutures)	24	29	27	23	*ca.* 40?	(28)	33?	33??
Horiz. circum.	492*						521?	
Sagittal arc	(345)						367?	
Frontal arc	109??						128?	
Parietal arc	124	(135)					124	
Occipital arc	(112)	108?		116			115	
Vault length, gl.-op.	178?	175??					181	
Height, auric.-vert.	111?	115		142?			118?	
Vault breadth	139*	132					142	
Minimum frontal br.	95*				(104)	(98)	99	
Bigonial breadth			92				102?	120?
Minimum ramus br.							36	34
Chin height			30		34	31	33	38
Cranial index	78.06*	75.43??					78.45	
Mean auricular	70.03*	74.92??					73.06	
Fronto-parietal	68.34*						69.71	
Morphology	B1	A3					A2	

* derived by doubling measurement on one side only to midplane.

TABLE 2. SKULL MEASUREMENTS AND AVERAGE INDICES OF MALE SAMPLES IN THE AEGEAN REGION FOR COMPARISON WITH LATE NEOLITHIC KEPHALA

Period	Late Neolithic		Early Bronze				Late Neolithic		Early Bronze		E. & M. Minoan		Late Neolithic		Early Bronze	
Area	Mainland Greece		Attica		Corinth		Keos Island		Central Cyclades		East Crete		South-central Cyprus		Lycia	
Site	Servia Tsangli Athens Astakos Ayior-yitika		Ayios Kosmas		Chelio-tomylos		Kephala		Paros & Antiparos		Palai-kastro Patema Ay. Nik.		Sotira and Erimi		Karataş	
Horiz. circumference	504.8	6	518.9	10	510.4	7	525.5	6	513.1	7	515.9	21	513.0	4	512.8	44
Sagittal arc	374.3	3	381.8?	5	368.5	4	367.0	1	356.8	5			366.5	4	372.2	40
Frontal arc	124.2	6	129.8	8	128.4	5	127.8	4	126.0	6			132.5	4	126.3	50
Parietal arc	128.2	6	131.1	9	123.7	7	130.6	7	123.2	5			128.5	6	129.8	46
Occipital arc	117.5	4	118.7	6	113.4	5	116.5	2	116.4	5			113.4	5	116.5	39
Vault length, gl.-op.	180.3	6	186.6	10	184.3	7	185.9	7	177.9	7	186.4	64	184.8	6	182.6	52
Height, auric.-vert.	114.2	5	119.2	9	116.2	6	113.9	7	116.8	6	118.9	25	117.3	6	118.7	52
Vault breadth	134.6	6	141.1	13	140.0	7	139.9	8	142.4	7	136.8	50	141.8	6	139.4	49
Minimum frontal breadth	94.2	6	97.3	10	95.2	6	98.3	7	95.2	6	95.7	10	99.0	3	96.8	61
Bizygomatic face br.	124.3	3	(127.4)	8	127.0	2	129.0	1	128.8	5	122.5	5	128.3	3	130.5	33
Bigonial breadth	94.6	3	98.0	5	90.8	6	(103.0)	6	(99.5)	2			99.3	3	101.8	36
Minimum ramus br.	32.3	4	29.0	4	31.0	4	33.4	5	31.5	2			34.3	4	31.5	67
Upper face height	67.0	2	(70.1)	7	71.0?	3	65.0	1	67.4	5	65.0	13	69.3	3	69.4	33
Chin height	35.6	3	31.9	7	32.5	6	35.8	12	33.5	2			35.8	5	34.6	69
Nose height	47.0	2	(50.8)	6	48.3?	3	47.0	1	49.2	6	48.9	13	53.0	2	49.8	34
Nose breadth	23.0	2	(23.5)	6	23.5	4	23.0	1	23.7	6	24.2	10	24.7	3	24.6	31
Cranial index	74.8	6	76.2	10	76.0	7	75.7	7	80.2	7	73.4	*	77.0	6	76.8	47
Mean auricular height	72.5	*	72.7	*	71.6	*	70.5	6	72.9	*	73.6	*	71.9	6	73.7	47
Fronto-parietal	70.0	6	69.0	10	68.3	6	70.1	7	66.9	6	70.0	*	68.3	3	68.9	47
Upper facial	53.9	2	(54.7)	6	55.9	*	50.4	1	52.4	5	51.6	*	54.1	3	53.4	28
Orbital index	80.5	2	88.9	5	84.1	2	79.5	1	85.3	6	80.2	*	87.7	3	80.9	35
Nasal index	49.5	2	(46.3)	6	48.9	3	48.9	1	48.2	6	49.5	*	(46.4)	3	49.5	31

( ) based in part on uncertain measurements.
* calculated by means of measurements rather than individual values.

TABLE 3. BASIC DATA ON ALL SKELETONS (Ages all approximate)

Grave number	I (14)									
Skeleton number	*1 KeK*		*4 KeK*		*4a KeK*		*4b KeK*		*2 KeK*	
Sex and age	M	30?	M?	29?	M?	Adult	M?	Adult	F	28?
Bone shaft shape:	L	R	L	R	L	R	L	R	L	R
Humerus, maximum	–	20	20	–	–	–	–	–	–	19
minimum	–	18	17	–	–	–	–	–	–	16
Femur, platymeric index	75.8		74.2		80.6		–		75.9	
A–P	25	–	22	24	–	31	–	–	22	22–
Transverse	33	–	31	31	–	25	–	–	29	29
Pilastric index	115.4		116.0		108.7		110.3		113.0	
A–P	31	29	29	29	24	26	26	28	28	25
Transverse	26	26	25	25	23	23	25	24	23	24
Tibia, cnemic index	63.9		–		–		–		75.9	
A–P	–	36	–	–	–	–	–	–	–	29
Transverse	–	23	–	–	–	–	–	–	–	22
Cross-section*	II	V	II		–	–	–	–	–	V
Sciatic notch	–		–		–		–		–	
Arthritis: vertebrae, limb	–	–	–	–	–	–	–	–	–	–
Mastoid height	32	–	–	–	–	–	–	–	–	–
Chin height	36?		–		–		–		–	
Teeth loss	0		–		–		–		–	
Caries	0		–		–		–		–	
Abscesses	0		–		–		–		–	
Lesions	0		–		–		–		–	
Post-mortem loss	7		–		–		–		–	
Alveoli preserved	13		–		–		–		–	
Teeth wear	++		–		–		–		–	
Browridges	++		–		–		–		–	
Occipital curve	slight		slight		–		–		slight	
Remarks	lower molar cusps 4–4–5		–		–		–		–	

* Tibia shaft: form of cross-section:
I Prismatic
II Oblique prism
III Concave prism (lat.)
IV Rhomboid
V Convex prism (post.)
VI Plano-convex

TABLE 3, cont.

I (14)		II (31)				IV (26)		V (20)					
3 KeK		*5 KeK*		*5a KeK*		*6 KeK*		*9 KeK*		*10 KeK*		*12 KeK*	
F 27?		Inf. 4 m.		Inf. 0		M? 34?		M 39		M 30+		M 35	
L	R	L	R	L	R	L	R	L	R	L	R	L	R
16	–	8	–	–	–	–	–	22	23	–	–	–	–
15	–	7	–	–	–	–	–	20	21	–	–	–	–
78.5		–		–		–		71.6		65.6		78.8	
21	23	–	–	–	–	–	–	24	23	21	21	26	–
28	28	–	–	–	–	–	–	32	33	32	32	33	–
108.7		–		–		–		94.5		100.0		116.4	
24	26	–	–	–	–	–	–	25	27	25	26	32	32–
23	23	–	–	–	–	–	–	27	28	26	25	28	27
–		–		–		–		64.9		61.0		64.1	
–	–	–	–	–	–	–	–	37	(36)	–	41	–	39
–	–	–	–	–	–	–	–	24	24	–	25	–	25
II		–	–	–	–	–	–	IV	IV	–	IV	III	
++?		–		–		–		v. small		–		+–	
–	–	–	–	–	–	sl.	–	sl.	sl.	–	–	Abs.	Abs.?
–	–	–	–	–	–	–	–	26	–	–	–	27	–
–		–		–		–		38		38		40+	
–		–		–		0??		0		–		1	
–		–		–		1		0		–		0	
–		–		–		0		0		–		0	
–		–		–		1?		0		–		1	
–		–		–		0?		8		–		8	
–		–		–		6?		14		Few		15	
–		–		–		++		+		–		+	
–		–		–		–		++		–		++	
+		–		–		slight		+		+		slight	
–		Perhaps twins				Diploë		A3		(A)		C5 – F3	
		Frontal		Temporal		very		Robust					
		diploë		only		thick		Phase VII		Phase V			
		4 mm.											

TABLE 3, cont. BASIC DATA ON ALL SKELETONS (Ages all approximate)

Grave number	V (20)									
Skeleton number	*7 KeK*		*8 KeK*		*11 KeK*		*13 KeK*		*13a KeK*	
Sex and age	F	23?	F	25?	F	30?	F?	39?	Mid-Adult	
Bone shaft shape:	L	R	L	R	L	R	L	R	L	R
Humerus, maximum	–	–	21	22	20	–	–	–	–	–
minimum	Frags.		17	17	16	–	–	–	–	–
Femur, platymeric index	67.7		77.4		–		–		–	
A–P	21	–	–	24	–	–	–	–	–	–
Transverse	31	–	–	31	–	–	–	–	–	–
Pilastric index	–		–		100.0		–		–	
A–P	–	–	–	–	25	–	–	–	–	–
Transverse	–	–	–	–	25	–	–	–	–	–
Tibia, cnemic index	–		–		68.8		–		–	
A–P	–	–	–	–	–	32	–	–	–	–
Transverse	–	–	–	–	–	22	–	–	–	–
Cross-section*	–	–	–	–	–	V	–	–	–	–
Sciatic notch	–		–		++?		–		–	
Arthritis: vertebrae, limb	–	–	Abs?	Abs?	–	–	–	–	–	–
Mastoid height	–	–	–	–	–	–	–	–	–	–
Chin height	–		–		33		–		–	
Teeth loss	–		0		–		–		–	
Caries	–		0		–		–		–	
Abscesses	–		0		–		–		–	
Lesions	–		0		–		–		–	
Post-mortem loss	–		1		3		–		–	
Alveoli preserved	–		3?		3		–		–	
Teeth wear	–		+		–		–		–	
Browridges	–		–		–		–		–	
Occipital curve	–		–		–		–		–	
Remarks	Thin skull frags.		Left clavicle 135		–		Rugged cheek bone acromion 39 mm.		Ramus, br. 30, long coronoid	

* Tibia shaft: form of cross-section:
I Prismatic
II Oblique prism
III Concave prism (lat.)
IV Rhomboid
V Convex prism (post.)
VI Plano-convex

TABLE 3, cont.

V (20)	VI (16)				VII (6)	IX (11)
12a KeK	*15 KeK*	*14 KeK*	*15a KeK*	*15b KeK*	*16 KeK*	*17 KeK*
Adolescent	M 24	F? 29?	Ch. 7?	M? 4+	M 30?	M 34
L R	L R	L R	L R	L R	L R	L R
Frags.	22 –	– –	– –	– –	Frags.	– –
– –	19 –	– –	– –	– –	– –	– –
–	–	75.8	–	–	–	74.2
– –	– –	23 –	– –	– –	– –	– 23
– –	– –	33 –	– –	– –	– –	– 31
–	Frags.	–	–	–	115.4	107.7
– –	– –	– –	Frags.	– –	30 –	– 28
– –	– –	– –	– –	– –	26 –	– 26
–	–	–	–	–	–	–
23 –	– –	– –	– –	– –	Frags.	– –
16 –	– –	– –	– –	– –	– –	– –
– –	– –	– –	– –	– –	– –	– –
–	sm.	$+^-$	–	$+^-$	–	–
– –	sl. Abs?	sl. –	– –	– –	– –	– –
– –	28 –	– –	– –	– –	– –	– –
–	–	34	–	–	36?	39
–	0	0	–	–	0	0
–	0	0	–	–	0	0
–	0	0	–	–	0	0
–	0	0	–	–	0	0
–	7	11	–	–	1	10
–	11	14	–	–	6	22
–	sl.	+	–	–	sl.	sl.
–	–	+	–	–	–	++
–	+	–	–	–	–	?
–	A2?	Long coronoid	Lumbar arches fused	Ilium: brim 22 post. 34	Molars 5–4–5	E2 R. frontal wound

TABLE 3, cont. BASIC DATA ON ALL SKELETONS (Ages all approximate)

Grave number	X (9)				XI (12)				XII (10)	
Skeleton number	*18 KeK*		*18a KeK*		*19 KeK*		*19a KeK*		*20 KeK*	
Sex and age	F 37		F? Adult		F? 20?		Child		F 24?	
Bone shaft shape:	L	R	L	R	L	R	L	R	L	R
Humerus, maximum	19	–	–	–	–	–	–	–	16	–
minimum	18	–	–	–	–	–	–	–	15	–
Femur, platymeric index	–		–		–		–		–	
A–P	–	–	–	–	–	–	–	–	–	–
Transverse	–	–	–	–	–	–	–	–	–	–
Pilastric index	104.7		–		–		–		100.0	
A–P	22	–	–	–	–	–	–	–	23	–
Transverse	21	–	–	–	–	–	–	–	23	–
Tibia, cnemic index	–		–		–		–		–	
A–P	–	–	–	–	–	–	–	–	–	–
Transverse	–	–	–	–	–	–	–	–	–	–
Cross-section*	–	–	–	–	–	–	–	–	–	–
Sciatic notch	–		–		–		–		–	
Arthritis: vertebrae, limb	sl.	–	–	–	–	–	–	–	–	–
Mastoid height	–	–	–	–	–	–	–	–	–	–
Chin height	–		–		–		–		–	
Teeth loss	–		–		–		–		–	
Caries	–		–		–		–		–	
Abscesses	–		–		–		–		–	
Lesions	–		–		–		–		–	
Post-mortem loss	–		–		–		–		–	
Alveoli preserved	–		–		–		–		–	
Teeth wear	–		–		–		–		–	
Browridges	–		–		–		–		–	
Occipital curve	+		–		–		–		–	
Remarks	–		Extra occiput		Slender frags.		V. thin skull		Thin skull	

* Tibia shaft: form of cross-section:
I Prismatic
II Oblique prism
III Concave prism (lat.)
IV Rhomboid
V Convex prism (post.)
VI Plano-convex

TABLE 3, cont.

XIII (7)						
23 KeK	*25 KeK*	*27 KeK*	*28 KeK*	*29 KeK*	*21 KeK*	*22 KeK*
M Adult	M 44	M 33	M 45?	M 42	F 24	F 30
L R	L R	L R	L R	L R	L R	L R
– –	– –	– –	– –	– 23	– –	– –
– –	– –	– –	– –	– 21	– –	– –
–	–	–	–	–	67.6	–
– –	– –	– –	– –	– –	– 23	– –
– –	– –	– –	– –	– –	– 34	– –
125.0	–	119.3	140.0	–	108.3	–
– 35	– –	31 –	35 –	– –	– 26+	– –
– 28	– –	26 –	25 –	– –	– 24	– –
–	57.9	–	low	–	–	–
– –	38+ –	– –	– –	– –	– –	– –
– –	22 –	– –	– –	– –	– –	– –
– –	V –	– –	III –	– –	– –	– –
–	sm?	–	–	–	–	–
– –	– –	– –	– –	– –	– –	– –
– –	– –	(28) –	– –	33 –	27 –	24 –
–	33+?	–	(32)	33–	–	–
–	0	1	4	0	0	0
–	?	0	0	0	0	0
–	0	0	0	0	0	0
–	–	1	4	0	0	0
–	5	2	3	8	3+	4
–	5	7	7	13(15)	8	14
–	–	+	–	+	+	++
–	++	++	–	++	+	+
–	+	+	–	+	+	+
Robust	A1 like *27 KeK*	A2	Robust	E1 Bruise M_3 suppressed	B1–C5	A3 Upper Pm_2 rotated 90°

TABLE 3, cont. BASIC DATA ON ALL SKELETONS (Ages all approximate)

Grave number	XIII (7)									
Skeleton number	*23a KeK*		*24 KeK*		*24a KeK*		*27a KeK*		*23b KeK*	
Sex and age	F? 22?		F? 27?		F? Adult		F Adult		Child 2+	
Bone shaft shape:	L	R	L	R	L	R	L	R	L	R
Humerus, maximum	–	–	–	20	–	–	–	–	–	–
minimum	–	–	–	16	–	–	–	–	–	–
Femur, platymeric index	–		–		75.0		–		–	
A–P	–	–	–	–	24	–	–	–	–	–
Transverse	–	–	–	–	32	–	–	–	–	–
Pilastric index	–		108.7		108.0		–		–	
A–P	–	–	–	25	27	–	–	–	–	–
Transverse	–	–	–	23	25	–	–	–	–	–
Tibia, cnemic index	70.6		–		–		–		–	
A–P	34	–	–	–	–	–	–	–	–	–
Transverse	24	–	–	–	–	–	–	–	–	–
Cross-section*	–	–	–	–	–	–	–	–	–	–
Sciatic notch	–		–		–		++		–	
Arthritis: vertebrae, limb	Abs?	–	–	–	–	–	–	–	–	–
Mastoid height	–	–	–	–	–	–	–	–	–	–
Chin height	–		30		?		–		–	
Teeth loss	–		2		–		–		–	
Caries	–		0		–		–		–	
Abscesses	–		0		–		–		–	
Lesions	–		2		–		–		–	
Post-mortem loss	–		7		–		–		–	
Alveoli preserved	–		16		–		–		–	
Teeth wear	–		+		–		–		–	
Browridges	–		–		–		–		–	
Occipital curve	–		sl.		?		–		–	
Remarks	–		–		Extra occiput		Ilium, talus		Skull vault normal 2–3 mm. thickness	

* Tibia shaft: form of cross-section:
I Prismatic
II Oblique prism
III Concave prism (lat.)
IV Rhomboid
V Convex prism (post.)
VI Plano-convex

TABLE 3, cont.

XIII (7)		XVII (8)		XVIII (3)				XIX (1)					
26 KeK		*29a KeK*		*30 KeK*		*30a KeK*		*32 KeK*		*34 KeK*		*31 KeK*	
Child 2+		F?? 8fm.		F 23		Adult		M? 37?		M 40?		F 26?	
L	R	L	R	L	R	L	R	L	R	L	R	L	R
–	–	–	–	–	21	–	–	–	–	–	–	–	–
–	–	–	–	–	15	–	–	–	–	–	–	–	–
–		–		75.0		–		–		–		–	
–	–	–	–	–	21	–	–	–	–	–	–	–	–
–	–	–	–	–	28	–	–	–	–	–	–	–	–
–		–		100.0		–		–		–		114.3	
–	–	–	–	–	26	–	–	–	–	–	–	24	–
–	–	–	–	–	26	–	–	–	–	–	–	21	–
–		–		61.3		–		–		–		–	
–	–	–	–	31	–	–	–	–	–	–	–	–	–
–	–	–	–	19	–	–	–	–	–	–	–	–	–
–	–	–	–	IV	–	–	–	–	–	–	–	–	–
–		++–		–		–		–		–		–	
–	–	–	–	Abs?	?	–	–	–	–	–	–	–	–
–	–	–	–	–	–	–	–	–	–	–	–	28	–
–		–		–		–		–		34		30	
–		–		–		–		–		1		0	
–		–		–		–		–		0		0	
–		–		–		–		–		0		0	
–		–		–		–		–		1		0	
–		–		–		–		–		14		12	
–		–		–		–		–		28		22	
–		–		–		–		–		+		sl.	
–		–		–		–		+		+		+	
–		–		+		–		sl.		–		sl.	
		Foetus		(A or E?)		Scraps		(C?)		Large?		(C?)	
Fragments M_2 has Carabelli cusp													

TABLE 3, cont. BASIC DATA ON ALL SKELETONS (Ages all approximate)

Grave number	XIX (1)						XX (13)			
Skeleton number	*32a KeK*		*33 KeK*		*31a KeK*		*35a KeK*		*35 KeK*	
Sex and age	F? Y. Adult		F	31?	Adult		M? Adult		F	30?
Bone shaft shape:	L	R	L	R	L	R	L	R	L	R
Humerus, maximum	–	–	–	–	–	–	–	–	19	–
minimum	–	–	–	–	–	–	–	–	15	–
Femur, platymeric index	–		–		–		–		–	
A–P	–	–	–	–	–	–	–	–	frag.	
Transverse	–	–	–	–	–	–	–	–	–	–
Pilastric index	–		–		–		frag.		–	
A–P	–	–	–	–	–	–	–	–	–	–
Transverse	–	–	–	–	–	–	–	–	–	–
Tibia, cnemic index	–		71.0		–		–		–	
A–P	–	–	–	31	–	–	–	–	–	–
Transverse	–	–	–	22	–	–	–	–	–	–
Cross-section*	–	–	–	II	–	–	–	–	–	–
Sciatic notch	–		–		–		–		–	
Arthritis: vertebrae, limb	–	–	–	–	–	–	–	–	–	–
Mastoid height	–	–	–	–	–	–	–	–	–	–
Chin height	–		–		–		–		–	
Teeth loss	–		–		–		–		0	
Caries	–		–		–		–		0	
Abscesses	–		–		–		–		0	
Lesions	–		–		–		–		0	
Post-mortem loss	–		–		–		–		0	
Alveoli preserved	–		–		–		–		4	
Teeth wear	–		–		–		–		sl.	
Browridges	–		+		–		–		absent	
Occipital curve	(+)		–		–		–		–	
Remarks	++ alveolar prognathism		–		Extra palate, jaw		–		–	

* Tibia shaft: form of cross-section:
I Prismatic
II Oblique prism
III Concave prism (lat.)
IV Rhomboid
V Convex prism (post.)
VI Plano-convex

TABLE 3, cont.

XXII (4)	XXV (25)	XXVI (24)	XXVII (2)	XXIX (22)	XXXII (23)	XXXV (37)
36 KeK	*37 KeK*	*38 KeK*	*39 KeK*	*40 KeK*	*41 KeK*	*42 KeK*
M? 28?	M 31?	F? 33?	M?? 3	Ch. 3–	Inf. 6m.	M?? 12–
L R	L R	L R	L R	L R	L R	L R
– –	– –	– –	– –	– –	– –	– –
– –	slivers	– –	– –	– –	– –	– –
–	–	–	–	–	–	–
slivers	– –	frag.	– –	– –	frag.	– –
– –	– –	slender	– –	– –	– –	– –
–	–	–	scraps	– –	– –	– –
– –	– –	– –	– –	– –	– –	– –
– –	– –	– –	– –	– –	– –	– –
–	–	–	–	–	frag.	–
– –	– –	– –	– –	– –	– –	– –
– –	– –	– –	– –	– –	– –	– –
– –	– –	– –	– –	– –	– –	– –
–	–	–	–	broken	–	$+^-$
– –	– –	– –	– –	– –	– –	– –
– –	++	– –	– –	– –	– –	– –
31	–	33?	22	–	–	–
0	–	0	0	–	–	–
0	–	0	0	–	–	–
0	–	0	0	–	–	–
0	–	0	0	–	–	–
3	–	2	0	–	–	–
16	–	6	20	–	–	–
sl.	–	sl.$^+$	milk sl.$^-$	–	–	–
–	+++	–	absent	–	–	+
–	++	–	sl.	–	–	–
Milk m_2 retained in jaw	(A2–C5?)	–	(C) Thin bone	Thin bone	–	–

TABLE 3, cont. BASIC DATA ON ALL SKELETONS (Ages all approximate)

Grave number	XXXVI (34)	XXXVII (39)	XXXVIII (32)	XXXIX (36)	XL (35)
Skeleton number	*43 KeK*	*68 KeK*	*69 KeK*	*70 KeK*	*71 KeK*
Sex and age	F 27	M 32	Inf. 8m.	F? 38?	M 33
Bone shaft shape:	L R	L R	L R	L R	L R
Humerus, maximum	– –	– 25	– –	20 –	22 23
minimum	– –	– 20	– –	14 –	17 19
Femur, platymeric index	65.4	82.3	–	75.9	80.9
A–P	17 –	27 29?	– –	22 –	28 27
Transverse	26 –	33 35?	– –	29 –	34 34
Pilastric index	100.0	108.9	–	104.2	107.3
A–P	22 –	29 32	– –	25 –	30 29
Transverse	22 –	28 28	– –	24 –	28 27
Tibia, cnemic index	–	71.8?	–	–	60.3
A–P	– –	– 39?	– –	– –	38 40
Transverse	– –	– 28	– –	– –	23 24
Cross-section*	– –	– V	– –	– –	V
Sciatic notch	–	(sl.)	–	–	sl.
Arthritis: vertebrae, limb	– –	Abs. Abs.	– –	– –	Abs. Abs.
Mastoid height	– –	32 –	– –	– –	25? –
Chin height	(32)	33–	Frags.	–	38
Teeth loss	0	1	–	–	1 broken
Caries	0	0	–	–	0
Abscesses	0	1–	–	–	0
Lesions	0	1	–	–	1
Post-mortem loss	0	9	–	–	0
Alveoli preserved	3	30	–	–	17
Teeth wear	sl.+	sl.+	–	–	+
Browridges	–	++	–	–	–
Occipital curve	++	+	–	++	sl.
Remarks	Lower molar cusps: 4–4–4	A3 Phase 6	Thin skull vault	Occipital diploë 5 mm.	(C5) Massive jaw Ankle hurt

* Tibia shaft: form of cross-section:
- I Prismatic
- II Oblique prism
- III Concave prism (lat.)
- IV Rhomboid
- V Convex prism (post.)
- VI Plano-convex

TABLE 4. SKELETAL MEASUREMENTS

Grave number	V (20)	VI (16)	XXXVII (39)	XL (35)	I (14)	
Skeleton number	*9 KeK*	*15 KeK*	*68 KeK*	*71 KeK*	*2 KeK*	*3 KeK*
Sex	M	M	M	M	F	F
Estimated age (sutures)	39	24	(31)	33	28?	27?
Humerus length	318	(310–20)	(330)	(306)		
Femur length	(410)		446?	430		(360–80)
Tibia length	(360)		(410)	360??	(315)	
Talus length	56		51	52		
Talus breadth	44		43	40		
Talus height	32		31	31		
Stature	<170.00			166.60	(152.88)	
Platymeric index	72.35		82.33	80.88		
Pilastric index	94.51		108.93	107.27		
Robusticity index	(13.48)		13.18	13.08		
Cnemic index	64.86		71.79			

TABLE 4, cont.

Grave number	V (20)		XIII (7)	XVIII (3)	XIX (1)	XX (13)
Skeleton number	*8 KeK*	*11 KeK*	*24 KeK*	*30 KeK*	*33 KeK*	*35 KeK*
Sex	F	F	F	F	F	F
Estimated age (sutures)	25??	*ca.* 30	27	23	(30)	30
Humerus length	(290)	(290)		(280)		(275)
Femur length			(410)			
Tibia length		(300+)			(340)	
Talus length						
Talus breadth						
Talus height						
Stature						
Platymeric index						
Pilastric index						
Robusticity index						
Cnemic index						

BIBLIOGRAPHY

Acsady, Gy. and Nemeskeri, J. (1970), *History of Human Life Span and Mortality*, Budapest (Akadémiai Kiadó).

Allison, A. C. (1964), "Polymorphism and Natural Selection in Human Populations," *Cold Spring Harbor Symposia on Quantitative Biology* 29, pp. 137–149.

Angel, J. Lawrence (1951), *Troy. Excavations Conducted by the University of Cincinnati, 1932–1938*, Supplementary Monograph I, *The Human Remains*, Princeton.

— (1959), "Early Helladic Skulls from Aghios Kosmas." Appendix in G. E. Mylonas, *Aghios Kosmas, an Early Bronze Age Settlement and Cemetery in Attica*, Princeton, pp. 167–179.

— (1966), "Porotic Hyperostosis, Anemias, Malarias and Marshes in the Prehistoric Eastern Mediterranean," *Science* 153 (No. 3737), pp. 760–763.

— (1968), "Ecological Aspects of Palaeodemography," *Symposia of the Society for the Study of Human Biology*, No. 8, *The Skeletal Biology of Earlier Human Populations* (ed. D. R. Brothwell), Oxford, pp. 263–270.

— (1969a), "The Bases of Paleodemography," *American Journal of Physical Anthropology*, n.s. 30, pp. 427–437.

— (1969b), "Paleodemography and Evolution," *American Journal of Physical Anthropology*, n.s. 31, pp. 343–353.

— (1969c), "Human Skeletal Material from Franchthi Cave," Appendix II, pp. 380–381 in T. W. Jacobsen, "Excavations at Porto Cheli and Vicinity, Preliminary Report, II: The Franchthi Cave, 1967–1968," *Hesperia* 38, pp. 343–381.

— (1970), "Human Skeletal Remains at Karataş," Appendix, pp. 253–259 in M. J. Mellink, "Excavations at Karataş-Semayuk and Elmalı in Lycia, 1969," *A.J.A.* 74, pp. 245–259.
— (1971a), *Lerna*, II, *The People*, Princeton (issued separately as *The People of Lerna, Analysis of a Prehistoric Aegean Population* by the Smithsonian Institution Press, Washington).
— (1971b), "Early Neolithic Skeletons from Çatal Hüyük: Demography and Pathology," *Anat. Stud.* 21, pp. 77–98.
— (1972), "Biological Relations of Egyptian and Eastern Mediterranean Populations during Pre-dynastic and Dynastic Times," *Journal of Human Evolution* 1, pp. 307–313.
Bruce-Chwatt, L. J. (1965), "Paleogenesis and Paleo-epidemiology of Primate Malaria," *Bulletin of the World Health Organization* 32, pp. 363–387.
Butzer, K. W. (1971), *Environment and Archaeology, an Introduction to Pleistocene Geography*, 2nd ed., Chicago.
Hadjimarkos, D. M. and Bonhorst, C. W. (1962), "Fluoride and Selenium Levels in Contemporary and Ancient Greek Teeth in Relation to Dental Caries," *Nature* 193, pp. 177–178.
Morant, G. M. (1925), "A Study of Egyptian Craniology from Prehistoric to Roman Times," *Biometrika* 17, pp. 1–52.
Woo, T. L. (1930), "A Study of Seventy-one Ninth Dynasty Egyptian Skulls from Sedment," *Biometrika* 22 pp. 65–93.

APPENDIX 6: OTHER SITES IN KEOS

Two other sites which were discovered in Keos by the Cincinnati expedition appear to have been roughly contemporary with Kephala. They are known only from unstratified surface finds.

PAOURA

A settlement situated on a rocky ridge at the northern end of the island within sight of Kephala (Pl. 1; visible on the far horizon in Pls. 52, e, 53, c). A brief description by Caskey (1971a, p. 392) is here repeated:

> On information from our foreman and one of the local workmen in 1968 we explored the surface of a lofty perch on a great outcropping of rock about two kilometers due east of Kephala, beyond the bay of Otzias. Locally it goes by the name of Paoura. . . . A conspicuous ridge of rock descends gradually to it from still higher ground on the south; to the north the descent is steep to the sea and on the east there is a sheer drop to a modern quarry half the way down. Otzias provides a sandy beach and a partly protected cove where small craft can lie. Closer to Paoura is a tiny indentation at the foot of a ravine, approachable from the sea in fair weather. The climb from either landing place is a weary one. We were told that water flows in winter from a spring below the ridge, not far from the site; in summer it is now dry.
>
> People settled at this picturesque, remote and unsheltered spot in very early times. Potsherds and obsidian on the surface are like those found at Kephala. Here and there one can make out the lines of walls, some straight, some curving. On the western side of the northern extremity a large expanse of native rock is nearly level; perhaps once occupied, it is now bare. In it there are a few small cavities which may have held the ends of upright timbers.

Most of the sherds are prehistoric and may be dated to the Neolithic period; some have already been published (Caskey, 1972, p. 358). A considerable number of sherds have also been found which may be dated to the Classical period, at which time the site was apparently occupied by a house or lookout station. Nothing was found to indicate any human activity at any other periods than these.

Further surface finds are illustrated on Plate 95. The numbers here assigned continue the sequence begun by Caskey (*ibid.*). The first group of finds are undoubtedly of Neolithic date.

OBSIDIAN (Pl. 95, **P 19–40**)

All from Melos, to judge by the physical appearance, which is like that of the Kephala obsidian (above, p. 5). The categories are those defined above (pp. 6–8).

POINTED TOOLS (Category 4)

P 19, blade sharpened to a point; broken at proximal end (i.e. that opposite point); triangular in section; secondary working at edge and on lower surface around point. **P 20**, intact; pointed at both ends; triangular in section; some working at edges. **P 21**, base missing; oval in section; much secondary working. **P 22**, base missing; oval in section; much secondary working but cruder than the preceding. **P 23**, base missing; flattened oval in section; secondary working especially at edges and around point. **P 24**, probably pointed at the ends, both of which are slightly broken; flattened oval in section; extensive fine secondary working. **P 25**, slightly broken at base, which may have an incipient tang; oval to triangular in section; extensive secondary working. **P 26**, broken at base, but with incipient tang; oval in section; extensive secondary working. **P 27**, intact or slightly broken; crude tang, triangular to ovel in section; extensive secondary working. **P 28**, tip chipped; well-defined tang, perpendicular shoulders; lentoid in section; extensive fine secondary working; this is the most carefully worked of all the obsidian found at Paoura. **P 29**, tip missing; almost pointed tang; sloping shoulders; lentoid to oval in section; extensive secondary working. **P 30**, intact; broad tang; sloping shoulders; flat and blade-like, triangular to trapezoidal in section; extensive secondary working at edges.

PARALLEL-SIDED BLADES (Category 1 a)

P 31–35, one or both ends missing, triangular to trapezoidal in section; secondary working at one or both edges.

SCRAPERS (Category 3)

P 36–38, one or both ends missing; triangular to trapezoidal in section; secondary working along at least one edge; **P 37** is also worked around one end.

USED CORE (Category 5)

P 39, one edge missing; roughly circular in outline and triangular in section.

WASTE

P 40, a piece from the shoulder of a core, struck off to facilitate the production of further tools.

POTTERY (Pl. 95, **P 41–44**)

The categories are those defined above (pp. 13–19).

C 1

P 43, from a scoop strut, round in section with shallow diagonal incisions.

OTHER SHERDS

P 41, from a fairly large vessel with an impressed band. **P 42, P 44**, from fairly large vessels with grooved decoration.

The following three pieces may be assigned with less certainty to the prehistoric period; nevertheless they are similar to finds from Kephala (see above, pp. 3–4 and Appendix 1) and are probably Neolithic.

COPPER AND COPPER WORKING

P 45, a small shapeless piece of copper or copper oxide. **P 46**, a piece of copper-rich slag. **P 47**, another piece of slag.

The foregoing finds (and those already published) are closely similar to those from Kephala. The obsidian suggests that there was a similar local industry at Paoura; the higher incidence of small, finely finished points may be fortuitous. The three tanged points **P 28–30** recall points from Saliagos (Evans and Renfrew, 1968, figs. 62, nos. 2, 8, 9; 63, no. 8; pl. 37). The pottery from Paoura is also similar to that from Kephala; the only feature which is not matched at Kephala is the rim with internally thickened ridge (Caskey, 1972, p. 359, P 2) and this has parallels at the Kitsos cave (Lambert, 1971, p. 711) in levels which must be about contemporary with Kephala (see above, Chapter IV).

SYKAMIA (AKROTERION SYKAMIAS)

A high ridge forms a promontory at the steep northeastern side of the island (Pl. 1; Caskey, 1972, p. 358). Next to it is a small sandy beach with a ravine and a tiny valley leading down to it. The sides of the ridge are abrupt and the top narrow, with bedrock almost everywhere exposed. Sherds and obsidian are scattered about the top and sides of the ridge. There are remains of a wall at one end, more than one meter high in places, which ran across the ridge and set it off from a saddle leading to higher ground at the northwest. Here and there traces of other walls can be distinguished, and there are cavities in the rock similar to those found at Paoura (and also at Ayia Irini, where they date probably to the Early Bronze Age; Caskey, 1964, p. 319).

The pottery collected (a selection of which has been published in Caskey, 1972, pl. 76, S 1–9) indicates that the ridge was inhabited at the time of Kephala, in the Early Bronze Age, and in the Late Bronze Age. Classical sherds were also found on a ridge at the other side of the little bay.

John E. Coleman

CONCORDANCES

1. KEPHALA INVENTORY NUMBERS: CATALOGUE NUMBERS

Inv. No.	*Cat. No.*	*Inv. No.*	*Cat. No.*	*Inv. No.*	*Cat. No.*	*Inv. No.*	*Cat. No.*
.1	**99**	1.5	**14**	3.27	**150***	4.29	**78***
.2	**98**	1.7	**109**	3.28	**151***	4.30	**79***
.4	**9***	1.8	**161***	3.29	**152***	4.31	**80***
.5	**106**	1.9	**100**	3.20	**157***	4.32	**178**
.6	**134**	1.1	**93***	3.31	**158***	4.33	**190**
.7	**146**	1.11	**92***	3.32	**131**	4.34	**212***
.8	**105**	1.12	**90***	3.33	**132**	4.35	**210***
.9	**104**	1.13	**89***	3.34	**129**	4.36	**38***
.10	**102**	1.14	**5***	3.35	**145**	4.37	**32***
.11	**137**	1.15	**3***	3.36	**111**	4.38	**33***
.12	**167***	1.16	**2**	3.37	**115**	4.39	**36**
.13	**135**	1.17	**6**	3.38	**123**	4.40	**24**
.14	**34***	1.18	**7***	3.39	**121**	4.41	**25**
.16	**97**	1.19	**4***	3.40	**143**	4.42	**133**
.17	**213***	1.20	**13**	3.41	**118**	4.43	**211***
.18	**165***	1.21	**125**	3.42	**156***	4.44	**20**
.19	**164***	1.22	**12**	3.43	**153***	4.45	**21**
.20	**138**	1.23	**122**	3.44	**155***	4.46	**30***
.21	**201**	1.24	**120**	4.1	**29***	4.47	**206**
.22	**173**	1.25	**113**	4.2	**28***	5.1	**94***
.23	**170**	1.26	**116**	4.4	**91***	6.1	**196**
.24	**76***	3.1	**124**	4.5	**202**	6.4	**182**
.25	**174**	3.2	**119**	4.6	**171**	6.5	**197**
.26	**74**	3.5	**101**	4.7	**23**	6.6	**176**
.27	**10**	3.6	**117**	4.8	**77***	6.7	**65**
.28	**64**	3.7	**86***	4.9	**81***	6.8	**66**
.29	**11***	3.8	**162***	4.10	**16**	6.9	**192**
.30	**148***	3.9	**130**	4.11	**26**	6.10	**53**
.31	**62**	3.10	**126**	4.12	**15**	6.11	**49**
.32	**37**	3.11	**127**	4.13	**85***	6.12	**54**
.33	**136**	3.12	**160***	4.14	**96A***	6.13	**191**
.34	**107**	3.13	**128**	4.15	**17**	6.14	**47**
.35	**75**	3.14	**112**	4.16	**18**	6.15	**50**
.36	**166***	3.15	**147***	4.17	**35**	6.16	**48**
.37	**175**	3.16	**108**	4.18	**22**	6.17	**198**
.38	**204**	3.17	**163***	4.19	**19**	6.18	**172**
.39	**203**	3.18	**114**	4.20	**39***	6.19	**169**
.40	**27**	3.19	**144**	4.21	**40***	6.20	**168**
.41	**63**	3.20	**139**	4.22	**41***	6.21	**194**
0.1	**88***	3.21	**140**	4.23	**42***	6.22	**195**
0.2	**87***	3.22	**142**	4.24	**43***	6.23	**208**
1.1	**103**	3.23	**141**	4.25	**45***	6.24	**209**
1.2	**110**	3.24	**154***	4.26	**46***	6.25	**193**
1.3	**1***	3.25	**159***	4.27	**44***	6.26	**199**
1.4	**8**	3.26	**149***	4.28	**31***	6.27	**200**

Inv. No.	*Cat. No.*	*Inv. No.*	*Cat. No.*	*Inv. No.*	*Cat. No.*	*Inv. No.*	*Cat. No.*
6.28	**51**	6.37	**68**	6.46	**207**	6.55	**181**
6.29	**55**	6.38	**73**	6.47	**185**	6.56	**189**
6.30	**70**	6.39	**56**	6.48	**183**	7.1	**95***
6.31	**72**	6.40	**57**	6.49	**184**	9.1	**82***
6.32	**52**	6.41	**58**	6.50	**177**	9.2	**83***
6.33	**60**	6.42	**59**	6.51	**187**	71.1	**84***
6.34	**67**	6.43	**61**	6.52	**188**	73.1	**96B***
6.35	**69**	6.44	**205**	6.53	**180**	*also*	
6.36	**71**	6.45	**179**	6.54	**186**	.3	p.82

2. PLATE NUMBERS: PAGE AND PLATE CROSS REFERENCES FOR UNINVENTORIED POTTERY AND OBJECTS

Plate		*Page*	*Plate Ref.*
Frontispiece			
	A	*25*	40 G; 86 F, L
	B	*69*	40 B; 86 B
	C	*69*	40 A; 86 E
	D	*81*	40 C; 86 G
	E	*69*	87 F
	F	*25*	87 P
	G	*40*	43 E; 87 N
	H	11, *70*	41 L; 86 P
	J	11, *70*	41 G; 86 S
	K	*70*	41 J; 86 W
	L	*25*	86 AL
	M	11, *28*, 102[21]	42 A; 86 AN
	N	11, *70*, 102[21]	42 E; 86 AO
	O	*70*	42 B; 86 AQ
27	A	*95*	75 B
	B	*81*	
	C	*69*	75 E
	D	13, *91*	75 H
	E	13, 19, *69*	75 A
	F	13, *69*	
	G	13, *69*	
28	A	14, 29, *69*	75 AC
	B	*91*	75 W
	C	14, *91*	75 AU
	D	*69*	75 AE
	E	*69*, 98[4]	75 Y
	F	14, 19, *81*, 98[2]	75 Z
	G	14, *81*	75 AS
	H	*33*	75 AK
	J	*81*	75 AJ
	K	*69*	
	L	*27*, 69	
	M	*91*	75 X
	N	9, *69*	75 Q
29	A	*81*	
	B	14, *69*	
	C	14, *29*	
	D	14, *69*	
	E	14, *81*, 102[19]	75 AR
	F	14, *69*	
	G	14, *69*	75 AA
	H	14, *81*	
	J	14, *69*	75 AF
	K	14, *69*	75 AB
	L	*69*	
	M	*97*	89 AK
	N	14, *69*	75 AP
(29)	O	*91*	75 AW
	P	14, *91*	75 AX
30	A	14, *91*	75 AZ
	B	14, *70*, 98[4]	75 AY
	C	15, *77*	75 BJ
	D	15, *91*	75 BA
	E	14, *77*, 100[12]	75 AV
	F	15, *70*, 100[12]	75 AT
	G	*77*	76 A
31	A	13, 15, *70*	77 K
	B	13, 15, *91*	77 O
	C	13, 15, *82*	77 P
	D	15, *40*	77 R
	E	15, *70*	77 S
	F	15, *70*	77 V
	G	15, 19, *23*, 98[2]	77 N
	H	15, *82*	
	J	15, *70*	77 A
	K	15, *70*, 71	
	L	15, *70*	77 L
	M	15, *23*	77 Q
	N	15, *70*	77 M
	O	15, *82*	
	P	15, *82*	77 Y
	Q	15, *37*	77 AB
	R	15, *82*	77 W
	S	15, *23*	77 T
	T	15, 69, *71*	77 Z
	U	15, 69, *71*	77 X
	V	15, 69, *71*	77 AG
32	A	12, 15, *97*	77 AA
	B	15, *71*	
	C	15, *71*	77 AW
	D	15, *71*	77 AV
	E	15, *71*	77 AH
	F	9, 12, 15, *71*	77 AS
	G	12, 15, *91*	77 AR
	H	15, *82*	77 AN
	J	15, *91*	77 AF
	K	15, *82*	77 AM
	L	15, *77*	77 AP
	M	15, *71*	77 AQ
	N	12, 15, *71*	
	O	*71*	77 G
	P	15, *71*, 100	77 AJ
	Q	15, *82*, 107[39]	
33	A	16, *71*	

Plate	*Page*	*Plate Ref.*
(33) B	16, 18, *37*	80 B
34 A	16, *23*, 98[2]	81 AG
B	16, *71*	81 Q
C	16, *33*	
D	16, *71*	
E	*28*	
F	*77*	
G	16, *33*	
H	16, *82*	81 T
J	*71*, 99[6]	
K	16, *82*	81 AA
36 A	17, *92*	83 R
B	17, *82*	83 Q
C	15, 17, *92*	83 AD
D	17, *82*, 92	83 V
E	*72*	83 AN
F	12, 17, *72*, 102[21]	83 AG
G	*72*, *102*[19]	
37 A	18, *72*	84 AJ
B	17, 37, 65, *72*	84 W, X
C	18, *25*, 100[12]	84 O
D	18, *25*, 100[12]	84 Q
E	18, *72*, 100[12]	84 P
F	17, *72*, 100[12]	84 C
G	17, *30*, 100[12]	84 D
H	17, *96*, 100[12]	84 B
J	17, 18, *72*, 100[12]	84 F
K	17, 18, *72*, 100[12]	84 J
L	17, *30*, 100[12]	84 V
M	18, *72*	84 AF
N	18, *82*	84 AG
O	18, *72*	84 AE
38 A	18, *25*, 100[12]	84 BB
B	18, *25*, 100[12]	84 BA
C	10, 18, *38*	84 BD
D	*73*	
E	18, *73*	
F	18, *97*	84 BC
G	18, *73*	84 AQ
H	18, *97*	84 AX
J	18, *92*	84 AV
K	19, *83*, 107[43]	
L	14, 19, *69*, 107[43]	85 AK
M	14, 19, *69*, 107[43]	85 AL
N	14, 19, *69*	85 AN
O	14, 19, *41*	85 AQ
P	14, 19, *69*	85 AT
39 A	19, *73*, 100[11]	85 F
B	19, *77*, 100[11]	85 E
C	19, *73*, 100[11]	85 C
D	19, *73*, 100[11]	84 BR
E	19, *73*, 100[11]	84 BQ
F	19, *83*	85 AY
G	19, *73*	85 AZ
H	19, 73, *83*	
J	19, *73*	
(39) K	19, *73*	
L	19, *83*	
M	19, *40*	
N	19, *73*	85 AX
O	19, *78*	
P	19, *40*	85 BB
Q	19, *83*	
R	19, *81*	85 BC
S	*93*	91 S
T	*83*	91 Q
U	17, 19, *28*	89 AC
V	12, *77*	89 AD
40 A	*69*	Fr.C; 86 E
B	*69*	Fr.B; 86 B
C	*81*	Fr.D; 86 G
D	*81*	86 A
E	*91*	86 C
F	*81*	86 D
G	14, *25*	Fr.A; 86 F, L
H	14, *69*	86 M
J	14, *91*	86 N
K	*69*	87 C
L	*28*	87 D
41 A	*69*	86 Y
B	11, *69*, 102[21]	86 AA
C	12, *81*, 107[42]	86 Z
D	*70*	86 X
E	*27*	86 AG
F	*81*	86 O
G	11, *70*	Fr.J; 86 S
H	*70*	86 U
J	*70*	Fr.K; 86 W
K	70, *81*	86 Q
L	11, *70*	Fr.H; 86 P
42 A	11, 14, *28*, 102[21]	Fr.M; 86 AN
B	14, *70*	Fr.O; 86 AQ
C	14, *70*	86 AR
D	12, 14, 69, 70, *81*	86 R
E	11, 14, *70*, 100, 102[21]	Fr.N; 86 AO
F	11, 14, *70*	87 H
G	11, 14, *91*	87 G
43 A	15, *23*	87 K
B	15, *70*	87 L
C	15, *71*	87 J
D	16, *82*	87 R
E	16, *40*	Fr.G; 87 N
44 A	12, *91*, 100[12]	88 B
B	12, *70*, 100, 100[12]	88 A
C	12, 13, *70*, 100[12]	88 W
D	12, 13, *81*, 100[12]	
E	12, 13, *77*, 100[12], 102[19]	88 P
F	12, *81*, 100[12]	
G	12, *81*, 100[12], 102[19]	88 H
H	12, *81*, 100[12], 102[19]	88 C
J	12, 15, *85*	88 AN
K	12, 15, 38, *82*	88 AO

Plate	*Page*	*Plate Ref.*
(44) L	12, *73*	88 AR
M	12, *73*, 100[12]	89 S
N	12, *73*	89 L
45 A	*93*	75 M
B	*24*	75 K
C	*97*	75 L
D	*28*	
E	*93*	75 N
F	*73*	
G	*32*	
H	*74*	91 O
J	*82*	81 W
K	82, *83*	77 BA
L	*78*	77 BE
M	*73*, 93	77 BG
46 A	*83*	89 U
B	12, *73*, 85, 99[6], 100[12], 102[21]	89 AS
C	*83*	77 BC
D	12, 16, *23*, 107[39]	80 A
E	115	
F	119	
G	119	
H	119, 120	
J	119, 120	
K	119	
75 A	19, *69*	27 E
B	*95*	27 A
C	*23*	
D	*81*	
E	*69*	27 C
F	18, 71, *77*	
G	18, *71*, 77	
H	13, *91*	27 D
J	*97*	
K	*24*	45 B
L	*97*	45 C
M	*93*	45 A
N	*93*	45 E
O	*91*	
P	*91*	
Q	9, *69*	28 N
R	*27*	
S	*69*	
T	*28*	
U	*28*	
V	*28*	
W	18, *91*	28 B
X	*91*	28 M
Y	18, *69*, 98[4]	28 E
Z	14, 19, *81*, 98[2]	28 F
AA	18, *69*	29 G
AB	14, 18, *69*	29 K
AC	14, 29, *69*	28 A
AD	14, 29, 69, *81*	
AE	18, *69*	28 D
AF	*69*	29 J

Plate	*Page*	*Plate Ref.*
(75) AG	18, *25*	
AH	15, *70*	
AJ	*81*	28 J
AK	*33*	28 H
AL	*69*	
AM	*91*	
AN	14, 70, *91*	
AO	14, *97*	
AP	14, *69*	29 N
AQ	*91*	
AR	14, *81*, 102[19]	29 E
AS	14, *81*	28 G
AT	15, *70*, 100[12]	30 F
AU	14, *91*	28 C
AV	14, *77*, 100[12]	30 E
AW	*91*	29 O
AX	14, *91*	29 P
AY	14, *70*, 98[4]	30 B
AZ	14, *91*	30 A
BA	15, *91*	30 D
BB	*91*	
BC	*70*	
BD	*85*	
BE	*91*	
BF	*77*	
BG	*70*	
BH	*70*	
BJ	15, *77*	30 C
BK	15, *70*	
BL	15, *91*	
BM	*70*	
BN	*91*	
BO	*91*	
BP	*81*	
BQ	15, *70*	
BR	*70*, 100[12]	
BS	14, 15, *91*	
BT	15, *91*	
BU	14, 15, *70*, 100[12]	
BV	14, 15, *70*, 100[12]	
BW	15, 91	
BX	15, *85*	
76 A	*77*	30 G
77 A	15, *70*	31 J
B	15, *70*	
C	15, *96*	
D	15, *97*	
E	15, *91*	
F	15, *82*	
G	15, *71*	32 O
H	15, *91*	
J	15, *91*	
K	15, *70*	31 A
L	15, *70*	31 L
M	15, *70*	31 N
N	15, 19, *23*, 98[2]	31 G

Plate	Page	Plate Ref.
(77) O	15, *91*	31 B
P	15, *82*	31 C
Q	15, *23*	31 M
R	15, *40*	31 D
S	15, 18, *70*	31 E
T	15, 18, *23*	31 S
U	15, 18, *82*	
V	15, 18, *70*	31 F
W	15, 18, *82*	31 R
X	15, 69, *71*	31 U
Y	15, *82*	31 P
Z	15, 69, *71*	31 T
AA	12, 15, *97*	32 A
AB	15, *37*	31 Q
AC	15, *71*	
AD	15, *71*	
AE	15, *82*	
AF	15, *91*	32 J
AG	69, *71*	31 V
AH	15, *71*	32 E
AJ	15, *71*, 100	32 P
AK	15, *91*	
AL	15, *77*	
AM	15, *82*	32 K
AN	15, *82*	32 H
AO	15, *91*	
AP	15, *77*	32 L
AQ	12, 15, *71*	32 M
AR	12, 15, *91*	32 G
AS	9, 12, 15, *71*	32 F
AT	*91*	
AU	12, *91*	
AV	15, *71*	32 D
AW	15, *71*	32 C
AX	*82*	
AY	*73*	
AZ	*73*	
BA	82, *83*	45 K
BB	*73*	
BC	*83*	46 C
BD	*83*	
BE	*78*	45 L
BF	*93*	
BG	*73*, 93	45 M
80 A	12, 16, 18, *23*, 107[39]	46 D
B	16, 18, *37*	33 B
C	16, *82*	
81 A	10, *23*	
B	*72*	
C	16, *28*	
D	16, *71*	
E	16, *91*	
F	*33*	
G	16, *33*	
H	*23*	
J	*25*	

Plate	Page	Plate Ref.
(81) K	16, *92*	
L	*23*	
M	*28*	
N	*91*	
O	*92*	
P	*91*	
Q	16, *71*	34 B
R	*23*	
S	16, *91*	
T	16, *82*	34 H
U	*97*	
V	*37*	
W	*82*	45 J
X	*72*	
Y	*72*	
Z	*23*	
AA	16, *82*	34 K
AB	*96*	
AC	*82*	
AD	*71*	
AE	16, *91*	
AF	*71*	
AG	*23*, 98[2]	34 A
AH	16, *71*	
AJ	16, *91*	
AK	16, *91*	
AL	16, *28*	
AM	16, *23*	
AN	*91*	
AO	*28*	
AP	*71*	
AQ	*71*	
AR	*37*	
83 A	*72*	
B	*41*	
C	17, *92*	
D	*92*	
E	17, *82*	
F	17, *92*	
G	*72*	
H	*72*	
J	*72*	
K	*72*	
L	17, *92*	
M	*92*	
N	17, *72*	
O	17, *92*	
P	*92*	
Q	17, *82*	36 B
R	17, *92*	36 A
S	*82*	
T	*72*	
U	*77*	
V	17, *82*, 92	36 D
W	*77*	
X	17, *29*	

Plate	*Page*	*Plate Ref.*
(83) Y	*92*	
Z	*96*	
AA	*96*	
AB	*92*	
AC	*92*	
AD	15, 17, *92*	36 C
AE	*92*	
AF	*72*	
AG	12, 17, *72*, 102[21]	36 F
AH	*92*	
AJ	*92*	
AK	*92*	
AL	17, *72*, 101[14]	
AM	17, *72*, 101[14]	
AN	*72*	36 E
AO	*77*	
AP	*72*	
AQ	17, *29*	
AR	*77*	
AS	*92*	
AT	17, *72*, 93	
AU	17, *28*, 77, 82, 93	
AV	63, *82*	
84 A	17, *92*, 100[12]	
B	17, *96*, 100[12]	37 H
C	17, *72*, 100[12]	37 F
D	17, *30*, 100[12]	37 G
E	17, 18, *96*, 100[12]	
F	17, 18, *72*, 100[12]	37 J
G	17, 18, *92*, 100[12]	
H	17, 18, *28*, 100[12]	
J	17, *72*, 100[12]	37 K
K	17, *72*, 100[12]	
L	17, *85*, 100[12]	
M	17, *92*, 100[12]	
N	17, *85*, 100[12]	
O	18, *25*, 100[12]	37 C
P	18, *72*, 100[12]	37 E
Q	18, *25*, 100[12]	37 D
R	17, *72*, 100[12]	
S	17, *72*, 100[12]	
T	17, *30*, 100[12]	
U	17, *28*, 100[12]	
V	17, *30*, 100[12]	37 L
W	17, *72*	37 B
X	17, *72*	37 B
Y	17, *37*	
Z	17, *72*	
AA	18, *92*	
AB	18, *37*	
AC	18, *92*	
AD	18, *77*	
AE	18, *72*	37 O
AF	18, *72*	37 M
AG	18, *82*	37 N
AH	*37*	

Plate	*Page*	*Plate Ref.*
(84) AJ	18, *72*	37 A
AK	18, *83*, 98[2]	
AL	18, *73*, 98[2], 100[11]	
AM	18, *73*, 98[2]	
AN	18, *33*, 98[2]	
AO	12, 18, *43*, 98[2], 100[11]	
AP	12, 18, *73*, 98[2], 100[11]	
AQ	18, *73*	38 G
AR	18, *73*	
AS	*73*	
AT	18, *83*	
AU	18, *93*	
AV	18, *92*	38 J
AW	18, *93*	
AX	18, *97*	38 H
AY	18, *92*	
AZ	18, *30*	
BA	18, *25*, 100[12]	38 B
BB	18, *25*, 100[12]	38 A
BC	18, *97*	38 F
BD	10, 18, *38*	38 C
BE	18, *73*, 98[2], 100[11], 102[19]	
BF	18, 30, *92*, 98[2], 100[11], 102[19]	
BG	30, *93*, 98[2], 100[11], 102[19]	
BH	30, *31*, 98[2], 100[11], 102[19]	
BI	—	
BJ	*96*	
BK	*30*	
BL	*33*	
BM	19, *43*	
BN	18, *24*, 71	
BO	12, 19, *92*, 96, 100[11]	
BP	12, 19, *28*, 96, 100[11]	
BQ	12, 19, *73*, 96, 100[11]	39 E
BR	12, 19, *73*, 96, 100[11]	39 D
BS	18, *73*	
BT	12, 19, *77*, 96, 100[11]	
BU	12, 19, *77*, 96, 100[11]	
85 A	*92*, 100[11]	
B	*92*, 100[11]	
C	19, *73*, 100[11]	39 C
D	*73*, 100[11]	
E	19, *77*, 100[11]	39 B
F	19, *73*, 100[11]	39 A
G	*28*, 100[11]	
H	*73*	
J	*73*, 98[2]	
K	*92*, 98[2]	
L	*31*, 98[2]	
M	*24*, 98[2]	
N	*93*, 100[12]	
O	*93*, 100[12]	
P	*93*, 100[12]	
Q	*93*, 100[12]	
R	*93*, 100[12]	
S	93, *97*	

Plate	*Page*	*Plate Ref.*
(85) T	27, 41, *73*	
U	27, 41, *73*	
V	*92*	
W	18, *28*, 93	
X	18, *28*, 93	
Y	*28*	
Z	*73*	
AA	*73*	
AB	*91*	
AC	*91*	
AD	19, *30*	
AE	19, *97*	
AF	19, *92*	
AG	19, *92*	
AH	19, *77–78*	
AJ	19, *73*	
AK	14, 19, *69*, 107[43]	38 L
AL	14, 19, *69*, 107[43]	38 M
AM	19, *69*	
AN	14, 19, *69*	38 N
AO	19, *92*	
AP	19, *93*	
AQ	14, 19, *41*	38 O
AR	19, *83*	
AS	19, *41*	
AT	14, 19, *69*	38 P
AU	19, *73*	
AV	19, *97*	
AW	*97*	
AX	*73*	39 N
AY	*83*	39 F
AZ	*73*	39 G
BA	*93*	
BB	19, *40*	39 P
BC	19, *81*	39 R
BD	19, *93*	
BE	19, *93*	
BF	19, *78*	
BG	19, *78*	
BH	19, *93*	
BJ	19, *73*	
BK	9, 19, *24*	
BL	9, 19, *30*	
86 A	14, *81*	40 D
B	14, *69*	Fr.B; 40 B
C	14, *91*	40 E
D	14, *81*	40 F
E	14, *69*	Fr.C; 40 A
F	14, *25*	Fr.A; 40 G
G	14, *81*	Fr.D; 40 C
H	14, *69*	
J	14, *23*	
K	14, *77*	
L	14, *25*	Fr. A; 40 G
M	14, *69*	40 H
N	14, *91*	40 J
(86) O	14, *81*	41 F
P	11, 14, *70*	Fr.H; 41 L
Q	14, *81*	41 K
R	12, 14, *81*	42 D
S	11, 14, *70*	Fr.J; 41 G
T	14, *27*, *95*	
U	14, *70*	41 H
V	14, *23*	
W	14, *70*	Fr.K; 41 J
X	14, *70*	41 D
Y	14, *69*	41 A
Z	12, 14, *81*, 107[42]	41 C
AA	11, 14, *69*, 102[21]	41 B
AB	14, *81*	
AC	14, *70*	
AD	14, *70*	
AE	14, *70*	
AF	14, *70*	
AG	14, *27*	41 E
AH	14, *70*	
AJ	14, *70*	
AK	14, *81*	
AL	14, *25*	Fr. L
AM	14, *70*	
AN	11, 14, *28*, 102[21]	Fr.M; 42 A
AO	11, 14, *70*, 100, 102[21]	Fr.N; 42 E
AP	14, *70*	
AQ	14, *70*	Fr.O; 42 B
AR	14, *70*	42 C
AS	14, *70*	
AT	14, *70*	
87 A	14, *72*	
B	14, *97*	
C	14, *69*	40 K
D	14, *28*	40 L
E	14, *69*	
F	14, *69*	Fr.E
G	11, 14, *91*	42 G
H	11, 14, *70*	42 F
J	15, *71*	43 C
K	15, *23*	43 A
L	15, *70*	43 B
M	*72*	
N	16, *40*	Fr.G; 43 E
O	*72*	
P	*25*	Fr. F
Q	*23*	
R	16, *82*	43 D
88 A	12, *70*, 100, 100[12]	44 B
B	12, *91*, 100[12]	44 A
C	12, *81*, 100[12], 102[19]	44 H
D	12, *70*, 100[12]	
E	12, *77*, 100[12]	
F	12, *70*, 100[12]	
G	12, *91*, 100[12]	
H	12, *81*, 100[12], 102[19]	44 G

Plate	*Page*	*Plate Ref.*
(88) J	12, *70*, 100[12]	
K	12, *28*, 100[12]	
L	12, *70*, 100[12]	
M	12, *37*, 100[12]	
N	12, *70*, 100[12]	
O	12, *70*, 100[12]	
P	12, 13, *77*, 100[12], 102[19]	44 E
Q	12, *95–96*, 100[12]	
R	12, *77*, 100[12]	
S	12, *77*, 100[12]	
T	12, *70*, 100[12]	
U	12, 14, *91*, 100[12]	
V	12, *91*, 100[12]	
W	12, 13, *70*, 100[12]	44 C
X	12, *96*, 100[12]	
Y	12, *92*, 100[12]	
Z	12, *70*, 100[12]	
AA	12, *92*, 100[12]	
AB	12, *92*, 100[12]	
AC	12, *70*, 100[12]	
AD	12, *70*, 100[12]	
AE	12, *96*, 100[12]	
AF	12, *28*, 100[12]	
AG	12, *92*, 100[12]	
AH	12, *28*, 100[12]	
AJ	12, *91*, 100[12]	
AK	12, *70*, 100[12]	
AL	12, *91*, 100[12]	
AM	*92*	
AN	12, 15, *85*	44 J
AO	12, 15, 38, *82*	44 K
AP	*92*	
AQ	12, *72*	
AR	12, *73*	44 L
AS	12, 70, 91, *92*	
AT	12, *72*	
AU	*73*	
AV	*72*	
AW	*97*	
AX	*92*	
AY	*73*	
AZ	*73*	
89 A	*73*	
B	*30*	
C	*92*	
D	*82*	
E	*73*	
F	*92*	
G	*28*	
H	*97*	
J	*73*	
K	*77*	
L	12, *73*	44 N
M	*82*	
N	*30*	
O	*82*	
(89) P	*82–83*	
Q	*73*, 100[12]	
R	*96*	
S	12, *73*, 100[12]	44 M
T	*28*	
U	*83*	46 A
V	*82*	
W	*72*	
X	12, *96*	
Y	12, *31*	
Z	12, *72–73*	
AA	*92*	
AB	*73*	
AC	17, 19, *28*	39 U
AD	12, *77*	39 V
AE	*77*	
AF	13, *83*	
AG	13, *83*	
AH	13, *28*	
AJ	13, *73*	
AK	13, *97*	29 M
AL	13, *73*	
AM	13, *92*	
AN	13, *83*	
AO	13, *83*	
AP	13, *73*	
AQ	*92*	
AR	*85*	
AS	12, *73*, 85, 99[6], 100[12], 102[21]	46 B
AT	13, *85*, 100[12], 102[21]	
AU	*43*, 100[12]	
AV	13, *43*, 100[12], 102[21]	
AW	13, *83*, 100[12]	
AX	13, *96*	
AY	*73*, 100[12]	
AZ	*83*, 100[12]	
BA	*97*, 100[12]	
BB	*73*, 100[12]	
BC	12, *73*, 100[12]	
BD	12, *73*, 100[12]	
BE	12, *85*, 100[12]	
BF	12, *92*, 100[12]	
BG	12, *73*, 100[12]	
BH	12, *28*, 100[12]	
BJ	12, *73*, 85, 100[12]	
BK	12, *73*, 85, 100[12]	
BL	12, *73*, 100[12]	
BM	12, *83*, 100[12]	
BN	12, *73*, 100[12]	
BO	12, *97*, 100[12]	
BP	12, *73*, 100[12]	
90 A	*73*, *121*	
B	*24*, *120*	
C	*25*, *121*	
D	*83*, *120*	
E	*28*, *121*	

Plate	*Page*	*Plate Ref.*
(90) F	*83, 120*	
G	*25, 121*	
H	*73, 120*	
J	*73, 121*	
K	10, *73*	
L	*93, 121*	
M	*97, 120*	
N	*73, 121*	
O	*83, 120–121*	
P	*73, 121*	
91 A	*73, 121*	
B	*24*, 120	
C	*23–24, 120*	
D	*24, 120*	

Plate	*Page*	*Plate Ref.*
(91) E	10, *24*	
F	10	
G	10, *40*	
H	9, *30*	
J	10, *24*	
K	*73–74*	
L	*96*	
M	*93*	
N	*93*	
O	*74*	45 H
P	*74*	
Q	*83*	39 T
R	*74*	
S	*93*	39 S

3. EXCAVATION GRAVE NUMBERS: TEXT GRAVE NUMBERS

Ex. No.	*Text No.*	*Page*
I	14	62
II	31	78
III	30	78
IV	26	75
V	20	64
VI	16	63
VII	6	57
VIII	21	65
IX	11	60
X	9	59
XI	12	61
XII	10	60
XIII	7	58
XIV	15	63
XV	17	63
XVI	18	63
XVII	8	59
XVIII	3	56
XIX	1	54
XX	13	61
XXI	5	57
XXII	4	57
XXIII	28	76
XXIV	27	75
XXV	25	75
XXVI	24	75
XXVII	2	56
XXVIII	29	78
XXIX	22	66
XXX	40	94
XXXI	19	64
XXXII	23	74
XXXIII	33	86
XXXIV	38	94
XXXV	37	93
XXXVI	34	86
XXXVII	39	94
XXXVIII	32	85
XXXIX	36	87
XL	35	87

INDEX

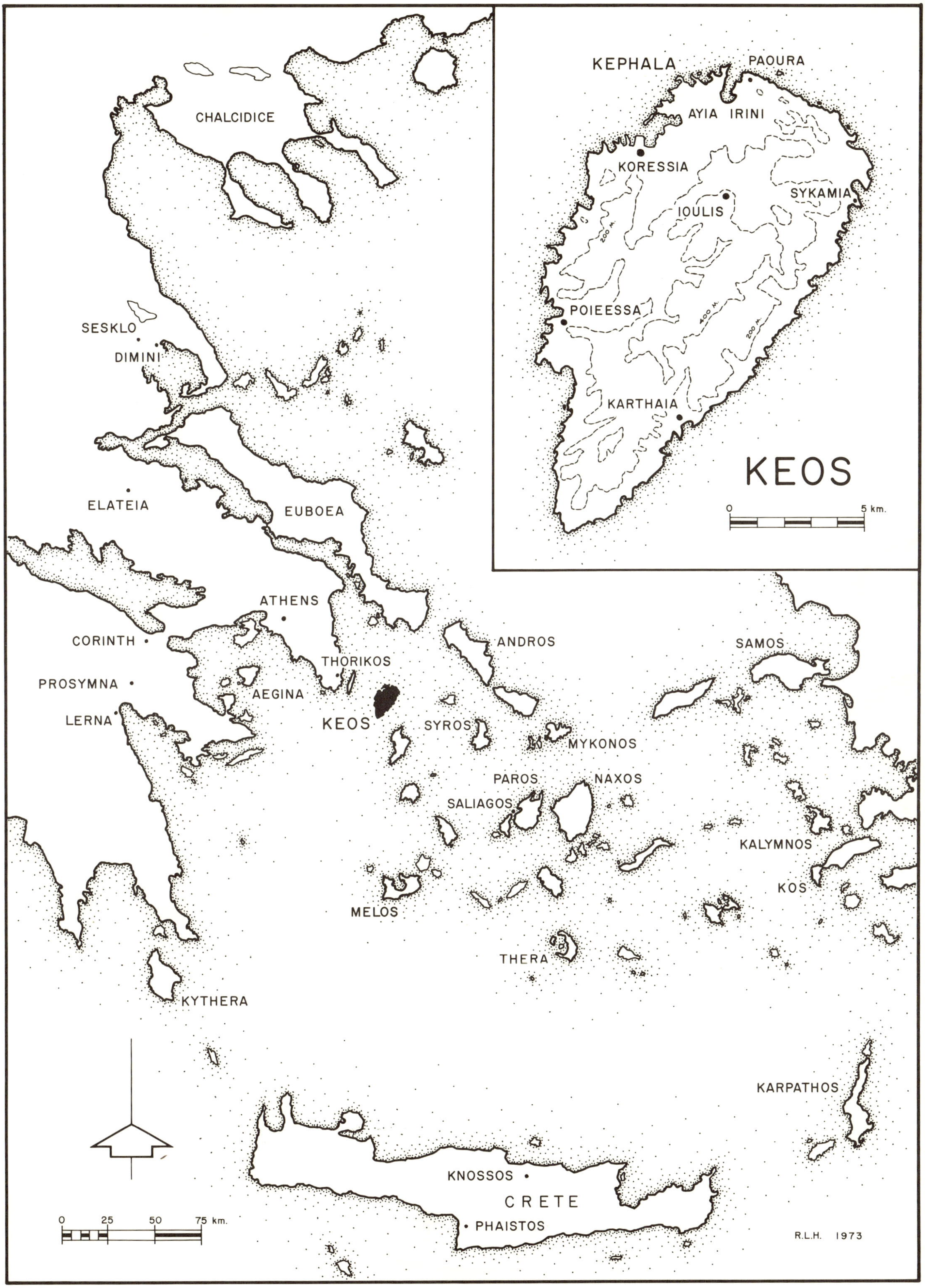

Maps of the central Aegean and Keos

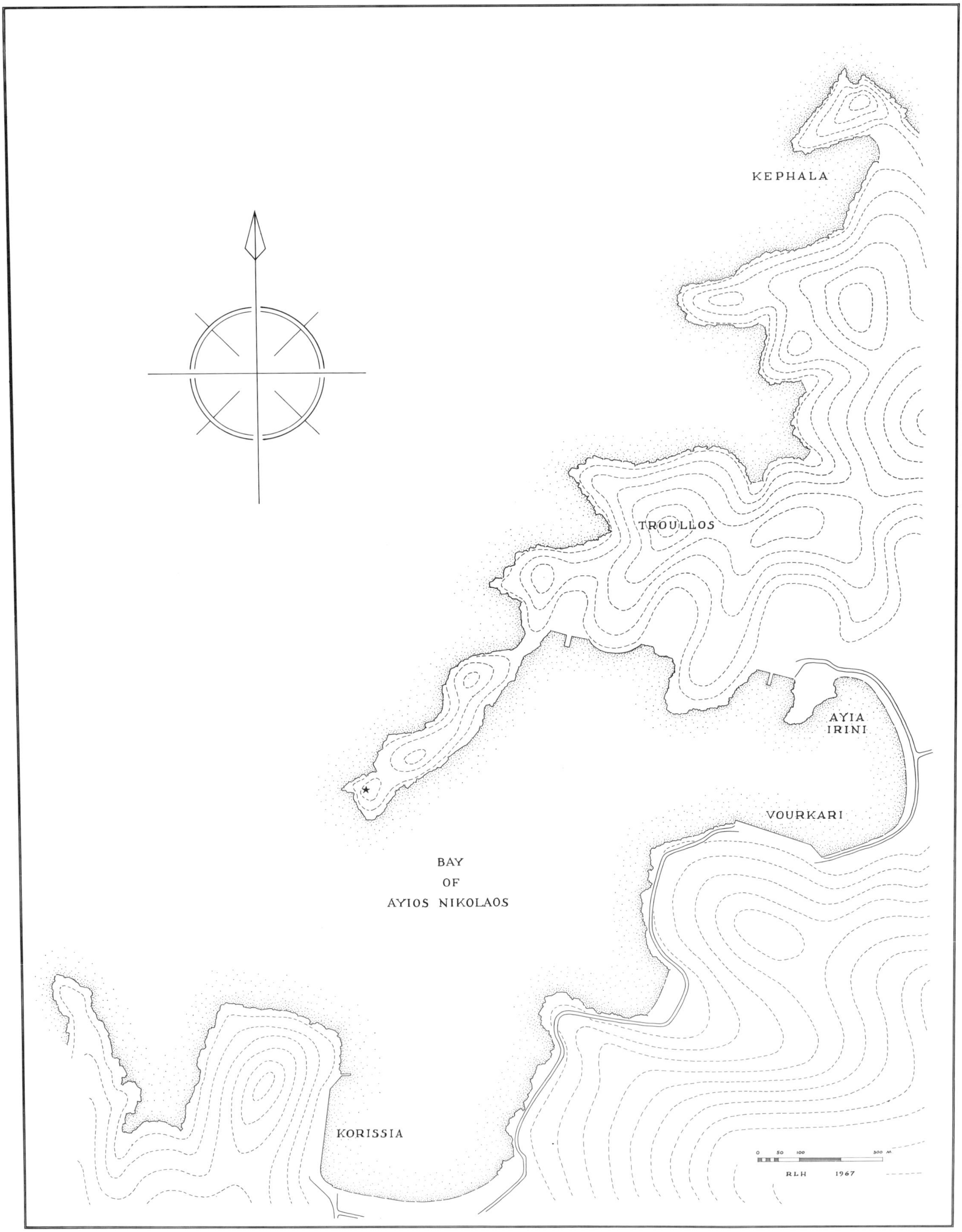

Map of part of northwest coast of Keos

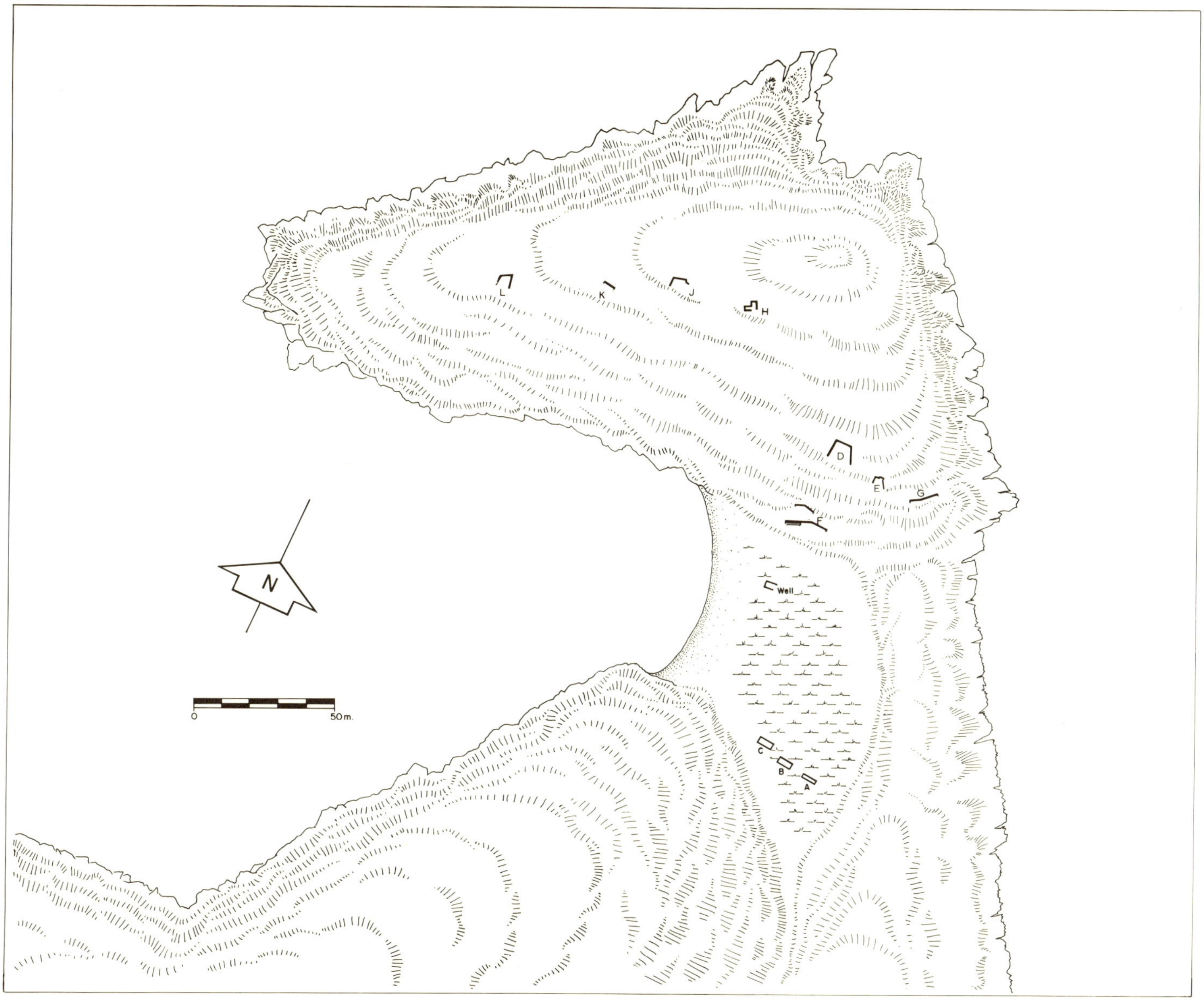

General plan of Kephala

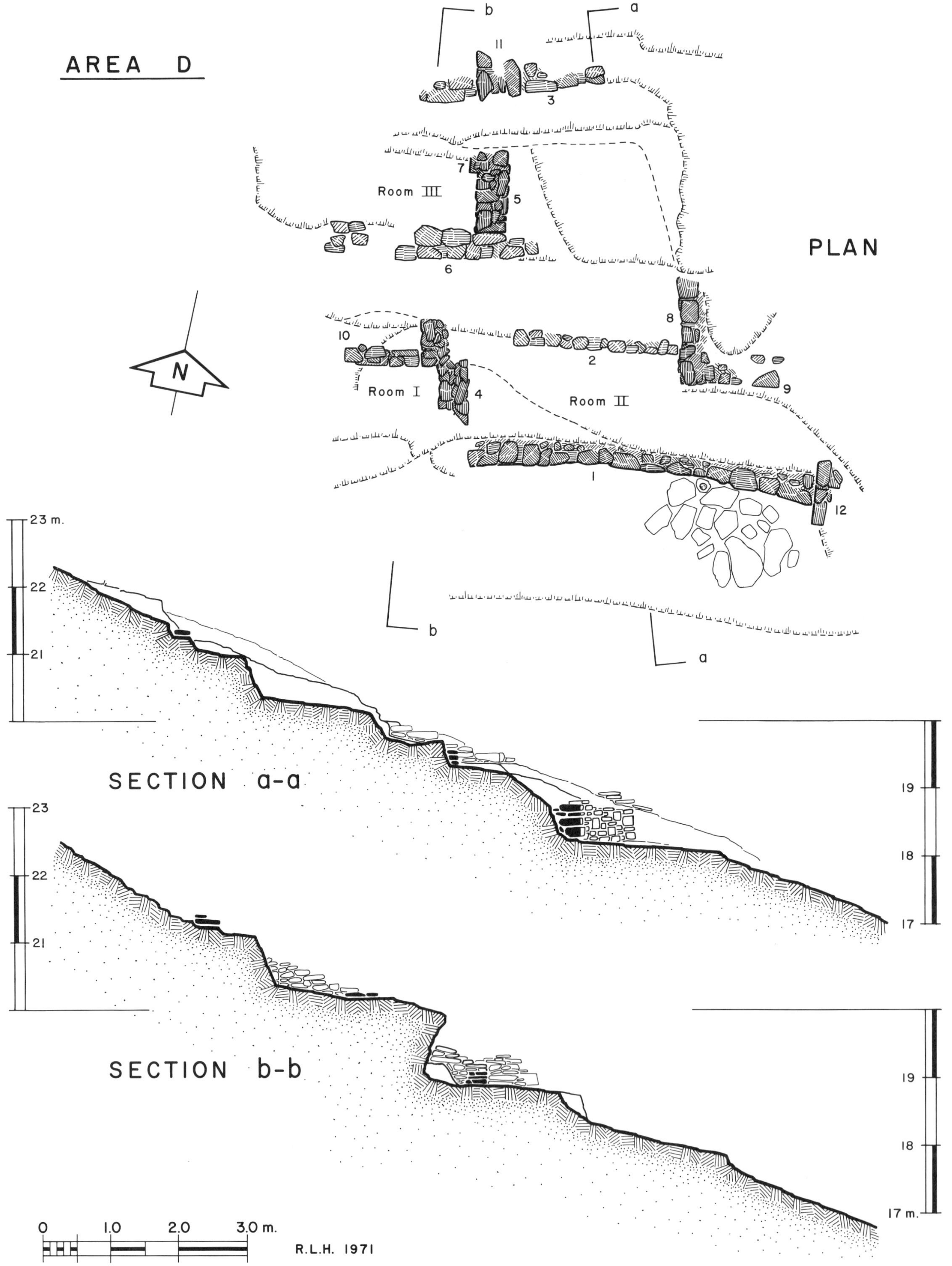

Plan and sections of Area D

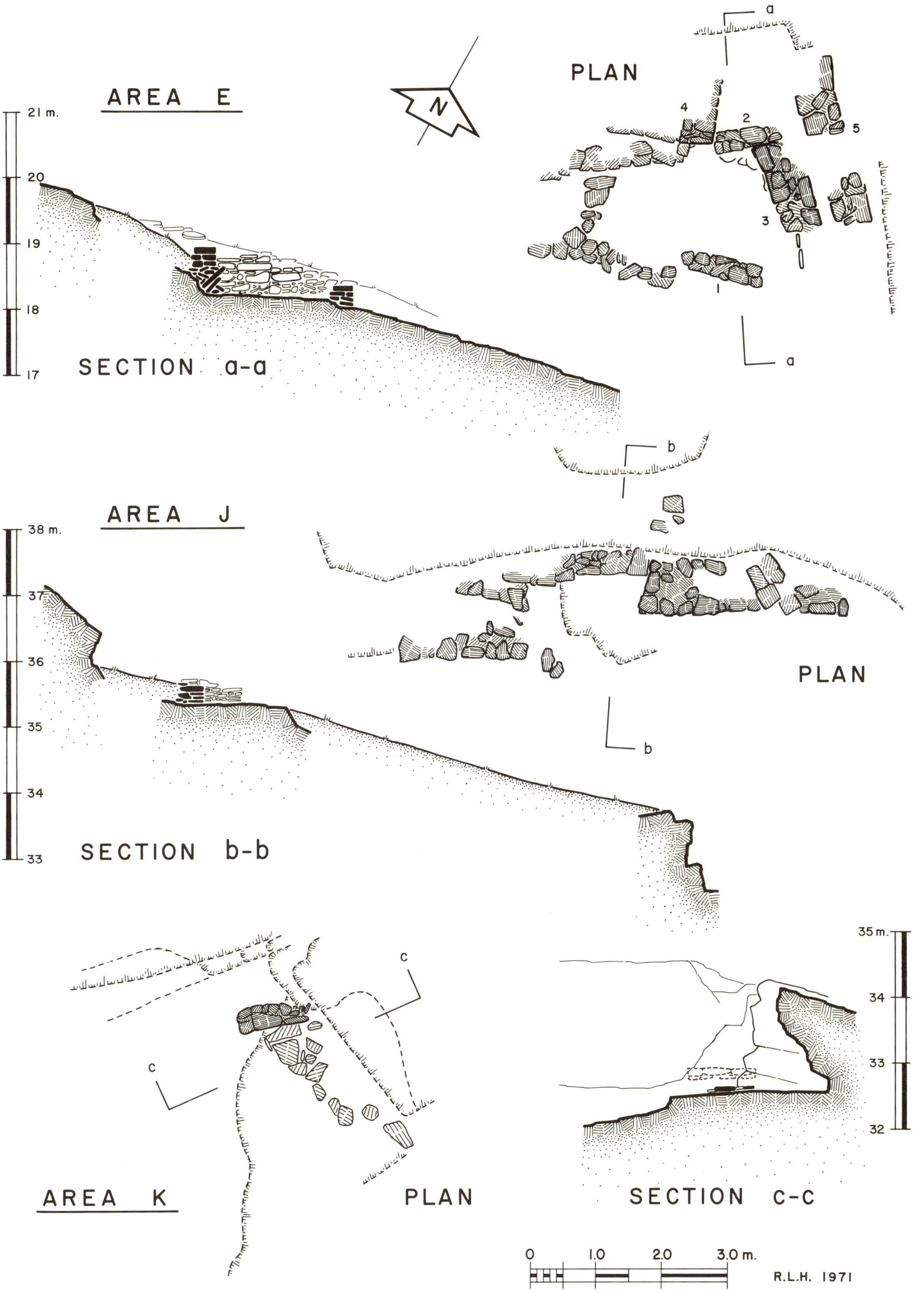

Plans and sections of Areas E, J and K

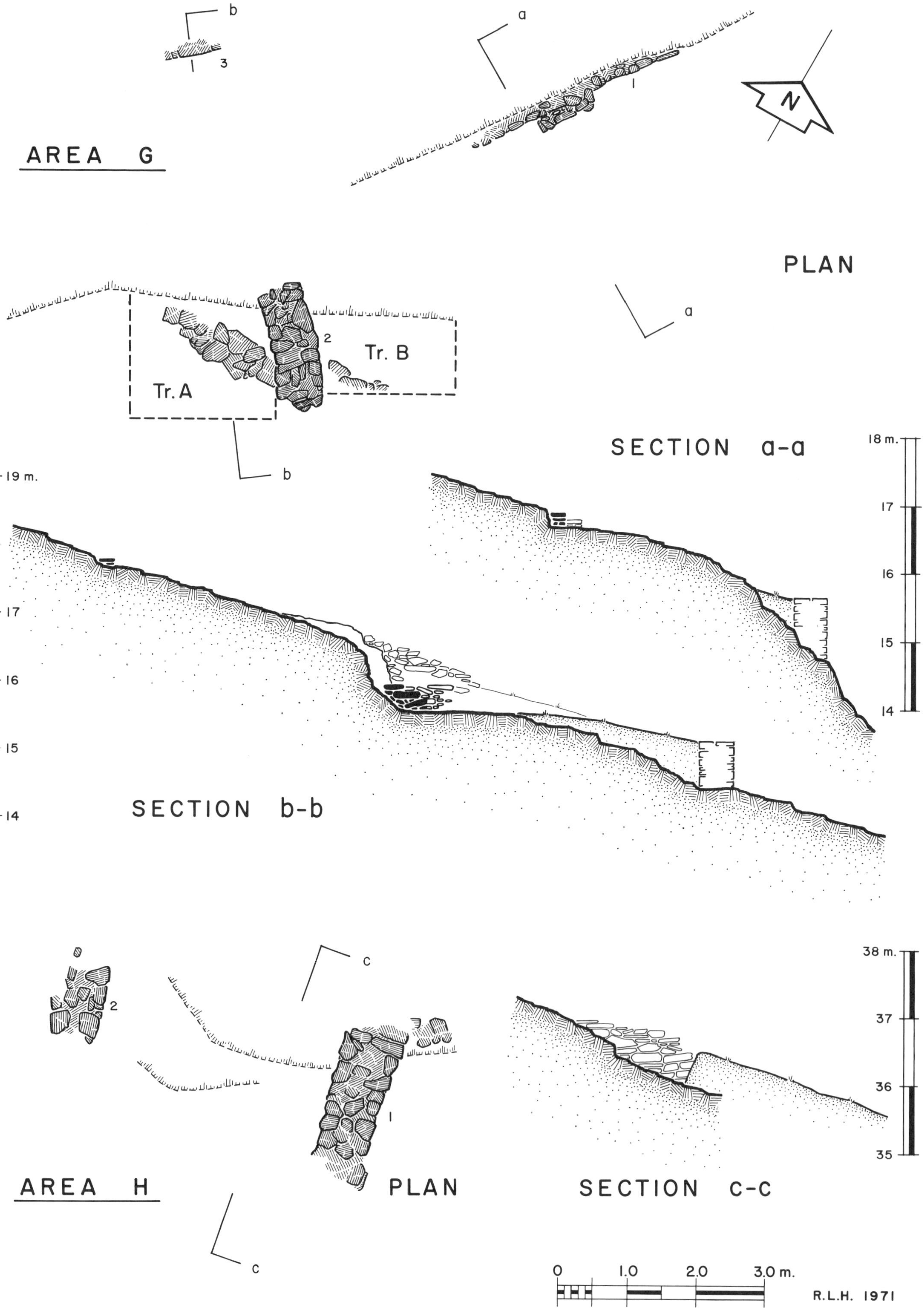

Plans and sections of Areas G and H

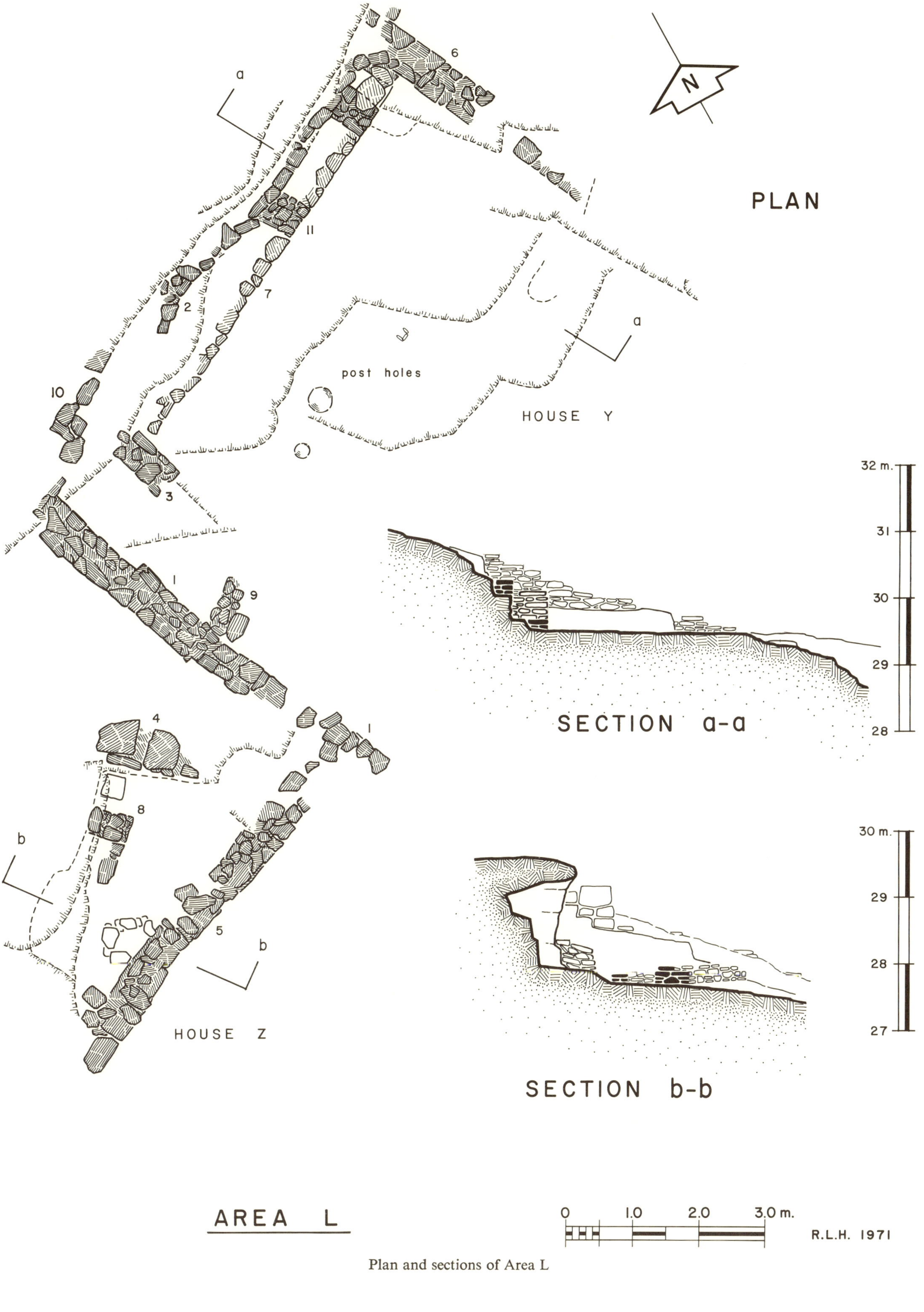

Plan and sections of Area L

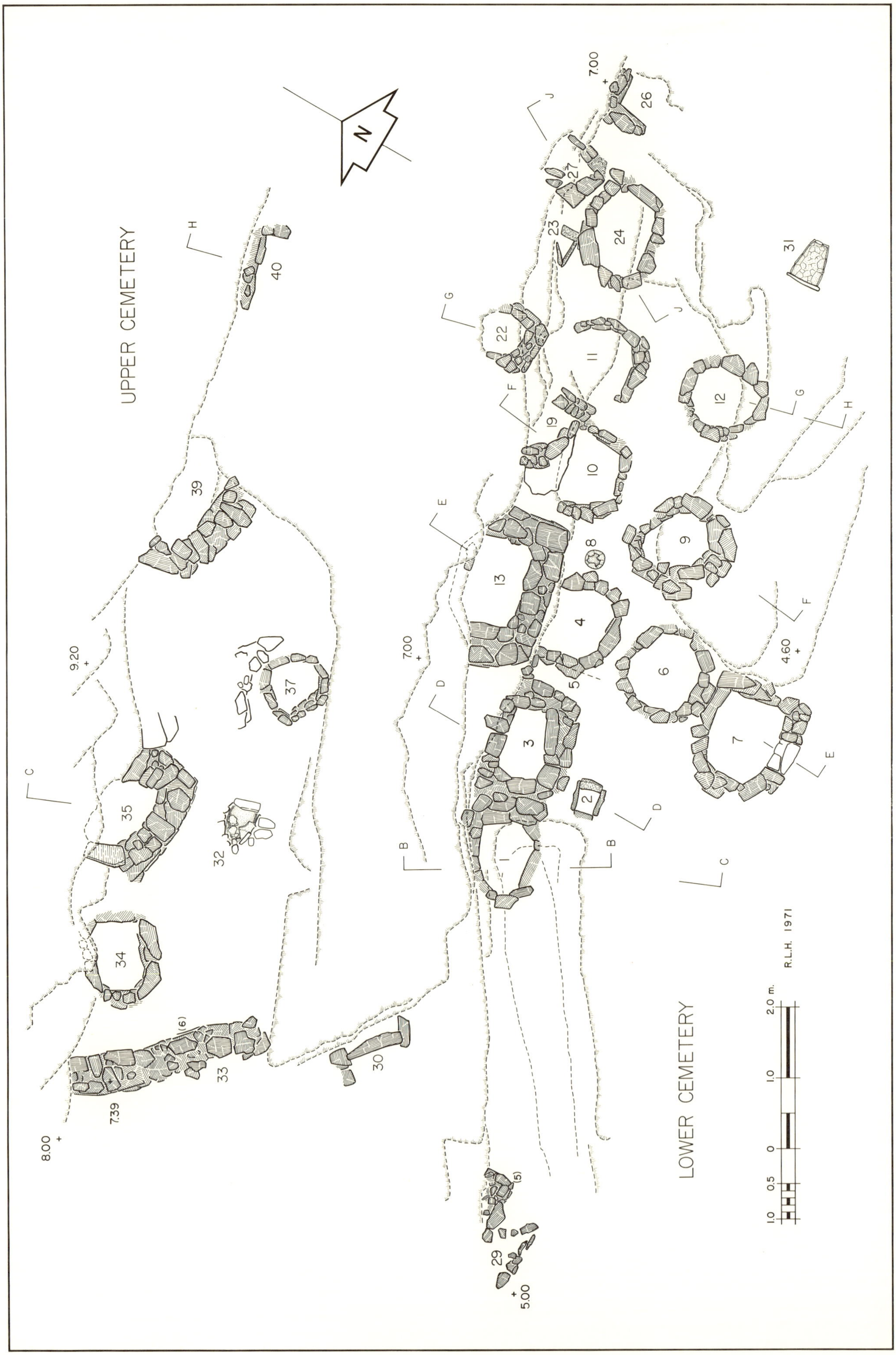

General plan of Cemetery (Area F)

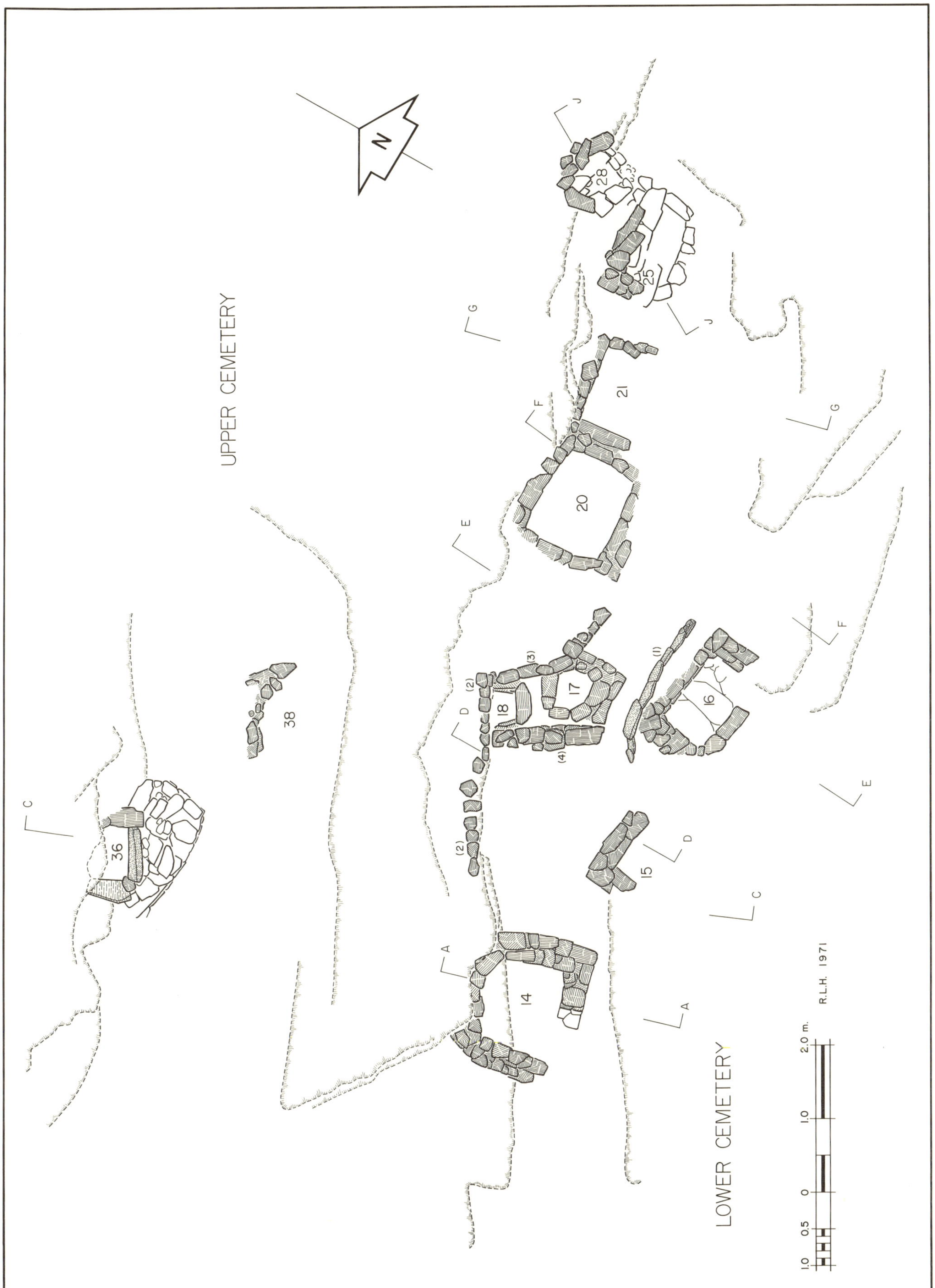

Plan of Cemetery (Area F) showing uppermost graves and walls

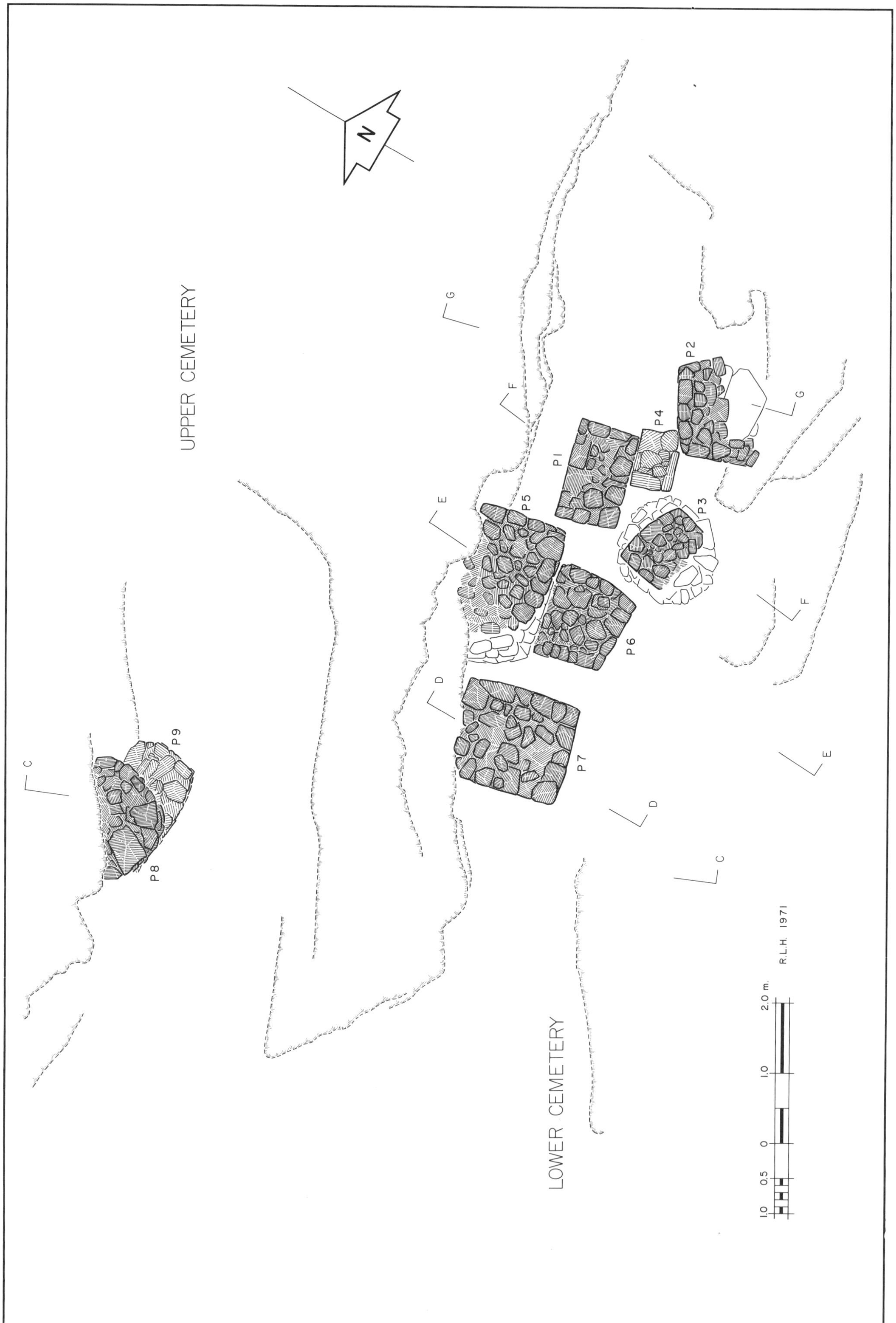

Plan of Cemetery (Area F) showing platforms

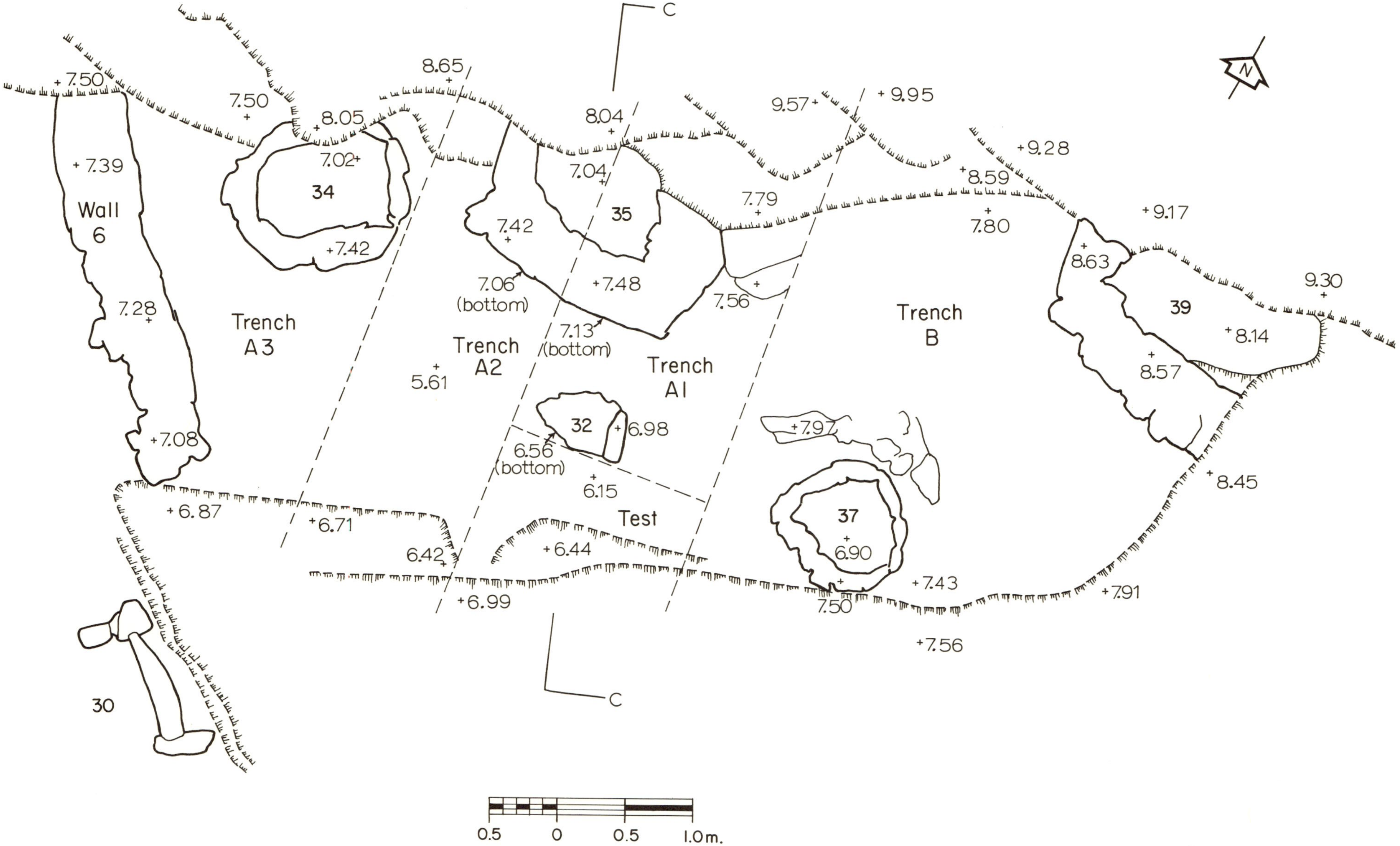

Plan of Upper Cemetery showing trenches and levels of graves and bedrock

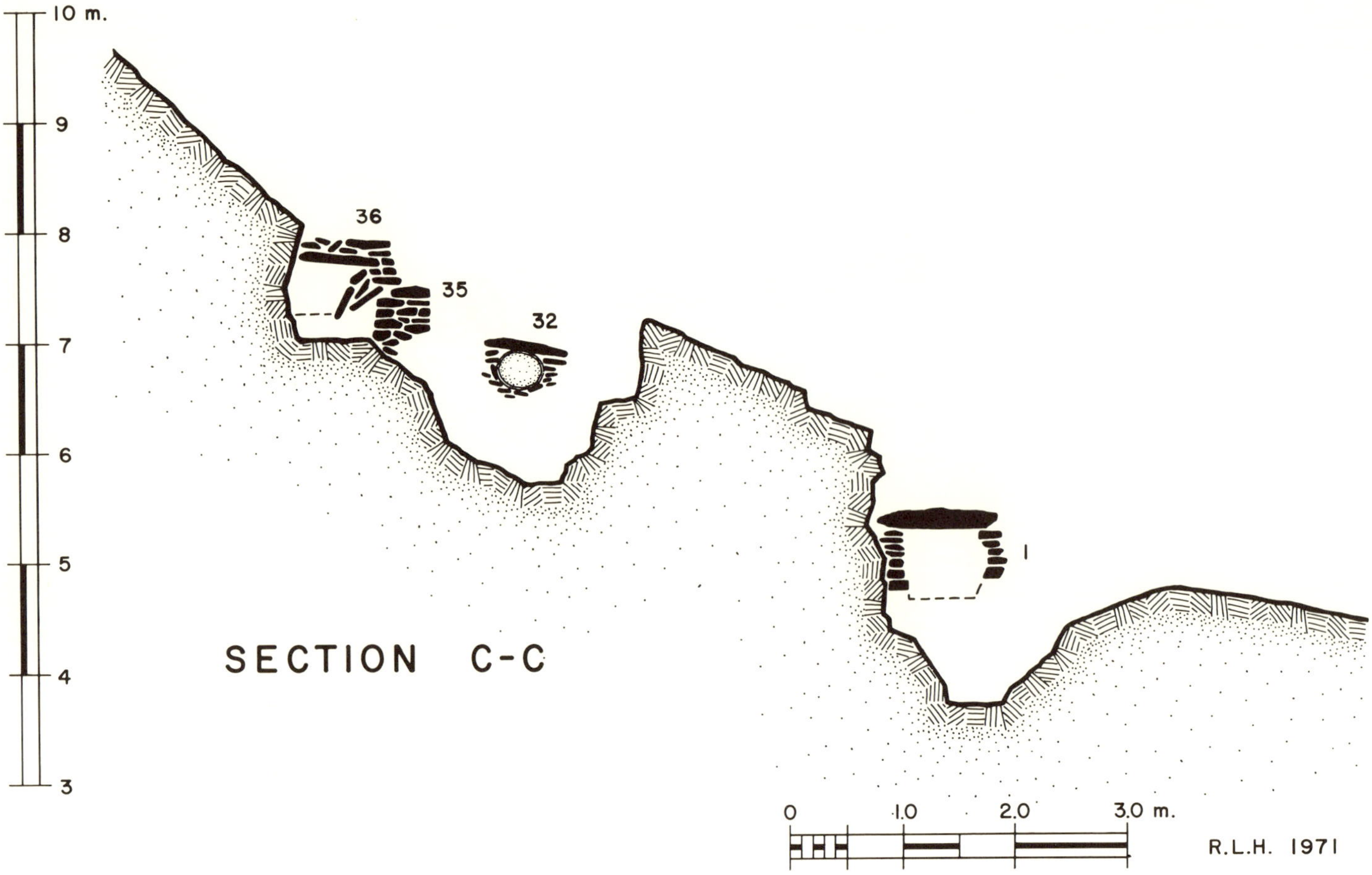

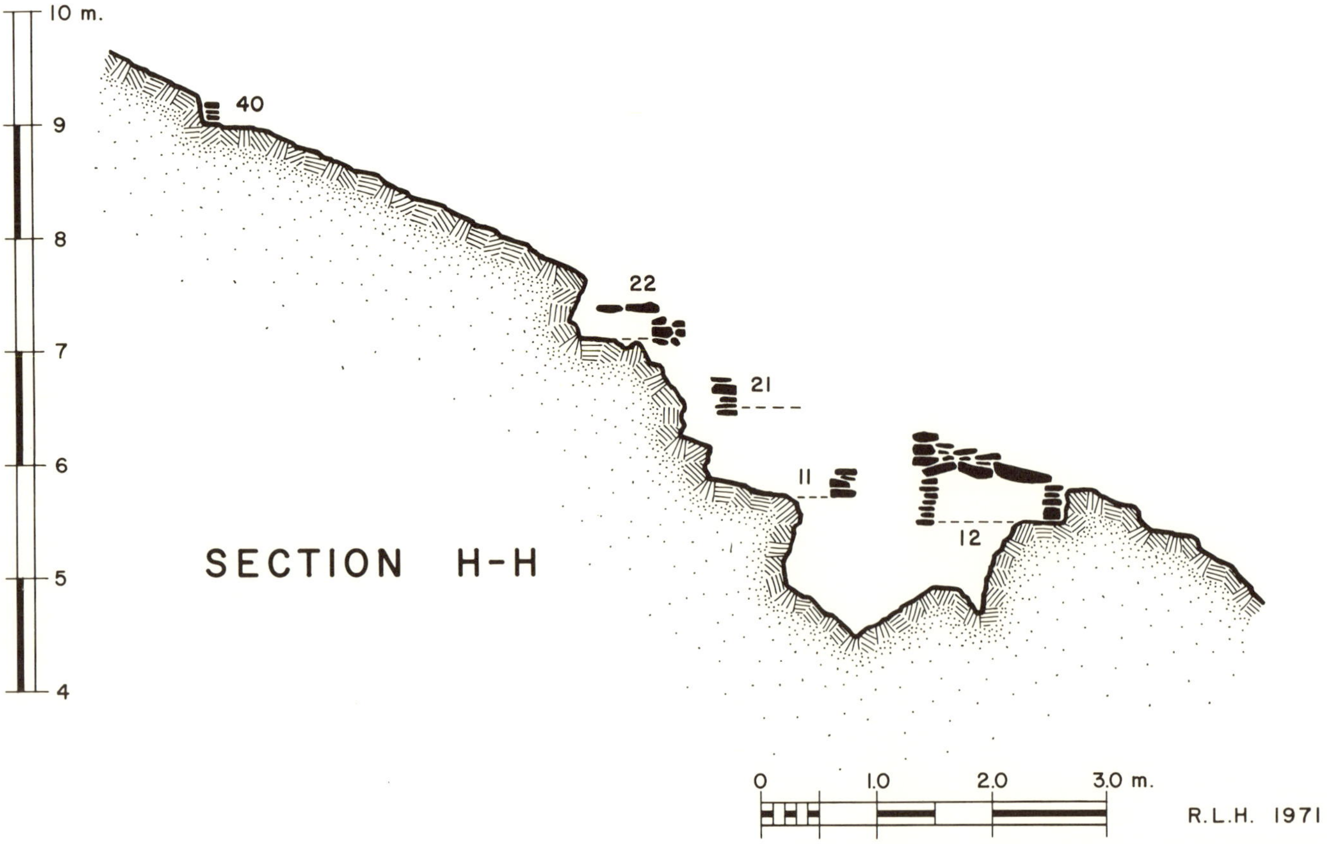

Cemetery, Sections C–C and H–H

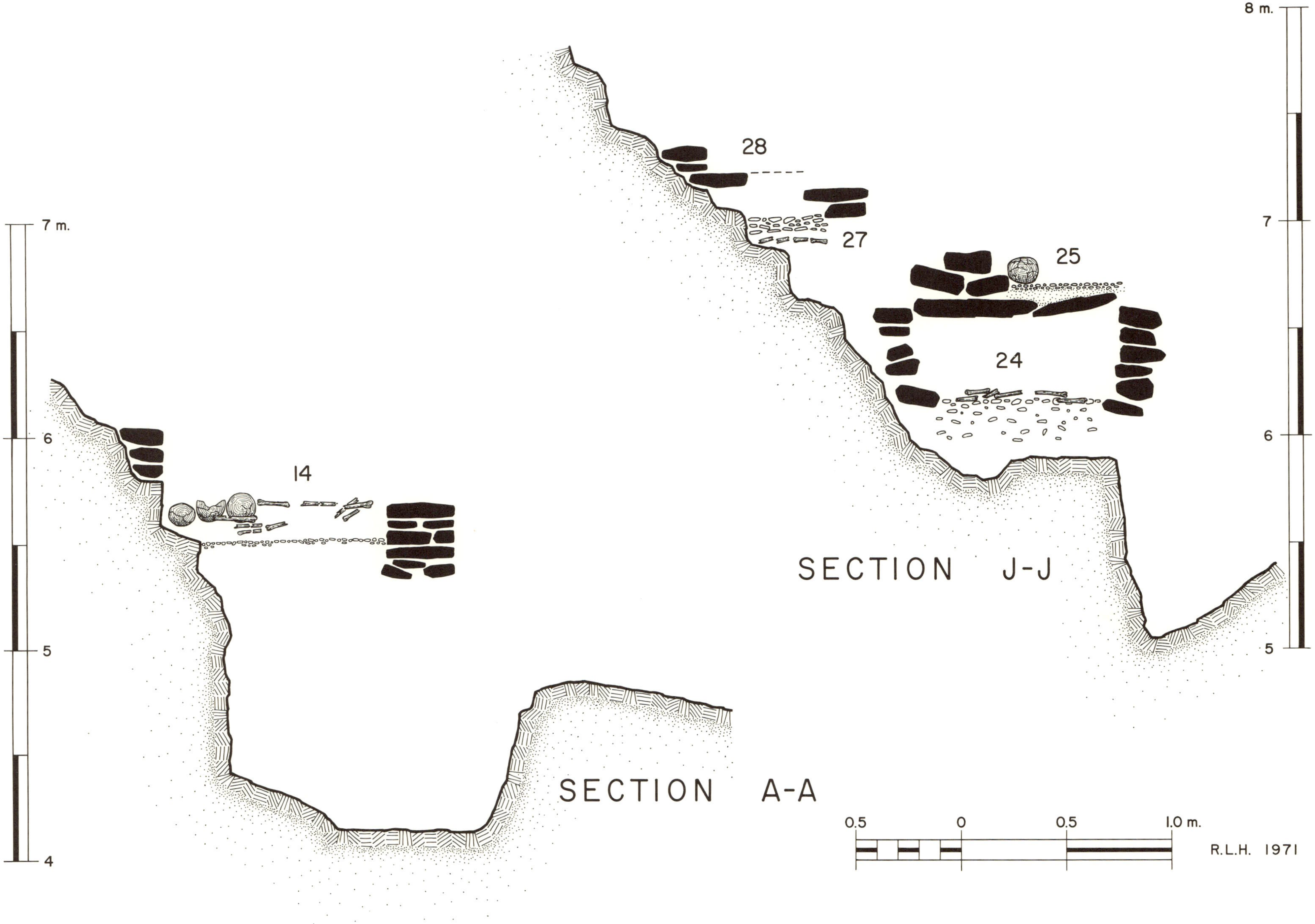

Lower Cemetery, Sections A–A and J–J

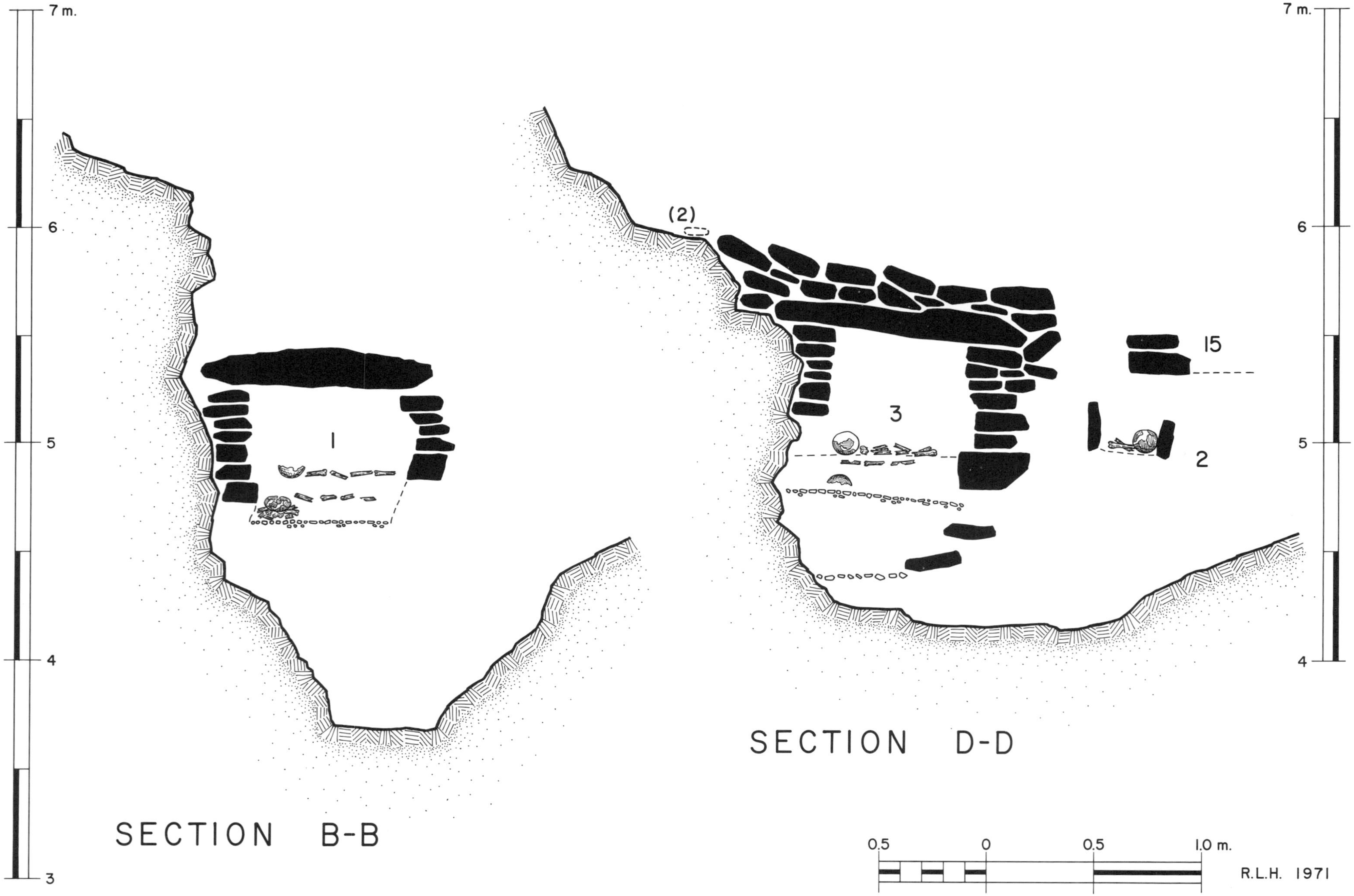

Lower Cemetery, Sections B–B and D–D

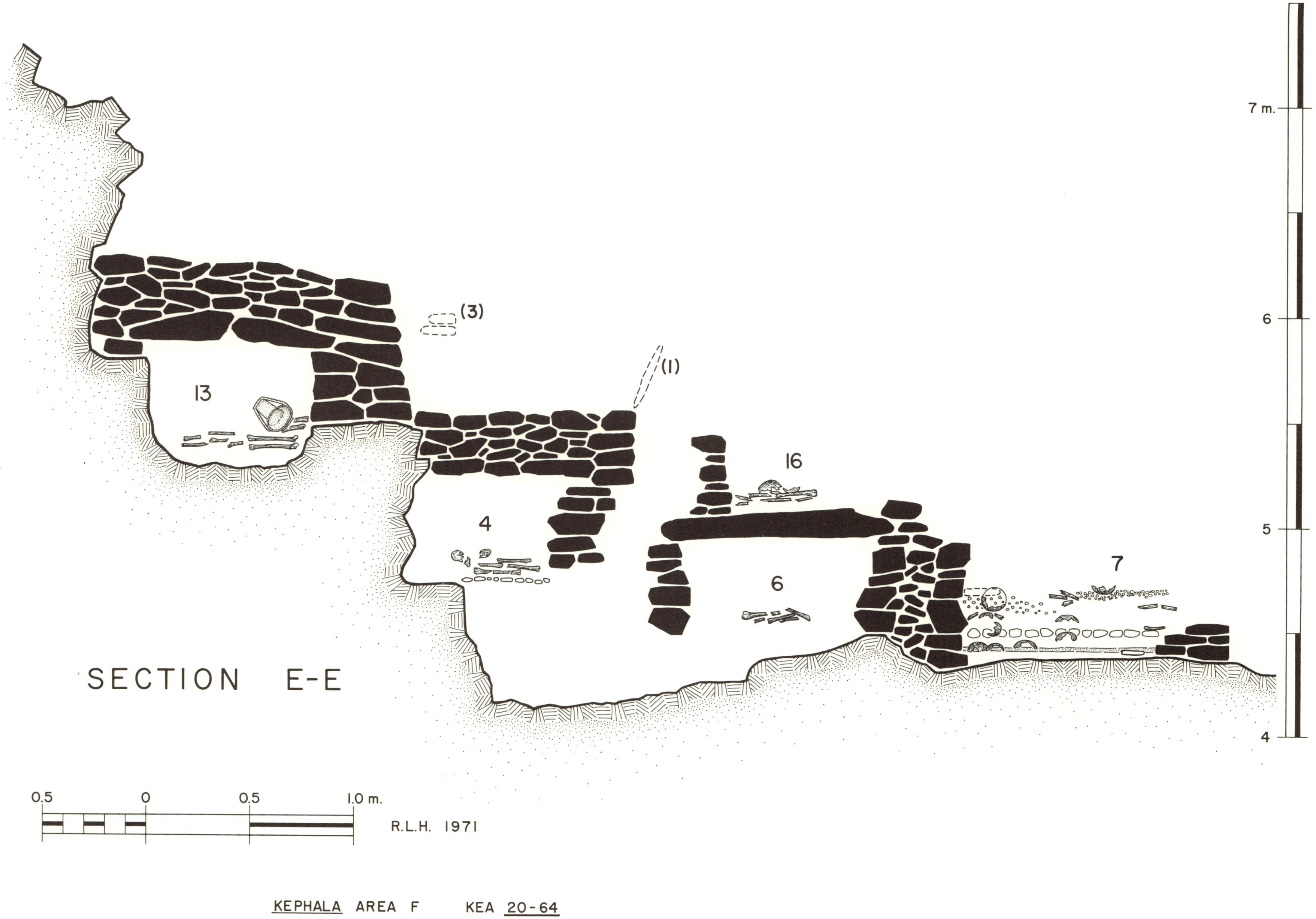

Lower Cemetery, Section E-E

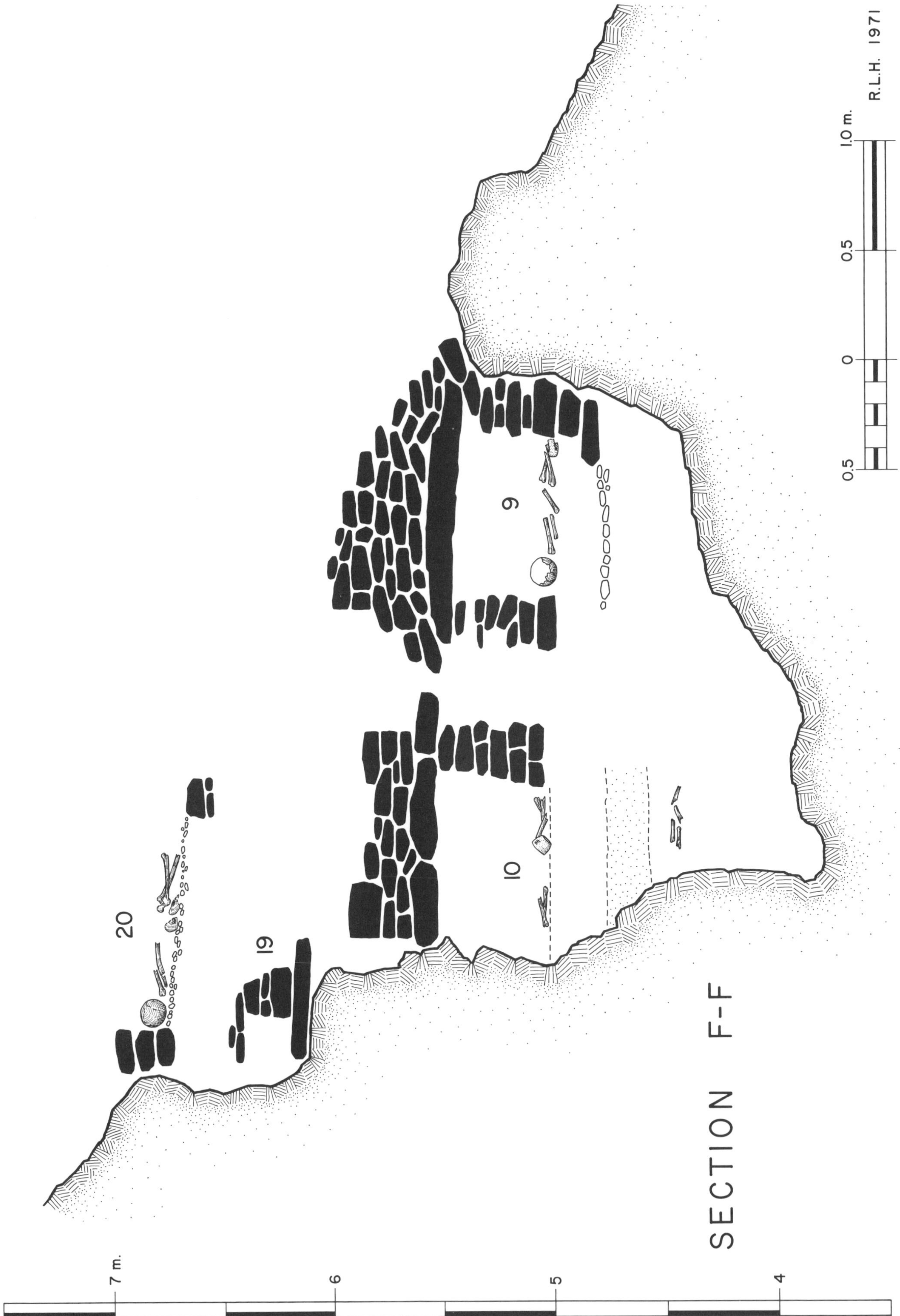

Lower Cemetery, Section F-F

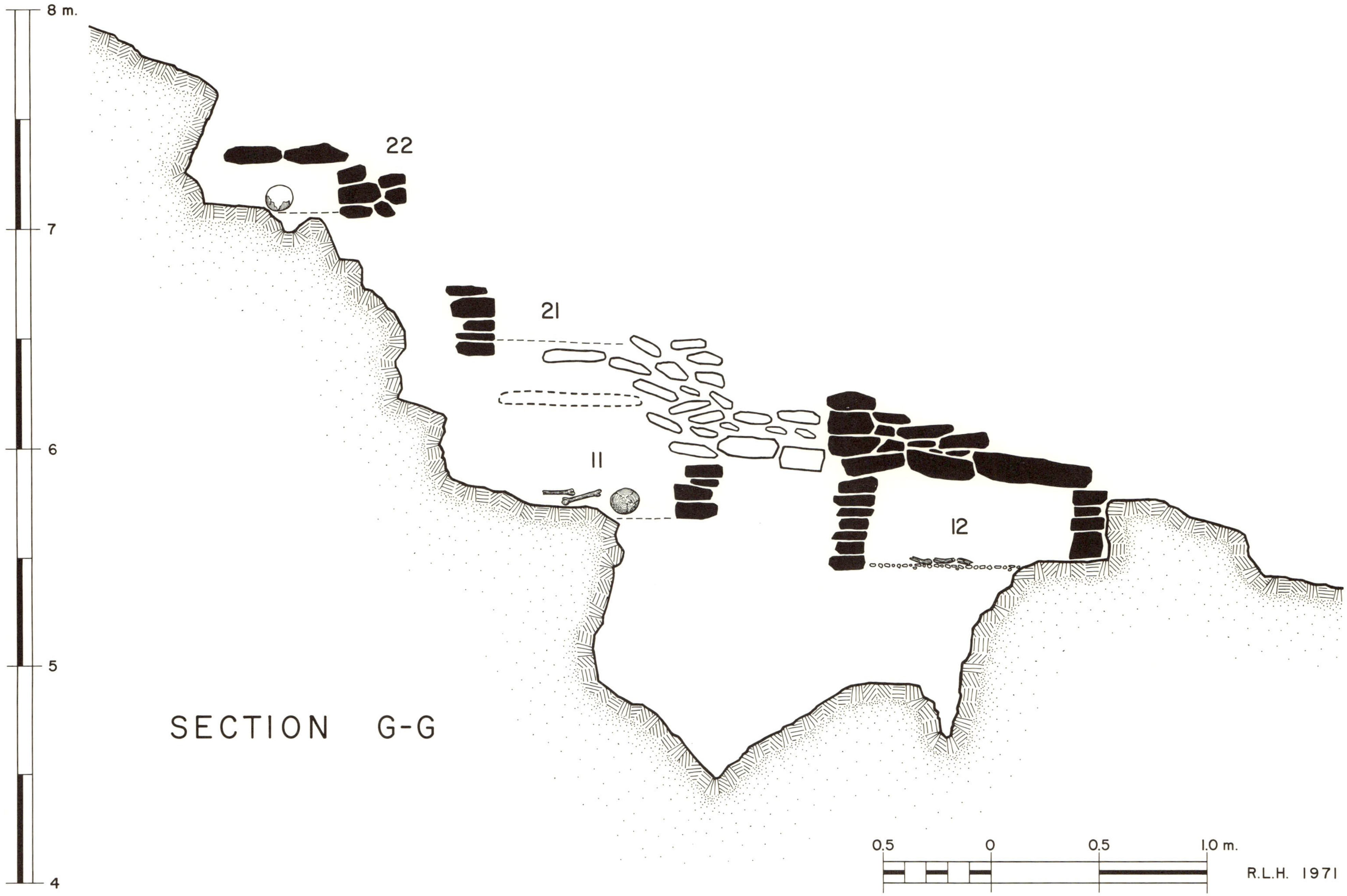

Lower Cemetery, Section G–G

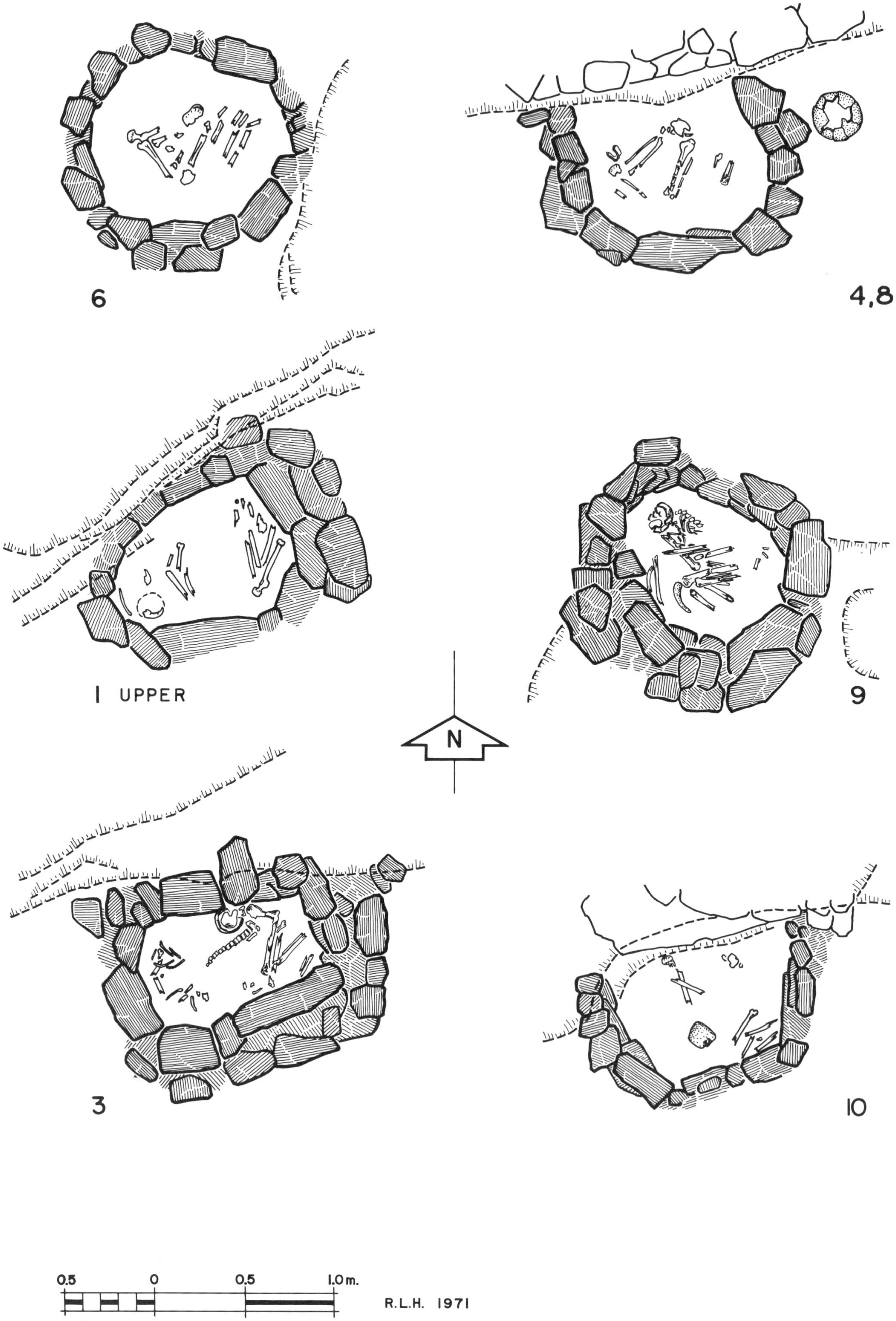

Plans of graves showing burials

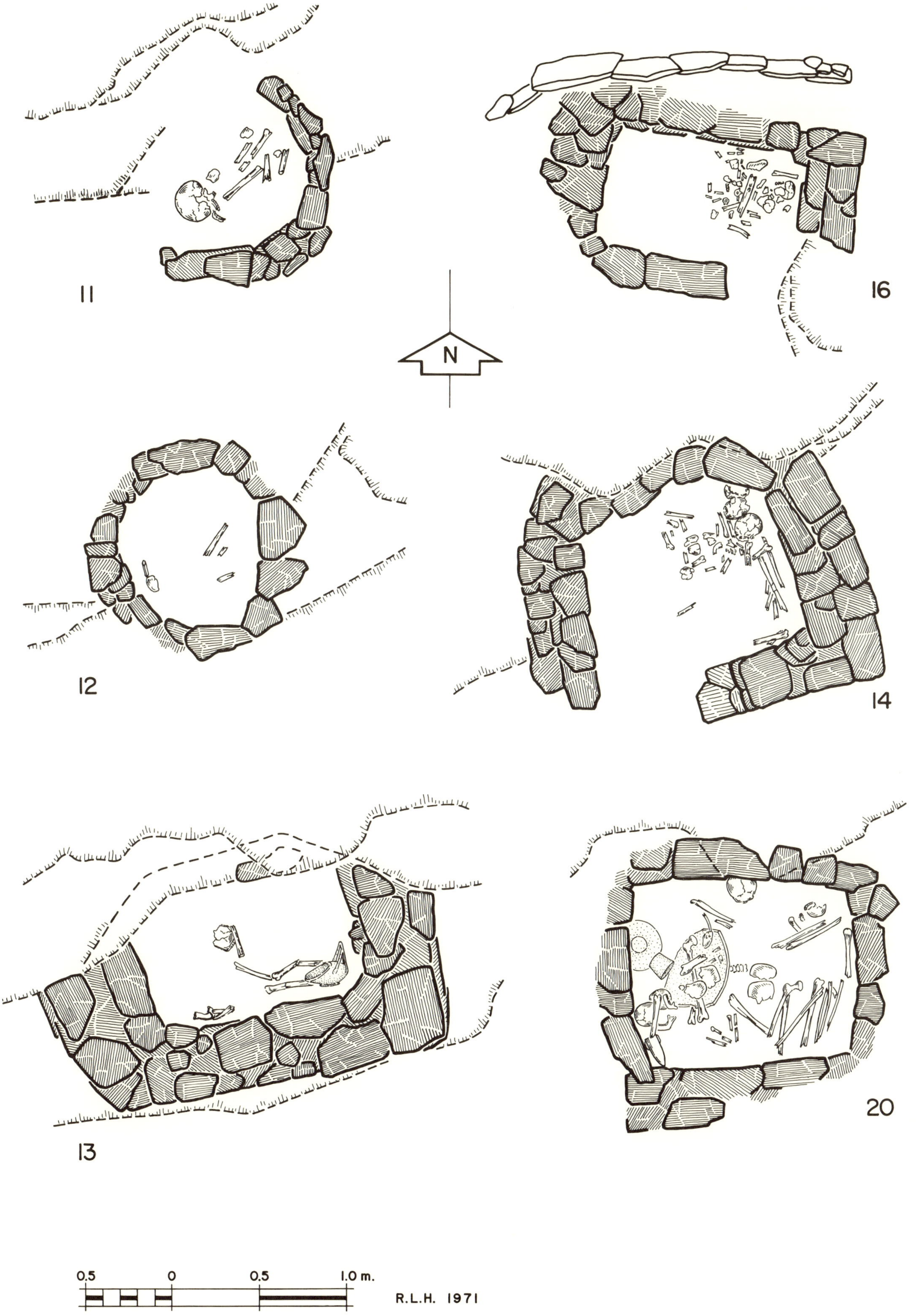

Plans of graves showing burials

7 UPPER

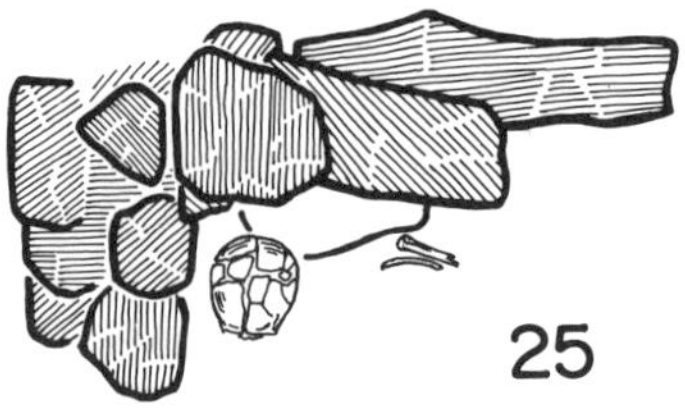

25

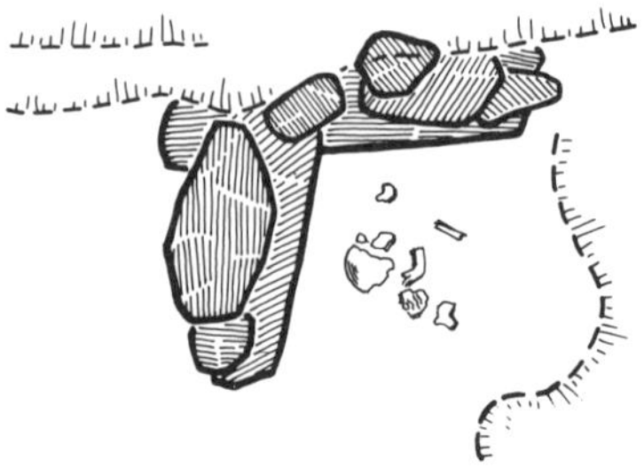

26

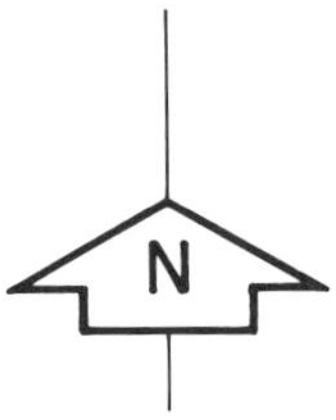

7 MIDDLE

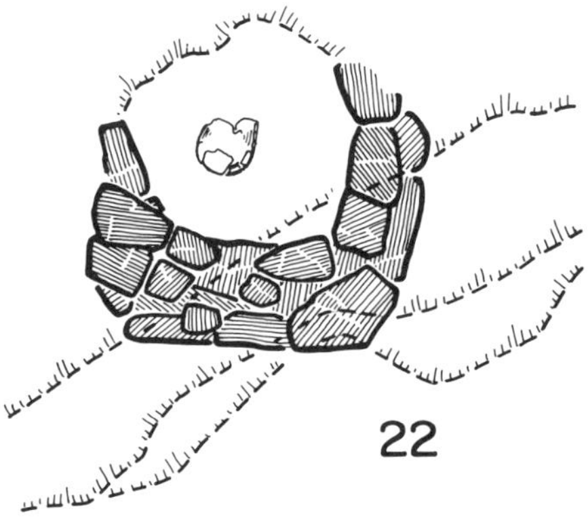

22

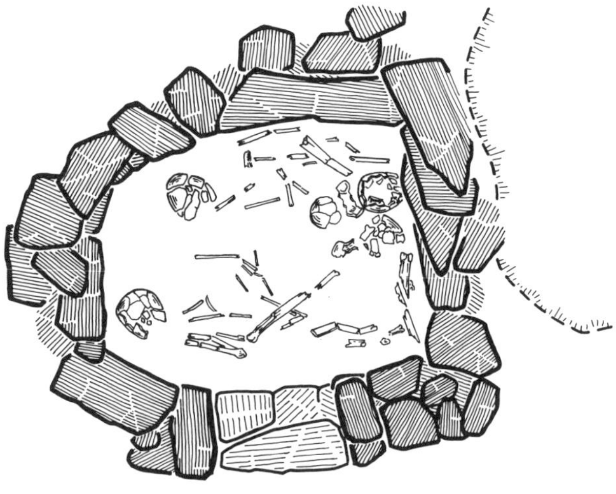

7 LOWER

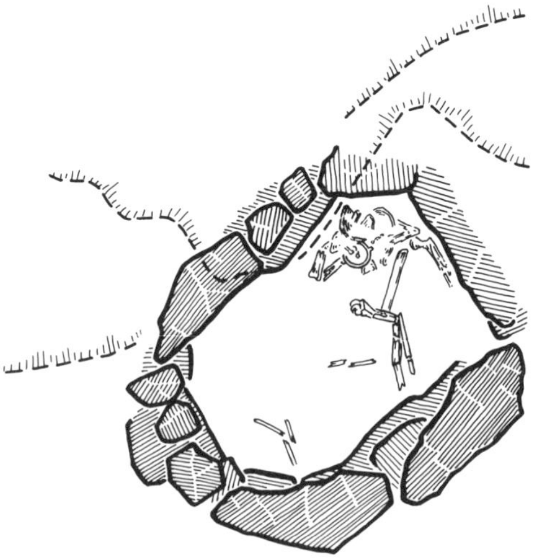

34

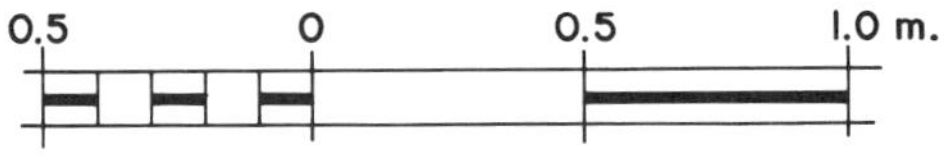

R.L.H. 1971

Plans of graves showing burials

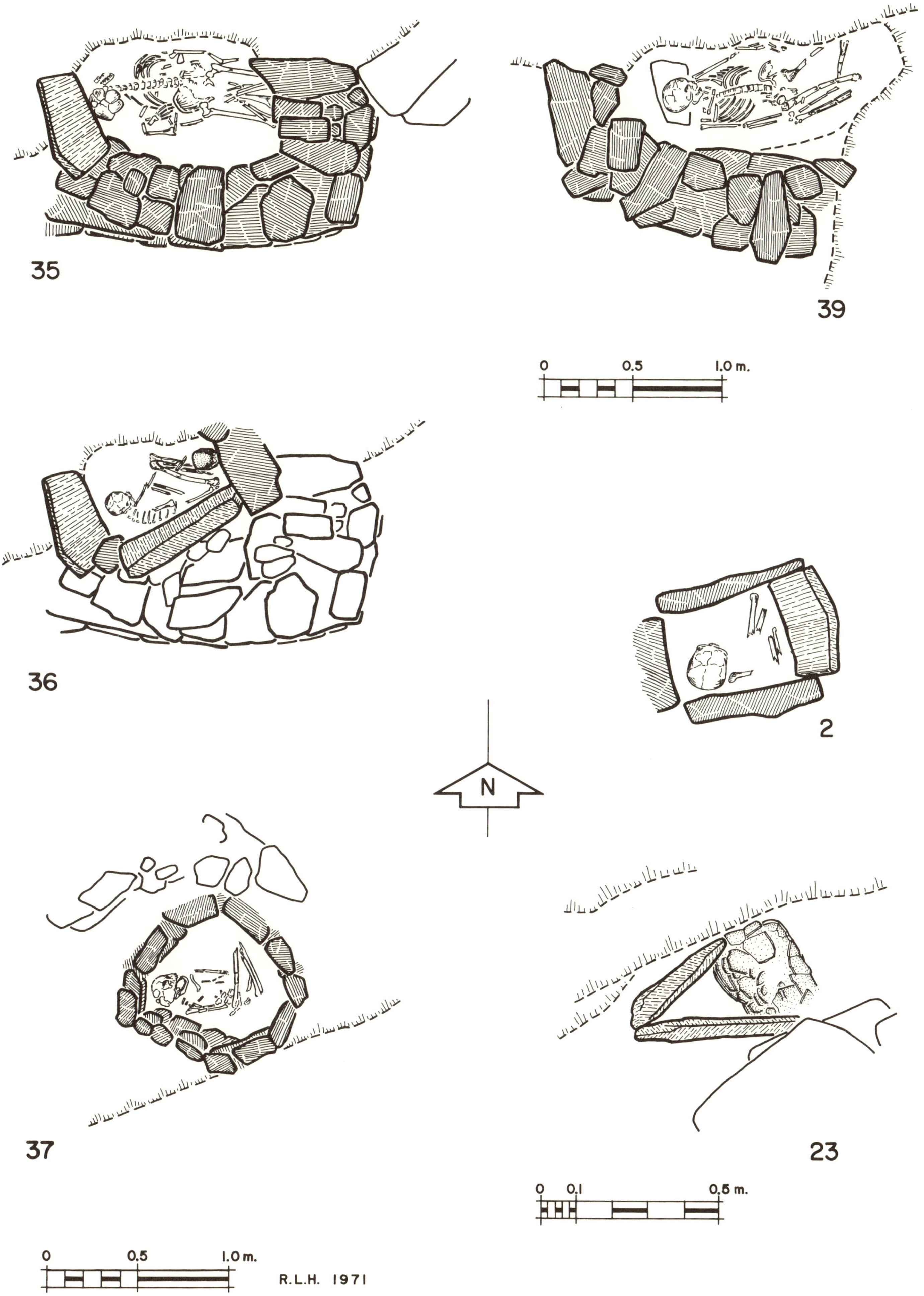

Plans of graves showing burials. (Grave 23 is shown after removal of northeast side)

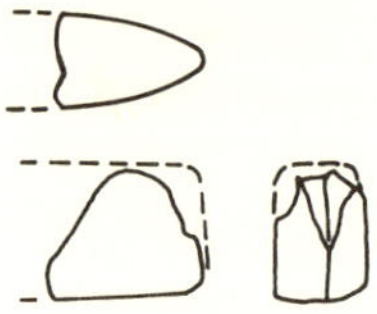
147*

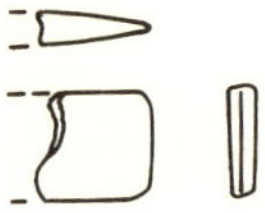
82*

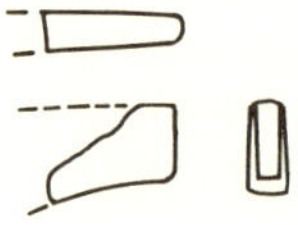
83*

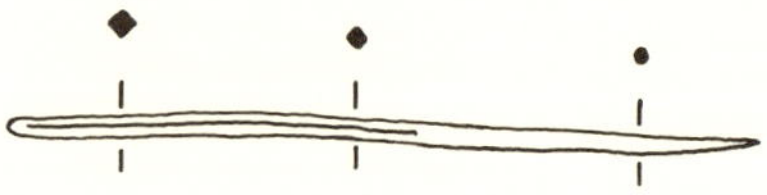
28*

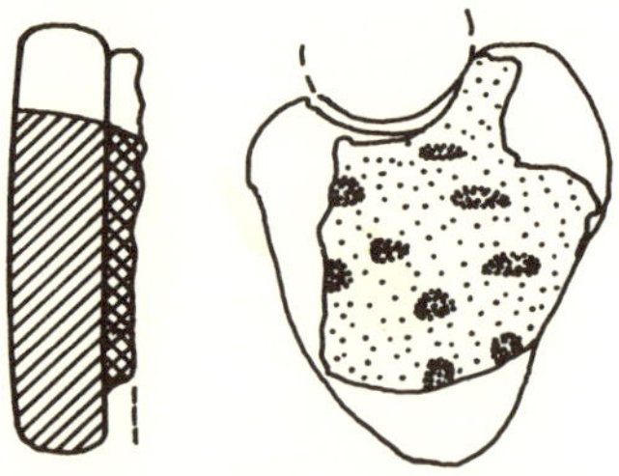
174

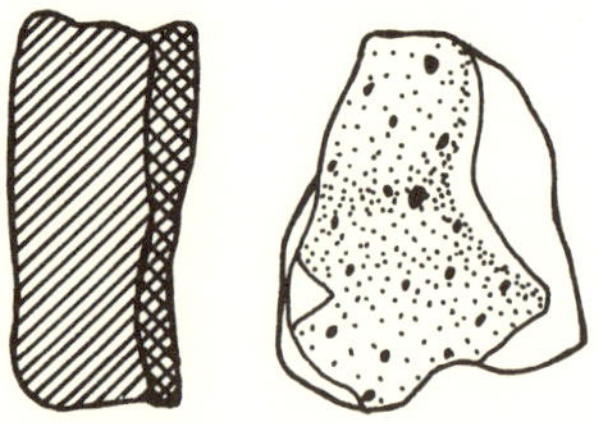
175

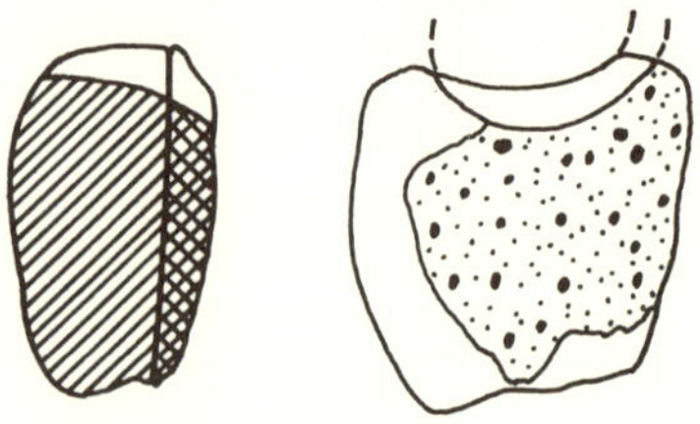
76*

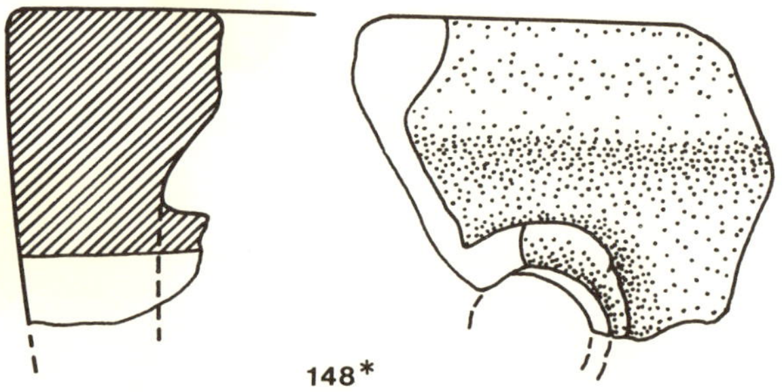
148*

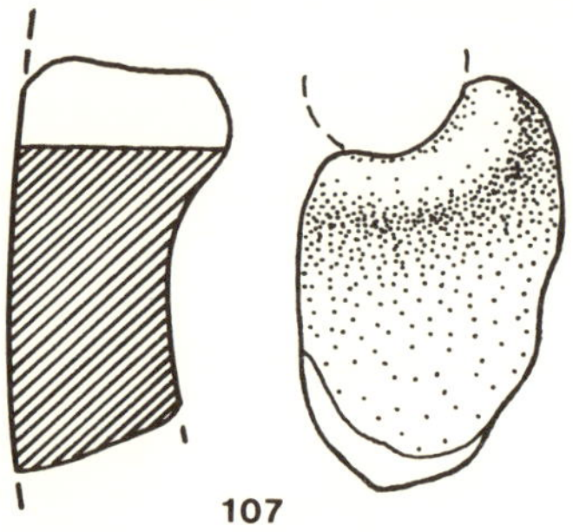
107

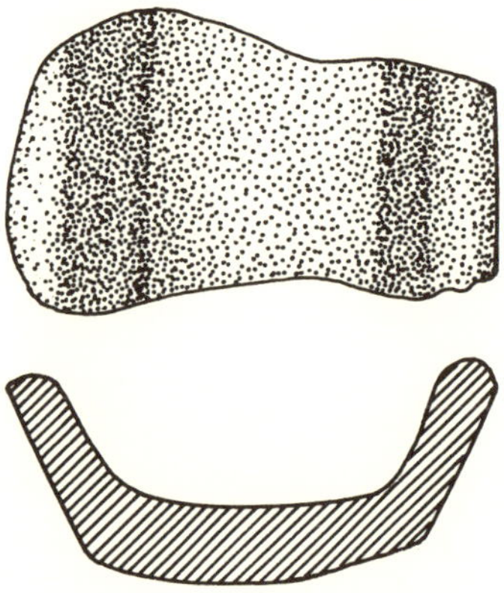
108

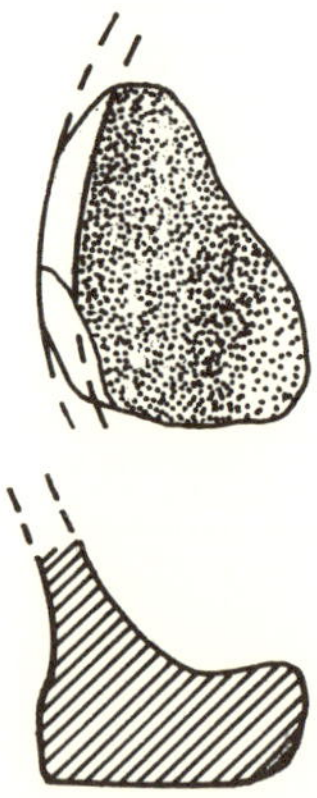
15

Copper and copper working

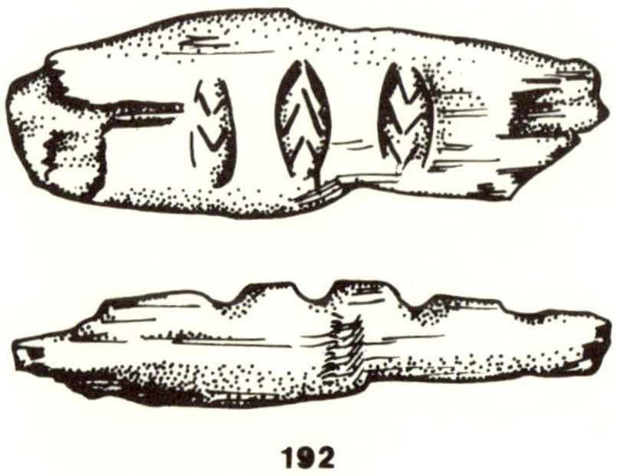
192

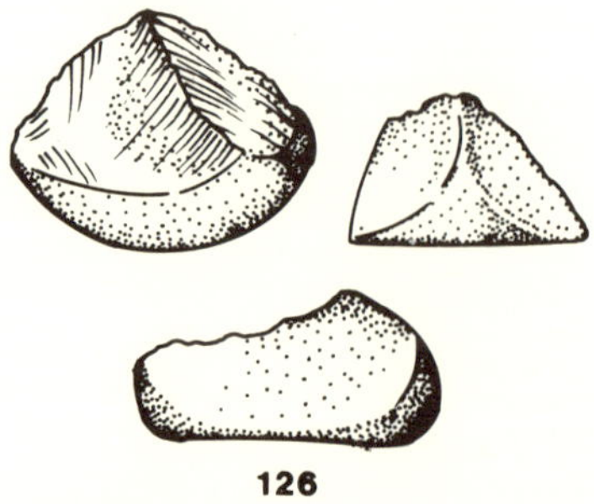
126

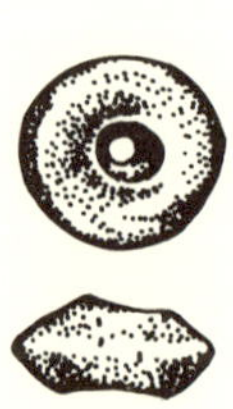
191

Stone

Scale *ca.* 3:5

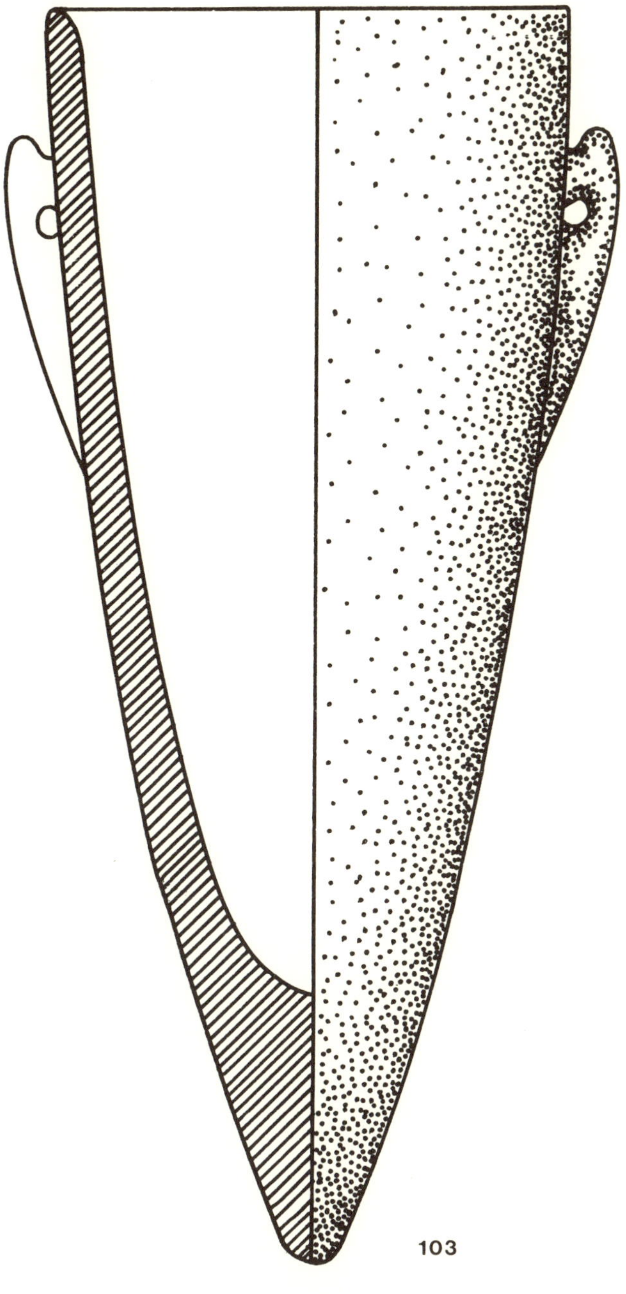

103

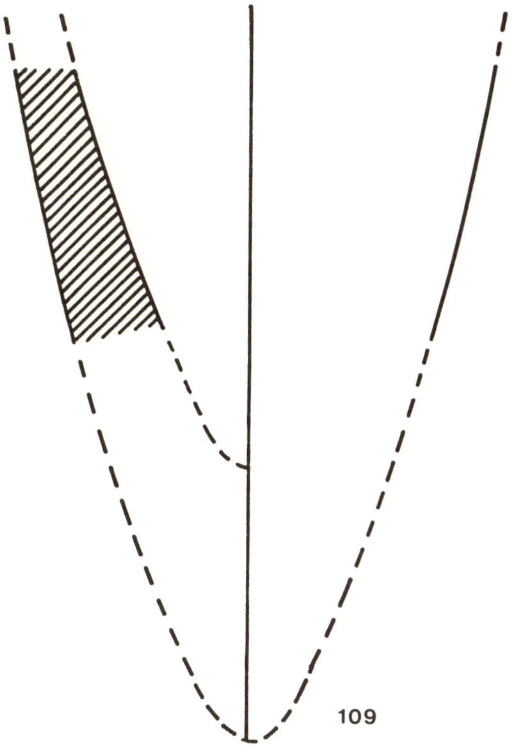

109

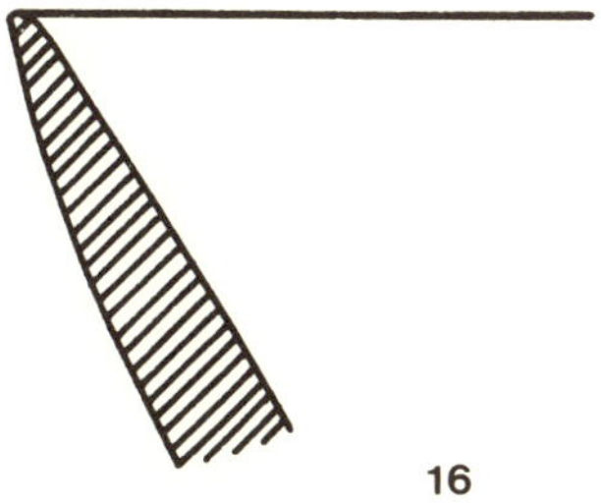

16

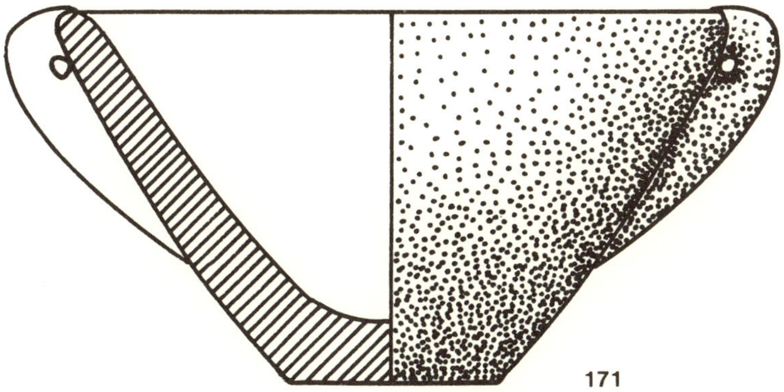

171

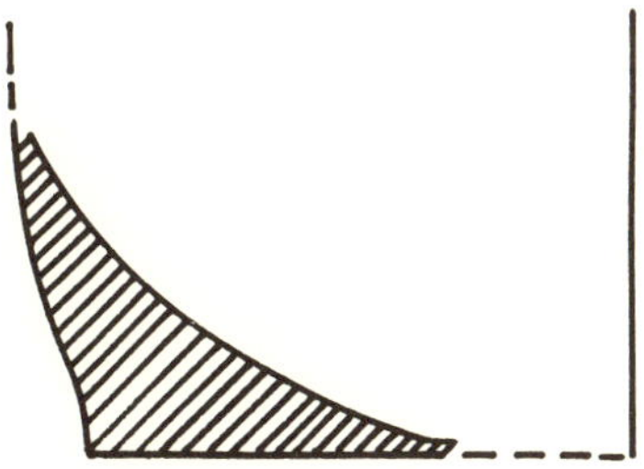

47

Marble vessels. Scale 1:1

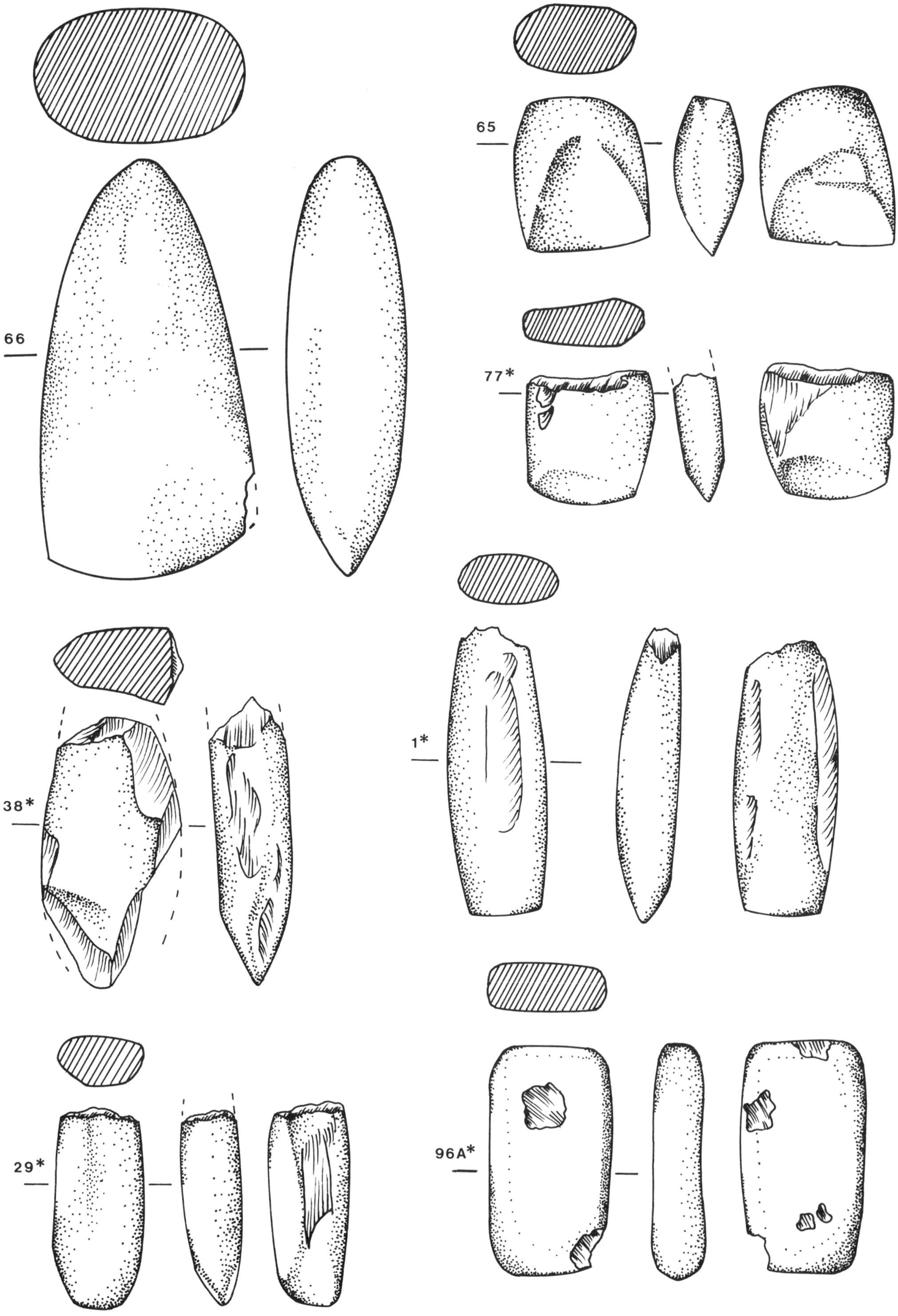

Stone celts and polisher (**96A***). Scale 1:1

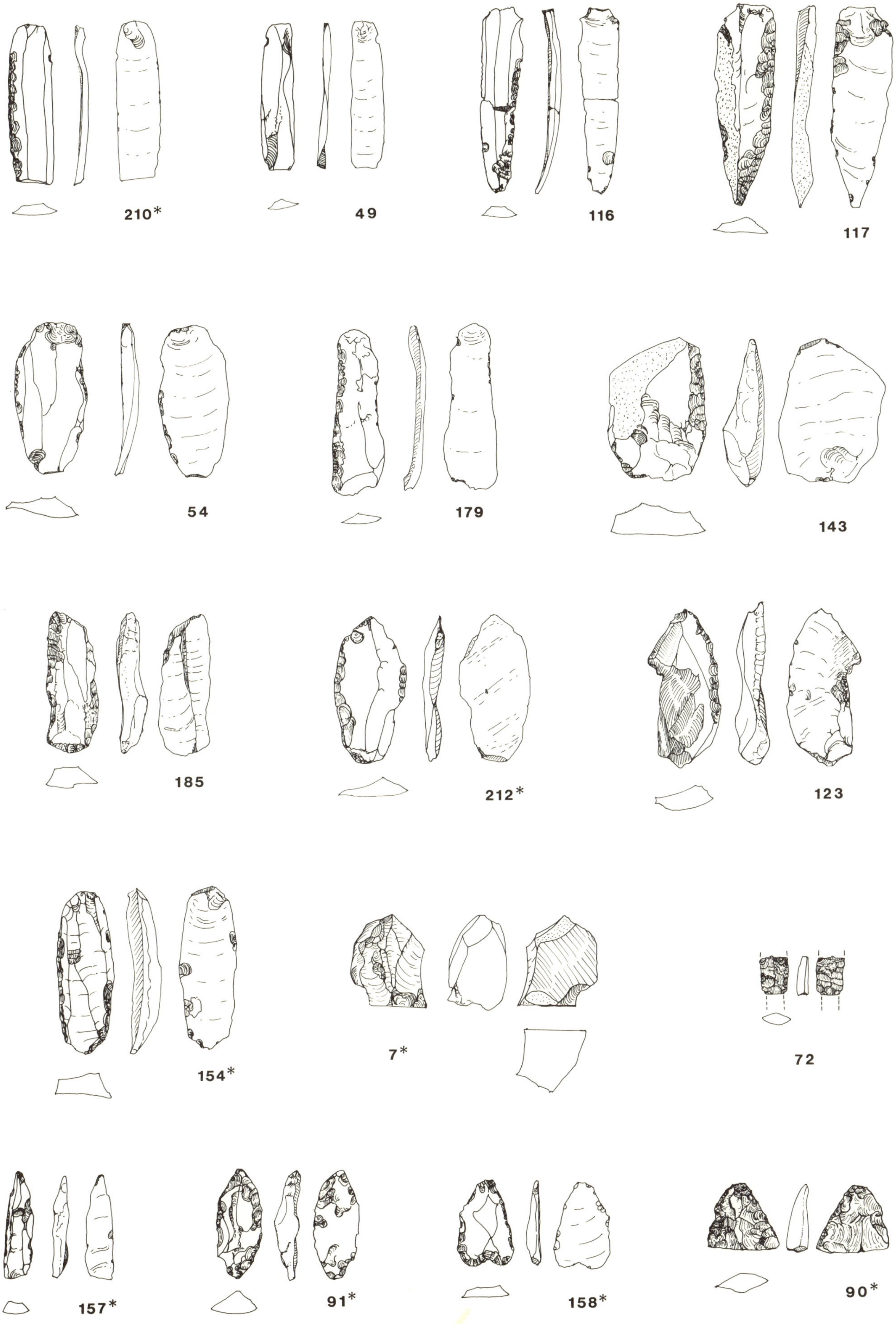

Objects of obsidian. Scale 1:2

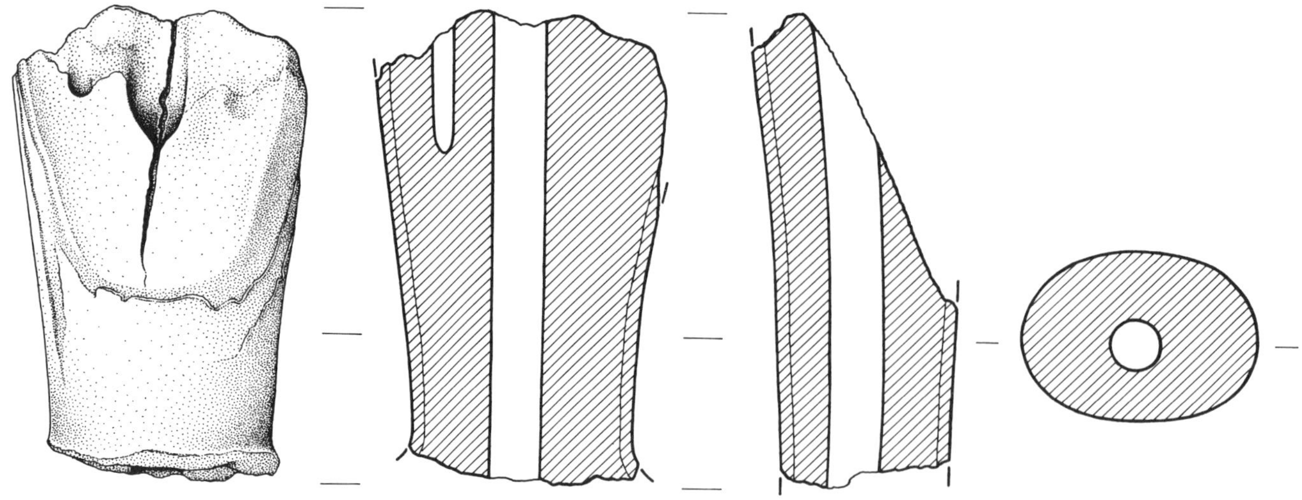

96 B*

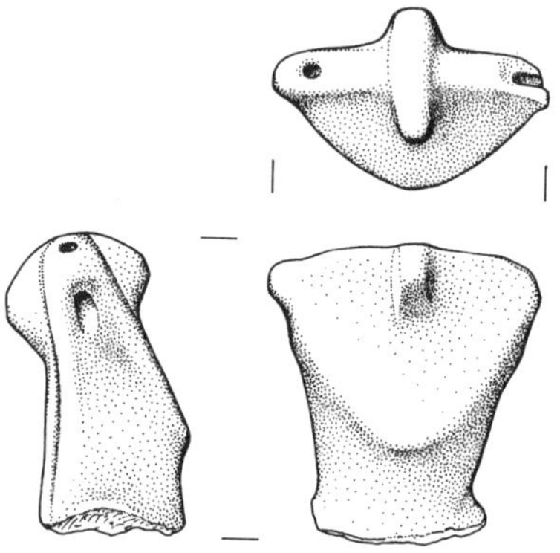

128

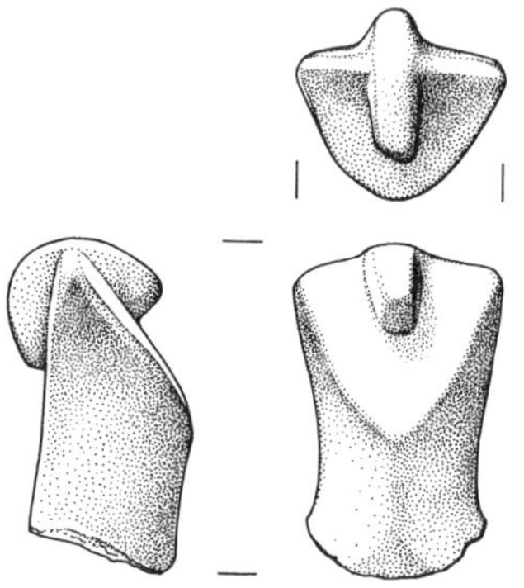

202

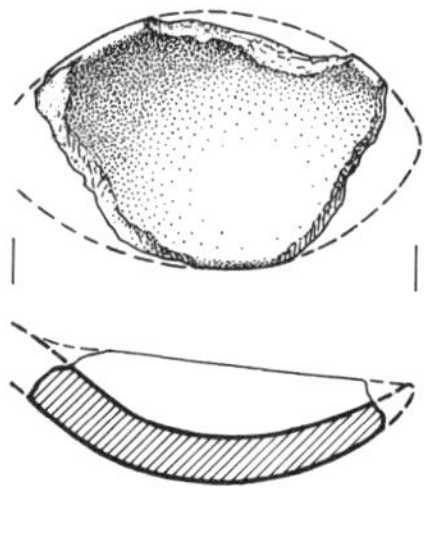

168

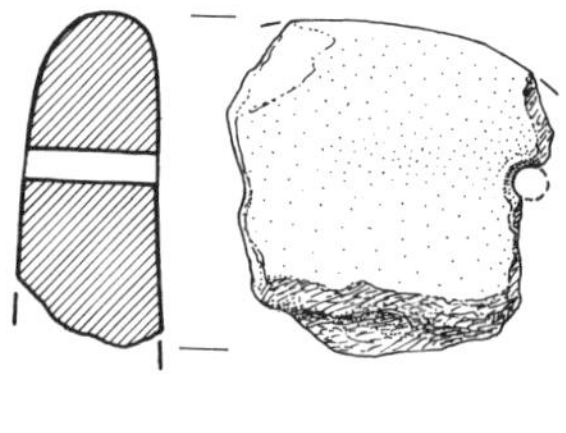

129

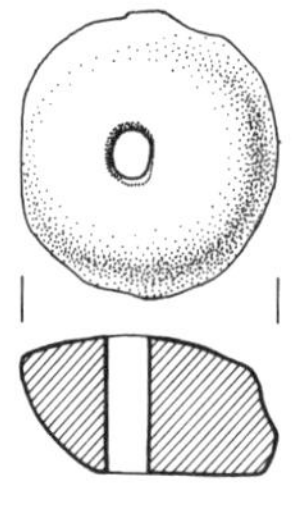

145

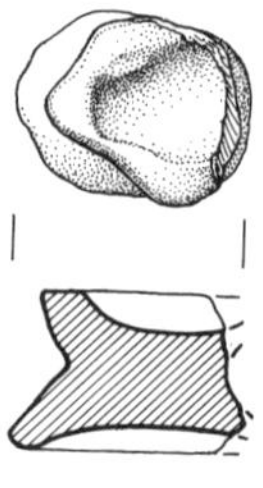

26

Objects of terracotta. Scale 1:2

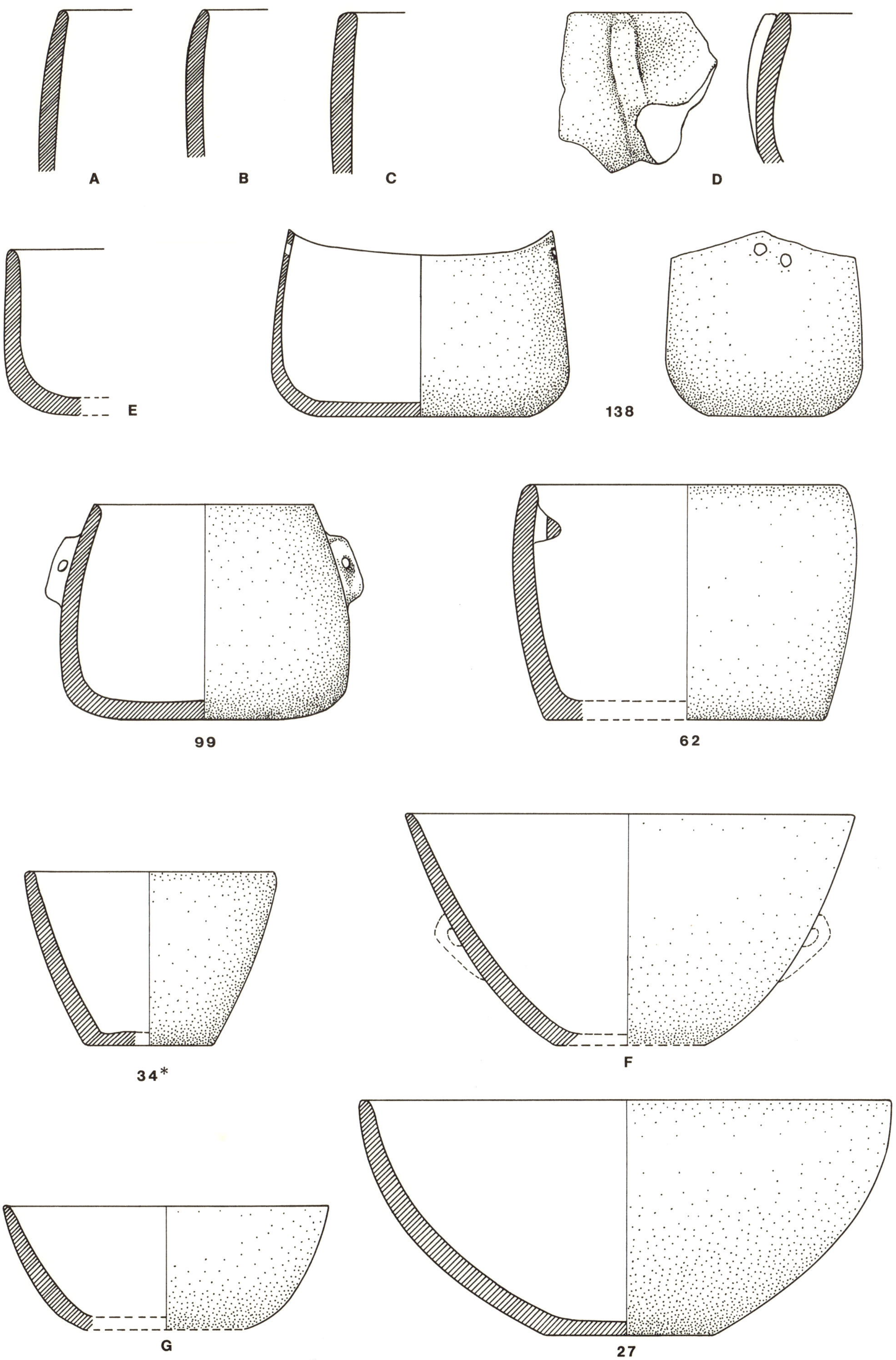

Bowls (Categories A 1 and A 2). Scale 1:2

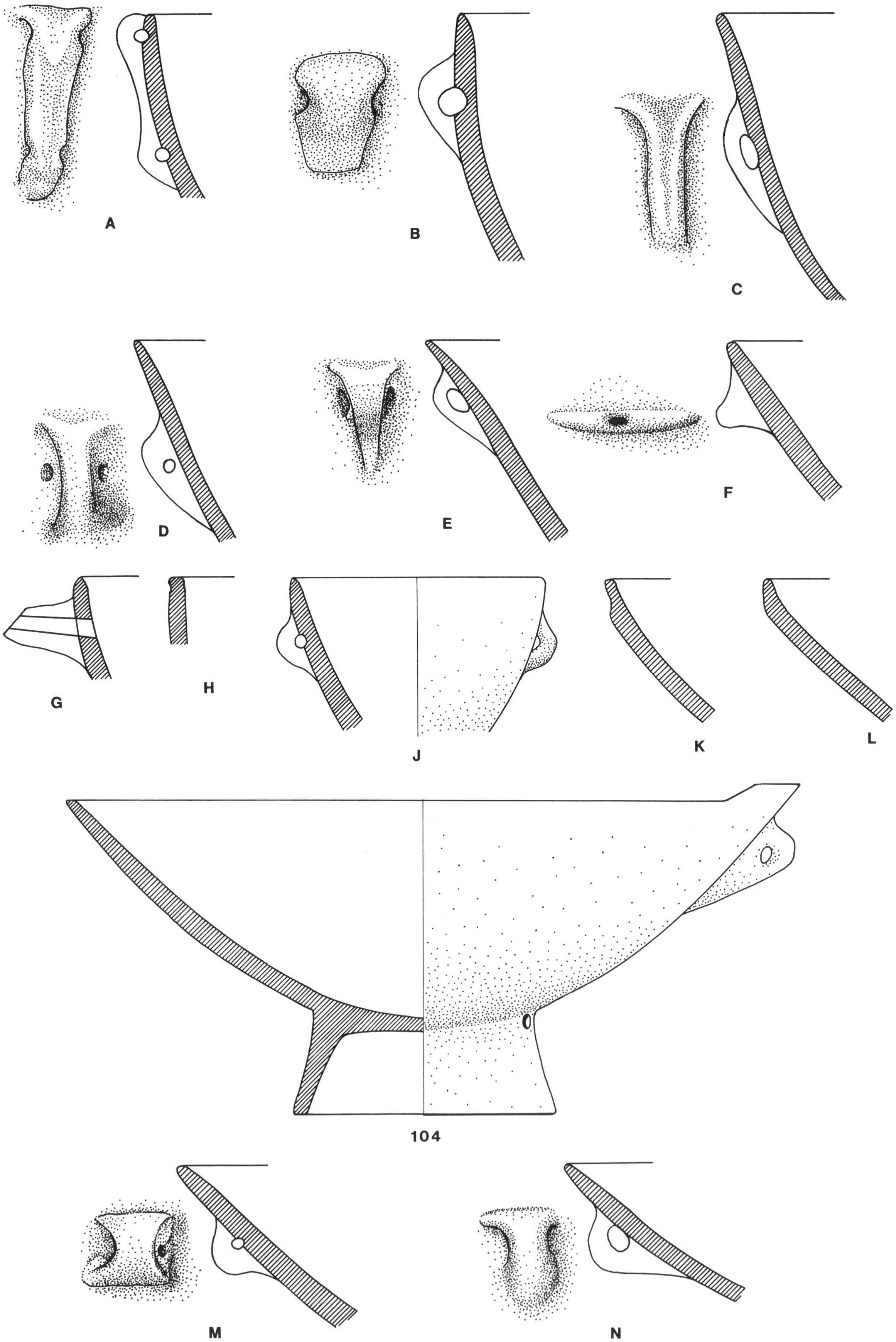

Bowls (Category A 2). Scale 1:2

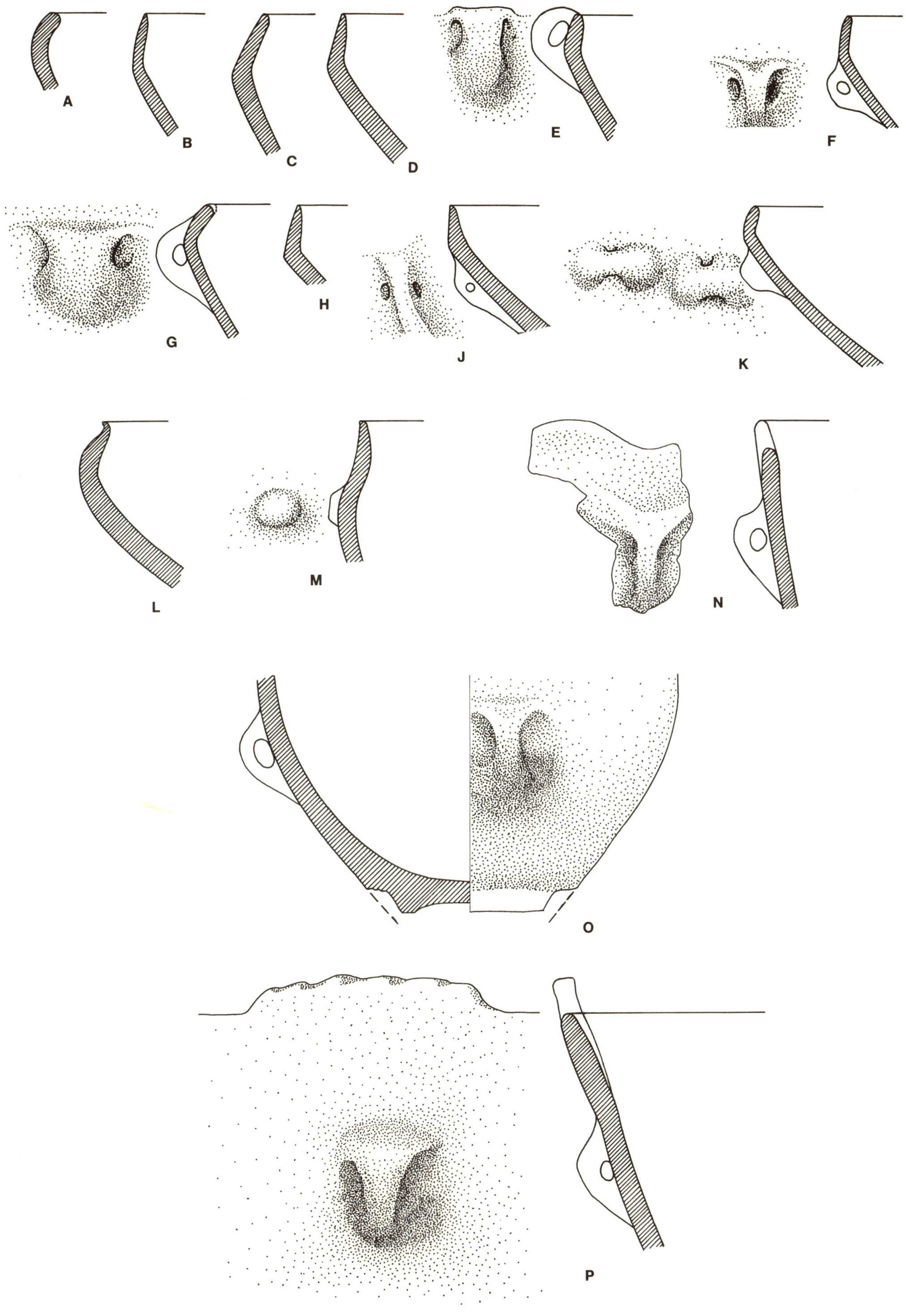

Bowls (Category A 2). Scale 1:2

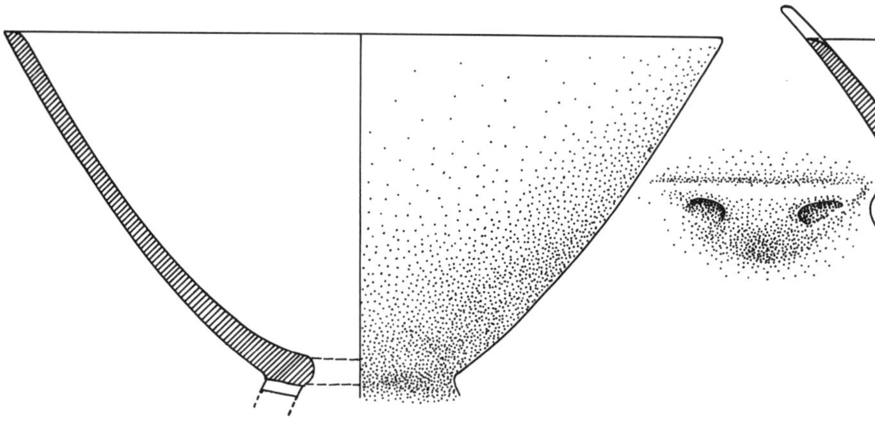

A

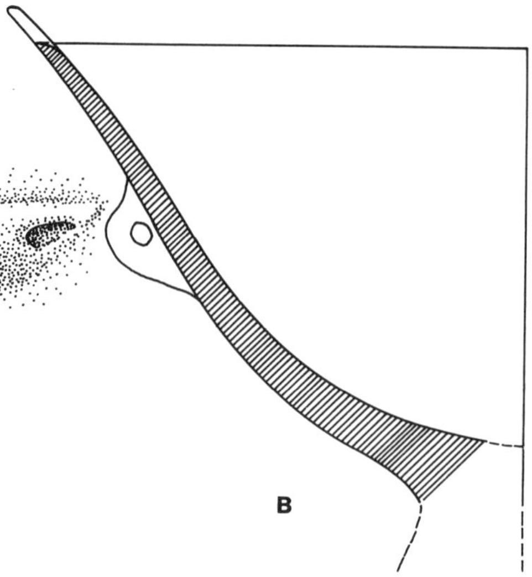

B

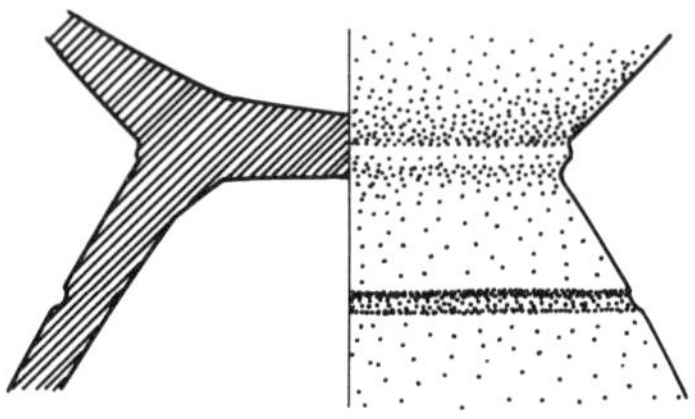

C

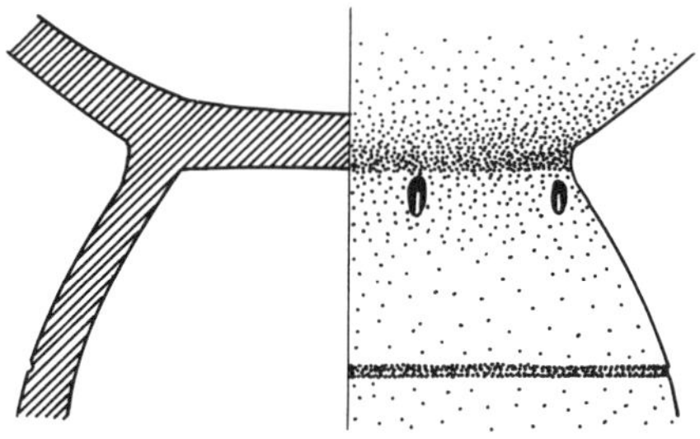

D

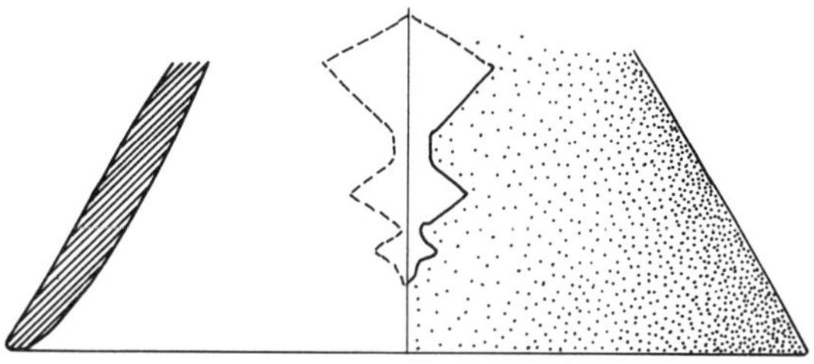

E

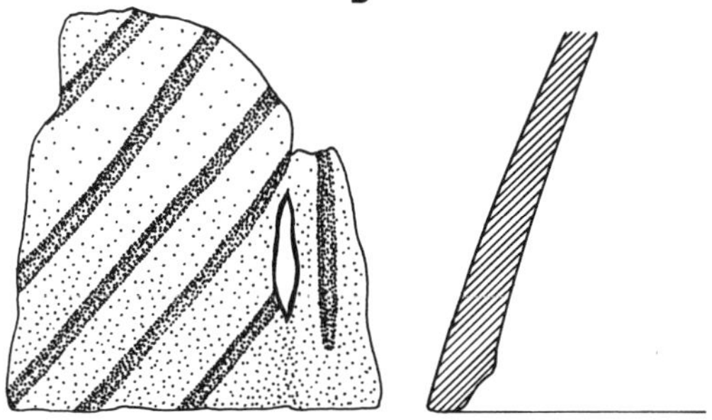

F

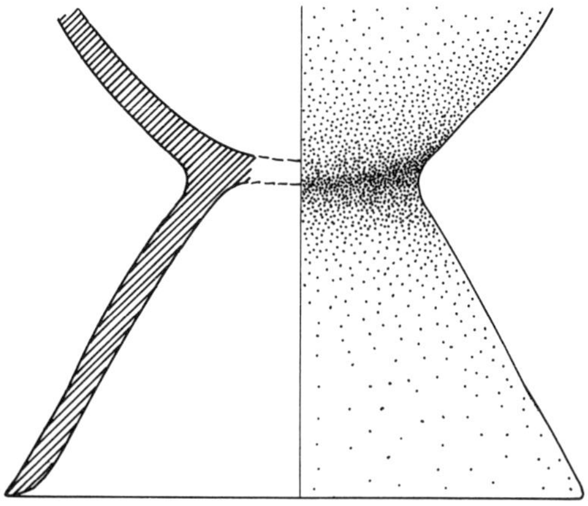

G

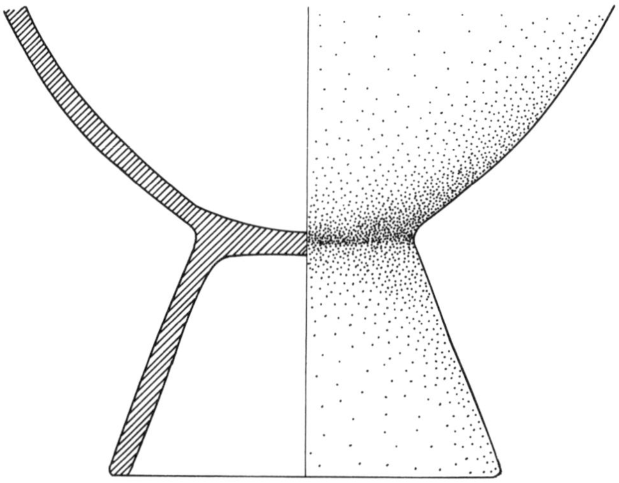

165*

Bowls (Category A 2: With Pedestals). Scale 1:2

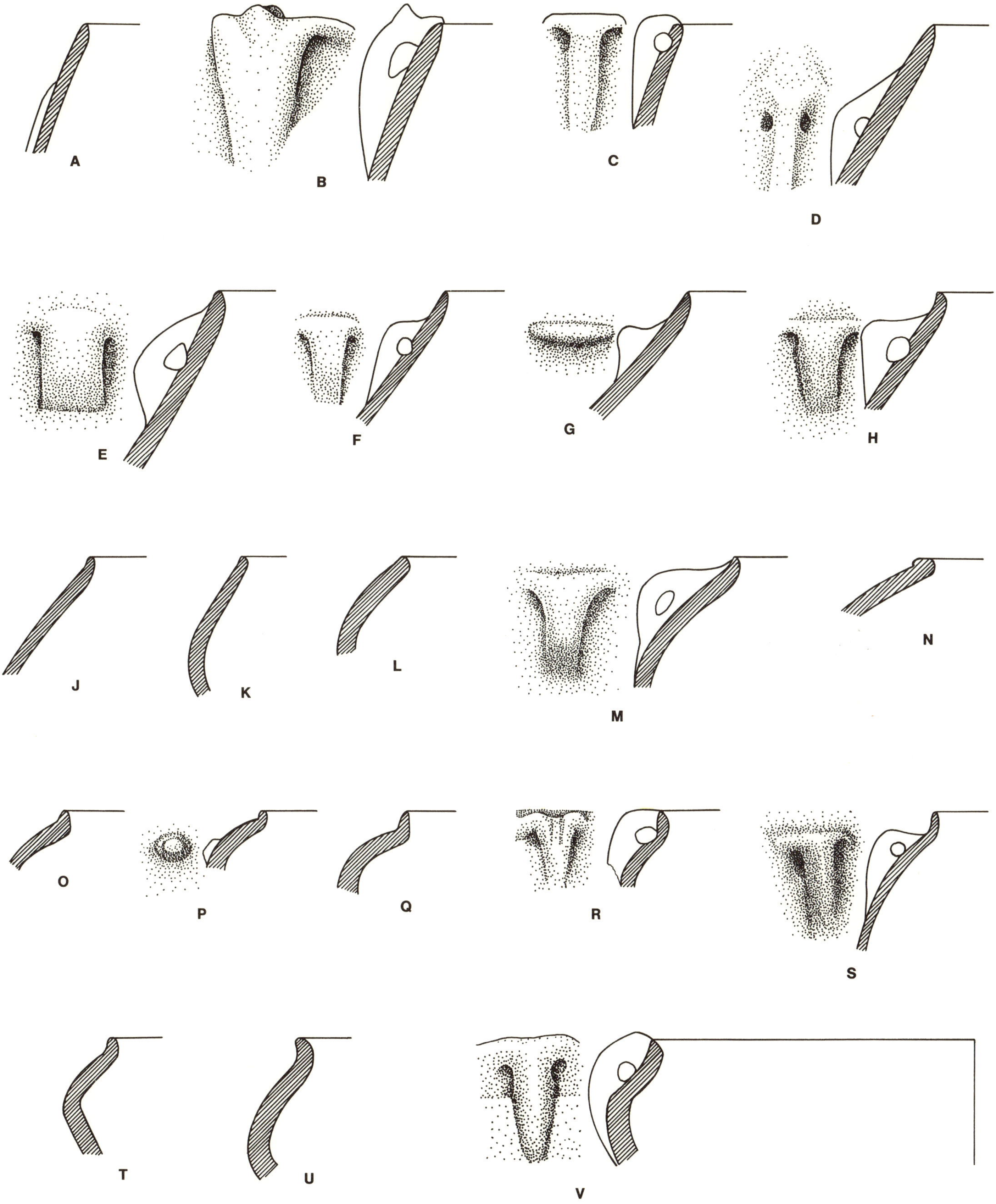

Small jars (Category B 1). Scale 1:2

PLATE 32

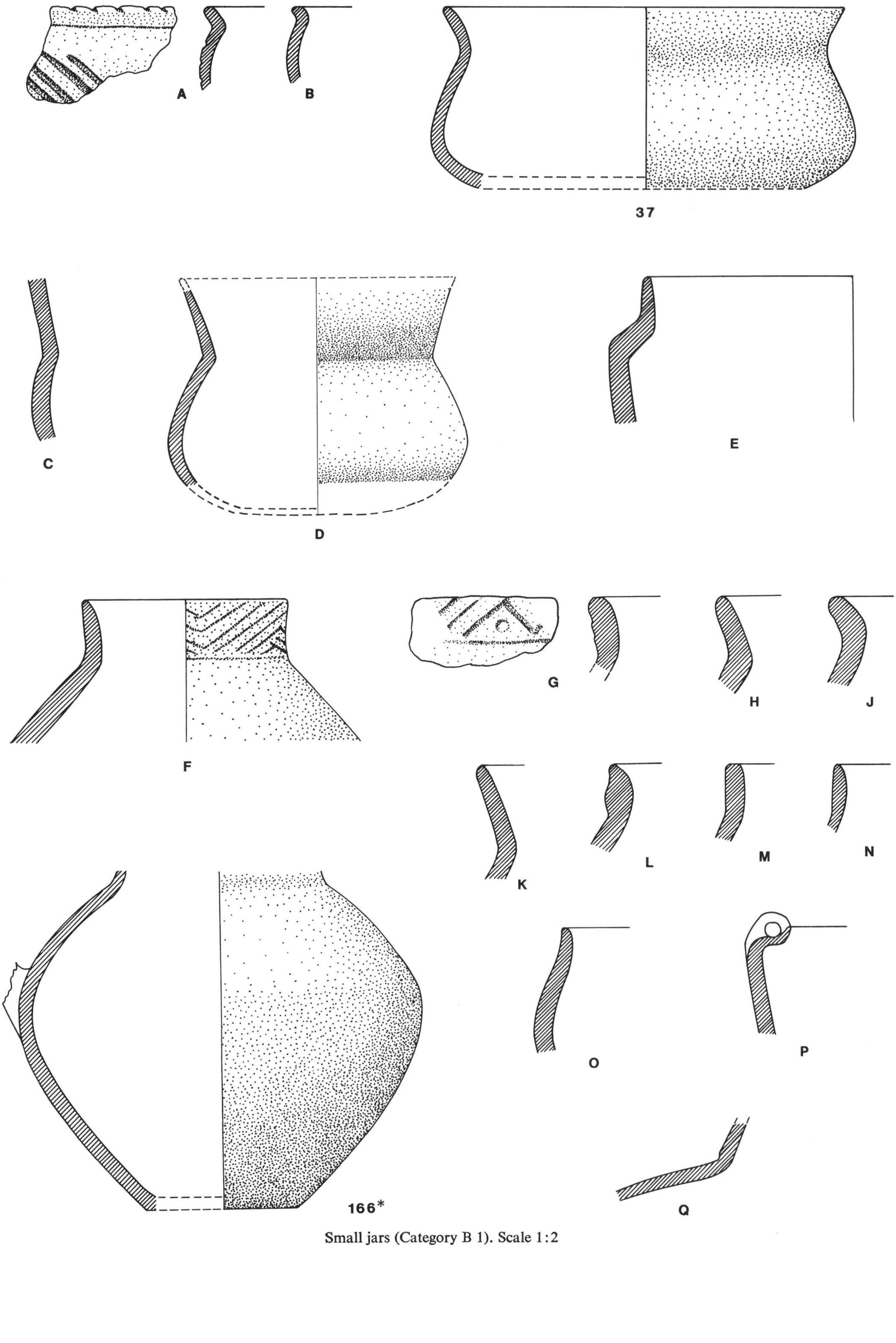

Small jars (Category B 1). Scale 1:2

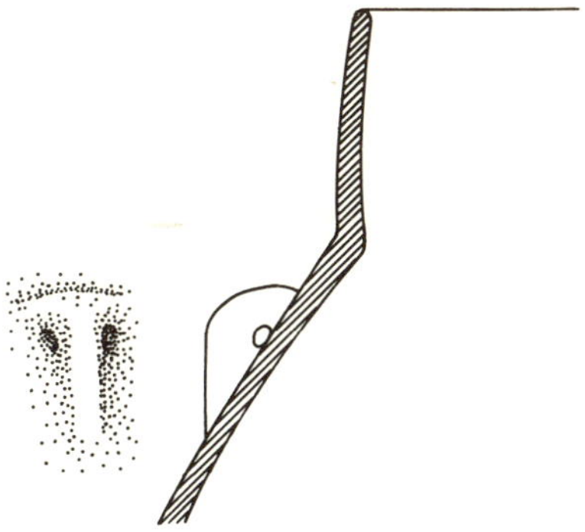

10

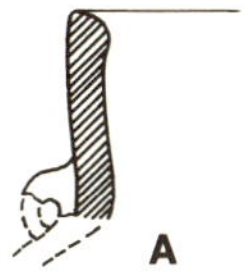

A

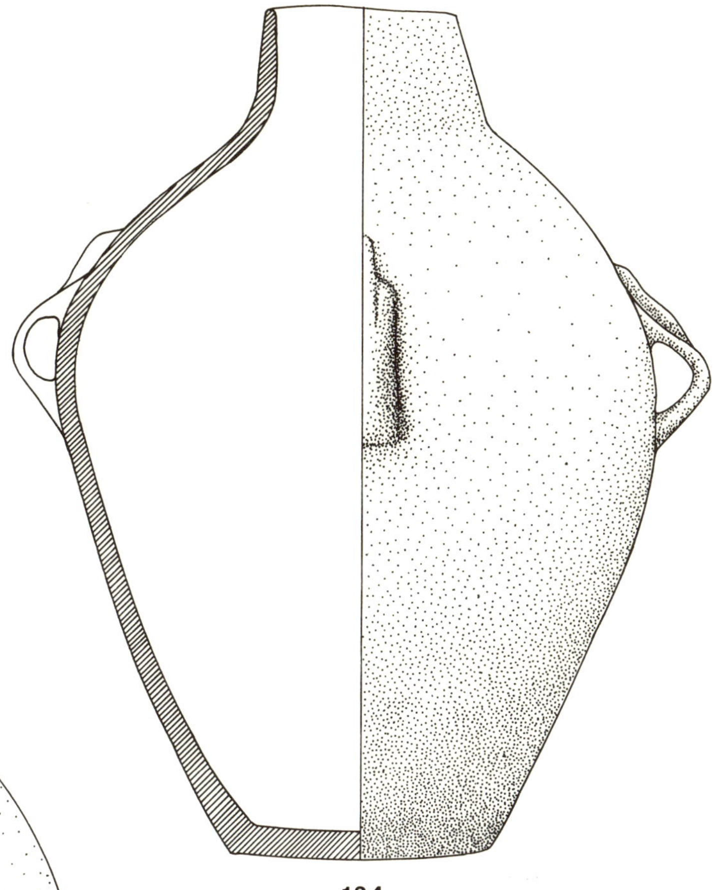

134

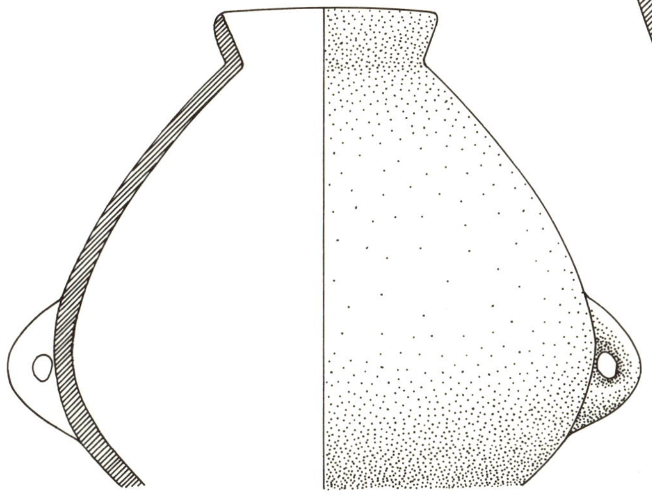

135

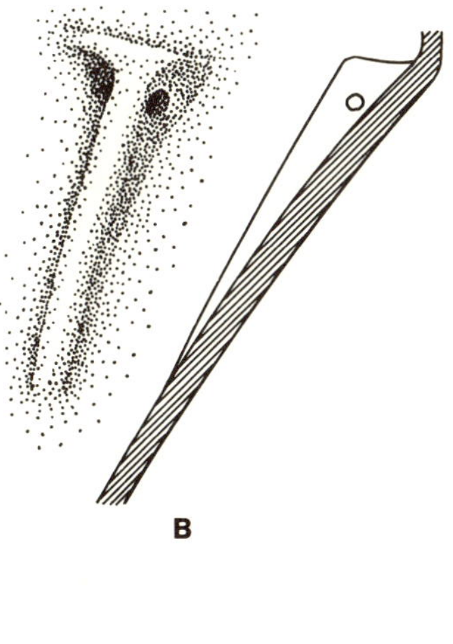

B

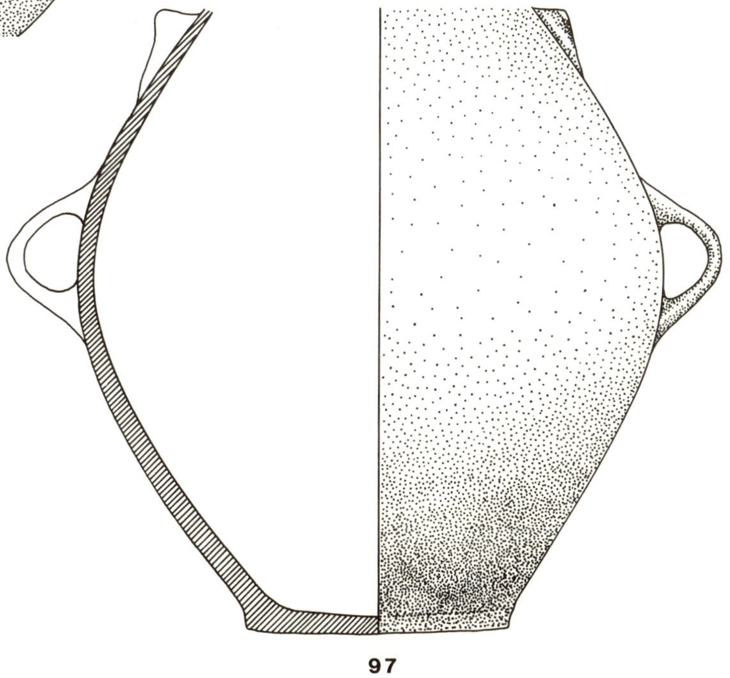

97

Large jars (Category B 2). Scale 1:4

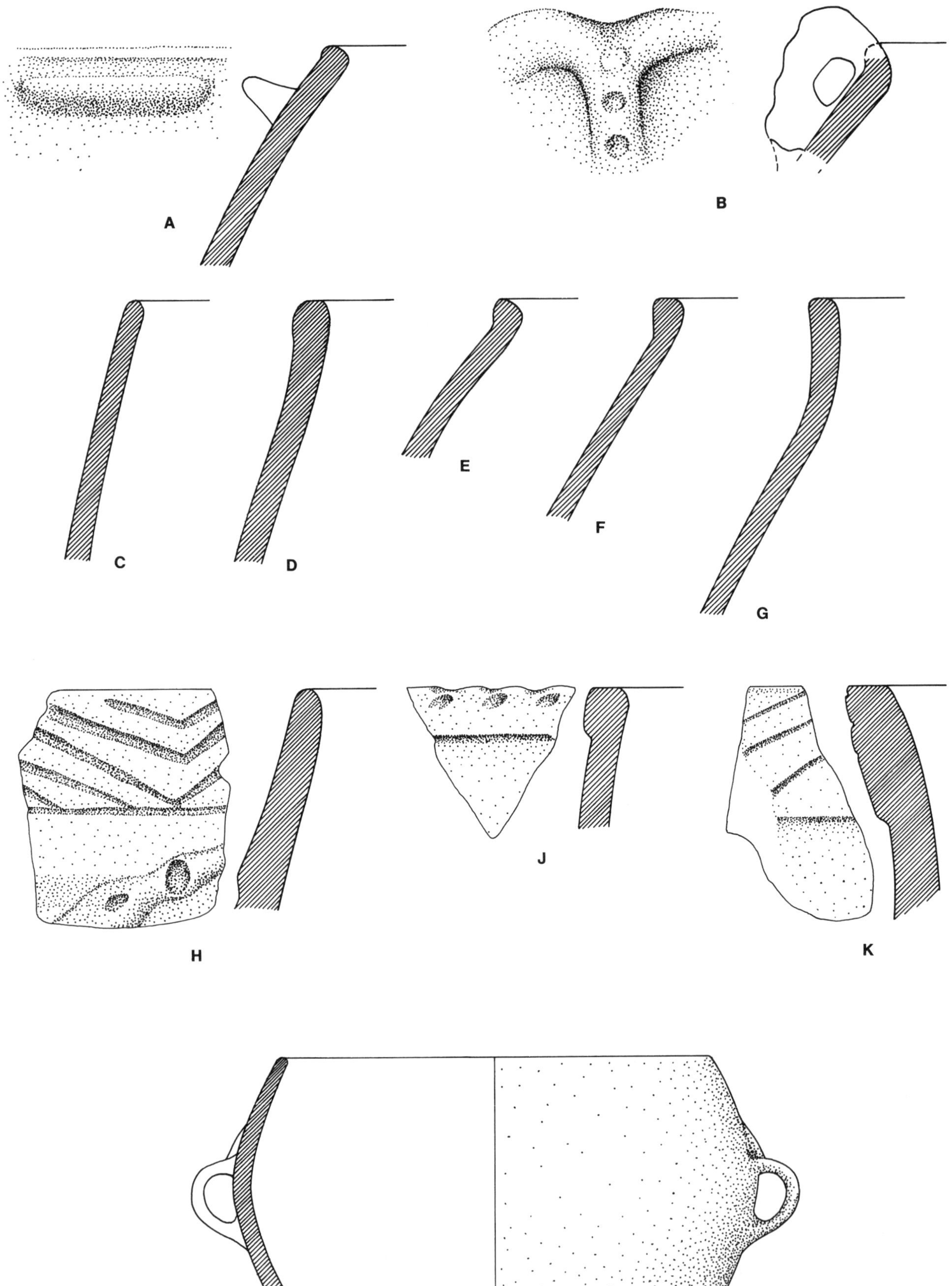

Large jars (Category B 2). Scales 1:2 (A–K), 1:4 (**74**)

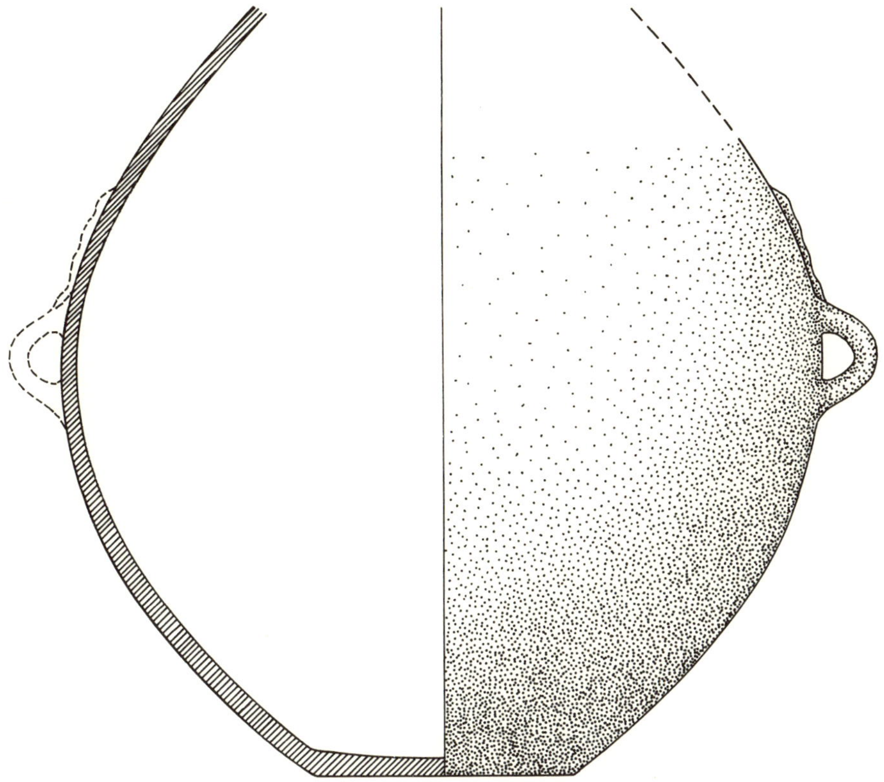

137

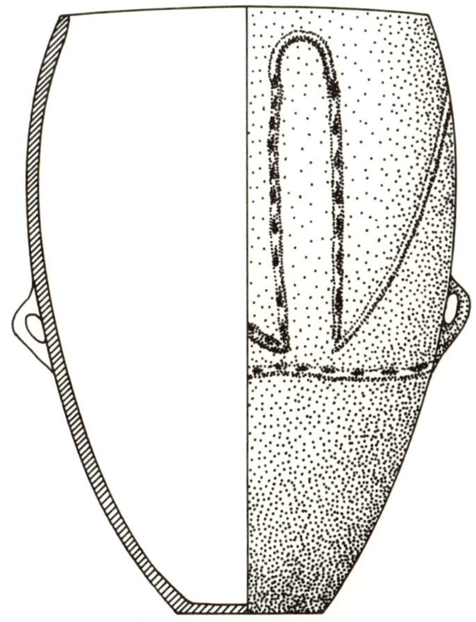

170

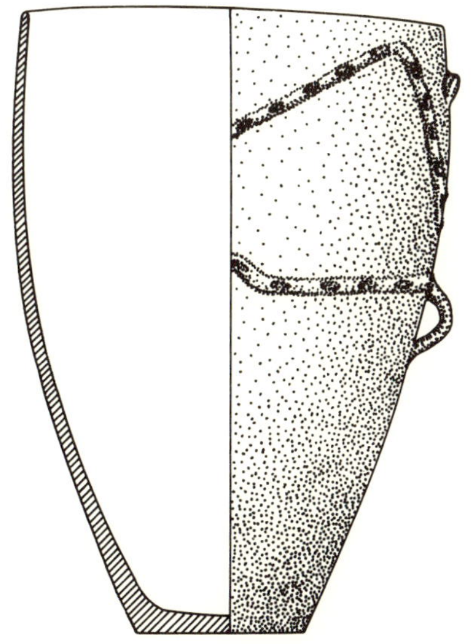

146

Large jars (Category B 2). Scales 1:4 (**137**), 1:8 (**146, 170**)

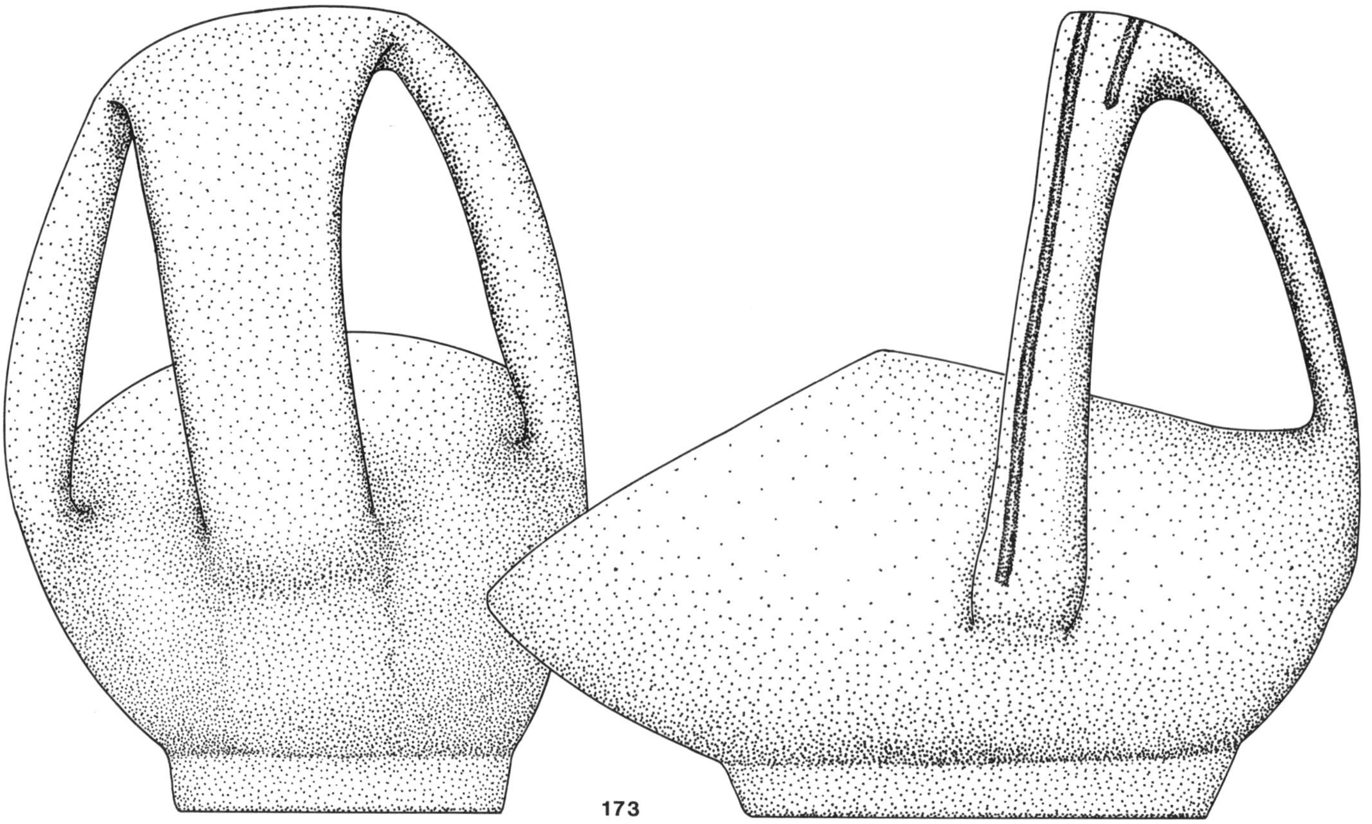

173

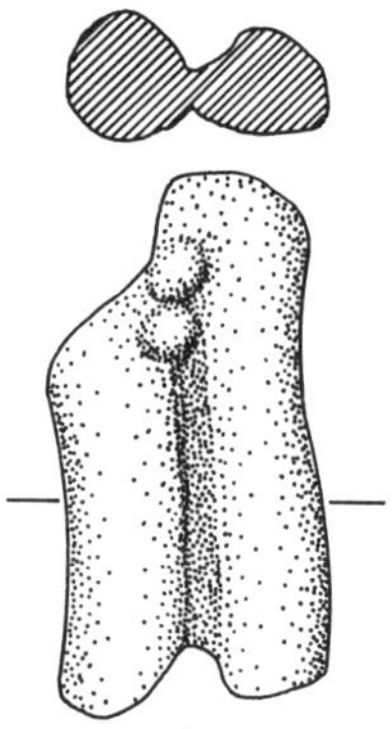

A

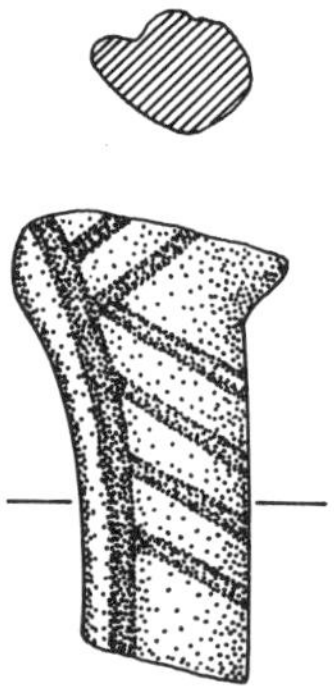

B

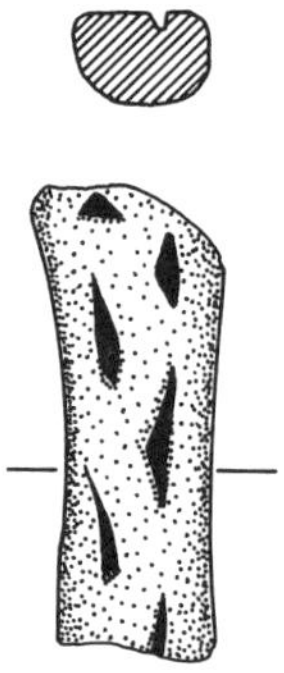

C

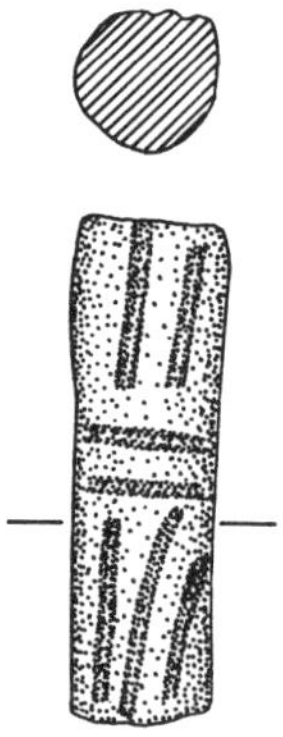

D

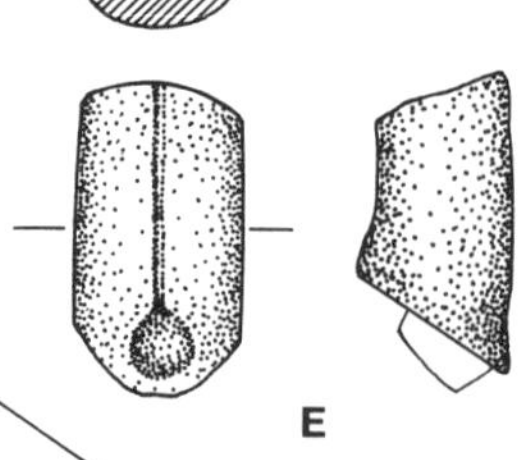

E

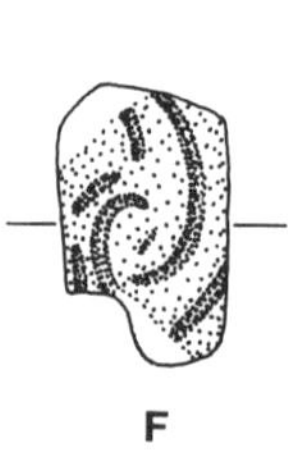

F

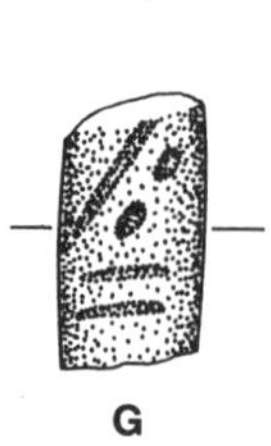

G

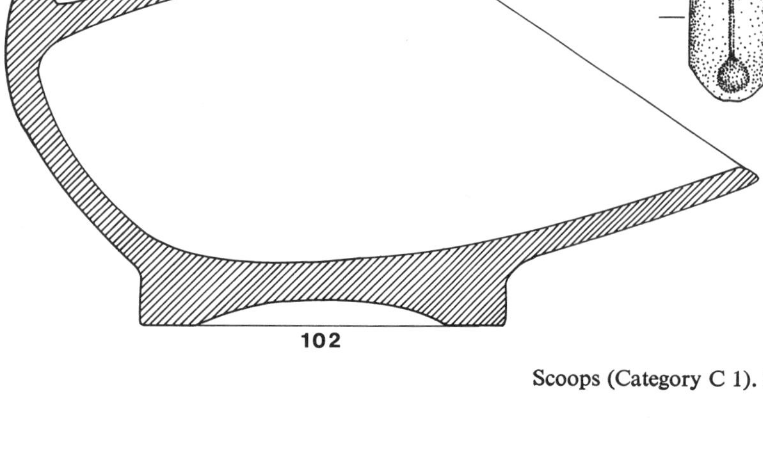

102

Scoops (Category C 1). Scale 1:2

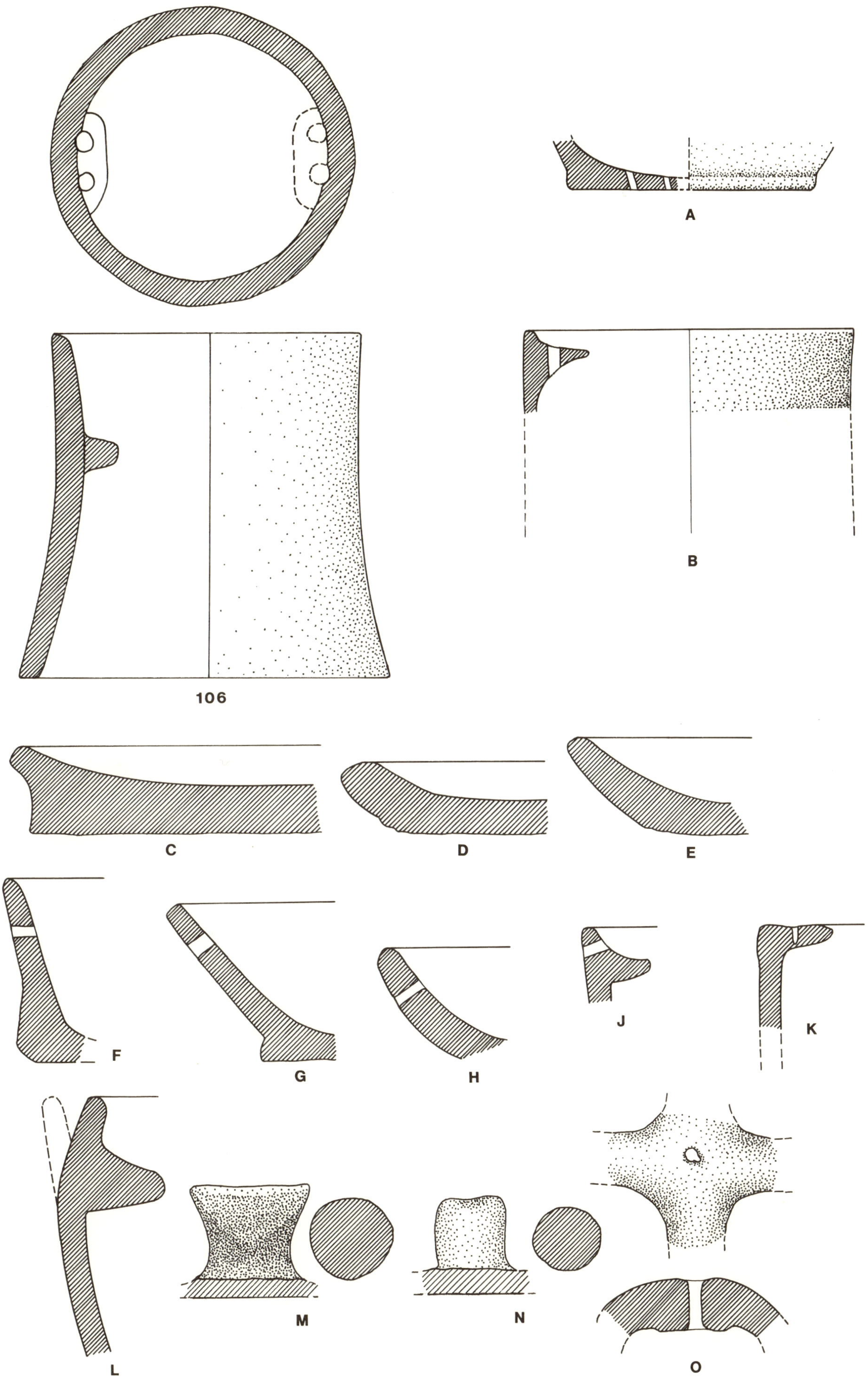

Miscellaneous vessels (Categories C 2– C 5). Scale 1:2

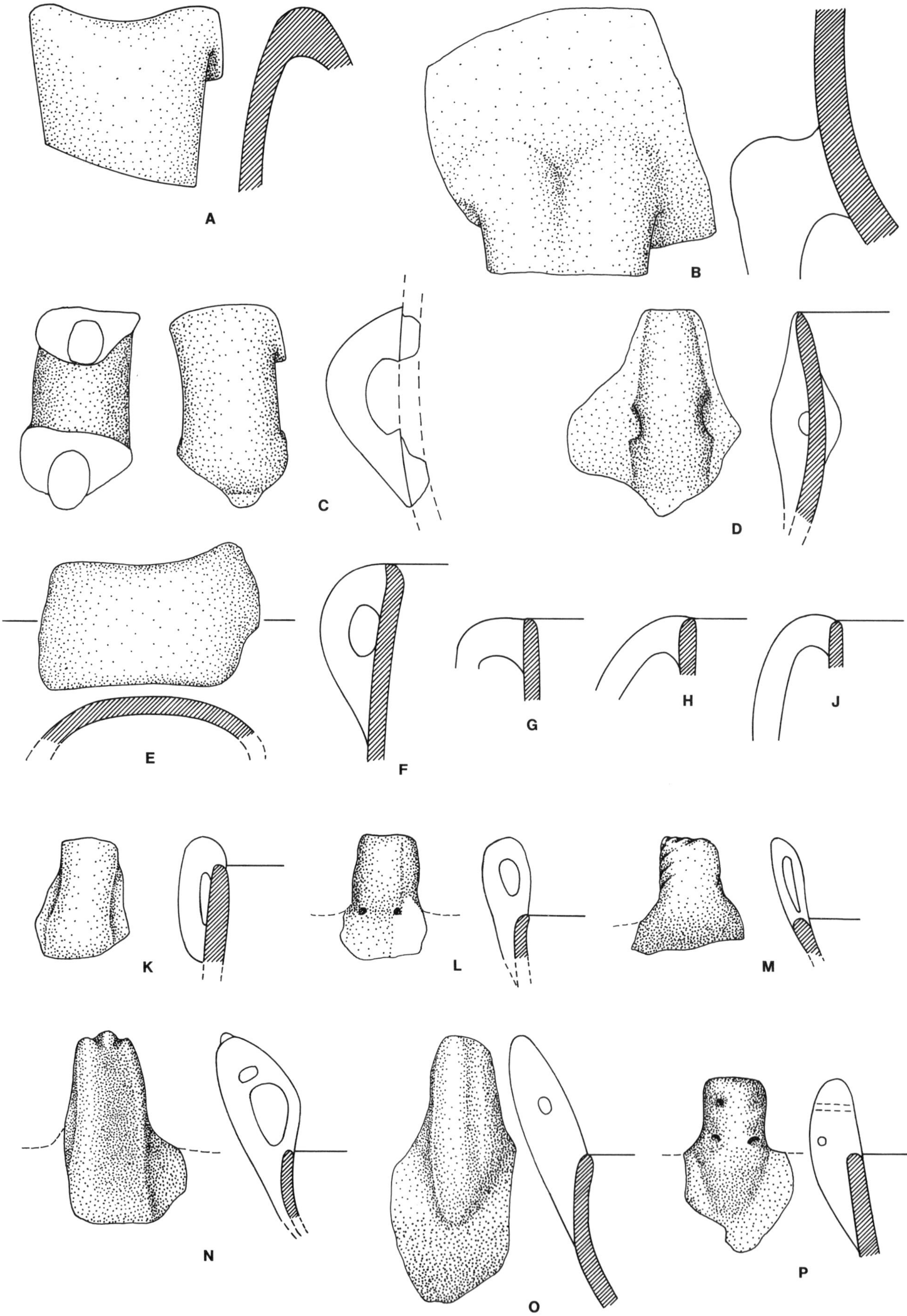

Handles and lug handles. Scale 1:2

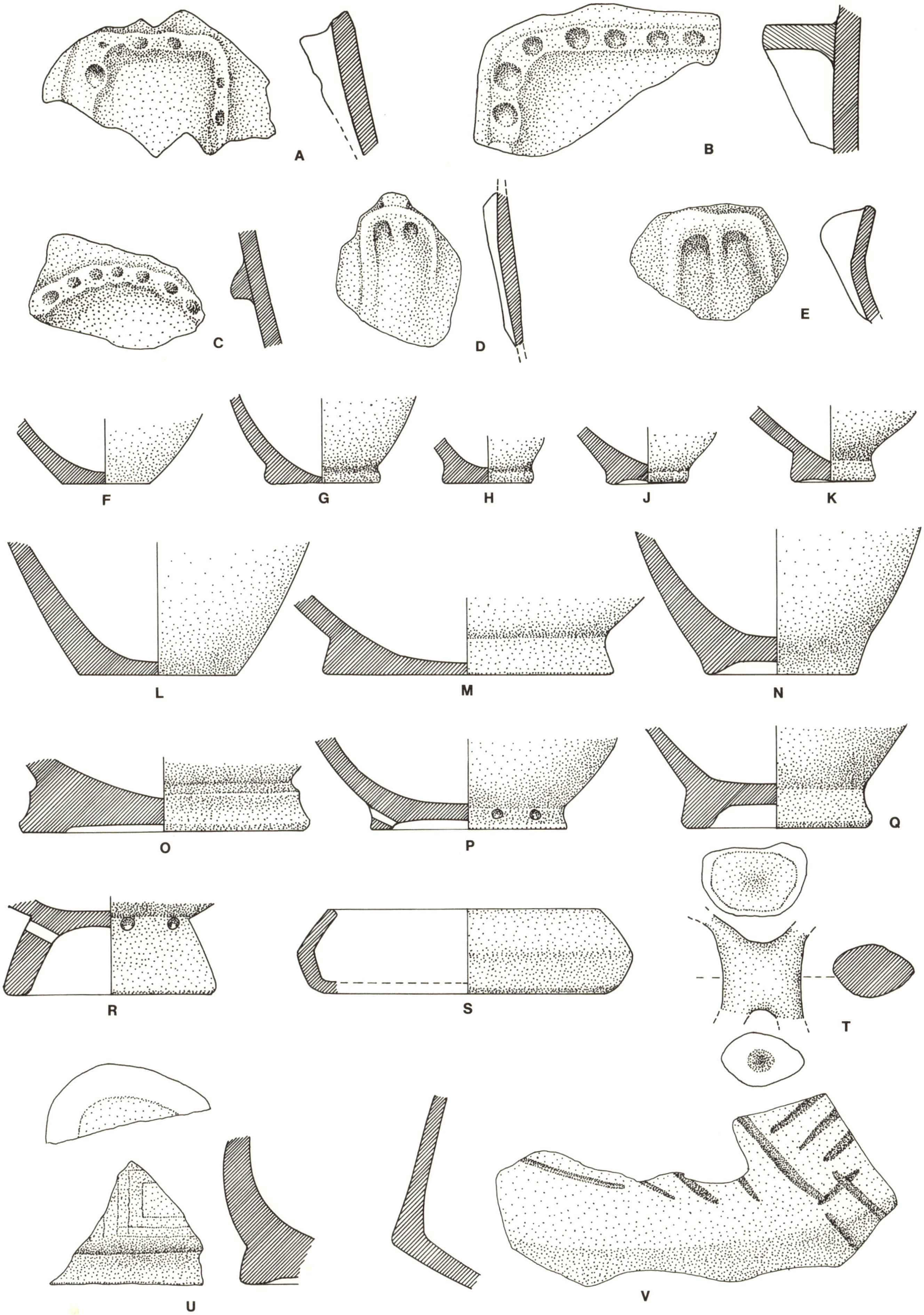

Lugs (A–E), bases (F–R) and oddments. Scale 1:2

Bowls (Category A 2) with pattern burnishing on the outside. Scale 1:2

Bowls (Category A 2) with pattern burnishing on the inside. Scale 1:2

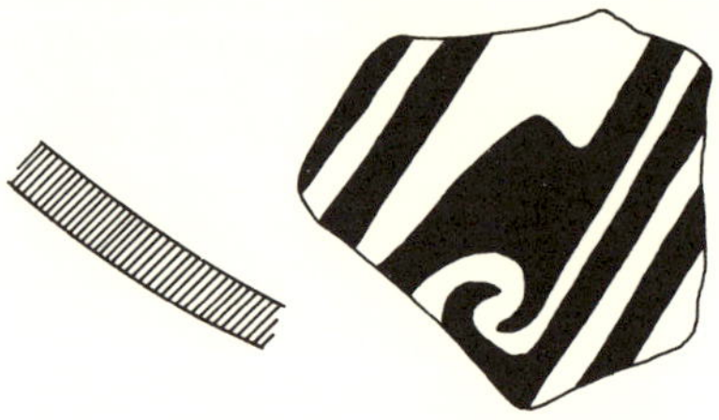

A

B

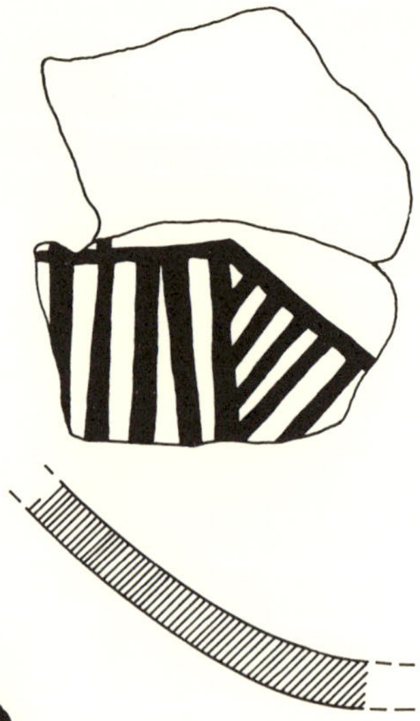

C

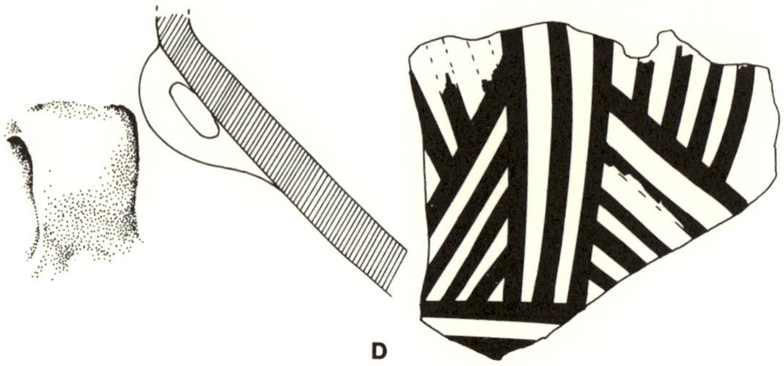

D

E

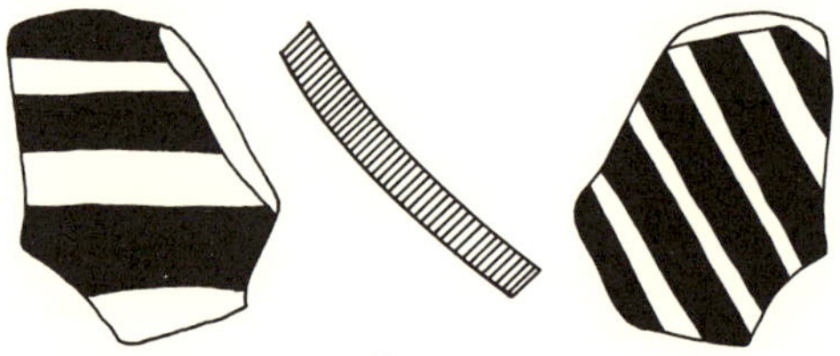

F

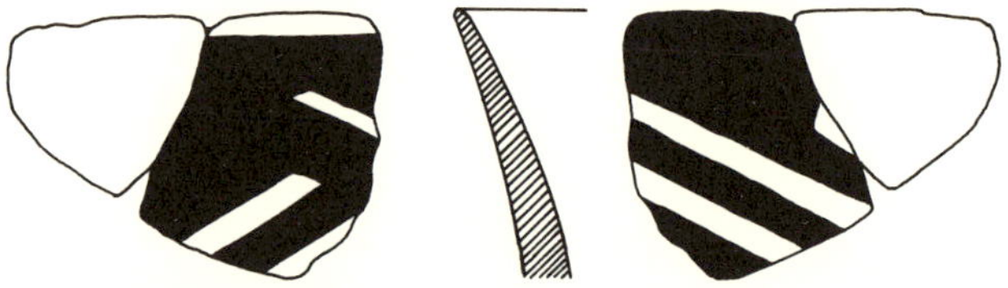

G

164*

Vessels with pattern burnishing. Scale 1:2

A

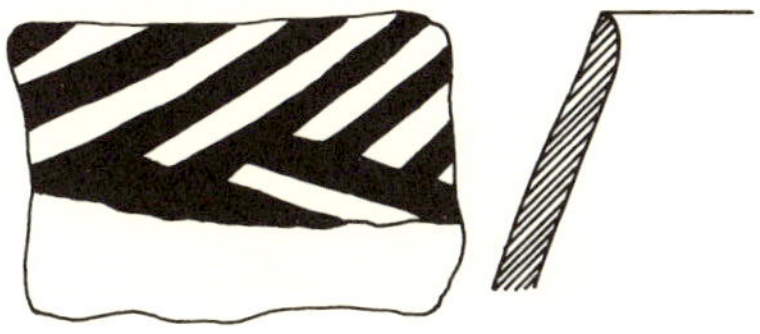
B

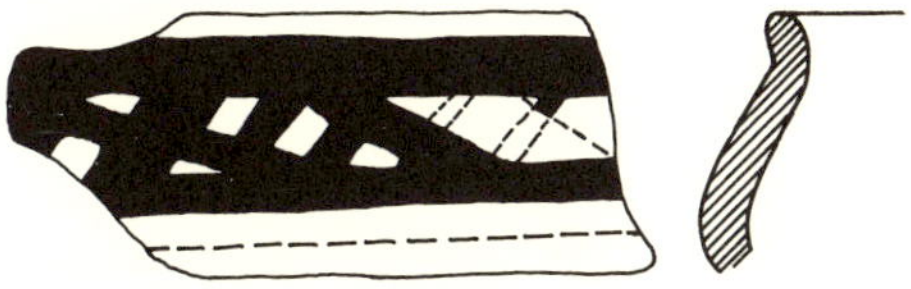
C

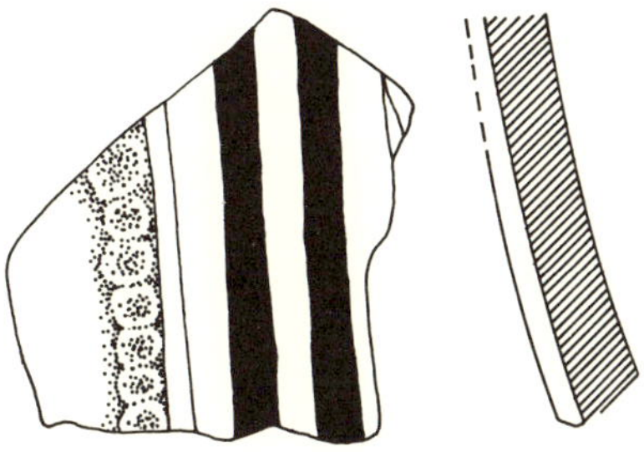
D

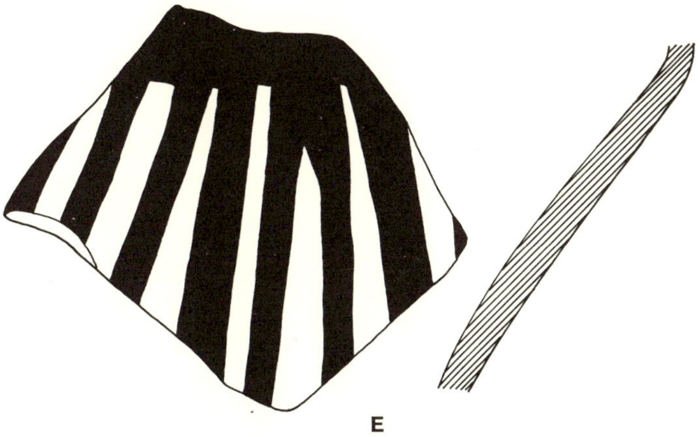
E

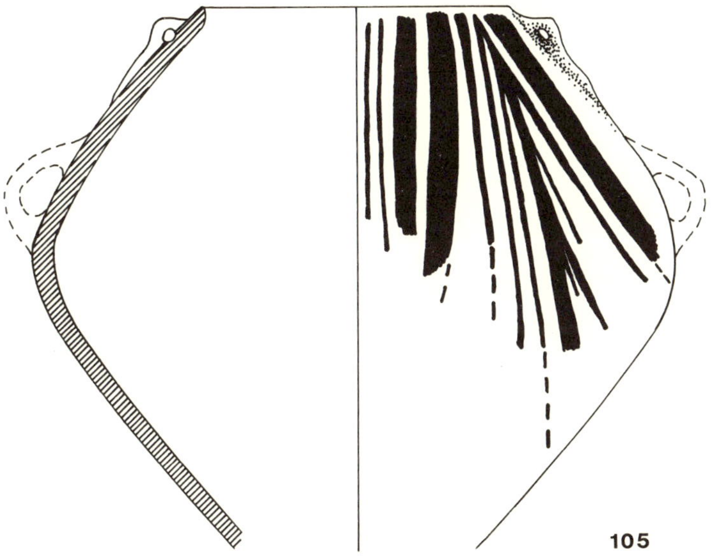
105

75

Jars (Categories B 1 and B 2) with pattern burnishing. Scales 1:2 (A–E), 1:4 (**75, 105**)

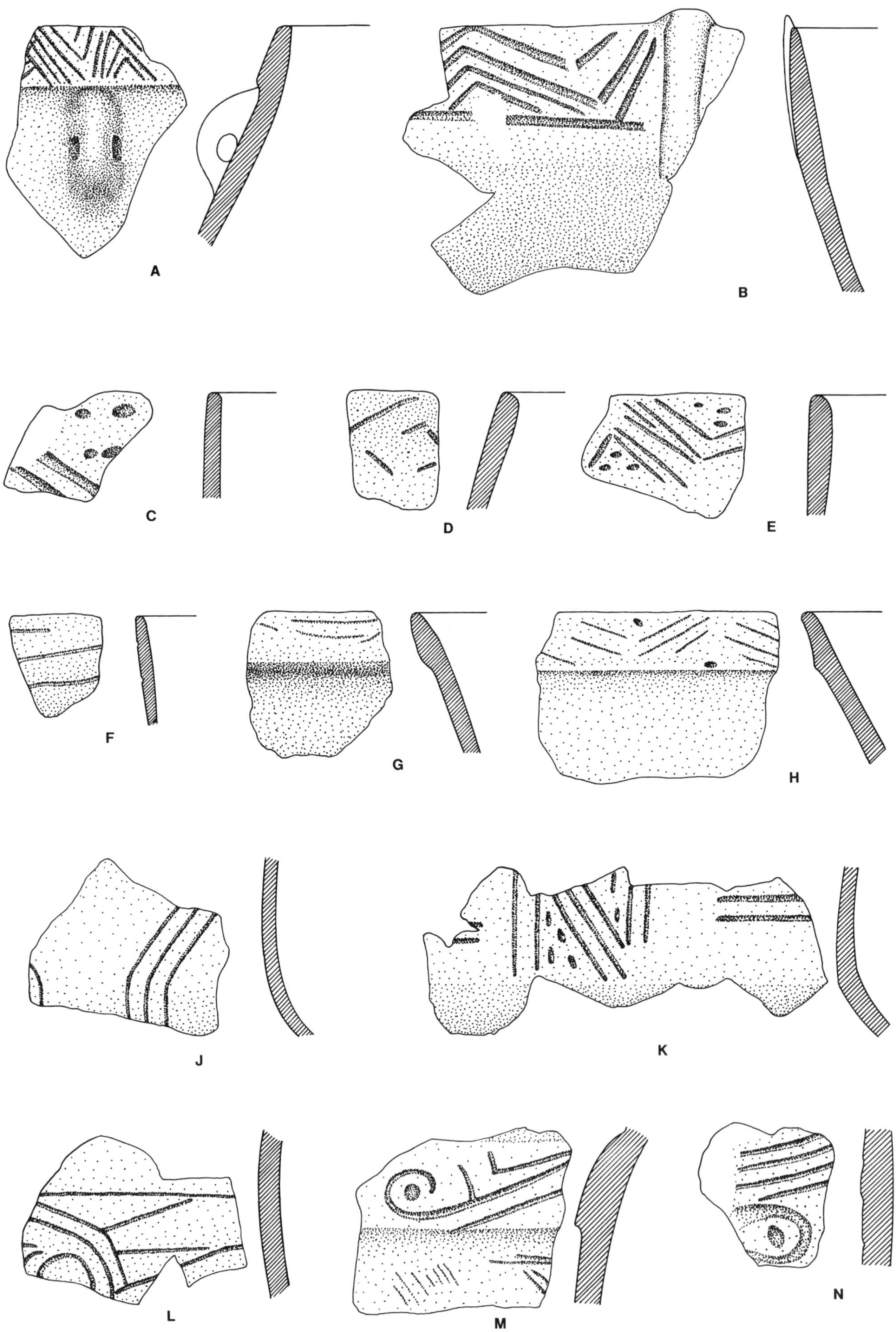

Vessels with incised decoration. Scale 1:2

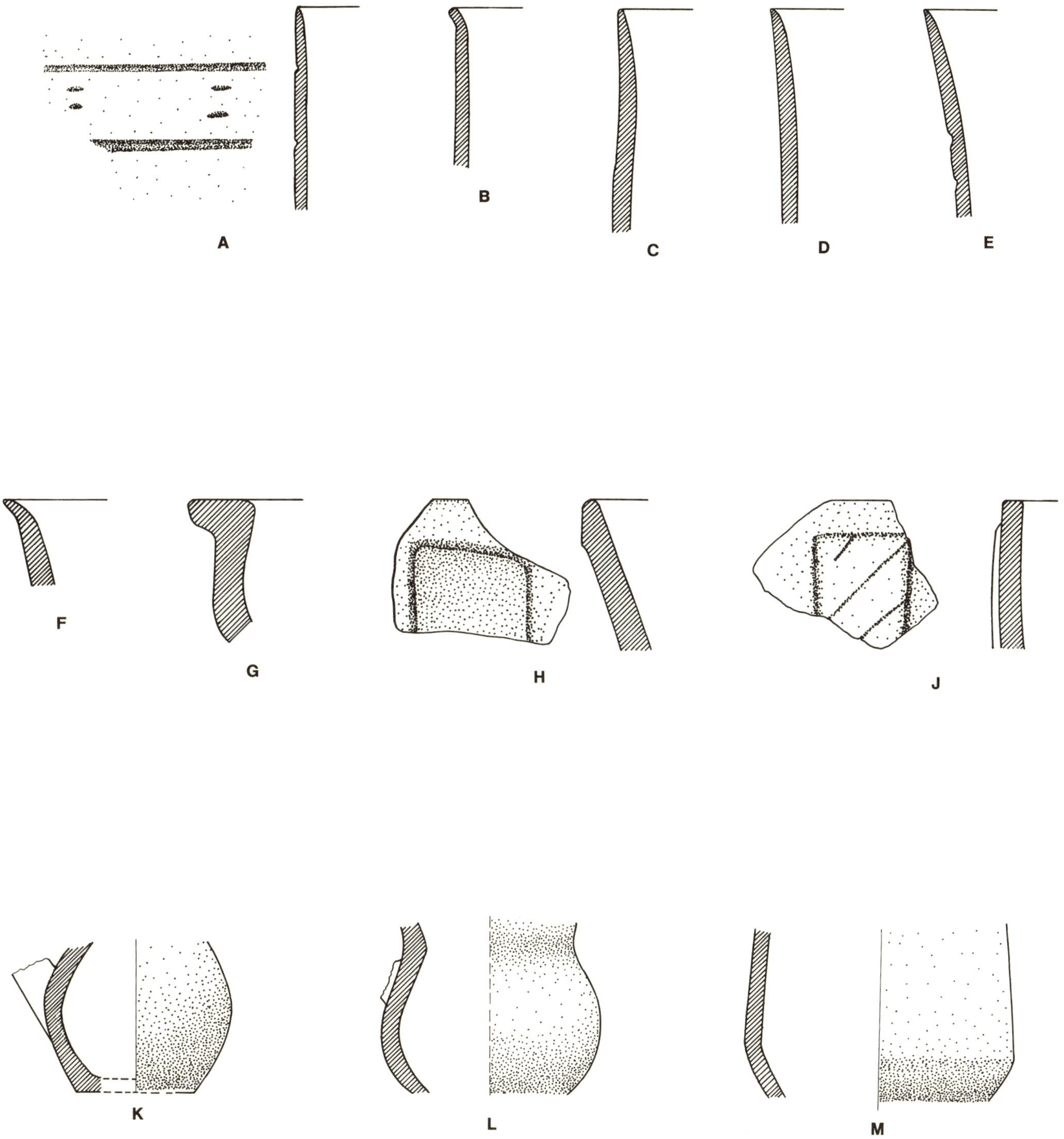

Other sherds. Scale 1:2

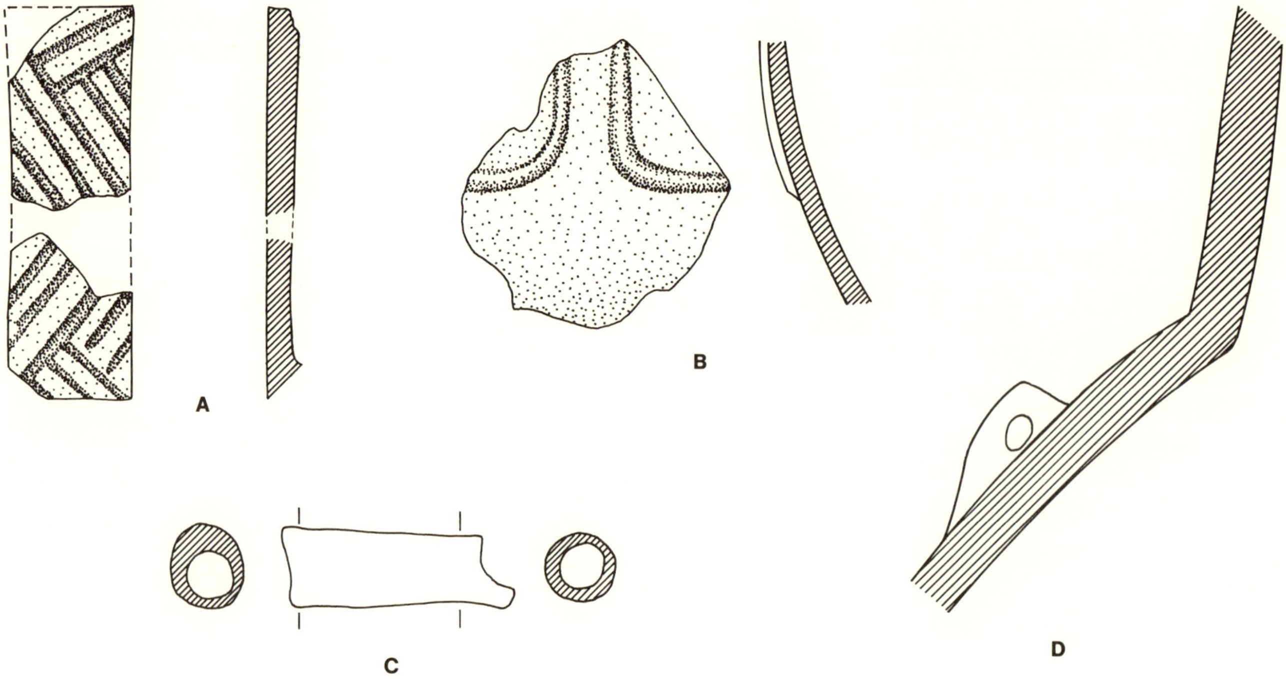

Miscellaneous sherds. Scale 1:2

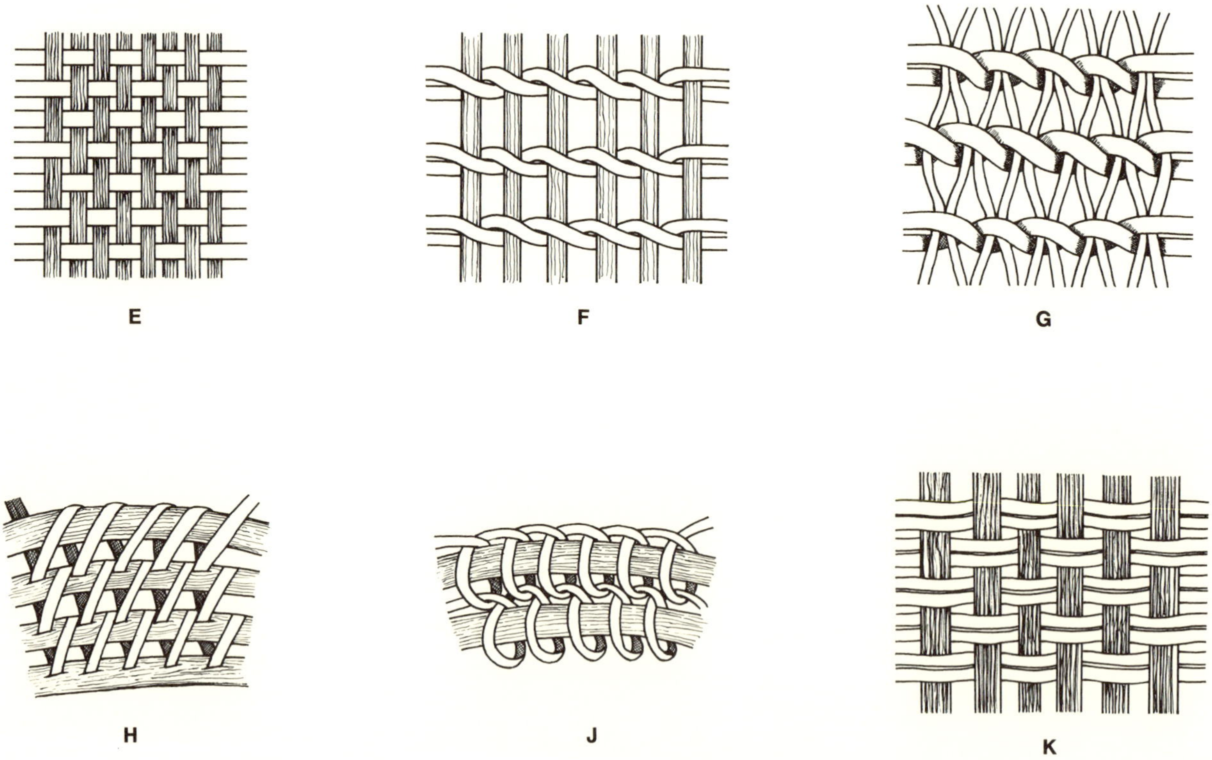

Schematic drawings of cloth and matting: E, plain cloth weave; F, simple twine matting; G, split twine matting; H, J, coiled matting; K, plain-weave matting

a. Promontory of Kephala from southwest

b. Promontory of Kephala from south

a. Bay and isthmus from northwest

b. Bay from east

a. Bay and promontory from south (1961)

b. Surface investigation east of Area H (1960) from west

c. Surface exploration in cemetery (1960) from east

d. View to southwest from summit of promontory. Excavation in Area H (1964)

e. Excavation in Lower Cemetery (1963) from southwest

f. Excavation in Lower Cemetery (1963) from south-southwest

a. Before excavation, from southwest

b. Wall 1 from southwest

c. Room I from south

d. Wall 4 with slabs against east side, from southeast

e. Wall 1 and terrace to south, from southwest

f. Paving south of Wall 1, from southwest

g. Stone with hole beside Wall 1, from south

h. Northern part from southeast; Wall 2 at lower right, Wall 3 at upper right

Area D

a. Area E from southwest

b. Area E from south; Wall 1 in foreground

c. Area G: Trench A and Wall 2, from west

d. Area G: Wall 1, center left, from southeast

e. Area G: Trench B and Wall 2, from east

a. Area H from northwest

b. Area H: Wall 1 from west

c. Area H: Wall 1 from west

d. Area J from southwest

e. South slope of promontory from west; Area K at upper left, Paoura in far distance

a. Area K: wall in upper stratum, from southwest

b. Area K after clearing, from southwest

c. Area L: House Y from west

d. Area L: House Y, northeast corner, from southwest

e. Area L: House Y, northeast corner, from southeast

a. Fallen stones, from southwest

b. View from northeast

c. View from east

d. Stones beside Wall 5, from northwest

e. Southwest side from northeast

f. Northeast side from southwest

Area L: House Z

a. View from southeast

b. Graves and platforms of Lower Cemetery from west

c. Graves of Lower Cemetery from northwest

d. *Dromos* from northeast

e. *Dromos* and graves of Lower Cemetery, from southwest

f. Graves of Lower Cemetery from northeast

a. Grave 1, lower burial, from northwest

b. Grave 1, upper burial, from north-northwest

c. Grave 2, burial, from south

d. Grave 3, cover, from west

e. Grave 3, burial, from east

Lower Cemetery

a. Central group from east; Grave 13, center right; Grave 8, lower center

b. Central group from east, after removal of P 5, P 7 and Grave 8

c. Grave 4, burial, from north

d. Grave 5 from north

e. Grave 6, cleared, from southwest

f. Grave 16 above cover of Grave 6, from south

Lower Cemetery

a. Grave 8 from east

b. Grave 8, cover, from south

c. Platforms from northeast: P 2, lower left; P 3, upper left; P 1, center right

d. Grave 9, burial, from northeast

e. Grave 10, cover, from south

f. Grave 10, cleared, from southwest

a. Upper burial level from south

b. Upper burial level from southwest

c. Between upper and middle burial levels, from south

d. Middle burial level from east

e. Stones below middle burial level, from south

f. Lower burial level from south

g. Detail of construction, from southeast

h. Grave cleared, from south

Grave 7

a. Grave 11, burial level, from northwest

b. Grave 11 below Grave 21, from southwest

c. Grave 13 from north

d. Grave 13, burial level, from north

e. Grave 13, cover, from south

f. Grave 12 from southeast

g. Grave 14, cleared, from southwest

h. Grave 14, burial level, from southwest

a. Grave 18, cleared, from south

b. Grave 18, left,and Grave 17, right, from southwest

c. Wall 1, above, and Grave 6, below, from south

d. Grave 17, cleared, with cover slab of Grave 5 beneath, from north

e. Grave 19 before opening, from south

f. Grave 19, cover slab, from east

a. Grave 15, upper middle, above stones over Grave 1, lower right, from north

b. Grave 20, cleared, from southwest

c. Grave 22, cover, from north

d. Grave 22, burial, from east

e. Grave 23, cover, center, and Grave 24, from northwest

f. Grave 23, opened, and Grave 24, from northwest

g. Grave 24, burial, from northwest

Lower Cemetery

a. Grave 28 above Grave 27, from north

b. Grave 27 with remaining cover slab at left, from west

c. Grave 25, burial, from east

d. Grave 31, cleared, from southeast

e. Grave 30, center, Grave 14, right, and Upper Cemetery before excavation, background, from southwest

f. Upper Cemetery during excavation, from northeast

g. Grave 34, burial level, from southwest

h. Grave 34, detail, from southwest

Upper and Lower Cemeteries

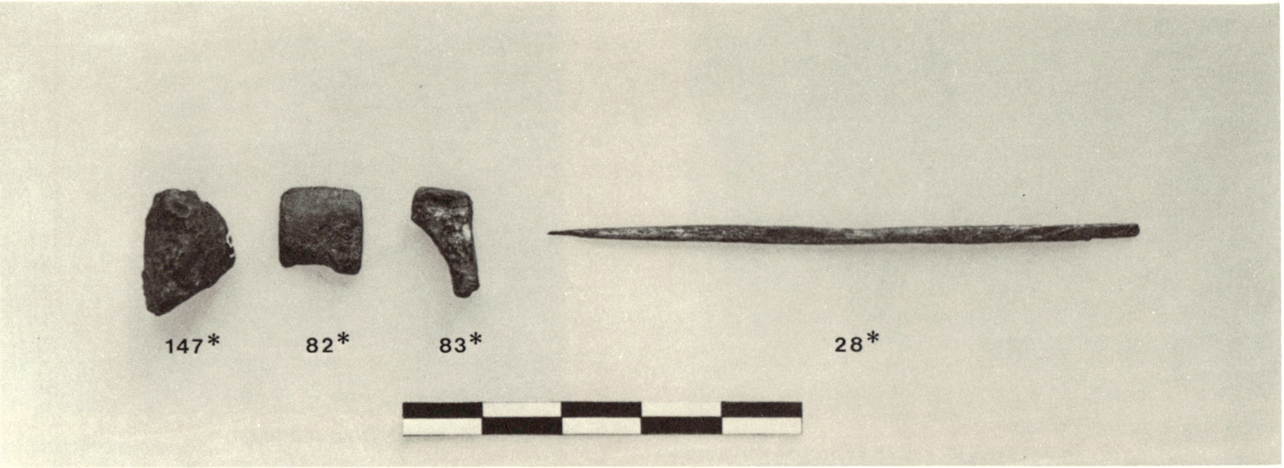

Copper and copper working

Lead

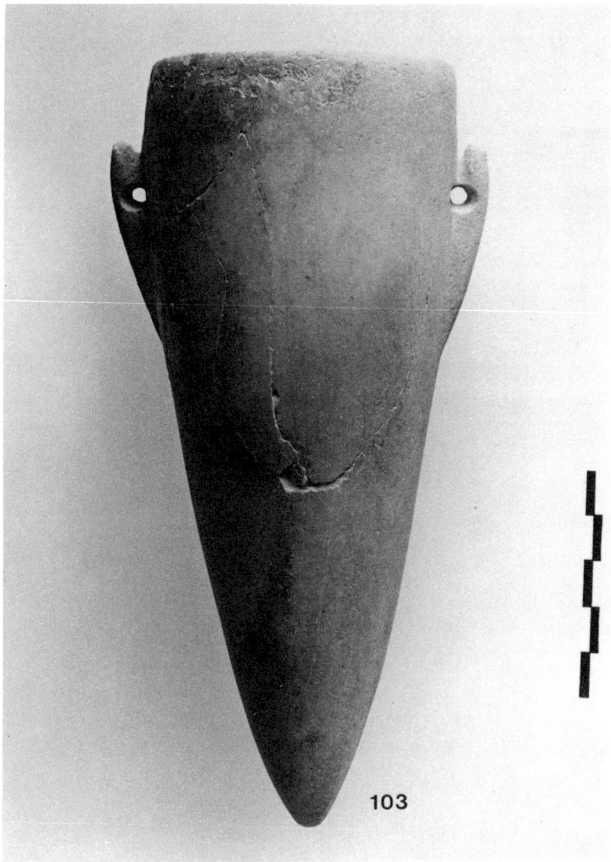

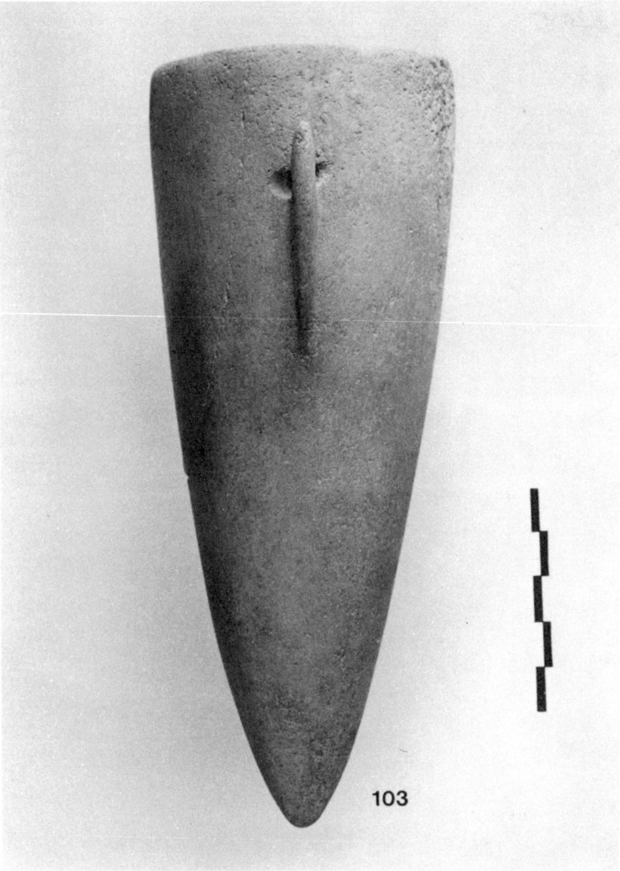

Marble vessels

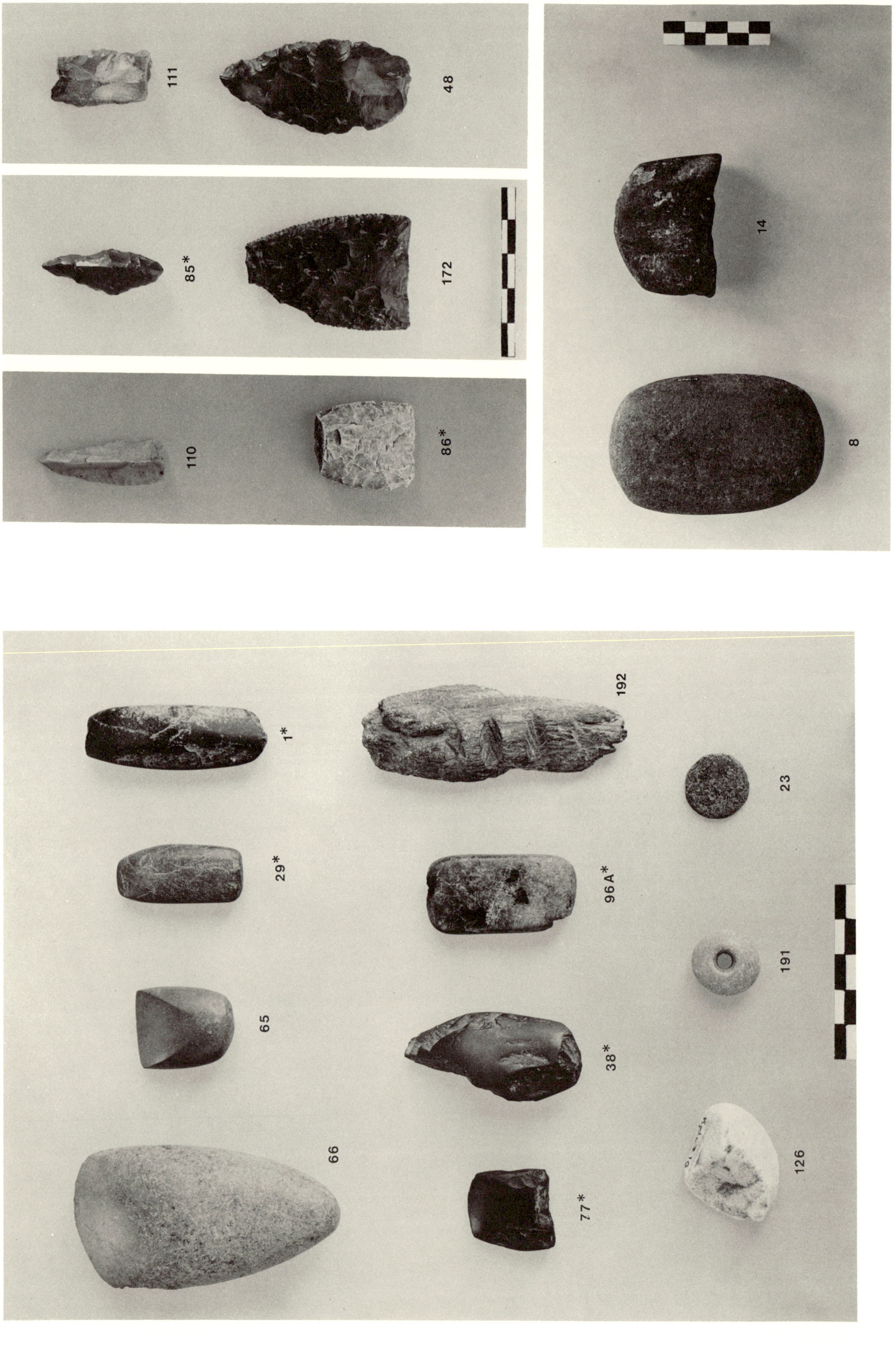

Celts, flint tools, and other objects of stone

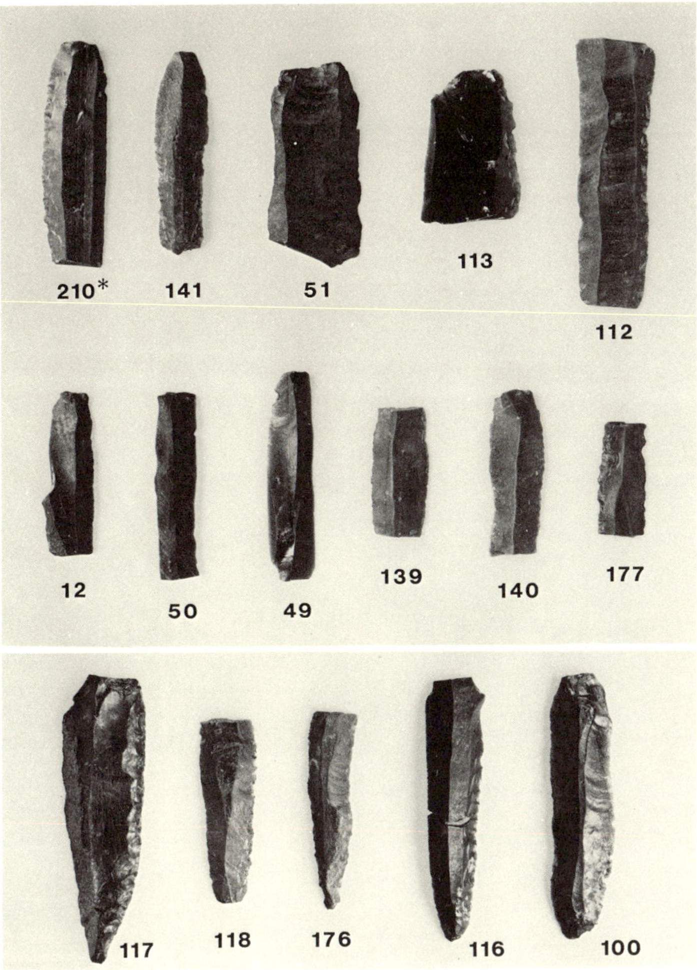

Category 1 a

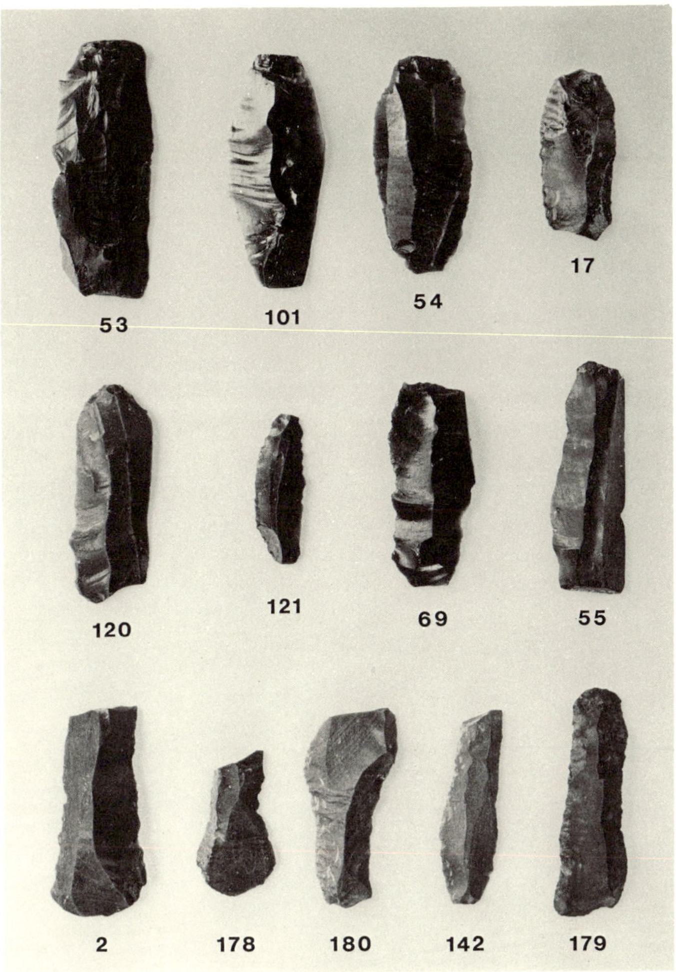

Category 1 b

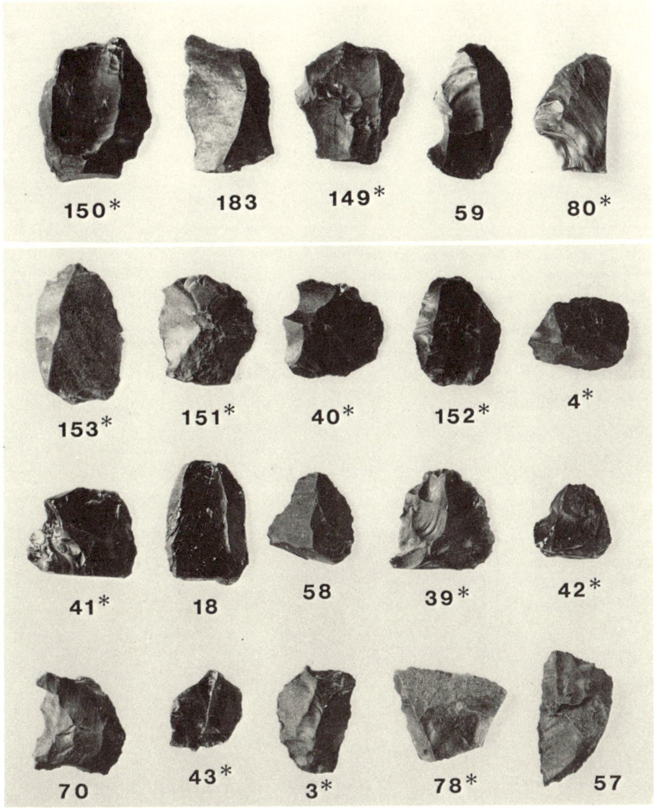

Category 2

Category 2

Obsidian tools. Scale 1:2

Category 3

Category 4

Category 5

Category 6

Waste cores

Waste

Obsidian tools and waste. Scale 1:2 except **93***, **94***, **95***, 1:4

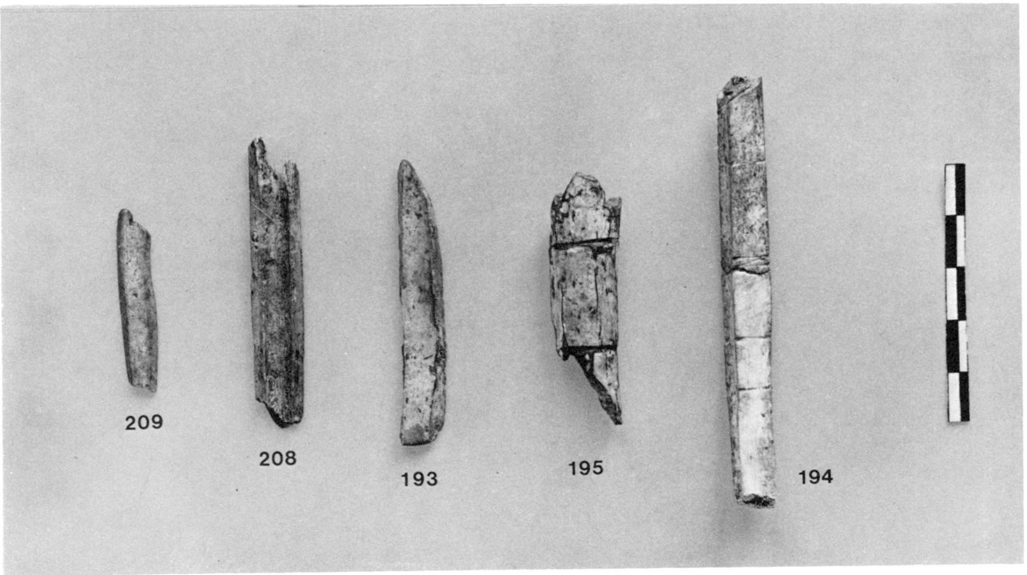

a. Bone tools

b. Terracotta rubbing-tools

c. Miscellaneous terracotta objects

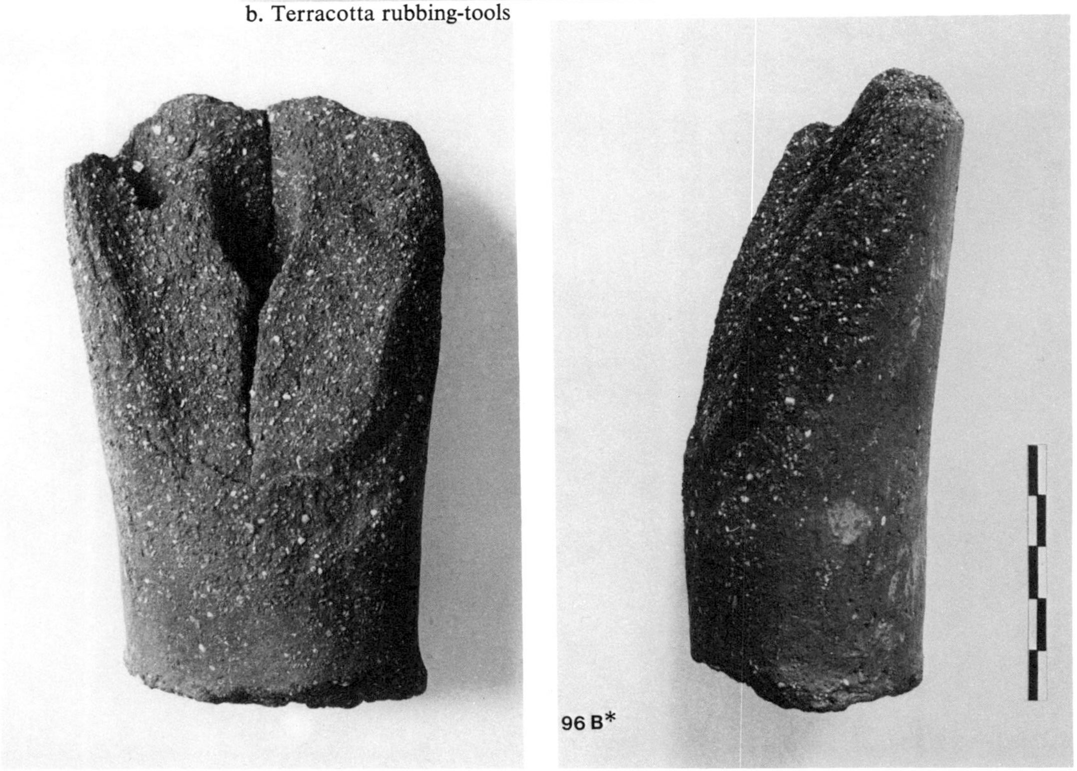

d. Terracotta figurine head

Terracotta figurines

160*

128

202

Terracotta figurines

138

99

62

62

34*

27

Bowls (Categories A 1 and A 2)

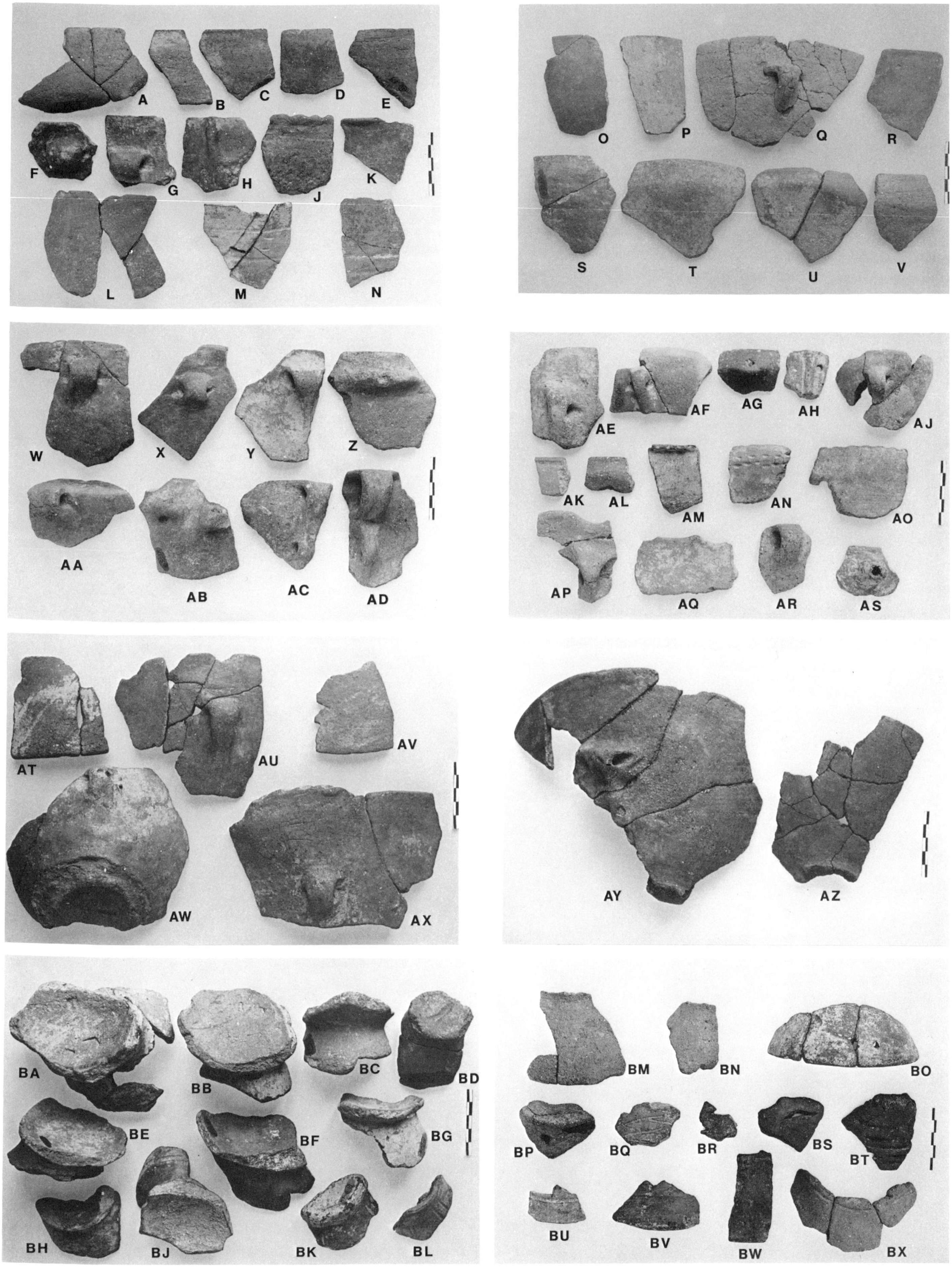

Bowls (Categories A 1 and A 2) and other small vessels (K–N)

104

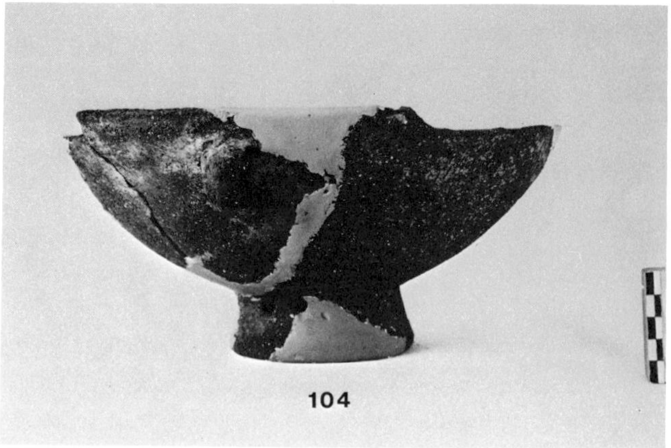
104

A

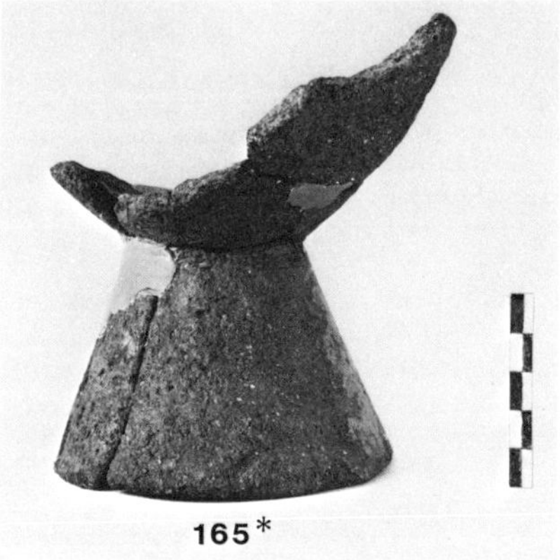
165*

37

164*

166*

Bowls (Category A 2) and small jars (Category B 1)

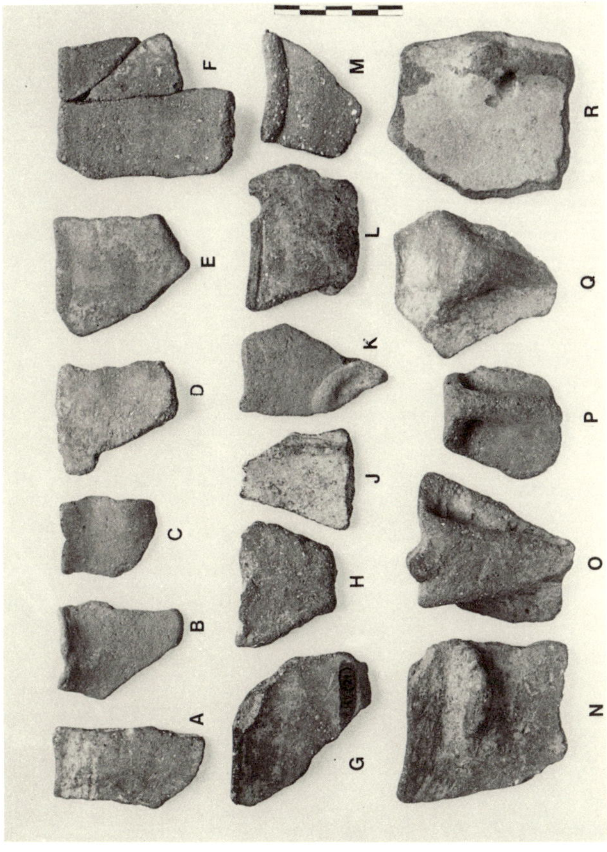

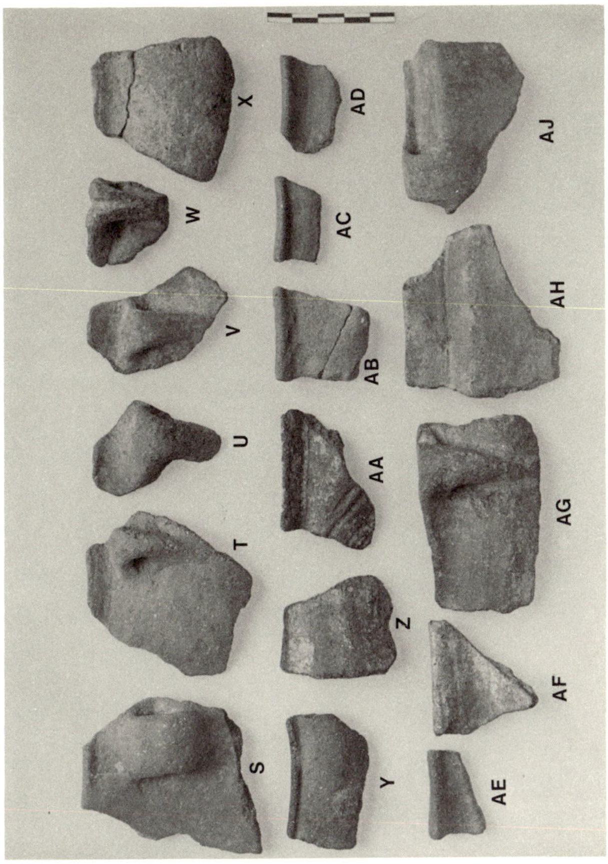

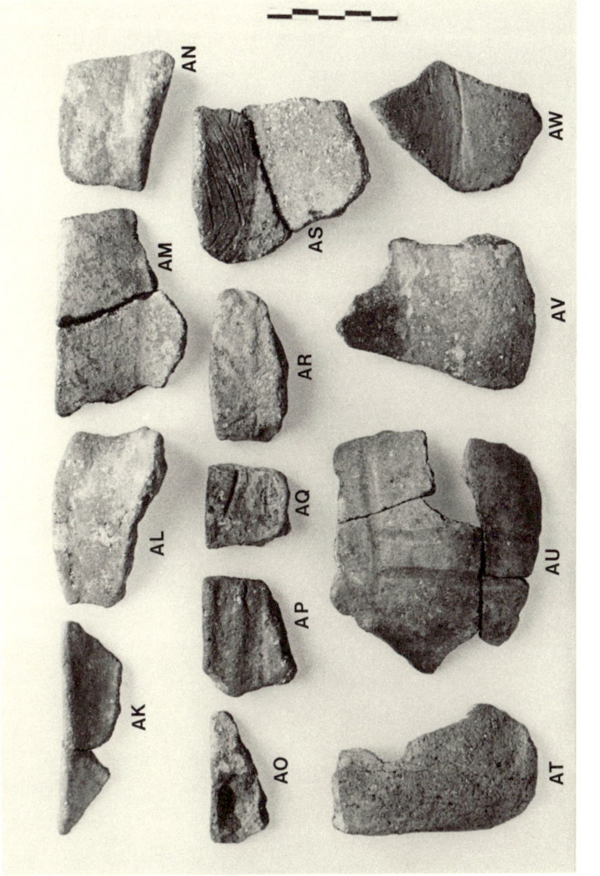

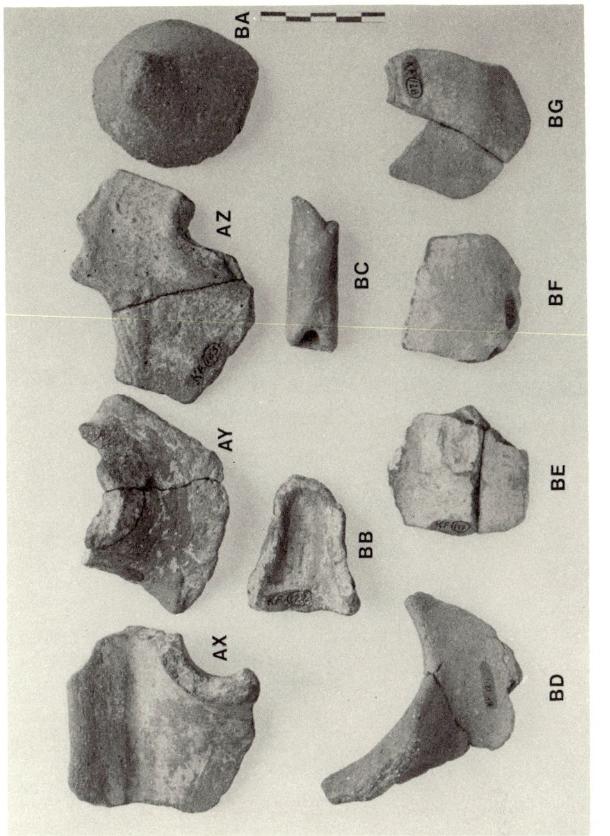

Small jars (Category B 1)

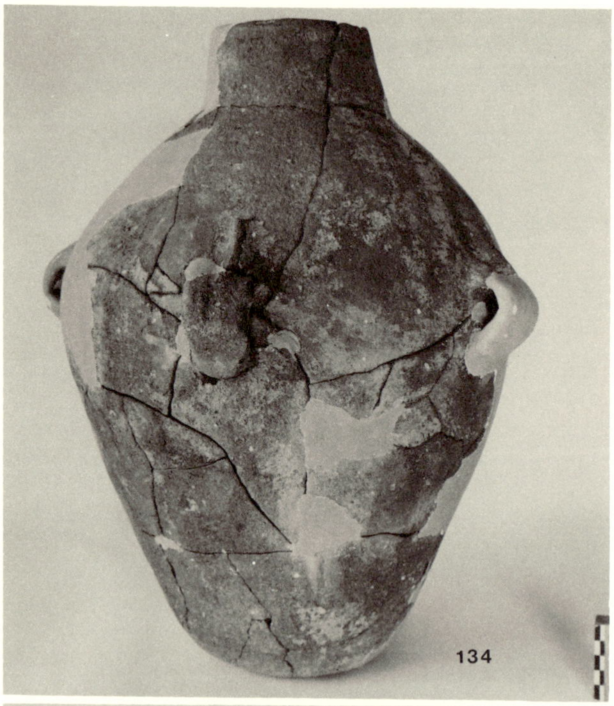

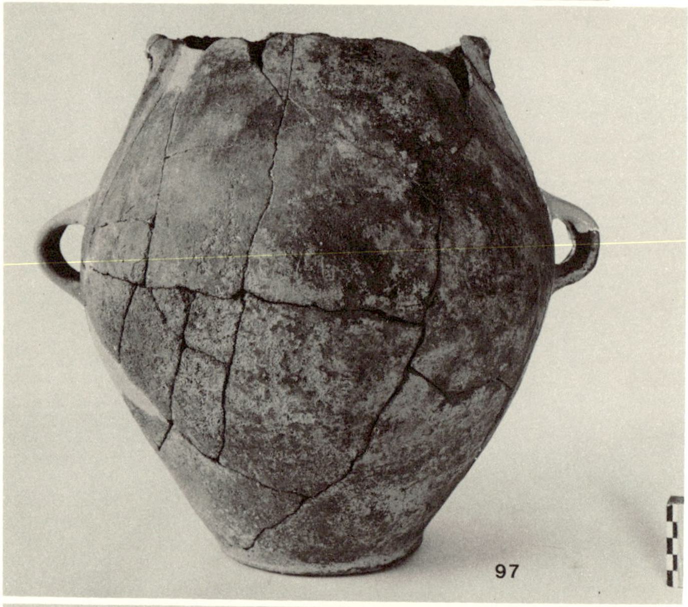

Large jars (Category B 2)

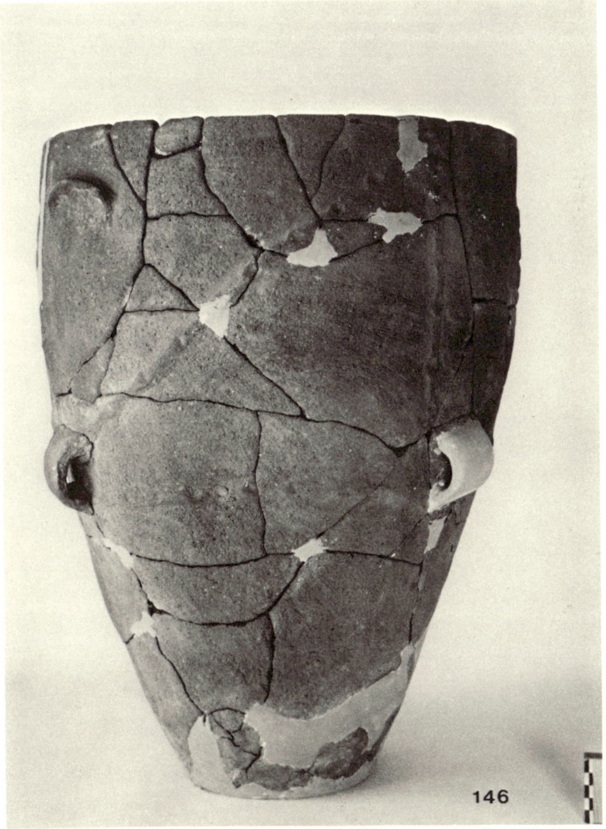

Large jars (Category B 2)

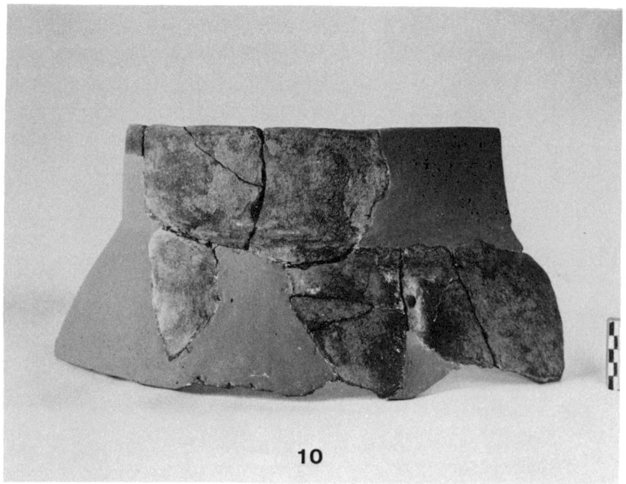

10

A

74

11*

B

64

136

C

Large jars (Category B 2)

Large jars (Category B 2)

PLATE 82

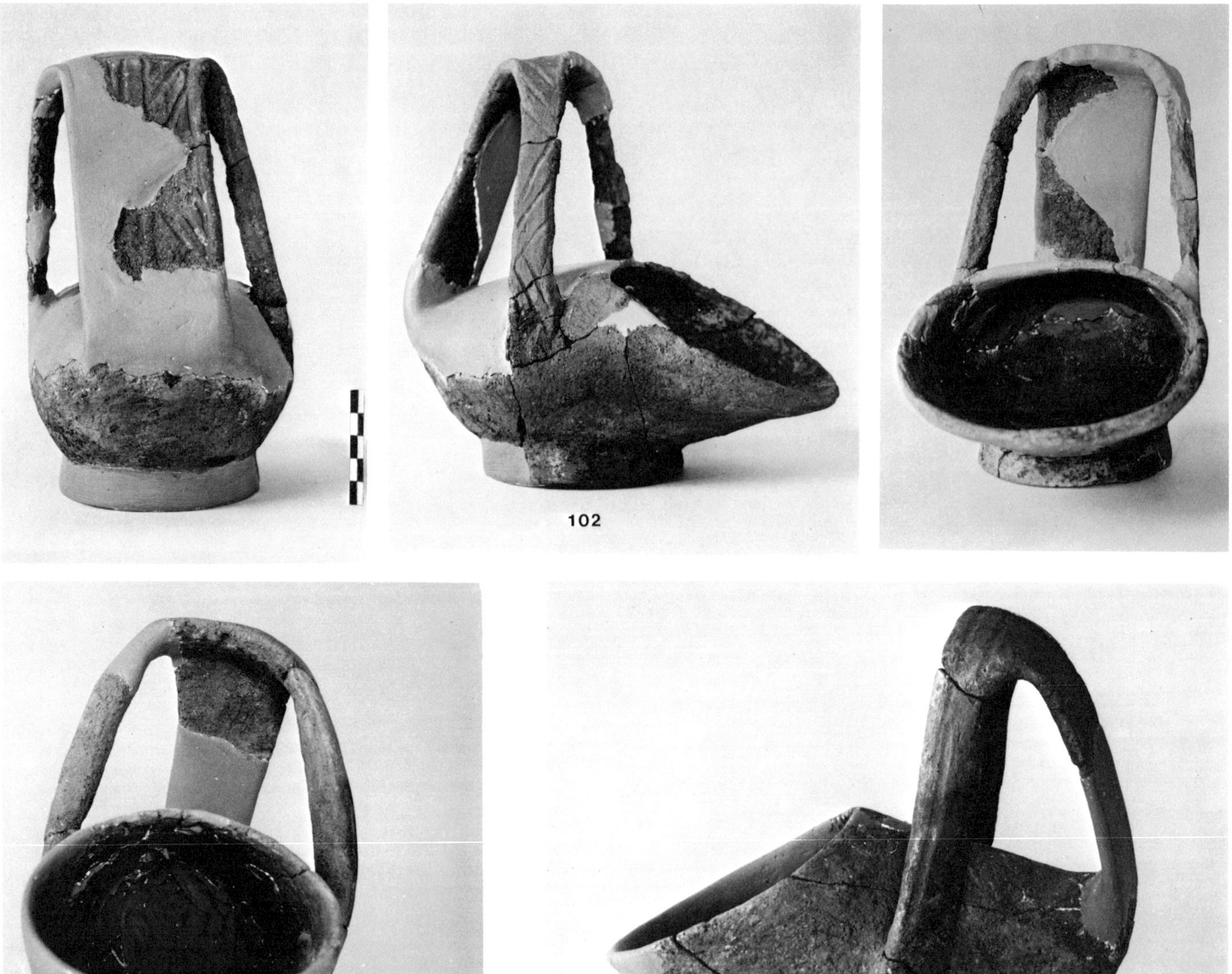

Scoops (Category C 1)

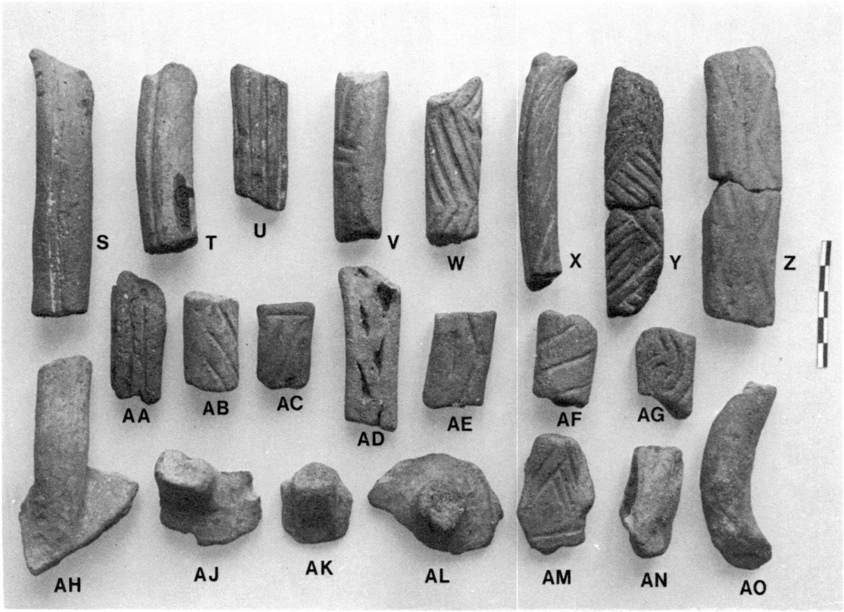

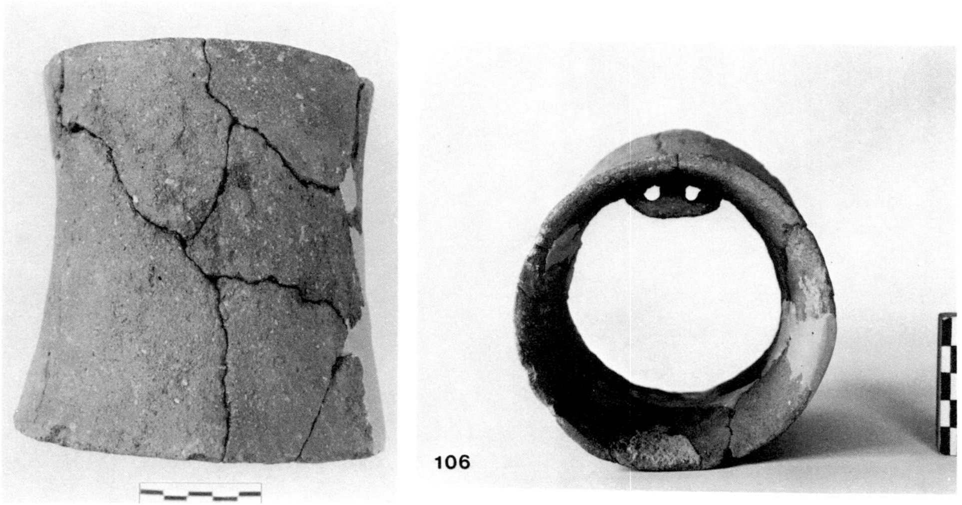

Scoops (Category C 1) and cylindrical vessel (Category C 2)

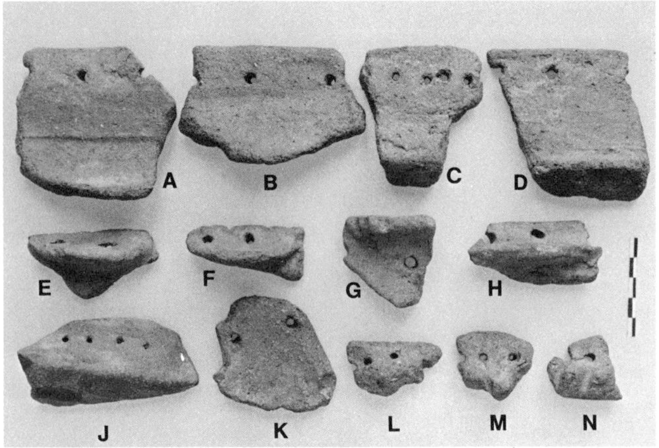

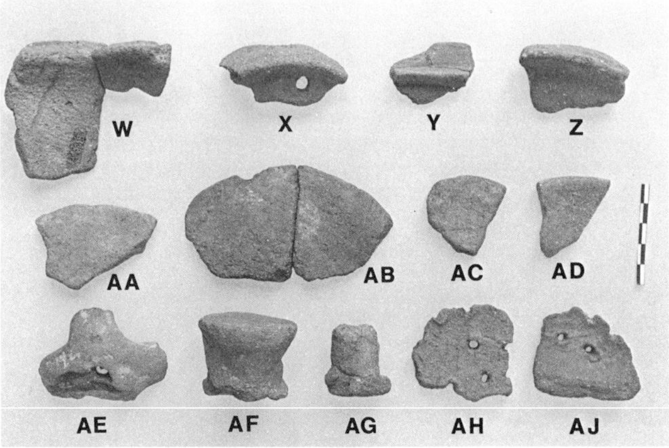

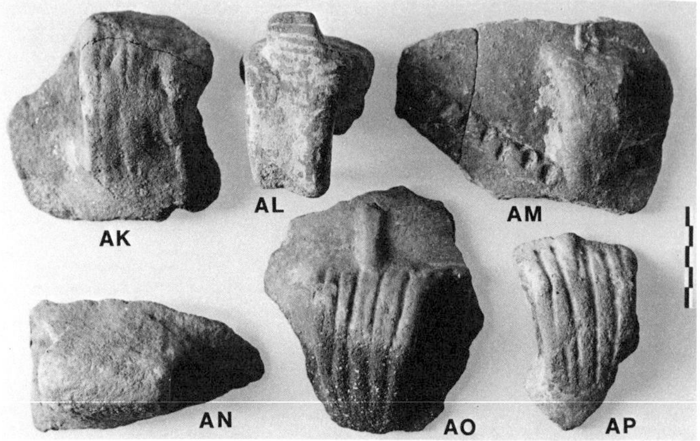

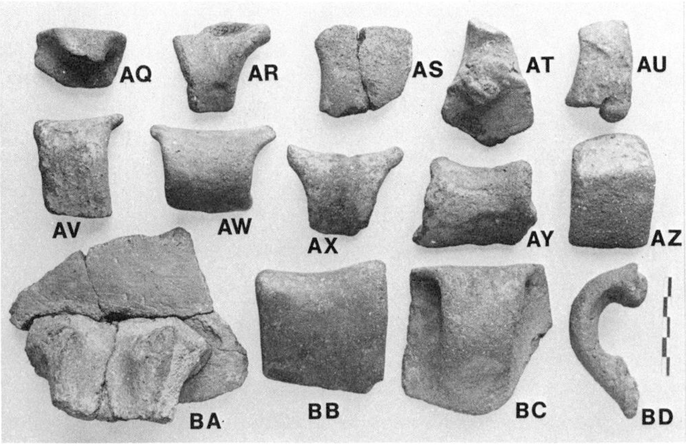

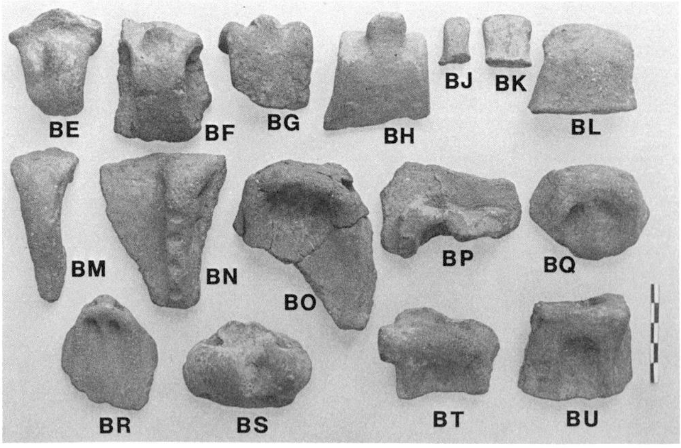

Cylindrical vessels (Category C 2: W–Z), baking pans (Category C 3: A–V), straining vessels (Category C 4: AH, AJ), lids (Category C 5: AA–AG) and handles (Other sherds: AK–BU)

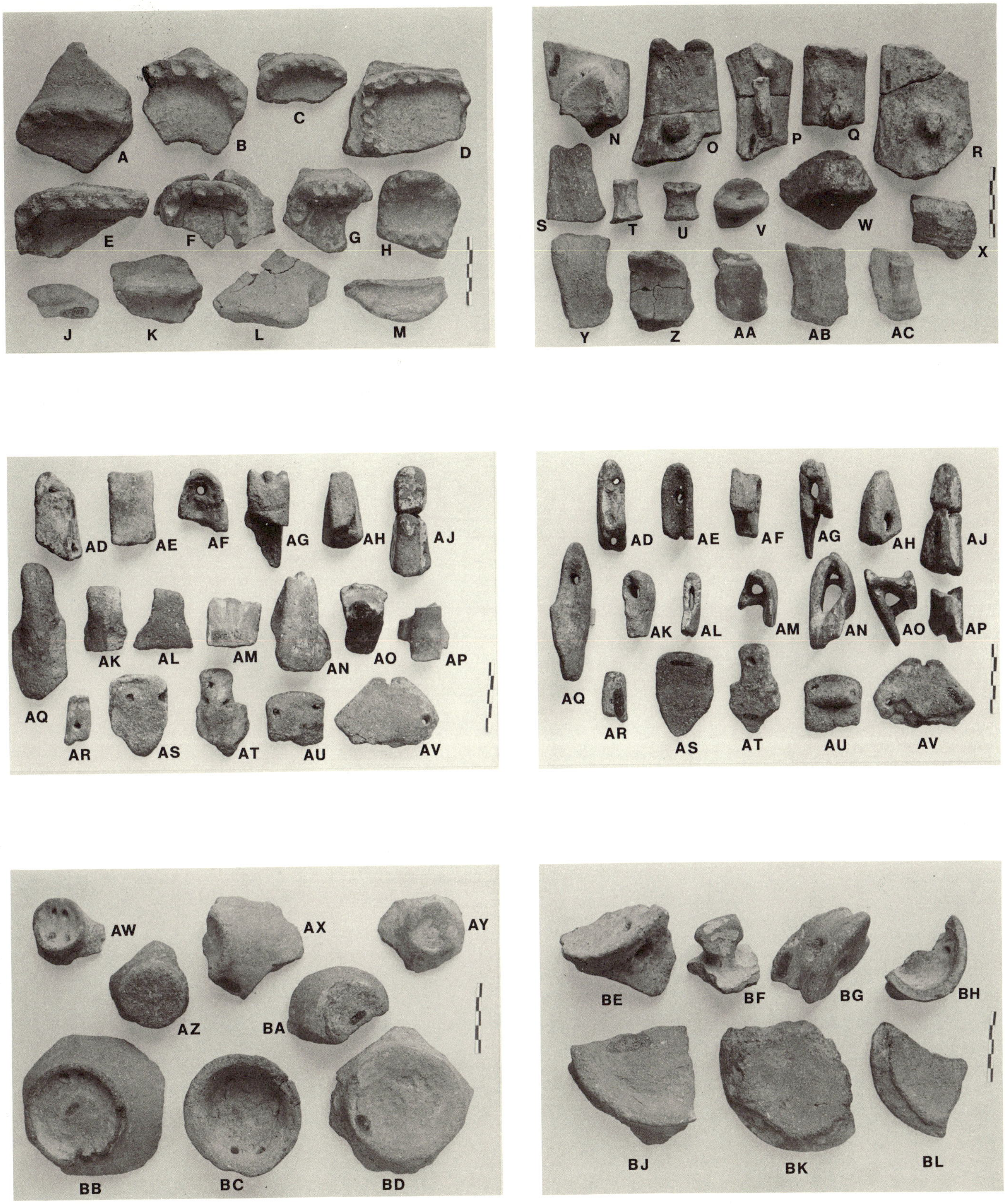

Other sherds: handles and bases

Bowls (Category A 2) with pattern burnishing on the outside (A–N) or inside (O–AT)

Bowls and jars with pattern burnishing

Jar with pattern burnishing (**75**) and vessels with incised decoration (A–AZ)

Sherds with incised (A–AE) and plastic (AF–BP) decoration

Cast of **167***

167*

Fragments A and B

Fragment A

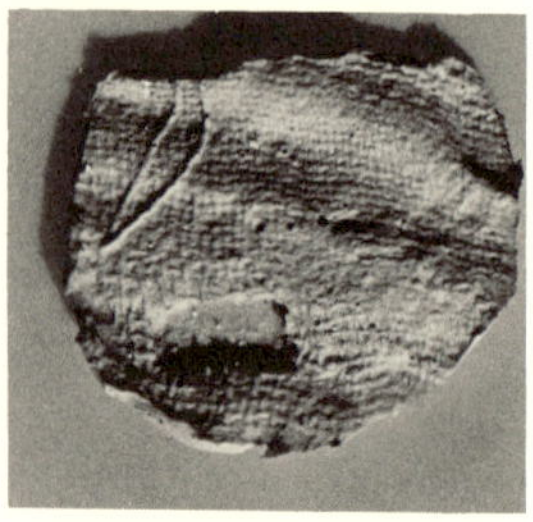

Cast of A

213*

Fragment B and cast

Fragment C and cast

Fragment D and cast

201

A

B

C

D E F G H J K L M N O P

Cloth, mat, and leaf impressions on pottery

Cast of D

Mat impressions (A–D) and other sherds

a. Barley (Hordeum Vulgare L.)

b. Lathyrus (Lathyrus Sativus L.)

(Scale in millimeters)

c. Cattle. Left: Bronze Age humerus, Ayia Irini. Right: distal humerus, Upper Cemetery

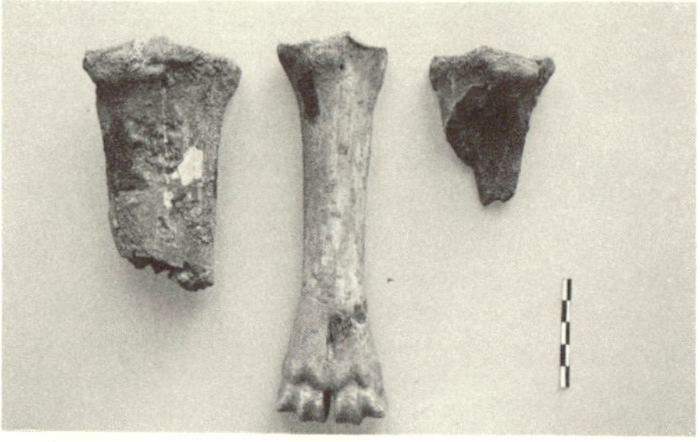

d. Cattle. Left: proximal metacarpus, Upper Cemetery. Center: typical Bronze Age metacarpus, Ayia Irini. Right: proximal metacarpus, Upper Cemetery

e. Goat-horn core, Lower Cemetery: anterior view to show keel

f. Goat-horn core, Lower Cemetery: mesial view

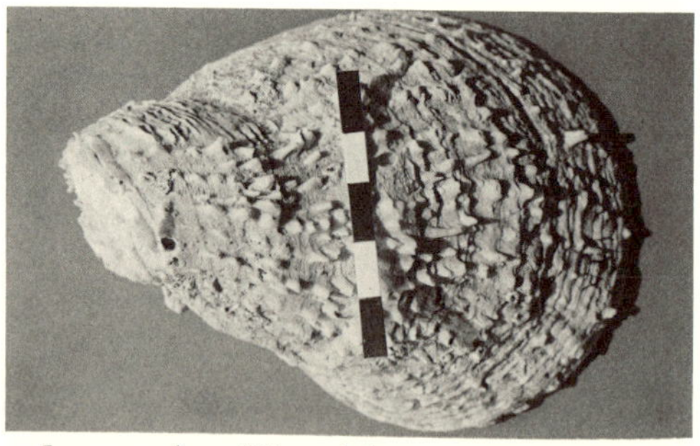

g. Lower valve of Spondylus

h. Triton fragments, Upper Cemetery

j. Opening of almost whole Triton, surface in Area G

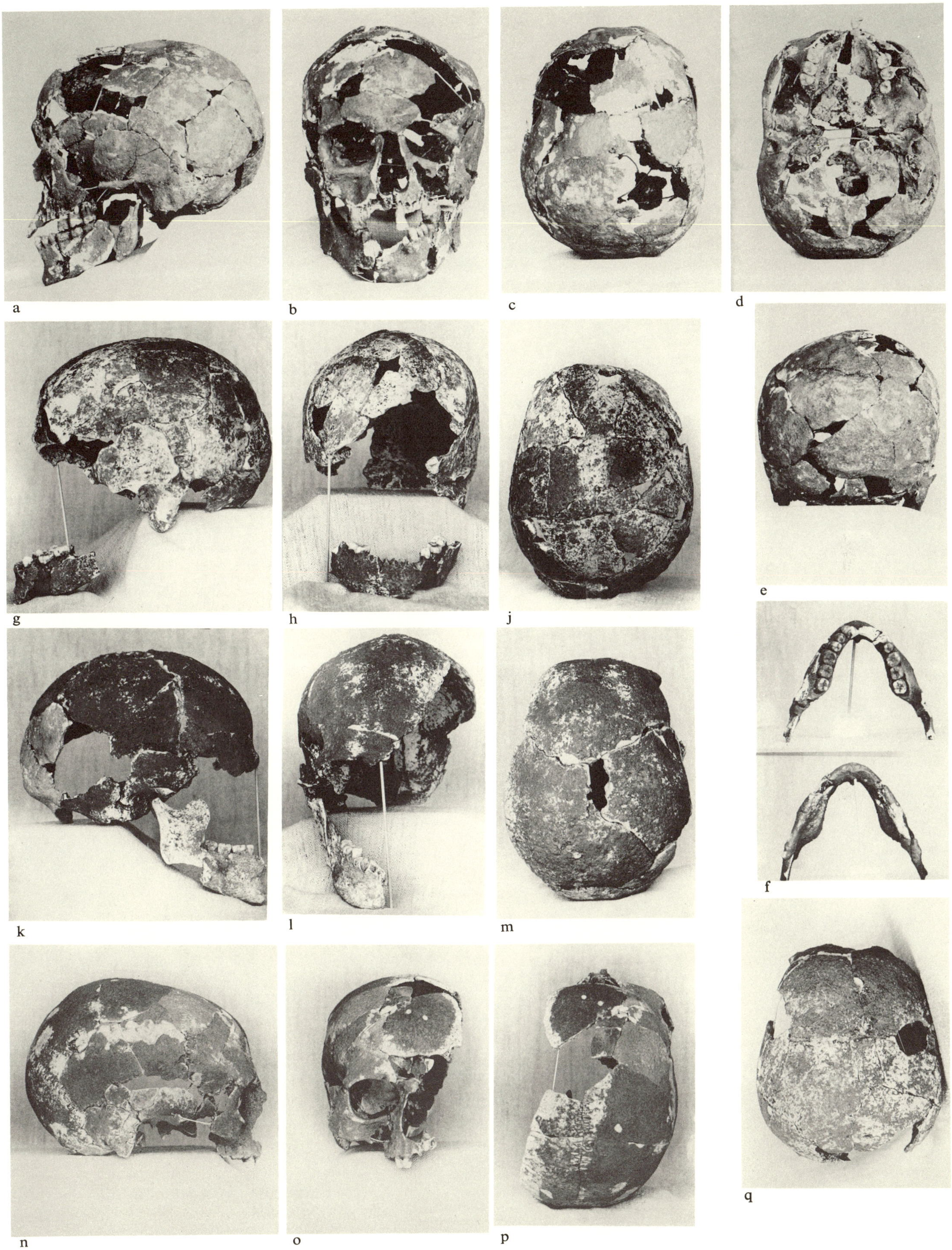

a–f. *68 Kek*, robust and low-faced male with excellent teeth. g–j. *29 Kek*, typical male. k–m. *9 Kek*, typical male. n–p. *21 Kek*, female.
q. top view of *12 Kek*: more laterally expanded, type C5 male, showing hole made after death

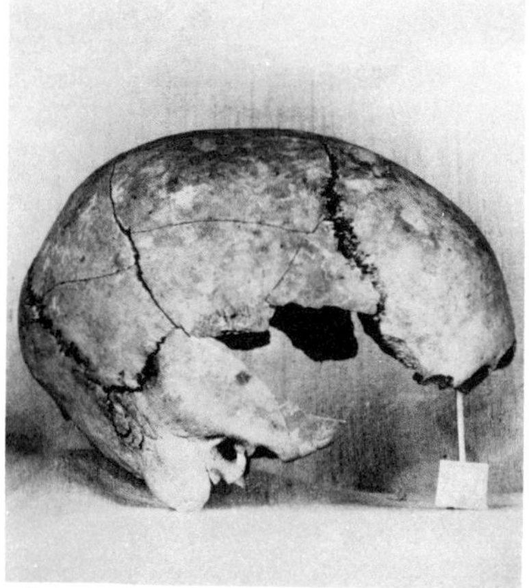
a

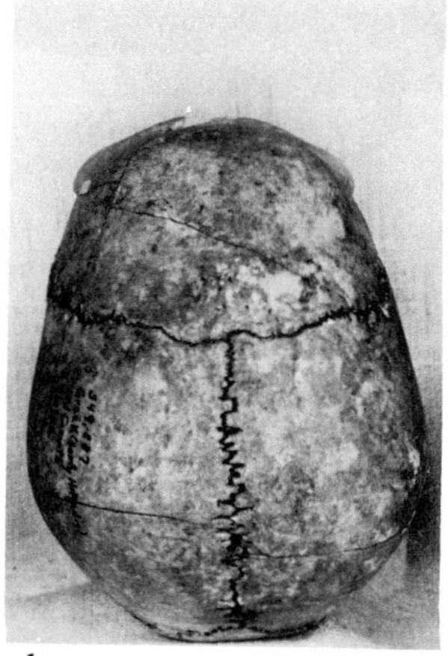
b

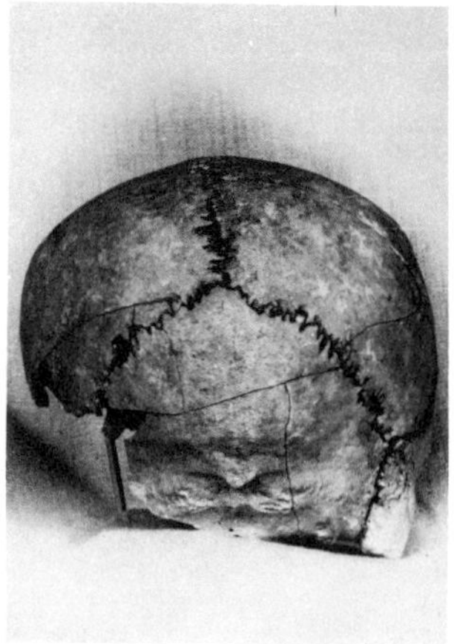
c

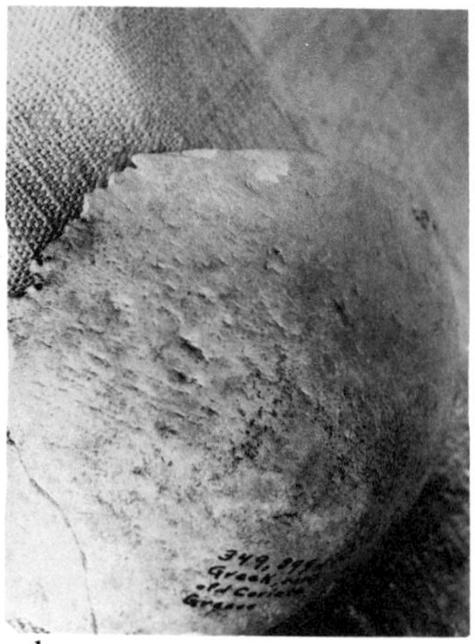
d

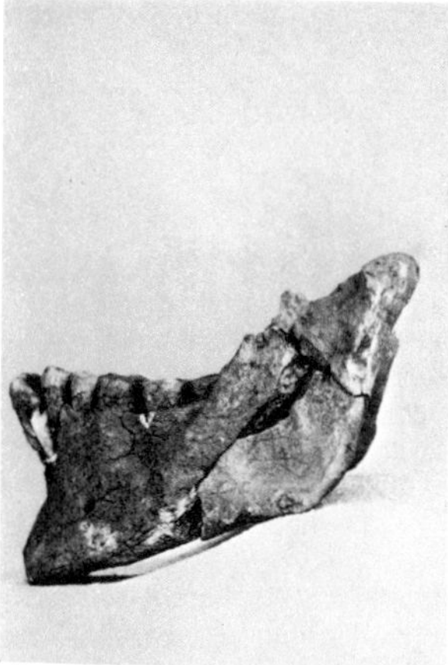
e

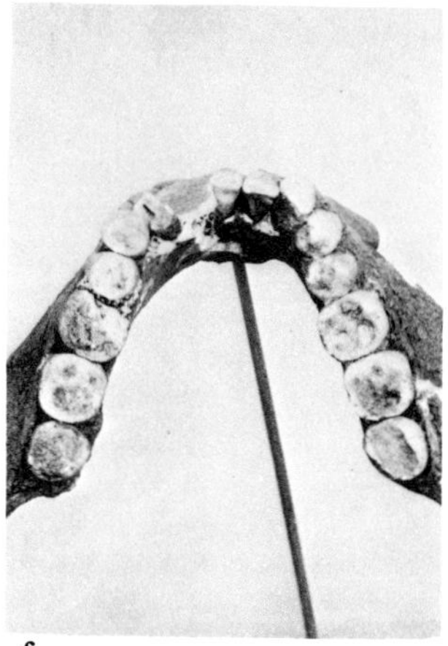
f

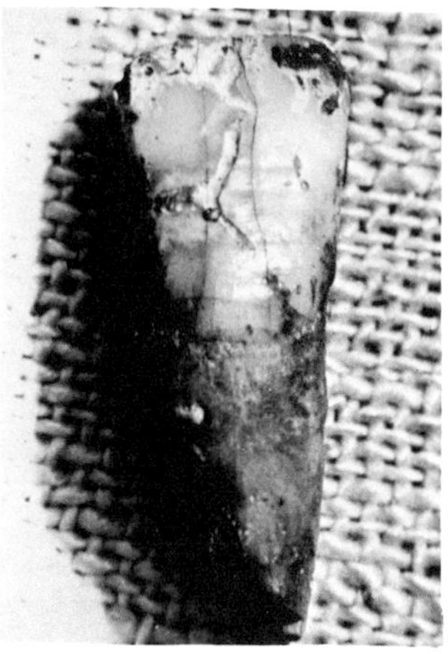
g

h

j

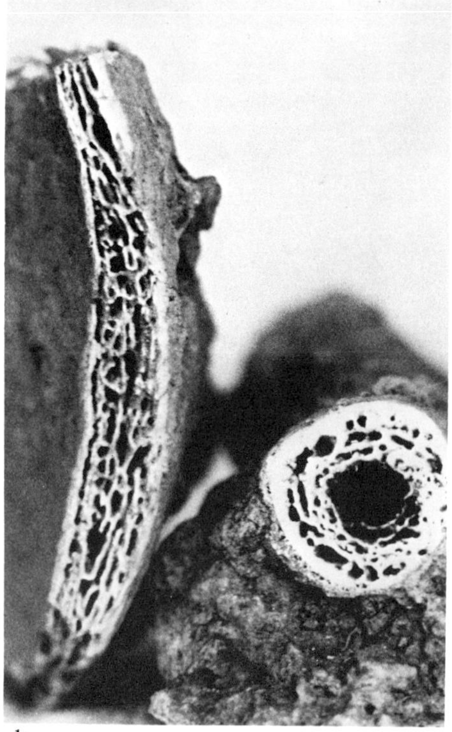
k

a–c. *12 C*, type A male from Cheliotomylos, Early Bronze Age Corinth. d. For comparison: porotic hyperostosis in *4 C*, child about 7 years old. e, f. *71 Kek*, male, to show teeth wear. g. *68 Kek*: upper central incisor tooth to show two sets of growth-arrest lines (hypoplasia) across enamel of crown. h. *68 Kek*: Phase 6 pubic symphysis. j. *17 Kek*, to show healed head wound (from spear or arrow?), inner and outer views, and its sequel, an inner layer of bone laid down between dura mater and inner table. k. *5 Kek* to show porotic hyperostosis well developed (enlargement of marrow space of skull diploë and of long bones from severe anemia, possible homozygous thalassemia) in an infant.

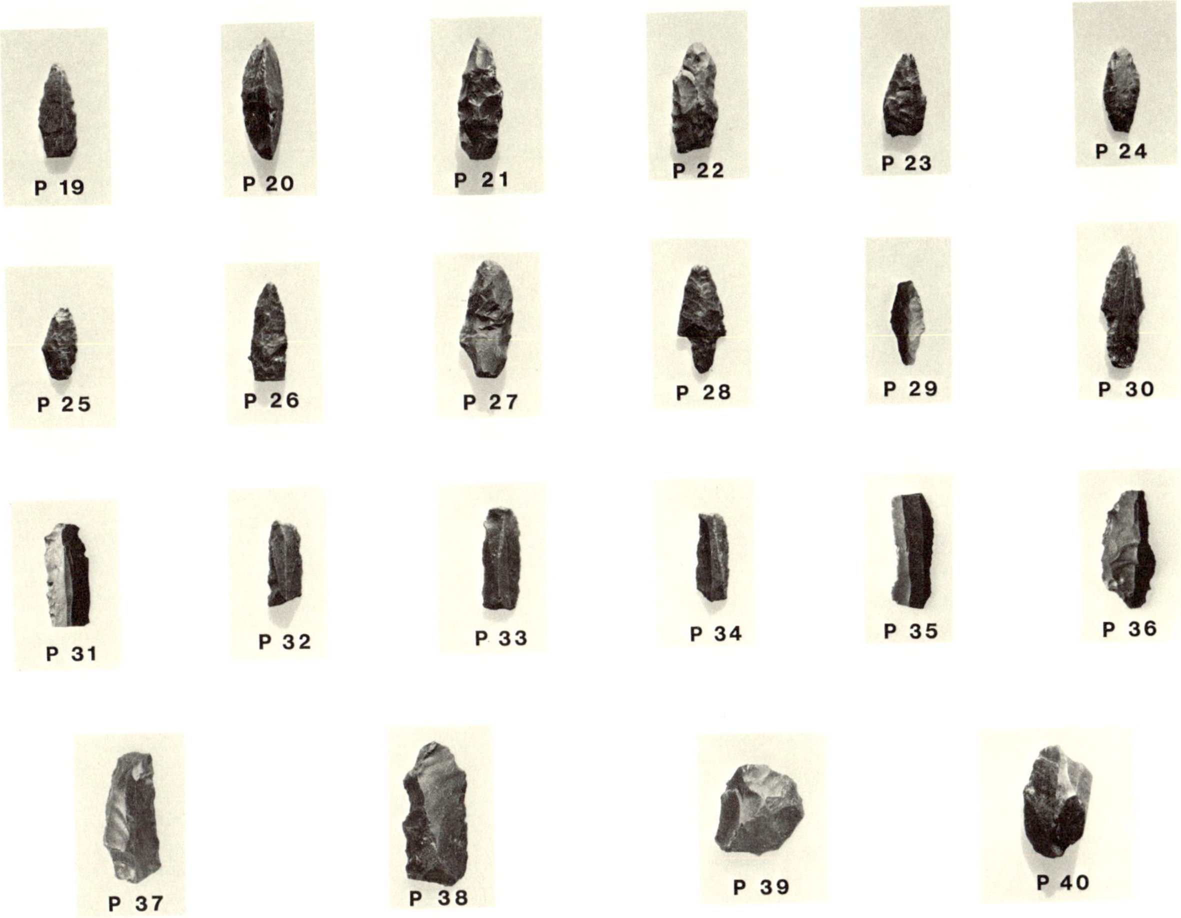

Obsidian

Pottery

Copper and copper working

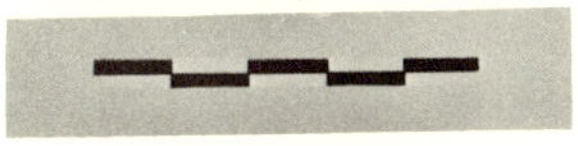

Paoura on Keos